Residential Possession Proceedings

Residential Possession Proceedings

9th Edition

Gary Webber
Mediator

Daniel Dovar
Barrister

SWEET & MAXWELL

THOMSON REUTERS

First Edition 1984
Fifth Edition 1997
Reprinted 1999
Sixth Edition 2001
Seventh Edition 2006
Eighth Edition 2008

Published in 2013 by
Sweet & Maxwell, 100 Avenue Road, London NW3 3PF,
part of Thomson Reuters (Professional) UK Limited
(Registered address in England & Wales, Company No. 1679046.
Registered Office and address for service: Aldgate House, 33 Aldgate High Street,
London EC3N 1DL).

For further information on our products and services, visit www.sweetandmaxwell.co.uk

Typeset by LBJ Typesetting Ltd
of Kingsclere
Printed in Great Britain by Ashford Colour Press, Gosport, Hants

A CIP catalogue record for this book
is available from the British Library.

ISBN 9780414024977

Preface

Previous editions noted the recommendations by the Law Commission to simplify housing law and to cut down the number of different residential tenancies. We expressed the view that these recommendations seemed increasingly unlikely to be adopted. What we didn't anticipate was the growing trend to increase the different types of tenancy. This new edition sees the introduction of the Flexible Tenancy, which joins the ranks of Family Intervention Tenancies, Starter Tenancies, Demoted Tenancies and Introductory Tenancies. The latest, the Flexible Tenancy, is the result of a shift to the philosophy behind social housing, from housing for life, to housing for those in need; a shift that has come about not only from political ideology but also because of the pressure of increasing demand on housing and growing waiting lists. The rise and fall of residential security of tenure in the private sector is now being followed in the public sector.

At the same time as public sector security of tenure is being lessened by domestic legislation, it has been given a new lease of life by European jurisprudence. The application of Article 8 of the European Convention on Human Rights has been widened and clarified by the decisions in *Manchester City Council v Pinnock* (2010) and London *Borough of Hounslow v Powell* (2011). The Equality Act 2010 has also made substantial changes, in particular in its attempt to address the difficulties created by *Lewisham v Malcolm* (2008) and we have dealt with this in a new chapter on discrimination.

There is also a new chapter on orders for sale, which includes charging orders and co-ownership cases, and the guidance provided by *Stack v Dowden* (2007) and *Jones v Kernott* (2011).

The new text incorporates the adjustments to the Tenancy Deposit Scheme introduced by the Localism Act 2011 as far as it relates to obtaining possession of assured shorthold tenancies.

We have decided to take out the chapter on social housing, preferring instead to incorporate the relevant points within different chapter headings.

The authors would very much like to thank Nigel Clayton, barrister, for all his help with the mortgages and orders for sale chapters. We of course remain responsible for any errors or omissions.

We have done our best to state the law as at January 2013. Monthly updates can be found at *www.propertylawuk.net*.

Gary Webber
Tanfield Chambers
www.propertylawuk.net

Daniel Dovar
Tanfield Chambers
www.tanfieldchambers.co.uk

Contents

Part I: Termination and the Right to Possession

Part II: Termination and the Right to Possession—Particular Cases

Part III: The Proceedings for Possession

Part IV: Appendices

Appendix 1: Two Rent/Housing Act Exceptions

Appendix 2: Statutory Extracts

Appendix 3: Housing and Regeneration Act 2008
Schedule 11 Part 2

List of Forms

Table of Cases

Table of Statutes

Table of Statutory Instruments

Table of Civil Procedure Rules

Part 1

Termination and the Right to Possession

Chapter 1

Has a Tenancy Been Created?

This chapter is concerned with preliminary matters that sometimes arise in **1.001**
possession proceedings relating to the existence or otherwise of a tenancy. The
distinction between a tenancy and a licence is dealt with in Ch.5. The basic
rules as to termination of tenancies and recovery of possession are dealt with in
Chs 2 and 3.

The requirement of certainty

A fundamental requirement of all leases and tenancy agreements is that the **1.002**
commencement date and the duration of the term must be certain. The parties
must be able to ascertain the date of commencement and the maximum duration
of the term at the outset of the tenancy. If it is not possible to do so the lease is
void. However, if the tenant takes possession and pays rent on a periodic basis in
accordance with the terms of the agreement, a periodic tenancy is created on the
terms of the agreement so far as they are consistent with a periodic tenancy. Such
a tenancy is certain because each party has the power to determine it by service of
an appropriate notice to quit (*Prudential Assurance Co Ltd v London Residuary
Body* [1992] 2 A.C. 386; [1992] 3 W.L.R. 279 HL; see also *Liverpool City Council
v Walton Group Plc* [2002] 1 E.G.L.R. 149 Ch D).

The requirement of certainty was raised in *Mexfield Housing Co-operative v
Berrisford* [2011] UKSC 52 where the agreement was stated to run "from month
to month until determined as provided in this agreement". The only term in relation to termination by the landlord was for re-entry in the event of default by the
tenant. As there was no ability for the landlord to determine the tenancy by a
notice to quit, it was for an uncertain term. However, it took effect as a 90 year
lease determinable on death (by virtue of s.149 of the Law of Property Act 1925),
which could otherwise only be determined in accordance with the right of re-
entry clause in the agreement. It could not be determined by a one-month notice
to quit.

Fixed terms: when is a deed required?

Where the tenancy is for a fixed term of more than three years it must be **1.003**
created by deed. If it is not created by deed it will be void (unless a periodic

tenancy can be implied or it operates as an equitable lease, see below (para.1.010)). A fixed term of three years or less may be granted either orally or in writing if it takes effect in possession (i.e. if it takes effect from the time it is created; see *Long v Tower Hamlets LBC* [1998] Ch. 197; [1996] 3 W.L.R. 317 Ch D) at the best rent which can be reasonably obtained without taking a fine (see ss.52 and 54(2) of the Law of Property Act 1925). A lease is regarded as being for a term of more than three years even if it contains a term permitting termination within that period (*Kushner v Law Society* [1952] 1 K.B. 264; [1952] 1 All E.R. 404 DC).

Formalities for creation of leases: Law of Property Act 1925 sections 52 to 55

52.—(1) All conveyances of land or of any interest therein are void for the purpose of conveying or creating a legal estate unless made by deed.

(2) This section does not apply to . . .

    (d)   leases or tenancies not required by law to be made in writing . . .

    (g)   conveyances taking effect by operation of law.

53.—(1) Subject to the provisions hereinafter contained with respect to the creation of interests in land by parol—

    (a)   no interest in land can be created or disposed of except by writing signed by the person creating or conveying the same, or by his agent thereunto lawfully authorised in writing, or by will, or by operation of law . . .

54.—(1) All interests in land created by parol and not put in writing and signed by the persons so creating the same, or by their agents thereunto lawfully authorised in writing, have, notwithstanding any consideration having been given for the same, the force and effect of interest at will only.

(2) Nothing in the foregoing provisions of this Part of this Act shall affect the creation by parol of leases taking effect in possession for a term not exceeding three years (whether or not the lessee is given power to extend the term) at the best rent which can be reasonably obtained without taking a fine.

55. Nothing in the last two foregoing sections shall . . . affect the right to acquire an interest in land by virtue of taking possession.

Executing the deed

Individuals

1.004 Since July 31, 1990 it has no longer been necessary for an individual to seal a deed. The deed is validly executed if it is duly signed and delivered. The procedure is governed by s.1 of the Law of Property (Miscellaneous Provisions) Act 1989.

Deeds and their execution: Law of Property (Miscellaneous Provisions) Act 1989 section 1

1.—(1) Any rule of law which—

    (a)   restricts the substances on which a deed may be written;

    (b)   requires a seal for the valid execution of an instrument as a deed by an individual; or

    (c)   requires authority by one person to another to deliver an instrument as a deed on his behalf to be given by deed, is abolished.

(2) An instrument shall not be a deed unless—

    (a)   it makes it clear on its face that it is intended to be a deed by the person making it or, as the case may be, by the parties to it (whether by describing itself as a deed or expressing itself to be executed or signed as a deed or otherwise); and
    (b) it is validly executed as a deed—

        (i)   by that person or a person authorised to execute it in the name or on behalf of that person, or
        (ii) by one or more of those parties or a person authorised to execute it in the name or on behalf of one or more of those parties.

(2A) For the purposes of subsection (2)(a) above, an instrument shall not be taken to make it clear on its face that it is intended to be a deed merely because it is executed under seal.

(3) An instrument is validly executed as a deed by an individual if, and only if—

    (a)   it is signed—

        (i)   by him in the presence of a witness who attests the signature; or
        (ii) at his direction and in his presence and the presence of two witnesses who each attest the signature; and

    (b) it is delivered as a deed.

(4) In subsections (2) and (3) above "sign", in relation to an instrument, includes

    (a)   an individual signing the name of the person or party on whose behalf he executes the instrument; and
    (b) making one's mark on the instrument,

and "signature" is to be construed accordingly.

(4A) Subsection (3) above applies in the case of an instrument executed by an individual in the name or on behalf of another person whether or not that person is also an individual.

(5) Where a solicitor or licensed conveyancer, or an agent or employee of a solicitor or licensed conveyancer, in the course of or in connection with a transaction, purports to deliver an instrument as a deed on behalf of a party to the instrument, it shall be conclusively presumed in favour of a purchaser that he is authorised so to deliver the instrument.

(6) In subsection (5) above—"purchaser" has the same meaning as in the Law of Property Act 1925;

(10) The references in this section to the execution of a deed by an individual do not include execution by a corporation sole . . .

(11) Nothing in this section applies in relation to instruments delivered as deeds before this section comes into force.

Companies

The law relating to execution of documents and deeds by companies registered with **1.005** the Companies Act is contained in ss.44 and 46 of the Companies Act 2006. Since April 6, 2008 a company can execute a document either by its common seal, by two authorised signatories or by a director whose signature is witnessed. Authorised signatories means every director of the company and a company secretary.

The execution of a deed by a company is governed by s.46:

Section 46 Execution of deeds

(1) A document is validly executed by a company as a deed for the purposes of section 1(2)(b) of the Law of Property (Miscellaneous Provisions) Act 1989 (c. 34) and for the purposes of the law of Northern Ireland if, and only if—

(a) it is duly executed by the company, and
(b) it is delivered as a deed.

(2) For the purposes of subsection (1)(b) a document is presumed to be delivered upon its being executed, unless a contrary intention is proved.

Finally, by s.47 the company may, by an instrument executed as a deed, empower a person to execute deeds on its behalf.

Where the deed or document was executed prior to that date, then the Companies Act 1985 ss.35 and 35AA are relevant.

For other corporations see s.74A of the Law of Property Act 1925.

Delivery of deeds

1.005A In *Longman v Viscount Chelsea* [1989] 2 E.G.L.R. 242 Nourse L.J. at 245E explained that there are three ways in which a deed may be "delivered":

"First, it may be delivered as an unconditional deed, being irrevocable and taking immediate effect. Second, it may be delivered as an escrow, being irrevocable but not taking effect unless and until the condition or conditions of the escrow are fulfilled. Third, it may be handed to an agent of the maker with instructions to deal with it in a certain way in a certain event, being revocable and of no effect unless and until it is so dealt with, whereupon it is delivered and takes effect."

Registration of leases

1.006 Since the coming into force of the Land Registration Act 2002 on October 13, 2003, it has been necessary to register all leases granted for more than seven years from the date of the grant (s.4(1)(c) of the 2002 Act). It has also been necessary to register the grant of a lease "to take effect in possession after the end of the period of three months beginning with the date of the grant" (s.4(1)(d)), the grant of any right to buy lease (s.4(1)(e)), the grant of any preserved right to buy lease, i.e. a person previously a secure tenant (s.4(1)(f)); and also the assignment of a lease with more than seven years to run at the date of the assignment (s.4(1)(a)). These provisions do not apply where the transfer takes effect by operation of law or to any assignment or surrender of a lease to the owner of the immediate reversion where the term is to merge in that reversion (s.4(3)(4)). If the registration requirement is not carried out the transfer, grant or creation becomes void (see further ss.7 and 8 of the 2002 Act). However, in situations where the tenant is in occupation under the void lease, the parties will generally be regarded in equity as being landlord and tenant and the landlord will be unable to recover possession. The issue of registration or lack of it takes on more importance where the landlord has assigned the reversion (see para.4.002).

In most cases, prescribed clauses must be inserted into a registrable lease granted out of a registered estate on or after June 19, 2006, i.e. the parties, the property, the term, restraints on alienation (see Land Registration Rules 2003 r.58A and Sch.1A).

Prior to the coming into force of the 2002 Act the general position was that a lease granted for a term of more than 21 years was required to be registered. See further ss.8, 22, 123 and 123A of the Land Registration Act 1925, as amended by the Land Registration Act 1997, in respect of leases granted on or after April 1, 1998. For leases granted before that date see ss.8, 22 and 123 prior to amendment by the 1997 Act.

If a lease which is required to be registered is not registered within the two-month period the transfer, grant or creation becomes void but takes effect as a contract made for valuable consideration to grant or create the legal estate concerned. An application can be made to the registrar either before or after the two months has elapsed seeking an extension of time. The Applicant must put forward a good reason why the extension should be granted (see ss.6(5) and 7 of the Land Registration Act 2002; see *also Rother Investments v Corke* [2004] 2 P. & C.R. 311, where there had been re-entry before registration of the transfer of the reversionary interest. This was held to have been a forfeiture by estoppel).

Periodic terms and tenancies at will

Periodic tenancies are tenancies that are granted on a yearly, monthly, weekly or indeed any other periodic basis. They are not tenancies just for the period specified, but are tenancies which continue from period to period indefinitely until determined by notice to quit (*Leek and Moorlands Building Society v Clark* [1952] 2 Q.B. 788 at 793). A periodic tenancy may be created by oral agreement (*Hammond v Farrow* [1904] 2 K.B. 332 at 335). **1.007**

A "tenancy at will exists where the tenancy is on terms that either party may determine it at any time" as opposed to a periodic tenancy which is one that "continues from period to period indefinitely until determined by proper notice" (*Javad v Aqil* [1991] 1 All E.R. 243, CA, per Nicholls L.J. at 244). A tenancy at will may, therefore, be determined by simply asking the tenant to leave, or by the service of proceedings for possession (*Martinali v Ramuz* [1953] 2 All E.R. 892). No special form of notice is required.

Estoppel between landlord and tenant

Where a person has been granted a tenancy both he and the landlord are estopped from denying its existence. The landlord cannot derogate from the tenant's grant and the tenant cannot dispute the landlord's title, even though the landlord has no interest in the land. Thus, if the landlord sues the tenant for possession the tenant cannot defend himself by saying "the property does not belong to you but to another" (*Industrial Properties (Barton Hill) Ltd v Associated Electrical Industries Ltd* [1977] Q.B. 580 at 596; *Stratford v Syrett* [1958] 1 Q.B. 107). **1.008**

The doctrine does not depend upon the grantor having purported to grant a tenancy. Even if he is purporting to grant a licence, if in fact it is a tenancy (see para.5.002), the grantor will be estopped from denying that there is a tenancy (*Bruton v London Housing Trust* [1999] 3 All E.R. 481 HL at 487):

> "... it is not the estoppel which creates the tenancy, but the tenancy which creates the estoppel. The estoppel arises when one or other of the parties wants to deny one of the ordinary incidents or obligations of the tenancy on the ground that the landlord had no legal estate. The basis of the estoppel is that having entered into an agreement which constitutes a lease or a tenancy, he cannot repudiate that incident or obligation" (*Bruton*, per Lord Hoffmann at 488c).

The principle applies whether the tenancy was created by deed, other writing or orally and whatever the length or period of the term. The estoppel applies to successors in title (*Mackley v Nutting* [1949] 2 K.B. 55).

As to whether the tenant can rely upon proof of termination of the landlord's title as a defence to a claim for possession brought by the landlord see *Halsbury's Laws of England and Wales*, 4th edn (London: Butterworths, 1985–1992), Vol.16(2), para.1035.

An estoppel between a landlord and a tenant does not prevent the true owner of the property with a better claim to possession from denying the tenancy. Where a tenant has been removed by such a person the tenant will only be able to sue his landlord for breach of the covenant for quiet enjoyment if the covenant is an unqualified one (*Halsbury's Laws of England and Wales*, 5th edn (2012), paras 657 and 658).

See also *Asher v Whitlock* (1865) LR 1 Q.B. 1 (referred to in *Wibberley Ltd v Insley* [1999] 2 All E.R. 897 HL at 901a) for the general principle "that possession is good against all the world except the person who can show a good title" which applies to all persons in possession including trespassers who can therefore evict subsequent trespassers.

> "The burden was upon Wibberley to show that it had a better title than Mr Insley. He was in possession and therefore needed to show no title at all. Possession is in itself a good title against anyone who cannot show a prior and therefore better right to possession: Asher v Whitlock" (per Lord Hoffmann).

Possession pursuant to agreement for lease or void lease

Introduction

1.009   Where a finally concluded agreement for a lease has been entered into (see para.1.011) but no lease has actually been granted, or where a lease is void because it was granted for a term of more than three years and was not made by deed (see para.1.003), the parties will nevertheless be regarded as landlord and tenant if the latter has actually entered into possession. However, the precise status of the occupant is different depending upon whether the common law applies or the rules of equity apply.

Difference between common law and equity

1.010   If the agreement provides for rent to be calculated on a yearly basis the tenant is regarded by the common law as being a tenant from year-to-year upon the terms of the intended lease but only so far as they are consistent with a yearly tenancy (*D'Silva v Lister House Development Ltd* [1970] 1 All E.R. 858). Thus, whatever the terms of the proposed lease, the tenancy is determinable by six months' notice to quit, although note that at the end of the intended term the tenancy comes to an end without the necessity of a notice. If the rent is calculated on a monthly or weekly basis the tenant has only a monthly or weekly tenancy (*Adler v Blackman* [1953] 1 Q.B. 146).

The rules of equity take the matter further. If the agreement is such that it is capable of being specifically enforced the tenant will be treated in equity as holding the property under the same terms as if the lease had been granted (*Walsh v Lonsdale* (1882) 21 Ch D 9). A void lease (i.e. a lease in respect of which the formal requirements have not been complied with) (see para.1.003) is treated for this purpose as being an agreement for a lease on the terms contained therein (*Parker v Taswell* (1858) 2 De G & J 559).

Where the *Walsh v Lonsdale* doctrine applies the tenant may rely upon it as a defence to a claim for possession whether the landlord commences proceedings in the county court or the High Court (*Kingswood Estate Co Ltd v Anderson* [1963] 2 Q.B. 169). However, an action for specific performance of the agreement may only be commenced in the county court if the value of the property (i.e. of the freehold interest) does not exceed the county court limit, presently £30,000 (s.23(d) of the County Courts Act 1984; *Foster v Reeves* [1892] 2 Q.B. 255; *Angel v Jay* [1911] 1 K.B. 666; *Amec Properties Ltd v Planning Research & Systems* [1992] 2 E.G.L.R. 70) unless the parties agree in writing to confer jurisdiction on the county court (s.24 of the 1984 Act).

The difference between the position at common law and in equity is unlikely to be of importance where the tenant has some statutory protection but may be crucial where he has no such protection. If, for example, the landlord serves a six-month notice to quit so as to terminate the tenancy at the end of the first year, he will not be entitled to possession at its expiry if the tenant can show that he has an equitable lease of more than one year.

Finally concluded agreement

It cannot be stressed too highly that there must be a finally concluded agreement. **1.011** The court will not order specific performance if there are any terms still being negotiated. For a case in which there was no finally concluded agreement see *Brent London Borough Council v O'Bryan* [1993] 1 E.G.L.R. 59, CA—agreement to let a scout hut on a monthly basis on terms to be laid down by valuers.

However, for the *Walsh v Lonsdale* doctrine to apply, it is not necessary that all the terms should have been agreed. What is required is agreement as to the "essential terms", that is, agreement as to the parties to the lease, the property to be let, the commencement and duration of the term and the rent or other consideration to be paid. If those terms have been agreed and no other terms have been offered but left unaccepted the court will, subject to any equitable reasons for not doing so, make an order for specific performance of a lease, such lease to contain "usual covenants" (see generally *Halsbury's Laws of England and Wales*, 5th edn (2012), Vol.62, paras 77 and 84; and see further note (7) below page 11).

Agreement to be in writing

By virtue of s.2 of the Law of Property (Miscellaneous Provisions) Act 1989 a **1.012** contract for the grant of a lease of more than three years (s.2(5)(a)), entered into on or after September 27, 1989 (the date upon which the Act came into force), can only be made in writing and all the terms which the parties have expressly agreed must be contained in one document which must be signed by or on behalf of each party to the contract. Where contracts are exchanged, all the express terms must be contained in each contract and one of the documents, but not necessarily the same one, must be signed by or on behalf of each party.

Law of Property (Miscellaneous Provisions) Act 1989 section 2

2.—(1) A contract for the sale or other disposition of an interest in land can only be made in writing and only by incorporating all the terms which the parties have expressly agreed in one document or, where contracts are exchanged, in each.

(2) The terms may be incorporated in a document either by being set out in it or by reference to some other document.

(3) The document incorporating the terms or, where contracts are exchanged, one of the documents incorporating them (but not necessarily the same one) must be signed by or on behalf of each party to the contract.

(4) Where a contract for the sale or other disposition of an interest in land satisfies the conditions of this section by reason only of the rectification of one or more documents in pursuance of an order of a court, the contract shall come into being, or be deemed to have come into being, at such time as may be specified in the order.

(5) This section does not apply in relation to—

(a) a contract to grant such a lease as is mentioned in s.54(2) of the Law of Property Act 1925 (short leases);

(b) a contract made in the course of a public auction; or

(c) a contract regulated under the Financial Services Act 1986;

and nothing in this section affects the creation or operation of resulting, implied or constructive trusts.

(6) In this section—"disposition" has the same meaning as in the Law of Property Act 1925; "interest in land" means any estate, interest or change in or over land or in or over the proceeds of sale of land.

(7) Nothing in this section shall apply in relation to contracts made before this section came into force.

(8) Section 40 of the Law of Property Act 1925 (which is superseded by this section) shall cease to have effect.

Notes

(1) Section 2 is only relevant to executory contracts. It has no relevance to contracts that have been completed. If parties choose to complete a contract that does not comply with the section they are free to do so (*Tootal Clothing Ltd v Guinea Properties Management Ltd* [1992] 2 E.G.L.R. 80).

(2) As to the meaning of "where contracts are exchanged" see *Commissioner for New Towns v Cooper (Great Britain) Ltd* [1995] 2 E.G.L.R. 113—exchange of letters not good enough).

(3) Any variation of the contract which is material to the disposition of the land must also comply with the provisions of the Act (*McCausland v Duncan Lawrie* [1996] 4 All E.R. 995 CA—variation of the completion date).

(4) The printing or typing of a name is not a signature within the meaning of s.2(3). Under the 1989 Act the term "signed" has the meaning an ordinary person would understand it to have (*Firstpost Homes Ltd v Johnson* [1995] 4 All E.R. 355).

(5) An agreement for the grant of an option falls within s.2 and must therefore be signed by, or on behalf of, all parties to the contract, but a letter exercising the option is not a "sale or other disposition of an interest in land" and so need only be signed by the purchaser (*Spiro v Glencrown Properties Ltd* [1991] 1 All E.R. 600).

(6) The section does not apply where the lease is to be for a term of three years or less. Nor does it apply to auction sales or contracts regulated by the Financial Services Act 1986.

(7) Section 2(1) of the 1989 Act requires all terms "which the parties have expressly agreed" to be in one document or, where contracts are exchanged, in each. The authors' understanding of this section is that it does not affect the old rule that it is only necessary expressly to agree the essential terms (see above para.1.011) and that the court will still make an order for specific performance so long as the requirements of the section have been complied with in relation to those terms. However, all terms that have been agreed, whether material or not, need to be in the written agreement. If they are not the agreement will not be valid unless it can be shown that either (i) the omitted terms were actually part of a separate contract, or (ii) the written agreement can be rectified to include the omitted terms (*Ali Oun v Ishfaq Ahmad* [2008] EWHC 545 (Ch)).

(8) An oral compromise of a dispute containing a term which stated that "the property be sold with vacant possession at the best price available" was not a contract for the sale or other disposition of an interest in land. It amounted only to an agreement to enter into a contract and could not, therefore, amount to a contract to sell or dispose of an interest in land (*Nweze v Nwoko* [2004] EWCA Civ 379).

(9) Nothing in s.2 affects the creation or operation of resulting, implied or constructive trusts (s.2(5)). There is also such a close relationship between constructive trusts and estoppel—particularly in the area of joint enterprise for the acquisition of land—that the doctrine can operate to give effect to an agreement rendered void by the section (*Yaxley v Gotts* [2000] 1 All E.R. 711 CA—see also para.5.013).

(10) Where the agreement was entered into before September 27, 1989 the provisions of s.40 of the Law of Property Act 1925 apply to the contract.

Minors

Section 1(6) of the Law of Property Act 1925 prohibits minors from holding a **1.013** legal estate in land. Further, para.1(1) of Sch.1 to the Trusts of Land and Appointments of Trustees Act 1996 provides that any attempt to grant a legal estate to a minor will result in the grantor holding the land on trust for the minor. See further para.21.031.

Chapter 2

Forfeiture

A written tenancy agreement will usually contain a clause enabling the landlord to **2.001** forfeit the term if the tenant is in breach of one of the covenants in the lease: for example, for the payment of rent or service charges, the carrying-out of repairs or the prohibition of subletting.

Forfeiture brings the tenancy, and all interests derived from the tenancy (i.e. sub-tenancies, mortgages and other charges), to an end so that the landlord is immediately entitled to possession (*Official Custodian for Charities v Mackey* [1984] 3 All E.R. 689). If the tenant wishes to retain possession he will have to apply for relief from forfeiture which will invariably require payment of any arrears and the remedying of any breach of covenant. As forfeiture brings the tenancy to an end the landlord ceases to be entitled to rent that would otherwise become payable and may no longer rely upon the tenant's covenants in the lease, although he may sue in respect of past arrears and breaches.

If the landlord elects to pursue an alternative remedy and to waive the right to forfeit in respect of a particular breach he will not subsequently be allowed to forfeit in respect of that breach. "Waiver" is dealt with in detail below, para.2.048.

This chapter deals with the common law and statutory rules that generally apply in all forfeiture cases. The position was substantially changed by the Commonhold and Leasehold Reform Act 2002 which introduced major changes relating to long residential leases and can be summarised as follows:

- A requirement to serve notices demanding rent in prescribed form.

- A restriction on the ability to forfeit a lease for small sums unless they have been outstanding for a long period of time.

- Restrictions on forfeiture (including service of s.146 notices) unless the breach has first been established.

It should also be noted that the rules relating to forfeiture are modified in certain types of tenancy. The special rules that apply in any particular case are dealt with in the appropriate chapter. Note in particular that the normal rules of forfeiture do not apply to assured tenancies (see para.6.015).

Forfeiture clauses

Introduction

2.002   The usual name for the clause in a lease entitling the landlord to bring the tenancy
to an end prior to its originally intended expiry date is the "proviso for re-entry".
The proviso operates by entitling the landlord to re-enter the property if one of a
number of stated events occurs and goes on to declare that upon re-entry the lease
comes to an end; hence, the other title used: "forfeiture clause". By re-entry the
landlord forfeits the lease.

Where there is no express forfeiture clause in a lease, no such clause will be
implied. The landlord may, however, be able to forfeit without a forfeiture clause if an
event occurs which is specified as being a condition of the term (see s.146(7) of the
Law of Property Act 1925 at para.2.015, and see *Woodfall: Landlord and Tenant*,
(London: Sweet & Maxwell) para.17.058. Impugning the landlord's title might
amount to a repudiation of the lease which, if accepted by the landlord, is a breach of
an implied condition entitling the landlord to forfeit. However, the form or content of
a statement of case denying the landlord's title will not normally be a proper basis for
a landlord to forfeit a lease (*Crisp v Eastaugh* [2007] EWCA Civ 638 at paras 44–47).

Where the tenant holds over after the expiry of a fixed term so that he becomes
a periodic tenant (para.3.021), the forfeiture clause in the fixed term is carried
over into the periodic term (*Thomas v Packer* (1857) 1 H&N 699). A landlord who
has assigned the right to recover rent to a third party, may still rely on a forfeiture
clause for non-payment of rent (*Kataria v Safeland Plc* [1998] 1 E.G.L.R. 39).

Disguising the forfeiture clause so as to avoid relief provisions

2.003   The purpose of the forfeiture clause is to provide the landlord with security for
performance of the terms of the lease. The courts "lean against forfeiture" and if
the tenant remedies the breach he will invariably be able to obtain relief from
forfeiture. Any attempt, therefore, to exclude the court's equitable and statutory
jurisdiction to grant relief by dressing up a forfeiture clause as something else will
fail (*Richard Clarke & Co Ltd v Widnall* [1976] 1 W.L.R. 845 CA—a clause
providing for termination of the lease on non-payment of rent which required the
landlord to serve a termination notice in that event did not deprive the clause of its
status as a forfeiture clause and the tenant did not lose his right to claim relief).
But a clause requiring notice of termination upon default will only operate as a
forfeiture clause if it brings the lease to an end before its natural termination date
(*Clays Lane Housing Co-operative v Patrick* (1984) 49 P. & C.R. 72).

Furthermore, s.146(12) of the Law of Property Act 1925 expressly provides
that the relief provisions of that section will have effect notwithstanding any
stipulation to the contrary (para.2.015). A forfeiture in the guise of a surrender
remains a forfeiture for the purposes of the section (*Plymouth Corporation v
Harvey* [1971] 1 All E.R. 623).

Demands for Payment

Formal demands for rent

2.004   The common law requires a formal demand to be made for the rent before the
landlord can forfeit in respect of non-payment unless the lease dispenses with the

requirement. The modern forfeiture clause in dealing with non-payment of rent does dispense with the requirement for a formal demand. It provides for re-entry if the rent is more than, say, 21 days in arrears, whether or not the landlord has made a formal demand for overdue rent.

Statutory rent notices

However, s.166(1) of the Commonhold and Leasehold Reform Act 2002 applies **2.004A** to long leases of dwellings (i.e. leases granted for a term of years certain exceeding 21 years plus some others, such as right to buy and right to acquire leases (see ss.76 and 77 of the 2002 Act)). In these cases the tenant will

> "not be liable to make a payment of rent under the lease unless the landlord has given him a notice relating to the payment; and the date on which he is liable to make the payment is that specified in the notice" (s.166(1)).

The notice is in prescribed form (The Landlord and Tenant (Notice of Rent) (England) Regulations 2004 (SI 2004/3096)—see Form 1 of this book, p.16). The date specified in the notice must be:

- not less than 30 days before nor more than 60 days after the day on which the notice is given; and

- not before that on which he would have been liable to make it in accordance with the lease.

If the date on which the tenant is liable to make the payment is after that on which he would have liable to make it in accordance with the lease, any provisions of the lease relating to non-payment of rent (e.g. forfeiture clauses or clause relating to interest on late payments) will have effect accordingly (s.166(4)).

It is possible to send the notice by post (s.166(5)). If sent by post it must be addressed to

> "a tenant at the dwelling unless he has notified the landlord in writing of a different address in England and Wales at which he wishes to be given notices"

under the section in which case the notice must be addressed to him there (s.166(6)). Section 7 of the Interpretation Act 1978 applies so that service will be deemed to have taken place if the envelope is properly addressed and the correct postage paid unless a contrary intention appears; with deemed delivery in the ordinary course of post.

If the forfeiture clause does not dispense with the requirement of a formal demand and s.166 does not apply (because it is not a long lease) then the common law provides that such a demand must be made at the place specified in the lease or, if none is specified, at the demised premises. It must be made before sunset on the last day for payment and should only relate to the sum due in respect of the last rental period. However, the strict common law position is ameliorated by statute. In the county court, service of the "summons" in the action will count as a demand where there is one half year's rent in arrear and no sufficient distress is found on the premises (s.139(1) of the County Courts Act 1984; see para.2.083; presumably, since the CPR, service of the "claim form" will be sufficient). Where proceedings are commenced in the High Court see s.210 of the Common Law Procedure Act 1852.

Form 1: Ground Rent Notice

2.005

COMMONHOLD AND LEASEHOLD REFORM ACT 2002, SECTION 166

NOTICE TO LONG LEASEHOLDERS OF RENT DUE

To (*insert name(s) of leaseholder(s)*):
.... **(note 1)**

This notice is given in respect of (*address of premises to which the long lease relates*)
....

It requires you to pay rent of £ .... on (*insert date*) .... **(note 2)**

This rent is payable in respect of the period (*state period*).......

[In accordance with the terms of your lease the amount of £ .... is/was due on ....
(*insert date on which rent due in accordance with the lease*).] **(note 3)**

Payment should be made to (*insert name of landlord(s) or, if payment to be made to an agent, name of agent*) at (*insert address*)
....
....

This notice is given by (*insert name of landlord(s) and if not given above, address*)

NOTES FOR LEASEHOLDERS
Read this notice carefully. It sets out the amount of rent due from you and the date by which you must pay it. You are advised to seek help immediately, if you cannot pay, or dispute the amount. Those who can help you include a citizens' advice bureau, a housing advice centre, a law centre and a solicitor. Show this notice and a copy of your lease to whoever helps you.

The landlord may be able to claim additional sums from you if you do not pay by the date specified in this notice. You have the right to challenge the reasonableness of any additional sums at a leasehold valuation tribunal.

Section 167 of the Commonhold and Leasehold Reform Act 2002 and regulations made under it prevent your landlord from forfeiting your lease for non-payment of rent, service charges or administration charges (or a combination of them) if the amount owed is £350 or less, or none of the unpaid amount has been outstanding for more than three years.

NOTES FOR LANDLORDS
1. If you send this notice by post, address it to the leaseholder at the dwelling in respect of which the payment is due, unless he has notified you in writing of a different address in England and Wales at which he wishes to be given notices under section 166 of the Commonhold and Leasehold Reform Act 2002.
2. This date must not be *either* less than 30 days or more than 60 days after the day on which this notice is given *or* before that on which the leaseholder would have been liable to make the payment in accordance with the lease.
3. Include this statement only if the date for payment is not the same as the date determined in accordance with the lease.

Service charge, maintenance, insurance, etc. reserved as rent

2.006 Many leases contain covenants requiring the tenant to contribute to the cost of insuring the building of which the demised premises form part, and to pay service charges, etc. and these payments are expresssly deemed by the lease to be payable as rent. They are normally called "insurance rent", "additional rent", "maintenance rent" or some other similar term. Each covenant of this type and its relationship to the forfeiture clause must be construed according to the terms of the lease. However, the effect is usually that the service charge is recoverable as rent (*Escalus Properties Ltd v Robinson* [1995] 4 All E.R. 852 at 857 CA). It follows that, the landlord will not have to serve a notice under s.146 of the Law of Property Act 1925 in respect of the failure to pay these sums and that the relief provisions relating to non-payment of rent will apply (para.2.083), rather than s.146(2) of the 1925 Act which deals with relief in other cases (para.2.094). Morrit VC in *Freeholders of 69 Marina, St Leonards–on–Sea, Robinson, Simpson & Palmer v John Oram &*

Mohammed Ghoorun [2011] EWCA Civ 1258 suggested that in all service charge cases a s.146 notice does need to be served. It should be noted that *Escalus* was not cited to the Judge as so it may not be correct. However, in light of this decision, practitioners may consider it advisable to serve a s.146 notice in all service charge cases in order to avoid potential difficulties. A s.146 notice for use where these sums are not reserved and payable as rent is to be found at p.29 (Form 3).

In the context of exercising the discretion to grant relief, there is no difference in substance between a service charge payable as rent and a service charge payable pursuant to some other covenant. The same principles apply to both. They are covenants to pay money secured by the right of forfeiture and relief will invariably be granted if the tenant pays the arrears and costs (*Khar v Delbounty Ltd* [1996] E.G.C.S. 183 CA); although note that there are certain mandatory minimum requirements for relief where the proceedings are for non-payment of rent in the county court (s.138 of the County Courts Act 1984, see para.2.083). Prescribed information must also be included in the Particulars of Claim. (See para.25.016.)

Service charge demands—summary-tenant's rights and obligations

Each demand for a service charge must be accompanied by a summary of the **2.007** tenant's rights and obligations in relation to service charges. The tenant has a right to withhold payment if proper notice is not given (s.21B of the Landlord and Tenant Act 1985. The demand must comply with the Service Charges (Summary of Rights and Obligations, and Transitional Provision) (England) Regulations 2007; the Service Charges (Summary of Rights and Obligations, and Transitional Provisions) (Wales) Regulations 2007 (SI 2007/3160 (W.271))

Administration charge demands—summary of tenant's rights and obligations

An "administration charge" means an amount payable by a tenant of a dwelling as **2.007A** part of or in addition to the rent which is payable, directly or indirectly–

- for or in connection with the grant of approvals under his lease, or application for such approvals,

- for or in connection with the provision of information or documents by or on behalf of the landlord or a person who is a party to his lease otherwise than as landlord or tenant,

- in respect of a failure by the tenant to make a payment by the due date to the landlord or a person who is party to his lease otherwise than as landlord or tenant, or

- in connection with a breach (or alleged breach) of a covenant or condition in his lease.

(Section 158 and Sch.11 of the 2002 Act).

Each demand for an administration charge must have with it a summary of the tenant's rights and obligations in relation to administration charges. The tenant has a right to withhold payment if proper notice is not given (para.4, Sch.11 of the Commonhold and Leasehold Reform Act 2002). It is necessary for the demand to comply with the The Administration Charges (Summary of Rights and Obligations)

(England) Regulations 2007 (SI 2007/1258); The Administration Charges (Summary of Rights and Obligations, and Transitional Provisions) (Wales) Regulations 2007 (SI 2007/3162 (W.273)).

Restrictions on forfeiture

2.008 As stated in the introduction, the Commonhold and Leasehold Reform Act 2002 introduced major changes to the law on forfeiture. The provisions under discussion in this section are designed to prevent forfeiture (or even service of a s.146 notice—see para.2.013) where the sums in arrears are modest. There are also provisions designed to prevent forfeiture until the landlord has established the non-payment of service or administration charges or other breach of covenant.

Not for small sums unless unpaid for a long time

It is not possible to forfeit a long lease of a dwelling (see ss.76 and 77 of the 2002 Act for the definition of a long lease—essentially for a term exceeding 21 years) "for failure by a tenant to pay an amount consisting of rent, service charges or administration charges (or a combination of them) ('the unpaid amount') unless the unpaid amount (a) exceeds the prescribed sum, or (b) consists of or includes an amount which has been payable for more than a prescribed period" (s.167(1)).

The sum prescribed is £350 (subs.(2)). The prescribed period is three years. Thus, a landlord cannot forfeit for a sum of £350 or less unless it or a part of it is outstanding for a period of more than three years (the Rights of Re-entry and Forfeiture (Prescribed Sum and Period) (England) Regulations 2004 (SI 2004/3086)).

If the tenant is liable to pay an administration charge (see below) in respect of his failure to pay any part of the unpaid amount, that "default charge" is not included in determining the amount of the unpaid amount. This will stop landlord's from adding the default charge to the unpaid sum so as to take it over the prescribed limit (s.167(2)).

Service charges and administration charges

2.009 The restrictions in relation to service and administration charges are contained in s.81 of the Housing Act 1996. The definition of an administration charge is dealt with at para.2.007.

Housing Act 1996 section 81

2.010 Section 81 of the Housing Act 1996 (as amended by the 2002 Act on February 28, 2005 in England and May 31, 2005 in Wales) provides as follows:

> (1) A landlord may not, in relation to premises let as a dwelling, exercise a right of re-entry or forfeiture for failure by a tenant to pay a service charge or administration charge unless—
>
> > (a) it is finally determined by (or on appeal from) a leasehold valuation tribunal or by a court, or by any arbitral tribunal in proceedings pursuant to a post-dispute arbitration agreement, that the amount of the service charge or administration charge is payable by him; or
> >
> > (b) the tenant has admitted that it is so payable.

(2) The landlord may not exercise a right of re-entry or forfeiture by virtue of subs.1(a) until after the end of the period of 14 days beginning with the day after that on which the final determination is made.

(3) For the purposes of this section it is finally determined that the amount of a service charge or administration charge is payable—

    (a)   if a decision that it is payable is not appealed against or otherwise challenged at the end of the time for bringing an appeal or other challenge; or

    (b)   if such a decision is appealed against or otherwise challenged and not set aside in consequence of the appeal or other challenge at the time specified in subsection (3A).

(3A) The time referred to in subs.3(b) is the time when the appeal or other challenge is disposed of—

    (a)   by the determination of the appeal or other challenge and the expiry of the time for bringing a subsequent appeal (if any); or

    (b)   by its being abandoned or otherwise ceasing to have effect.

(4) The references in subsection (1) to premises let as a dwelling does not include premises let on—

    (a)   a tenancy to which Part 11 of the Landlord and Tenant Act 1954 applies (business tenancies);

    (b)   a tenancy of an agricultural holding within the meaning of the Agricultural Holdings Act 1986 in relation to which that Act applies, or

    (c)   a farm business tenancy within the meaning of the Agricultural Tenancies Act 1995.

(4A) References in this section to the exercise of a right of re-entry or forfeiture include the service of a notice under s.146(1) of the Law of Property Act 1925 (restriction on re-entry or forfeiture).

(5) In this section:

    (a)   "administration charge" has the meaning given by Pt 1 of Sch.11 to the Commonhold and Leasehold Reform Act 2002; [see para.2.007]

    (b)   "arbitration agreement", "arbitral tribunal" have the same meaning as in Pt 1 of the Arbitration Act 1996 and "post-dispute arbitration agreement", in relation to any matter, means an arbitration agreement made after a dispute about the matter has arisen;

    (c)   "dwelling" has the same meaning as in the Landlord and Tenant Act 1985;

    (d)   "service charge" means a service charge within the meaning of s.18(1) of the Landlord and Tenant Act 1985, other than one excluded from that section by s.27 of that Act (rent of dwelling registered and not entered as variable).

(6) Nothing in this section affects the exercise of a right of re-entry or forfeiture on other grounds.

Housing Act 1996 section 95

(1) Any jurisdiction expressed by a provision to which this section applies to be conferred on the court shall be exercised by a county court. **2.011**

(2) There shall also be brought in a county court any proceedings for determining any question arising under or by virtue or any provision to which this section applies.

(3) Where, however, other proceedings are properly brought in the High Court, that court has jurisdiction to hear and determine proceedings to which subs.(1) or (2) applies which are joined with those proceedings.

(4) Where proceedings are brought in a county court by virtue of subs.(1) or (2), that court has jurisdiction to hear and determine other proceedings joined with those proceedings despite the fact they would otherwise be outside its jurisdiction.

(5) The provisions to which this section applies are—

(a) section 81 (restrictions on termination of tenancy for failure to pay service charge) . . .

Landlord and Tenant Act 1985 section 18

2.012

(1) In the following provisions of this Act "service charge" means an amount payable by a tenant of a dwelling as part of or in addition to the rent—

(a) which is payable, directly or indirectly, for services, repairs, maintenance, improvements or insurance or the landlord's costs of management; and

(b) the whole or part of which varies or may vary according to the relevant costs.

Notes

(1) Subsection (1)(b) of s.81 of the Housing Act 1996 does not state that the admission must be in writing. Therefore, although in theory an oral admission or agreement will be sufficient, in practice the landlord will almost invariably be best advised to seek a determination unless he has a written admission.

(2) The right to forfeit is not exercisable until 14 days have elapsed after the determination. See further s.81(2), (3) and (3A) of the 1996 Act as substituted by s.170 of the 2002 Act.

(3) The phrase "exercise of a right of re-entry or forfeiture" includes service of a notice under s.146(1) of the 1925 Act. Thus, where the lease requires service of a s.146 notice, it is not possible to serve that notice until after the final determination of the dispute (s.81(4A) as inserted by s.170(5) of the 2002 Act).

(4) Where the landlord wishes the county court to determine the amount of the service charges he should probably do so by suing for the sum due. Simply seeking a declaration will not leave him with any other enforceable remedy if he subsequently decides not to forfeit. A judgment in default is a "determination" for the purposes of s.81 (*Southwark London Borough Council v Tornaritis* [1999] 7 C.L. 220, Cty Ct). In practice in most cases a determination will be made by the Leasehold Valuation Tribunal and cases started in the county courts are often transferred to the Tribunal (see para.2.014). They are a specialist tribunal with particular experience of service charge disputes. Enforcement is then by way of the county court. With that in mind it will usually be best to start out in the Tribunal.

(5) One of the effects of s.81 is that a lending institution with a charge on the property will no longer (or at least should not) pay the alleged arrears of service charges to the landlord unless it has some clear evidence that the tenant agrees or admits that the service charges are due or that there has been a county court or arbitral determination. Landlords should consider

whether or not it is appropriate, depending on the circumstances, to join a lender to such an application or at least to give them notice.

(6) As a general rule a landlord will not be able to forfeit a lease of a dwelling by peaceable re-entry, although there is no reason why he should not do so if there is clearly no one residing on the premises (Protection from Eviction Act 1977 s.2, para.2.072). However, the effect of s.81 is that he cannot re-enter even if the property is vacant unless the service charges have been agreed, admitted or determined.

(7) It is the service of the proceedings which operates as a forfeiture (para.2.074). Thus, in theory, it would seem that the landlord may issue proceedings but may not serve them until the service charges are agreed, admitted or determined. However, it is suggested that proceedings are not actually issued until after that time.

Other breaches—no section 146 notice unless liability first established (section 168)

By virtue of s.168 of the Commonhold and Leasehold Reform Act 2002 landlords **2.013** may not serve a notice under s.146(1) of the Law of Property Act 1925, in respect of any other breach, on a tenant unless:

- it has been finally determined on an application to the Leasehold Valuation Tribunal that a breach has occurred; or

- the tenant has admitted the breach; or

- a court in any proceedings, or an arbitral tribunal in proceedings pursuant to a post-dispute arbitration agreement, has finally determined that the breach has occurred.

As with the similar provisions in relation to service and administration charges (above) note that s.168 does not require an admission to be in writing. However, common sense dictates that it will not usually be advisable for the landlord to serve a s.146 notice if he is relying upon an alleged oral admission.

The landlord may not serve a notice until after the end of the period of 14 days beginning with the day after the date on which the final determination is made (i.e. in the case of a Leasehold Valuation Tribunal, court or arbitration determination); see s.169(2) and (3) for determining time.

Section 168 gives the LVT power to hear an application by a landlord for a determination that a breach has occurred (s.168(4)). But the landlord may not make such an application if the dispute has been:

- or is to be referred to post-dispute arbitration;

- determined by a court;

- has been determined by an arbitrator subject to a post-dispute agreement.

Landlords cannot manipulate the system by providing for the dispute to be determined in a particular manner or on particular evidence. Any agreement to that effect—except in a post-dispute arbitration agreement—is void (s.169(1)).

Leasehold Valuation Tribunals

2.014 The Leasehold Valuation Tribunal (LVT) has jurisdiction to deal with disputes between landlords and tenants in relation to service and administration charges. It may determine the reasonableness of a service charge and whether it is payable; by whom, to whom, the amount, the date and the manner payable. (Sections 19 and 27A of the 1985 Act). The jurisdiction applies "whether or not any payment has been made" (s.27A(2)). There are similar provisions that apply to "administration charges" (Sch.11 para.5). The LVT may also determine whether or not a service charge would be payable if costs were incurred on repairs, etc. (s.27A(3)). This is a useful tool for landlords on major projects who want to ensure that all the money will be recoverable after the works are done.

In determining whether a breach has occurred, the LVT has jurisdiction to decide whether the landlord has waived the covenant (*Swanston Grange (Luton) Management Limited v Langley-Essen* [2008] L. & T.R. 20, LT).

If there are proceedings before a court dealing with matters that fall within the LVT's jurisdiction, the court will be able to transfer those matters to the LVT; and is likely to do so (2002 Act Sch.12 para.3). For the procedure on transfer see CPR PD 56 para.15.1.

Section 146 notices

Introduction

2.015 If a landlord has established a breach of covenant in accordance with the provisions explained in paras 2.010 or 2.013 above (other than a covenant to pay rent: see s.146(11) of the Law of Property Act 1925) the landlord cannot (subject to certain limited exceptions set out in s.146(9) of the 1925 Act, see para.2.047) exercise any right of re-entry in the lease in respect of that breach unless he has first served a notice under s.146(1) of the 1925 Act. The notice must be in writing (s.196(1) of the Act; para.2.027).

Law of Property Act 1925 section 146

> (1) A right of re-entry or forfeiture under any proviso or stipulation in a lease for a breach of any covenant or condition in the lease shall not be enforceable, by action or otherwise, unless and until the lessor serves on the lessee a notice—
> (a) specifying the particular breach complained of; and
> (b) if the breach is capable of remedy, requiring the lessee to remedy the breach; and
> (c) in any case, requiring the lessee to make compensation in money for the breach;
>
> and the lessee fails, within a reasonable time thereafter, to remedy the breach, if it is capable of remedy, and to make reasonable compensation in money, to the satisfaction of the lessor, for the breach.
> (5) For the purposes of this section—

(a) "Lease" includes an original or derivative underlease; also an agreement for a lease where the lessee has become entitled to have his lease granted; also a grant at a fee farm rent, or securing a rent by condition.

(b) "Lessee" includes an original or derivative underlessee, and the persons deriving title under a lessee; also a grantee under any such grant as aforesaid and the persons deriving title under him.

(c) "Lessor" includes an original or derivative underlessor, and the persons deriving title under a lessor; also a person making such grant as aforesaid and the persons deriving title under him.

(d) "Underlease" includes an agreement for an underlease where the underlessee has become entitled to have his underlease granted.

(e) "Underlessee" includes any person deriving title under an underlessee.

(7) For the purposes of this section a lease limited to continue as long only as the lessee abstains from committing a breach of covenant shall be and take effect as a lease to continue for any longer term for which it could subsist, but determinable by a proviso for re-entry on such a breach.

(11) This section does not, save as otherwise mentioned, affect the law relating to re-entry or forfeiture or relief in case of non-payment of rent.

(12) This section has effect notwithstanding any stipulation to the contrary.

(13) The county court has jurisdiction under this section.

As the purpose and effect of a s.146 notice is to operate as a preliminary to forfeiture, service of such a notice cannot be an unequivocal affirmation of the existence of the lease and, therefore, does not operate to waive a right to forfeit (*Church Commissioners for England v Nodjoumi* (1986) 51 P. & C.R. 155; see para.2.051); but a notice served under s.146 should not contain a demand for arrears of rent accruing since the breach complained of in the notice. This is because the demand may possibly waive that breach, it not being necessary to serve a s.146 notice in respect of arrears of rent. **2.016**

Where the breach of covenant is a continuing one (see para.2.051), for example where the tenant is failing to keep the premises in good repair, and the landlord has waived the right to forfeit in respect of the earlier stages of the breach but is seeking to forfeit in respect of the stages that have occurred since the waiver, he does not need to serve a fresh s.146 notice if such a notice was served prior to the waiver and if there has been no change in the condition of the premises (*Greenwich London Borough Council v Discreet Selling Estates Ltd* [1990] 2 E.G.L.R. 65).

"It seems to me that a notice under section 146 asserts not only that the tenant is presently in breach but also that he will continue to be in breach unless and until he carries out the repairs required. It must necessarily assert that, if the landlord is to be able to rely at the trial on further delay which will have occurred up to the commencement of proceedings. In those circumstances I see no practical need for any fresh notice if a landlord wishes to rely on that continuing breach as a ground of forfeiture in the future and no legal reason why a fresh notice should be required in respect of the same defects" (*Greenwich LBC v Discreet Selling Estates Ltd*, per Staughton L.J. at 68).

Form 2: Section 146 notice—assignment

2.017

NOTICE SERVED PURSUANT TO section 146 OF THE LAW OF PROPERTY ACT 1925

Re: [*address of property*]

To: [*name of the assignee*]

I, [*name and address of the landlord*] hereby give you notice that:

1. The above-mentioned premises were let under a lease dated the [*insert date*] and made between [*state names*] for a term of [*insert number*] years commencing on the [*insert date*].

2. The lease contains a covenant not to assign, sublet or part with possession of the said premises without the written permission of the landlord.

3. This covenant has been broken in that on or about [*insert date*] [*name the original tenant*] assigned the lease to you without my previous consent.

4. I require you to remedy the breach if the same is capable of remedy.

DATED   [*signed by the landlord*]

Contents of the notice

2.018 Section 146(1) of the Law of Property Act 1925 requires that the notice should:

(1) specify the breach complained of; and

(2) if the breach is capable of remedy, require the tenant to remedy it; and

(3) in any case, require the tenant to make compensation in money for the breach.

The notice does not need to refer to the statute (*Van Haarlam v Kasner* [1992] 2 E.G.L.R. 59 Ch D).

A s.146 notice must be served even if the breach is not capable of remedy. The notice has a two-fold purpose; first, to give the tenant the opportunity to remedy the breach (if it is capable of remedy) before the landlord forfeits and second, to give the tenant the opportunity to apply to the court for relief (*Expert Clothing and Sales Ltd v Hillgate House Ltd* [1985] 2 All E.R. 998).

"In a case where the breach is 'capable of remedy' . . . the principal object of the notice procedure . . . is to afford the lessee two opportunities before the lessor actually proceeds to enforce his right of re-entry, namely (1) the opportunity to remedy the breach within a reasonable time after service of the notice and (2) the opportunity to apply to the court for relief from forfeiture. In a case where the breach is not 'capable of remedy', there is clearly no point in affording the first of these two opportunities; the object of the notice procedure is thus simply to give the lessee the opportunity to apply for relief" (*Expert Clothing*, per Slade L.J. at 1005c).

Each of the three requirements will be looked at in turn. Examples of s.146 notices are to be found above at p.24, Form 2 and p.29, Form 3.

Specify the breach

2.019 The breach complained of should clearly be set out in the notice. The usual practice is to set out the terms of the lease that have allegedly been breached and then to give details of the breach by reference to those terms. The notice will be invalid if it refers to the wrong covenant (*Jacob v Down* [1900] 2 Ch 156). The notice should precisely specify the breaches of covenant alleged. If it fails to do so it will be invalid and any entry pursuant to the notice unlawful (*Akici v LR Butlin Ltd* [2005] EWCA Civ 1296—notice accused the tenant of "parting" with possession when it should have alleged "sharing" possession!).

Remedy the breach

If a breach can be remedied, remedial action must be required of the tenant in the **2.020** notice but, notwithstanding the wording of s.146, it is not necessary to require the tenant to remedy the breach if it is not capable of remedy within a reasonable time after service of the notice (*Expert Clothing* at 1009f).

Whether a breach of covenant is "capable of remedy" for the purposes of s.146(1)(b) depends on whether the harm suffered by the landlord by the relevant breach is capable of being remedied in practical terms. The breach of a positive covenant, whether continuous or once and for all, is ordinarily remediable provided the remedy is carried out within a reasonable time. The amount of time that is to be regarded as reasonable will depend upon the particular circumstances of the case (*Expert Clothing* at 1008c).

The position, so far as negative covenants are concerned, is not quite so clear. Although there may be negative covenants that are capable of being remedied (*Scala House and District Property Co Ltd v Forbes* [1974] Q.B. 575 at 585), they are less likely to be remediable than positive ones. Fortunately, there are authorities in respect of some negative covenants. For example, if the tenant assigns, sublets or parts with possession in breach of covenant he commits an act which is incapable of remedy (*Scala House v Forbes*). Breach of a covenant not to use the premises for illegal or immoral purposes is a breach that is incapable of remedy if a stigma is thereby attached to the premises (*Rugby School (Governors) v Tannahill* [1935] 1 K.B. 87; *British Petroleum Pension Trust Ltd v Behrendt* [1985] 2 E.G.L.R 97 CA); but for the position where the sub-tenant has used the premises in an immoral or illegal way without the knowledge of the tenant, *see Glass v Kencakes Ltd* [1966] 1 Q.B. 611.

There is a definite move in the authorities towards holding that breaches are remediable. For example in *Akici v LR Butlin Ltd* [2005] EWCA Civ 1296 the court held that the proper approach should be "practical rather than technical" and that a breach of the covenant against sharing or parting with possession where it fell short of creating or transferring a legal interest (as in *Scala House*) was remediable.

If the mischief caused by the breach can be removed the breach is capable of **2.021** remedy for the purposes of the section. Thus, a covenant not to display trade or business signs can be remedied by taking the sign down (*Savva v Hussein* [1996] 2 E.G.L.R. 65 CA):

> "In my judgment, except in a case of breach of covenant not to assign without consent, the question is: whether the remedy referred to is the process of restoring the situation to what it would have been if the covenant had never been broken, or whether it is sufficient that the mischief resulting from a breach of covenant can be removed. When something has been done without consent, it is not possible to restore the matter wholly to the situation it was in before the breach. The moving finger cannot be recalled. That is not to my mind what is meant by a remedy, it is a remedy if the mischief caused by the

breach can be removed. In the case of a covenant not to make alterations without consent or not to display signs without consent, if there is a breach of that, the mischief can be removed by removing the signs or restoring the property to the state it was in before the alterations" (per Staughton L.J. at 66H).

If the landlord is not sure whether the breach is one that is capable of remedy his notice should require the tenant to remedy it "if it is capable of remedy" (*Glass v Kencakes Ltd* and see Form 2, p.24).

Although not required by s.146(1) it is common practice to state the time in which the breach is to be remedied, which must be a reasonable one. Three months will be sufficient in most cases (see *Gulliver Investments v Abbott* [1966] EGD 299—a repairs case, and para.2.029) but obviously every case will depend upon its own facts and in many cases a much shorter period will be all that is required (see *Courtney Lodge Management Ltd v Blake* [2005] L. & T.R. 2 CA, where the four days given to respond to the notice were held to be insufficient and therefore forfeiture had not been effected). A reasonable time to carry out repairs only commences from the date that the landlord enables access to the property (*Target Home Loans v Iza Ltd* [2000] 1 E.G.L.R. 23 CLCC overruled on another point in *Smith v Spaul* [2003] Q.B. 983, see para.2.036). Where the breach is incapable of remedy and the only purpose of the notice is to give the tenant the opportunity to apply for relief an extended period will not be necessary.

Compensation

2.022 Notwithstanding the terms of s.146(1)(c), the landlord need not include a provision in the notice requiring compensation if he does not in fact desire to be compensated (*Rugby School (Governors) v Tannahill*); but if he does not ask for it in the notice he will not be entitled to recover compensation in the proceedings (*Lock v Pearce* [1893] 2 Ch 271).

Surveyors' and solicitors' costs

2.023 Many leases contain specific provision for payment of professional fees incurred in the preparation and service of a s.146 notice even if forfeiture of a lease is avoided without a court order. However, even if there is no such clause in the lease s.146(3) provides for recovery of such costs.

Section 146(3) of the Law of Property Act 1925

2.024   (3) A lessor shall be entitled to recover as a debt due to him from a lessee, and in addition to damages (if any), all reasonable costs and expenses properly incurred by the lessor in the employment of a solicitor and surveyor or valuer, or otherwise, in reference to any breach giving rise to a right of re-entry or forfeiture which, at the request of the lessee, is waived by the lessor, or from which the lessee is relieved, under the provisions of this Act.

Service of the notice: upon whom

2.025 The notice should be served upon the tenant. If there is more than one tenant all the tenants must be served (*Blewett v Blewett* [1936] 2 All E.R. 188). Where the lease has been assigned, the notice should be served on the assignee and not the assignor, even if the assignment is unlawful. This is because the assignment, although unlawful, is effective to transfer the tenancy to the assignee. He is now the tenant and the person who is interested in avoiding the forfeiture (*Old Grovebury Manor Farm Ltd v W Seymour Plant Sales and Hire Ltd (No.2)* [1979] 1 W.L.R. 1397). It is not necessary to serve the notice on sub-tenants or mortgagees (*Egerton v Jones* [1939] 2 K.B. 702; *Church Commissioners for England v Ve-Ri-Best Manufacturing Co Ltd* [1957] 1 Q.B. 238).

Mode of service

Having said that the landlord must serve the notice on the tenant, it is not actually **2.026** necessary to search out the tenant and place the notice in his hand. The provisions of s.196 of the Law of Property Act 1925 (see below), as extended by s.1 of the Recorded Delivery Act 1962, apply. The effect of these sections is as follows:

(1) A s.146 notice is sufficiently served if it is sent by registered letter or recorded delivery addressed to the tenant by name at the tenant's last known place of abode or business in the United Kingdom. If the letter is not returned through the post office undelivered, service is deemed to be made at the time at which the letter would in the ordinary course of post be delivered (s.196(4)). To prove service the landlord need only show that the letter was prepaid, properly addressed and actually posted.

(2) The landlord may also serve the s.146 notice by leaving it at the tenant's last known place of abode or business in the United Kingdom or affixing it or leaving it for him on the land or on any house or building comprised in the lease (s.196(3)). If this method is used it is sufficient if it is addressed to "the lessee" (s.196(2)).

In either of the above two cases the landlord will not need to show that the tenant actually received the s.146 notice (*Re 88 Berkeley Road, London NW9* [1971] Ch 648). In *Van Haarlam v Kasner* [1992] 2 E.G.L.R. 59, a notice which was served at the property pursuant to s.196(3) was held to be good service even though at the date of service the landlord knew that the tenant was in prison and unlikely to receive it. See also *Blunden v Frogmore Investments Ltd* [2002] EWCA Civ 573; where the building was destroyed by a bomb and the notices sent to various addresses by recorded delivery were returned: nevertheless service was good.

The methods of service set out in s.196 are permissive. They do not have to be used. If the notice is in fact served by some other method, and it can be proved, that will be sufficient.

The notice may also be left at the tenant's property with some person provided that it is reasonable to suppose that it will be passed on to the tenant (*Cannon Brewery Co Ltd v Signal Press Ltd* (1928) 139 L.T. 384).

Law of Property Act 1925 section 196; service of notices

(1) Any notice required or authorised to be served or given by this Act shall be in **2.027** writing.

(2) Any notice required or authorised by this Act to be served on a lessee or mortgagor shall be sufficient, although only addressed to the lessee or mortgagor by that designation, without his name, or generally to the persons interested, without any name, and notwithstanding that any person to be affected by the notice is absent, under disability, unborn, or unascertained.

(3) Any notice required or authorised by this Act to be served shall be sufficiently served if it is left at the last-known place of abode or business in the United Kingdom of the lessee, lessor, mortgagee, mortgagor, or other person to be served, or, in case of a notice required or authorised to be served on a lessee or mortgagor, is affixed or left for him on the land or any house or building comprised in the lease or mortgage, or, in case of a mining lease, is left for the lessee at the office or counting-house of the mine.

(4) Any notice required or authorised by this Act to be served shall also be sufficiently served, if it is sent by post in a registered letter addressed to the lessee, lessor, mortgagee, mortgagor, or other person to be served, by name, at the aforesaid place of abode or business, office, or counting-house, and if that letter is not returned by the postal operator (within the meaning of the Postal Services Act 2000) concerned undelivered; and that service shall be deemed to be made at the time at which the registered letter would in the ordinary course be delivered.

(5) The provisions of this section shall extend to notices required to be served by an instrument affecting property executed or coming into operation after commencement of this Act unless a contrary intention appears.

(6) This section does not apply to notices served in proceedings in the court.

Tenant's action on receipt of notice

2.028 A tenant in receipt of a s.146 notice (who wishes to retain his lease) has three choices:

(1) He may remedy the breach complained of within the time stated, if the breach is capable of remedy.

(2) If he suspects that the landlord will re-enter without taking proceedings for possession, he may apply to the court for an injunction to prevent the landlord from so doing (see Ch.35). He may wish to apply for an injunction where the landlord has not established the breach in accordance with the provisions explained in paras 2.010 to 2.013 above or where the landlord specifies a time in which to remedy the breach which the tenant considers to be unreasonably short.

(3) He may apply for relief from forfeiture. He is entitled to make the application immediately on receipt of the notice and does not need to wait for the landlord to commence proceedings for possession (see para.2.095).

Depending upon the circumstances of the case, the tenant may wish to combine two or more of these courses of action, but where it is clear that the landlord will only forfeit by taking proceedings it will not be necessary to seek an injunction or to apply for relief prior to service of those proceedings.

Tenant's failure to comply with notice

2.029 If the tenant fails, within a reasonable time of service of the notice, to remedy the breach (if it is capable of remedy) and to make reasonable compensation in money to the landlord's satisfaction (if the landlord has required compensation), the landlord may re-enter the property and thereby forfeit the lease. If there is a person lawfully residing in the premises he may only do so by the issue and service of proceedings (see para.2.072). The landlord must not commence proceedings until a reasonable time has elapsed. This is the position even where the breach is incapable of remedy for even in these circumstances the tenant needs time to consider his position and to decide whether to apply for relief, and to take such action as will assist his claim (*Scala House*—14 days held sufficient in the circumstances of the case; and see *Expert Clothing* and *Courtney Lodge Management Ltd*, above, para.2.020).

Form 3: Section 146 notice–service charges

2.030

NOTICE PURSUANT TO section 146 OF THE LAW OF PROPERTY ACT 1925

To: [*name of tenant*]

Re: [*address of property*]

I, [*state name and address of the landlord*], hereby give you notice that:

1. The above-mentioned premises were let to you by me under a lease dated the [*insert date*] for a term of [*state number*] years commencing on the [*state date*].

2. By clause [*state number of clause*] of the lease you covenanted to pay service charges calculated in accordance with schedule [*state number of schedule*] to the lease on the usual quarter days.

3. In breach of this clause you failed to pay the sum of £ [*state amount*] due in respect of service charges on [*insert date*].

4. I require you to remedy the breach by paying the said sum within 7 days of service of this notice. If you fail to do so I shall take proceedings to forfeit your lease.

DATED   [*signed by the landlord*]

IMPORTANT NOTE

Section 81 of the Housing Act 1996 applies to this notice. By virtue of that section—A landlord may not, in relation to premises let as a dwelling, **exercise a right of re-entry or forfeiture** for failure by a tenant to pay a service charge or administration charge unless—(a) it is finally determined by (or on appeal from) a **leasehold valuation tribunal** or by a **court**, or by any arbitral tribunal in proceedings pursuant to a **post-dispute arbitration agreement**, that the amount of the service charge or administration charge is payable by him, or (b) the tenant had **admitted** that it is so payable.

Where the amount is the subject of a determination, the landlord may not exercise a right of re-entry or forfeiture until after the end of the period of 14 days beginning with the day after that on which that final determination is made.

For these purposes it is finally determined that the amount of a service or administration charge is payable—
(a)   if a decision that it is payable is not appealed against or otherwise challenged, at the end of the time for bringing an appeal or other challenge, or
(b)   if such a decision is appealed against or otherwise challenged and not set aside in consequence of the appeal or other challenge at the expiry of the 'relevant time' mentioned below.

The 'relevant time' is when the appeal or other challenge is disposed of—
(a)   by the determination of the appeal or other challenge and the expiry of the time for bringing a subsequent appeal (if any) or
(b)   by its being abandoned or otherwise ceasing to have effect.

Repairing covenants

Particular rules apply where the landlord is seeking to forfeit for breach of the **2.031** covenant to repair. In certain cases the landlord's right to recover possession is limited by the provisions of the Leasehold Property (Repairs) Act 1938 (see para.2.040 for the provisions of the Act). In all cases special rules apply in relation to service of s.146 notices.

Section 146 notices in repair cases

All s.146 notices in repair cases must, in accordance with the usual requirement to **2.032** specify the breach complained of, give details of the repairs that have not been carried out. The usual and most sensible practice is to attach a schedule of dilapidations prepared by a surveyor to the notice. However, it is not necessary to specify in the minutest detail the items that need repairing so long as the tenant clearly knows what he has to do to avoid forfeiture. The schedule of dilapidations will normally set out the work that is required to put the property into good repair, but it is not in fact necessary to specify the acts required to remedy the breach (*Fox v Jolly* [1916] 1 A.C. 1, 11), particularly, when the tenant knows or ought to know what is needed to be done (*Adagio Properties v Ansari* [1998] 2 E.G.L.R. 69 CA—where the tenant had turned one flat into two). The notice is not invalid if it alleges some breaches which were not in fact committed (*Blewett v Blewett* [1936] 2 All E.R. 188).

Where the lease was originally granted for a term of seven years or more, and more than three years or more remain unexpired at the date of service of the notice, the provisions of the Leasehold Property (Repairs) Act 1938 apply (see para.2.040). In those circumstances the landlord must serve the s.146 notice at least one month before he intends to re-enter and must inform the tenant in the notice of his right to serve a counter-notice. If the tenant does serve a counter-notice the landlord may not forfeit without the leave of the court (s.1 of the 1938 Act). As to the application for leave see para.2.037.

Service of the notice

Landlord and Tenant Act 1927 section 18

2.033   **18.**—(2) A right of re-entry or forfeiture for a breach of any such covenant or agreement as aforesaid [i.e. any covenant or agreement to keep or put premises in repair during the currency of a lease, or to leave or put premises in repair at the termination of a lease: see s.18(1) at para.2.044] shall not be enforceable, by action or otherwise, unless the lessor proves that the fact that such a notice as is required by s.146 of the Law of Property Act 1925 had been served on the lessee was known either—

    (a) to the lessee; or
    (b) to an underlessee holding under an underlease which reserved a nominal reversion only to the lessee; or
    (c) to the person who last paid the rent due under the lease either on his own behalf or as agent for the lessee or underlessee.

and that a time reasonably sufficient to enable the repairs to be executed had elapsed since the time when the fact of the service of the notice came to the knowledge of any such person.

Where a notice has been sent by registered post addressed to a person at his last known place of abode in the United Kingdom, then, for the purposes of this subsection, that person shall be deemed, unless the contrary is proved, to have had knowledge of the fact that the notice had been served as from the time at which the letter would have been delivered in the ordinary course of post.

This subsection shall be construed as one with s.146 of the Law of Property Act 1925.

2.034   Service of s.146 notices was dealt with in general terms at para.2.026. However, where one is concerned with breach of a repairing covenant there are further requirements imposed on the landlord in relation to service of the notice (s.18 of the Landlord and Tenant Act 1927). He may not exercise his right to re-enter unless he proves that service of the notice was known either:

    (1) to his tenant;
    (2) to a sub-tenant holding under a sub-lease which reserved only a nominal reversion to the tenant; or
    (3) to the person who last paid the rent,

and that a reasonable time has elapsed since the time when the fact of service was known to such a person.

However, the landlord's position is ameliorated by the fact that where the notice is sent by registered post or recorded delivery to a person at his last known place of abode in the United Kingdom, proof of posting means that the notice is deemed to have come to his knowledge in the ordinary course of post unless the contrary is proved (s.18(2) of the 1927 Act; s.1(1) of the Recorded Delivery Service Act 1962).

Tenant's action on receipt of the notice; counter-notice

The tenant has 28 days in which to serve a counternotice. If he serves the counter- **2.035**
notice within this period the landlord will (if the 1938 Act applies; see para.2.040) have to apply to the court for leave to re-enter the property, which the court will only grant in limited circumstances. If the tenant fails to serve a counter-notice within this period he will lose his rights under the Act. The counter-notice should inform the landlord that he claims the benefit of the 1938 Act.

Form 4: Application for leave under 1938 Act

2.036

Part 8 claim form

Note: these are the details to be inserted under the heading "details of claim"
I [*Name of the landlord*] of [*address*] applies to the Court for an order in the following terms.

1. Leave under section 1 of the Leasehold Property (Repairs) Act 1938 to take proceedings for the enforcement of its right of re-entry by reason of breaches of the repairing covenants contained in a Lease granted by the Applicant to the Respondent on _____ whereby the dwelling known as [*address of dwelling*] was demised to the Respondent for a term of _____ years from _____.

2. Leave under section 1 of the 1938 Act to take proceedings for damages for breaches of the said repairing covenants;

3. A direction under section 2 of the 1938 Act that the Applicant do have the benefit of section 146(3) of the Law of Property Act 1925 in relation to the costs and expenses incurred in reference to the said breaches; and

4. An order that the Respondent do pay the costs of this application.

The grounds upon which the Applicant claims to be entitled to the order are that the property is in a state of disrepair and that subs [*(a) and (d)*] of section 1(5) of the 1938 Act apply. Full particulars of the said grounds are set out in the witness statement of _____ dated _____ and filed with this application.

There is no prescribed form and a simple letter will suffice. A mortgagee in possession cannot serve a counternotice as they are not liable to the lessor to remedy the breach or to make compensation (see *Smith v Spaul* [2003] Q.B. 983, CA).

Section 23(2) of the Landlord and Tenant Act 1927, which authorises a tenant to serve documents on the person to whom he has been paying rent, applies in relation to service of the counternotice (s.51 of the Landlord and Tenant Act 1954).

Landlord's application for leave to enforce right of re-entry

The landlord will only be granted leave to re-enter the property (whether by **2.037**
proceedings or otherwise: s.1(1)(3)) if the landlord proves one of the five grounds set out in s.1(5) of the 1938 Act. The full subsection is at para.2.040. The grounds may be summarised as follows:

(a) immediate remedying of the breach is required to prevent substantial diminution in value of reversion, or substantial diminution has occurred;

(b) immediate remedying of the breach is required to comply with statute, bye-law, court order, etc.;

(c) immediate remedying of the breach is required in interests of occupiers other than the tenant;

(d) immediate remedying of the breach is cheap compared to result of delay.

CPR Pt 56 governs the claim for leave to re-enter. Paragraph 1 of CPR PD 56 states that the claimant must use the Pt 8 procedure as modified by Pt 56 and CPR PD 56. The claim form should therefore be a Pt 8 claim form (Form N208; see Form 4 above). The claim must be brought in the county court unless there are exceptional circumstances (CPR r.56.2; CPR PD 56 para.2.2). The witness statement relied on by the landlord will usually be made by the landlord's surveyor who, in addition to exhibiting the s.146 notice, should exhibit the original schedule of dilapidations served with the notice. It should also state the grounds in s.1(5) of the 1938 Act relied upon and the circumstances necessary to establish those grounds (see Form 5, page 36 for a precedent).

2.038   It is not good enough for the landlord to show that he has an arguable or prima facie case. He must prove on a balance of probabilities that one or more of the grounds set out in s.1(5) of the 1938 Act applies as at the date of hearing (*Associated British Ports v CH Bailey Plc* [1990] 1 All E.R. 929 HL; *Landmaster Properties Ltd v Thackeray Properties Service Ltd* [2003] 2 E.G.L.R. 30 QBD). Thus, if a dispute arises as to whether or not any of the grounds apply it will be necessary to have a full trial of the issue with oral evidence given.

The court may, in granting or refusing leave, impose on the landlord or the tenant such terms and conditions as it thinks fit (s.1(6)).

An application under the 1938 Act for leave to commence proceedings for forfeiture of a lease is a "pending land action" within the meaning of s.17(1) of the Land Charges Act 1972 and is, therefore, registrable as a "pending action" under s.5 of the 1972 Act (*Selim Ltd v Bickenhall Engineering Ltd* [1981] 3 All E.R. 210). Where the land is registered the action is protected by entry of a unilateral notice under s.34(2)(b) of the Land Registration Act 2002 (see also s.87(1)(a)).

Recovery of landlord's costs

2.039 Section 146(3) of the Law of Property Act 1925 gives the landlord the right to recover as a debt due to him all reasonable costs and expenses properly incurred in the employment of a solicitor and surveyor or valuer in reference to any breach giving rise to a right of re-entry which, at the request of the tenant, is waived by the landlord or for which the tenant is relieved under the provisions of the Act (see para.2.023). However, a landlord on whom a counternotice has been served under s.1 of the 1938 Act may not rely on s.146(3) unless he makes an application for leave under that section (s.2 of the 1938 Act).

Leasehold Property (Repairs) Act 1938

2.040   **1.**—(1) Where a lessor serves on a lessee, under subs.(1) of s.146 of the Law of Property Act 1925, a notice that relates to a breach of a covenant or agreement to keep or put in repair during the currency of the lease all or any of the property comprised in the lease, and at the date of the service of the notice three years or more of the term of the lease remain unexpired, the lessee may within 28 days from that date serve on the lessor a counternotice to the effect that he claims the benefit of this Act.

(2) A right to damages for a breach of such a covenant as aforesaid shall not be enforceable by action commenced at any time at which three years or more of the term of the lease remain unexpired unless the lessor has served such a notice as is specified in subs.(1) of s.146 of the Law of Property Act 1925, and where a notice is served under this subsection, the lessee may, within 28 days from the date of the service thereof, serve on the lessor a counternotice to the effect that he claims the benefit of this Act.

(3) Where a counternotice is served by a lessee under this section, then, notwithstanding anything in any enactment or rule of law, no proceedings, by action or otherwise, shall be taken by the lessor for the enforcement of any right of re-entry or forfeiture under any proviso or stipulation in the lease for breach of the covenant or agreement in question, or for damages for breach thereof, otherwise than with the leave of the court.

(4) A notice served under subs.(1) of s.146 of the Law of Property Act 1925 in the circumstances specified in subs.(1) of this section, and a notice served under subs.(2) of this section shall not be valid unless it contains a statement, in characters not less conspicuous than those used in any other part of the notice, to the effect that the lessee is entitled under this Act to serve on the lessor a counternotice claiming the benefit of this Act, and a statement in the like characters specifying the time within which, and the manner in which, under this Act a counternotice may be served specifying the name and address for service of the lessor.

(5) Leave for the purposes of this section shall not be given unless the lessor proves—

(a) that the immediate remedying of the breach in question is requisite for preventing substantial diminution in the value of his reversion, or that the value thereof has been substantially diminished by the breach;

(b) that the immediate remedying of the breach is required for giving effect in relation to the premises to the purposes of any enactment, or of any byelaw or other provision having effect under any enactment or for giving effect to any order of a court or requirement of any authority under any enactment or any such byelaw or other provision as aforesaid;

(c) in a case in which the lessee is not in occupation of the whole of the premises as respects which the covenant or agreement is proposed to be enforced, that the immediate remedying of the breach is required in the interests of the occupier of those premises or of part thereof;

(d) that the breach can be immediately remedied at an expense that is relatively small in comparison with the much greater expense that would probably be occasioned by postponement of the necessary work; or

(e) special circumstances which, in the opinion of the court, render it just and equitable that leave should be given.

(6) The court may, in granting or in refusing leave for the purposes of this section, impose such terms and conditions on the lessor or on the lessee as it may think fit.

2. A lessor on whom a counternotice is served under the preceding section shall not be entitled to the benefit of subs.(3) of s.146 of the Law of Property Act 1925 (which relates to costs and expenses incurred by a lessor in reference to breaches of covenant), so far as regards any costs or expenses incurred in reference to the breach in question, unless he makes an application for leave for the purposes of the preceding section, and on such an application the court shall have power to direct whether and to what extent the lessor is to be entitled to the benefit thereof.

3.   This Act shall not apply to a breach of a covenant or agreement in so far as it imposes on the lessee an obligation to put premises in repair that is to be performed upon the lessee taking possession of the premises or within a reasonable time thereafter.

7.—(1) In this Act the expressions "lessor", "lessee" and "lease" have the same meanings assigned to them respectively by ss.146 [see para.2.011] and 154 of the Law of Property Act 1925, except that they do not include any reference to such a grant as is mentioned in the said s.146, or to the person making, or to the grantee under such a grant, or to persons deriving title under such a person; and "lease" means a lease for a term of seven years or more, not being a lease of an agricultural holding within the meaning of the Agricultural Holdings Act 1986.

(2) The provisions of s.196 of the said Act [i.e. Law of Property Act 1925] (which relate to the service of notices) shall extend to notices and counternotices required or authorised by this Act.

Landlord and Tenant Act 1954 section 51

2.041   (3) The said Act of 1938 shall apply where there is an interest belonging to Her Majesty in right of the Crown or to a Government department, or held on behalf of Her Majesty for the purposes of a Government department, in like manner as if that interest were an interest not so belonging or held.

Damages for failure to repair

2.042 Where the landlord forfeits for breach of the repairing covenant it is also likely that he will wish to recover damages for breach of that covenant. A full discussion of the subject is beyond the scope of this book, but the following points are particularly worth noting.

Limitation on amount of damages

2.043 The sum that the landlord may recover for damages for breach of covenant to repair is limited by s.18(1) of the Landlord and Tenant Act 1927 to the amount by which the value of the landlord's interest in the property is damaged by the breach. The section also precludes the landlord from recovering damages if the landlord intended to pull down the premises or make structural alterations which would render the repairs valueless.

Landlord and Tenant Act 1927 section 18

2.044   (1) Damages for breach of a covenant or agreement to keep or put premises in repair during the currency of a lease, or to leave or put premises in repair at the termination of a lease, whether such covenant or agreement is expressed or implied, and whether general or specific, shall in no case exceed the amount (if any) by which the value of the reversion (whether immediate or not) in the premises is diminished owing to the breach of such covenant or agreement as aforesaid; and in particular no damage shall be recovered for a breach of any such covenant or agreement to leave or put premises in repair at the termination of a lease, if it is shown that the premises, in whatever state of repair they might be, would at or shortly after the termination of the tenancy have been or be pulled down, or such structural alterations made therein as would render valueless the repairs covered by the covenant or agreement.

If appropriate, the cost of repairs may be used as a guide to the amount of the diminution in value of the property (*Jones v Herxheimer* [1950] 2 K.B. 106), but if the repairs are not actually going to be carried out the cost of them is unlikely to be a good guide (*Smiley v Townshend* [1950] 2 K.B. 311). However, it does not necessarily follow that where repairs are not going to be done the damages will be nominal (*Culworth Estates Ltd v Society of Licensed Victuallers* [1991] 2 E.G.L.R. 54). In *Craven (Builders) Ltd v Secretary of State for Health* [2000] 1 E.G.L.R. 128 Ch D it was held that if the landlord was not going to carry out the repairs, the burden of proof that the cost of repairs is the measure of damages lies on the landlord. In that case the value of the property unrepaired was £245,000 and the cost of reinstatement would have been £312,000; however, there was no market for the property in good repair and the diminution in value was reduced to £40,000.

Even if there is evidence of disrepair and evidence of the cost to remedy the disrepair, no amount will be awarded if the disrepair has no material affect on the value of the property (*Ultraworth Ltd v General Accident Fire and Life* [2000] 2 E.G.L.R. 115, QBD, TCC). Further, if there were alternative and realistic uses for the property which would have reduced the affect of the disrepair on the value, this may reduce the amount of damages (*Sun Life Assurance Plc v Racal Traces Ltd* [2000] 1 E.G.L.R. 138, QBD, TCC and *P & O Property Holdings Ltd v Secretary of State for the Environment* (2000) February 16, TCC H.H. Judge Thornton QC (unreported)).

Date at which damages are assessed

Where the landlord has forfeited the lease by proceedings and is claiming damages **2.045** for failure to deliver up the property in good repair, the date at which damages are assessed is the date upon which proceedings in the forfeiture action were served. This is because the covenants in the lease are suspended on that date and, if the property is eventually forfeited and possession given, the tenant will have remained in occupation as a trespasser. If the ex-tenant has caused further damage after service of the claim the landlord should seek to recover his loss by claiming damages in tort (*Associated Deliveries Ltd v Harrison* (1984) 50 P. & C.R. 91, CA; see also para.2.074).

Form 5: Witness statement in support of application under 1938 Act

2.046

[*Name of Witness*] (1)
Dated ____________
Filled on behalf of the Claimant
[Refer to attachments]

IN THE COUNTY COURT

In the matter of the Leasehold Property (Repairs) Act 1938

BETWEEN:

[*Name of the Claimant*] *Claimant*

—AND—

[*Name of The Defendant*] *Defendant*

I, [*Name of the Claimant surveyor*], FRICS. Chartered Surveyor, of [*address*] will say as follows:

1. I make this witness statement with the authority of the Claimant and in support of its application for leave to take the proceedings referred to in the Claim dated ____________ and for the other relief sought in that application. I have been a qualified surveyor for ____________ years and am a partner in the firm of ____________ Chartered Surveyors, of ____________. The facts stated herein are within my own knowledge and belief.

2. The counterpart of the Lease dated ____________ between ____________ and ____________ referred to in the Claim is now produced and shown to me marked " ____________ I". Under the terms of the Lease the Claimant granted the Defendant a tenancy of the property known as ____________ for a term of ____________ years from ____________.

3. By Clause ____________ of the Lease, the Defendant covenanted with the Claimant to keep the Properly in good and proper repair. By Clause ____________ of the Lease the Defendant covenanted to pay to the Claimant the legal costs and surveyor's fees incurred by the Claimant in preparing a notice under section 146 of the Law of Property Act 1925.

4. On ____________ I visited the Property and subsequently prepared a Schedule of Dilapidation. I confirm that it is necessary to carry out the remedial works listed in the Schedule. I served a copy of my Schedule together with a notice under section 146 of the Law of Property Act 1925 and section 1 of the Leasehold Property (Repairs) Act 1938 upon the Defendant by recorded delivery on ____________. A copy of the notice and attached Schedule are now produced and shown to me marked " ____________ 2". A counternotice was served by the Defendant on ____________. A copy of that notice is now produced and shown to me marked " ____________ 3".

5. There are a large number of items in the Schedule. The items upon which the Claimant relies for the purpose of this application are marked with an asterisk on the copy exhibited to this witness statement. *All the items so marked relate to dampness. The property is being severely damaged by the ingress of water through the roof, and by rising damp around the foundations. If the remedial works are not carried out immediately there is a grave risk that the structural timbers could be affected by the damp penetration. It is, therefore, most urgent that steps are taken to eliminate dump penetration. The cost of the works listed in the Schedule connected with remedying the problem of damp is approximately ____________. If the works are left for any period and the structural timbers are affected the cost of remedying the defects will be greatly increased.*

6. Having regard lo the above, I consider that subsections (a) and (d) of section 1(5) of the Leasehold Property (Repairs) Act 1938 apply, namely:

(a) that the breaches must be remedied immediately in order to prevent substantial diminution in the value of the Claimant's reversion; and

(b) that the breach can be immediately remedied at an expense that is relatively small in comparison with a much greater expense that would probably be occasioned by postponement of the necessary work.

7. On ____________ I returned to the property. Notwithstanding service of the notice, the necessary repairs have not been carried out.

Statement of Truth etc.

Insolvency

2.047 Subsections (9) and (10) of s.146 are relevant on the bankruptcy of the tenant. Where the tenant is a corporation the term "bankruptcy" means the winding up of the company (s.205(1) of the Law of Property Act 1925).

Law of Property Act 1925 section 146(9)(10); Bankruptcy of the lessee

(9) This section does not apply to a condition for forfeiture on the bankruptcy of the lessee or on taking in execution of the lessee's interest if contained in a lease of—

(a) agricultural or pastoral land;

(b) mines or minerals;

(c) a house used or intended to be used as a public-house or beer-shop;

(d) a house let as a dwelling-house, with the use of any furniture, books, works of art, or other chattels not being in the nature of fixtures;

(e) any property with respect to which the personal qualifications of the tenant are of importance for the preservation of the value or character of the property, or on the ground of neighbourhood to the lessor, or to any person holding under him.

(10) Where a condition of forfeiture on the bankruptcy of the lessee or on taking in execution of the lessee's interest is contained in any lease, other than a lease of any of the classes mentioned in the last subsection then—

(a) if the lessee's interest is sold within one year from the bankruptcy or taking in execution, this section applies to the forfeiture condition as aforesaid;

(b) if the lessee's interest is not sold before the expiration of that year, this section only applies to the forfeiture condition aforesaid during the first year from the date of the bankruptcy or taking in execution.

The effect of those subsections is that, save in the limited circumstances set out in subs.(9), s.146 applies:

(1) forever, if the lease is sold within one year from the bankruptcy or winding-up;

(2) for a period of one year only, if the lease is not sold within that year.

Nothing in subs.(9) or (10) affects the right of sub-tenants to apply for an order under s.146(4) (s.1 of the Law of Property (Amendment) Act 1929), as to which see para.2.107.

Note that the Insolvency Act 1986 (as amended by the Insolvency Act 2000 and the Enterprise Act 2002) imposes restrictions on forfeiture, whether by peaceable re-entry or proceedings, against companies or individuals that are insolvent or facing insolvency. The restrictions in relation to individuals are set out in ss.252 to 254 of the 1986 Act. For companies in administration or in respect of which an application for administration has been made see paras 43 and 44 of Sch.B1 to the 1986 Act.

Waiver

Introduction

When a landlord becomes entitled to forfeit a lease, it only becomes forfeit **2.048** at his option. He can therefore either elect to continue with the lease or determine it.

> "[C]ommon law waiver, or waiver by election, proceeded upon the premise that the party said to be fixed by the waiver must have possessed two or more substantive but inconsistent rights, and his choice by overt act communicated to the other party to rely on one such right precluded him from later claiming the benefit of another" (per Laws L.J. in *Oliver Ashworth (Holdings) Ltd v Ballard (Kent) Ltd* [2000] Ch.12 at 32 CA).

The landlord waives the right to forfeit if, after becoming aware of the breach, he does any act which unequivocally recognises the continued existence of the tenancy:

> "The basic principle is that the court leans against forfeitures. Therefore, if a landlord, after he knows of a breach of covenant entitling him to forfeit a lease, either communicates to the tenant his election to treat the tenancy as continuing, or does any act which recognises the existence of the tenancy or is inconsistent with its determination, he is deemed to have waived the forfeiture. It is for the lessee to establish the facts which in law constitute the waiver" (*David Blackstone Ltd v Burnetts (West End) Ltd* [1973] 3 All E.R. 782, per Swanwick J. at 790f).

2.049 There is no waiver if at the time of the landlord's act he has no actual or implied knowledge of the breach (see *Official Custodian for Charities v Parway Estates Development Ltd* [1984] 3 All E.R. 679). The landlord must have knowledge of the breach before he can be said to have waived his right to forfeit. The knowledge required to put the landlord to his election is the knowledge of the basic facts which in law constitute the breach of covenant entitling him to forfeit the lease. Where the landlord suspects the breach but feels unable to prove it, see *Van Haarlam v Kasner* [1992] 2 E.G.L.R. 59 at 63. If he wishes to forfeit he will usually be best advised not to demand rent or take any other steps that may be construed as a waiver while he investigates the position.

Once the landlord or his agent, such as an employee working at the premises, has the requisite knowledge any appropriate act by the landlord or his agent will in law effect a waiver or a forfeiture (*David Blackstone Ltd v Burnetts (West End) Ltd* [1973] 3 All E.R. 782; *Metropolitan Properties Co Ltd v Cordery* (1979) 39 P. & C.R. 10):

> "It is also clear . . . that a principal is affected by the knowledge of his agent and that he cannot escape the consequences of an act done by one agent by saying that it was not that agent but another that had the actual knowledge . . . the knowledge required to put a landlord to his election is knowledge of the basic facts that in law constitute a breach of covenant entitling him to forfeit the lease. Once he or his agent knows these facts, an appropriate act by himself or any agent will in law effect a waiver or a forfeiture. His knowledge or ignorance of the law is . . . irrelevant" (per Swanwick J. at 789h, 795c).

2.050 The landlord does not need to know all the facts. It is sufficient if he knows that there has been a breach or if he is aware of facts that pointed to a breach of covenant or which should put him on inquiry as to the nature of the breach (*Metropolitan Properties Ltd v Cordery* [1979] 2 E.G.L.R. 78; *Cornillie v Saha* (1996) 72 P. & C.R. 147). Where the tenant has sublet the landlord need only know that there has been a sub-letting or parting with possession. He does not need to know the name of the sub-tenant or the length of the term, nor the rent payable (*Cornillie v Saha*).

However, simply allowing the tenant, to commit the breach without doing anything to prevent it is not sufficient to amount to a waiver (*Perry v Davies* (1858) CB(NS) 769).

To constitute a waiver the election must be communicated to the tenant:

"The landlord has an election whether to waive or to forfeit, and it seems to me as at present advised that a statement or act by the landlord which is neither communicated to the tenant nor can have any impact on the tenant should not be taken to be an election to waive the forfeiture" (*London & County (A&D) Ltd v Wilfred Sportsman Ltd* [1971] Ch 764, per Russell L.J. at 782A; see also Swanwick J. at 793c in *David Blackstone Ltd v Burnetts (West End) Ltd* [1973] 3 All E.R. 782).

"Continuing" and "once and for all" breaches

In considering whether or not a breach has been waived it is necessary to distin- **2.051** guish between "continuing" and "once and for all" breaches. Where the breach is a continuing one (for example, where the tenant is failing to keep the premises in good repair), the landlord will not be able to forfeit in respect of the earlier stage of the breach that he has waived, but he may forfeit for any continuation of the breach that has occurred since the waiver. Thus, if the tenant continues to fail to repair the premises after the waiver the landlord may forfeit. If a notice under s.146 of the Law of Property Act 1925 has previously been served in respect of the breach there is no need to serve a further notice if there has been no change in the condition of the premises (*Greenwich London Borough Council v Discreet Selling Estates Ltd* [1990] 2 E.G.L.R. 65; see para.2.016).

In most cases there is no difficulty in distinguishing between "continuing" and "once and for all" breaches. For example, failure to pay rent is a "once and for all" breach that can be waived by subsequent action (*Church Commissioners for England v Nodjoumi* (1986) 51 P. & C.R. 155). Breach of the covenant to repair is a "continuing" breach (*Penton v Barnett* [1898] 1 Q.B. 276; *Greenwich London Borough Council v Discreet Selling Estates Ltd* [1990] 2 E.G.L.R. 65); as is breach of the covenant to use the premises as a private residence (*Segal Securities v Thoseby* [1963] 1 Q.B. 887) or only for business use (*Cooper v Henderson* (1982) 263 E.G. 592 at 594).

The landlord may, of course, forfeit in respect of any breach that has occurred since the waiver whether the new breach is a "continuing" or "once and for all" breach. Waiver of the breach does not waive the existence of the covenant (see below, para.2.068).

Waiver by acceptance, etc. of rent

Acceptance of rent

Acceptance of rent payable in arrears, as a matter of law, waives the right to **2.052** forfeit. The landlord may not protect his position by accepting the rent "without prejudice" to that right. He must make an election: forfeiture or acceptance of the rent. He cannot have both (*Segal Securities v Thoseby* [1963] 1 Q.B. 887 at 898).

Acceptance of future rent payable in advance waives a "once and for all" breach which has occurred in the past (*Segal Securities* at 901) and apparently a breach which occurs in the period covered by the rent (*Segal Securities* at 901). So far as "continuing" breaches are concerned the acceptance of rent in advance can only waive those breaches that are at the time of the demand known to be "continuing" and will only waive them for such periods as it is definitely known they will continue:

" . . . I now turn to the important and decisive question as to the circumstances in which a demand for or acceptance of rent payable in advance constitutes a waiver of breaches during the period covered by the rent demanded. Clearly it cannot be a waiver of future breaches of which the landlord has no advance knowledge . . . Equally clearly, an acceptance of rent in advance does waive a once and for all—that is to say, a non-continuing—breach in the past: such a waiver applies both to the past and to the period covered by the rent.

As regards continuing breaches, it seems to me that, in the absence of express agreement, the acceptance of rent in advance can at highest only waive those breaches that are at the time of demand known to be continuing, and to waive them for such period as it is definitely known they will continue" (*Segal Securities Ltd v Thoseby* [1963] 1 Q.B. 887 per Sachs J. at 901).

2.053   Where rent is due in respect of two or more periods, a demand for rent in respect of the later period waives the breach in respect of the earlier period. For example, if the tenant fails to pay rent on the September quarter day and on the December quarter day, a demand for both lots of rent will waive the right to forfeit in respect of the failure to pay the September quarter. However, the demand for the December quarter will not waive the right to forfeit in respect of the failure to pay that sum. The landlord may demand and bring proceedings in respect of the rent for that quarter and obtain judgment for it; and if the tenant fails to pay still forfeit in respect of it (*Re Debtors Nos 13A10 and 14A10 of 1995* [1996] 1 All E.R. 691 Ch D).

"In my judgment, in the context of a lease containing a right of re-entry in the common form, as that in the present case, once an instalment of rent has not been paid in the period allowed by the lease for payment, there is nothing inconsistent between the landlords re-entering and their claiming or receiving the rent concerned. Their right of re-entry arises once the rent is unpaid within the specified period and by virtue of that non-payment. It is unaffected by demand for or acceptance of that instalment of rent outside the period permitted for payment" (per Rattee J. at 697b).

It is important to note that acceptance after the event giving the landlord the right to forfeiture of the rent that accrued prior to that date does not waive the right to forfeit in respect of that breach (*Stephens v Junior Army and Navy Stores Ltd* [1914] 2 Ch.516 at 523) – for an alternative view see Rix L.J. at para.31 in *Osibanjo v Seahive Investments Ltd* [2008] EWCA Civ 1282).

Where a landlord receives a cheque from a tenant which covers both rent and some other sum owing to the landlord, the landlord may cash the cheque and repay the balance relating rent without waiving the right to forfeit. This would seem to follow from *Osibanjo v Seahive Investments Ltd* [2008] EWCA Civ 1282, where it was held that acceptance of a cheque tendered by the tenant to discharge an outstanding bankruptcy sum and as part payment for arrears of rent, where the landlord returned the balance relating to rent and stated that "[f]or the avoidance of doubt the clearance of your cheque through this firm's client account should not be regarded as a waiver by our client of his right to forfeit the lease" did not amount to an act of waiver. Mummery L.J.:

" . . . the processing of the cheque is not in itself conclusive of the question whether the payment was accepted as rent. The processing is evidence of payment to Seahive, but for waiver of forfeiture it must also be shown that the payment was accepted and that it was accepted as rent by the landlord. In this case only part of the sum realised by the processing of the cheque was accepted. That sum related to the bankruptcy debt, which

Mr Osibanjo paid in order to secure the dismissal of the bankruptcy petition. It was
accepted on that basis and it was used to achieve that end. In my judgment, that was not
an acceptance of the balance by Seahive as rent." (para.22).

Where, in order to avoid waiver of the breach, the landlord refuses to accept rent **2.054**
he will subsequently be able to claim mesne profits (damages for use and occupation) in proceedings for possession and may seek an order for an interim payment
in those proceedings (CPR r.25.7(i)(d)).

Where the landlord delays in returning rental payments he may be held to have
accepted the rent and waived the right to forfeit. However, if the rent is returned
within a reasonable time of receipt he will not be regarded as having done so.
Some delay will be acceptable particularly if the landlord has written stating that
he will not accept rent. Every case will turn upon its own facts, the issue in each
case being whether or not the landlord can be said to have accepted the rent (*John
Lewis Properties Plc v Viscount Chelsea* [1993] 2 E.G.L.R. 77 Ch D).

Appropriation of payment to specific debt

Where several distinct debts are owing by a debtor to his creditor, the debtor **2.055**
has the right when he makes a payment to appropriate the money to any of the
debts that he pleases, and the creditor is bound if he takes the money, to apply
it in the manner directed by the debtor. If the debtor does not make any appropriation at the time when he makes the payment, the right of appropriation
devolves on the creditor (see generally *Chitty on Contracts*, edited by H.G. Beale,
31st edn (London: Sweet & Maxwell, 2012), Vol.1, paras 21.060–21.062). This
can be important where a landlord sues for rent and obtains a judgment. The
tenant goes into arrears again and the landlord decides to forfeit. If the tenant
then makes a payment and appropriates it to the latest sum due the landlord has no
right to forfeit. He cannot appropriate it to the earlier sums that were due. However,
if the tenant fails to appropriate the payment to the current rent the landlord
may appropriate it to the arrears. For an example of appropriation in a landlord
and tenant context see *Milverton Group Ltd v Warner World Ltd* [1995] 32
E.G. 70, CA.

"The relevant principles relating to appropriation are as follows. (1) The question is to
be decided as if it arose solely between the creditor and the person making the payment
[such as a surety: author's note]. The fact that someone else is liable for a debt to which
the payment could have been appropriated is irrelevant. (2) Appropriation is in the first
instance a matter for agreement between the creditor and the debtor. (3) If the agreement
contains no express or implied appropriation, the debtor may appropriate at the time
when he pays. (4) If the debtor does not appropriate at the time when he makes the
payment, the right of application devolves on the creditor. (5) The creditor may appropriate at any time thereafter. (6) Appropriation by the creditor depends upon his intention, express or implied or presumed. It is not governed by fixed rules, eg deeming the
payment to be appropriate to the first debt incurred" (*Milverton Group Ltd v Warner* per
Hoffmann, L.J. at 73).

See also *Thomas v Ken Thomas Ltd* [2006] EWCA Civ 1504 where, in a telephone
conversation, the landlord made it clear that he would not accept the appropriation
made on behalf of the tenant. The sums were paid by CHAPS directly into the
landlord's bank account and not returned. It was held that the landlord could not
do this. A creditor cannot unilaterally reject an appropriation made by a debtor.

If the landlord had not wished to accept the tenant's appropriation he needed to return the money. Neuberger L.J. at [28] after referring to the law on appropriation as set out in Chitty stated:

". . . (4) That law, properly applied, shows that, if he exercises the right, it is the tenant debtor who can appropriate, and that it is only if he does not do so that the creditor landlord is entitled to appropriate. (5) If the creditor landlord is unhappy with the appropriation to the extent of not being prepared to accept the money on the basis that it is offered, he can refuse it or if, as in this case, it is paid by CHAPS or a similar system, he can return it within a reasonable time. (6) Once the money is accepted or retained on the basis selected by the tenant, then, subject to any question of contrary agreement, estoppel or the like, the recipient of the money, the landlord, is as a matter of law fixed with the appropriation–and with its consequences in terms of waiver of forfeiture, which do not depend on what he intended."

Demand for rent

2.056 An unambiguous demand for rent that has accrued since the right to forfeit has arisen is no different from acceptance of rent. It amounts in law to an election to treat the tenancy as continuing and waives the right to forfeit if at the time it is made the landlord has sufficient knowledge (see above) of the facts to put him to his election. It does not matter that the demand was sent by mistake by a person employed by the landlord or his agent who has no personal knowledge of the breach. Likewise, the mere fact that the landlord did not intend to waive the breach is irrelevant (*David Blackstone v Burnetts (West End) Ltd* [1973] 3 All E.R. 782; *Central Estates (Belgravia) Ltd v Woolgar (No.2)* [1972] 3 All E.R. 610).

Unlike a demand for rent, a demand for payment of insurance sums which are not reserved as rent under the lease will not amount to a waiver, unless it amounts to an unequivocal acknowledgement of the continuation of the lease (see *Yorkshire Metropolitan v Co-operative Retail Service* [2001] L. & T.R. 298, Ch D).

Distress for rent

2.057 The general rule is that a distraint for rent does waive a prior breach (*Doe d David v Williams* (1835) 7 C&P 322). However, where the lease provides that a landlord may not forfeit for non-payment of rent until he has attempted to distrain for the rent, any such act of distraint does not operate as a waiver (*Shepherd v Berger* [1891] 1 Q.B. 597). In that case, part of the arrears were recovered by the distraint but that did not prevent the landlord from being able to forfeit in respect of the balance (see also s.139(1) of the County Courts Act 1984, para.2.083 and s.210 of the Common Law Procedure Act 1852 where the proceedings are in the High Court). Note that it is not possible to distrain in respect of various statutorily protected tenancies without leave of the county court (s.147 of the Rent Act 1977; s.8 of the Rent (Agriculture) Act 1976; s.19 of the Housing Act 1988).

Proceedings for rent

2.058 To bring a straightforward claim for rent is clearly no different from a demand for rent and thus waives the right to forfeit (*Dendy v Nicholl* (1858) 4 CB(NS) 376).

However, it often occurs that the tenant is in breach of covenant. The landlord serves a notice under s.146 of the Law of Property Act 1925, but before he commences proceedings a further quarter's rent falls due. If the rent is tendered and accepted the landlord waives the right to forfeit. If no rent is tendered may the landlord seek to forfeit in respect of both the earlier breach and the non-payment of rent and may he claim the arrears in the proceedings? The arguments each way are as follows.

On the one hand, the service of proceedings for possession is an unequivocal election to forfeit and anything else done or claimed in the proceedings cannot amount to a waiver (*Ivory Gate v Spetale* (1999) 77 P. & C.R. 141). On the other hand, a claim based upon non-payment of rent implies that the landlord considers the lease to be in existence on the date upon which the rent falls due. Such a claim is therefore inconsistent with an election to treat the lease as forfeited.

The decision in *Dendy v Nicholl* is sometimes cited as authority for the proposi- **2.059** tion that one may not make a claim for possession based upon forfeiture and claim arrears of rent. However, in *Penton v Barnett* [1898] 1 Q.B. 276 it was stated that *Dendy v Nicholl* is simply authority for the proposition that an action for rent is as good as a waiver of forfeiture as an action of possession is a forfeiture of the tenancy. In *Penton v Barnett* the lease contained a covenant to repair and the landlord served a s.146 notice requiring the tenant to repair within three months. Three days after the expiration of the notice a quarter's rent became due. No repairs having been carried out the landlord brought an action for possession based on the breach of covenant and non-payment of rent and in the proceedings claimed the quarter's rent (the defendant paid the rent into court). The Court of Appeal held that as the breach of covenant was a continuing one the claim for rent did not affect the right to possession in respect of non-repair after the date when the rent fell due. The implication is that the claim for rent in the proceedings did waive the failure to repair up to the date upon which the rent fell due and that if the breach had been a "once and for all" breach the claim for rent would have waived the breach.

> "The position on January 14, 1897 would be that as nothing had been done since the notice as to repairs, the plaintiff had the right to determine the tenancy by the issue of the writ, and to sue in respect of such rights as had accrued to him during the tenancy . . . Then he brought his action for possession, and in it he claimed for a quarter's rent due on the previous December 25. In my opinion, this claim does not constitute a waiver of the forfeiture. All that was laid down in Dendy v Nicholl was that an action for rent was as good as a waiver of forfeiture as an action of ejectment was as a determination of the tenancy. If there had not been a recurring breach, but something which had happened once and for all, the state of things might have been different; but in this case, in my opinion, there is nothing in the statement of claim inconsistent with an election to determine the lease from December 25" (*Penton v Barnett* [1898] 1 Q.B. 276 per Rigby L.J. at 280–281).

In conclusion, therefore, it would seem that a claim for arrears of rent that is **2.060** included in proceedings for possession based upon forfeiture for breach of covenant will waive the breach if it is a "once and for all" breach but not if it is a "continuing" breach (see also the discussion of *Penton v Barnett* in *Greenwich LBC v Discreet Selling Estates Ltd* [1990] 2 E.G.L.R. 65 at 67).

After re-entry has occurred the landlord is entitled to bring a claim for the rent that accrued prior to the re-entry (*Hartshorne v Watson* (1838) 4 Bing NC 178). Perhaps, therefore, the solution is to commence proceedings for possession based upon forfeiture for the breach of covenant with an alternative claim based upon forfeiture for non-payment of rent but not to include a claim for those arrears. Once those proceedings have been served (i.e. once the re-entry is deemed to have taken place; see para.2.074) a claim for rent up to the date of service of the proceedings (i.e. the date of re-entry) and for mesne profits thereafter can be issued and served. The two actions can then be consolidated.

Waiver by other means

2.061 Where no demand for rent is involved different considerations apply. The general principle was set out in *Expert Clothing Service and Sales Ltd v Hillgate House Ltd* [1985] 2 All E.R. 998.

> "In the present case where no acceptance of rent (or demand for rent) is involved, the court is, I think, free to look at all the circumstances of the case to consider whether [the landlord's act] was so unequivocal that, when considered objectively, it could only be regarded as having been done consistently with the continued existence of a tenancy" (per Slade L.J. at 1012c).

This general principle should always be borne in mind but there are also authorities dealing with particular circumstances.

Service of a notice to quit

2.062 Service of a valid notice to quit recognises the continuing existence of the lease and thus waives the right to forfeit (*Marche v Christodoulakis* (1948) 64 T.L.R. 466).

Service of a section 146 notice

2.063 As the purpose and effect of a s.146 notice is to operate as a preliminary to actual forfeiture (see para.2.016), service of such a notice cannot be an unequivocal affirmation of the existence of the lease and therefore does not operate to waive a right to forfeit (*Church Commissioners for England v Nodjoumi* (1986) 51 P. & C.R. 155); but a notice served under s.146 should not contain a demand for arrears of rent accruing since the breach complained of in the notice because the demand may possibly waive that breach, it not being necessary to serve a s.146 notice in respect of arrears of rent.

Negotiations that recognise the continued existence of the tenancy

2.064 In *Expert Clothing* the sending of a letter enclosing a proposed deed of variation was not, on the facts, regarded as a waiver but it was recognised that in certain circumstances the proffering of a mere negotiating document might amount to an unequivocal recognition of the existence of a presently subsisting tenancy (at 1012). But it seems that it will be necessary to know the terms of the negotiations before it will be held that the right to forfeit has been waived. The mere fact that negotiations have taken place will be insufficient and the court will not have regard to the contents of "without prejudice" negotiations (*Re National Jazz Centre Ltd* [1988] 2 E.G.L.R. 57).

"The test that was adopted by Slade L.J. in Expert Clothing ... was whether the sending of a letter in the course of negotiations could be reasonably understood as unequivocally indicating the landlord's intention to treat the lease as subsisting on the date of the letter.

The facts of that case were much stronger than the present case in favour of the tenant's submission of the existence of the lease, in that a draft had been proffered which referred to the continuation of a lease. Nevertheless, the Court of Appeal held that there had been no such waiver. That case in itself demonstrates that the mere existence of negotiations is not sufficient to show that the landlord participating in the negotiations is accepting that the tenancy does not exist and that there has been no forfeiture. It is true that if rent is proffered and accepted without prejudice, the court will look at the fact of acceptance of the rent and will hold that is sufficient to constitute an admission of the existence of the lease and a waiver of any forfeiture said to have occurred prior to that date. But I cannot see that there is any similarity between the acceptance of a rent without prejudice and the mere entering into of negotiations. It is impossible, in my judgment, to reach a conclusion that there has been an unequivocal acceptance of the existence of a lease by the entering into of negotiations, without looking at what occurred in the [without prejudice] negotiations themselves, and that, it is quite clear . . . is something which the court cannot do" (per Gibson J. at 58H).

Form 6: Letter accepting mesne profits

2.065

Dear

RE: _____

Please find enclosed a claim form claiming possession of the property which you occupy at _____ .

All further payments in respect of your occupation of the property should be sent to _____ at _____. These payments will be accepted by your landlord as damages for your use and occupation of property whilst the proceedings continue, it being clearly understood that acceptance by the landlord of such sums does not give rise to the creation of a new tenancy.

Yours etc

Grant of a reversionary lease

The grant of a reversionary lease "subject to and with the benefit" of the tenant's **2.066** lease does not waive the right to forfeit. It is not an unequivocal act of recognition of the pre-existing lease and as a statement or act which is neither communicated to nor could have any impact on the tenant is not an election to waive a right to forfeit (*London & County (A&D) Ltd v Wilfred Sportsman Ltd* [1971] 1 Ch D 764).

Court proceedings; injunction claim

A claim in forfeiture proceedings for possession and an injunction restraining the **2.067** tenant from continuing with the breaches will waive the right to forfeit. However, the landlord may seek an injunction in the alternative without waiving the right to forfeit (*Calabar Properties Ltd v Seagull Autos Ltd* [1969] 1 Ch. 451). For an example of where the landlord waived his right to forfeit by seeking an injunction (as well as demanding rent) see *Iperion Investments Corporation v Broadwalk House Residents Ltd* [1992] 2 E.G.L.R. 235).

And in *Cornillie v Saha* (1996) 72 P. & C.R. 147 commencement of proceedings seeking access to a flat under the terms of the tenancy waived the right to forfeit even though the purpose of seeking access was to confirm that the tenant had sub-let.

Waiver of breach does not waive the covenant

2.068 It is sometimes thought that a waiver of a breach amounts to a waiver of the cove-nant, for example, that a waiver by the landlord of a particular sub-letting in breach of covenant prevents the landlord from complaining about sub-lettings that may occur in the future. This view is incorrect. Section 148 of the Law of Property Act 1925 expressly provides that this is not so "unless a contrary intention appears".

Section 148 of the Law of Property Act 1925

(1) Where any actual waiver by a lessor or the persons deriving title under him of the benefit of any covenant or condition in any lease is proved to have taken place in any particular instance, such waiver shall not be deemed to extend to any instance, or to any breach of covenant or condition save that to which such waiver specially relates, nor operate as a general waiver of the benefit of any such covenant or condition.

(2) This section applies unless a contrary intention appears . . .

However, circumstances may arise where the landlord is estopped from relying on a term of the lease (*Central London Property Trust Ltd v High Trees House Ltd* [1947] K.E. 130; *Brikom Investments Ltd v Carr* [1979] 2 All E.R. 753).

Clauses that attempt to avoid waiver

2.069 Some leases contain a proviso to the effect that the right to forfeit will continue notwithstanding the acceptance of or demand for rent by the landlord with knowl-edge of the breach. However, the consequences of an act, relied on by a tenant as a wavier, are a matter of law and not of intention (*David Blackstone v Burnetts (West End) Ltd* [1973] 3 All E.R. 782 at 789h). It is, therefore, submitted that any clause in a lease which seeks to permit the landlord to forfeit notwithstanding an act waiving the breach is of no effect.

No waiver after service of proceedings

2.070 Once the landlord has unequivocally elected to re-enter, whether by service of a claim for possession or otherwise, no subsequent act will be treated as waiving the right to forfeit (*Civil Service Co-operative Society v McGrigor's Trustee* [1923] 2 Ch. 347 at 358). Further receipt of "rent" may, however, give rise to an inference that a new tenancy has been created (*Evans v Wyatt* (1880) 43 L.T. 176).

The landlord should not, therefore, accept any monies until after he has served his claim form and if he does so he is best advised to do so expressly on the basis that the payments are being accepted as mesne profits (damages for occupation) and that there is no intention to create a new tenancy. (For a specimen letter see Form 6, page 45.) Receipt of monies in such circumstances does not create a new tenancy because there is no intention to create legal relations (see discussion of *Street v Mountford*, Ch.5). See also the ability to apply for interim payments in respect of mesne profits (CPR r.25.6).

The act of re-entry

Where an event has occurred permitting the landlord to forfeit, he must do some **2.071**
act evidencing his intention to re-enter. Service of a claim for possession is equivalent to an act of re-entry and this is the normal method by which a landlord of
residential premises forfeits a lease (see para.2.074). Two other methods of
re-entry are as follows.

Peaceable re-entry

At common law peaceable re-entry brings the lease to an end, but a landlord is not **2.072**
permitted to enforce a right of re-entry where the premises were "let as a dwelling"
otherwise than by proceedings in court while any person is lawfully residing in
them or part of them (s.2 of the Protection from Eviction Act 1977).

Protection from Eviction Act 1977

> 2. Where any premises are let as a dwelling on a lease which is subject to a right of
> re-entry or forfeiture it shall not be lawful to enforce that right otherwise than by proceed-
> ings in the court while any person is lawfully residing in the premises or part of them.

Where the property is let for mixed residential and business purposes, for example
where it consists of a shop with a flat above, the property is to be regarded as
having been "let as a dwelling". That phrase means "let wholly or partly as a
dwelling". The landlord will not therefore be entitled to forfeit the lease of the
whole by re-entering the shop (*Patel v Pirabakaran* [2006] EWCA Civ 685).

Self-help is, therefore, only a practical proposition where it is clear that no-one
is living in the premises.

For a peaceable re-entry to be effective the landlord must actually re-enter the
property with the intention of terminating the tenancy but he does not need to be
in possession for any substantial period of time (*Billson v Residential Apartments
Ltd* [1992] 1 All E.R. 141 HL).

It is the intention to re-enter which is important. So long as the landlord intends to
bring the lease to an end it does not matter that he has made a mistake as to the identity of the tenant (*Eaton Square Properties Ltd v Beveridge* [1993] E.G.C.S. 91).

Where a landlord with a right to forfeit does an act which is inconsistent with
the continued existence of the lease, such as taking possession, it is not open to
him later to argue that he did not intend to forfeit the lease (*Re AGB Research Plc*
[1994] E.G.C.S. 73 Ch D). However, not every act that initially looks like a
re-entry is so. For example, if the circumstances are such that the tenant appears
to have disappeared from the property and the landlord has merely re-entered for
the purpose of securing the premises the lease will not have been brought to an
end (*Relvok Properties Ltd v Dixon* (1972) 25 P. & C.R. 1, CA).

Dealing with sub-tenants and other persons in actual occupation

In principle, it is possible to effect a re-entry of premises, where the person in **2.073**
occupation is a sub-tenant or trespasser as against the tenant, by coming to an
arrangement with the occupier whereby that person remains in occupation as the
immediate tenant of the landlord on the terms of a new tenancy (*London & County
(A&D) Ltd v Wilfred Sportsman Ltd* [1970] 2 All E.R. 600; *Ashton v Sobelman*

[1987] 1 All E.R. 755 at 763f and 764h; *Hammersmith and Fulham London Borough Council v Top Shop* [1989] 2 All E.R. 655 at 669e). See also *Redleaf Investments Ltd v Talbot, The Times*, May 5, 1994, Ch D. In that case the tenant was a company in administration. It was in arrears of rent and was no longer in occupation. The landlord granted an immediate lease to a third party. This grant was held to operate as a forfeiture of an existing lease and not the grant of a reversionary lease. However, where any such person is lawfully residing in the dwelling any such arrangement would, it is submitted, amount to a breach of s.2 of the Protection from Eviction Act 1977 and is not permitted (see para.2.072).

Forfeiture claims

Introduction

2.074   In nearly all cases a landlord of residential premises will seek to forfeit the lease by taking proceedings for possession (see above). Where he does so it is the service of the claim form (not its issue), which operates as the decisive election to forfeit and which is equivalent to re-entry (*Ivory Gate v Spetale* (1999) 77 P. & C.R. 141, CA). This has two consequences where possession is granted and there is no relief from forfeiture. First, rent is payable by the tenant up until the date of service of the proceedings. From that date the landlord is entitled to recover payments for the occupation of the land from the ex-tenant as trespasser, as mesne profits (damages for use and occupation), see *Canas Property Co Ltd v KL Television Services Ltd* [1970] 2 All E.R. 795, CA. See further Ch.28, Rent Cases (see reference to *Maryland v Josephs* (1998), para.2.084, where relief is granted). Second, from the date of service of the proceedings the tenant is no longer bound by any of the other covenants in the lease, such as the covenant to repair. If after that date the ex-tenant damages the property the landlord's remedy will be in tort (*Associated Deliveries Ltd v Harrison* (1984) 50 P. & C.R. 91, CA).

> ". . . in appropriate proceedings it seems to me that the landlord could well have a very adequate remedy in a claim for damages for wrongful occupation of the land . . . the authorities seem to indicate that in appropriately constituted proceedings the damages recoverable could extend beyond mere payment for the use and occupation of land, to include any loss within the ordinary rules of remoteness of damage which the plaintiff has suffered from being denied possession of the property and so unable to secure and occupy the property for his own purposes" (per Dillon L.J. at 103).

Form 7: Defence and counterclaim for relief from forfeiture

2.075

Form N11

DEFENCE

Note: insert the details below after "I dispute the claimant's claim because:—"

1. to 5. [*admit and deny the allegations in the Particulars of Claim as appropriate*]

COUNTERCLAIM

6. If, which is denied, the said lease has become liable to be forfeited the Defendant seeks to be relieved from the forfeiture on such terms as the court shall think fit.

AND the Defendant counterclaims for relief from forfeiture upon such terms as the court shall think fit.

The particulars of claim

The particulars of claim must be indorsed with the name and address of any **2.076** person entitled to claim relief against forfeiture as undertenant, including a mortgagee (CPR PD 55 para.2.4(1) and an equitable chargee, see *Croydon (Unique) Ltd v Wright* [2001] Ch 318, CA, see further para.2.117); and where such particulars are stated an extra copy of the particulars of claim should be filed with the court for service on that person (CPR PD 55 para.2.4(2)); see further Ch.26 in respect of proceedings.

Where the person concerned is a sub-tenant in occupation the landlord may **2.077** well wish to join him as a party to the proceedings in any event.

The claim form should not include a claim for an injunction in addition to the claim for possession as this may be construed as a waiver of the right to forfeit, although a claim in the alternative may be added (see above, para.2.067).

Where the tenant was a protected tenant under the Rent Act 1977 it is necessary for the landlord to obtain an order for possession based upon one of the Rent Act grounds, in addition to the forfeiture, but both the forfeiture and the Rent Act claims should be dealt with together (see para.8.024). For the position in relation to assured tenancies see para.6.009, and for the position in relation to secure tenancies see para.10.009.

Registration of the action

A claim for the forfeiture of a lease is a "pending land action" within the meaning **2.078** of s.17(1) of the Land Charges Act 1972 and is, therefore, registrable as a "pending action" under s.5 of the 1972 Act (*Selim Ltd v Bickenhall Engineering Ltd* [1981] 3 All E.R. 210). Where the land is registered the claim may be protected by entry of an unilateral notice under s.34(2)(b) of the Land Registration Act 2002 (see also s.87(1)(a)).

Summary judgment

A landlord cannot claim summary judgment against a defendant in proceedings **2.079** for possession of residential premises where he or she is holding over after the end of the tenancy and the occupation is protected within the meaning of Rent Act 1977 or the Housing Act 1988 (CPR r.24.3). However, even in other cases the nature of the procedure is likely to make such a step unnecessary; i.e. the summary nature of an undefended possession claim. Further, those acting for the tenant should bear in mind the case of *Liverpool Properties Ltd v Oldbridge Investments Ltd* [1985] 2 E.G.L.R. 111. It was held that a claim for relief is inextricably linked to the landlord's claim for possession and that if genuine and arguable it amounts to an arguable defence precluding the making of an order for possession on an application for summary judgment. There will be few cases where the court comes to the conclusion that the tenant's application for relief is bound to fail (*Sambrin Investment Ltd v Taborn* [1990] 1 E.G.L.R. 61 per Gibson J. at 63A).

Company in liquidation; the "Blue Jeans" order

If the letting was a "company let" and the tenant is a company in liquidation under **2.080** a winding-up order which has no defence to a claim for possession based upon forfeiture the landlord may, instead of issuing a claim (which would require leave from the companies court) and making an application for summary judgment, seek an order for possession in the winding-up (*Re Blue Jeans Sales Ltd* [1979] 1 All E.R. 641—possession was sought on the ground that the lease was forfeit by reason of non-payment of rent. It was not disputed that there were substantial arrears).

In *Re Blue Jeans Sales Ltd* the company had sub-let and there were sub-tenants in occupation. The question arose as to their protection as they were obviously not a party to the proceedings. The court held that the parties in actual occupation were protected by RSC O.45, r.3 (see para.34.001) which precludes the Companies Registrar from giving leave to issue a writ of possession until notice to the occupiers has been given enabling them to apply for relief from forfeiture.

Landlord seeking to withdraw the claim after tenant's admission

2.081 Where a landlord serves a claim form unequivocally electing to forfeit a lease and the landlord's claim is admitted by the tenant the landlord cannot subsequently withdraw the claim and argue that the lease remains in existence (*GS Fashions Ltd v B & Q Plc* [1995] 4 All E.R. 899 Ch D; see also *Kingston upon Thames Borough Council v Marlow* (1995) *The Times*, October 25, QBD). In an appropriate case the landlord will be able to avoid the problem by claiming an injunction as an alternative to forfeiture because proceedings making such a claim do not constitute an unequivocal election to determine the lease (see para.2.067).

> "In this case the landlord by its writ, after pleading a breach of the covenant against parting with possession, made the immediate election to forfeit. In law this was equivalent of the landlord peaceably re-entering and taking possession. Thereupon the tenant by its defence admitted and agreed the commission of the breach and the forfeiture, and the landlord's right to possession, and made no claim to relief. It seems to me that at this stage on the pleadings alone there is agreement resolving or obviating any dispute as to the landlord's entitlement to forfeit, and the forfeiture effected by service of the writ no longer remained open to challenge or question by the landlord. The lease is to be treated as determined by forfeiture as the parties intended" (*GS Fashions Ltd* per Lightman J. at 904f).

The limitations of the decision in *GS Fashions Ltd* were set out by Lightman J. at 906d:

> "I should emphasise certain limitations on the proposition of law on which I have founded this judgment. (1) I am concerned only with the rights inter se as between lessor and lessee. I am not here concerned only with the situation where there is a sub-tenant or mortgagee of the lease. Confirmation or validation of a forfeiture by the lessee alone may not prejudice the entitlement of a sublessee or mortgagee to challenge the validity of the forfeiture and accordingly to maintain the continued subsistence of their interests. (2) I do not have to consider the position where after service of the writ the lessee in its defence denies the entitlement to forfeit and how far it is open to the parties and in particular the lessor to challenge his pleadings and position thereafter. But as it seems to me, by parity of reasoning, if the lessee alleges that the forfeiture was invalid, the lessor should be able to concede and agree the lessee's contention and on that basis withdraw his claim to forfeiture. (3) The lessor can avoid the situation arising in this

case by claiming in the alternative in his writ forfeiture and relief (e.g. an injunction restraining or remedying breaches of covenant) which presupposes the continued existence of the lease, leaving his election between remedies (unless previously exercised) to the trial."

Dismissal or discontinuance of a forfeiture claim—no admission

The dismissal of a forfeiture claim, whether by compromise or otherwise, has the consequence that the forfeiture has not been established and the lease, whatever its status might have been during the action, is fully restored (*Hynes v Twinsectra Ltd* [1995] 2 E.G.L.R. 69, CA): **2.082**

> "The order made was that that action should be dismissed, and it seems to me impossible to contend, once that has happened, that any conclusion follows other than that the forfeiture has not been established. The lease, whatever may have been its status pending that action, must, in my judgment, be taken to have been fully restored when the action was dismissed ... In my view, once the forfeiture proceedings were dismissed, the contention that the lease did not exist cannot be accepted. There was no need for a grant of relief to restore the lease from the shadowy slate it had enjoyed to a full existence; the dismissal of the claim that had driven it into the shadows had that effect" (per Hutchinson L.J. at 73D).
> ... the authorities establish that service of proceedings for possession is an election by the lessor to treat the lease as forfeited. Further, it is to be taken as notional re-entry and thus forfeiture; but the act of forfeiture is subject to determination by the court of the validity of the claim. The lease is potentially good and the process of forfeiture is not complete until the proceedings are determined, which may include determination of an application for relief from forfeiture, but it will be a nullity if the proceedings do not succeed, or there is relief from forfeiture" (per Aldous L.J. at 73k).

The position is the same where the landlord has discontinued the claim before the tenant has admitted that forfeiture had taken place (*Mount Cook Ltd v Media Business Centre Ltd* [2004] EWHC 346, Ch).

Relief from forfeiture; non-payment of rent

County court

Sections 138 to 140 of the County Courts Act 1984 (as amended) contain the rules relating to relief from forfeiture where proceedings are brought in the county court. Section 138 applies where the landlord has commenced proceedings for possession. Section 139(2) applies where the landlord has re-entered the property without taking proceedings. **2.083**

County Courts Act 1984 sections 138–140

> **138.**—(1) This section has effect where a lessor is proceeding by action in a county court (being an action in which the county court has jurisdiction) to enforce against a lessee a right of re-entry or forfeiture in respect of any land for non-payment of rent.

(2) If the lessee pays into court or to the lessor not less than five clear days before the return day all the rent in arrear and the costs of the action, the action shall cease, and the lessee shall hold the land according to the lease without any new lease.

(3) If—

  (a) the action does not cease under subs.(2); and

  (b) the court at the trial is satisfied that the lessor is entitled to enforce the right of re-entry or forfeiture

the court shall order possession of the land to be given to the lessor at the expiration of such period, not being less than four weeks from the date of the order, as the court thinks fit, unless within that period the lessee pays into court or to the lessor all the rent in arrear and the costs of the action.

(3A) . . .

(4) The court may extend the period specified under subs.(3) at any time before possession of the land is recovered in pursuance of the order under that subsection.

(5) If—

  (a) within the period specified in the order; or

  (b) within that period as extended under subs.(4), the lessee pays into court or to the lessor—

    (i)   all the rent in arrear; and

    (ii) the costs of the action,

he shall hold the land according to the lease without any new lease.

(6) Subsection (2) shall not apply where the lessor is proceeding in the same action to enforce a right of re-entry or forfeiture on any other ground as well as for non-payment of rent, or to enforce any other claim as well as the right of re-entry or forfeiture and the claim for arrears of rent.

(7) If the lessee does not—

  (a) within the period specified in the order; or

  (b) within that period as extended under subs.(4), pay into court or to the lessor—

    (i)   all the rent in arrear; and

    (ii) the costs of the action

the order shall be enforceable in the prescribed manner and so long as the order remains unreversed the lessee shall, subject to subss.(8) and (9A), be barred from all relief.

(8) The extension under subs.(4) of a period fixed by a court shall not be treated as relief from which the lessee is barred by subs.(7) if he fails to pay into court or to the lessor all the rent in arrear and the costs of the action within that period.

(9) Where the court extends a period under subs(4) at a time when—

  (a) that period has expired; and

  (b) a warrant has been issued for the possession of the land,

the court shall suspend the warrant for the extended period; and, if, before the expiration period, the lessee pays into court or to the lessor all the rent in arrear and all the costs of the action, the court shall cancel the warrant.

(9A) Where the lessor recovers possession of the land at any time after the making of the order under subs.(3) (whether as a result of the enforcement of the order or otherwise) the lessee may, at any time within six months from the date on which the lessor recovers possession, apply to the court for relief; and on any such application the court may, if it thinks fit, grant to the lessee such relief, subject to such terms and conditions, as it thinks fit.

(9B) Where the lessee is granted relief on an application under subs.(9A) he shall hold the land according to the lease without any new lease.

(9C) An application under subs.(9A) may be made by a person with an interest under a lease of the land derived (whether immediately or otherwise) from the lessee's interest therein in like manner as if he were the lessee; and on any such application the court may make an order which (subject to such terms and conditions as the court thinks fit) vests the land in such a person, as lessee of the lessor, for the remainder of the term of the lease under which he has any such interest as aforesaid, or for any lesser term.

In this subsection any reference to the land includes a reference to part of the land.

(10) Nothing in this section or s.139 shall be taken to affect—

    (a) the power of the court to make any order which it would otherwise have power to make as respects a right of re-entry or forfeiture on any ground other than non-payment of rent; or

    (b) section 146(4) of the Law of Property Act 1925 (relief against forfeiture).

139.—(1) In a case where s.138 has effect, if—

    (a) one-half-year's rent is in arrear at the time of the commencement of the action; and

    (b) the lessor has a right to re-enter for non-payment of that rent; and

    (c) no sufficient distress is to be found on the premises countervailing the arrears then due,

the service of the summons in the action in the prescribed manner shall stand in lieu of a demand and re-entry.

(2) Where a lessor has enforced against a lessee, by re-entry without action, a right of re-entry or forfeiture as respects any land for non-payment of rent, the lessee may, at any time within six months from the date on which the lessor re-entered, apply to the county court for relief, and on any such application the court may, if it thinks fit, grant to the lessee such relief as the High Court could have granted.

(3) Subsections (9B) and (9C) of s.138 shall have effect in relation to an application under subs.(2) of this section as they have effect in relation to an application under subs.(9A) of that section.

140.—For the purposes of ss.138 and 139—

"lease" includes—

    (a) an original or derivative underlease;

    (b) an agreement for a lease where the lessee has become entitled to have his lease granted; and

    (c) a grant at a fee farm rent, or under a grant securing a rent by condition;

"lessee" includes—

    (a) an original or derivative underlessee;

    (b) the persons deriving title under a lessee;

    (c) a grantee under a grant at a fee farm rent, or under a grant securing a rent by condition; and

    (d) the person deriving title under such a grantee;

"lessor" includes—

    (a) an original or derivative underlessor;

    (b) the person deriving title under a lessor;

    (c)   a person making a grant at a fee farm rent, or a grant securing a rent by condition; and

    (d)   the person deriving title under such a grantor;

"underlease" includes an agreement for an underlease where the underlessee has become entitled to have his underlease granted; and "underlessee" includes any person deriving title under an underlessee.

Particular points to note are as follows:

2.084

(1) Relief granted by virtue of s.138 is restricted to cases of forfeiture for non-payment of rent. It has no application where there are arrears of service charges which are not deemed by the lease to be payable as additional rent (*Escalus Properties Ltd v Robinson* [1995] 4 All E.R. 852, CA).

(2) Under s.138 there is an automatic grant of relief if all the arrears and costs are paid into court not less than five clear days before the return date (s.138(2)). The words "all rent in arrears" includes the rent that has accrued since the proceedings began (see *Maryland Estates Ltd v Joseph* [1999] 1 W.L.R. 83 CA—a case on subs.(3) but which surely applies to this subsection). Relief is retrospective and the tenant is not obliged to pay anything further, such as mesne profits (*United Dominions Trust Ltd v Shellpoint Ltd* [1993] 4 All E.R. 310, CA; *Escalus Properties Ltd v Robinson* [1995] 4 All E.R. 852, CA).

(3) The "return date" referred to in s.138(2) is the date stated on the claim form for the hearing of the claim for possession. Thus, if the hearing does not go ahead on that date the tenant may not take advantage of this provision by paying the arrears and fixed court fee and fixed solicitor's costs not less than five clear days prior to the actual hearing (*Swordheath Properties Ltd v Bolt* [1992] 2 E.G.L.R. 68 CA). He will have to rely upon the other relief provisions in the section and pay any further costs that have been incurred in the meantime and that he may be ordered to pay.

(4) Where the money is not paid into court more than five clear days prior to the return date so that the case proceeds the court must give the tenant at least four weeks to pay the arrears and costs (s.138(3)). The phrase "all the rent in arrear" in s.138(3) includes an amount for the period between service of the claim and the date of the order for relief (*Maryland Estates Ltd v Joseph*).

(5) See *Thomas v Ken Thomas Ltd* [2006] EWCA Civ 1504, where Neuberger L.J. stated obiter "rent in arrears" does not include rent for which the right to forfeit had been lost. It only includes the specific rent arrears upon which the landlord has retained a right to forfeit. If so, this means that landlords have to be very careful about letting large arrears accrue and waiving the right to forfeit in respect of those historical sums.

(6) The order for possession is in County Court Form N27 or N27(2).

(7) An application for an extension under s.138(4) should be made on notice (CPR r.23).

(8) The words "the lessee shall be barred from all relief" in subs.(7) mean barred from relief in all courts. The tenant may not, therefore, attempt

to obtain relief in the High Court relying upon that court's inherent jurisdiction (*Di Palma v Victoria Square Property Co Ltd* [1985] 2 All E.R. 676), but by virtue of subs.(9A) the tenant may apply for relief in the county court at any time within six months from the date on which the landlord recovers possession.

(9) For the exercise of the discretion in cases where an application for relief is made under s.138(9A) or s.139(2) after physical re-entry see the cases mentioned below in relation to High Court applications for relief (para.2.085). See Form 9, p.58 for an order granting relief.

(10) Sub-tenants and mortgagees may apply for relief under s.138(9C)—see further para.2.107 et seq.

(11) Where the tenancy is in joint names it is probably necessary for any application under s.138(9C) or by a tenant pursuant to s.139(2) to be made by all the joint tenants (cf. *TM Fairclough & Sons Ltd v Berliner* [1931] 1 Ch. 60; *Jacobs v Chaudhuri* [1968] 2 Q.B. 470).

(12) Where relief is granted pursuant to subss.(9A) and (9B) the order is retrospective. The effect is that the tenant is obliged to pay only the arrears of rent and costs. However, it is likely to be the arrears of rent up until the date of the hearing (cf. *Maryland Estates v Joseph*). The court will not order the tenant to pay mesne profits from the date the proceedings were served (which may be higher than the rent) (*United Dominions Trust Ltd v Shellpoint Ltd* [1993] 4 All E.R. 310, CA; *Escalus Properties Ltd v Robinson* [1995] 4 All E.R. 852, CA).

(13) If a party cannot claim relief pursuant to s.138 or s.146 Law of Property Act 1925, proceedings can be transferred to the High Court, where the court can exercise its inherent jurisdiction to grant relief (s.42 of the County Courts Act 1984 and *Bland v Ingrams Estates Ltd* [2001] 2 W.L.R. 1638 CA—a charging order case).

(14) Where the landlord has peaceably re-entered and the tenant wishes to make a claim for relief from forfeiture, CPR Pt 55 applies and he must use Claim Form N5A. Note in particular r.55.3(1) and CPR PD 55 para.1 which require the claim to be made in the county court in nearly all cases.

Relief: high court

Senior Courts Act 1981 section 38

(1) In any action in the High Court for the forfeiture of a lease for nonpayment of rent, the court shall have power to grant relief against forfeiture in a summary manner, and may do so subject to the same terms and conditions as to the payment of rent, costs or otherwise as could have been imposed by it in such an action immediately before the commencement of this Act. **2.085**

(2) Where the lessee or a person deriving title under him is granted relief under this section, he shall hold the demised premises in accordance with the terms of the lease without the necessity for a new lease.

It will only be very rarely that a claim for possession will be brought in the High Court or that it will be appropriate to claim relief in the High Court (see para.25.012). However, in such a case the following will apply.

Time limits for applications

2.086 Where there are at least six months' rent in arrears, if at any time before the trial of the landlord's claim for possession the tenant pays or tenders to the landlord or pays into court all the rent and arrears due, together with the costs, the proceedings are automatically discontinued, and the tenant holds the property without any need for a new lease (s.212 of the Common Law Procedure Act 1852; *Standard Pattern Co Ltd v Ivey* [1962] Ch. 432).

If the tenant fails to pay this sum before the trial he may apply for relief thereafter (s.38 of the Senior Courts Act 1981). The application must, however, be made within six months of the order for possession being executed. After six months have elapsed he is barred from applying for relief (s.210 of the Common Law Procedure Act 1852).

Where the tenant owes less than six months' rent or the landlord has re-entered without the benefit of a court order the tenant may apply for relief at any time after the order has been made. There is no six-month time-limit but the court will take into account any delay when deciding whether or not relief should be granted (*Thatcher v Pearce & Sons* [1968] 1 W.L.R. 748).

Method of application

2.087 The tenant may begin a claim for relief using Form N5A. CPR r.55 applies to such a claim. However, it should be noted that it is highly unlikely to be appropriate to bring a claim in the High Court (CPR r.55.3). If the landlord has brought proceedings for possession the application for relief may presumably still be made by way of counterclaim or informally during the course of the hearing of the landlord's claim (*Lam Kee Ying Sdn Bhd v Lam Shes Tong* [1974] 3 All E.R. 137) notwithstanding the introduction of CPR r.55.

Where the tenancy is in joint names it is probably necessary for all the joint tenants to join in the application for relief together (see *TM Fairclough & Sons Ltd v Berliner* [1931] 1 Ch. 60; *Jacobs v Chaudhuri* [1968] 2 Q.B. 470).

Exercise of discretion to grant relief

2.088 The court may grant relief on such terms and conditions as to the payment of rent, costs or otherwise as the court thinks fit (s.38 of the Senior Courts Act 1981). It is well settled law that the purpose of including in a lease a right of re-entry for non-payment of rent is to secure payment of rent and that:

> ". . . save in exceptional circumstances, the functions of the court in exercising this equitable jurisdiction is to grant relief when all that is due for rent and costs has been paid up, and (in general) to disregard any other causes of complaint that the landlord may have against the tenant" (*Gill v Lewis* [1956] 2 Q.B. 1 at 13).

Form 8: Claim form for relief against forfeiture

2.089

Claim form for relief against forfeiture	**In the**
	Claim No.

SEAL

Claimant
(name(s) and address(es))

Defendant(s)
(name(s) and address(es))

The claimant is interested in the lease dated   20   , of the property:

The defendant, as the person entitled to the reversion on the lease, on   20   , forfeited or served notice of intention to forfeit the lease.

The claimant seeks relief from that forfeiture so that the lease can continue.

Full particulars of the claim are [overleaf][attached].

The claim will be heard on: **20**   **at**   **am/pm**

at

Defendant's name and address for service			
		Court fee	£
		Solicitor's costs	£
		Total amount	£
		Issue date	

N5A Claim form for relief against forfeiture (10.01)   Printed by The Court Service Publications Branch

Form 9: Order granting relief under section 146

2.090

IN THE	COUNTY COURT	Claim No

BETWEEN

[*Name of landlord*]   *Claimant*

—AND—

[*Name of tenant*]   *Defendant*

Upon the application of the Defendant[1] for relief from forfeiture dated_____

And upon hearing Counsel for the Claimant and for the Defendant

It is ordered that

1. Upon payment by the Defendant to the Claimant of the sums referred to below within_____ days of the date hereof the Defendant be granted relief from forfeiture of the lease dated_____ 20_____ of the premises known as _____ and that the Defendant thereafter do hold the premises according to the lease without the grant of a new lease. The sums referred to are as follows:

    (1) £ _____ in respect of rent and service charges for the whole of the period up to the date hereof; and

    (2) £ _____ on account[2] of the Claimant's costs of the action including the costs occasioned by the Defendant's application for relief from forfeiture.

2. The Defendant do pay the Claimant's costs of the application for relief to be subject to a detailed assessment if not agreed.

3. If the Defendant fails to pay the sums referred to in paragraph 1 to the Claimant within the said period of _____ days (or within such further period or periods as the parties may agree or the Court may allow) the Defendant's application for relief from forfeiture shall stand dismissed and the Defendant shall pay the Claimant's costs summarily assessed at £ _____

DATED

Notes:

  (1) This form assumes that the application is made in the landlord's proceedings for possession (see 2.097). If made by way of separate proceedings it will need to be adapted accordingly.

  (2) As the landlord will have obtained an order for costs in the possession claim it is not necessary to make an order for such costs here.

2.091 The fact that the tenant has been a bad payer in the past is not even a good reason for refusing relief; nor is the fact that the tenant is insolvent (*Re Brompton Securities Ltd (No.2)* [1988] 3 All E.R. 677 Ch D):

> "The case for Langham House [the landlord], in substance, is that it is unfair and unjust that Langham House should have to continue to look for payment of rent and performance of the other covenants in the lease to a company which is admittedly insolvent and which is, in effect, a trustee of the benefit of the lease for another. I do not think that that is a ground for refusing relief. Once arrears are brought up to date Langham House will be in no different position from any other lessor with an impecunious tenant. It would be an entirely new departure for the court to decline to grant relief on the ground that a tenant has been a bad payer in the past and is likely to continue to be a bad payer in the future" (per Vinelott at 680j).

The period of payment must be within the immediately foreseeable future.

Relief ought not be granted when the only potential means of payment is a Pt 20 claim against the landlord (*Inntrepreneur Pub Co v Langton* [2000] 1 E.G.L.R. 34 Ch D).

The courts will generally be reluctant to refuse relief where the landlord will receive a windfall. However, in *Greenwood Reversions Ltd v World Environment Foundation Ltd* [2008] EWCA Civ 47 the Court of Appeal upheld a refusal to grant relief on the basis that although the lease was still a valuable asset, the Defendant's liability to the Claimant effectively wiped out its value. Further, the Defendant had demonstrated over the years through his "woefully and wilful bad behaviour" that he was not a respectable tenant.

Effect of relief; mesne profits

Where relief is granted the order is retrospective. The tenant holds the demised **2.092** premises in accordance with the terms of the lease and without the necessity for a new lease (Common Law Procedure Act 1852 s.212; Senior Courts Act 1981 s.38). The effect is that the tenant is obliged to pay the arrears of rent and costs up to the date of the order. He will not be ordered to pay mesne profits (which may be higher) (*United Dominions Trust Ltd v Shellpoint Ltd* [1993] 4 All E.R. 310 CA; *Escalus Properties Ltd v Robinson* [1995] 4 All E.R. 852, CA).

Tenant altering position and third parties

Where, however, the parties have altered their position prior to the application for **2.093** relief the court may refuse relief, particularly where third parties have acquired rights and the effect of the order would be to defeat those rights or would be unfairly prejudicial to the landlord (*Gill v Lewis* [1956] 2 Q.B. 1; *Silverman v AFCO (UK) Ltd* [1988] 1 E.G.L.R. 51, CA).

> " . . . where parties have altered their position in the meantime, and in particular where the rights of third parties have intervened, relief ought not to be granted where the effect of it would be to defeat the new rights of third parties or be unfair to the landlord having regard to the way in which he has altered his position." (*Gill v Lewis*, per Jenkins L.J. at p.10).

Where the court considers it appropriate to grant relief notwithstanding the grant of a new tenancy by the landlord to a third party the tenant (who has applied for relief) will be put into the position of immediate reversioner to the new tenant's lease and entitled to payment of rent from the new tenant (*Fuller v Judy Properties Ltd* [1992] 1 E.G.L.R. 75 CA). Compare *Bank of Ireland Home Mortgages v South Lodge Developments* [1996] 14 E.G. 92 where Lightman J. took the view that *Fuller v Judy Properties* was authority for the proposition that relief may be granted "either in reversion upon the new lease or with priority to and unincumbered by the new lease". In deciding whether it is appropriate the court in each case has regard to whether or not the new tenant had or should have had notice of the application for relief. In *Khar v Delbounty Ltd* [1996] E.G.C.S. 183 CA, the court ordered the original tenant's lease to be sold with the landlord taking the amount due to him out of the proceeds of sale and paying the balance to the tenant. The sale was postponed while the new tenant, who had an assured short-hold tenancy, remained in occupation.

See also *Bland v Ingram Estates (No.2)* [2001] 50 E.G. 92 CA where it was held that the consequence of the grant of relief was that the new lease took effect as a lease of the reversion, the new tenants were interposed as the intermediate landlord between the landlord and the original tenant. It was therefore the new tenants who were entitled to receive the rent arrears which had accrued since the new lease was granted. In deciding how much to pay to the new tenants, credit was given for the fact that they had enjoyed occupation of the premises from the date of the new lease until the date of the grant of relief. The amount of credit they had to give was a full occupation rent this cancelled out the rent due from the date of the new lease.

Relief from forfeiture; other covenants

2.094 Where the landlord brings proceedings for forfeiture of a lease or forfeits by actual re-entry in respect of a breach of covenant other than by non-payment of rent, the tenant may apply for relief pursuant to s.146(2) of the Law of Property Act 1925. Where relief is granted to the tenant the relief reinstates the lease as if there had never been a forfeiture (*Official Custodian for Charities v Mackey* [1984] 3 All E.R. 689 at 694f).

Relief from forfeiture; section 146(2) of the Law of Property Act 1925

> (2) Where a lessor is proceeding, by action or otherwise, to enforce such a right of re-entry or forfeiture, the lessee may, in the lessor's action, if any, or in any action brought by himself, apply to the court for relief; and the court may grant or refuse relief, as the court, having regard to the proceedings and conduct of the parties under the foregoing provisions of this section, and to all the other circumstances, thinks fit; and in case of relief may grant it on such terms, if any, as to costs, expenses, damages, compensation, penalty, or otherwise, including the granting of an injunction to restrain any like breach in the future, as the court, in the circumstances of each case, thinks fit.
> . . .
> (13) The county court has jurisdiction under this section.

Time for applying

2.095 The wording of subs.(2) of s.146 states that the tenant may apply for relief where the landlord "is proceeding by action or otherwise to enforce" his right of re-entry. The landlord is proceeding the moment he serves his s.146 notice (*Pakwood Transport Ltd v 15 Beauchamp Place Ltd* (1977) 245 E.G. 309). The tenant may therefore apply for relief upon receipt of the notice.

In *Rogers v Rice* [1892] 2 Ch. 170 the landlord had forfeited by bringing proceedings. It was held that the words "is proceeding" mean that the tenant may apply for relief at any time up until the time the landlord has actually re-entered pursuant to the order for possession. After that date it is no longer possible to make an application under s.146(2). If the landlord has obtained a judgment for possession but has not actually re-entered the landlord is still "proceeding" and the tenant may still apply for relief (*Egerton v Jones* [1939] 2 K.B. 702).

The decision in *Rogers v Rice* does not apply where the landlord has forfeited by peaceable re-entry, in which case the tenant may apply for relief after actual re-entry (*Billson v Residential Apartments Ltd* [1992] 1 All E.R. 141 HL).

Joint tenants and equitable assignees

2.096 Where the lease is in joint names all the tenants must join in the application for relief (*TM Fairclough & Sons Ltd v Berliner* [1931] 1 Ch. 60).

An equitable assignee (i.e. a person who has agreed to take the lease from an existing tenant) as well as the assignor is entitled to apply for relief (*High Street Investments Ltd v Bellshore Property Investments Ltd* [1996] 2 E.G.L.R. 40 CA).

Method of application

The tenant may apply for relief by the following methods: **2.097**

(1) By application in the landlord's proceedings (CPR r.23).

(2) By counterclaim in the landlord's claim for possession (see Form 7 on p.48).

(3) By application at the hearing of the landlord's claim for possession (*Lam Kee Ying Sdn Bhd v Lam Shes Tong* [1974] 3 All E.R. 137).

(4) By claim form N5A under CPR r.55 (see Form 8 on p.57).

Exercise of discretion to grant relief to the tenant

The first point to bear in mind when considering whether or not a tenant is likely **2.098** to be granted relief is the width of the discretion granted to the court by s.146(2). The position was clearly stated by the Lord Chancellor, Lord Loreborn, in the leading case of *Hyman v Rose* [1912] A.C. 623 (in relation to the statutory predecessor to s.146):

". . . the discretion given by the section is very wide. The court is to consider all the circumstances and the conduct of the parties. Now it seems to me that when the Act is so express to provide a wide discretion, meaning, no doubt, to prevent one man from forfeiting what in fair dealing belongs to some one else, by taking advantage of a breach from which he is not commensurately and irreparably damaged, it is not advisable to lay down any rigid rules for guiding that discretion . . . It is not safe I think to say that the court must and always will insist upon certain things when the Act does not require them, and the facts of some unforeseen case may make the court wish it had kept a free hand" (*Hyman v Rose* [1912] A.C. 623; per Lord Loreborn at 631).

Some of the reported cases (including some referred to below) come close to losing sight of this general principle and this needs to be borne in mind when looking at the authorities. For a case in which the above statement of Lord Loreborn was considered and applied, see *Southern Depot Co Ltd v British Railways Board* [1990] 2 E.G.L.R. 39—referred to below, para.2.100.

Remedying the breach as a condition of relief

"In the ordinary way relief is almost always granted to a person who makes good the **2.099** breach of covenant and is able and willing to fulfil his obligations in the future" (*Bathurst (Earl) v Fine* [1974] 2 All E.R. 1160, per Lord Denning at 1162 h).

In accordance with the principle that the court's discretion under s.146(2) is unfettered, there is no rule of law that the breach must be remedied prior to the hearing of the application for relief. However, unless there is some good reason why the breach has not been remedied by that date or, at least, that all reasonable steps have been taken to remedy the breach, the court will usually take a dim view of the tenant's case and may exercise its discretion in refusing to grant relief. It will almost invariably require the breach to be remedied as a condition precedent to relief. See *Cremin v Barjack Properties Ltd* [1985] 1 E.G.L.R. 30 at 32 CA. Where the tenant makes good the breach and is able and willing to fulfil his obligations in the future he will usually be granted relief.

"Wilful" breaches

2.100 It is sometimes argued that the court will not grant relief against forfeiture to a tenant who is in "wilful breach", except in exceptional circumstances (see *Rope-maker Properties Ltd v Noonhaven Ltd* [1989] 2 E.G.L.R. 50). The following passage of Lord Wilberforce in *Shiloh Spinners v Harding* [1973] A.C. 691 at 725 is usually relied upon.

> "Established and, in my opinion, sound principle requires that wilful breaches should not, or at least should only in exceptional cases, be relieved against, if only for the reason that the assignor should not be compelled to remain in a relation of neighbour-hood with a person in deliberate breach of his obligations."

However, *Shiloh Spinners v Harding* was not a case concerned with relief from forfeiture of a lease and in *Southern Depot Co Ltd v British Railways Board* [1990] 2 E.G.L.R. 39 Morritt J. refused to hold that relief was confined to exceptional cases where the tenant had been in wilful breach. The court granted relief on stringent terms which included payment of the landlord's costs of the action on an indemnity basis:

> "There can be no doubt that the wilfulness of the breach is a relevant consideration and that the court should not in exercising its discretion encourage a belief that parties to a lease can ignore their obligations and buy their way out of any consequential forfeiture. But to impose a requirement that relief under section 146(2) should be granted only in an exceptional case seems to me to be seeking to lay down a rule for the exercise of the court's discretion which the decision of the House of Lords in Hyman v Rose [1912] AC 623 said should not be done. Certainly Lord Wilberforce in Shiloh Spinners v Harding did not purport to do so in cases under the statute. Accordingly, in my judgment, although I should give considerable weight to the fact that two out of the three breaches were wilful, I am not required to find an exceptional case before granting relief from forfeiture" (*Southern Depot Co Ltd v British Railways Board* [1990] 2 E.G.L.R. 39; per Morritt J. at 43M to 44A).

For a case where Southern Depot was applied see *Mount Cook Land Ltd v Hartley* [2000] E.G.C.S. 26 Ch D where it was held that consideration should be given to the proportionality between the extent of the breach and the potential windfall for the landlord.

Serious breaches

2.101 Relief may be granted where a serious breach is involved, such as using the premises as a brothel in breach of a covenant against immoral user (*Central Estates (Belgravia) Ltd v Woolgar (No.2)* [1972] 1 W.L.R. 1048). It has been stated that it is the established practice of the court not to grant relief in cases where the breach involves immoral user "save in very exceptional circumstances" (*GMS Syndicate Ltd v Gary Elliott Ltd* [1982] Ch.1), although to be quite so definite may be to lay down a "rigid rule" that fetters the court's discretion (see dicta of Lord Loreborn in *Hyman v Rose*, para.2.098, above).

Personal qualifications of the tenant

Where the personal qualifications of the tenant are of importance for the preserva- **2.102**
tion of the value or character of the property, those qualifications may be taken
into account by the court in determining whether to exercise its discretion to grant
relief against forfeiture (*Earl Bathurst v Fine* [1974] 2 All E.R. 1160).

Relief in respect of part of the premises

The court has power to grant relief in respect of only part of the premises (*GMS* **2.103**
Syndicate Ltd—the tenant was not granted relief in respect of the other part used
by sub-tenants for immoral purposes).

Tenant altering position and third parties affected

Where the landlord has altered his position before the application for relief, or **2.104**
where a third party has acquired an interest in the property prior to that date, relief
will invariably not be granted if the landlord or the third party would be unfairly
prejudiced by the order (*Gill v Lewis* [1956] 2 Q.B. 1—a rent case; see further
para.2.093 above).

Where a landlord has recovered possession pursuant to a court order and the
tenant subsequently has the order set aside or successfully appeals and makes an
application for relief in the continuing proceedings the court, in deciding whether
or not to grant relief, will take into account any consequences of the original order
and repossession and any delay on the part of the tenant (*Billson v Residential
Apartments* Ltd [1992] 1 All E.R. 141 HL).

Terms and conditions of relief

The court may (and usually does) grant relief on such terms as to costs, expenses, **2.105**
damages, compensation, penalty or otherwise, including the grant of an injunction
to restrain any like breach in the future, as the court thinks fit (s.146(2) of the Law
of Property Act 1925). See Form 9, p.58 for a specimen order. Different parties
may be granted relief on different terms (*Duke of Westminster v Swinton* [1948] 1
K.B. 524). The order is retrospective and is by reinstatement of the lease. The
effect is that the tenant is obliged to pay only the arrears of rent and costs. He will
not be required to pay mesne profits (which could be higher than the rent) as a
condition of relief (*Escalus Properties Ltd v Robinson* [1995] 4 All E.R. 852 CA).

Where relief is granted subject to a condition as to the doing of something
within a certain time the court may extend the time for compliance (*Starside
Properties Ltd v Mustapha* [1974] 1 W.L.R. 816). Where the parties have entered
into a consent order specifying terms and conditions for relief, the court has jurisdiction to vary the terms but will do only in exceptional circumstances (*Fivecourts
Ltd v JR Leisure Development Co Ltd* [2001] L. & T.R. 47 HC; *Ropac v Inntrpreneur
Pub Co* [2001] L. & T.R. 93, HC). Where the landlord alleges that the tenant has
failed to comply with the condition he may not apply for leave to enforce the order
for possession without notifying the tenant of the application (see para.35.001).

Costs

Where relief from forfeiture is granted, the tenant will normally be required to pay **2.106**
the landlord's costs on an indemnity basis as a condition of relief, notwithstanding

comments to the contrary by Lord Templeman in *Billson v Residential Apartments Ltd (No 1)* [1992] 1 A.C. 494 at 541. In *CB Patel & PC Patel v K&J Restaurants Ltd* [2010] EWCA Civ 1211 paras 98 to 104, the Court of Appeal considered that Lord Templeman had misunderstood the effect of an order for indemnity costs.

> "I have come to the conclusion that the indemnity basis should apply as a general principle, despite what Lord Templeman said, and that there is nothing in the circumstances of the present case to make it appropriate either to adopt the standard basis or to disallow some part of the Claimants' costs. As it seems to me, the factors which led the Court of Appeal in Egerton v Jones to decide in favour of a more generous basis of costs than party and party (which seems to me to be the equivalent of the modern standard basis) are still relevant as a general principle, and that normally this should require that the applicant for relief should pay the landlord's costs on the indemnity basis, rather than only on the standard basis. I therefore consider that K&J should be required K&J to pay the Claimants' costs of the proceedings at first instance on the indemnity basis as a condition of obtaining relief against forfeiture." (para 104).

The mere fact that someone is publically funded, and therefore has some costs protection, does not necessarily mean that they will not be required to pay the landlord's costs as a condition of relief. See *Crisp v Eastaugh* [2007] EWCA Civ 638, Arden L.J., para 27:

> "At the time when the judge gave his judgment Mr Eastaugh was publicly funded. He is no longer publicly funded. However, it is clear from the judge's findings that Mr Eastaugh is entitled to not insubstantial assets. In my judgment, nothing in Section 11 of the Access to Justice Act 1999, which protects publicly funded litigants, prevents this court from providing that as a condition of obtaining relief from forfeiture Mr Eastaugh should pay not merely the costs which could be ordered against him under Section 11, but the difference between those costs and the percentage of the costs which the Landlord has incurred. In my judgment it would be fair, in these circumstances, to make an order to that effect for the reasons that I have given. In concluding that relief from forfeiture should be given, I take into account that the sums due to Mr Crisp are relatively minor and in addition that the lease has a considerable period yet to run."

In order to minimise the costs payable, the tenant should make an offer under CPR r.36, preferably no later than the date upon which he serves his application, setting out his proposed terms which should include an offer to pay the costs to date. If the offer is rejected but the court subsequently makes an order for relief in the proposed terms (or better) the court may well order the landlord to pay the tenant's costs from the date of the offer (see *Mount Cook v Hartley* [2000] E.G.C.S. 26 Ch D).

Relief to sub-tenants and mortgagees; rent and other covenants

Introduction

2.107   Forfeiture of a lease brings any sub-lease or other derivative interest to an end. Where an order is made granting the tenant relief from forfeiture all derivative interests are automatically reinstated (*Dendy v Evans* [1910] 1 K.B. 263). Where, however, the tenant has not been granted or has not applied for relief the sub-tenant may wish to make his own application. If the lease was subject to a mortgage the mortgagee may also wish to make an application for relief.

   Depending on the circumstances, relief may be obtained under s.138 of the County Courts Act 1984 (rent cases only), s.38 of the Senior Courts Act 1981 (rent cases only, High Court) or s.146 of the Law of Property Act 1925 (rent and other covenants, either court).

County court rent cases

Where proceedings have been commenced in the county court, based upon nonpay- **2.108** ment of rent, a sub-tenant may obtain automatic relief by the payment of arrears of rent and costs pursuant to s.138(2) or (5) (see para.2.083) even though the landlord has brought the claim against the tenant, and the sub-tenant is not itself a party to the proceedings (*United Dominions Trust Ltd v Shellpoint Trustees Ltd* [1993] 4 All E.R. 310 CA—because the term "lessee" in s.138(2) and (5), by virtue of s.140, includes an underlessee). If automatic relief is granted by reason of payment by the sub-tenant of all the arrears (see para.2.084) all the leasehold interests in the property, including the tenant's, are restored unconditionally. The sub-tenant is not additionally required to pay mesne profits (which may be greater than the rent) to the landlord for the period between service of the proceedings and the date of the order. This is a consequence of the lease being restored (*United Dominions Trust Ltd* at 316f and 318j; *Escalus Properties Ltd v Robinson* [1995] 4 All E.R. 853 at 858d).

Form 10: Sub-tenant's application for a vesting order

2.109

FORM N244

Insert the details below at Part A

I, [*state name of Applicant*], of [*state address*] wish to apply to be joined in the proceedings and for an order vesting the property comprised in the lease referred to in the Particulars of Claim in myself for the remainder of the said term upon such conditions as to the execution of any deed or other document and the payment of rent and costs, or such other conditions as the court may think fit.

The grounds upon which I make this application are that:

   (1) By an agreement dated the [*insert date*] the Defendant sublet the whole of the said property to me for a term of years.

   (2) I am prepared to pay to the claimant all the sums claimed in the Particulars of Claim.

   (3) I am prepared to pay the rent and service charges payable under the terms of the said lease and to perform all the other covenants contained therein.

   (4) I am entitled to make this application under section 146(4) of the Law of Property Act 1925.

If automatic relief has not been obtained by the tenant or a sub-tenant pursuant to **2.110** s.138(2) or (5) and the landlord obtains possession an application for a vesting order may be made pursuant to s.138(9C) at any time within six months from the date on which the landlord recovers possession (para.2.083). The court's power to make an order under this section is discretionary. If made, a vesting order does not reinstate the interests derived from the original underlease or mortgage but gives rise to a new interest (see further below in relation to vesting orders made under s.146(4)). If the sub-tenant fails to make an application within the six-month time-limit he will thereafter be barred from all relief in both the county court and High Court (s.138(7); *United Dominions Trust Ltd v Shellpoint Trustees Ltd*).

High Court rent cases

In exceptional cases relief may be sought in the High Court (CPR r.55.3), in a rent **2.111** case, pursuant to s.38 of the Senior Courts Act 1981 (para.2.085). The application may be made after the landlord has enforced the order, but if the rent is six months or more in arrears s.210 of the Common Law Procedure Act 1852 applies so that the application must be made within six months of the date of execution.

If relief is granted by reason of payment of the rent and costs all the leasehold interests in the property, including the tenant's, are restored unconditionally. The sub-tenant cannot be required to pay mesne profits to the landlord for the period between the service of the writ and the date of the order as a condition of relief (*Escalus Properties Ltd v Robinson* [1995] 4 All E.R. 853 at 859).

County Court or High Court; rent or other covenants

2.112 A vesting order may also be sought pursuant to s.146(4) of the Law of Property Act 1925 both in the county court and High Court. This subsection applies to rent cases as well as to breaches of other covenants.

Section 146(4) of the Law of Property Act 1925

> Where a lessor is proceeding by action or otherwise to enforce a right of re-entry or forfeiture under any covenant, proviso, or stipulation in a lease, or for nonpayment of rent, the court may, on application by any person claiming as under-lessee any estate or interest in the property comprised in the lease or any part thereof, either in the lessor's action (if any) or in any action brought by such person for that purpose, make an order vesting, for the whole term of the lease or any less term, the property comprised in the lease or any part thereof in any person entitled as underlessee to any Estate Or Interest in such property upon such conditions as to execution of any deed or other document, payment of rent, costs, expenses, damages, compensation, giving security, or otherwise, as the court in the circumstances of each case may think fit, but in no case shall any such underlessee be entitled to require a lease to be granted to him for any longer term than he had under his original sublease.

Exercise of discretion

2.113 An order made pursuant to s.146(4) does not restore the original underlease. A new lease is created and vested in the sub-tenant (see *Cadogan v Dimovic* [1984] 2 All E.R. 168 at 172). The position is the same where a mortgagee is granted a new lease under s.146(4) save that the new lease is held subject to the equity of redemption in the mortgagor (*Chelsea Estates Investment Trust Co Ltd v Marche* [1955] 1 All E.R. 195).

The court's power under s.146(4) is discretionary. When making an order under s.146(4) the court's discretion is very wide and the new lease may be different from that which he originally held. The position is explained by Warner J. in *Hammersmith and Fulham LBC v Top Shop Centres Ltd* [1989] 2 All E.R. 655 at 664–665:

> "The court may not under that subsection vest in the applicant a new lease beginning before the date of its order or ending later than the original underlease would have done; but the discretion is otherwise unfettered . . . Thus the court may, under s.146(4), order that the new lease should be at a rent different from that reserved by the original underlease . . . It may order that the new lease should be for a term ending sooner than the term granted by the original underlease. It may order that the new lease should contain different covenants and it may, on my reading of the subsection, order that the new lease should comprise a lesser part of the property demised by the forfeited lease than was comprised in the original underlease."

Form 11: Mortgagee's application for a vesting order

2.114

Form N244

Insert the details below at Part A

MONASTERY BUILDING SOCIETY ("the Society") of _____ wishes to apply for.

1. An order that it be joined in these proceedings pursuant to CPR 19.2 and
2. An order that [*the property referred to in the Particulars of Claim*] be vested in the Society pursuant to section 146(4) of the Law of Property Act 1925.

The grounds upon which the Society makes the application are that it is a mortgagee of the said property under a first charged dated _____ that it is entitled to make this application under the said statutory provision and that it is willing to comply with such conditions as the court may think fit.

However, the court is unlikely to grant a lease containing terms less stringent than those in the head lease (*Hill v Griffin* [1987] 1 E.G.L.R. 81—vesting order refused because the sub-tenant was not prepared to accept a lease containing a repairing covenant which was as onerous as in the head lease). It should also be noted that there is sometimes a reluctance to grant relief from forfeiture to a sub-tenant "because it thrusts upon the landlord a person whom he has never accepted as tenant and creates … a contract between them" (*Fivecourts Ltd v JR Leisure Development Co Ltd* [2001] L. & T.R. 47, HC); although such an argument is less likely to have as much weight where the sub-tenancy was created pursuant to a consent expressly granted by the landlord. It is an invariable condition that the sub-tenant pay the landlord's costs of the proceedings (on a standard basis: see para.2.106). The fact that the sub-tenant is legally aided does not prevent the court from imposing such a condition (*Factors (Sundries) Ltd v Miller* [1952] 2 All E.R. 630, CA). But see Pt 36 offers at para.2.106.

Alternative application under subsection (2)

A sub-tenant may also apply for relief pursuant to s.146(2) of the 1925 Act (see **2.115** para.2.094). The subsection, although usually used by tenants, also applies to sub-tenants. If relief is granted pursuant to this subsection the order is retrospective and operates by reinstatement of the lease. There is therefore no requirement made to pay mesne profits as a condition of relief (*Escalus Properties Ltd v Sinclair* [1995] 4 All E.R. 853 CA). If the application is made under subs.(4) the court is likely to make an order that it be a condition of the grant of a vesting order that mesne profits be paid in respect of the period between service of the proceedings and the date of the order. If the amount of the market rent is greater than the current rent the sub-tenant may therefore wish to make the application under subs. (2) with an alternative application for a vesting order under subs.(4). The advantage of having a vesting order is that on the grant of the new lease to the sub-tenant the head lease is not restored.

If the sub-tenant does make an alternative application under subs.(2) the court has a discretion to choose between ordering relief under that subsection or making a vesting order under s.146(4); and where a vesting order together with an order for mesne profits would give the landlord a windfall the court is likely to make an order for relief under subs.(2) (*Escalus Properties v Sinclair*).

Time for the application

2.116 The decision of the House of Lords in *Billson v Residential Apartments Ltd* [1992] 1 All E.R. 141 (see para.2.095), that a tenant may apply for relief after peaceable re-entry but not after a landlord has recovered possession pursuant to a court order (unless that order is set aside), applies to applications made pursuant to s.146 by any person claiming as underlessee (*Rexhaven Ltd v Nurse* (1995) 28 H.L.R. 241, Judge Colyer QC sitting as a judge of the Chancery Division). Thus, if a sub-tenant or mortgagee is served with proceedings or otherwise discovers that the landlord has served a s.146 notice on the tenant he will usually be best advised to make an application under s.146(4) immediately (see further under "court procedure", para.2.118).

If an order for possession is obtained and executed without the sub-tenant or mortgagee knowing about it an application (i) to be joined in the proceedings and (ii) for the order for possession and execution thereon to be set aside, will need to be applied for. However, it has been held that in the absence of special circumstances a mortgagee, who has been notified of the proceedings and then neglects to intervene until after judgment has been obtained and executed by the landlord, will be unable successfully to impugn the judgment on the ground that it seeks to do so in order to mount a claim for relief (*Rexhaven v Nurse* (above)—the mortgagee had been sent a copy of the writ seeking possession but had mistakenly filed it away).

Persons who may apply: sub-tenants and mortgagees

2.117 Sub-tenants may clearly apply for relief under the various provisions, including unlawful sub-tenants (*Southern Depot Co Ltd v British Railways Board* [1990] 2 E.G.L.R. 39 at 42M–43A).

An equitable assignee of an underlease (i.e. a person who has agreed to take the underlease from the existing sub-tenant) as well as the assignor is entitled to apply for relief (*High Street Investments Ltd v Bellshore Property Investments Ltd* [1996] 2 E.G.L.R. 40 CA).

As the vesting of a new lease in a sub-tenant or mortgagee, pursuant to s.146(4) of the 1925 Act or s.138(9C) of the 1984 Act, does not reinstate the interests derived from the sub-lease or mortgage any sub-undertenant must make his own application for a vesting order even if the sub-tenant has made an application (*Hammersmith and Fulham LBC v Top Shop Centres Ltd* [1989] 2 All E.R. 655).

Mortgagees, whether legal or equitable, of the tenant's interest are persons who derive title under a tenant and so may apply for relief (s.140 of the 1984 Act; s.38 of the 1981 Act; s.146(4) of the 1925 Act; see *Belgravia Insurance Co Ltd v Meah* [1963] 3 All E.R. 828—general principles and legal mortgages; *Good v Wood* [1954] 1 All E.R. 275—equitable mortgages). See Forms 11 and 12 (pp.67 and 69) for an application for relief and witness statement in support to be used by a mortgagee, and Form 13 at p.70 for a vesting order.

The holder of a charging order is entitled to apply for relief under s.138 (9C). However, such a person is not an underlessee for the purposes of s.146 and as he does not have a right to possession he cannot rely on the High Court's inherent jurisdiction. Should the chargee find that he cannot rely on s.138 (i.e. the landlord is not proceeding by action in the county court (see s.138(1)), he may be able to rely on an indirect claim for relief. An indirect claim is based upon the ex-tenant/ chargor's implied obligation to protect the security by compelling them to claim relief. This would necessitate the joining of the ex-tenants if they were not already a party (*Bland v Ingrams Estates Ltd* [2001] 2 W.L.R. 1638 CA and *Croydon (Unique) Ltd v Wright* [2001] Ch. 318 CA).

Where the landlord has forfeited for non-payment of rent and the sub-tenant or mortgagee applies for relief under the Senior Courts Act 1981 he should join the original tenant in the proceedings (or, if the lease was assigned, the assignee), or if it is not possible to do so the absence of that party should be explained (*Hare v Elms* [1893] 1 Q.B. 604; *Humphreys v Morten* [1905] 1 Ch. 739). Lord Denning has stated, obiter, that it is not necessary to join the tenant (or his assignee) where the sub-tenant claims relief under s.146(4) of the Law of Property Act 1925 (*Belgravia Insurance Co Ltd* at 832H), but it is advisable to do so (or at least to notify him of the application) unless it is not possible, in which case his absence should be explained.

Court procedure

A sub-tenant or mortgagee who has been joined by the landlord in a claim to possession may make an application for a vesting order by way of counterclaim, or by application in the landlord's claim under Pt 23. If he is not an original defendant he may also apply to be joined as a party pursuant to CPR r.19.2. See Forms 10 and 11 for the details to insert on the application form (N244), Form 12 for a witness statement in support and Form 13 for a draft order to attach. Alternatively, he may issue his own claim. Part 55, which relates to relief from forfeiture strictly speaking, would not seem to apply to an application for a vesting order and the wording of Form N5A which is the prescribed claim form for relief under Pt 55 is not suitable. It would therefore seem that an application for a vesting order should be made under Pt 8, because there is unlikely to be a substantial dispute of fact (CPR r.8.1(2)(a)).

2.118

Form 12: Witness statement in support of application for a vesting order

2.119

IN THE	COUNTY COURT		Claim No

BETWEEN:

[*Name of landlord*]   Claimant

—AND—

[*Name of tenant*]   Defendant

WITNESS STATEMENT

[*name*], Solicitor, of [*address*] will say as follows:

1. I am the solicitor acting on behalf of Monastery Building Society. I make this witness statement, with due authority from my client, in support of the Society's application to be joined in these proceedings and for a vesting order. Save where otherwise appears the facts stated herein are within my own knowledge and belief.

2. The Claimant's claim is for possession of the dwelling known as [*address*]. The dwelling is held by the Defendant under a lease for a term of 99 years granted to him by the Claimant's on _____ A copy of the lease is now produced and shown to me marked "_____1". This lease is subject to a legal mortgage in favour of the Society. A copy of the Charge Certificate is now produced and shown to me marked "_____2".

3. The Defendant fell into arrears with his mortgage and the Society took possession on_____ 1994 pursuant to an order for possession in this court dated_____ 1994. The amount outstanding to the Society on the mortgage at today's date is £_____. The Society is in the process of selling the dwelling although a buyer has not yet been found.

4. The Society has been served with these proceedings pursuant to CPR PD 55, para.2.4. It is in these circumstances that the Society applies to be joined in the proceedings and seeks a vesting order pursuant to the statutory provisions referred to in the application. The Society is ready, able and willing to comply with such conditions as the court may consider it proper to impose.

Statement of truth etc.

2.120 As stated above, if the landlord re-enters the property pursuant to an order for possession made after service of a s.146 notice (i.e. for breach of covenant other than payment of rent), any such sub-tenant or mortgagee has no right to apply for relief until he has had that order set aside. Nor may he apply under s.138(9C) in a rent case outside the six-month time-limit (para.2.083). If the landlord does manage to obtain and enforce an order for possession in the county court without the knowledge of the sub-tenant or a mortgagee, any such person should apply to have the order for possession set aside to be joined in the action and for an order pursuant to s.146(4) in the continuing proceedings.

Form 13: Vesting order in favour of mortgagee

2.121

IN THE   COUNTY COURT   Claim No

BETWEEN:

[Name of landlord]

Claimant

—AND—

(1) *[Name of tenant]*
(2) MONASTERY BUILDING SOCIETY   *Defendants*

ORDER

UPON the application of Monastery Building Society

AND UPON HEARING solicitors for the Claimant and for Monastery Building Society

IT IS ORDERED THAT:

1. The Monastery Building Society be joined as a Second Defendant to these proceedings.

2. The dwelling known as *[address]* be vested in the Second Defendant pursuant to section 146(4) of the Law of Property Act 1925 upon the terms of the draft lease attached to this Order provided that the Second Defendant do within 28 days hereof:

    (1) Pay to the Claimant the sum of £ _____ in respect of rent, mesne profits and service charges outstanding:
    (2) Pay the Claimant £ _____ in respect of the costs of its action against the First Defendant and the costs of and occasioned by the Second Defendant's application dated_____ .
    (3) Execute a lease in the terms of the draft annexed hereto.

3. If the Second Defendant fails to comply with the said conditions within the said period of 28 days or within such further period or periods as the parties may agree or the Court may allow the Second Defendant's application for a vesting order shall stand dismissed and the Second Defendant shall pay the Claimant's costs of and occasioned by the Second Defendant's application summarily assessed at £_____

4. Liberty to apply.

DATED

2.122 Where the landlord has proceeded by action in the High Court and has obtained an order for possession he may not enforce the order without leave, and leave will not be given unless it is shown that every person in actual possession has sufficient notice of the proceedings to enable him to apply for relief (RSC O.45, r.3(3)). The sub-tenant or mortgage will, therefore, have an opportunity to make an application for relief. (There is no equivalent provision in the county court). As stated above, if the landlord re-enters the property pursuant to an order for possession made after service of a s.146 notice (i.e. for breach of covenant other than payment of rent), any such sub-tenant or mortgagee has no right to apply for relief unless the order is set aside. Thus, if the sub-tenant or mortgagee is notified of the order pursuant to RSC O.45, r.3(3) he should immediately make an application for relief.

Chapter 3

Other Methods of Termination

At common law a tenancy may be brought to an end in a number of ways. The most **3.001** important are by forfeiture, notice to quit, effluxion of time and surrender. Forfeiture was dealt with in the last chapter. This chapter deals with the other methods. However, it should be noted that many modern tenancies are governed by specific statutory provisions and require specific notices to be served. For example, an assured tenancy under the Housing Act 1988 requires a "notice of intention to commence proceedings for possession" to be served. The special rules that apply to the termination of specific tenancies are dealt with in the appropriate chapter.

It is also worth bearing in mind that in some cases it may be an act of discrimination or a breach of a tenant's human rights, to bring a tenancy to an end (see Chs 23 and 24).

Notice to quit by landlord

Service of a notice to quit is appropriate where the tenancy the landlord wishes to **3.002** determine is a periodic one (oral or written). A notice to quit may not be used to determine a fixed-term tenancy unless the lease contains an express clause (commonly known as a "break clause") permitting the landlord to bring it to an end in this way.

The notice

As a general rule a notice to quit premises let as a dwelling will only be valid **3.003** if it is in writing and contains such information as may be prescribed by statutory instrument, presently The Notices to Quit etc. (Prescribed Information) Regulations 1988 (SI 1988/2201); s.5(1)(a) of the Protection from Eviction Act 1977. However, the notice need not be in writing and need not contain the prescribed information if the premises are let on an "excluded tenancy" (see para.22.008) which was entered on or after the date on which the Housing Act 1988 came into force (January 15, 1989) unless it was entered into pursuant to a contract made before that date (s.5(1B) of the 1977 Act).

Protection from Eviction Act 1977 section 5

    (1) Subject to subs.(1B) below no notice by a landlord or a tenant to quit any premises let (whether before or after the commencement of this Act) as a dwelling shall be valid unless—

   (a)   it is in writing and contains such information as may be prescribed; and
   (b)   it is given not less than four weeks before the date on which it is to take effect.

(1A) . . .

(1B) Nothing in subs.(1) . . . above applies to—

   (a)   premises let on an excluded tenancy which is entered into on or after the date on which the Housing Act 1988 came into force unless it is entered into pursuant to a contract made before that date.

Premises let as an agricultural holding upon which there is a dwelling are not "premises let as a dwelling" for the purposes of s.5 (*National Trust v Knipe* [1997] 4 All E.R. 627 CA).

Section 5 was held to apply to a licence to occupy where the occupier although not paying any "rent" did have an obligation to repair the property during their occupation as that amounted to a licence granted for money's worth and was therefore not an excluded licence (*Polar Park Enterprises v Allason* [2007] EWHC 1088 (Ch)). Conversely, it has been held that short term accommodation provided by local authorities while they investigate whether they have any duty to house an individual under the Housing Act 1996, is not a dwelling for the purposes of the Act (see *Rogerson v Wigan MBC* [2004] EWHC 1677; *Mohamed v Manek* (1995) 27 H.L.R. 439 CA and *Desnousse v Newham* [2006] EWCA Civ 547).

Where the notice is required to contain the prescribed information it will not be invalid merely because the exact words used in the regulations are not used in the notice. So long as the words used clearly impart the information that is prescribed the notice will be valid (see *Wilsher v Foster* [1981] C.L.Y. 1546; compare *Meretune Investments v Martin* [1984] C.L.Y. 1917—county court cases coming to opposite conclusions on the use of out of date standard forms).

See Form 14 (p.76) for a specimen notice to quit containing the prescribed information.

Every notice to quit must relate to the whole of the premises let and must be served the proper period before its expiry.

Appropriate notice periods

3.004 The appropriate period of notice and the date upon which a notice to quit is to expire may be provided for in the tenancy agreement. If so the notice to quit should be served in accordance with the tenancy (but subject to the minimum requirement of four weeks' notice where s.5(1)(b) of the Protection from Eviction Act 1977 applies (see below)). Where there are no such terms the following rules apply.

Where by virtue of s.5(1)(a) of the Protection from Eviction Act 1977 a notice to quit is required to be in writing and to contain prescribed information (see above) the notice to quit must be given not less than four weeks before the date on which it is to take effect (s.5(1)(b)). Thus, in the usual case a weekly tenant must be given at least four weeks' notice. However, if s.5(1) does not apply he may be given only a week's notice.

Section 5(1) of the 1977 Act only provides for a minimum period of notice. If the tenancy is of a type that requires longer notice such longer notice must be given. Thus, a monthly tenancy requires at least a calendar months' notice and a quarterly tenancy requires at least one quarter's notice.

A yearly tenancy requires at least six months' notice. Usually this means 183 days but if the tenancy is to end on one of the quarter days (March 25, June 24, September 29 and December 25) then at least two quarters' notice must be given. A tenancy is a yearly tenancy if expressed to be yearly even if the rent is payable quarterly, monthly, etc. (*Adler v Blackman* [1953] 1 Q.B. 147).

In calculating the minimum notice period required include the day of service **3.005** and exclude the day of expiry (*Schnabel v Allard* [1967] 1 Q.B. 627). The date of expiry must be at the end of a complete period of the tenancy or the first day of a new period (*Sidebotham v Holland* [1895] 1 Q.B. 378; *Crate v Miller* [1947] K.B. 946). Unless there is an indication in the lease to the contrary a tenancy stated to be "from" a particular date commences immediately after midnight the following day (*Ladyman v Wirral Estates* [1968] 2 All E.R. 197). If the tenancy is a monthly tenancy and the notice is given on the last day of the month it should be dated to expire on the last day of the next month even where that month is a shorter month. The notice should not give a particular time in the day before which the tenant must leave.

Examples

(a) If a weekly tenancy commences on a Monday the notice to quit must expire **3.006** on a Sunday (or a Monday) and must be given by the Sunday (or, if it is to expire on a Monday, by the Monday) four weeks beforehand (unless s.5(1) (b) of the Protection from Eviction Act 1977 does not apply in which case it may be given one week beforehand).

(b) If a monthly tenancy commences on the 20th of a month, the notice to quit must be given by the 19th (or 20th) of any particular month to expire on the 19th (or 20th) of the next month. If a monthly tenancy commences on January 31, the notice to quit can be given to expire on February 28 (or February 29 in a leap year). Where the landlord served a notice on September 30, 1978 under the business tenancy provisions of the Landlord and Tenant Act 1954 and the tenant had four months from the date of service to apply for a new tenancy and did so on January 31, 1979 it was held that as the term "month" meant a calendar month the notice ended on January 30, 1979 and the tenant's application was dismissed (*Dodds v Walker* [1980] 1 W.L.R. 1061).

(c) If a yearly tenancy is granted on May 1, 1982 the notice to quit must be given by October 29, 1982 to determine on April 30, 1983 or May 1, 1983 (i.e. 183 days).

In order to ensure that the notice expires on the proper day the landlord may insert the following clause in the notice to quit:

"I hereby give you notice to quit on the day of or at the expiration of the period of your tenancy which shall expire next after the expiration of four weeks from the service upon you of this notice".

However, use of such a formula will be sufficient only if the expiry date can clearly be ascertained by reference to it (*Chez Auguste Ltd v Cottat* [1951] 1 K.B. 293; *Allam & Co Ltd v Europa Poster Services Ltd* [1968] 1 All E.R. 826).

In *Hussain v Bradford Community Housing Limited* [2009] EWCA Civ 763 an assured weekly tenancy contained a clause that the tenants should give the landlord "not less than 28 days written notice expiring on any Friday should he/she wish to terminate". The weekly periodic tenancy ended on a Friday. One of the two joint tenants served a notice to quit on January 24, 2007 "with effect from Sunday 25/02/2007 or the day on which a complete period of your tenancy expires next after the end of four weeks from the date of this notice". The remaining joint tenant argued that the notice to quit was ineffective as it gave two alternative dates. The judge disagreed. Patten L.J. at para.11:

> "It is true that the notice gives two possible termination dates, but only one complies with the requirements of clause 2.2 of the tenancy agreement and that date, which is Friday February 23, is the first in time. In my judgment, there is no basis for construing the notice so as to exclude the operation of the catch-all provision. It was obviously inserted to ensure that the notice expired at the end of a contractual period of the tenancy if that was not Sunday 25 February and it would have been read by the respondent as intending to terminate the tenancy in accordance with clause 2.2 of the tenancy agreement: see *Mannai Investment Co Ltd v Eagle Star Life Assurance Co Ltd* [1997] AC 749. For these reasons, in my judgment, the notice to quit took effect at the end of Friday 23 February"

No doubt the same applies to two alternative dates in a s.21 notice—see para.7.022.

3.007   Unless the above requirements are strictly complied with the notice will generally be ineffective. Only minor clerical errors will not invalidate a notice to quit, if the meaning would be clear to a reasonable tenant. The test is: "Is the notice quite clear to a reasonable tenant reading it? Is it plain that he cannot be misled by it?" (*Carradine Properties Ltd v Aslam* [1976] 1 W.L.R. 442: approved is *Mannai Investment Co Ltd v Eagle Star Life Assurance Co Ltd* [1997] 2 W.L.R. 945 HL). For example, a notice to quit dated in error 1894 when the landlord clearly meant 1994 will not invalidate the notice. If proceedings for possession have been commenced on the basis of a defective notice to quit, they will be dismissed and the landlord will have to serve a valid notice before fresh proceedings can be commenced.

It should be noted that the landlord must never commence proceedings until the notice to quit has expired. If he does so the proceedings are premature and will be dismissed.

Who may give a notice

3.008 The notice must be given by or on behalf of the tenant's immediate landlord at the time of the notice. Thus a prospective purchaser cannot serve a notice to quit, but once a landlord has given the tenant notice his successors in title may rely upon it (*Doe d. Earl of Egremont v Forwood* (1842) 3 Q.B. 627). A notice to quit given by one of two or more joint landlords is valid if the tenancy is a periodic one (*Parsons v Parsons* [1983] 1 W.L.R. 1390; see also *Hammersmith and Fulham LBC v Monk* [1992] 1 All E.R. 1 HL—a decision relating to the termination by one of two joint tenants without the consent of the other). However, if the tenancy is for a fixed term with a clause providing for termination by a notice to quit (i.e. a break clause), all of the joint owners must agree to service of the notice to quit unless the lease otherwise provides (cf. *Hounslow LBC v Pilling* [1994] 1 All E.R. 432 CA—a decision relating to termination by joint tenants).

Notice given by agents

It is worth bearing in mind that the purpose of the rules contained in this para- **3.009** graph is to ensure that the tenant can rely upon the notice to quit; that he can be sure that it comes from the landlord. The first rule is that a person such as a managing agent, who has been given a general authority to deal with a property on behalf of a landlord, may give a tenant a notice to quit in his own name without having to show a specific authority to determine the tenancy. The notice is even valid if it is given by the agent as if he were the landlord and fails to disclose his own agency (*Doe d. Earl Manvers v Mizem* (1837) 2 Mood & R56); *Harmond Properties Ltd v Gajdzis* [1968] 3 All E.R. 263; *Townsend Carriers Ltd v Pfizer Ltd* (1977) 33 P. & C.R. 361). Such an agent may also commence proceedings for possession.

The second rule is that all other persons (e.g. rent collectors, solicitors, the landlord's husband or wife) may only give a notice to quit on behalf of the land-lord if they have the landlord's actual authority to do so at the time the notice is given (*Jones v Phipps* (1868) L.R. 3 Q.B. 567). A landlord may not subsequently ratify the notice and thereby validate it. The fact of the agency should be expressed on the notice which should be expressly given on behalf of the landlord, who should be named or otherwise identified (*Lemon v Lardeur* [1946] 2 All E.R. 329; *Divall v Harrison* [1992] 2 E.G.L.R. 64 CA). There is, of course, nothing to prevent a solicitor or a wife having a general authority to manage the property in which case the first rule set out above will apply.

Service upon whom?

The landlord must serve the notice to quit on his immediate tenant. He may not **3.010** serve an assignor of the tenancy nor an undertenant. An assignment of the tenancy in breach of covenant, although unlawful, is effective, and so even in these circumstances the notice to quit should be served on the assignee (*Old Grovebury Manor Farm Ltd v W Seymour Plant Sales and Hire Ltd (No.2)* [1979] 1 W.L.R. 1397). If the tenancy is held by joint tenants but only one of them is in occupation, service on the occupying tenant is sufficient unless the lease provides that all must be served (*Doe d. Bradford (Lord) v Watkins* (1806) 7 East 551); it is safer, however, to address it to both.

It sometimes occurs that the person in occupation is not the original tenant. If the tenancy was in writing, and contained a provision requiring a notice to quit to be served to terminate the tenancy, there should be no real problems about service because the provisions of s.196 of the Law of Property Act 1925 will be available (see below). However, if the section does not apply service of a notice addressed to the tenant but given to a sub-tenant or simply left at the premises will not be sufficient, although if they are truly sub-tenants it should usually be possible to find out to whom they pay their rent and thus to find the tenant. Where there has been no sub-letting the persons who are left in occupation will, in the absence of any evidence to the contrary, be assumed to be the tenant's assignees and notice to quit may be given to them (*Doe d. Morris v Williams* (1826) 6 B & C 41; see also *Egerton v Rutter* [1951] 1 K.B. 472). Compare

Form 14: Notice to quit by landlord

NOTICE TO QUIT

(BY LANDLORD OF PREMISES LET AS A DWELLING)

Name and
Address of
Tenant

To. ....

of ....

....

Name and
Address of
Landlord

[I][We][as][on behalf of] your landlord[s]...

of ....

*Me/them or as
appropriate
†Address of
premises

give you NOTICE TO QUIT and deliver up possession to* ....

of † ....

....

‡Date for
possession

on‡ .... 20 .... or the day on which a complete period of your

tenancy expires next after the end of four weeks from the service of this notice.

Date of notice

Dated .... 20 ....

Signed ....

Name and
Address of Agent
if Agent served
notice

....

....

....

INFORMATION FOR TENANT
(See *Note 2 below*)

1. If the tenant or licensee does not leave the dwelling, the landlord or licensor must get an order for possession from the court before the tenant or licensee can lawfully be evicted. The landlord or licensor cannot apply for such an order before the notice to quit or notice to determine has run out.

2. A tenant or licensee who does not know if he has any right to remain in possession after a notice to quit or a notice to determine runs out can obtain advice from a solicitor. Help with all or part of the cost of legal advice and assistance may be available under the Legal Aid Scheme. He should also be able to obtain information from a Citizens' Advice Bureau, a Housing Aid Centre or & Rent Officer.

NOTES

1. Notice to quit premises let as a dwelling must be given at least four weeks before it takes effect, and it must be in writing (Protection from Eviction Act 1977, section 5 as amended).
2. Where a notice to quit is given by a landlord to determine a tenancy of any premises let as a dwelling, the notice must contain this information (the Notices to Quit etc (Prescribed Information) Regulations 1988).
3. Some tenancies are excluded from this protection: see Protection from Eviction Act 1977, as 3A and 5(1B).

Chamberlaine v Scalley (1992) 26 H.L.R. 26 where the tenant had left her "common law husband" in occupation upon whom the notice to quit was served. It was held that this was insufficient.

Mode of service for written tenancies

Law of Property Act 1925 section 196(5)

3.011   The provisions of this section shall extend to notices required to be served by any instrument affecting property executed or coming into operation after the commencement of this Act unless a contrary intention appears.

Where the tenancy is in writing the provisions of s.196 of the Law of Property Act 1925, as extended by s.1 of the Recorded Delivery Service Act 1962 (see para.2.027) may apply. However, s.196(5) of the Law of Property Act 1925 will not extend s.196 to notices unless the tenancy agreement makes express provision for service of a notice to quit (*Wandsworth LBC v Attwell* [1996] 1 E.G.L.R. 57 CA—weekly tenancy agreement contained in informal documents—the notice to quit was not "required" by the "instrument" but by the general law). By the same reasoning s.196 does not apply to notices served pursuant to s.8 or s.21 of the Housing Act 1988 (see paras 6.020 and 7.028).

Further, s.196 will not apply if "a contrary intention appears" in the agreement.

The effect of s.196 where it does apply is as follows:

(1) A notice to quit is sufficiently served if it is sent by registered letter or recorded delivery addressed to the tenant by name at the tenant's last known place of abode or business in the United Kingdom. If the letter is not returned through the post office undelivered, service is deemed to be made at the time at which the letter would in the ordinary course of post be delivered (s.196(4)). To prove service the landlord need only show that the letter was prepaid, properly addressed and actually posted.

(2) The landlord may also serve the notice to quit by leaving it at the tenant's last known place of abode or business in the United Kingdom or affixing it or leaving it for him on the land or on any house or building comprised in the lease (s.196(3)). If this method is used it is sufficient if it is addressed to "the lessee" (s.196(2)).

See further para.2.027.

Mode of service for oral tenancies and written tenancies to which section 196 does not apply

Where the tenancy is an oral one or a written one to which s.196 does not apply the **3.012** notice to quit must come to the tenant's attention before the notice period begins to run. Personal service is not required. The notice may be sent by post and if the tenant is living at the premises the court will as a matter of practice presume that the notice was delivered in the ordinary course of post. However, the presumption may be rebutted by evidence from the tenant that the notice was not in fact received. Simply leaving the notice to quit at premises that are known to be empty will not be sufficient unless the landlord can show (whether by the tenant's admission or otherwise) that it came to the tenant's attention prior to commencement of the notice period.

Where the notice is served by post the landlord is probably best advised to serve the notice by registered letter or recorded delivery. Whatever the method of service it is also sensible to send the tenant a copy of the notice (in addition to the original) indorsed with a memorandum of service upon it. The tenant should be asked to sign, date and return the copy on the date of receipt. He may not always do so but if he does it should prevent arguments about service at a later date.

If for any reason a tenancy granted by a housing authority is not secure (see para.10.003) it cannot rely upon s.233 of the Local Government Act 1972 in relation to service of a notice to quit. Thus, in the absence of an express provision in the tenancy agreement the authority cannot rely upon service of the notice at the tenant's last known address unless it can be shown that the notice was actually received by the tenant (*Enfield LBC v Devonish* [1996] E.G.C.S 194).

Where difficulties arise in relation to service of a notice to quit upon a tenant who has disappeared it may be possible to determine the tenancy by an application to the county court pursuant to s.54 of the Landlord and Tenant Act 1954 (see para.3.031).

Service of notice to quit where the tenant has died

3.013 Where the tenant was an individual who has died service of the notice to quit will depend upon various factors:

(1) If there are executors of the tenant's estate the notice should be addressed and served on them. If the provisions of s.196 of the Law of Property Act 1925 apply (see s.196(5); see para.3.011) the notice to quit may be served by affixing it to the premises or leaving it for them there pursuant to s.196(3) (see para.2.027). Their names can be discovered by doing a probate search.

(2) If there are executors but no grant has been filed at the Principal Registry (so that the names of the executors are not known) the notice may be served on the Public Trustee (s.18(1), (2) of the Law of Property (Miscellaneous Provisions) Act 1994).

(3) If there are no executors or if the tenant died intestate and no administrators have yet been appointed the property vests in the Public Trustee (see para.4.021) and (subject to anything in the agreement) the notice to quit should be addressed to the personal representatives of the deceased (naming him) and left at or sent by post to his last known place of residence or business in the United Kingdom and a copy of it, similarly addressed, should be served on the Public Trustee at the Public Trust Office, 81 Chancery Lane, London WC2A 1DD (020 7911 7127) DX 0012 London Chancery Lane (See s.18 of 1994 Act; *Practice Direction* [1995] 3 All E.R. 192). The Public Trustee keeps a register of all notices served on him. To enter a notice on the register it should be accompanied by Form NL(1) of The Public Trustee (Notices Affecting Land) (Title on Death) Regulations 1995 (SI 1995/1330). A search of the register may be made against the name of the deceased person by using Form NL(2). In the event that the search shows an entry a copy of the document will be sent to the person requesting the search (reg.4 of the 1995 Regulations).

(4) Once personal representatives have been appointed any notice to quit should be served on them. In order to discover their names the landlord can lodge an application for a standing search at the Probate Registry.

(5) Once the property is vested in beneficiaries the notice to quit should be served upon them (s.36 of Administration of Estates Act 1925).

Where a person serving a notice to quit had no reason to believe that the tenant was dead and serves the notice as if he were alive that service is valid even though he has in fact died (s.17 of the 1994 Act, see below).

For the position generally on the death of a tenant see para.4.021.

Law of Property (Miscellaneous Provisions) Act 1994 sections 17 and 18

3.014   17—(1) Service of a notice affecting land which would be effective but for the death of the intended recipient is effective despite his death if the person serving the notice has no reason to believe that he has died.

(2) Where the person serving a notice affecting land has no reason to believe that the intended recipient has died, the proper address for the purposes of s.7 of the Interpretation Act 1978 (service of documents by post) shall be what would be the proper address apart from his death.

(3) ...

18—(1) A notice affecting land which would have been authorised or required to be served on a person but for his death shall be sufficiently served before a grant of representation has been filed if—

(a) it is addressed to "The Personal Representatives of" the deceased (naming him) and left at or sent by post to his last known place of residence or business in the United Kingdom; and

(b) a copy of it, similarly addressed, is served on the Public Trustee.

(2) The reference in subs.(1) to the filing of a grant of representation is to the filing at the Principal Registry of the Family Division of the High Court of a copy of a grant of representation in respect of the deceased's estate or, as the case may be, the part of his estate which includes the land in question.

(3) The method of service provided for by this section is not available where provision is made—

(a) by or under any enactment; or

(b) by an agreement in writing,

requiring a different method of service, or expressly prohibiting the method of service provided for by this section, in the circumstances.

Proof of service

See para.27.004.   **3.015**

Payment of rent after notice to quit

If the landlord accepts rent after expiry of the notice to quit a new tenancy will not **3.016** necessarily be implied and all the circumstances must be looked at to show the parties' true intentions (*Clarke v Grant* [1950] 1 K.B. 104; *Marcroft Wagons Ltd v Smith* [1951] 2 K.B. 496). In order to ensure that no intention to create a new tenancy is found a landlord requiring rent after service of a notice to quit should demand payment of mesne profits (equal to the rental sum) without prejudice to the effect of the notice to quit. In the circumstances the court will probably hold that there has been no tenancy created on the basis that there was no intention to create legal relations (see *Street v Mountford* [1985] 2 All E.R. 289, Ch.5). Receipt of rent by the landlord of a tenant who has held over after the expiry of the notice to quit, as a statutory tenant under the Rent Act 1977, does not raise any implied agreement to a renewal of the contractual tenancy; the landlord has no option but to accept the rent (*Davies v Bristow* [1920] 3 K.B. 428—see further para.8.016).

Withdrawal of notice to quit

Withdrawal will only be effective if both parties consent to it and it will result in **3.017** a new tenancy commencing from the expiry of the notice; the old tenancy does not continue (see generally *Woodfall: Landlord and Tenant* (London: Sweet & Maxwell), para.17.264).

Notice to quit by tenant

Periodic tenancies and break clauses

3.018 Except where the premises are let on an "excluded tenancy" (see para.22.008) which was entered into on or after the date on which the Housing Act 1988 came into force (January 15, 1989) (and which was not entered into pursuant to a contract made before that date), a tenant of a contractual periodic tenancy must give his landlord notice to quit in writing. The notice need not be in any particular form (because no information has been prescribed by statutory instrument) but it must state the date on which the tenancy is to be determined and the notice must be given at least four weeks before that date (s.5 of the Protection from Eviction Act 1977). However, as with notices given by landlords, a monthly tenancy requires one month's notice, a quarterly tenancy requires a quarter's notice and a yearly tenancy requires six months' notice. The notice should be made to expire on the last day of the tenancy or the anniversary of the tenancy (cf. para.3.004). The landlord may waive the notice requirements of the tenancy or s.5 and treat a defective notice as valid (*Hackney LBC v Snowden* [2001] L.&T.R. 6—"the recipient of a notice which does not comply with section 5 is free to ignore it").

A periodic joint tenancy held by two or more joint tenants may be determined by a notice to quit given by one of the joint tenants without the concurrence of the others unless the terms of the tenancy provide otherwise (*Hammersmith and Fulham LBC v Monk* [1992] 1 All E.R. 1 HL). Failure by one of the joint tenants to consult the others prior to service of a notice is not a breach of trust and encouragement by the landlord to the tenant to give the notice does not invalidate it (*Crawley BC v Ure* (1995) 27 H.L.R. 524 CA; *Notting Hill Housing Trust v Brackley* [2001] 18 E.G. 175 (CS) CA). Nor is a notice invalid by virtue of the fact that it was served by one joint tenant against whom a domestic violence injunction has been made; even if (according to Lord Hoffmann) the injunction includes an order restraining the joint tenant from terminating the tenancy (*Harrow LBC v Johnstone* [1997] 1 All E.R. 929 HL). For the considerations as to whether the Human Rights Act 1998 might apply to this situation see para.23.015.

If the tenancy was a protected tenancy a statutory tenancy will arise after termination by the notice (*Lloyd v Sadler* [1978] 2 All E.R. 529; see para.8.012).

3.019 A notice served pursuant to a break clause in a lease (as opposed to a notice to quit) must be served by all the joint tenants unless the lease expressly provides for it to be determined by one of them (*Re Viola's Indenture of Lease* [1909] 1 Ch. 244; *Hounslow LBC v Pilling* [1994] 1 All E.R. 432 CA). If notice is required to be given by all the tenants but the notice is signed by one only, it may still be effective if that tenant has the other tenants' authority to give notice as their agent. Thus a landlord before acting on a notice signed by one joint tenant should enquire directly of the other joint tenants to learn whether the signing tenant had their authority so to do.

If there is a break clause the tenant should be careful to ensure that the notice complies with the requirements of the lease. However, as with notices to quit, minor errors where the meaning is clear will not invalidate the notice. If the notice unambiguously conveys a decision to determine the tenancy in accordance with the lease the court may ignore immaterial errors which would not have misled a reasonable landlord receiving the notice (*Mannai Investment Co Ltd v Eagle Star Life Assurance Co Ltd* [1997] 3 All E.R. 352 HL).

If the tenancy is regulated the landlord may seek to recover possession under Case 5 of Sch.15 to the Rent Act 1977 if the tenant refuses to leave at the end of the notice period.

A tenant's notice may be served in accordance with the provisions of s.196 of the Law of Property Act 1925 (if the tenancy is in writing and contains a provision for termination by notice to quit and s.196 is not excluded; see s.196(5); para.3.011) by service at an address furnished by the landlord in accordance with s.48 of the Landlord and Tenant Act 1987 or, if no such address has been furnished, at the last address furnished in accordance with s.47 of that Act (s.49 of the 1987 Act; as to ss.47 and 48, see para.28.008).

Landlord and Tenant Act 1987 section 49

In Section 196 of the Law of Property Act 1925 (regulations respecting notices), any reference in subss.(3) or (4) to the last known place of abode or business of the person to be served shall have effect, in its application to a notice to be served by a tenant on a landlord of premises to which this Part applies, as if that reference included a reference to—

(a) the address last furnished to the tenant by the landlord in accordance with s.48; or

(b) if no address has been so furnished in accordance with s.48, the address last furnished to the tenant by the landlord in accordance with s.47.

Fixed-term tenancies

3.020 The tenant cannot terminate before the end of a fixed term unless there is a specific clause in the lease allowing him to do so. The tenant need not give notice to the landlord that he is leaving on the last day of a fixed term.

Expiration of fixed term

3.021 Unless the lease provides otherwise, it is not necessary for the landlord or the tenant to serve the other party with a notice to quit at the end of the fixed term (cf. assured and secure tenancies). The tenant has until midnight on the last day before he need leave (*Re Crowhurst Park* [1974] 1 W.L.R. 583 at 588).

At common law a tenant who remains in occupation without the landlord's consent does so as a tenant at sufferance, and is liable to the landlord for damages for use and occupation (*Bayley v Bradley* (1848) 5 C.B. 396 at 406; see further para.28.042). It is not necessary to serve a notice to terminate a tenancy at sufferance. The landlord may simply commence proceedings for possession. A tenant who remains in possession with the landlord's consent, however, is a tenant at will. The landlord must demand possession from a tenant at will before he commences proceedings for possession although it is not necessary to give four weeks' notice under s.5 of the Protection from Eviction Act 1977 (*Crane v Morris* [1965] 1 W.L.R. 1104). A tenant who remains in possession paying rent on a periodic basis becomes a periodic tenant so long as it is proper to infer that the parties reached an agreement for a new tenancy from all the circumstances, including payment of rent (*Longrigg, Burrough and Trounson v Smith* [1979] 2 E.G.L.R. 42; *Dreamgate Properties Ltd v Arnot* [1997] E.G.C.S. 121). Unless there is an agreement to the contrary the terms of the periodic tenancy will be the same as the terms that applied to the fixed term so far as they are consistent with a periodic tenancy. In particular this means that any forfeiture clause in the fixed term carries over into the periodic term (*Thomas v Packer* (1857) 1 H & N 669) but that the tenancy may also be determined by giving notice appropriate to the period of the tenancy.

The above rules are the general common law rules that apply in the absence of agreement to the contrary. The parties may agree, however, that after the tenancy has come to an end the tenant should become a licensee under either a revocable or irrevocable licence (see *Foster v Robinson* [1951] 1 K.B. 149). The question

"in each case is quo animo the parties have so acted: depending upon the circumstances, their conduct may give rise to a new tenancy, a licence or some other arrangement" (*Burrows v Brent LBC* [1996] 4 All E.R. 577, per Lord Browne-Wilkinson at 583f).

Surrender and abandonment

3.022   A tenancy is brought to an end by surrender when the landlord and tenant both agree that the tenant should yield up the term to the landlord. If the tenancy is a joint tenancy all the joint tenants must agree to the surrender for it to be effective (*Leek and Moorlands Building Society v Clark* [1952] 2 Q.B. 788). Where the tenants owe a substantial amount of rent and one of the joint tenants has been absent for a long period it may be possible to infer that he has given an authority to the other to surrender on behalf of them all (*Preston Borough Council v Fairclough* (1982) 8 H.L.R. 72; cf. *Cooper v Varzdari* (1986) 18 H.L.R. 299). The surrender may be express or by operation of law. However, the general rule is that one of two or more joint tenants cannot surrender a tenancy (cf. *Hounslow LBC v Pilling* [1994] 1 All E.R. 432 CA).

Express surrender

3.023   An express surrender must be made by deed unless the lease is granted for a term of three years or less at the best rent that could reasonably be obtained without taking a fine in which case the lease may be surrendered in writing (ss.52(1), 52(2)(d) and 54(2) of the Law of Property Act 1925). When presented with a document that is expressed to be a surrender it is necessary to ensure that that is exactly what it is. A forfeiture that is disguised as a surrender in order to prevent the tenant from being able to take advantage of the provisions relating to relief against forfeiture will nonetheless be treated as a forfeiture (*Plymouth Corporation v Harvey* [1971] 1 W.L.R. 549).

Surrender by operation of law

3.024   It is much more common, when one is dealing with possession of residential premises, to find surrenders operating as a matter of law. The essence of a surrender by operation of law is the consensual giving up of possession of the premises to the landlord by the tenant.

A surrender of a lease by operation of law occurs where the parties have acted towards each other in a way that is inconsistent with the continuation of the tenancy. Surrender by operation of law does not depend on the intention of the parties, but rather on their conduct, and is founded in estoppel. The burden of proof lies on the party claiming that there has been a surrender: *Artworld Financial Corporation v Safaryan* [2009] EWCA Civ 303. Dyson L.J. (para.29) agreeing with the trial judge and quoting at length from her judgement set out the principles:

"(1) The issue of whether there has been a surrender by operation of law after a tenant's abandonment of the leased premises must be determined by evaluating the effect of the landlord's conduct as a whole (cf *London Borough of Brent v Sharma* (1992) 25 HLR 257 at 259). ... the totality of such acts can amount to a resumption of possession even though individual acts might each be only equivocal. With this in mind –

(2) The test is whether the landlord's conduct is 'so' inconsistent (*Oastler v Henderson* (1877) 2 QBD 575 at 577) with the continuation of the tenant's lease that it could only be justified as being lawful on the basis that the landlord has accepted the tenant's implied offer to give back possession, and has taken possession of the premises beneficially for himself.

(3) Accepting back the keys without more will always be equivocal. As a matter of practicality and common sense, one party has to hold the keys to prevent an absurd situation in which they are passed back and forth because neither party wants to risk it being suggested that it has made an admission by holding them.

(4) Any act of the landlord which is consistent with its rights under the lease, such as entering the premises to inspect or to repair them, will not in itself give rise to a surrender because, by definition, it is not inconsistent with the lease continuing.

(5) Any further act of the landlord which amounts to protecting or preserving the property, such as taking security measures or doing necessary repairs, will not in itself give rise to a surrender because such self-help, necessary to preserve the landlord's interest in the value of his property, is a reasonable response to the tenant's evinced intention not to perform the obligations of the tenancy: cf *McDougall's Catering Foods Ltd v BSE Trading Ltd* (1998) P & CR 312; *Relvok Properties Ltd v Dixon* (1972) 25 P & CR 1, at p 7.

(6) Similarly, any act of the landlord which amounts to the landlord's performing the tenant's covenants under the lease, such as keeping the garden tidy, would not necessarily amount to a resumption of possession as it is not inconsistent with holding the defaulting tenant to performing the lease.

(7) Any further act of the landlord referable to the landlord's seeking to re-let the premises will not necessarily give rise to a surrender by operation of law, as it is no more than what the landlord might reasonably be expected to do in the circumstance for the potential benefit of all parties: *Oastler v Henderson* [1877] 2 QBD 575. The landlord must be entitled to seek to mitigate the damage caused in reality (even if not yet technically in law so long as the lease remains extant) by the tenant's abandoning the lease, by seeking to obtain another tenant, without thereby losing his rights against the original tenant if he is unable to do so.

(8) However, if the landlord goes further and uses the premises for his own benefit beyond the totally trivial - and certainly, in my judgment, if such use amounts to occupation of the premises - then he re-takes possession of the premises inconsistently with the continuance of the lease. This will give rise to a surrender by operation of law, since it is only on the basis of having accepted such a surrender that the landlord's acts would be lawful."

3.025   If the tenant has abandoned the premises the landlord may accept the surrender by changing the locks and re-letting the premises (*R. v London Borough of Croydon Ex p. Toth* (1988) 20 H.L.R. 576), but any landlord that does so is taking quite a risk. He may be mistaken. The tenant may not have absconded the premises at all. He may just be on an extended holiday. The landlord may find himself being accused of committing the offence of unlawful eviction, although he does have a defence if he can prove that he believed, and had reasonable cause to believe, that the tenant had ceased to reside in the premises (s.1(2) of the Protection from Eviction Act 1977). By far the safest solution is to terminate by some other method, such as a notice to quit (if possible), and then to commence proceedings for possession. See also below for the procedure under s.54 of the Landlord and Tenant Act 1954 where the tenant has been missing for over six months (para.3.031).

3.026   Where the parties enter into a new tenancy during the currency of an existing tenancy a surrender of the old tenancy comes about; but only where the parties intend that the tenancy should have a new tenancy on different terms from those of the former tenancy (*Jenkin R Lewis & Son Ltd v Kerman* [1970] 3 All E.R. 414 at 419; *Take Harvest Ltd v Liu* [1993] 2 All E.R. 459 PC).

> "If a tenant holding land under a lease accepts a new lease of the same land from his landlord he is taken to have surrendered his original lease immediately before he accepts the new one. The landlord has no power to grant the new lease except on the footing that the old lease is surrendered and the tenant by accepting the new lease is estopped from denying the surrender of the old one. This 'surrender by operation of law' takes effect whether or not the parties to the new lease intend it to take effect. Moreover, even if there is no express grant of a new lease the old lease will be surrendered by operation of law if the arrangements made between the landlord and the tenant are such as can only be carried out so as to achieve the result which they have in mind if a new tenancy is in fact created." (*Jenkin R Lewis & Son Ltd v Kerman*, per Russell L.J. at 419.)

> "The substantial result which the landlord and tenant 'have in mind' in making their arrangements in the hypothetical case postulated by Russell L.J. is that the tenant shall have a new tenancy of the premises on different terms from those of his former tenancy, whether or not they realise that the law would analyse their agreement as having the effect of the grant of a new tenancy and a surrender of the former tenancy. In cases where the parties do not have this substantial result in mind, the grant of a new tenancy (with a consequent surrender by operation of law) will not be inferred" (*Take Harvest Ltd v Liu per Sir Christopher Slade* at 468d).

3.027 A variation of the terms of the lease which affect the legal estate either by increasing the extent of the premises demised or the term for which they are held operates as a surrender of the old tenancy and the grant of a new one. Other changes, however substantial, do not have this effect (*Friends Provident Life Office v British Railways Board* [1996] 1 All E.R. 336—deed of variation substantially increasing the rent and making it payable in advance instead of in arrear, and alterations to the alienation and user clauses did not effect a surrender and re-grant). In particular, an increase in rent will not be sufficient to give rise to a new tenancy and a surrender of the old (*Jenkin R Lewis & Son v Kerman* [1970] 3 All E.R. 414 CA applied in Friends' Provident).

> "Viewing the matter apart from authority it is difficult to see why the fiction of a new lease and a surrender by operation of law should be necessary in this case; for by simply

increasing the amount of rent and providing that the additional rent shall be annexed to the reversion, one is not altering the nature of the pre-existing item of property" (*Jenkin R Lewis & Son v Kerman* [1970] 3 All E.R. 414 CA per Russell L.J. at 420b).

An agreement adding a new person as a joint tenant constitutes an agreement to vary the existing contract and does not operate as a surrender and re-grant (*Francis Perceval Sounders Dec'd. Trustees v Ralph* (1993) 28 E.G. 129, QBD). However, an agreement to substitute a new tenant for the old tenant will operate as a surrender and re-grant (*London Borough of Tower Hamlets v Ayinde* (1994) 26 H.L.R. 631 CA—secure tenants gave notice to landlord that they were leaving the country and purported to transfer their tenancy to the defendant who moved into the property. The landlord regarded her as unlawful occupier but continued to accept rent from her for five years. Held: there had been a surrender and regrant to the defendant who was entitled to remain in occupation). See also *Camden LBC v Alexandrou* (1997) 30 H.L.R. 534 CA where the wife took over the husband's tenancy after he wrote to the landlord saying that he did not object to her doing so because he could not afford the rent and he was leaving. Where there are negotiations between a landlord and a prospective new tenant for the grant of a lease which are ultimately *unsuccessful*, this is *not* an unequivocal acceptance by the parties to the existing lease that it has come to an end. The mere fact that the tenant has stopped using the property will not be sufficient (*QFS Scaffolding Ltd v Sable* [2010] EWCA Civ 682).

There is a surrender where the landlord and tenant agree that the tenant is to occupy the premises in the future as a licensee (*Foster v Robinson* [1951] 1 K.B. 149) assuming of course that the new agreement is truly a licence (see Ch.5). See also *Dibbs v Campbell* (1988) 20 H.L.R. 374—surrender of a protected tenancy intended to be a protected shorthold tenancy followed by grant of a valid protected shorthold tenancy; and *Bolnore Properties Ltd v Cobb* (1996) 29 H.L.R. 202 CA—surrender of statutory tenancy followed 24 hours later by the grant of a new protected shorthold tenancy.

Evidence of abandonment

It is not uncommon for the landlord to seek an immediate order for possession at **3.028** the hearing on the basis that the tenant has not turned up and that he has abandoned the premises. He will try to rely upon evidence of conversations that he has had with neighbours, the milkman, etc. who have told him that the tenant has disappeared. This evidence is hearsay and if the landlord wishes to rely upon it he will have to call these people or adduce their evidence under the provisions of the Civil Evidence Act 1995, see para.27.008.

Effect of surrender

Where the tenant surrenders by actually giving up possession to the landlord it is **3.029** obviously not necessary to obtain an order for possession. But if the surrender was an express one and the tenant refuses to give up possession it will be necessary to obtain a court order before the landlord can recover possession unless the tenancy is an "excluded tenancy" (see para.22.008) entered into on or after commencement of the Housing Act 1988 (January 15, 1989) otherwise than pursuant to a contract entered into before that date (s.3 of the Protection from Eviction Act 1977).

For the effect on sub-tenants, see para.4.015.

Rent

3.030 If the tenant abandons the premises his liability for rent continues until the landlord accepts the surrender. The onus is on the tenant to show that the landlord's act amounts to an unequivocal acceptance of the surrender if he wishes to avoid paying rent for the period after he left (*Relvok Properties Ltd v Dixon* (1973) 25 P. & C.R. 1; *Boyer v Warbey* [1953] 1 Q.B. 234—a statutory tenant who did not give notice as required by s.3 of the Rent Act 1977).

Difficulty in serving notice to quit; Landlord and Tenant Act 1954 section 54

3.031   There is also a procedure under section 54 of the Landlord and Tenant Act 1954 to bring the tenancy to end when the landlord has been unable to serve a notice to quit and the tenant has been missing for six months.

Landlord and Tenant Act 1954 section 54

3.032   Where a landlord, having power to serve a notice to quit, on an application to the county court satisfies the court—

(a) that he has taken all reasonable steps to communicate with the person last known to him to be the tenant, and has failed to do so;

(b) that during the period of six months ending with the date of the application neither the tenant nor any person claiming under him has been in occupation of the property comprised in the tenancy or any part thereof; and

(c) that during the said period either no rent was payable by the tenant or the rent payable has not been paid,

the court may if it thinks fit by order determine the tenancy as from the date of the order.

Note:

(1) A notice pursuant to a break clause is a notice to quit (s.69).

(2) The procedure is under CPR Pt 8 as modified by CPR 56 and PD 56.

Frustration and repudiation

3.033 A lease may be determined by frustration (*National Carriers Ltd v Panalpina (Northern) Ltd* [1981] 1 All E.R. 161 HL).

It has also been held (in the county court) that a lease can be terminated by a repudiatory breach and acceptance of that repudiation (*Hussein v Mehlman* [1992] 2 E.G.L.R. 87—breach of landlord's repairing covenant treated by the tenant as a repudiatory breach entitling him to terminate. In *Chartered Trust Plc v Davies* [1997] 2 E.G.L.R. 83 Hussein was treated as being correct but there was no argument upon it. See also *Abidogun v Frolan Health Care Ltd* [2001] EWCA Civ 1821 at para.2.002; and *Reichman v Beveridge* [2006] EWCA Civ 1659 at [10]).

Recovery of possession—limited power to postpone

Once the tenancy has come to an end the landlord may recover possession, but **3.034** only by way of court proceedings unless the tenancy is an "excluded tenancy" (see para.22.008) entered into on or after the commencement of the Housing Act 1988 (January 15, 1989) otherwise than pursuant to a contract made before that date (s.3 of the Protection from Eviction Act 1977). Where the tenant has no statutory security of tenure, the court has power at common law to postpone the order for possession. This power has, however, been severely limited by the Housing Act 1980. The effect is that the order may only be postponed for a maximum of 14 days unless such a short order would cause exceptional hardship in which case the court may postpone the date for possession for up to six weeks (s.89 of the Housing Act 1980). The only exception to this rule is where the lease has been brought to an end by forfeiture in which case the tenant may be able to obtain relief against the forfeiture (s.89(2) of the Housing Act 1980). The limitations imposed on the court's discretion by s.89 apply when proceedings are in the High Court as well as the county court (*Boyland and Son Ltd v Rand* [2006] EWCA Civ 1860) but do not apply to a Court exercising appellate jurisdiction during the appeal process so that a warrant can be stayed pending appeal (*Admiral Taverns (Cygnet) Ltd v Daniel* [2008] EWHC 1688).

Housing Act 1980 section 89

(1) Where a court makes an order for the possession of any land in a case not falling within the exceptions mentioned in subsection (2) below, the giving up of possession shall not be postponed (whether by the order or any variation, suspension or stay of execution) to a date later than fourteen days after the making of the order, unless it appears to the court that exceptional hardship would be caused by requiring possession to be given up by that date; and shall not in any event be postponed to a date later than six weeks after the making of the order.

(2) The restrictions in subsection (1) above do not apply if—

    (a) the order for possession is made in an action by a mortgagee for possession; or

    (b) the order is made in an action for forfeiture of a lease; or

    (c) the court had power to make the order only if it considered it reasonable to make it; or

    (d) the order relates to a dwelling house which is the subject of a restricted contract (within the meaning of section 19 of the 1977 Act); or

    (e) the order is made in proceedings brought as mentioned in section 88(1) above (rental purchase agreements).

See para.23.017 for the relationship between s.89 and the Human Rights Act 1998.

Chapter 4

Leases: Assignment, Sub-letting, Bankruptcy and Death

Assignment by landlord

In this section, we are concerned with the sale of the landlord's interest in the **4.001** property, i.e. the assignment of the reversion.

Binding nature of tenancy on new landlord

Where a lease was registered under the Land Registration Act 1925 or the Land **4.002** Registration Act 2002 the interest is deemed to be vested in the lessee (ss.9, 12 and 23 of the 1925 Act and s.12 of the 2002 Act; Sch.12 para.1 of the 2002 Act) and any purchaser of the landlord's interest will take subject to the lease.

Where a lease was "granted for a term" of 21 years or less prior to October 13, 2003 (when the 2002 Act came into force) it will constitute an overriding interest under s.70(1)(k) of the 1925 Act and will continue to bind purchase of the landlord's estate (2002 Act, Sch.12 para.12) whether or not the tenant is in occupation (*City Permanent Building Society v Miller* [1952] Ch. 840 at 848).

The position in respect of overriding interests is different where the lease was granted on or after October 13, 2003. The general position is that the tenancy will constitute an overriding interest if it was granted for a term of seven years or less (see further Sch.1 para.1 and Sch.3 of the 2002 Act). For other interests that might be binding as overriding interests (such as an agreement for a lease held by a person in occupation) see para.2 of each of those Schedules.

Where the tenant's interest was not an overriding one it may, under the 1925 Act, have been protected by an entry on the register of a notice or a caution and remains protected (1925 Act s.59(2); 2002 Act, Sch.12 paras 1 and 2). Under the 2002 Act a lease may not be protected by a notice if it was granted for a term of three years or less from the date of the grant and is not required to be registered (s.33(b)). It will have to rely upon its overriding status. If a lease is protected by a notice under the 2002 Act it ceases to have priority as an overriding interest (s.29(3)).

If the land is unregistered the purchase takes subject to any tenant with a legal estate. If the tenant only has an equitable interest (i.e. an agreement for a lease operating in equity as a lease) the purchase is bound by it if it is registered under the Land Charges Act 1972.

If the new landlord is bound by the tenant's interest he will not be able to obtain possession unless the old landlord would have been able to.

Rights of new landlord against tenant

4.003 The law is governed by two sets of rules depending upon the date upon which the tenancy was granted. Generally speaking, where the tenancy was granted before January 1, 1996, s.141 of the Law of Property Act applies ("old tenancies"). Where it was granted on or after that date the provisions of the Landlord and Tenant (Covenants) Act 1995 generally apply ("new tenancies"); see s.30(4) of the 1995 Act. (For a more precise definition see s.1 of the 1995 Act.)

Old tenancies

4.004 On assignment of the reversion, the right to sue the tenant in respect of all future and any outstanding breaches committed prior to the date of the assignment passes to the new landlord (s.141 of the Law of Property Act 1925). This provision applies to all tenancies including oral ones (see definition of lease in s.205(xxii) of the 1925 Act; *Re King, Robinson v Gray* [1963] 1 All E.R. 781 at 792) and to a specifically enforceable agreement for lease (*Rickett v Green* [1910] 1 K.B. 253).

Law of Property Act 1925 section 141

(1) Rent reserved by a lease, and the benefit of every covenant or provision therein contained, having reference to the subject matter thereof, and on the lessee's part to be observed or performed, and every condition of re-entry and other condition therein contained, shall be annexed and incident to and shall go with the reversionary estate in the land, or in any part thereof, immediately expectant on the term granted by the lease, notwithstanding severance of that reversionary estate, and without prejudice to any liability affecting a covenantor or his estate.

(2) Any such rent, covenant or provision shall be capable of being recovered, received, enforced, and taken advantage of, by the person from time to time entitled, subject to the term, to the income of the whole or any part, as the case may require, of the land leased.

(3) Where that person becomes entitled by conveyance or otherwise, such rent, covenant or provision may be recovered, received, enforced or taken advantage of by him notwithstanding that he becomes so entitled after the condition of re-entry or forfeiture has become enforceable, but this subsection does not render enforceable any condition of re-entry or other condition waived or released before such person becomes entitled as aforesaid.

New tenancies

4.005 If the original landlord has assigned the reversion the original tenant is liable to the current landlord in respect of all future breaches because the benefit of the covenant goes with the reversionary estate (s.3(1) of the 1995 Act). However, the effect of s.23 of the 1995 Act is that the right to sue for the pre-assignment arrears remains with the assignor (*Edlington Properties Ltd v JH Fenner & Co Ltd* [2006] EWCA Civ 403 at [48]) unless there is an express assignment of the chose in action under s.136 of the Law of Property Act 1925.

Whether the tenancy is a new or old one, see para.28.056 in relation to the requirement for notice of the assignment.

Landlord and Tenant (Covenants) Act 1995 section 3

(1) The benefit and burden of all landlord and tenant covenants of a tenancy—

    (a) shall be annexed and incident to the whole, and to each and every part, of the premises demised by the tenancy and of the reversion in them; and

    (b) shall in accordance with this section pass on an assignment of the whole or any part of those premises or of the reversion in them.

Liabilities of old and new landlord after assignment

As above, the law is governed by two sets of rules depending upon the date upon which the tenancy was granted.

Old tenancies

By virtue of s.142 of the Law of Property Act 1925, the new landlord becomes **4.006** liable to comply with the obligations under the lease on the assignment of the reversion; but he is not liable in damages for breaches that occurred prior to the date of the assignment of the landlord's interest (*Duncliffe v Caerfelin Properties Ltd* [1989] 2 E.G.L.R. 38 QBD). The tenant will, therefore, have to sue the old landlord in respect of any such breaches. However, the tenant may set off against a rent debt which has passed to the new landlord under s.141 (see para.4.004) any damages due to him as a result of the assignor's breach of his repairing obligations because the debt vests in the new landlord as assignee subject to all equities which are available to the tenant as assignor (*Smith v Muscat* [2003] EWCA Civ 962, per Sedley L.J. at [28] and [33]).

Law of Property Act 1925 section 142

(1) The obligation under a condition or of a covenant entered into by a lessor with reference to the subject-matter of the lease shall, if and as far as the lessor has power to bind the reversionary estate immediately expectant on the term granted by the lease, be annexed and incident to and shall go with that reversionary estate, or the several parts thereof, notwithstanding severance of that reversionary estate, and may be taken advantage of and enforced by the person in whom the term is from time to time vested by conveyance, devolution, in law or otherwise; and, if and as far as the lessor has power to bind that person from time to time entitled to that reversionary estate, the obligation aforesaid may be taken advantage of and entered against any person so entitled.

This section takes effect without prejudice to any liability affecting a covenantor or his estate.

Section 142 applies to obligations in a side letter and will therefore bind the **4.007** new landlord after an assignment if on the letter's true construction the parties intended that the obligation should run with the land (*System Floors Ltd v Ruralpride Ltd* [1995] 1 E.G.L.R. 48 CA—agreement in a letter given to the tenant at the same time as the grant of a lease, whereby the tenant was given the right to surrender the lease after each rent review, was binding on purchaser of the landlord's interest. The letter contained no reference to successors in title but commercial reality required the concession to be construed as binding on successors otherwise the concession could have been easily circumvented by assigning the reversion). See also *Lotteryking Ltd v AMEC Properties Ltd* [1995] 2 E.G.L.R. 13 Ch D where it was held that the obligations assumed by the landlord under two collateral agreements, to carry out repairs, were assumed by reference to the demised premises and accordingly ran with the reversion.

By virtue of the contract between them an original landlord continues to be liable to an original tenant on his covenant after assignment of the reversion (see final sentence of s.142).

Where the landlord is an assignee of the reversion, in principle, he ceases to be liable after a further assignment of the reversion because there is no longer any privity of estate between that landlord and the tenant.

New tenancies

4.008 The rights and liabilities of the new landlord are set out in ss.2, 3 and 23 of the 1995 Act. After the assignment he becomes liable on the landlord covenants in the lease whether or not they have reference to the subject-matter of the tenancy, i.e. whether or not they "touch and concern the land" (s.2(1)). The old landlord is not automatically released from his covenants when he assigns the reversion. If he wishes to be released he needs to serve an appropriate notice (see further ss.6, 7 and 8 of the 1985 Act). The old landlord remains liable for breaches that occurred prior to the assignment (*Edlington Properties Ltd v JH Fenner & Co Ltd* [2006] EWCA Civ 403).

Whether the tenancy is a new or old one specific regard must be had to s.3 of the Landlord and Tenant Act 1985. The liability of the old landlord does not actually cease until the tenant has been notified of the new landlord's name and address in accordance with s.3 (s.3(3A)).

Landlord and Tenant Act 1985 section 3

(1) If the interest of the landlord under a tenancy of premises which consist of or include a dwelling is assigned, the new landlord shall give notice in writing of the assignment, and of his name and address, to the tenant not later than the next day on which rent is payable under the tenancy or, if that is within two months of the assignment, the end of that period of two months.

(2) If trustees constitute the new landlord, a collective description of the trustees of the trust in question may be given as the name of the landlord, and where such a collective description is given—

(a) the address of the new landlord may be given as the address from which the affairs of the trust are conducted; and

(b) a change in the persons who are for the time being the trustees of the trust shall not be treated as an assignment of the interest of the landlord.

(3) A person who is the new landlord under a tenancy falling within subsection (1) and who fails, without reasonable excuse, to give the notice required by that subsection, commits a summary offence and is liable on conviction to a fine not exceeding level 4 on the standard scale.

(3A) The person who was the landlord under the tenancy immediately before the assignment ("the old landlord") shall be liable to the tenant in respect of any breach of any covenant, condition or agreement under the tenancy occurring before the end of the relevant period in like manner as if the interest assigned were still vested in him; and where the new landlord is also liable to the tenant in respect of any such breach occurring within that period, he and the old landlord shall be jointly and severally liable in respect of it.

(3B) In subsection (3A) "the relevant period" means the period beginning with the date of the assignment and ending with the date when—

(a) notice in writing of the assignment, and of the new landlord's name and address, is given to the tenant by the new landlord (whether in accordance with subsection (1) or not); or

(b) notice in writing of the assignment, and of the new landlord's name and last known address, is given to the tenant by the old landlord

whichever happens first.

(4) In this section—

(a) "tenancy" includes a statutory tenancy; and

(b) references to the assignment of the landlord's interest include any conveyance other than a mortgage or charge.

Date upon which assignment takes effect

Where the landlord's interest is a freehold or a lease of more than three years the **4.009** assignment of the interest must be made by deed (ss.52 and 54 of the Law of Property Act 1925). Section 141 of the Law of Property Act 1925 or ss.2, 3 and 23 of the 1995 Act does not, therefore, come into operation, and the new landlord may not enforce the covenants or forfeit, until the legal estate is conveyed to him by the deed.

Where the landlord's estate is registered it is the registration which confers on the new landlord the interest transferred together with all rights, including the rights and interests which would, under the Law of Property Act 1925, have been transferred if the land had not been registered (s.20 of the Land Registration Act 1925 in the case of freeholds, and ss.22 and 23 of that Act in the case of leaseholds; *Brown & Root Technology Ltd v Sun Alliance & London Assurance Co Ltd* [1997] 1 E.G.L.R. 39 CA). Thus, in the case of registered land the new landlord may not take steps to enforce the covenants or forfeit until the disposition of the estate has been registered.

If proceedings are commenced by the old landlord the new landlord can be substituted as claimant once the legal interest has been vested in the new landlord.

Assignment by tenant

Has there been an effective assignment?

An assignment is ineffective to pass the tenant's legal estate to the proposed **4.010** assignee unless it is made by deed (s.52(1) of the Law of Property Act 1925). This is the position even where the tenancy is a yearly or other periodic tenancy (*Crago v Julian* [1992] 1 All E.R. 744). However, a deed is not necessary where the landlord expressly or impliedly agrees to the assignee becoming the tenant and accepts him in the place of the former tenant. There is, strictly speaking, no assignment but a surrender and a new tenancy which can be created orally

(*Crago v Julian* at 749b), but note that the old tenant must also expressly or impliedly agree to the new arrangement (see further Surrender, para.3.027).

An assignment of a registered leasehold interest is not effective to pass the legal estate until it is registered (ss.6 and 7 of the Land Registration Act 2002; *E.ON UK Plc v Gilesports Ltd* [2012] EWHC 2172 (Ch)).

4.011 A contract for the assignment of a lease will, as between the contracting parties, vest an equitable interest in the assignee if it is capable of being specifically enforced (see the doctrine of *Walsh v Lonsdale*, para.1.010). An assignee in possession will, therefore, invariably have an effective interest in the property as against the assignor, whether the assignment was made by deed or not. However, the agreement to assign is not binding on the landlord (*Cox v Bishop* (1857) 8 De GM & G 815). Furthermore, the fact that the intended assignee has paid the rent does not of itself mean that the landlord is estopped from denying the assignment, for the rent could be paid by him as agent for the real tenant (*Official Trustee of Charity Lands v Ferriman Trust* [1937] 3 All E.R. 85).

Although the landlord may not be bound to accept an equitable assignee as the assignee of the lease he may wish to do so, particularly if he wishes to serve a notice to quit. In the absence of evidence to the contrary there is a presumption that the occupier is an assignee, thus permitting the landlord to serve a notice to quit upon him (see cases cited at para.3.010). Furthermore, where a licence to assign is granted at the request of the tenant and the assignee enters into possession pursuant to the licence he may be estopped from denying that a valid assignment has been made (*Rodenhurst Estates v Barnes* [1936] 2 All E.R. 3).

Assignment in breach of covenant

4.012 An assignment is effective and transfers the tenancy to the assignee, even if it is made in breach of an absolute or qualified covenant prohibiting assignments (*Old Grovebury Manor Farm v W Seymour Plant Sales and Hire Ltd (No.2)* [1979] 3 All E.R. 504 CA; *Governors of Peabody Donation Fund v Higgins* [1983] 3 All E.R. 122) unless the assignment of the lease is registrable and has not been registered (*E.ON UK Plc v Gilesports Ltd* [2012] EWHC 2172 (Ch)). However, if the assignment has taken place in breach of any such covenant and there is a right of re-entry provided for in the lease the landlord may forfeit. An assignment is not unlawful unless it is committed in breach of a term of the tenancy agreement (*Allcock v Moorhouse* (1882) 9 Q.B.D. 366—a periodic tenancy), but it may still give rise to a ground for possession (*Case 6*, Rent Act 1977; see para.A2.019). See further *RC Glaze Properties Ltd* in relation to sub-lettings (para.4.015).

Unreasonable refusal to consent to assignment

4.013 Where the covenant against assignment is a qualified covenant, i.e. a covenant not to assign without consent, the landlord may not unreasonably refuse his consent (s.19(1) of the Landlord and Tenant Act 1927). If his consent is requested and he unreasonably refuses the landlord will not be able to rely upon the covenant to obtain possession. For guidance as to whether or not the landlord's consent is unreasonable see in particular *International Drilling Fluids Ltd v Louisville Investments (Uxbridge) Ltd* [1986] 1 All E.R. 312 (general principles); *Dong Bang Minerva (UK) v Davina Ltd* [1996] 2 E.G.L.R. 31 (landlord's costs) and *Kened Ltd v Connie Investments Ltd* [1997] 04 E.G. 141 at 142 (burden of proof); *Go West Ltd v Spigarolo* [2003] EWCA Civ 17.

Effect of assignment

Once the lease has been assigned the assignee is liable to the landlord on the **4.014** covenants that touch and concern the land pursuant to the principle of "privity of estate", i.e. he is liable so long as he holds the estate. However, he will cease to be liable after he has himself assigned the lease to someone else unless he previously entered into an agreement with the landlord (usually pursuant to a licence to assign permitting him to take the lease) to remain liable.

The new tenant is not liable in damages for breaches committed by his predecessor (*Parry v Robinson-Wyllie* [1987] 2 E.G.L.R. 133) unless the breach is a continuing one, in which case he will be liable for that continuing breach. However, the landlord will be entitled to forfeit in respect of any breaches that have not been remedied or waived and the new tenant will have to apply for relief from forfeiture (see Ch.2).

A tenant who assigns his lease retains the right to sue the landlord for breaches of covenant that occurred before the assignment. The right to sue in respect of past breaches does not pass to the assignee, but if the breach is a continuing one the new tenant may sue in respect of that continuing breach (*City & Metropolitan Properties v Greycroft* [1987] 3 All E.R. 839 QBD).

Sub-letting

Unless there is a covenant against sub-letting the tenant may sub-let all or part of **4.015** the premises without the risk of prejudicing his tenancy. In the absence of a written tenancy agreement it is often difficult to determine whether or not the tenant is prohibited from sub-letting. In *RC Glaze Properties Ltd v Alabdinboni* (1993) 25 H.L.R. 150, the Court of Appeal held that the county court judge was entitled to infer the presence of a term prohibiting sub-letting where a rent book used consistently by the landlord stated in bold type that sub-letting was prohibited. It is a question of fact in every case whether such a term can be inferred.

However, once the landlord lawfully determines the tenancy by service of a valid notice to quit the sub-tenancy disappears along with the head lease whether or not it was lawfully granted. Or, as it is often graphically expressed "the branch falls with the tree" (see *Moore Properties (Ilford) Ltd v McKeon* [1976] 1 W.L.R. 1278 where the tenants were in fact unlawful). The sub-tenancy comes to an end even if the notice to quit has been served with the consent of the head-tenant (*Barrett v Morgan* [2000] UKHL 1). The position is the same at the end of a fixed-term tenancy.

Where the tenancy is unlawful, i.e. created in breach of covenant, the landlord may bring the tenancy to an end by forfeiting it provided that the lease contains a forfeiture clause. If the landlord does forfeit the lease the sub-tenancy will once again also disappear. The tenant and the sub-tenant will, however, have the right to claim relief against forfeiture (see paras 2.094 and 2.117).

If the landlord does not wish to forfeit the lease he may seek an injunction either in anticipation of an intended breach or in some cases afterwards. In *Hemingway Securities v Dunraven Ltd* [1995] 1 E.G.L.R. 61 an injunction was granted against a tenant and sub-tenant for breach of the covenant against sub-letting. The sub-tenant was ordered to surrender the tenancy. (See also *Crestfort Limited v Tesco Stores Limited* [2005] EWHC 805 (Ch)). The landlord may also sue for damages for breach of the covenant.

4.016   The position is rather different where the tenant surrenders his term. In that case the "branch does not fall with the tree" because a tenant by voluntarily surrendering his term will not be permitted to destroy the sub-tenancy that he has created (*Parker v Jones* [1910] 2 K.B. 32; *Cow v Casey* [1949] 1 K.B. 474 at 478). Instead the tenant in effect becomes the tenant of the landlord on the terms of the sub-tenancy unless the surrender was with a view to the grant of a new lease (s.139 of the Law of Property Act 1925) in which case the sub-tenant once again becomes a sub-tenant and his rights and obligations continue as if nothing had occurred (s.150 of the Law of Property Act 1925). For a modern example, in the context of a secure tenancy, see *Basingstoke and Deane BC v Paice* (1995) 27 H.L.R. 433 CA. If the landlord was aware of the sub-tenancy at the time that he accepted the surrender he may not even forfeit if the sub-letting was in breach of covenant (*Parker v Jones*—query whether he may forfeit if he was not aware of the breach at the time that he accepted the surrender). Where, however, the tenant terminates his tenancy by a notice to quit upon the landlord, service of the notice will destroy the sub-tenancy (*Pennell v Payne* [1995] 2 All E.R. 592 CA) even if it has been served as a result of an agreement with the landlord. That agreement may expose the head tenant to a claim for damages for breach of the covenant against derogation from grant but it does not invalidate the notice to quit (*Barrett v Morgan* [2000] UKHL).

A sub-letting of the whole term operates as an assignment, so that the tenant loses his interest in the property and will not be able to claim possession from the sub-tenant (*Milmo v Carreras* [1946] K.B. 306). But in a case where the tenant held under a periodic tenancy and sub-let for a fixed term that was greater than the period an assignment was not deemed to have taken effect (*Curteis v Corcoran* (1947) 150 E.G. 44).

Bankruptcy

Bankruptcy of the landlord

4.017   Where the landlord is the freehold owner of the premises the tenant's position is unaffected if the landlord goes bankrupt. The reversion simply becomes vested in the landlord's trustee in bankruptcy/liquidator unless and until he assigns the property to someone else. If the landlord was himself a tenant the sub-tenant's position is slightly different and is dealt with below.

Bankruptcy of the tenant (Insolvency Act 1986 sections 283, 306, 308A, 315–321)

4.018   The general position is that upon the bankruptcy of a tenant the tenant's interest in the dwelling-house vests, as part of his estate (s.283), in the trustee in bankruptcy immediately on the trustee's appointment taking effect (s.306 of the Insolvency Act 1986). However, it should be noted that certain assured, protected, agricultural and secure tenancies and occupancies do not form part of the estate unless a specific notice is served upon the bankrupt by the trustee (ss.283(3A) and 308A as introduced by s.117 of the Housing Act 1988—see the relevant chapter in relation to each type of tenancy). In the case of a continuation tenancy under Pt 1 of the 1954 Act (which would now be under Sch.10 of the Local Government and

Housing Act 1989—see Ch.16) this was held to be part of the bankrupt's estate (*De Rothschild v Bell* [2000] Q.B. 33).

Where the tenant's interest in the dwelling-house does vest in the trustee in bankruptcy s.315 of the 1986 Act provides that the trustee may, by the giving of a prescribed notice (i.e. prescribed by rules made under ss.384 and 412), disclaim the tenancy. He may do so notwithstanding that he has taken possession of the property, endeavoured to sell it or otherwise exercised rights of ownership in relation to it (see s.315(1), (2)(b)). In addition to serving a notice upon the landlord, the trustee must also (so far as he is aware of their addresses) serve a copy of the disclaimer on every person claiming under the bankrupt as sub-tenant or mortgagee and upon every person in occupation or claiming a right to occupy the dwelling-house. In these circumstances the disclaimer will take effect if there is no application made for a vesting order under s.320 (see below) within a period of 14 days beginning with the day on which the last notice was served or, if there is such an application, the court directs that the disclaimer is to take effect (see ss.317 and 318).

The trustee may not disclaim where a "person interested in the property" has **4.019** applied in writing to the trustee to ask him whether he will disclaim or not and the trustee has not served a notice of disclaimer within the period of 28 days beginning with the date of that application (s.316).

Where the trustee does disclaim the disclaimer operates "so as to determine, as from the date of the disclaimer, the rights, interests and liabilities of the bankrupt and his estate in or in respect of the property disclaimed" but does not affect third party rights "except so far as is necessary for the purpose of releasing the bankrupt, the bankrupt's estate and the trustee from any liability" (s.315(3)); see further *Hindcastle Ltd v Barbara Attenborough Associates Ltd* [1996] 1 All E.R. 737, in particular per Lord Nicholls at 747g–j).

Any person who claims an interest in the disclaimed dwelling-house, any person who is under any liability in respect of it, and any person in occupation or claiming a right to be in occupation may seek a vesting order pursuant to s.320. The terms upon which a vesting order may be made are set out in s.321.

If the trustee is entitled to and does disclaim, the original tenant has no right to remain on the premises and if he continues to do so without the consent of the landlord proceedings for possession may be taken (*Smalley v Quarrier* [1975] 2 All E.R. 688 CA). The landlord may not, however, recover possession from the bankrupt tenant's sub-tenant (*Smalley v Hardinge* (1881) 7 Q.B.D. 524). The subtenants are released from their obligations to the tenant but they must perform the obligations which the tenant originally owed to his landlord. If they do not do so and there is a proviso for re-entry the landlord may forfeit (*Re Finley Ex p. Clothworkers' Co* (1888) 21 Q.B.D. 475 at 486; *Re Levy Ex p. Walton* (1881) 17 Ch D 746 and see para.2.047 in relation to restrictions on forfeiture). If any subtenant wishes to regularise the position he may apply for an order vesting the tenant's interest in himself, pursuant to s.320 of the 1986 Act.

If the bankrupt is an assignee of the term the lease continues in existence after disclaimer and the landlord can claim the rent from the original tenant who may apply for an order vesting the estate in himself (*Warnford Investments Ltd v Duckworth* [1979] Ch. 127). Thereafter the original tenant will once again be able to occupy the premises.

Some leases contain a clause permitting the landlord to forfeit the lease on the tenant's bankruptcy and if the trustee does not disclaim the lease the landlord may seek to recover possession by commencing forfeiture proceedings (s.146(9) and (10) of the Law of Property Act 1925; see further para.2.047).

Death

Death of landlord

4.020 The tenant's position is unaffected by the death of the landlord. During the administration of his estate the landlord's interest will vest in his personal representatives and eventually the beneficiary of the original landlord's estate will become the lessor. These changes do not, however, give any of these persons the right to claim possession of the premises in circumstances other than those which would have given the deceased landlord the right to claim possession. See para.25.006 for the rights of personal representatives to sue for possession.

Death of the tenant

4.021 The death of the tenant does not terminate the tenancy (ss.1 and 3(1) of the Administration of Estates Act 1925). The tenant's interest, whether it be for a fixed or periodic term, vests in the personal representatives who are liable to pay the rent from the estate (*Youngmin v Heath* [1974] 1 All E.R. 461).

Where the tenant has left a will and the named executors are alive and prepared to administer the estate, the tenancy will vest in them from the date of death if they have obtained a grant of probate (*Re Crowhurst Park* [1974] 1 W.L.R. 583). Where there is a will but no executor with power to obtain a grant the estate vests in the Public Trustee (Administration of Estates Act 1925 s.9, as amended). Where the tenant has died intestate the estate vests in the Public Trustee until administrators are appointed (Administration of Estates Act 1925 s.9, as amended).

Administration of Estates Act 1925 section 9

> (1) Where a person dies intestate, his real and personal estate shall vest in the Public Trustee until the grant of administration.
> (2) Where a testator dies and—
>
> > (a) at the time of his death there is no executor with power to obtain probate of the will; or
> > (b) at any time before probate of the will is granted there ceases to be any executor with power to obtain probate;
>
> the real and personal estate of which he disposes by the will shall vest in the Public Trustee until the grant of representation.
> (3) The vesting of real or personal estate in the Public Trustee by virtue of this section does not confer on him any beneficial interest in, or impose on him any duty, obligation or liability in respect of, the property.

4.022 Once letters of administration have been granted the estate vests in the administrators from the date of the grant. Their title to the property does not relate back to the date of death as with executors (*Long (Fred) and Sons Ltd v Burgess* [1950] K.B. 115).

The beneficiaries become entitled to hold the tenancy when it has been vested in them by an assent (s.36 of the Administration of Estates Act 1925). If the title is registered the beneficiary should register as proprietor (s.41(4) of the Land Registration Act 1925).

As a periodic tenancy continues notwithstanding the death of the tenant, failure to terminate the tenancy by notice to quit will leave the tenancy in being (*Wirral Borough Council v Smith and Cooper* (1982) 43 P. & C.R. 312—landlord unable to bring possession proceedings against squatters because of failure to determine the periodic tenancy).

As to service of a notice to quit after the death of a tenant see para.3.013.

Although the death of the tenant does not automatically terminate the tenancy it may give the landlord the right to forfeit the lease if there is a forfeiture clause in the agreement allowing him to do so.

Chapter 5

Licence Agreements

It is usually important to know whether an agreement is a tenancy or a licence. A **5.001**
licensee cannot be an assured tenant (under the Housing Act 1988) or a regulated
tenant (under the Rent Act 1977) and his rights in relation to the property which
he occupies are likely to be very limited; although see para.10.004 in relation to
secure tenancies and in some cases, a licensee will have the limited protection of
the Protection from Eviction Act 1977 (see para.22.003). This chapter considers
the circumstances in which a person is a licensee, the termination of licences
(other than those that are secure tenants) and recovery of possession from
licensees.

In the past there was much litigation on this subject culminating in decisions of
the House of Lords. In *Street v Mountford* [1985] 2 All E.R. 289 the traditional
view that, save for certain limited exceptions, an occupier of land for a term at a
rent is a tenant provided that the occupier is granted exclusive possession was
reaffirmed. The position where two or more persons occupy one property under
separate agreements which purport to be "licences" was considered by the House
of Lords in *AG Securities v Vaughan* and *Antoniades v Villiers* [1988] 3 All E.R.
1058.

In each of these cases the leading judgment was given by Lord Templeman.
The quotations in this chapter are taken from his judgments.

Distinction between leases and licences

Generally

"The traditional view that the grant of exclusive possession for a term creates a tenancy **5.002**
is consistent with the elevation of a tenancy into an estate in land. The tenant possessing
exclusive possession is able to exercise the rights of an owner of land, which is in the
real sense his land albeit temporarily and subject to certain restrictions. A tenant armed
with exclusive possession can keep out strangers and keep out the landlord unless the
landlord is exercising limited rights reserved to him by the tenancy agreement to enter
and view and repair. A licensee lacking exclusive possession can in no sense call the
land his own and cannot be said to own any estate in the land. The licence does not
create an estate in the land to which it relates but only makes an act lawful which would
otherwise be unlawful" (*Street* at 292d to e).

"... the traditional distinction between a tenancy and a licence of land lay in the grant
of land for a term at a rent with exclusive possession" (*Street* at 292g).

After the decision of the Court of Appeal in *Somma v Hazelhurst* [1978] 1 W.L.R. 1014 the courts, when dealing with written agreements for the occupation of land, had adopted the practice of analysing their provisions for the purpose of assigning some of them to the category of terms which are usually thought to be found in tenancy agreements and of assigning others to the category of terms which are usually thought to be found in licences. In *Street v Mountford* Lord Templeman stated that this was the wrong way to assess such agreements. The proper approach is to analyse each agreement in order to decide whether exclusive possession has been granted (299h).

5.003   Furthermore, the label that the parties attach to an agreement is not conclusive. The mere fact that they call it a licence does not necessarily mean that it is a licence. If upon its true construction the agreement is a tenancy, i.e. it gives a right to exclusive possession for a fixed or periodic term at a rent, the court will hold that it is a tenancy whatever the parties might say about their intentions.

> "The consequences in law of the agreement, once concluded, can only be determined by consideration of the effect of the agreement. If the agreement satisfied all the require- ments of a tenancy, then the agreement produced a tenancy and the parties cannot alter the effect of the agreement by insisting that they only created a licence. The manufacture of a five-pronged implement for manual digging results in a fork even if the manufac- turer, unfamiliar with the English language, insists that he intended to make and has made a spade" (*Street* at 294j).
>
> ". . . the only intention which is relevant is the intention demonstrated by the agree- ment to grant exclusive possession for a term at a rent" (*Street* at 300b; see further below, "Shams" and "Pretences").

Application of the rule to residential premises

5.004 "In the case of residential accommodation there is no difficulty in deciding whether the grant confers exclusive possession. An occupier of residential accommodation at a rent for a term is either a lodger or a tenant. The occupier is a lodger if the land- lord provides attendance or services which require the landlord or his servants to exercise unrestricted access to and use of the premises. A lodger is entitled to live in the premises but cannot call the place his own . . . If on the other hand residential accommodation is granted for a term at a rent with exclusive possession, the land- lord providing neither attendance nor services, the grant is a tenancy; any express reservation to the landlord of limited rights to enter and view the state of the premises and to repair and maintain the premises only serve to emphasise the fact that the grantee is entitled to exclusive possession and is a tenant" (*Street* at 293g to j).

> ". . . in my opinion, in order to ascertain the nature and quality of the occupancy and to see whether the occupier has or has not a stake in the room or only permission for himself personally to occupy, the court must decide whether on its true construction the agreement confers on the occupier exclusive possession" (*Street* at 299a).

A lodger will very often be a person who lives in a house with a family using one bedroom and sharing the other accommodation. Meals may be provided and perhaps his room will be cleaned for him. However, there are other cases where occupiers of single rooms will be held to be licensees rather than tenants. In *Marchant v Charters* [1977] 3 All E.R. 918 a bed-sitting room was occupied on terms that the landlord cleaned the rooms daily and provided clean linen each week. Lord Templeman stated that the court's decision that the occupier was a licensee and not a tenant was sustainable on the grounds that the occupier was a lodger and did not enjoy exclusive possession (*Street* at 298g). In *Abbeyfield (Harpenden) Society Ltd v Woods* [1968] 1 All E.R. 352 the occupier of a room in an old people's home was held to be a licensee and not a tenant. Besides occupying one room, the occupier was provided with services, meals and a resident housekeeper. Lord Templeman stated that as far as he understood the decision "the court came to the conclusion that the occupier was a lodger and was therefore a licensee and not a tenant" (*Street* at 298a to c).

The retention of a key, by itself, is not decisive in determining whether or not the landlord retains exclusive possession (*Aslan v Murphy (Nos 1 and 2)* [1989] 3 All E.R. 130; *Family Housing Association v Jones* [1990] 1 All E.R. 385).

As to flat sharing see Ch.14.

Written licence agreements: genuine cases

The question of whether or not the agreement confers upon the occupier exclusive **5.005** possession has caused most difficulty in cases where there have been two or more occupiers who are in occupation pursuant to written agreements which are expressed to be licence agreements.

In *Crancour Ltd v Da Silvaesa* [1986] 1 E.G.L.R. 80 the accommodation concerned was bed-sit type accommodation in a large house. The occupiers had entered into written agreements that were called "licences". Clause 1 licensed the occupiers to use the furnished room provided

> "on each day between the hours of midnight and 10.30 am and between noon and midnight but at no other time for a period of 26 weeks . . . for the purpose of temporary accommodation for the licensee's personal use only . . ."

The agreement also contained the following clauses:

> "2. The possession, management and control of the flat remains vested in the licensor, who is the occupier for all purposes including taxation and rating. The licensor will retain the keys to the flat and has an absolute right of entry at all times for the purpose of exercising such management and control and . . . for the purpose of providing the attendance mentioned in clause 9 hereof or for the purpose of removing or substituting such articles of furniture from the flat as the licensor may see fit.
> 3. The licensee shall pay the licensor a fee of £110 per fortnight for his use of the flat . . .
> 4. The licensor may for any reason and at any time require the licensee forthwith to vacate the flat and move into any other flat of comparable size in the building which the licensor may offer the licensee . . .
> 5. This licence agreement confers upon the licensee merely a personal privilege to use the flat.
>   . . .
> 9. The licensor will provide the following attendance for the licensee: (i) Housekeeper; (ii) Lighting of common parts; (iii) Cleaning of common parts; (iv) Window cleaning; (v) Service to front door; (vi) Telephone; (vii) Cleaning of flat; (viii) Collection of rubbish; (ix) Provision and laundering of bed linen; (x) Hot water."

The Court of Appeal held that the provision relating to the times at which the room **5.006** could be used (in cl.1) and as to the right to remove furniture were arguably "sham" provisions and that the case was not therefore sufficiently clear to justify a summary order for possession. However, it also held that if the written agreements represented the true agreement of the parties the occupants were lodgers and not tenants. (In relation to cl.4 of the agreement compare *Dresden Estates v Collinson* [1987] 1 E.G.L.R. 45—a case concerned with business premises.)

Genuine non-possession agreements are not confined to bed-sitter/hostel type accommodation. They may also exist, for example, in flat-sharing cases. In *AG Securities v Vaughan* [1988] 3 All E.R. 1058 the property consisted of six living rooms, a kitchen and bathroom. Four rooms were furnished as bedrooms, a fifth as a lounge and a sixth as a sitting room. The owner entered into separate agreements with each occupant. Each agreement was in the same form and described the occupier as a licensee who had

> "the right to use in common with others who have or may from time to time be granted the like right the flat known as (Flat 25) but without the right to exclusive possession of any part of the said flat".

The flat was kept fully occupied; whenever one agreement was terminated the owner of the property invited applications to fill the vacancy. The monthly sum payable by each applicant was not necessarily the same as the monthly sum payable by any of the continuing occupiers of the flat. The four occupiers at the time of the proceedings were all in occupation under agreements of different dates and were each paying different sums. The House of Lords held that each occupier was a licensee of the whole flat. There was no unity of interest, no unity of title, no unity of time and no unity of possession (see Lord Oliver at 1074j). It was impossible to hold that they were joint tenants. For similar cases, where the occupiers were held to be licensees, see *Stribling v Wickham* (1989) 21 H.L.R. 318 and *Mikeover Ltd v Brady* [1989] 3 All E.R. 618.

5.007   Note that in *AG Securities v Vaughan* it was not contended that any individual occupier had a tenancy of a particular room in the flat with a right to use the remainder in common with the tenants of other rooms: see Lord Oliver at 1074b. In other circumstances this may be the situation in which case the occupiers will be entitled to the protection afforded by s.22 of the Rent Act 1977 or, as the case may be, s.10 of the Housing Act 1988 (see further para.14.004).

In *Westminster City Council v Clarke* [1992] 1 All E.R. 695 the local authority provided homeless persons with temporary accommodation in a hostel while dealing with their applications for permanent accommodation under the Housing Act 1985. Those persons occupied bed-sitting rooms under agreements which negatived exclusive possession. The grant of exclusive possession would have been inconsistent with the purposes for which the council provided the accommodation and the House of Lords held that the agreements were genuine licences. However, Lord Templeman pointed out that the case was a very special one which was unlikely to have more than limited application (at 703f).

An agreement in respect of a room in a hostel providing that the occupier could be moved to another room at any time in order to facilitate better management of the hostel was held to be a genuine licence (*Brennan v Lambeth BC* (1997) 30 H.L.R. 481 CA).

Written "licence" agreements: "shams" and "pretences"

5.008 The House of Lords considered this type of agreement in *Antoniades v Villiers* [1988] 3 All E.R. 1058. In that case the accommodation comprised a bedroom, a bed-sitting room, kitchen and bathroom. The occupiers, a man and a woman, had spent three months looking for a flat where they could live together. When they were shown the flat by the owner the bedroom lacked a bed. They expressed a preference for a double bed and this was provided. The occupiers entered into separate "licence agreements" in standard form whereby "the licensor licenses the licensee to use (but not exclusively) all those rooms etc." In particular cl.16 of the agreement was in the following terms:

> "16. The licensor shall be entitled at any time to use the rooms together with the licensee and permit other persons to use all of the rooms together with the licensee."

The two agreements were clearly interdependent. Both would have been signed or neither. In those circumstances the court held that the two agreements should be read together:

> "Mr Villiers and Miss Bridger applied to rent the flat jointly and sought and enjoyed an exclusive occupation of the whole of the flat. They shared the rights and the obligations imposed by the terms of their occupation. They acquired joint and exclusive occupation of the flat in consideration of periodical payments and they therefore acquired a tenancy jointly. Mr Antoniades required each of them, Mr Villiers and Miss Bridger, to agree to pay one-half of each aggregate periodical payment, but this circumstance cannot convert a tenancy into a licence. A tenancy remains a tenancy even though the landlord may choose to require each of two joint tenants to agree expressly to pay one-half of the rent. The tenancy conferred on Mr Villiers and Miss Bridger the right to occupy the whole flat as their dwelling. Clause 16 reserved to Mr Antoniades the power at any time to go into occupation of the flat jointly with Mr Villiers and Miss Bridger. The exercise of that power would at common law put an end to the exclusive occupation of the flat by Mr Villiers and Miss Bridger, terminate the tenancy of Mr Villiers and Miss Bridger and convert Mr Villiers and Miss Bridger into licensees. But the powers reserved to Mr Antoniades by cl 16 cannot be lawfully exercised because they are inconsistent with the provisions of the Rent Acts (1066e) . . . Where a landlord creates a tenancy of a flat and reserves the right to go into exclusive occupation at any time of the whole or part of the flat with or without notice, that reservation is inconsistent with the provisions of the Rent Acts and cannot be enforced without an order of the court under section 98. Where a landlord creates a tenancy of a flat and reserves the right to go into occupation of the whole or part of the flat with or without notice, jointly with the existing tenants, that reservation also is inconsistent with the provisions of the Acts. Were it otherwise every tenancy agreement would be labelled a licence and would contract out of the Rent Acts by reserving power to the landlord to share possession with the tenant at any time after the commencement of the term" (at 1067c).

Earlier in his judgment Lord Templeman had said: **5.009**

> "Parties to an agreement cannot contract out of the Rent Acts; if they were able to do so the Acts would be a dead letter because in a state of housing shortage a person seeking residential accommodation may agree to anything to obtain shelter. The Rent Acts protect a tenant but they do not protect a licensee. Since parties to an agreement cannot contract out of the Rent Acts, a document which expresses the intention, genuine or bogus, of both parties or of one party to create a licence will nevertheless create a tenancy if the rights and obligations enjoyed and imposed satisfy the legal requirements of a tenancy. A person seeking residential accommodation may concur in any expression of intention in order to obtain shelter. Since parties to an agreement cannot contract out of the Rent Acts, a document expressed in the language of a licence must nevertheless be examined and construed by the court in order to decide whether the rights and obligations enjoyed and imposed create a licence or a tenancy. A person seeking residential

accommodation may sign a document couched in any language in order to obtain shelter. Since parties to an agreement cannot contract out of the Rent Acts, the grant of a tenancy to two persons jointly cannot be concealed, accidentally, or by design, by the creation of two documents in the form of licences. Two persons seeking residential accommodation may sign any number of documents in order to obtain joint shelter. In considering one or more documents for the purpose of deciding whether a tenancy has been created, the court must consider the surrounding circumstances, including any relationship between the prospective occupiers, the course of negotiations and the nature and extent of the accommodation and the intended and actual mode of occupation of the accommodation" (at 1064f).

In deciding whether or not the terms of a so-called "licence agreement" in fact create a tenancy the court does not simply ask itself whether the agreement is a sham. It also considers whether in the light of all the circumstances its provisions truly represent the agreement between the parties or whether they are a "pretence" (*AG Securities v Vaughan*, per Lord Templeman at 1067h; *Aslan v Murphy (Nos 1 and 2)* [1989] 3 All E.R. 130). And see *Family Housing Association v Jones* [1990] 1 All E.R. 385 where a term in the agreement which expressly stated that exclusive possession was not granted was held to be a "pretence".

Cases where occupier with exclusive possession is not a tenant

5.010 There can be no tenancy unless the occupier enjoys exclusive possession but there are exceptional cases where an occupier with exclusive possession is not a tenant; exceptional circumstances may exist which negative the prima facie intention to create a tenancy:

> "There can be no tenancy unless the occupier enjoys exclusive possession; but an occupier who enjoys exclusive possession is not necessarily a tenant. He may be the owner in fee simple, a trespasser, a mortgagee in possession, an object of charity or a service occupier. To constitute a tenancy the occupier must be granted exclusive possession for a fixed or periodic term certain in consideration of a premium or periodical payments. The grant may be express, or may be inferred where the owner accepts weekly or other periodic payments from the occupier" (*Street* at 294a).
>
> "The intention to create a tenancy was negatived if the parties did not intend to enter into legal relationships at all, or where the relationship between the parties was that of vendor and purchaser, master and service occupier, or where the owner, a requisitioning authority, had no power to grant a tenancy" (*Street* at 295j to 296a).

Thus, one can see from the judgment of Lord Templeman in *Street v Mountford* that the following cases are examples where notwithstanding an agreement granting the occupant the right to exclusive possession for a term at a rent no tenancy has been granted:

(a) Where there has been no intention to create legal relations, for example where there has been in the circumstances such as a family arrangement, an act of friendship or generosity (see Lord Templeman at 294e; 295b, j; 296c; 298f); but note that the mere fact of family relationship or act of friendship, etc. will not necessarily prevent the creation of legal relations. There are many cases where one member of a family grants to another a tenancy of premises.

(b) Service occupancies (see Ch.17).

(c) Occupancy by reference to the holding of an office (see Lord Templeman at 300d).

(d) Body conferring right to exclusive possession having no power to grant a tenancy (Lord Templeman at 295j).

(e) Contract between vendor and purchaser for the sale of land (see para.21.016).

In *Sharp v McArthur* (1987) 19 H.L.R. 364 CA, the owner of a flat which was for **5.011** sale let the occupier, who was in urgent need of accommodation, into possession as a favour pending the sale. Rent was paid. It was held that there were exceptional circumstances that rebutted the presumption of a tenancy.

In *Westminster CC v Basson* [1991] 1 E.G.L.R. 277 CA, an unlawful occupier was told that proceedings had been commenced and that until they were determined she would be expected to pay damages for use and occupation. The letter concluded:

"In making the payments as Use and Occupation Charges this arrangement is not intended as the creation of a tenancy or a licence akin to a tenancy in any way whatsoever".

It was held that the intention to create a tenancy was negatived by that sentence. At 278B Mustill L.J. said:

"The sense of the letter is perfectly clear . . . The council were saying 'We desire you to vacate the premises. We trust that you will do so voluntarily. If not we shall take steps to remove you. Meanwhile we are not going to let you remain in there free of charge and to make sure that we are paid we shall expect to receive payment at the stated rate in the stated manner until we succeed in regaining possession'".

In *Gray v Taylor* (1998) 31 H.L.R. 262 CA a person occupying an almshouse was held to be a licensee.

However, the mere fact that the landlord is performing socially valuable functions, that it has agreed with the head landlord from whom it has obtained the building not to grant sub-tenancies and that is itself a licensee is not a special circumstance negativing the grant of a tenancy (*Bruton v London & Quadrant Housing Trust* [1999] 3 All E.R. 481 HL).

Irrevocable licences

Most licences may be determined in accordance with the terms of the agreement **5.012** or upon the giving of reasonable notice (see below). This section is concerned with those licences that may not be so revoked by the licensor.

In *DHN Food Distributors v London Borough of Tower Hamlets* [1976] 3 All E.R. 462 at 467a Lord Denning stated that

"a contractual licence under which a person has the right to occupy premises indefinitely gives rise to a constructive trust under which the legal owner is not allowed to turn out the licensee".

Whether or not a licence is revocable depends upon the terms of the agreement (*Millennium Productions Ltd v Winter Garden Theatre (London) Ltd* [1946] 1 All E.R. 680 per Lord Greene M.R.; *Hounslow London Borough Council v Twickenham Garden Developments Ltd* [1971] Ch. 233).

A licensee does not necessarily have to show that there is a contract before he can argue that he has an irrevocable licence. He may instead be able to rely upon the equitable doctrine of estoppel. Where the licensor has made a promise that the licensee may live on the premises for a certain period of time and the licensee has acted in reliance upon the promise and thereby suffered a detriment, the licensor is estopped from revoking the licence before that period has passed (see *Errington v Errington and Woods* [1952] 1 K.B. 290). It is important to remember where the burden of proof lies in these cases. The licensee must show that the licensor made a representation intending that the licensee should act upon it. There is then a presumption that the licensee relied upon it. If the licensor is to succeed he must show that there was no reliance (see *Greasley v Cooke* [1980] 3 All E.R. 710). The licensee must show that he has suffered a detriment as a result of the reliance (*Stevens & Cutting v Anderson* [1990] 1 E.G.L.R. 95). The licensor may be able to resist the licensee's claim for an estoppel by showing that the licensee has not come to court with "clean hands" (*Williams v Staite* [1979] Ch. 291; *Willis & Son v Willis* (1985) 277 E.G. 1133).

5.013   If the court comes to the conclusion that the property owner is estopped from turning out the licensee "an equity arises" and the court will then consider how to satisfy that equity. There is a wide range of relief that may be granted. The licensee is usually given a right to remain in the property for the period promised but in extreme cases outright ownership might be transferred (see, e.g. *Greasley v Cooke; Inwards v Baker* [1965] 2 Q.B. 29; *Dillwyn v Llewelyn* (1862) 4 De GF & J 517). Each case will depend upon its own facts and will turn upon the nature of the promise, the way in which the licensee acted in reliance upon it and the detriment that was sustained (*Yaxley v Gotts* [2000] 1 All E.R. 711 CA at 720f). For the considerations that apply when deciding how to satisfy the equity see *Burrows & Burrows v Sharp* (1989) 23 H.L.R. 82 CA. The fact that an estoppel has arisen does not automatically mean that a remedy will be given (*Sledmore v Dalby* (1996) 72 P. & C.R. 196 CA—the person with the benefit of the estoppel had lived in the house rent-free for 18 years and the elderly owner of the house now had a greater need for it—the equity had expired).

For constructive trust cases where the defendant in a possession claim claims to be the sole or joint beneficial owner of the property, see Ch. 33.

Termination and recovery of possession

Termination

5.014   Subject to the requirement to give not less than four weeks' notice in the case of periodic licences (see below), a licensor wishing to revoke a revocable licence should give such notice as is required by the terms of the agreement. Where there are no such terms the licensor should give the licensee a reasonable amount of time to leave (*Minister of Health v Bellotti* [1944] K.B. 298; *Vaughan v Vaughan* [1953] 1 Q.B. 762). Whether the amount of time given is sufficient is a question of fact in each case. The periods in respect of which the licence fees are paid will be relevant, as will the length of time the licensee has been in occupation. For example see *Earl of Macclesfield v Parker* (2003) July 24 (unreported) Ch D— where two years' notice was considered reasonable to leave a castle. For guidance on how to ascertain what term is likely to be implied see *Sandhu v Farooqui* [2003] H.L.R. (Case 55) 817 CA.

However, no notice by a licensor (or licensee) to determine a periodic licence to occupy premises as a dwelling is valid, unless it is in writing and contains such information as may be prescribed by statutory instrument (presently the Notices to Quit etc. (Prescribed Information) Regulations 1988 (SI 1988/2201)) and is given not less than four weeks before the date on which it is to take effect (s.5(1A) of the Protection from Eviction Act 1977). As emphasised, this provision only applies to periodic licences (*Norris v Checksfield* [1991] 4 All E.R. 327—as the right of an employee/licensee to remain in occupation comes to an end on termination of the employment (see para.17.002), the licence is not a periodic licence and it is not necessary to serve a notice to quit in accordance with s.5(1A)). Furthermore, s.5(1A) need not be complied with where the premises are occupied under an "excluded licence" (s.5(1B), see para.22.008 for definition of excluded licence).

Protection from Eviction Act 1977 section 5

(1A) Subject to subsection (1B) below, no notice by a licensor or a licensee to determine a periodic licence to occupy premises as a dwelling (whether the licence was granted before or after the passing of this Act) shall be valid unless—

(a) it is in writing and contains such information as may be prescribed; and
(b) it is given not less than four weeks before the date on which it is to take effect.

(1B) Nothing in . . . subsection (1A) above applies to—

(a) [　]
(b) premises occupied under an excluded licence.

5.015 For a form of notice to be served by a licensor, containing the prescribed information, see Form 15, p.110. No information has been prescribed in relation to notices to be given by licensees.

Where a valid notice has been served in accordance with s.5 of the Protection from Eviction Act 1977 (if applicable) but a reasonable amount of time has not been given the court will nevertheless make an order for possession if a reasonable amount of time had elapsed by the date proceedings were commenced. It is submitted that as the licence is revoked immediately the notice is given the court also has power to make an order for possession if a reasonable amount of time has elapsed at the date of the hearing even if it had not done so on the date the proceedings were commenced (*Minister of Health v Bellotti*).

One of two joint licensors may revoke an *oral licence* without the consent of the other (see *Annen v Rattee* [1986] 1 E.G.L.R. 136). Where however the licence agreement is *in writing*, whether or not one of the licensors may do so depends upon the proper construction of the licence agreement (*Fitzhugh v Fitzhugh* [2012] EWCA Civ 694).

For a discussion as to whether an irrevocable licence may be revoked by the licensor where it would be inequitable to permit the licensee to continue to rely upon it see *Williams v Staite* [1979] Ch. 291 and *Willis & Son v Willis* (1985) 277 E.G. 113.

Proceedings for possession

5.016   Unless the licence is an "excluded licence" the licensor may only recover possession by way of court proceedings (s.3(2B) and s.3A of the Protection from Eviction Act 1977; see para.22.003).

Form 15: Notice to quit by licensor

NOTICE TO QUIT

(BY LANDLORD OF PREMISES LET AS A DWELLING)

Name and Address of Tenant	To. .... of ....
Name and Address of Landlord	[I][We][as][on behalf of) your landlord[s].. of ....
*Me/them or as appropriate †Address of premises	give you NOTICE TO QUIT and deliver up possession to* .... of‡ ....
‡Date for possession	on‡ .... 20 .... or the day on which a complete period of your tenancy expires next after the end of four weeks from the service of this notice.
Date of notice	Dated .... 20 .... Signed ....
Name and Address of Agent if Agent served notice	....

INFORMATION FOR TENANT
(See *Note 2 below*)

1. If the tenant or licensee does not leave the dwelling, the landlord or licensor must get an order for possession from the court before the tenant or licensee can lawfully be evicted. The landlord or licensor cannot apply for such an order before the notice to quit or notice to determine has run out.

2. A tenant or licensee who does not know if he has any right to remain in possession after a notice to quit or a notice to determine runs out can obtain advice from a solicitor. Help with all or part of the cost of legal advice and assistance may be available under the Legal Aid Scheme. He should also be able to obtain information from a Citizens' Advice Bureau, a Housing Aid Centre or & Rent Officer.

NOTES

1. Notice to quit premises let as a dwelling must be given at least four weeks before it takes effect, and it must be in writing (Protection from Eviction Act 1977. section 5 as amended).

2. Where a notice to quit is given by a landlord to determine a tenancy of any premises let as a dwelling, the notice must contain this information (the Notices to Quit etc (Prescribed Information) Regulations 1988).

3. Some tenancies are excluded from this protection: see Protection from Eviction Act 1977. as 3A and 5(1B).

A former licensee is a trespasser within the meaning of CPR r.55.1(b) so that the provision that allows for early hearing dates in trespasser claims will apply (55.5(2)—see further Ch.31).

Licensees, like tenants, may not dispute the title of their "landlords" (*Government of Penang v Oon* [1972] A.C. 425 at 433E). Thus, a licensee will not be able to avoid an order for possession by arguing that the licensor has no interest in the property.

Most contractual licensees in the private sector given the right to occupy prior to the commencement of the Housing Act 1988 will have been in occupation under restricted contracts. In these cases the court has power to suspend the order for possession for up to three months upon certain conditions as to the payment of sums for use and occupation, etc. (see Ch.9). In all other cases the county court will only be able to postpone the date for possession for up to 14 days, unless such a short order would cause exceptional hardship in which case the court will have the power to suspend the order for up to six weeks (s.89 of the Housing Act 1980; see para.3.034).

For licensees who are protected under the Rent (Agriculture) Act 1976, see Ch.18, and for licensees in the public sector, see Ch.10.

Assignment, sub-letting, bankruptcy and death

Revocable licences

As an ordinary contractual licence creates no interest in land it is automatically **5.017** determined by the bankruptcy or death of the licensor or by the licensor voluntarily assigning the land over which the licence is exercised (see *Terunnanse v Terunnanse* [1968] A.C. 1086, per Lord Devlin at 1095G).

A licensee may not assign the benefit of the agreement unless there is a term in the agreement, express or implied, permitting him to assign (*Dorling v Honnor Marine Ltd* [1964] Ch. 560 and see s.136 of the Law of Property Act 1925).

A licensee may not sub-let as such (i.e. so as to bind the licensor in any way) but as between the licensee and the "sub-tenant" a tenancy by estoppel will have been created (see para.1.008; *Bruton v London and Quadrant Housing Trust* [1999] 3 All E.R. 481 HL). The tenancy by estoppel will be brought to an end if the licence is terminated and there are no grounds for encumbering the licensor's title with the tenancy by estoppel. The fact that the licensor knew that the licensee would grant a tenancy does not of itself mean that the licensor has authorised that grant. (See *Kay v London Borough of Lambeth* [2006] UKHL 10—where it also did not matter that the licensee became a tenant after the occupier had been granted his tenancy.)

Where a licensee goes bankrupt or dies the licence automatically comes to an end (*Coleman v Foster* (1856) 1 H & N 37—compare secure tenancies (Ch.10) and agricultural accommodation (Ch.18)).

Irrevocable licences

Irrevocable licences have been held to bind a purchaser of the licensor's interest **5.018** in the land who had notice of the licence (*Binions v Evans* [1972] Ch. 359), a licensor's trustee in bankruptcy (*Re Sharpe (a bankrupt)* [1980] 1 W.L.R. 219), and the personal representatives and beneficiaries of a licensor's estate (*Errington v Errington and* Woods [1952] 1 K.B. 290; *Inwards v Baker* [1965] 2 Q.B. 29). But all these cases should now be read in the light of *Ashburn Anstalt v Arnold* [1988] 2 All E.R. 147 CA (overruled on another point in *Prudential Assurance Co* *v London Residuary Body* [1992] 3 All E.R. 504 HL) where it was held that a contractual licence was not an interest in land capable of binding a purchaser even where that purchaser had notice; and that the only circumstances in which the licence may be binding upon third parties is where a constructive trust is imposed and that the court will not impose such a trust unless it is satisfied that the conscience of the purchaser is affected. See also *Habermann v Koehler* (1996) 72 P. & C.R. D10, where the issue was discussed in relation to s.70(1)(g) of the Land Registration Act 1925 but unfortunately without any clear conclusion.

Where the licensor has died those acting for the licensee should consider whether the client has any rights under the Inheritance (Provision for Family and Dependants) Act 1975. Under that Act it may be possible to obtain an interest in the property giving the licensee a right to live there (see s.2(1)(c),(d)). The application under the Act should be made within six months from the date on which representation with respect to the estate of the deceased is first taken out (s.4). If the personal representatives are seeking to obtain an order for possession the licensee should apply for the possession proceedings to be adjourned until after the application under the 1975 Act has been determined.

Part 2

Termination and the Right to Possession—Particular Cases

Chapter 6

Assured Tenancies

The assured tenancy and the assured shorthold tenancy (see Ch.7) were created by **6.001** the Housing Act 1988. Parliament in 1988 did not repeal the Rent Act 1977; Rent Act tenancies in existence at the date of the commencement of the 1988 Act (January 15, 1989) continue to exist. However, all private sector tenancies (save for a few transitional exceptions) created on or after that date are either assured or assured shorthold tenancies.

Broadly speaking, private sector tenancies created on or after January 15, 1989 and before February 28, 1997 are ordinary assured tenancies, unless the tenancy was granted for a term in excess of six months and a notice of an assured shorthold tenancy was served at the appropriate time in which case the tenancy is an assured shorthold (see para.7.001).

A fundamental change took place on February 28, 1997 when s.96 of the Housing Act 1996 came into force. Any tenancy entered into on or after that date is, with certain limited exceptions, automatically an assured shorthold tenancy. If one of the exceptions does apply the tenancy is an ordinary assured tenancy (see further para.7.006).

The landlord under an assured tenancy may not recover possession unless he **6.002** can prove a ground for doing so, except where it is a shorthold, in which case he need only serve an appropriate notice (see Ch.7).

A periodic assured tenancy may be determined only by an order of the court after a notice of intention to commence proceedings has been served (unless the notice requirement is dispensed with). Notices to quit are irrelevant and of no effect.

Fixed-term assured tenancies do come to an end at the expiry of the term but thereupon a "statutory periodic tenancy" automatically arises. This periodic tenancy like other assured periodic tenancies may not be determined by the landlord without service of a notice of intention to commence proceedings (unless dispensed with) and an order of the court. A statutory periodic tenancy under the 1988 Act is a true interest in land capable of assignment (s.5(3); s.15(3) of the 1988 Act).

Definition of assured tenancies

The basic rules: section 1 of the Housing Act 1988

Housing Act 1988 section 1

6.003
1.—A tenancy under which a dwelling house is let as a separate dwelling is for the purposes of this Act an assured tenancy *if and so long as*—

(a) the tenant or, as the case may be, each of the joint tenants is an individual; and

(b) the tenant or, as the case may be, at least one of the joint tenants occupies the dwelling house as his only or principal home; and

(c) the tenancy is not one which, by virtue of subsection (2) or subsection (6) below, cannot be an assured tenancy.

Note the words in italics. If one of the conditions ceases to apply the tenancy will cease to be assured. The exceptions referred to in subs.(c) are dealt with below.

A "dwelling-house" may be a house properly so called or part of a house: s.45. Where a dwelling-house is let together with other land the land is treated as part of the dwelling-house and therefore assured if and so long as the main purpose of the letting is the provision of a home for the tenant or, where there are joint tenants, at least one of them: s.2(1)(a) (unless the land is agricultural land exceeding two acres in which case the letting cannot be assured: Sch.1 para.6). However, the tenancy will not be assured if and so long as the main purpose of the letting is not the provision of a home for the tenant or, where there are joint tenants, at least one of them (s.2(1)(b)). See further paras 8.004 and 17.014.

6.004 The letting of a houseboat cannot be a tenancy of a dwelling-house unless the boat is sufficiently annexed to the land so as to become part of the land (*Chelsea Yacht & Boat Co Ltd v Pope* [2000] L.&T.R. 401 CA):

> "Here the houseboat rested periodically on the riverbed below it and was secured by ropes and perhaps to an extent the services to other structures. It is difficult to see how attachments in this way to the pontoons, the anchor in the riverbed and the rings in the embankment wall could possibly make the houseboat part of the land. One is bound to ask 'which land?' There is in my judgment no satisfactory answer to this question. More importantly, however, all these attachments could simply be undone. The houseboat could be moved quite easily without injury to itself or the land . . . It is common sense that a house built on land is part of the land. . . . So too it is common sense that a boat on a river is not part of the land. A boat, albeit one used as a home, is not the same genus as real property" (per Tuckey L.J.).

Where the houseboat is on the land it might be sufficiently annexed to give rise to a tenancy (see *Elitestone Ltd v Morris* [1997] 1 W.L.R. 687 in relation to Rent Act tenancies; para.8.003). However, in *Mew v Tristmire Ltd* [2011] EWCA Civ 912 houseboats resting on wooden platforms had not become annexed to the land. They were structures that could have been removed without being dismantled or destroyed in the process. The occupants of the houseboats were therefore licensees rather than assured tenants. *Elitestone Ltd v Morris* was distinguished. Patten L.J. at para.41:

> "A structure like the bungalow in *Elitestone* which is positioned on a residential site for which a rent or licence fee is paid has, from the start, all the attributes of a house and none of the features of removability inherent in, for example, a caravan or a boat. The

fact that it is not bolted as such on to the pillars which support it is immaterial. By its very nature it is intended to be a permanent feature of the site. The bungalow was constructed on site from components brought in for that purpose. It was not readily transportable as a unit and its removal would always have involved its demolition or destruction. In these circumstances, it is much easier to infer that the purpose of its annexation was that it should become part of the site."

Even if it is sufficiently annexed so as to become part of the land, rather than remain as a chattel, it is still necessary to determine whether it contains all the features necessary to make it a house (*Chelsea Yacht & Boat Co Ltd v Pope*—as to which see para.8.003).

A "dwelling" is a place where one lives, regarding and treating it as one's home. A dwelling can consist of a single room and the absence of cooking facilities does not of itself deprive the place of its status as a dwelling. Whether the premises do qualify as a dwelling depends on all the circumstances to be judged at the time proceedings are commenced (*Uratemp Ventures Ltd v Collins* [2001] 3 W.L.R. 806 HL). In *Mew v Tristmire*, even if there had been tenancies they would not have been assured as "a tenancy of the plot and supporting platform alone does not attract any statutory protection and would have been determined by one of the sets of notices served" (para.43).

The requirement that the tenant be an individual means that a letting to a company cannot be an assured tenancy (see further para.17.021). Note the require-ment that the dwelling be occupied by the tenant "as his only or principal home". The test is stricter than the test of residence under s.2 of the Rent Act 1977. The court should not look at the tenant's subjective intention to return when he has ceased to occupy but should look at the intention objectively based on the observ-able facts (*Ujima Housing Association v Ansah* (1997) 30 H.L.R. 831 CA—tenant sub-let the whole of the property on an assured shorthold and left no personal possessions—held the tenant ceased to be assured). It is of the "most enormous importance" whether the tenant sleeps at the property. However, the fact that the tenant intends to move out or cease using the property as his only or principal home at some time in the future, is not material (*Sumeghova v McMohan* [2003] 35 H.L.R. (case 26) 349 CA). See further the detailed guidance given by Etherton L.J. in *Islington London Borough Council v Boyle* [2011] EWCA Civ 1450, which is set out in the Secure Tenancies chapter at para.10.006.

For further assistance with the definition of the assured tenancy compare para.8.003 in relation to protected tenancies. See Ch.14 for the position where the tenant shares some of his accommodation.

The exceptions (section 2(2), (6) of and Schedule 1 to the 1988 Act)

The main exceptions are to be found in Pt 1 of Sch.1 to the Housing Act 1988, **6.005** the full text of which is set out in Appendix 2. They may be summarised as follows:

(1) Tenancies entered into before the commencement of the Housing Act 1988 or pursuant to contracts made before that date.

(2) Tenancies of dwelling-houses with high rateable values/high rents (see Appendix 1—see also para.2A of Sch.1 to the 1988 Act, para.A2.050; see further this paragraph below).

(3) Tenancies at a low rent (see Appendix 2—see also paras 3A, 3B and 3C; para.A2.050).

(4) Business tenancies (see Ch.17).

(5) Licensed premises (see para.17.008).

(6) Tenancies of agricultural land.

(7) Tenancies of agricultural holdings (see Ch.18).

(8) Lettings to students (see Ch.19).

(9) Holiday lettings (see Ch.19).

(10) Resident landlords (see Ch.14).

(11) Landlord's interest belonging to the Crown, save where the property is under the management of the Crown Estate Commissioners.

(12) Landlord a local authority, etc. (see Ch.10).

(13) Transitional cases (see below).

Note that the tenancy only ceases to be assured "*if and so long as*" the exception applies.

A tenancy under which the rent payable for the time being is payable at a rate exceeding £100,000 is not assured (Sch.1, para.2(1)(b); see para.A2.050). (Prior to October 1, 2010 in England and December 1, 2011 in Wales the figure was £25,000 (the Assured Tenancies (Amendment)(England) Order 2010; the Assured Tenancies (Amendment of Rental Threshold) (Wales) Order 2011).

Note that it is not the date the tenancy commences that matters (as long as it was entered into after April 1, 1990: para.2(1)(b) of Sch.1 to the 1988 Act); and the tenancy can go in and out of the Act if the rent changes. Thus, if the tenancy is assured at one stage during the tenancy because the rent does not exceed £100,000 it will cease to be assured if the rent does subsequently exceed that figure. However, note also that it is not possible to use a rent review provision at the end of the term deliberately to avoid the Act: *Bankway Properties Ltd v Penfold-Dunsford* [2001] EWCA Civ 528. In that case the Court of Appeal struck down a rent review clause which sought to increase the rent to £25,000 at the end of the term. The initial rent was £4,680 and the "annual rent of £25,000 substantially exceeded what any tenant of this property could hope to pay" and was well above what it could genuinely have been expected to be the market rent at the review date. In this case the tenancy in fact remained assured because the rent did not exceed £25,000 (the threshold then in force) but the effect of it would have been to prevent the tenant from having the protection of the Act because it was known from the outset that the tenant would not be able to pay such a high rent. It was therefore held to be invalid.

Temporary housing of homeless persons

6.006 There is a further exception which relates to the situation where a local authority makes an arrangement with another person to provide temporary accommodation for a homeless person (see s.209 of the Housing Act 1996).

Where the tenancy is not assured and no other statutory protection applies (e.g. in resident landlord cases), the common rules set out in Chs 2 and 3 as to termination will apply. Thus, in the case of a periodic tenancy a standard note to quit should be served (para.3.002).

Assured tenancies under the Housing Act 1980

Sections 56–58 of the Housing Act 1980 created a form of tenancy called an **6.007** "assured tenancy" which could only be granted by certain approved bodies. These tenancies were subject to the provisions of the Landlord and Tenant Act 1954 Pts II and IV (the business tenancy code) as modified by the Housing Act 1980 so as to be applicable to residential premises. This form of assured tenancy came to an end with the enactment of the Housing Act 1988.

By virtue of s.37 of the 1988 Act any tenancy entered into on or after the commencement of the 1988 Act cannot be an assured tenancy for the purposes of ss.56–58 of the Housing Act 1980. Furthermore, by virtue of s.1(3) of the 1988 Act at the commencement of the 1988 Act all 1980 Act assured tenancies became assured tenancies under the 1988 Act.

There is a limited exception. Where before the commencement of the 1988 Act a tenant under a 1980 Act assured tenancy had made an application to the court for the grant of a new tenancy and at the commencement the tenancy was continuing by virtue of s.24 or any provisions of Pt IV of the 1954 Act it continues to be a 1980 Act assured tenancy. However, any new tenancy granted will be a 1988 Act assured tenancy: see s.37(2), (3), (6)—see also subss.(4) and (5) for further transitional provisions.

In the case of 1980 Act assured tenancies that have become 1988 Act assured tenancies Pt 1 of Sch.1 to the 1988 Act (the list of exceptions) has effect as if it consisted only of paras 11 (Crown) and 12 (other public bodies). In the case where the landlord is and was prior to commencement a fully mutual housing association (see Housing Associations Act 1985 Pt I) para.12 of Sch.1 is also amended so as to delete the reference to such associations (sub-para.1(h): s.4(5)).

Transitional provisions

There are four types of tenancy created after the commencement of the **6.008** Housing Act 1988 that may be protected (under the Rent Act 1977) rather than assured:

(a) a tenancy entered into in pursuance of a contract made before the commencement of the 1988 Act;

(b) a tenancy granted to a person who, immediately before the tenancy was granted, was a protected or statutory tenant (except for shorthold cases) of the landlord;

(c) certain tenancies granted after an order for possession made pursuant to s.98 of the Rent Act 1977 on the ground that suitable alternative accommodation is available to the tenant;

(d) cases where the tenancy has been transferred from a new town corporation to the private sector pursuant to s.38 of the Act.

See further para.8.009 in relation to protected and statutory tenancies and para.15.003 in relation to protected shorthold tenancies. See also s.35 of the 1988 Act in relation to "housing association tenancies".

Termination by landlord

Housing Act 1988 section 5(1)(2) and section 45(4)

6.009   **5.**—(1) An assured tenancy cannot be brought to an end by the landlord except by—

    (a) obtaining—

        (i)   an order of the court for possession of the dwelling-house under sections 7 or 21; and

        (ii) the execution of the order;

    (b) obtaining an order of the court under section 6A (demotion order); or

    (c) in the case of a fixed term tenancy which contains power for the landlord to determine the tenancy in certain circumstances, by the exercise of that power;

and, accordingly, the service by the landlord of a notice to quit is of no effect in relation to a periodic assured tenancy.

(1A) Where an order of the court for possession of the dwelling-house is obtained, the tenancy ends when the order is executed.

(2) If an assured tenancy which is a fixed term tenancy comes to an end otherwise than by virtue of—

    (a) an order of the court of the kind mentioned in subsection (1)(a) or (b) or any other order of the court; or

    (b) a surrender or other action on the part of the tenant,

then, subject to section 7 and Chapter II below, the tenant shall be entitled to remain in possession of the dwelling house let under that tenancy and, subject to subsection (4) below, his right to possession shall depend upon a periodic tenancy arising by virtue of this section . . .

45.—(4) For the avoidance of doubt, it is hereby declared that any reference in this Part of this Act (however expressed) to a power for a landlord to determine a tenancy does not include a reference to a power of re-entry or forfeiture for breach of any term or condition of the tenancy.

Introduction

6.010 The rules set out in this section only apply to termination by landlords (for termination by the tenant, see para.6.031).

Furthermore, they do not apply where the proceedings for possession are brought by a mortgagee who has lent money on the security of the assured tenancy: s.7(1).

Nor do these rules apply where the tenancy was originally assured but has ceased to be so, perhaps because the dwelling house ceased to be the tenant's principal home. In these circumstances, it becomes an ordinary common law tenancy. If the tenancy is a periodic tenancy it may be determined in the normal way, i.e. by notice to quit. If it is a fixed term it will expire at the end of the term, or it may be possible to determine it during the fixed term by forfeiture.

Periodic tenancies

6.011 A landlord may not bring an assured tenancy which is a periodic tenancy to an end by service of a notice to quit (s.5(1)). It may only be determined by an order of the court and the court may not "entertain the proceedings for possession" unless the landlord has served a "notice of intention to commence proceedings for possession" (or the court considers it just and equitable to dispense with the requirement of such a notice—s.8(1)(b) see para.6.023).

Expiry of fixed terms and statutory periodic tenancies

A fixed-term assured tenancy will come to an end at the expiry of the term. **6.012** However, on the coming to an end of such a tenancy, otherwise than by virtue of (a) an order of the court, or (b) surrender or other action on the part of the tenant, a statutory periodic tenancy arises (s.5(2), (3), (7)) unless, on the coming to an end of the fixed term, the tenant is entitled, by virtue of the grant of another tenancy, to possession of the same or substantially the same dwelling-house as was let to him under the fixed-term tenancy (s.5(4)).

A statutory periodic tenancy, like any other assured periodic tenancy, may not be brought to an end by notice to quit but only by court proceedings initiated by a notice seeking possession (unless the requirement for such a notice is dispensed with; see para.6.023).

(The landlord cannot prevent a periodic tenancy from arising by requiring the tenant, on or before the date the fixed-term tenancy is entered into or the periodic tenancy arises, (a) to enter into an obligation to do any act which will cause the tenancy to come to an end, or (b) to execute, sign or give any surrender, notice to quit or other document which has the effect of bringing the tenancy to an end, at a time when it is an assured tenancy: s.5(5).)

Terms of statutory periodic tenancies; section 5(3), section 6

Where a statutory periodic tenancy arises the periods of the tenancy are the same as **6.013** those for which rent was last payable under the fixed term and the terms are (subject to certain other provisions, for example ss.15 and 16) the same as those of the fixed term except that any term which makes provision for determination by the landlord or the tenant has no effect while the tenancy remains an assured tenancy (s.5(3)(d), (e)), unless the terms are varied in accordance with the procedure set out in s.6.

Termination during fixed term; break clauses

The landlord may exercise a break clause in a lease so as to bring the fixed term to **6.014** an end (s.5(1)), but if he does so a statutory periodic tenancy automatically arises (s.5(2)), unless a new tenancy is granted (s.5(4)). If the landlord wishes to obtain an order for possession by reliance upon a break clause see s.7(6) at para.6.028.

Termination during fixed term; "forfeiture"

The landlord will not be able to obtain an order for possession during the fixed **6.015** term unless:

(a) the ground relied upon by the landlord is one of a number of specified grounds—see para.6.024; and

(b) there is a forfeiture clause in the lease or some other provision for it to be brought to an end on the ground in question (s.7(6); see further para.6.026).

Although the provision in the tenancy agreement relied upon is often a forfeiture clause, the court order terminating the tenancy is not in fact a true "forfeiture". It is an order made under s.5(1) of the 1988 Act. It is not therefore necessary to serve a notice under s.146 of the Law of Property Act 1925, in addition to a s.8 notice, and the usual rules relating to relief from forfeiture do not apply (*Artesian Residential Investments Ltd v Beck* [1999] 3 All E.R. 113 CA).

Notice of intention to seek possession; section 8

6.016 Where there are joint landlords not all of them need serve the notice. It is validly served so long as it is served by at least one of them (s.8(1)(a)).

The court has a discretion to dispense with the requirement for a notice (see para.6.023). However, unless it does so the notice must comply with the following requirements:

(1) It must be in prescribed form or in a form substantially to the same effect (see reg.2 and Form No.3 of The Assured Tenancies and Agricultural Occupancies (Forms) Regulations 1997; Form 16 of this book, p.124). (The form refers to licensees because it is also to be used in the case of assured agricultural occupancies, see para.18.010.)

(2) The notice must specify the landlord's ground for possession in para.3 of the notice (see para.6.024 for the various grounds); but the grounds specified in the notice may be altered or added to with the leave of the court (s.8(2)—see para.6.021). When setting out the ground relied upon, it is not necessary to state the full text of the relevant ground, but the landlord must set out the substance of the ground so that the notice gives "the tenant the information which the provision requires to be given in the notice to enable the tenant to consider what she should do and, with or without advice, to do that which is in her power and which will best protect her against the loss of her home" (*Mountain v Hastings* [1993] 2 E.G.L.R. 53, per Ralph Gibson at 55H; notice stating:—"Ground 8. At least three months rent is unpaid"—not good enough). "It is difficult to think of any good reason why a person, given the task of settling a form of notice, should choose to use words different from those in the statute" (per Ralph Gibson at 55M).

(3) The landlord must also give a full explanation of why each ground is relied upon (para.4 of the notice). The particulars given should be sufficiently stated that the tenant knows what he has to do to put matters right. For example, if the ground for possession is based upon arrears of rent, the amount of the arrears should be stated or the notice must contain sufficient information so as to enable the tenant to calculate the amount that is due (*Marath v MacGillivray* (1996) 28 H.L.R. 486 CA). Compare similar provisions in the Housing Act 1985; see para.10.012.

(4) The notice must inform the tenant that the proceedings will not begin earlier than the date specified in the notice. The date that must be specified varies depending upon the ground or grounds that are relied upon:

6.017   (a) In most cases the date specified must not be earlier than the expiry of the period of two weeks from the date of service of the notice.

(b) However, if the notice specifies any of the Grounds 1, 2, 5, 6, 7, 9 or 16 (whether without other grounds or with any ground other than Ground 14; i.e. the nuisance ground—see below) the date specified in the notice must not be earlier than (i) two months from the date of service of the notice; and (ii) if the tenancy is a periodic tenancy, the earliest date on which if it were an ordinary common law tenancy it could be brought to an end by a notice to quit given by the landlord on the same date as the date of service of the notice.

(c) If the notice specifies Ground 14 (nuisance—see para.29.003) (with or without other grounds) the date specified in the notice "shall not be earlier than the date of the service of the notice". Thus, if a tenant or visitor is causing a nuisance the landlord does not have to wait until before commencing proceedings (sections 8(3)(b); (4)–(4B) as amended by s.151 of the 1996 Act).

(5) It must inform the tenant that the proceedings will not begin later than 12 months from the date of service of the notice.

(6) Where there are joint landlords not all of them need serve the notice. It is validly served so long as it is served by at least one of them (s.8(1)(a)); although note that para.6 of the form states: "If there are joint landlords each landlord or agent must sign unless one signs on behalf of the rest with their agreement". (Query: whether this is correct, given the terms of s.8(1) (a)?) The parties can agree that longer notice than the statute requires be given but the court can still dispense with the requirement for notice in an appropriate case (*North British Housing Association Ltd v Sheridan* (1999) 32 H.L.R. 346).

Fixed terms: statutory periodic tenancies

The landlord may serve a notice of intention seeking possession at a time when **6.018** the dwelling-house is let on a fixed term, or after a fixed-term tenancy has come to an end but in relation (in whole or in part) to events occurring during that tenancy. If he does so the notice has effect notwithstanding that the tenant becomes or has become a tenant under a statutory periodic tenancy arising on the coming to an end of the fixed term. It is not necessary to serve another notice to determine the periodic tenancy (s.8(6)).

6.019   **Form 16: Notice by landlord seeking possession**

Housing Act 1988 section 8 as amended by section 151 of the Housing Act 1996

Notice seeking possession of a property let on an Assured Tenancy or an Assured Agricultural Occupancy

- Please write clearly in black ink.

- Please tick boxes where appropriate and cross out text marked with an asterisk (*) that does not apply.

- This form should be used where possession of accommodation let under an assured tenancy, an assured agricultural occupancy or an assured shorthold tenancy is sought on one of the grounds in Schedule 2 to the Housing Act 1988.

- Do not use this form if possession is sought on the "shorthold" ground under section 21 of the Housing Act 1988 from an assured shorthold tenant where the fixed term has come to an end or, for assured shorthold tenancies with no fixed term which started on or after 28 February 1997, after six months has elapsed. There is no prescribed form for these cases, but you must give notice in writing.

---

1. To: ....

Name(s) of tenant(s)licensee(s)*

---

2. Your landlord/licensor* intends to apply to the court for an order requiring you to give up possession of:

....

....

....

Address of premises

---

3. Your landlord/licensor* intends to seek possession on ground(s) .... in Schedule 2 to the Housing Act 1988, which read(s):

....

....

....

Give the full text (as set out in the Housing Act 1988 as amended by the Housing Act 1996) of each ground which is being relied on. Continue on a separate sheet if necessary.

---

4. Give a full explanation of why each ground is being relied on:

....

....

Continue on a separate sheet if necessary.

Notes on the grounds for possession

- If the court is satisfied that any of grounds 1 to 8 is established, it must make an order (but see below in respect of fixed term tenancies).

- Before the court will grant an order on any of grounds 9 to 17, it must be satisfied that it is reasonable to require you to leave. This means that, if one of these grounds is set out in section 3. you will be able to suggest to the court that it is not reasonable that you should have to leave, even if you accept that the ground applies.

- The court will not make an order under grounds 1, 3 to 7, 9 or 16, to take effect during the fixed term of the tenancy (if there is one) and it will only make an order during the fixed term on grounds 2. 8, 10 to 15 or 17 if the terms of the tenancy make provision for it to be brought to an end on any of these grounds.

- Where the court makes an order for possession solely on ground 6 or 9, the landlord must pay your reasonable removal expenses.

5. The court proceedings will not begin until after:

....

Give the earliest date on which court proceedings can be brought

- Where the landlord is seeking possession on grounds 1, 2, 5 to 7, 9 or 16, court proceedings cannot begin earlier than two months from the date this notice is served on you (even where one of grounds 3, 4, 8, 10 to 13, 14A, 15 or 17 is specified) and not before the date on which the tenancy (had it not been assured) could have been brought to an end by a notice to quit served at the same time as this notice.

- Where the landlord is seeking possession on grounds 3, 4, 8, 10, to 13, 14A, 15 or 17, court proceedings cannot begin earlier than two weeks from the date this notice is served (unless one of 1, 2, 5 to 7, 9 or 16 grounds is also specified in which case they cannot begin earlier than two months from the date this notice is served).

contd

contd

- Where the landlord is seeking possession on ground 14 (with or without other grounds), court proceedings cannot begin before the date this notice is served.
- Where the landlord is seeking possession on ground 14A, court proceedings cannot begin unless the landlord has served, or has taken all reasonable steps to serve, a copy of this notice on the partner who has left the properly.
- After the date shown in section 5, court proceedings may be begun at once but not later than 12 months from the date on which this notice is served. After this time the notice will lapse and a new notice must be served before possession can be sought.

6. Name and address of landlord/licensor*

To be signed and dated by the landlord or licensor or his agent (someone acting for him). If there are joint landlords each landlord or the agent must sign unless one signs on behalf of the rest with their agreements.

Signed .... *Date* ....
....

Please specify whether: landlord □ licensor □ joint landlords □ landlord's agent □

Name(s) (Block Capitals) ....
....

Address
....
....
....

Telephone—Daytime .... *Evening* ....

What to do if this notice is served on you

- This notice is the first step requiring you to give up possession of your home. You should read it very carefully.
- Your landlord cannot make you leave your home without an order for possession issued by a court. By issuing this notice your landlord is informing you that he intends to seek such an order. If you are willing to give up possession without a court order, you should tell the person who signed this notice as soon as possible and say when you are prepared to leave.
- Whichever grounds are set out in section 3 of this form, the court may allow any of the other grounds to be added at a later date. If this is done, you will be told about it so you can discuss the additional grounds at the court hearing as well as the grounds set out in section 3.
- If you need advice about this notice, and what you should do about it. take it immediately to a citizens' advice bureau, a housing advice centre, a law centre or a solicitor.

Service of the notice

The 1988 Act does not specify any general requirements in relation to how **6.020** s.8 notices are to be served (compare para.7.028). Nor is there any general requirement to serve the notice upon anyone other than the tenant. However, where the landlord is relying upon Ground 14A (domestic violence; see para.30.002) the court may not entertain the proceedings unless the s.8 notice has been served on the partner who has left or the landlord has "taken all reasonable steps to serve a copy of the notice on that partner" or "the court considers it just and equitable to dispense with such requirements as to service." See para.6.023. Where the s.8 notice is amended with leave after commencement to include Ground 14A, the proceedings cannot continue until the partner who has left has been served with notice or reasonable steps have been taken to serve notice on him, or the requirement for such a notice is dispensed with (s.8A of the 1988 Act).

Housing Act 1988 sections 8 and 8A (as amended)

8.—(1) The court shall not entertain proceedings for possession of a dwelling house let **6.021** on an assured tenancy unless—

    (a) the landlord or, in the case of joint landlords, at least one of them has served on the tenant a notice in accordance with this section and the proceedings are begun within the time limits stated in the notice in accordance with subsection (3) to (4B) below; or

    (b) the court considers it just and equitable to dispense with the requirement of such a notice.

(2) The court shall not make an order for possession on any of the grounds in Schedule 2 to this Act unless that ground and particulars of it are specified in the notice under this section; but the grounds specified in such a notice may be altered or added to with the leave of the court.

(3) A notice under this section is one in the prescribed form informing the tenant that—

    (a) the landlord intends to begin proceedings for possession of the dwelling house on one or more of the grounds specified in the notice; and

    (b) those proceedings will not begin earlier than a date specified in the notice in accordance with subsection (4) to (4B) below; and

    (c) those proceedings will not begin later than twelve months from the date of service of the notice.

(4) If a notice under this section specifies in accordance with subsection (3)(a) above Ground 14 in Schedule 2 to this Act (whether with or without other grounds), the date specified in the notice as mentioned in subsection (3)(b) above shall not be earlier than the date of the service of the notice.

(4A) If a notice under this section specifies in accordance with subsection (3)(a) above, any of Grounds 1, 2, 5 to 7, 9 and 16 in Schedule 2 to this Act (whether without other grounds or with any ground other than Ground 14), the date specified in the notice as mentioned in subsection (3)(b) above shall not be earlier than—

    (a) two months from the date of service of the notice; and

    (b) if the tenancy is a periodic tenancy, the earliest date on which, apart from section 5(1) above, the tenancy could be brought to an end by a notice to quit given by the landlord on the same date as the date of service of the notice under this section.

(4B) In any other case, the date specified in the notice as mentioned in subsection (3)(b) above shall not be earlier than the expiry of the period of two weeks from the date of the service of the notice.

(5) The court may not exercise the power conferred by subsection (1)(b) above if the landlord seeks to recover possession on Ground 8 in Schedule 2 to this Act.

(6) Where a notice under this section—

    (a) is served at a time when the dwelling house is let on a fixed term tenancy; or

    (b) is served after a fixed term tenancy has come to an end but relates (in whole or in part) to events occurring during that tenancy,

the notice shall have effect notwithstanding that the tenant becomes or has become tenant under a statutory periodic tenancy arising on the coming to an end of the fixed term tenancy.

8A.—(1) Where the ground specified in a notice under section 8 (whether with or without other grounds) is Ground 14A in Schedule 2 to this Act and the partner who has left the dwelling house as mentioned in that ground is not a tenant of the dwelling house, the court shall not entertain proceedings for possession of the dwelling house unless—

    (a) the landlord or, in the case of joint landlords, at least one of them has served on the partner who has left a copy of the notice or has taken all reasonable steps to serve a copy of the notice on that partner; or

    (b) the court considers it just and equitable to dispense with such requirements as to service.

(2) Where Ground 14A in Schedule 2 to this Act is added to a notice under section 8 with the leave of the court after proceedings for possession are begun and the partner who has left the dwelling house as mentioned in that ground is not a party to the proceedings, the court shall not continue to entertain the proceedings unless—

    (a) the landlord or, in the case of joint landlords, at least one of them has served a notice under subsection (3) below on the partner who has left or has taken all reasonable steps to serve such a notice on that partner; or

    (b) the court considers it just and equitable to dispense with the requirement of such a notice.

(3) A notice under this subsection shall—

    (a) state that proceedings for the possession of the dwelling house have begun;

    (b) specify the ground or grounds on which possession is being sought; and

    (c) give particulars of the ground or grounds.

Proceedings for possession

Commencing proceedings

The landlord must commence proceedings (see Ch.22) after the date specified in **6.022** the notice of intention to commence proceedings for possession but before 12 months from the date specified have elapsed. If he does not do so, the court may not entertain proceedings for possession (s.8(1)(a)).

Note: Where the landlord's claim for possession is based upon or includes an allegation of non-payment of rent the particulars of claim must set out certain prescribed information (see para.25.016).

Dispensing with requirement of a notice: section 8(1)(b)

Section 8(1) of the 1988 Act provides that the court shall not entertain proceed- **6.023** ings for possession of a dwelling-house let on an assured tenancy unless the landlord serves a notice of proceedings for possession or the court considers it just and equitable to dispense with the requirement of such a notice (subs.(b); para.6.021).

In deciding whether or not to dispense with the notice the court must consider all the circumstances from the point of view of both the landlord and tenant and must have regard to matters at the date of the hearing (see *Knowsley Housing Trust v Revell* [2003] 35 H.L.R. (case 63) 958 CA; where the importance of assessing the facts of each individual case was stressed). The court may take into account events that have occurred since commencement of the proceedings (*Kelsey Housing Association v King* (1996) 28 H.L.R. 270 CA—the landlord relied upon Grounds 12 (breach of obligation) and 14 (nuisance) but failed to serve a s.8 notice. The defendants waited for five months after service of their defence before taking the point, and not until shortly before the hearing. The requirement for the notice was dispensed with):

"The purpose of the requirement of the statutory notice is to enable the relevant party to take steps to remedy the complaints so that he can be in as good a position as possible to avoid eviction. However, the statutory framework makes it clear that in certain circumstances the statutory notice can be dispensed with. Thus, the mere fact that the appropriate particulars have not been given does not mean that proceedings will be struck out. There is a residual jurisdiction provided for in s.8(1)(b) for the court to dispense with the requirements of notice in circumstances where it is just and equitable to do so. *Even if the failure to give the statutory notice does create prejudice*, that may not be conclusive. The statutory requirement placed upon the court is to consider what is just and equitable and in no way can it avoid carrying out that duty by coming to a conclusion that one or other of the parties has been prejudiced. The requirements of the court are to weigh all the factors before it . . . .

Every case will depend upon its own facts and the pleaded ground or grounds relied on in the notice. The court must take all the circumstances into account, both from the view of the landlord and the tenant, and decided whether it is just and equitable to dispense with the required particulars . . . .

It was submitted . . . that the judge wrongly took into account facts that occurred after the proceedings had started. . . . However, the court is given the power to dispense with the requirements of notice, provided that it is just and equitable to do so. Thus, although there may potentially, and probably will, be prejudice if the appropriate notice is not given, that cannot be conclusive. The judge in every case must look at the facts and decide the matter *at the time when the proceedings come before him*" (per Aldous L.J. at 275, 276 and 277; authors' emphasis in each case).

The court may not dispense with the requirement where the ground for possession is Ground 8 (eight weeks' rent arrears, etc.); s.8(5).

The grounds for possession

6.024   The court is not permitted to make an order for possession of a dwelling-house let under an assured tenancy except on one or more of the 18 grounds for possession set out in Sch.2 to the 1988 Act. There are two categories of ground: those where the court must make an order for possession (Grounds 1 to 8) and those where the court possesses a discretion as to whether or not to make an order (Grounds 9 to 17). As shown above, the ground relied upon must be specified in the notice of intention to commence proceedings. If it is not, the court may not make an order for possession on that ground. The grounds specified in the notice may be altered or added to with the leave of the court (s.8(2)) but the court may well not give leave where extensive amendments to the notice are required (for example, where it is necessary in effect to add a schedule of dilapidations: *South Buckinghamshire County Council v Francis* [1985] C.L.Y. 1900—a secure tenancy case, see para.10.018).

There is no clear guidance in the Act or elsewhere as to how the grounds are to be altered or added. It is suggested that a further draft notice including the amendments be served or that the proposed amendments should be set out in the particulars of claim. Much will depend on the time at which it becomes apparent that the landlord may wish to alter or add to the grounds in the notice. In any event as much notice as possible should be given to the tenant of the intention to obtain leave. Note, also, the power of the court to dispense with the requirement for a notice and the way in which the discretion is exercised (para.6.023).

(None of these provisions relate to proceedings brought by a mortgagee who has lent money on the security of the assured tenancy: s.7(1).)

The mandatory grounds: Grounds 1 to 8

6.025   If the court is satisfied that any of these grounds is established the court must make an order for possession (s.7(3)). The grounds, which are set out in Pt 1 of Sch.2 to the 1988 Act (see Appendix 2), may be summarised as follows:

(1) Owner has lived in or wishes to live in the property (see para.30.016).

(2) Mortgagee requiring possession in order to exercise power of sale (see para.32.082).

(3) Holiday homes let out of season (see para.19.007).

(4) Student accommodation let during vacation (see para.19.001).

(5) Ministers of religion (see para.21.024).

(6) Demolition, reconstruction or substantial works.

(7) Death of the tenant—periodic tenancy (and fixed term for tenancies of a dwelling house in England) (see para.6.036).

(8) Substantial arrears of rent (see generally Ch.28; in particular para.28.023).

Grounds 1 to 5 require a notice to have been served not later than the beginning of the tenancy (unless, in the case of Grounds 1 and 2, the court is of the opinion that it is just and equitable to dispense with the requirement of notice: cf. cases under the Rent Acts—see para.30.013). Where such a notice is required Pt IV of Sch.2 applies to those notices. Where there are joint landlords the notice is sufficiently served, so long as it is served by at least one of the joint landlords. Further, notice served in relation to initial tenancies will usually be effective in relation to later tenancies of the same kind.

The discretionary grounds: Grounds 9 to 16

If the court is satisfied that any of these grounds is established then the court **6.026** may make an order for possession if it considers it reasonable to do so. The grounds, which are set out in Pt II of Sch.2 to the 1988 Act, may be summarised as follows:

(9)   Suitable alternative accommodation (see para.30.019).

(10)   Some arrears of rent (see Ch.28).

(11)   Persistent delay in paying rent (see Ch.28).

(12)   Breach of obligation of tenancy.

(13)   Deterioration of dwelling-house or common parts.

(14)   Nuisance, annoyance, immoral or illegal user (see para.29.001).

(14A) Domestic violence where the landlord is a "social landlord" (see para.30.002).

(15)   Deterioration of furniture (see para.30.001).

(16)   Tenancy resulting from employment by landlord—employment has ceased.

(17)   False statement b.y the tenant.

Where the tenancy agreement incorporates the statutory grounds in force at the time the tenancy is deemed to incorporate any subsequent statutory amendments (*North British Housing Association Ltd v Sheridan* (1999) 32 H.L.R. 346).

Reasonableness

6.027 When the court is considering whether or not it is reasonable to make an order for possession on Ground 14 (nuisance and annoyance cases) the court is given specific instructions as to how to exercise its discretion (s.9A of the 1988 Act). This is dealt with in Ch.29 (anti-social behaviour).

Fixed terms (section 7(6), (7))

6.028 The court may not make an order for possession of a dwelling-house to take effect at a time when it is let on an assured fixed-term tenancy unless:

   (a) the ground for possession is Ground 2, 7 (for dwelling houses in England only), 8, 10, 11, 12, 13, 14, 14A, 15, or 17; and

   (b) the terms of the tenancy make provision for it to be brought to an end on the ground in question (whether that provision takes the form of a provision for re-entry, for forfeiture, for determination by notice or otherwise): s.7(6).

The usual provisions for relief will not apply where the landlord has relied upon a forfeiture clause, see para.6.015.

Where the court makes an order for possession on grounds relating to a fixed-term tenancy which has come to an end any statutory periodic tenancy which has arisen on the ending of the fixed term automatically comes to an end (without any notice and regardless of the period) when the order is executed (s.7(7) as amended by the Housing and Regeneration Act 2008).

Housing Act 1988 section 7(6), (7)

   (6) The court shall not make an order for possession of a dwelling house to take effect at a time when it is let on an assured fixed term tenancy unless—

   (a) the ground for possession is Ground 2 or Ground 8 in Part I of Schedule 2 to this Act or any of the grounds in Part II of that Schedule, other than Ground 9 or Ground 16; and

   (b) the terms of the tenancy make provision for it to be brought to an end on the ground in question (whether that provision takes the form of a provision for re-entry, for forfeiture, for determination by notice or otherwise).

   (6A) In the case of a dwelling-house in England, subsection (6)(a) has effect as if it also referred to Ground 7 in Part 1 of Schedule 2 to this Act.

   (7) Subject to the preceding provisions of this section, the court may make an order for possession of a dwelling house on grounds relating to a fixed term tenancy which has come to an end; and where an order is made in such circumstances, any statutory periodic tenancy which has arisen on the ending of the fixed term tenancy shall end (without any notice and regardless of the period) on the day in accordance with section 5(1A).

The order for possession

6.029 Where the landlord is relying upon any of the discretionary grounds for possession (i.e. Grounds 9 to 17 of Sch.2) the court may, on the making of an order for possession or at any time before execution of such an order, stay or suspend the execution of the order or postpone the date for possession for such period or periods as the court thinks just (s.9). If any such stay, suspension or postponement is ordered the court must, unless it considers that to do so would cause exceptional hardship or would otherwise be unreasonable, impose conditions with regard to payment by the tenant of arrears of rent (if any) and rent and may impose such other conditions as it thinks fit. The court may, if it thinks it appropriate, discharge or rescind the order for possession (s.9(4)).

The court has no such discretion where the ground for possession is one of the mandatory grounds contained in Pt I of Sch.2 to the 1988 Act. In these cases the court may not postpone the order for possession for more than 14 days (six weeks in cases of exceptional hardship) (s.89 of the Housing Act 1980) (see para.3.034).

Where an order for possession is made on Ground 6 (demolition, reconstruction or substantial works) or Ground 9 (suitable alternative accommodation) the landlord is required to pay to the tenant a sum equal to the reasonable removal expenses likely to be incurred by the tenant in removing from the dwelling-house (s.11(1)). Any question as to the amount to be paid is determined by agreement between the landlord and the tenant or, in default of agreement, by the court (s.11(2)). Any sum so payable to the tenant is recoverable as a civil debt from the landlord (s.11(3)).

Housing Act 1988 section 9

(1) Subject to subsection (6) below, the court may adjourn for such period or **6.030** periods as it thinks fit proceedings for possession of a dwelling-house let on an assured tenancy.

(2) On the making of an order for possession of a dwelling-house let on an assured tenancy or at any time before the execution of such an order, the court, subject to subsection (6) below, may—

    (a)   stay or suspend execution of the order; or
    (b)   postpone the date of possession,

for such period or periods as the court thinks just.

(3) On any such adjournment as is referred to in subsection (1) above or on any such stay, suspension or postponement as is referred to in subsection (2) above, the court, unless it considers that to do so would cause exceptional hardship to the tenant or would otherwise be unreasonable, shall impose conditions with regard to payment by the tenant of arrears of rent (if any) and rent and may impose such other conditions as it thinks fit.

(4) If any such conditions as are referred to in subsection (3) above are complied with, the court may, if it thinks fit, discharge or rescind any such order as is referred to in subsection (2) above.

(6) This section does not apply if the court is satisfied that the landlord is entitled to possession of the dwelling-house—

    (a)   on any of the grounds in Part I of Schedule 2 to this Act; or
    (b)   by virtue of subsection (1) or subsection (4) of section 21 below.

Termination by tenant

There are no special provisions in the Housing Act 1988 directly governing termi- **6.031** nation by the tenant. An assured tenant may therefore determine the tenancy in the usual way, i.e. by surrender and, in the case of a periodic tenancy, by service of notice to quit (see Ch.3). The fact that it may do so is apparent from the following provisions. Indeed it would be absurd if he could not:

- Section 5(1) states that an assured tenancy cannot be brought to an end by the landlord except by obtaining an order of the court and execution of the order (see para.6.009). It also states that "the service by the landlord of a notice to quit shall be of no effect in relation to a periodic assured tenancy". It does not prevent a tenant serving a notice to quit. (*Laine v Cadwallader* [2001] L. & T.R. 81 CA at [12]).

- Section 5(2) states: "If an assured tenancy which is a fixed term tenancy comes to an end otherwise than by virtue of (a) an order of the court, or (b) a surrender or other action on the part of the tenant the tenant shall be entitled to remain in possession" after the end of a fixed-term tenancy (para.6.009). Conversely, therefore, the tenant is not entitled to remain in possession if he surrenders or brings the assured tenancy to an end by any "other action" such as a notice to quit.

- Section 5(5) deals with the situation where "on or before the date on which a tenancy is entered into" the tenant serves a notice to quit or does some other act which is intended to bring the tenancy to an end. In such circumstances the notice to quit, etc. is of no effect. It is implicit that a notice to quit or surrender at any other time is perfectly valid.

(See also the position in relation to secure tenancies where it has been held that the similar provisions of the Housing Act 1985 do not prevent the tenant from terminating by service of notice to quit or surrender, para.10.009).

If the tenant leaves on or before the end of the fixed term there is no difficulty for the landlord. He has his property back. What is the position if the tenant serves a notice to quit but then refuses to leave? Section 7 states that the court shall not make an order for possession "let on an assured tenancy" except where one of the grounds specified in Sch.2 applies and a s.8 notice has been served. However, if the tenancy has been brought to an end by the tenant, it is no longer let on any tenancy. Further, (it is submitted) by virtue of s.5(2)—referred to above—the tenant is no longer "entitled to remain in possession". The landlord is therefore entitled to possession without proving any of the grounds or serving a s.8 notice.

6.032   If the tenant remains in possession after the end of the fixed term, a statutory periodic tenancy arises "immediately on the coming to an end of the fixed term tenancy" (s.5(3)(a)). The tenant should not therefore remain in occupation a moment longer if he wishes to avoid a continuation of the tenancy. If he does stay longer he will need to serve a valid notice to quit (*Laine v Cadwallader* [2001] L. & T.R. 81 CA at [12]). The periods of the statutory periodic tenancy will be "the same as those for which rent was last payable under the fixed term tenancy" (s.5(3)) and an appropriate notice to quit in respect of that period will need to be served. It will also be necessary to comply with s.5 of the Protection from Eviction Act, which requires a minimum of four weeks' notice (see further para.3.018).

Housing Act 1988 section 5(5)

(5) If, on or before the date on which a tenancy is entered into or is deemed to have been granted as mentioned in subsection (3)(b) above, the person who is to be the tenant under that tenancy—

(a) enters into an obligation to do any act which (apart from this subsection) will cause the tenancy to come to an end at a time when it is an assured tenancy; or

(b) executes, signs or gives any surrender, notice to quit or other document which (apart from this subsection) has the effect of bringing the tenancy to an end at a time when it is an assured tenancy,

the obligation referred to in paragraph (a) above shall not be enforceable or, as the case may be, the surrender, notice to quit or other document referred to in paragraph (b) above shall be of no effect.

Assignment, sub-letting, bankruptcy and death

Assignment, sub-letting and parting with possession: Housing Act 1988 section 15

Subject to what is written in the next paragraph, it is an implied term of every **6.033** assured tenancy which is a periodic tenancy that, except with the consent of the landlord, the tenant shall not (a) assign the tenancy (in whole or in part), or (b) sub-let or part with possession of the whole or any part of the dwelling-house let on the tenancy (s.15(1)). Section 19 of the Landlord and Tenant Act 1927 does not apply to this implied term. The landlord therefore has an absolute right to refuse such an assignment, sub-letting or parting with possession. He does not have to show that his refusal was reasonable (s.15(2)).

However, there is no such implied term in the case of a periodic tenancy which is not a statutory periodic tenancy (i.e. not a periodic tenancy that has arisen after the end of a fixed term: see para.6.012) if:

(a) there is a provision (whether contained in the tenancy or not) under which the tenant is prohibited (whether absolutely or conditionally) from assigning or sub-letting or parting with possession or is permitted (whether absolutely or conditionally) to assign, sub-let or part with possession; or

(b) a premium is required to be paid on the grant or renewal of the tenancy: s.15(3).

The term "premium" includes (a) any fine or other like sum; (b) any other pecuniary consideration in addition to rent; and any sum paid by way of deposit, other than one which does not exceed one-sixth of the annual rent payable under the tenancy immediately after the grant or renewal in question (s.15(4)).

There are no provisions in the 1988 Act relating to fixed-term tenancies. Thus, the right of the tenant to assign, sub-let or part with possession will depend upon the terms of the agreement and s.19 of the 1927 Act will apply. After expiry of the fixed term the tenant will become a statutory periodic tenant and the provisions of s.15(1) of the 1988 Act will apply (see above) (i.e. the implied covenant against assigning, etc. without consent). A tenant of a social landlord has, under s.158 of the Localism Act 2011, a right in certain circumstances to a transfer of their tenancy.

If the tenant does assign, sub-let or part with possession in breach of a term of the tenancy the landlord may rely upon that fact as a ground for possession

(Ground 12, which is a discretionary ground). But note that in the case of an assignment the assignment is effective to transfer the tenancy (Ch.4, para.4.012) and that the notice of intention to commence proceedings for possession should therefore be served upon the assignee.

Note also *Ujima Housing Association v Ansah* (1997) 30 H.L.R. 831 CA—assured tenant who sub-let the whole and ceased to occupy ceased to be assured (dealt with at para.6.004).

Termination of head tenancy: effect on assured tenancy

6.034 The common law provides that where a tenancy is determined all sub-tenancies automatically come to an end unless the superior tenancy has been determined by surrender (see para.4.016). Section 18 of the 1988 Act nullifies this rule in relation to assured sub-tenancies lawfully granted by providing that where the superior tenancy is determined any such assured sub-tenancy shall continue in existence. The person who would but for the assured tenancy be entitled to possession of the dwelling-house becomes the new landlord: s.18(1). This rule will not apply if the person who would be the new landlord is entitled to rely upon one of the exclusions contained in Sch.1 to the 1988 Act (s.18(2)).

Bankruptcy of the tenant

6.035 Section 283(3A) of the Insolvency Act 1986 (as introduced by s.117 of the Housing Act 1988) provides that an assured tenancy the terms of which inhibit an assignment as mentioned in s.127(5) of the Rent Act 1977 does not form part of a bankrupt tenant's estate. Thus, the assured tenancy does not automatically vest in the trustee in bankruptcy under s.306 of the Insolvency Act 1986 on the bankruptcy of the tenant (see generally para.4.018). However, s.308A of the Insolvency Act 1986 (as introduced by s.117 of the 1988 Act) provides that where the trustee serves a notice in writing upon the bankrupt under s.308A the assured tenancy vests in the trustee as part of the bankrupt's estate; and except against a purchaser in good faith, for value and without notice of the bankruptcy, the trustee's title to that tenancy has relation back to the commencement of the bankruptcy.

If the trustee in bankruptcy does serve a notice under s.308A so that the tenancy becomes vested in him the former tenant, who remains in occupation of the dwelling-house, does so as a licensee of the trustee. If the trustee disclaims the tenancy the original tenant will have no right to remain in occupation and will be a trespasser (*Smalley v Quarrier*, see para.4.019).

Death of the tenant

Fixed-term tenancies

6.036 The general law applies. Where a fixed term is held by joint tenants the survivors become the tenants. If a sole tenant dies the tenancy devolves according to his will or on intestacy (see generally para.4.021). In England the landlord can seek to recover possession by relying on Ground 7 (see further para.6.039).

Periodic tenancies: joint tenancies

In the case of an assured tenancy which is a periodic tenancy (including a statu- **6.037** tory periodic tenancy) held by joint tenants where one of the joint tenants dies the general law applies and the survivors become the tenants.

Periodic tenancies: spouse or civil partner living with sole tenant

Where the tenant was a sole tenant and immediately before the tenant's **6.038** death the tenant's spouse or civil partner was occupying the dwelling-house as his or her only or principal home the tenancy vests in the spouse or civil partner and not according to the tenant's will or intestacy. However, the tenancy will not vest in the spouse or civil partner if the deceased tenant was "himself a successor" as defined in subs.(2) or subs.(3) of s.17. The effect of these subsections is that the tenancy will not vest in the spouse or civil partner by virtue of s.17 where:

(1) the tenancy becomes vested in the original tenant by virtue of s.17 (i.e. as a spouse or civil partner on the death of his or her former spouse or civil partner) under the will or intestacy of a previous tenant;

(2) at some time before his death the original tenant was a joint tenant and prior to his death he became the sole tenant by survivorship;

(3) the original tenant became entitled to an assured periodic tenancy after the death of a regulated tenant under the Rent Act 1977 pursuant to s.39(5) of the Housing Act 1988 (see para.8.050).

Subsection 3 deals with the situation where the deceased tenant was a successor by virtue of subs.(2) in relation to one tenancy and he has subsequently entered into a tenancy agreement of the same or substantially the same premises. In order to ensure that there is a transfer to the spouse or civil partner under s.17 in these circumstances subs.(3) provides that a tenant (i.e. the deceased tenant) is also a successor in relation to a tenancy "(the new tenancy)" which was granted to him (alone or jointly with others) if:

(a) at some time before the grant of the new tenancy, he was, by virtue of subs. (2), a successor in relation to an earlier tenancy of the same or substantially the same dwelling-house as is let under the new tenancy; and

(b) at all times since he became such a successor he has been a tenant (alone or jointly with others) of the dwelling-house which is let under the new tenancy or of a dwelling-house which is substantially the same as that dwelling-house.

From April 1, 2012, private registered providers of social housing may make express provision in an assured tenancy granting additional succession rights so that even though the deceased tenant was a successor, another party will be entitled to take over the tenancy on their death (s.17(1E)).

A person who was living with the tenant as his or her wife or husband is treated as the tenant's spouse or person who was living with the tenant as if they were civil partners shall be treated as the tenant's civil partner (s.17(4)). Where there is more than one person who was a "spouse" or "civil partner" of the tenant occupying the dwelling-house immediately before the death of the tenant the person who is entitled to succeed is the person who is decided upon by agreement or in default by decision of the county court (s.17(5))!

Periodic tenancy: sole tenant—no spouse or civil partner entitled to succeed

6.039   Where there is no succession of the tenancy to a spouse or civil partner pursuant to s.17 the tenancy will devolve under the will or on intestacy but the landlord will be entitled to recover possession under Ground 7 if he begins proceedings not later than 12 months after the death of the former tenant or, if the court so directs, after the date on which, in the opinion of the court, the landlord or, in the case of joint landlords, any one of them became aware of the former tenant's death. The reference to "proceedings for recovery of possession" refers to court proceedings, not service of the s.8 notice. The period of 12 months is therefore calculated from the date the proceedings are commenced (*Shepping v Osada* [2000] L. & T.R. 489 CA).

Ground 7 is a mandatory ground for possession and so the court must make an order without considering the reasonableness of the landlord's request for possession.

Ground 7 expressly states that for the purposes of that ground the acceptance by the landlord of rent from a new tenant after the death of the former tenant shall not be regarded as creating a new periodic tenancy, unless the landlord agrees in writing to a change (as compared with the tenancy before the death) in the amount of the rent, the period of the tenancy, the premises which are let or any other term of the tenancy.

Note that if the tenant (i.e. the personal representative or the beneficiary, as the case may be) is not occupying "the dwelling as his only or principal home" the tenancy will cease to be assured (para.6.003) and it will not be necessary to rely upon Ground 7. The tenancy will be an ordinary common law tenancy terminable by a notice to quit.

Chapter 7

Assured Shorthold Tenancies

All assured tenancies entered into on or after February 28, 1997 are (save for a **7.001** few limited exceptions) automatically assured shortholds. The landlord does not have to serve a notice in advance; the tenancy does not need to be in writing and there is no six-month minimum period for the tenancy (see s.19A of the Housing Act 1988 introduced by s.96 of the 1996 Act; the Housing Act 1996 (Commencement No.7 and Savings) Order 1997 SI 2007/225).

An assured shorthold tenancy is a type of assured tenancy. The rules in Ch.6 relating to assured tenancies therefore apply to shortholds unless they conflict with the provisions explained in this chapter. The purpose of the assured shorthold tenancy is to enable the landlord to let his property with the knowledge that he will be able to recover possession at the end of the contractual term or thereafter without having to rely upon the usual assured tenancy grounds.

There is a limited control on rent increases, in that in certain circumstances the tenant may refer the rent to a rent assessment committee in order to determine the correct market rent. Rent control in respect of assured shorthold tenancies is dealt with in ss.22 and 23 of the 1988 Act (as amended) (see further para.28.053).

In this chapter assured shorthold tenancies created prior to February 28, 1997 are referred to as "old" shortholds and those created on or after that date are referred to as "new" shortholds.

Assured agricultural occupancies are dealt with in Ch.18 (para.18.010).

Starter tenancies

"Starter tenancies" are used by housing associations in the same way that **7.001A** local authorities use introductory tenancies. It allows them to evict a tenant if the tenant causes problems soon after he moves in. Starter tenancies are not creatures of statute but are simply assured shorthold tenancies. They are granted for a fixed term. At the end of that period, if everything is satisfactory, a normal assured tenancy is granted.

Definition of assured shorthold tenancy; "old" shortholds

The basic rule: section 20 of the 1988 Act

7.002 An "assured shorthold tenancy" is an "assured tenancy" (see para.6.003):

(a) which is a fixed-term tenancy granted for a term certain of not less than six months. (In *Bedding v McCarthy* (1994) 41 E.G. 151 CA, the tenancy agreement was expressed to be for a period of six months. The tenant was given the s.20 notice a few hours before he entered into the tenancy agreement on the same day. The tenant argued that agreement was not for a full period of six months. However, the court held that the law ignored hours. It was therefore for a period of six months. In *Goodman v Evely* [2001] P.L.S.C.S. 17; [2001] EWCA Civ 104 it was held that a tenancy for "a term certain of one year and . . . thereafter from month to month" was a fixed term for the purpose of s.20(1)(a)); and

(b) in respect of which there is no power for the landlord to determine the tenancy at any time earlier than six months from the beginning of the tenancy (other than by a power of re-entry or forfeiture for breach of the tenancy (s.45(4)); para.6.009); and

(c) in respect of which an assured shorthold notice in prescribed form (or in a form "substantially to the same effect") was served by the landlord (or, in the case of joint landlords, at least one of them; s.20(6)(a) upon the tenant (or in the case of joint tenants upon all of them; s.45(3)) before the tenancy was entered into stating that the assured tenancy to which it related was to be an assured shorthold (reg.2 and Form 7 of the Assured Tenancies and Agricultural Occupancies (Forms) Regulations 1988 (as amended)—Form 17 on p.139).

7.003 In *Ravenseft v Hall* the landlord had inserted the incorrect starting date for the tenancy. The notice stated that the tenant was to remain in the dwelling-house for at least six months from June 24, 1996, whereas she was in fact entitled to remain for at least six months from August 28, 1996. In *White v Chubb* the s.20 notice contained an error as to the expiry date in the tenancy. It was stated to be May 1, 1994, whereas the correct date was April 1, 1994. In *Kasseer v Freeman* there were mistakes in the wording of the information on the form used.

The Court of Appeal (giving judgment in these three cases together—*Ravenseft Properties Ltd v Hall; White v Chubb; Kasseer v Freeman* [2001] EWCA Civ 2034) held that in deciding whether or not each notice was valid the question was simply whether, notwithstanding any errors or omissions, the notice was substantially to the same effect (applying *Mannai Investment Co Ltd v Eagle Star Life Assurance*). The approach adopted in the earlier cases of *Panyai v Roberts* and *York v Casey* [1998] 30 E.G. 110 of asking whether or not the error was an obvious one was not followed.

The notices had accomplished their statutory purpose of informing the proposed tenants of the special nature of the assured shorthold tenancy and were "substantially to the same effect" as the prescribed form.

Two other decisions have dealt with problems arising through agency. The landlord need not give his particulars on the s.20 form if his agent has provided their details (*Osborn v Dior* [2003] EWCA Civ 281). Notice can also be served on an agent of the tenant (*Yenula Properties Ltd v Naidu* [2002] EWCA Civ 719).

Form 17: Notice of an assured shorthold tenancy

© 1993 *OYEZ* Form No 7 of the Assured
Tenancies and Agricultural Occupancies
(Forms) Regulations 1988 (as amended)

HOUSING ACT 1988
Section 20
Notice of an Assured Shorthold Tenancy

- Please write clearly in black ink.
- If there is anything you do not understand you should get advice from a solicitor or a Citizens' Advice Bureau, before you agree to the tenancy.
- The landlord must give this notice to the tenant before an assured shorthold tenancy is granted. It does not commit the tenant to take the tenancy.
- **THIS DOCUMENT IS IMPORTANT. KEEP IT IN A SAFE PLACE.**

(1) Name of proposed tenant if a joint tenancy is being offered enter the names of the joint tenant(s)

To(¹):

1. You are proposing to take a tenancy of the dwelling known as:

(2) The tenancy must be for a term certain of at least six months

(²) from the ... day of ... 19
to the ... day of ... 19

2. This notice is to tell you that your tenancy is to be an *assured shorthold tenancy*. Provided you keep to the terms of the tenancy, you are entitled to remian in the dwelling for at least the first six months of the fixed period agreed at the start of the tenancy. At the end of this period, depending on the terms of the tenancy, the landlord may have the right to repossession if he/she wants.

3. The rent for this tenancy is the rent we have agreed. However, you have the right to apply to a rent assessment committee for a determination of the rent which the committee considers might reasonably be obtained under the tenancy. If the committee considers (i) that there is a sufficient number of similar properties in the locality let on assured tenancies and that (ii) the rent we have agreed is significantly higher than the rent which might reasonably be obtained having regard to the level of rents for other assured tenancies in the locality, it will determine a rent for the tenancy. That rent will be the legal maximum you can be required to pay from the date the committee directs. If the rent includes a payment for council tax, the rent determined by the committee will be inclusive of council tax.

To be signed by the landlord or his/her agent (someone acting for him/her). If there are joint landlords each must sign, unless one signs on behalf of the rest with their agreement.

Signed:

Name(s) of landlord(s):

Address of landlord(s):

Telephone:

If signed by agent, name and address of agent

Telephone: ... Date: ... 19

SPECIAL NOTE FOR EXISTING TENANTS
- Generally, if you already have a protected or statutory tenancy and you give it up to take a new tenancy in the same or other accommodation owned by the same landlord, that tenancy cannot be an assured tenancy. It can stilll be a protected tenancy.
- But if you currently occupy a dwelling which was let to you as a protected shorthold tenant, special rules apply.
- If you have assured tenancy which is not shorthold under the Housing Act 1988, you cannot be offered an assured shorthold tenancy of the same or other accommodation by the same landlord.

Reproduced for illustrative purposes only by kind permission of The Solicitors' Law Stationery Society Limited. The Housing Acts 1988 and 1996 abolished the need to serve these notices when creating a new assured shorthold tenancy on or after February 28, 1997.

An exception: grant to existing assured tenant (section 20(3))

7.004 Notwithstanding that the above conditions apply a new tenancy will not be an assured shorthold tenancy where:

(a) immediately before the grant of the new tenancy the person to whom it is granted (or, if there are joint tenants, at least one of them) was tenant under an assured tenancy which was not a shorthold tenancy; and

(b) the new tenancy is granted by the person who, immediately before the beginning of the tenancy, was the landlord under the previous assured tenancy.

For a case where the landlord managed to get away with taking a surrender of a statutory tenancy and 24 hours later granting a new protected shorthold (see para.15.003) to the same tenant, see *Bolnore Properties Ltd v Cobb* (1996) 29 H.L.R. 202 (CA). However, it should be noted that the tenancy was subject to an order for possession and eviction was imminent. The tenant could only have avoided the eviction by surrendering the existing tenancy. The court therefore held that the surrender and re-grant 24 hours later of a protected shorthold were genuine. The court would no doubt apply similar considerations if the original tenancy had been an ordinary assured tenancy and the latter an assured shorthold. See also *Dibbs v Campbell* (1988) 20 H.L.R. 374 (referred to at para.15.003).

Persons who were protected shorthold tenants under the Rent Act 1977 (sections 34(2), (3))

7.005 Where a new tenancy was granted on or after the commencement of the Housing Act 1988 (January 15, 1989) to a person who immediately before the grant was:

(a) a tenant under a protected shorthold tenancy (i.e. pursuant to s.52 of the Housing Act 1980; see para.15.003); or

(b) a protected or statutory tenant of a dwelling-house which was let under a protected shorthold tenancy which ended before January 15, 1989

and in respect of which at that date either there had been no grant of a further tenancy or any grant of a further tenancy had been made to the person who immediately before that grant was in possession of the dwelling-house as a protected or statutory tenant and who fulfils all the requirements of an assured tenancy (para.6.003), the new tenancy is an assured shorthold tenancy even if the usual conditions for assured shorthold tenancies do not apply (see above) (s.34(3)). However, if the landlord (or, in the case of joint landlords, all of them: s.45(3)) served notice on the tenant that the new tenancy was not to be a shorthold tenancy (i.e. an assured shorthold) before the tenancy was entered into the tenancy will be an ordinary assured tenancy (s.34(3)).

"New" shortholds

Definition of "new" shortholds

7.006 A "new" shorthold (the authors' term) is an assured tenancy created on or after February 28, 1997. By virtue of s.19A of the Housing Act 1988 (introduced by s.96 of the 1996 Act) all such assured tenancies are automatically assured short-holds unless one of the exceptions set out below applies.

Exceptions

The exceptions may be summarised as follows: **7.007**

(1) A tenancy entered into pursuant to any contract made before February 28, 1997 (s.19A(b)).

(2) Where (i) the landlord serves the tenant with a notice that the tenancy is not to be or is no longer a shorthold or (ii) where the tenancy itself "contains a provision to the effect that the tenancy is not an assured shorthold tenancy" (Sch.2A, paras 1–3). In *Andrews v Cunningham* [2007] EWCA Civ 762 it was held that the words "Assured Tenancy" on the cover of a rent book did not amount to such a notice (because an assured shorthold tenancy is an assured tenancy); and stated obiter that any such "provision" almost certainly needs to be in writing. Where a landlord of an assured shorthold tenant mistakenly served such a notice, which on its face turned the tenancy into an ordinary assured tenancy, the notice was good and the tenancy became a non-shorthold at the end of the first year (*Saxon Weald Homes Ltd v Chadwick* [2011] EWCA Civ 1202.)

(3) A statutory periodic tenancy arising by virtue of s.5 of the 1988 Act (see para.6.012) on the expiry of a fixed-term assured tenancy will not be a shorthold (Sch.2A, para.8).

(4) Any assured tenancy entered into on or after February 28, 1997, which replaces a pre-existing assured tenancy which was not itself a short-hold, will not be a shorthold (i.e. a "replacement tenancy"; see para.7.013) unless the tenant serves a notice on the landlord in prescribed form saying it will be a shorthold (Sch.2A, para.7). A *Tomlin* order (see 25.040) reciting that T, who had been an assured non-shorthold tenant, would reside under a new tenancy as an assured shorthold tenant, was not sufficient to avoid the security provisions of the Housing Act 1988—the prescribed form must be used (*Kahlon v Isherwood* [2011] EWCA Civ 602, Patten L.J. at para.21: "the provision in the prescribed form is clearly part of the substance of the notice . . . it is no answer to its omission to say that the information it conveys was well known to the tenant at the relevant time").

(5) An assured tenancy by succession following on from a Rent Act tenancy (see s.39 of the 1988 Act; para.8.050) other than a protected shorthold will not be an assured shorthold (Sch.2A, para.4).

(6) An assured tenancy which became assured on ceasing to be a secure tenancy (Sch.2A, para.5).

(7) An assured tenancy arising at the end of a long tenancy by virtue of Sch.10 to the Local Government and Housing Act 1989 (Sch.2A, para.6).

(8) Assured agricultural occupancies unless a shorthold notice is served prior to the grant of the tenancy. It will not be possible to serve such a notice where the landlord and the tenant are the same as under a pre-existing assured tenancy (Sch.2A, para.9).

Duty of landlord to provide statement of terms

7.008 The rule that all new assured tenancies will automatically be shortholds without the need for anything in writing means that there are many informal, oral, tenancy agreements. Section 20A of the 1988 Act (as introduced by s.97 of the 1996 Act) therefore provides that the tenant may, by notice in writing, require the landlord under that tenancy to provide him with a written statement of any term of the tenancy which is not evidenced in writing and dealing with:

    (a) the date on which the tenancy began or, if it is a statutory periodic tenancy or tenancy to which s.39(7) applies (assured tenancy by succession to protected shorthold; see para.15.015), the date on which the tenancy came into being;

    (b) the rent payable and the dates on which it is payable;

    (c) any term relating to rent review; and

    (d) if the tenancy is for a fixed term, the length of that term.

Failure to provide such a statement is an offence (s.20A(4)). It is important to note that the statement is not to "be regarded as conclusive evidence of what was agreed by the parties to the tenancy in question" (s.20A(5)). The tenant may therefore challenge the landlord's statement as to the terms by calling oral or other written evidence in the normal way.

There are certain exceptions (see s.20A(3)).

Housing Act 1988 section 20A

7.009   (1) Subject to subsection (3) below, a tenant under an assured shorthold tenancy to which s.19A above applies may, by notice in writing, require the landlord under that tenancy to provide him with a written statement of any term of the tenancy which—

        (a) falls within subsection (2) below; and
        (b) is not evidenced in writing.

    (2) The following terms of a tenancy fall within this subsection, namely—

        (a) the date on which the tenancy began or, if it is a statutory periodic tenancy or a tenancy to which section 39(7) below applies, the date on which the tenancy came into being;
        (b) the rent payable under the tenancy and the dates on which that rent is payable;
        (c) any term providing for a review of the rent payable under the tenancy; and
        (d) in the case of a fixed term tenancy, the length of the fixed term.

    (3) No notice may be given under subsection (1) above in relation to a term of the tenancy if—

        (a) the landlord under the tenancy has provided a statement of that term in response to an earlier notice under that subsection given by the tenant under the tenancy; and
        (b) the term has not been varied since the provision of the statement referred to in para.(a) above.

    (4) A landlord who fails, without reasonable excuse, to comply with a notice under subsection (1) above within the period of 28 days beginning with the date on which he received the notice is liable on summary conviction to a fine not exceeding level four on the standard scale.

(5) A statement provided for the purposes of subsection (1) above shall not be regarded as conclusive evidence of what was agreed by the parties to the tenancy in question.

(6) Where—

(a) a term of a statutory periodic tenancy is one which has effect by virtue of section 5(3)(e) above; or

(b) a term of a tenancy to which subsection (7) of section 39 below applies is one which has effect by virtue of subsection (6)(e) of that section,

subsection (1) above shall have effect in relation to it as if paragraph (b) related to the term of the tenancy from which it derives.

(7) In subsections (1) and (3) above—

(a) references to the tenant under the tenancy shall, in the case of joint tenants, be taken to be references to any of the tenants; and

(b) references to the landlord under the tenancy shall, in the case of joint landlords, be taken to be references to any of the landlords.

Statutory periodic tenancies

After an assured tenancy (any assured tenancy), which is of a fixed term, comes **7.010** to an end, a statutory periodic tenancy automatically arises by virtue of s.5 of the 1988 Act (see para.6.012). An assured tenancy which comes into being pursuant to s.5 of the 1988 Act on the coming to an end of a tenancy which is automatically a shorthold by virtue of s.19A is also automatically a shorthold (s.19A(b) of the 1988 Act; s.96 of the 1996 Act).

However, an assured tenancy which comes into being on or after February 28, 1997 by virtue of s.5 in respect of a tenancy which was not a shorthold will itself not be a shorthold (para.8 of Sch.2A to the 1988 Act); i.e. any assured tenancy created prior to the coming into force of the 1996 Act will only give rise to another assured tenancy, not a shorthold.

Termination by landlord before fixed term has expired

Section 21(1) of the 1988 Act expressly preserves the landlord's right to recover **7.011** possession pursuant to Ch.1 of the 1988 Act. An assured shorthold tenancy, like any other assured tenancy, may therefore be brought to an end during the fixed term if:

(a) the ground for possession is any of the following grounds: 2 (mortgagee requiring possession), 8 (substantial arrears of rent), 10 (some rent due), 11 (persistent delay in paying rent), 12 (breach of the tenancy), 13 (deterioration of the dwelling-house or common parts), 14 (nuisance, annoyance, immoral or illegal user) or 15 (deterioration in condition of furniture); and

(b) the terms of the tenancy make provision for it to be brought to an end on the ground in question, whether that provision takes the form of a provision for re-entry, for forfeiture, for determination by notice or otherwise (s.7(6)).

In order to terminate the tenancy during the currency of the fixed term the landlord must carry out the procedure applicable to all assured tenancies. The statutory provisions relating to forfeiture do not apply where the landlord is relying upon a forfeiture clause, see para.6.015.

But note that if the tenancy contains a clause permitting the landlord to terminate the tenancy within the first six months on any of the above grounds the tenancy will not be an "old" assured shorthold tenancy unless that clause is "a power of re-entry or forfeiture for breach of any term or condition of the tenancy" (s.20(1)(b) and s.45(4); see para.7.002). This issue is most likely to arise where the tenancy permits the landlord to terminate the tenancy on Ground 2 (see para.A2.058).

Status of tenant after expiry of fixed term: subsequent tenancies

7.012 Where the tenant remains in occupation of the dwelling-house at the end of the fixed term he will usually do so as a statutory periodic tenant pursuant to s.5(2) of the 1988 Act, but as will be seen below, the landlord will be able to regain possession from such a tenant by service of a notice under s.21 of the 1988 Act.

In some cases the fixed term is followed by a contractual periodic tenancy pursuant to the terms of the original tenancy or the landlord grants the tenant a new tenancy. If, on the coming to an end of an "old" assured shorthold tenancy (including a tenancy which was an assured shorthold but ceased to be assured before it came to an end), a new tenancy of the same or substantially the same premises comes into being under which the landlord and the tenant are the same as at the coming to an end of the earlier tenancy, then if and so long as the new tenancy is an assured tenancy, it is an assured shorthold tenancy whether or not the three conditions set out in s.20(1) (para.7.002) are satisfied (s.20(4)). For an example see *Lower Street Properties Ltd v Jones* [1996] 2 E.G.L.R. 67 CA.

However, it will not be an assured shorthold if before the new tenancy is entered into (or, in the case of a statutory periodic tenancy, takes effect in possession) the landlord (or, in the case of joint landlords, at least one of them: s.20(6)(b) serves notice on the tenant that the new tenancy is not to be a shorthold tenancy. In the unlikely event that he does so, the tenancy will be an ordinary assured tenancy (s.20(5)).

Termination by section 21 notice

Housing Act 1988 section 21

7.013   (1)   Without prejudice to any right of the landlord under an assured shorthold tenancy to recover possession of the dwelling house let on the tenancy in accordance with Chapter I above, on or after the coming to an end of an assured shorthold tenancy which was a fixed term tenancy, a court shall make an order for possession of the dwelling house if it is satisfied—

      (a)   that the assured shorthold tenancy has come to an end and no further assured tenancy (whether shorthold or not) is for the time being in existence, other than an assured shorthold periodic tenancy (whether statutory or not); and

      (b)   the landlord or, in the case of joint landlords, at least one of them has given to the tenant not less than two months'notice in writing stating that he requires possession of the dwelling house.

(1A) Subsection (1B) applies to an assured shorthold tenancy of a dwelling house in England if—

    (a) it is a fixed term tenancy for a term certain of not less than two years, and
    (b) the landlord is a private registered provider of social housing.

(1B) The court may not make an order for possession of the dwelling-house let on the tenancy unless the landlord has given to the tenant not less than six months' notice in writing—

    (a) stating that the landlord does not propose to grant another tenancy on the expiry of the fixed term tenancy, and
    (b) informing the tenant of how to obtain help or advice about the notice and, in particular, of any obligation of the landlord to provide help or advice.

(2) A notice under paragraph (b) of subsection (1) above may be given before or on the day on which the tenancy comes to an end; and that subsection shall have effect notwithstanding that on the coming to an end of the fixed term tenancy a statutory periodic tenancy arises.

(3) Where a court makes an order for possession of a dwelling house by virtue of subsection (1) above, any statutory periodic tenancy which has arisen on the coming to an end of the assured shorthold tenancy shall end (without further notice and regardless of the period) in accordance with section 5(1A).

(4) Without prejudice to any such right as is referred to in subsection (1) above, a court shall make an order for possession of a dwelling house let on an assured shorthold tenancy which is a periodic tenancy if the court is satisfied—

    (a) that the landlord or, in the case of joint landlords, at least one of them has given to the tenant a notice in writing stating that, after a date specified in the notice, being the last day of a period of the tenancy and not earlier than two months after the date the notice was given, possession of the dwelling house is required by virtue of this section; and
    (b) that the date specified in the notice under paragraph (a) above is not earlier than the earliest day on which, apart from section 5(1) above, the tenancy could be brought to an end by a notice to quit given by the landlord on the same date as the notice under paragraph (a) above.

(4A) Where a court makes an order for possession of a dwelling-house by virtue of subsection (4) above, the assured shorthold tenancy shall end in accordance with section 5(1A).

(5) Where an order for possession under subsections (1) or (4) above is made in relation to a dwelling house let on a tenancy to which section 19A above applies, the order may not be made so as to take effect earlier than—

    (a) in the case of a tenancy which is not a replacement tenancy, six months after the beginning of the tenancy; and
    (b) in the case of a replacement tenancy, six months after the beginning of the original tenancy.

(5A) Subsection (5) above does not apply to an assured shorthold tenancy to which section 20B (demoted assured shorthold tenancies) applies.

(6) In subsection (5)(b) above, the reference to the original tenancy is—

    (a) where the replacement tenancy came into being on the coming to an end of a tenancy which was not a replacement tenancy, to the immediately preceding tenancy; and
    (b) where there have been successive replacement tenancies, to the tenancy immediately preceding the first in the succession of replacement tenancies.

(7) For the purposes of this section, a replacement tenancy is a tenancy—

    (a)   which comes into being on the coming to an end of an assured shorthold; and

    (b)   under which, on its coming into being—

        (i)   the landlord and tenant are the same as under the earlier tenancy as at its coming to an end; and

       (ii)   the premises let are the same or substantially the same as those let under the earlier tenancy as at that time.

Introduction

7.014 If the landlord wishes to regain possession in respect of an assured shorthold tenancy by reliance upon s.21 he must serve a notice in accordance with the provisions of that section. The 1988 Act does not specify how it should be served (see further para.7.028).

The notice must be in writing. However, there are no prescribed forms. Law Stationers do provide precedents (see Form 18, p.159 and Form 19, p.160) but so long as the notice complies with the terms of the relevant provision it may be in any form. As can be seen there are two different notices, one referred to in s.21(1) and the other in s.21(4). We shall discuss below which notice is required to be served in which set of circumstances.

In the case of joint landlords the notice must be given by at least one of them (s.21); and where there are joint tenants the notice must be given to all of them (s.45(3)).

An argument (in respect of a social landlord) that s.21 breaches arts 6 (fair trial) and 8 (family life) of the European Convention on Human Rights has failed in the Court of Appeal. The section is necessary in a democratic society, as some procedure has to be available for recovering possession of property at the end of the tenancy (*Donoghue v Poplar Housing & Regeneration Community Association Ltd* [2001] EWCA Civ 595).

In relation to tenancies granted from April 1, 2012, a private registered provider of social housing, must serve an additional notice at least six months prior to proceedings where the tenancy is for a fixed term of not less than two years. That notice must state that the landlord does not propose to grant another tenancy on the expiry of the fixed term and provide information to the tenant on how to obtain help and advice (see s.21(1B)).

Note s.75 of the Housing Act 2004 which prohibits the service of a s.21 notice by the unlicensed landlord of a house in multiple occupation and in certain tenancy deposit scheme cases; see para.7.029.

Relationship with section 8 notices

7.015 The right to terminate a tenancy by service of a s.21 notice is a right which is additional to the right to terminate the tenancy by service of a notice of intention to commence proceedings under s.8 where the landlord has a normal assured tenancy ground that he can rely upon (para.6.016). The fact that the two rights are concurrent is apparent from the words

"without prejudice to any right of the landlord under an assured tenancy to recover possession of the dwelling-house let on the tenancy in accordance with Chapter 1 above" (the opening words of s.21(1)).

Chapter 1 is the chapter of the Act that contains s.8 and which deals with assured tenancies generally. Section 21(4) also makes it clear that service of a notice under that subsection is "without prejudice to any such right".

Example The tenancy was originally for a fixed term of six months and the tenant has **7.016** held over as a statutory periodic tenant, paying rent weekly. There are now nine weeks' rent arrears. The landlord can choose whether to serve a s.8 notice and make a claim based upon the non-payment of rent or can serve a s.21 notice and then claim possession under that section. If he relies upon the non-payment of rent he can bring proceedings once 14 days have passed since service of the notice (para.6.017). If he is going to rely upon a s.21 notice he will have to wait at least two months for the notice to expire (see further below) and he will not be able to use the accelerated possession procedure if he also wants to claim the rent (para.26.002).

It is clearly not necessary to serve a notice of intention to commence proceedings under s.8 in addition to the s.21 notice when the landlord is only relying upon s.21. Section 8 notices "have no apparent relevance to the termination of an assured shorthold" (*Panayi v Roberts* (1993) 28 E.G. 125 CA per Mann L.J.).

See also s.5(1) and (2) which indicate that the court can make an order under Ch.1 (which includes s.8) or Ch.II (which includes s.21).

Notices under section 21(1)

It can be seen from subs (1) that the landlord serving a notice under it must give **7.017** "not less than two months' stating that he requires possession of the dwelling house". There is no requirement that the notice must terminate on any particular day. So long as the landlord gives the tenant not less than two months' written notice that he requires possession the notice will be valid. (As to whether or not he can commence proceedings before two months has passed see para.7.031).

Sometimes the tenancy contains an option to break during the fixed term. If the landlord wishes to break the term pursuant to that clause and give a notice under s.21 in the same document he may do so but he must make sure that the notice is properly drafted so as to be effective in both respects (*Aylward v Fawaz* (1997) 21 HLR 408 CA—a notice giving the tenant two months which stated "I give you notice that I require possession of the flat" was sufficiently clear on the facts to operate as an exercise of the break clause as well as a notice under s.21(1)(b)).

We shall consider below the circumstances in which a landlord may serve a notice under s.21(1) (para.7.023).

Notices under section 21(4)

Notices under subs. (4) are rather different. Where this subsection applies: **7.018**

- The notice must specify a date (which seems to imply that a calendar date must be used but see further *Lower Street Properties Ltd v Jones* below).

- The date specified must be the last day of a period of the tenancy. (For examples see below. Where the tenancy is a statutory periodic tenancy s.5(3)(d) of the 1988 Act provides that it is one "under which the periods of the tenancy are the same as those for which rent was last payable under the fixed term tenancy"—see further *Meya* below).

- The date specified must be not earlier than two months after the date the notice was given.

- The date specified must not be earlier than the earliest day on which the tenancy could have been brought to an end by a notice to quit given by the landlord on the same date if it were an ordinary contractual tenancy. For example, if the tenancy is a quarterly tenancy at least one quarters notice needs to be given.

- The notice must state that possession of the dwelling house is required by virtue of s.21 after the date specified—but note that in *Notting Hill Housing Trust v Roomus* [2006] EWCA Civ 407 the Court of Appeal held that a notice that stated that the landlord required possession "At the end of the period of your tenancy" meant the same thing and was a valid notice. (But never use the word "on"—see *McDonald v Fernandez* below).

- The notice must state that after the specified date possession of the dwelling-house is required by virtue of this section. Usually landlords do not use these words in the actual body of the notice but tend to head the notice with words something like "Notice under s.21(4) of the Housing Act 1988". This would seem to be sufficient but there is no good reason not to put the actual words required by the section into the body of the notice.

Periodic tenancies—some examples

7.019
- If the rent is payable weekly in advance on a Monday the landlord needs to have a s.21(4) notice with a "last day of the period" being a Sunday. If the rent is payable in arrears on a Sunday then again "the last day of the period" is a Sunday.

- If the rent is payable monthly on the 20th of the month the notice must have a "last day of the period" being the 19th of the relevant month.

- If the tenancy is a monthly tenancy and the rent is payable on the first day of the month the notice should have "a last day of the period" being the last day of a calendar month even where that month is a shorter month (*Dodds v Walker* [1980] 1 W.L.R. 1061).

Housing Act 1988 section 5

5(2) If an assured tenancy which is a fixed term tenancy comes to an end otherwise than by virtue of—

    (a) an order of the court of the kind mentioned in subsection (1)(a) or (b) or any other order of the Court; or

    (b) a surrender or other action on the part of the tenant,

then subject to section 7 and Chapter II below, the tenant shall be entitled to remain in possession of the dwelling-house let under that tenancy and, subject to subsection (4) below, his right to possession shall depend upon a periodic tenancy arising by virtue of this section.

  (3) The periodic tenancy referred to in subsection (2) above is one—

    (a) taking effect in possession immediately on the coming to an end of the fixed term tenancy;

    . . .

(d) under which the periods of the tenancy are the same as those for which rent was last payable under the fixed term tenancy; and

(e) under which, subject to the following provisions of this Part of this Act, the other terms are the same as those of the fixed term tenancy immediately before it came to an end, except that any term which makes provision for determination by the landlord or the tenant shall not have effect while the tenancy remains an assured tenancy.

. . .

(7) Any reference in this Part of this Act to a statutory periodic tenancy is a reference to a periodic tenancy arising by virtue of this section.

The requirement that the notice must expire on the last day of a period of the tenancy is a strict one: *McDonald v Fernandez* [2003] EWCA Civ 1219. The facts of this case provide a good example of the strict requirements of the section:

> **Example** The tenants were in occupation under a statutory periodic tenancy that ran **7.020** from the 4th of each month to the 3rd of each month. This meant that the notice needed to specify an expiry date that was the 3rd of the month. The landlord purported to serve a notice under s.21(4) on October 24, 2002. The date specified in the notice should therefore have been January 3, 2003. However, the date given was January 4, 2003. That one day (too many!) was fatal.

The position is absurd but that is what the sub-section says. The main judgment was given by Hale L.J. (as she then was) and contains the following passage (at paras 22 and 23):

> ". . . the statute requires the notice to specify a date which is the last date of the period. The statute does not require the landlord to specify a date on which he requires possession. This is not a notice to quit. The landlord will not get possession without the tenant's consent unless he goes to court. That is why the statute requires the landlord to state that possession is required 'after a date specified in the notice, being the last day of a period of the tenancy'. This is not a case where the legislation permits a form to be 'substantially to the same effect'. The subsection is clear and precise. Nor is it difficult for landlords to comply. They know when the period ends. Furthermore, this is not a case where the consequences of failure to comply are particularly serious for landlords: a defective notice can be cured the next day. Even if the defect is not noticed until the point is taken in court, a valid notice can then be given. The landlord is not unwillingly and unwittingly saddled with a tenant who has security of tenure, as would be the case with an invalid notice under section 20. One purpose of the subsection may be to alert tenants to the need to look for alternative accommodation, but another is to give the courts a clear and simple set of criteria, which trigger their mandatory duty to order possession".

Many landlords and practitioners will find these comments rather unhelpful. The failure to get the notice right is in fact easily done, especially by unrepresented landlords yet by reason of an unnecessary technicality they can be required to go through the process again, which will take time and which may possibly lead to a loss of rent.

A further twist

As stated above the date specified in a notice served under s.21(4) must end on the **7.021** last day of a period of the tenancy. There is some uncertainty as to what is the last day of a period when the fixed term ends in the middle of a rental period.

Example The tenant is in occupation under a six-month fixed term tenancy. The rent is payable weekly each Monday. The fixed term comes to end on a Thursday. The tenant then holds over under a statutory periodic tenancy pursuant to s.5(3)(d) of the 1988 Act. Do the periods under that periodic tenancy start on a Friday and end on a Thursday; or do they continue to run from each Monday so that they end each Sunday?

The point is not comprehensively answered in, but we can derive some assistance from, the case of *Church Commissioners for England v Meya* [2006] EWCA Civ 821. In that case the terms of the tenancy provided that "the rent" meant "a clear yearly rent of £17,680" and by way of a separate clause the tenant was obliged "to pay the rent to the landlords by equal quarterly payments in advance on the usual quarter day".

At common law a tenancy under which the rent is a "yearly rent" is a yearly tenancy requiring six months notice to quit ending on the last day of the period. Thus, if the periods of this statutory periodic tenancy were annual, six months notice requiring possession would have been required. But if the periods were quarterly only a quarter's notice was required (see s.21(4)(b)). The key dates were as follows:

- On December 30, 2004 the fixed term agreement expired. Thereafter the tenancy was a statutory periodic tenancy.

- On March 2, 2005 the landlord served a notice requiring possession under s.21(4).

- The notice stated that the landlord required possession "after the 30 May 2005 or at the end of that period of your tenancy which will end after the expiry of two months from the giving of this notice whichever is the later". If the tenancy was a quarterly tenancy, applying the "saving formula" (as to saving formulas see below) the date specified in the notice was the June quarter day.

- On July 4, 2005 the landlord issued a claim for possession.

If the tenancy was a quarterly tenancy the landlord was entitled to bring the claim on July 4. However, if the tenancy was an annual tenancy the proceedings were premature.

Where the tenancy is a statutory periodic tenancy s.5(3)(d) provides that the periodic tenancy "is one under which the periods of the tenancy are the same as those for which rent was last payable under the fixed term tenancy". The key word in s.5(3)(d) is the word "last". Ward L.J. at paras 21 and 22:

"It qualifies the word 'payable' by expressing a relation of time or manner or nature to what is payable. If the focus is on time, manner or nature of what is payable, then one has to ascertain first what payment of rent last fell due, in other words, what was the last payment of rent the respondent was obliged to make, and then secondly of course, ascertain the period covered by that last payment. Here the rent was an annual rent but it was expressly payable quarterly in advance. The last payment was £4,420 and it was payable in advance for the September quarter. So the period is a quarterly period."

The tenancy was therefore held to be a quarterly tenancy; and a quarters notice was sufficient.

There are actually two questions in cases like this: (i) what are the periods of the tenancy—the point specifically dealt with in *Meya*; and (ii) on what date does each period end? It is to be noted that the original fixed term tenancy in the case **ended on December 30, 2004**. This meant that the statutory periodic tenancy started on December 31 (see s.5(3)(a)—it took "effect immediately on the coming to an end of the fixed term tenancy"). However, the periods of the tenancy, by which the last day of the period was calculated, **ended at the end of each period; i.e. the last day of the quarter**. Thus, the Court of Appeal calculated the end of the period by reference to the June quarter day, not by reference to the ending of the original fixed term. Thus, in the example above it would seem clear that the last day of each period is a Sunday.

Saving formulae?

In order to avoid problems landlords often use a s.21(4) notice containing a **7.022** "saving formula". It might for example be in the following format:

"I give you notice that I require possession of the dwelling-house known as . . . after [calendar date or, if later,] the day on which a complete period of your tenancy expires next after the end of two months from the service of this notice".

However, the words in brackets can give rise to difficulties:

Example 1 The periods of the tenancy end on the 4th of each month. The notice is served on January 2, 2013. It requires possession "after 1 March 2013 or if later the day on which a complete period of your tenancy expires next after the end of two months from service of this notice". The complete period ending two months after service of the notice ends on March 4. The notice is therefore valid. However . . .

Example 2 Once again the periods end on the 4th of each month and the notice is served on January 2, 2013. However this time it requires possession "after 5 March or if later the day on which a complete period of your tenancy expires next after the end of two months from service of this notice". Again, the complete period ending two months after service of the notice ends on March 4. However, March 4, is not later than March 5! So as a matter of construction the notice is not valid. Nor would it help if the words "if later" were deleted as this would mean that the notice would be stating that it ends on "4 March or 5 March" which is not therefore specifying a single date. Nor can one say that the notice ends on April 4, because the next time that the period ends two months after service on January 2 is March 4, not April 4.

Example 3 One would think that the words "if later" need to be included. Otherwise there is no certainty with the date. However, in *Hussain v Bradford Community Housing Limited* [2009] EWCA Civ 763 an assured weekly tenancy contained a clause that the tenants should give the landlord "not less than 28 days written notice expiring on any Friday should he/she wish to terminate". The weekly periodic tenancy ended on a Friday. One of the two joint tenants served a notice to quit on 24 January 2007 "with effect from Sunday 25/02/2007 *or* the day on which a complete period of your tenancy expires next after the end of four weeks from the date of this notice." The remaining joint tenant argued that the notice to quit was ineffective as it gave two alternative dates. The judge disagreed. Patten L.J. at para.11:

"It is true that the notice gives two possible termination dates, but only one complies with the requirements of clause 2.2 of the tenancy agreement and that date, which is Friday February 23, is the first in time. In my judgment, there is no basis for construing the notice so as to exclude the operation of the catch-all provision. It was obviously inserted to ensure that the notice expired at the end of a contractual period of the tenancy if that was not Sunday 25 February and it would have been read by the respondent as intending to terminate the tenancy in accordance with clause 2.2 of the tenancy agreement: see *Mannai Investment Co Ltd v Eagle Star Life Assurance Co Ltd* [1997] AC 749. For these reasons, in my judgment, the notice to quit took effect at the end of Friday 23 February"

Perhaps the same applies to two alternative dates in a s.21 notice—although it is important to remember that a s.21 notice is not a notice to quit to which the Mannai principles clearly apply. It is a statutory requirement (see Hale L.J. in *McDonald v Fernandez* at para.7.020).

The Solution

7.022a   However, strange as it may seem, it is not actually necessary to put in a calendar date. In *Lower Street Properties Ltd v Jones* [1996] 2 E.G.L.R. 67 it was held that a notice which is stated to expire

"at the end of the period of the tenancy which will end after the expiry of two months from the service of the notice"

is a valid notice even if it is undated. Such a notice refers to the last day with sufficient specificity because it can readily be ascertained. The word "specified" means no more than made clear.

"Because of the wording of section 21(4) if an actual date is to be given in the notice it must be 'the last day of the period of the tenancy' and there is an obvious risk of a minor arithmetical error giving rise to the argument that the notice is invalid which is no doubt why the printed form suggests as a possible wording that the notice will expire 'at the end of the period of your tenancy which will end after the expiry of 2 months from the service upon you of this notice'. In my judgment, that is a form of words which does meet the requirements of section 21(4) because the tenant knows or can easily ascertain the date referred to" (Kennedy L.J. at 69M).

The date of service of the notice "can if necessary be proved by oral evidence, by agreement, or in any other way considered to be appropriate" (*Lower Street Properties* at 70B).

In *Notting Hill Housing Trust v Roomus* [2006] EWCA Civ 407, Dyson L.J. said of *Lower Street Properties v Jones*, at para.4:

". . . the importance of this decision is that it sanctioned the use of the formula as being sufficient to specify the last day of a period of a tenancy: *it is not necessary to specify a calendar date.*"

The authors therefore suggest that all notices under s.21(4) should use the formula approved by the Court of Appeal in these cases, i.e.:

"I give you notice that I require possession of the dwelling-house known as [the address] after the day on which a complete period of your tenancy expires next after the end of two months from the service of this notice".

Not all district judges like the use of such formulae and of course practitioners will want to make sure that the order for possession is made the first time it comes before the judge. Thus, when using the accelerated procedure (see Ch.26) the letter accompanying the application could contain a short sentence stating something like:

"Please ask the District Judge to note that the formula used by the landlord in the s.21(4) notice is that approved by the Court of Appeal in *Lower Street Properties v Jones* [1996] 2 EGLR 67 and *Notting Hill Housing Trust v Roomus* [2006] EWCA Civ 407".

Which notice?

So when is it necessary to serve a notice under s.21(1) and when is it necessary to   **7.023**
serve a notice under s.21(4)? There are four possible situations that may arise:

a. The shorthold tenancy is and always has been a periodic tenancy. This has been possible since February 28, 1997 (para.7.006). It is quite clear in this situation that it is necessary to serve a notice under s.21(4); in particular the date specified in the notice must be the last day of a period of a tenancy (para.7.018).

b. The tenancy was granted for a fixed term that has not yet expired. It is quite clear in this situation that a notice may be served under s.21(1), i.e. at least two months' written notice must be given by the landlord that he requires possession of the dwelling-house but the notice need not specify a date, let alone one ending on the last day of a period of a tenancy.

c. A contractual periodic tenancy has arisen by virtue of a clause in the fixed term. For example, a period of one year that has continued from month to month. In that case the tenancy has not "come to an end" as required by s.21(1)(a). It has continued in existence as a contractual periodic tenancy. It is therefore necessary to serve a notice under s.21(4).

d. The tenancy was originally granted for a fixed term that has expired and the tenant has remained in occupation under a statutory periodic tenancy. This last situation is not so clear. We shall now deal with it in some detail.

General consensus

The general consensus among commentators has been that in this last case a   **7.024**
notice under s.21(4) must be served. The principal reason given is that subs.(2) states that a notice "may be given" under s.21(1)(b) "before or on the day on which the tenancy comes to an end"; the implication being, it is suggested, that it may not be given after that date. (For example, see *Civil Procedure Rules* ("*White Book*") (London: Sweet & Maxwell, 2012) vol.2, para.3A-896). It is also the view generally held by district judges.

Arguments the other way

There are however arguments the other way: **7.025**

(1) Starting with subs.(1), that subsection states in plain terms: ". . . on or after the coming to an end of an assured shorthold tenancy which was a *fixed term* tenancy, a court shall make an order for possession of the dwelling-house if it is satisfied (a) that the assured shorthold tenancy has come to an end and no further assured tenancy (whether shorthold or not) is for the time being in existence, *other than* an assured shorthold periodic tenancy (whether statutory or not)".

A statutory periodic tenancy is one which takes effect "on the coming to an end of a fixed term tenancy". In other words, the sub-section clearly envisages that s.21(1) will apply in situations where the tenancy is a statutory periodic tenancy, so long as there was originally a fixed term.

(2) Subsection (2) of s.21 does not state that the notice may *only* be served before or on the day on which the tenancy comes to an end. Rather, it makes it clear (in our view) that a notice under subs.(1) can be served before or on that date even though it will take effect after that date.

(3) There is no logic in making a distinction between a case where a notice was served, say, a day or two before the term expired and another case where the notice was served a day or two afterwards. The date of service is really of no relevance. In both cases the tenancy will continue as a statutory periodic tenancy for almost the same period of time (H.H. Judge Brian Knight QC in *Brich Island Properties v Whyatt*, Central London County Court, September 29, 1999).

(4) Some commentators refer to the opening words of subs.(4): "Without prejudice to any such right as is referred to in subsection (1) above". They rely upon those words to argue that subss.(1) and (4) are mutually exclusive alternatives and that subs.(4) therefore applies to all periodic tenancies (including situations where there was originally a fixed term). Indeed this is the assumption made by Hale L.J. in *McDonald v Fernandez* (para.7.020). However, there are problems with this approach:

    a.   A careful reading of these words indicates that subs.(4) is not saying "without prejudice to subsection (1)", it is saying without prejudice to the right referred to in that subsection. As stated above the right referred to is the concurrent right to terminate by a s.8 notice (para.7.015).

    b.   The use of the words "without prejudice" does not mean that a person can only exercise one of two alternative rights. Rather, they make the two alternatives concurrent; i.e. you can use either of them.

    c.   If the two alternatives are mutually exclusive, the correct notice in relation to a statutory periodic tenancy that has previously been a fixed-term tenancy is (in our view) one under s.21(1).

(5) Subsection (4) has had a clear purpose since February 28, 1997 when it became possible to grant periodic assured tenancies; but what was its purpose prior to that date? Section 21(1)(a) as originally drafted only referred to statutory periodic tenancies. Thus, a contractual periodic tenancy could only be terminated under subs.(4). At that time it was necessary for the initial shorthold tenancy to be for a fixed-term (s.20(1)(a)). There were however at least two sets of circumstances in which a contractual periodic tenancy might arise. First, such a situation could where the

tenancy was originally for a fixed term with an express term providing for the tenancy to continue as a periodic tenancy thereafter. Second, a short-hold periodic tenancy might arise under s.20(4). In either of those circumstances, s.21(4) would have applied.

(6) The words "an assured shorthold periodic tenancy (whether statutory or not)" in s.21(1)(a), were introduced by s.194, Sch.11 para.103 of the Local Government and Housing Act 1989. There may be some contractual tenancies that are now covered by these words. However, the existence of subs.(4) does continue to ensure that all periodic tenancies can be brought to an end.

(7) Section 98 of the Housing Act 1996 is also sometimes relied upon to support the contention that a notice under s.21(4) must be served in respect of all periodic tenancies. However, s.98 of the 1996 Act did no more than insert a requirement in both s.21(1) and s.21(4) that the notice served must be in writing. It was not intended to contradict the clear words of s.21(1) referred to above.

A problem with the above

A problem with the above arguments relates to the facts of *McDonald v Fernandez*. **7.026** In that case the tenancy was originally a fixed-term tenancy, which continued as a statutory periodic tenancy. The Court of Appeal held that the notice that was served failed to comply with s.21(4) because the date specified in the notice was not the last day of a period of the tenancy (para.7.018). However, none of the above arguments were put to the court by the landlord. It was not suggested that the notice was valid under s.21(1). The arguments all related to s.21(4). The main point put by the landlord was that a notice under s.21(4) was akin to a common law notice to quit, which can be dated to expire on the first day of a period of the tenancy. It was also argued that *Mannai Investment Co Ltd v Eagle Star Assurance Co Ltd* [1997] A.C. 749 applied, i.e. that it was sufficiently clear to comply with the statutory requirements of subs.(4). It is these arguments that were rejected.

Conclusion

If the above arguments are correct it is permissible to serve a s.21(1) notice in any **7.027** case where the tenancy was originally for a fixed term and has continued as a statutory periodic tenancy. There is of course no harm in complying with the extra requirements of s.21(4). Indeed, this is the sensible course to take if the notice is served after the fixed term has expired, but in our view if the notice does not comply with those requirements the notice will still be valid.

Service of the notice

Practitioners will sometimes be uncertain as to whether or not to serve the notice **7.028** by post or personally. Unfortunately there are no statutory provisions to assist:

- There is nothing in the Housing Act 1988 itself that provide that service by post is deemed to be service (as for example with service of s.25 notices under the Landlord and Tenant Act 1954).

- Section 7 of the Interpretation Act 1978 which has a provision for deemed service in the event of proof of posting only applies where the statute "authorises or requires any document to be served by post". No such requirement or authorisation is to be found in s.21.

- Section 196 of the Law of Property Act 1925 which includes provision for service by registered letter (which includes recorded delivery: s.1 and Sch.1 para.1 of the Recorded Delivery Service Act 1962) does not apply because those provisions only apply where the relevant notice is required or authorised by the 1925 Act (s.196(2)) or is "required to be served by an instrument affecting property". Other statutes, such as the 1988 Act, are not instruments affecting property (*Wandsworth LBC v Attwell* [1996] 1 E.G.L.R. 57, Glidewell L.J. at [58]).

The decision in *Wandsworth LBC v Attwell* is sometimes cited in support of the proposition that if there is a provision in the tenancy agreement providing for service of the s.21 notice by post then it may be so served. However, this would appear to be a misreading of the case which only relates to notices to quit (see para.3.011). Even if s.196 is incorporated into the tenancy agreement that will not assist because the s.21 notice (as opposed to a notice to quit in a non-statutory tenancy) is required by s.21 of the 1988 Act, not by the tenancy agreement.

If the landlord wishes to have certainty then it is best to serve personally and get proof of the personal service. However, if the landlord serves many notices and is prepared to take the risk that service by post may be challenged in the odd case then service by post will usually be the most practical method. As a matter of evidence the notice will be presumed to have come to the tenant's attention unless challenged (see further para.3.012). Where a defendant has filed a defence form to the claim one should always look at it to see whether or not he is denying having received the notice. Service of the notice will usually be admitted.

Tenancy deposit schemes

Prohibitions on service of section 21 notices

7.029   Tenancy deposit schemes came into force on April 6, 2007. The idea behind the schemes is to safeguard tenancy deposits and to provide ADR methods of resolving disputes in relation to them. There is one "custodial scheme" into which deposits are paid and held in a separate account which is operated by the scheme administrator. There are also two "insurance based schemes" where the landlord retains the deposit and any failure on the part of the landlord to pay it to the tenant is covered by the scheme's insurance arrangements. Since April 6, 2007 it has been compulsory for the landlord to place any deposit taken in respect of an assured shorthold tenancy into one of the approved schemes.

The tenancy deposit provisions were substantially amended by the Localism Act 2011, which came into effect on April 6, 2012. The majority of the changes relate to the penalties that a landlord must pay if it fails to protect the deposit (for an outline see para.28.063). However, there were also amendments relating to the service of a s.21 notice.

If the deposit is not held within an authorised scheme the landlord cannot serve a s.21 notice (s.215(1) (a)).

Further, ss.(5) and (6) of s.213 require a landlord who has received a deposit to give the tenant certain prescribed information. If that information is not given a s.21 notice may not be served until the information is given (s.215(2)). The prescribed information that the landlord is required to give to a tenant when a deposit is taken is set out in the Housing (Tenancy Deposits) (Prescribed Information) Order 2007 (SI 2007/797).

A failure to adhere to either of these requirements within any time stipulated by the Act, does not mean that the landlord is for ever precluded from serving a s.21 notice. Once the landlord has complied, a s.21 notice can be served.

Alternatively, since April 6, 2012, a landlord who has failed to protect the deposit and provide the prescribed information can serve a s.21 notice if:

a)   the deposit is returned in full (or with deductions agreed with the tenant); or

b)   proceedings have been brought by the tenant in relation to the landlord's failure to protect a deposit, and those proceedings are either determined, withdrawn or settled. (see s.215(2A)).

See also para.7 of the revised form N5B (Accelerated procedure claim form) on p.399 which states:

"(a) was a money deposit received on or after 6th April 2007? If yes, at the date of the service of the Section 21 Notice: (i) The deposit was held under a Tenancy Deposit Scheme (TDS) authorised under Part 6 of the Housing Act 2004. My reference number is (ii) The initial requirements of the TDS have been complied with in relation to the deposit. (iii) The Claimant had given the defendant and anyone who paid the deposit on behalf of the defendant the prescribed information in relation to the deposit and the operation of the TDS".

Two particular points to note are as follows:

(1)   A "deposit" is defined in s.213(8) as "a transfer of property intended to be held (by the landlord or otherwise) as security for—(a) the performance of any obligations of the tenant, or (b) the discharge of any liability of his, arising under or in connection with the tenancy".

(2)   "No person may, in connection with a shorthold tenancy, require a deposit which consists of property other than money" (s.213(7)). If any such non-monetary deposit is taken "no s.21 notice may be given in relation to the tenancy until such time as the property in question is returned to the person by whom it was given as a deposit" (s.215(3)).

Recovery of possession

New Assured Shortholds—six-month restriction on recovery of possession

Section 20 of the 1988 Act provides, in relation to "old" assured shortholds, that **7.030** they must be granted for a term of at least six months. There is no such provision in relation to "new" shortholds. However, an order for possession cannot be made pursuant to s.21 in respect of a new shorthold "so as to take effect earlier than . . .

six months after the beginning of the tenancy" (s.21(5)(a)). (An order for possession can of course be made on one of the grounds specified in Sch.2 if the relevant conditions apply and a s.8 notice has first been served; see Ch.6.)

Where the tenancy is a "replacement tenancy" the order for possession cannot take effect until "six months after the beginning of the original tenancy" (s.21(5)(b)).

A replacement tenancy is one which comes into being on the coming to an end of an assured shorthold tenancy and under which, on its coming into being:

- the landlord and tenant are the same as under the earlier tenancy; and

- the premises let are the same or substantially the same as those let under the earlier tenancy.

Procedure

7.031   The accelerated possession procedure is available in respect of some assured shorthold tenancies determined in accordance with s.21 of the 1988 Act, i.e. where proceedings are being commenced after expiry of the fixed term. If the necessary conditions are satisfied the landlord will be able to obtain possession without a court hearing (see Ch.26). Note that the procedure is commenced by prescribed form (para.26.003).

Where the necessary conditions are not satisfied or where the landlord is seeking to obtain possession prior to expiry of the fixed term (see para.7.011) it will be necessary to utilise the standard procedure (Ch.25).

Quaere whether proceedings may be commenced before the date specified in the notice requiring possession. The usual rule that a claimant may not bring proceedings before he has a cause of action would not seem to apply because strictly speaking his cause of action, i.e. his right to possession, does not arise until the court makes the order for possession. Compare s.8(3)(b) in relation to assured tenancies that are not assured shortholds. See *Lower Street Properties Ltd v Jones* [1996] 2 E.G.L.R. 67 CA, in particular the judgment of Schiemann L.J. at 70, which suggests that it is not possible. The passage by Kennedy L.J. at 70E does seem to leave open the possibility although he also considered it to be highly undesirable. However, both comments were *obiter dicta*. Note also the reference to "on" in the phrase "on or after the coming to an end of an assured shorthold which was a fixed term tenancy" in s.21(1). In order for the court to make an order "on" that date it will have been necessary for the claim to have started before the s.21 notice expired.

Even if the landlord is not able to commence proceedings prior to expiry of a notice under s.21, the effect of s.19A in relation to "new" shortholds is probably that the proceedings may be commenced within the first six months (after expiry of the notice) even though the order can only take effect subsequently (see above).

If the court is satisfied that the notice complies with s.21 it must make an order for possession. The court may not postpone or suspend the order for possession for more than 14 days (or six weeks in the case of exceptional hardship: s.89 of the Housing Act 1980 (see para.3.034).

Form 18: Assured shorthold tenancy: notice requiring possession—expiry of fixed term tenancy

HOUSING ACT 1988

Section 21(1)(b)

Assured Shorthold Tenancy: Notice Requiring Possession:

Fixed Term Tenancy
(Note 1)

(1) Name and address of tenant

To(1)

of

(2) Name and address of landlord
(Note 2 overleaf)

From(2)

of

(3) Address of dwelling

I give you notice that I require possession of the dwelling house known as(3)

(4) Date of expiry (Note 3 overleaf)

after(4)

(5) Note 3 overleaf

Dated(5)   20

Landlord

(6) Name and address

Landlord's agent(6)

NOTES

1. On or after the coming to an end of a fixed term assured shorthold tenancy, a court must make an order for possession if the landlord has given a notice in this form.

2. Where there are joint landlords, at least one of them must give this notice.

3. The length of the notice must be at least two months and the notice may be given before or on the day on which the fixed term comes to an end.

Form 19: Assured shorthold tenancy: notice requiring possession— periodic tenancy

©W 1998 *Oyez*

HOUSING ACT 1988

Section 2l(4)(a)

Assured Shorthold Tenancy: Notice Requiring Possession: Periodic Tenancy
(Note 1)

(1) Name and address of tenant	To(^{1})
	of
(2) Name and address of landlord (Note 2 overleaf)	From(^{2})
	of
(3) Address of dwelling	I give you notice that I require possession of the dwelling house known as(^{3})
(4) Date of expiry (Note 3 overleaf)	after(^{4})
	Dated
	Landlord
(5) Name and address	[Landlord's agent](^{6})

NOTES

1. Where an assured shorthold tenancy has become a periodic tenancy, a court must make an order for possession if the landlord has given proper notice in this form.

2. Where there are joint landlords, at least one of them must give this notice.

3. The date specified must be:
   (a) the last day of a period of the tenancy;
   (b) at least two months after this notice is given; and
   (c) no sooner than the earliest day on which the tenancy could ordinarily be brought to an end by a notice to quit.

Chapter 8

Rent Act Tenancies

The Rent Act 1977 is concerned with two principal forms of tenancy: the **8.001** "protected tenancy" and the "statutory tenancy". Collectively they are referred to as "regulated tenancies" (s.18); more commonly known as Rent Act tenancies. As long as it is in existence a protected tenancy is contractual in nature and is determined according to contractual principles. Immediately upon termination, however, contractual principles cease to be of importance in relation to the landlord's right to recover possession and a so-called "statutory tenancy" arises. A statutory tenancy is not a tenancy in the strict sense. It is a personal right to occupy a dwelling-house until a court orders that the tenant should give up possession which the court will only do if it is satisfied that one of a number of specified grounds has been made out. As the terms "protected tenancy" and "statutory tenancy" are differently defined the tenant may be a protected tenant before the tenancy's determination but not a statutory tenant thereafter (e.g. if he does not actually live on the premises or if the tenant is a company). The consequences of such an outcome are that as a protected tenant he is able to take advantage of some of the rights that are available to regulated tenants (e.g. the ability to apply for a fair rent to be registered) but after termination he will not be able to take advantage of the provisions relating to security of tenure.

Where the occupier of the premises is not a regulated tenant he may nevertheless have some protection under s.19 of the Rent Act 1977 if his tenancy or licence is a restricted contract (see Ch.9).

Effect of the Housing Act 1988

Since the Housing Act 1988 came into force on January 15, 1989 it has not **8.002** been possible (save in a few limited cases: see below "Transitional provisions") to create a protected tenancy. The Act did not abolish Rent Act tenancies. A person who was a protected or statutory tenant prior to commencement of the 1988 Act continued to be entitled to remain in occupation pursuant to the Rent Act 1977. The major effect of the 1988 Act on existing Rent Act tenancies relates to the right to succeed to the tenancy on the death of the tenant (see para.8.050).

The protected tenancy

Rent Act 1977 section 1

8.003   1.   Subject to this Part of this Act, a tenancy under which a dwelling-house (which may be a house or part of a house) is let as a separate dwelling is a protected tenancy for the purposes of this Act. Any reference in this Act to a protected tenant shall be construed accordingly.

"House" is not defined in the Act but the words "which may be a house or part of a house" indicate that the section does not only apply to houses properly so called. A flat is a house for the purposes of the section. A single room within a house or a hostel can be "a house" (*Luganda v Service Hotels Ltd* [1969] 2 Ch. 209). Two separate properties may be a dwelling-house where the two are let together as one unit to be used as a single dwelling (*Langford Property Co Ltd v Goldrich* [1949] 1 K.B. 511; *Whitty v Scott-Russell* [1950] 2 K.B. 32). It has been held that a caravan may be a "house" within the meaning of the section if there is a sufficient degree of permanence (*R. v Rent Officer of Nottingham Registration Area Ex p. Allen* [1985] 2 E.G.L.R. 153). This is presumably correct given the House of Lords decision in *Elitestone Ltd v Morris* [1997] 2 All E.R. 513, where it was held that a chalet built out of wood, which rested by its own weight on concrete blocks without any attachment and which could only be removed by the process of demolition, was part of the land so that the 1977 Act applied. A caravan which can be towed away, however, cannot be a dwelling-house within the meaning of the Act (*Morgan v Taylor* (1949) 153 E.G. 3). Occupiers of mobile homes have a separate code of protection (see Ch.20). It is highly unlikely that a houseboat will be held to be sufficiently annexed to the land to be capable of being part of the land (see further para.6.004)

8.004   For the house to be "a dwelling house . . . let as a . . . dwelling" the premises to which the tenancy applies must be suitable for living in and the purpose of the tenancy must be that someone is to live there. A "dwelling" is a place where one lives, regarding and treating it as one's home. A dwelling can consist of a single room and the absence of cooking facilities does not of itself deprive the place of its status as a dwelling. Whether the premises do qualify as a dwelling depends on all the circumstances to be judged at the time proceedings are commenced (*Uratemp Ventures v Collins* [2001] 3 W.L.R. 806 HL). The fact that the tenant is unable to wash or use a toilet on the premises does not mean that the tenancy is thereby precluded from protection (*Cole v Harris* [1945] K.B. 474; *Goodrich v Paisner* [1957] A.C. 65—see also "Shared accommodation" in Ch.14).

An express term as to the purpose of the tenancy is conclusive evidence of the purpose (*Wolfe v Hogan* [1949] 2 K.B. 194). Where there is no such express term the court will look to the actual use to which the tenant puts the premises to ascertain the intention of the parties. The tenancy will not be protected unless the use of the premises concerned extends to all those activities which are essential to enable them to exhibit the characteristics of a complete home (*Kavanagh v Lyroudias* [1985] 1 All E.R. 560 at 562g to be read in the light of *Hampstead Way Investments Ltd v Lewis-Weare* [1985] 1 All E.R. 564). Thus, unless the tenant sleeps and eats at the premises on a regular basis the tenancy will not be protected. Simply carrying on one of these activities is insufficient:

"Where a person is a tenant of two different parts of the same house under different lettings by the same landlord, and carries on some of his living activities in one part of the house and the rest of them in the other part, neither tenancy will normally be protected. If, however, the true view of the facts is that there is, in substance, a single combined or composite letting of the two parts of the house as a whole, then the tenancies of both parts together will, or anyhow may, be protected" (*Hampstead Way* per Lord Brandon at 568h).

Note that it is not necessary for the tenant to live on the premises himself for the tenancy to be protected but once the contractual tenancy has been determined it will be necessary for him to live there if the tenancy is to be a statutory one (see below "The statutory tenancy").

The effect of the word "separate" is dealt with in Ch.14 (see "Shared accommodation"). **8.005**

Where land, such as a garden, is let together with the dwelling-house, that land is also treated as part of the house and therefore protected under s.1 unless it is agricultural land exceeding two acres (s.26). Distinguish cases where the house is incidentally let with the land in which case the dwelling-house will not be protected (s.6).

The exceptions

The words "subject to this Part of this Act" in the definition of a protected tenancy **8.006** refer to those tenancies that are not protected even though they fall within the definition contained in s.1 of the Rent Act. The exceptions are set out in ss.4-16 of the Rent Act:

(1) Dwelling-houses above certain rateable values/rents (ss.4 and 25—see Appendix 1).

(2) Tenancies where no rent or a low rent is payable (s.5—see Appendix 1).

(3) Dwelling houses let with land (s.6).

(4) Payments for board or attendance (s.7—see Ch.19).

(5) Lettings to students by specified institutions (s.8—see Ch.19).

(6) Holiday lettings (s.9—see Ch.19).

(7) Agricultural holdings (s.10—see Ch.18).

(8) Licensed premises (s.11—see Ch.17, para.17.008).

(9) Resident landlords (s.12—see Ch.14).

(10) Landlord's interest belonging to the Crown, save where the property is under the management of the Crown Estate Commissioners (s.13 as amended by s.73 of the Housing Act 1980).

(11) Landlord a local authority etc. (ss.14, 15 and 16—see Ch.10).

(12) See also the situation where the tenancy is a business tenancy within Pt II of the 1954 Act (para.17.012).

A protected tenancy obtained by fraud can be rescinded even after it has expired by effluxion of time thus preventing the tenant from obtaining a statutory tenancy (*Killick v Roberts* [1991] 4 All E.R. 289 CA).

Housing Act 1988: transitional provisions

8.007 The basic rule is that it has not been possible to create a protected tenancy since the commencement of the Housing Act 1988 (January 15, 1989); s.34(1) of that Act. There are, however, exceptions. In certain circumstances a tenancy of residential premises created on or after January 15, 1989 may be protected.

In order fully to understand the position it is necessary to remember that s.1 of the Rent Act 1977 has not been repealed. Thus, if there were no other provisions in the 1988 Act dealing with the situation a tenancy would be both assured and protected. To avoid such an absurdity para.13(1) of Sch.1 to the 1988 Act provides that if a tenancy is protected within the meaning of the Rent Act 1977 it cannot be assured. The exceptions are as follows:

Pre-commencement contracts

8.008 A tenancy which is entered into on or after the commencement of the 1988 Act pursuant to a contract made before the commencement of the 1988 Act, cannot be assured (Sch.1 para.1).

If it satisfies the requirements of a protected tenancy it will be protected under the 1977 Act (s.34(1)(a); Sch.1 para.13(1)).

Existing protected or statutory tenants

Housing Act 1988 section 34(1)(b)

8.009   34.—(1) A tenancy which is entered into on or after the commencement of this Act cannot be a protected tenancy, unless—

      (b) ... it is granted to a person (alone or jointly with others) who, immediately before the tenancy was granted, was a protected or statutory tenant and is so granted by the person who at that time was the landlord (or one of the joint landlords) under the protected or statutory tenancy.

This subsection clearly applies where the tenant is being granted a new tenancy of the same dwelling-house. The new tenancy is protected rather than assured. It also applies where the landlord grants, to his existing protected or statutory tenant, a tenancy of different premises. This subsection is intended to protect a tenant with Rent Act security who has been persuaded by his landlord to enter into a new tenancy after January 15, 1989. It stops him from losing his Rent Act protection by virtue of the voluntary surrender of his tenancy. However, where the court makes an order for possession the section has no application and subs.(c) applies—see below (*Laimond Properties Ltd v Al-Shakarchi* (1998) 30 H.L.R. 1107 CA at 1106–1107; *Arogol Co Ltd v Rajah* [2001] EWCA Civ 454). In *Truro Diocesan Board of Finance Ltd v Foley* [2008] EWCA Civ 1162 a Rent Act tenant lost his protection when he surrendered his tenancy and seven days later entered into an assured shorthold tenancy of the same property. The agreement for the new tenancy, although in place at the time the old tenancy was surrendered, did not provide sufficient continuity to bring the tenancy within s.34(1)(b) of the Housing Act 1988.

Where, after January 15, 1989, an existing Rent Act tenant, A, enters into a tenancy with the same landlord as before, but jointly with new tenant B, the new joint tenancy AB is a protected tenancy. However, if B subsequently takes a new tenancy on his own that will not be protected (*Secretarial and Nominee Co Ltd v Thomas* [2005] EWCA Civ 1008).

Pre-existing shorthold tenancies

The exception contained in s.34(1)(b) does not apply to a person who entered into **8.010** occupation prior to January 15, 1989 under a protected shorthold tenancy and who has entered into a new agreement after that date. His tenancy will be an assured tenancy (in fact an assured shorthold—for a full explanation see para.7.005).

Suitable alternative accommodation cases

Section 34(1)(c) (when read with s.1 of the Rent Act 1977 and para.13(1) of Sch.1 to **8.011** the 1988 Act) provides that a tenancy will be protected (rather than assured) if it was granted on or after January 15, 1989 to a person in the following circumstances:

(a) prior to the grant of the tenancy an order for possession was made against the tenant on the court being satisfied that suitable alternative accommodation was to be made available to him (either under the 1977 Act or the Rent (Agriculture) Act 1976); and

(b) the tenancy is of the suitable alternative accommodation as to which the court was satisfied; and

(c) in the proceedings for possession the court considered that, in the circumstances, the grant of an assured tenancy would not afford the required security and, accordingly, directed that the tenancy would be a protected tenancy.

For a case in which the court decided that an assured tenancy would afford the required security, so that a protected tenancy was not ordered see *Laimond Properties Ltd v Al-Shakarchi* (1998) 30 H.L.R. 1107 CA.

Tenancies transferred from public to private sector

This is a special exception relating to the transfer of tenancies from the commis- **8.012** sion for the New Towns or a development corporation to the private sector: see s.34(1)(d) and s.38(4) of the 1988 Act.

The statutory tenancy

Section 2(1)(a) of the Rent Act 1977 provides that **8.013** "after termination of a protected tenancy of the dwelling house the person who, immediately before that termination, was the protected tenant of the dwelling house shall, if and so long as he occupies the dwelling house as his residence, be the statutory tenant of it".

As explained in the introduction to this chapter, the protected tenancy is a contractual tenancy and is brought to an end by the ordinary contractual methods dealt with in Chs 2 and 3, i.e. notice to quit, forfeiture, expiration of fixed term or surrender. If the surrender is an express one (i.e. as opposed to a surrender by operation of law) and, notwithstanding the surrender, the tenant remains in occupation, he becomes a statutory tenant. A protected tenancy can also be converted into a statutory tenancy by service of a notice of increase in rent under s.49 of the Rent Act 1977 (see below).

Notice of increase (section 49 of the Rent Act 1977)

8.014 A protected tenancy is converted into a statutory tenancy where the landlord serves a notice of increase under s.45(2) or s.46 of the Rent Act 1977 (para.28.052) in circumstances where the tenancy could, by a notice to quit served by the landlord at the same time, be brought to an end before the date specified in the notice of increase (s.49(4)).

Rent Act 1977 section 49

8.015   49.—(1) Any reference in this section to a notice of increase is a reference to a notice of increase under section 45(2) or 46 of this Act.

(2) A notice of increase must be in prescribed form.

(3) Notwithstanding that a notice of increase relates to statutory periods, it may be served during a contractual period.

(4) Where a notice of increase is served during a contractual period and the protected tenancy could, by a notice to quit served by the landlord at the same time, be brought to an end before the date specified in the notice of increase, the notice of increase shall operate to convert the protected tenancy into a statutory tenancy as from that date.

(5) If the county court is satisfied that any error or omission in a notice of increase is due to a bona fide mistake on the part of the landlord, the court may by order amend the notice by correcting any errors or supplying any omission therein which, if not corrected or supplied, would render the notice invalid and, if the court so directs, the notice as so amended shall have effect and be deemed to have had effect as a valid notice.

(6) Any amendment of a notice of increase under subsection (5) above may be made on such terms and conditions with respect to arrears of rent or otherwise as appear to the court to be just and reasonable.

(7) No increase of rent which becomes payable by reason of an amendment of a notice of increase under subsection (5) above shall be recoverable in respect of any statutory period which ended more than six months before the date of the order making the amendment.

The court will not infer that a notice of increase in rent of sufficient length to convert the contractual tenancy into a statutory tenancy has been served merely by reason of the fact that there has been an increase in rent (*Trustees of Thomas Pocklington v Hill* [1989] 2 E.G.L.R. 97 at 99D–H). However, where a notice was served during the period prior to the revocation of the phasing provisions (see para.28.052), which was of insufficient length to convert the periodic tenancy into the statutory tenancy at the time of the first increase in rent, it will have been sufficient to operate the conversion at the time of the second increase (*Thomas Pocklington* at 99K-M).

Note that it is also possible to apply to the court to amend the notice under s.49(5) in certain limited circumstances.

A statement on a certified copy of the rent register that the tenancy is a statutory tenancy may be admitted in evidence of that fact (s.66(3) of the Rent Act 1977). See also *White v Wareing* [1992] 1 E.G.L.R. 271, where the tenancy was pleaded as a statutory tenancy and there was no defence filed (by the unrepresented tenant). In the Court of Appeal the defendant was represented by counsel who argued that there was no evidence that the contractual tenancy had been converted into a statutory tenancy. The court held that:

> "It is reasonable to assume, in the case of a tenancy lasting for a long time, as this had lasted, where there had been a number of references to the rent tribunal, among other things, that this was a tenancy that had converted to a statutory tenancy. . . . The majority of cases in the county court these days are statutory tenancies. It is, I would have thought, rare to have a contractual tenancy. When it is pleaded as a statutory tenancy it is perfectly reasonable for the judge so to assume it unless it is raised that it is not. Indeed, in this particular case, any other conclusion than a statutory tenancy would have been an absurd one" (per Butler-Sloss L.J. at 272G-H).

Payment of rent after termination of protected tenancy

If the landlord continues to accept rent after termination of the protected tenancy **8.016** whether by expiry of a fixed term or service of a notice to quit, a new contractual tenancy is not inferred even if the rent is an increased rent (*Morrison v Jacobs* [1945] K.B. 577; *Davies v Bristow* [1920] 3 K.B. 428). This is because the statutory tenant is entitled to remain in occupation until the court orders otherwise and the landlord is therefore entitled to the rent. There is no reason why a statutory tenancy should not continue for many years. A new contractual tenancy will, however, come into being if the parties genuinely intend to create one.

Where the landlord accepts rent after termination of the protected tenancy in circumstances where he is not sure whether the person in occupation is entitled to the protection afforded by the Rent Act and while he is considering his position the monies received will be considered as mesne profits if he subsequently goes on to take possession proceedings. Acceptance of the monies will not be treated as creating a new tenancy (*Marcroft Wagons Ltd v Smith* [1951] 2 K.B. 496, discussed by Lord Templeman in *Street v Mountford* [1985] 2 All E.R. 289 at 295).

Terms of the statutory tenancy

So long as he retains possession of the dwelling-house the statutory tenant must **8.017** observe, and is entitled to the benefit of, all the terms and conditions of the original contractual tenancy so far as they are consistent with the provisions of the Rent Act 1977 (s.3(1); e.g. in *Henry Smith's Charity v Willson* [1983] Q.B. 316 a covenant against sub-letting in the contractual tenancy was held to be a term of the statutory tenancy).

Termination of statutory tenancy by tenant

8.018 Where a protected tenancy has come to an end and the tenant has held over as a statutory tenant he must give the landlord notice to quit in writing (s.5 of the Protection from Eviction Act 1977) if he wishes to give up possession of the dwelling-house. The notice period is the same as may have been required by the protected tenancy (subject to s.5 of the Protection from Eviction Act 1977 which provides that the tenant must give at least four weeks' notice). Where the protected tenancy did not require any such notice the tenant must give three months' notice to determine the statutory tenancy (see s.3(3) of the Rent Act 1977). There is no prescribed form.

Where the tenant fails to leave at the end of the notice period the landlord may be able to recover possession under Case 5 of Sch.15 to the Rent Act 1977 if in reliance on the notice the landlord has contracted to sell or let the premises or has taken other steps as a result of which he would in the court's opinion be seriously prejudiced if he could not obtain possession. The landlord will only be able to rely on this case if the notice given by the tenant was a valid one (*De Vries v Sparks* (1927) 137 L.T. 411). A conditional contract to sell is not sufficient for there to be "serious prejudice" (*Hunt v Bliss* (1919) 89 L.J. K.B. 174).

Where a statutory tenant gives up possession without giving the requisite notice or properly surrendering, i.e. with the agreement of the landlord, he will cease to be a statutory tenant because he will no longer be occupying the dwelling-house as his residence (s.2 of the Rent Act 1977) but he will still be liable for the rent due in the notice period unless the landlord unequivocally accepts the tenant's abandonment as a surrender (*Boyer v Warbey* [1953] 1 Q.B. 234—see also para.3.030).

For surrender of statutory tenancies see *Hulme v Langford* (1985) 50 P. & C.R. 199.

Occupation as a residence

8.019 It is not always easy to determine whether the tenant is continuing to occupy the premises as his residence within s.2 of the Rent Act 1977. Two problems in particular arise.

Abandonment and temporary absence

8.020 If a person abandons a dwelling-house he clearly ceases to occupy it as his residence and he will therefore cease to be a statutory tenant. Prolonged absence (i.e. for five years) has been held to have been sufficient evidence of abandonment precluding the tenant from returning and claiming protection (*Moreland Properties v Dhokia* [2004] L. & T.R. 20 CA). A person may, however, leave the dwelling-house on a temporary basis with the intention of returning. The position was considered in the leading case of *Brown v Brash and Ambrose* [1948] 2 K.B. 247, where it was held that:

    (a) it is a matter of fact and degree as to whether the absence is sufficiently long or continuous so as to raise the inference that the occupation as a residence has ceased; if the period of absence is relatively brief the burden of proof that occupation as a residence has ceased lies on the landlord;

(b) if that inference is raised on the facts the onus is then on the tenant to show that his residence has not ceased—the tenant may show this by establishing a de facto intention to return after his absence (the *animus revertendi* or *possidendi*); the tenant must also show a formal, visible and outward sign of his intention to return (the *corpus possessionis*) e.g. by leaving his belongings or a caretaker on the premises;

(c) if the *corpus possessionis* ceases, e.g. by the tenant removing his belongings, the tenant ceases to occupy as his residence.

The tenant may thus be able to be absent for a long time but nevertheless remain a statutory tenant. (As to the onus of proof see also *Roland House Gardens v Cravitz* (1975) 29 P. & C.R. 432 at 438.)

Thus, a person who is ill in hospital for a temporary period, even a lengthy one, remains a statutory tenant (*Tickner v Hearn* [1961] 1 All E.R. 65), so does a sailor who is at sea for months on end (*Skinner v Geary* [1931] 2 K.B. 546 at 558) or a person who often goes away for the weekend. In *Richards v Green* (1983) 268 E.G. 443 the tenant left his home to nurse his sick parents but left his furniture, books, records and some clothing there. He spent over two years nursing his parents and when they died he stayed on at their home to arrange the sale of it. He always intended to return to his flat but in the meantime allowed two friends to live there from time to time. It was held that the tenant still treated the flat as his home and was still a statutory tenant. A "temporary" period may be many years (*Gofor Investments v Roberts* (1975) 29 P. & C.R. 366; *Brickfield Properties Ltd v Hughes* (1988) H.L.R. 108).

A husband tenant of a "deserted wife", though absent, is deemed to be in occu- **8.021** pation of the dwelling-house through the presence of his wife (*Griffiths v Renfree* (1989) 21 H.L.R. 338). See also Ch.21 for the rights of one spouse or civil partner to remain where the other is the statutory tenant and the right to have the tenancy transferred into his or her name under Sch.7 to the Family Law Act 1996. But if the tenancy is not transferred under that Act the husband will cease to be a statutory tenant and the wife will lose her right to remain in possession upon divorce (*Metropolitan Properties Co Ltd v Cronan* (1982) 44 P. & C.R. 1).

A statutory tenant who departs forever leaving behind a mistress does not, through her occupation, continue as a statutory tenant even if she has borne him children. She will therefore have to leave if required to do so (*Colin Smith Music v Ridge* [1975] 1 All E.R. 290).

It is possible for a person to be a statutory tenant of only part of the premises of which he had previously been the protected tenant of the whole (*Regalian Securities Ltd v Ramsden* [1981] 1 W.L.R. 611).

If one of two joint tenants leaves the other will be the statutory tenant (*Lloyd v Sadler* [1978] Q.B. 774).

Two homes

A person may have two dwelling-houses, each of which he occupies as his home, **8.022** so that, if either of them is let to him, his tenancy of it is protected by the Rent Act 1977; and where a person owns one dwelling-house which he occupies as his home for most of his time and is at the same time the tenant of another dwelling-house which he only occupies rarely or for limited purposes it is a question of fact and degree whether he occupies the latter dwelling-house as his second home (*Hampstead Way Investments Ltd v Lewis-Weare* [1985] 1 All E.R. 564 at 568 HL).

For examples of where the occupier was held to be a statutory tenant of the second property see *Langford Property Co Ltd v Athanassoglou* [1948] 2 All E.R. 722 (a home in the country and a property in London used during the week) and *Bevington v Crawford* (1974) 232 E.G. 191 (a home in France where the tenant spent most of his time and a home in England). For examples of where the occupier was held not to be a statutory tenant of the second property see *Regalian Securities Ltd v Scheuer* (1982) 263 E.G. 973 (tenant occupied the flat in question two months a year as a residence and spent some time there during the daytime for the rest of the year) and *Hampstead Way* (tenant owned a house half a mile away from the flat concerned and used the flat to sleep in when he worked late at night in a local club, so as not to disturb the family by arriving home in the early hours of the morning).

The question in every case will really be whether the dwelling-house can be said to be a home to the tenant (e.g. see *Hampstead Way* at 568d and 570f).

Surrender of statutory tenancy

8.023 It is not possible to contract out of the protection afforded by the Rent Act. Thus, an agreement to surrender is not enforceable (see further para.25.039 in relation to agreements to orders for possession). However, it is obviously possible actually to surrender such a tenancy. The tenant can hand over the keys and leave.

It is also possible in certain circumstances for the parties to agree that in the future the tenant shall continue to occupy under some other status such as a licensee (see *Foster v Robinson* [1951] 1 K.B. 149). Thereafter that will be his status. For a case where the landlord managed to get away with taking a surrender of a statutory tenancy and 24 hours later granting a new protected shorthold to the same tenant see *Bolnore Properties Ltd v Cobb* (1996) 29 H.L.R. 202 CA. However, it should be noted that the tenancy was subject to an order for possession and an eviction was imminent. The tenant could only have avoided the eviction by surrendering the existing tenancy. The court therefore held that the surrender was genuine. See also *Dibbs v Campbell* (1988) 20 H.L.R. 374.

Termination by the landlord and recovery of possession

8.024 The landlord will not be entitled to an order for possession unless he can show that the contractual tenancy has come to an end and that there is a ground for possession. The methods of determination, i.e. notice to quit, forfeiture, expiration and surrender are dealt with in Chs 2 and 3 (and see further para.8.013 above). Except in the case of forfeiture proceedings where it is the service of the proceedings that operates as the re-entry, the landlord must show that the contractual tenancy has come to an end prior to commencement of the action. This follows from the rule that the plaintiff must have a cause of action at the time of commencement. Thus, where the tenancy has been determined by a notice to quit the landlord should be very careful to ensure that the notice has expired before any further steps are taken. Service of a notice to increase rent pursuant to s.49(4) of the Rent Act 1977 also converts a periodic contractual tenancy into a statutory tenancy (see para.8.014). The landlord need take no steps to determine a statutory tenancy other than commence proceedings for possession (s.3(4) of the Rent Act 1977). However, "the lack of a letter before action or similar warning may affect the issue of reasonableness under section 98(1) and costs" (*White v Wareing* [1992] 1 E.G.L.R. 271 at 272J). Prior to commencing proceedings the landlord should therefore send the tenant a letter before action requiring the tenant to leave. A notice to quit, although not technically required, would be a "similar warning".

Where a landlord wishes to obtain possession of a dwelling-house that has been let on a protected tenancy the steps to be taken will therefore depend on whether the contractual tenancy was for a periodic or fixed term, whether forfeiture is appropriate and whether the contractual tenancy has already been determined.

(1) Fixed-term contractual tenancy that has expired: send a letter before action requiring the tenant to leave and then commence proceedings for possession.

(2) Fixed-term tenancy, containing forfeiture clause, that has not expired: if the tenant is in breach of covenant commence proceedings for possession based upon forfeiture, preceded if necessary by s.146 notice.

(3) Periodic contractual tenancy without forfeiture clause: serve appropriate notice to quit and when it has expired commence proceedings for possession.

(4) Periodic contractual tenancy with forfeiture clause: if tenant is in breach of covenant either commence proceedings for possession based upon the forfeiture, preceded if necessary by s.146 notice or serve appropriate notice to quit and then commence proceedings for possession (see further para.25.014).

(5) Periodic tenancy that was determined by a notice to quit at some earlier time thus giving rise to a statutory tenancy: if the landlord is able to prove service of the notice to quit send a letter before action and then commence proceedings for possession. If not, serve a fresh notice to quit and, after expiry, commence proceedings.

(6) Periodic contractual tenancy that has been converted into a statutory tenancy by service of a notice of increase in rent under s.49 of the Rent Act 1977: make sure that the notice complies with s.49(4) (see para.8.014) and if the landlord is able to prove service of the notice, send a letter before action and then commence proceedings for possession. If he is not able to do so, serve a notice to quit and after it has expired commence proceedings for possession.

The grounds

The grounds for possession are referred to in s.98 of the Rent Act 1977. They **8.025** consist of two types: the discretionary grounds and the mandatory grounds. Section 98(1) which deals with the discretionary grounds provides that the court shall not make an order for possession unless it considers it reasonable to make the order and either (i) suitable alternative accommodation is or will be available or (ii) one of the Cases set out in Pt I of Sch.15 applies (Cases 1–10). Section 98(2) which deals with the mandatory grounds provides that the court shall make an order for possession if one of the Cases in Pt II of Sch.15 applies (Cases 11–20).

The discretionary grounds

8.026 Where the landlord is relying upon one of the discretionary grounds the onus is on him to show that the court should make an order for possession (*Nevile v Hardy* [1921] 1 Ch. 404). He must show that it is reasonable to make the order having regard to the circumstances that exist at the date of the hearing (*Smith v McGoldrick* (1976) 242 E.G. 1047).

In deciding whether it is reasonable to make the order for possession the judge may not take into account the fact that the tenant has relied upon his statutory rights under s.11 of the Landlord and Tenant Act 1985 (implied repairing obligations), the Family Law Act 1996, the Rent Act 1977, or indeed any other statute (*Sopwith v Stuchbury* (1983) 17 H.L.R. 50).

The court must consider the question of overall reasonableness even where the case itself refers to this question (e.g. Case 9). Any failure to do so makes the decision appealable (*Peachey Property Corporation Ltd v Robinson* [1967] 2 Q.B. 543). But the issue of reasonableness is a matter of discretion for the county court and the Court of Appeal will not interfere if it has been properly considered, even though the latter court might have come to a different conclusion on the facts (*Fuggle (RF) Ltd v Gadsden* [1948] 2 K.B. 236 at 243). However, if the Court of Appeal considers that an appeal should be allowed on some other ground it can consider circumstances that have occurred since the date of the hearing (*King v Taylor* [1955] 1 Q.B. 150; *Alexander v Mohamedzadeh* [1985] 2 E.G.L.R. 161). As to appeals generally see para.25.045.

The mandatory grounds

8.027 Where the landlord seeks to rely upon one or more of the mandatory grounds it is not necessary for the landlord to show that it is reasonable for the court to make the order although he must show that he gave notice in writing that possession might be recovered under the relevant case not later than the "relevant date" (usually the date the tenancy commenced) unless it is "just and equitable" to grant the order for possession notwithstanding that no such notice was given (e.g. see para.28.017). Such a notice should be in writing.

The grounds

8.028 The full text of Sch.15 to the Rent Act is set out in Appendix 2. The grounds for possession set out in that schedule can be summarised as follows:

The discretionary grounds (Cases 1–10)

8.028A   (1)   Arrears of rent and breach of obligation (see Ch.28).

(2)   Nuisance, annoyance, immoral or illegal user (see Ch.29).

(3)   Deterioration of the dwelling-house (see Ch.30).

(4)   Deterioration of furniture (see Ch.30).

(5)   Tenant's notice to quit (see para.3.018).

(6)   Assigning or sub-letting without consent (see paras 8.034–8.036).

(7)   Repealed.

(8)   Dwelling-house required for employee (see para.17.009).

(9)   Dwelling-house required by landlord (see para.30.004).

(10) Overcharging sub-tenants.

The mandatory grounds (Cases 11–20)

(11) Owner-occupiers (see para.30.011).   **8.029**

(12) Retirement homes.

(13) Holiday homes let out of season (see Ch.19).

(14) Student accommodation let during the vacations (see Ch.19).

(15) Ministers of religion (see Ch.21).

(16) Required for agricultural employee (see Ch.18).

(17) Farmhouse after amalgamation (see Ch.18).

(18) Other farmhouses required for farmers (see Ch.18).

(19) Shortholds (see Ch.15).

(20) Serviceman's accommodation.

The order

Where the court makes an order for possession under one of the discretionary **8.030** grounds the court may stay or suspend execution of the order, or postpone the date for possession, for such period or periods as it thinks fit, at the time the order is made or at any time before the order is executed (s.100(2) of the Rent Act 1977). On any such stay, suspension or postponement the court must, unless it considers that to do so would cause exceptional hardship to the tenant or would otherwise be unreasonable, impose conditions with regard to the payment of arrears or rent (if any) and rent or mesne profits and may impose such other conditions as it thinks fit (s.100(3)). If any such conditions are complied with the court may, if it thinks fit, discharge or rescind the order for possession (s.100(4)).

Where the order for possession is made under one of the mandatory grounds the court may only postpone the date for possession for up to 14 days unless exceptional hardship would be caused by such a short order in which case the court may postpone the effect of the order for up to six weeks (s.100(5) of the Rent Act 1977; s.89 of the Housing Act 1980; see para.3.034).

For the effect of an order for possession on a spouse or civil partner of the defendant see para.21.002.

Enforcing the order

A statutory tenant remains a statutory tenant (so long as he occupies the dwelling- **8.031** house as his residence) between the time the order for possession is made and eviction pursuant to a warrant for possession. The landlord may not, therefore, resort to self-help to enforce the order for possession and if he does so will be liable to pay the tenant damages for unlawful eviction (*Haniff v Robinson* [1993] 1 All E.R. 185).

Assignment, sub-letting, bankruptcy and death

Assignment of landlord's interest

8.032 Where the tenancy is protected, i.e. a contractual tenancy, the provisions dealt with in Ch.4 at para.4.001 will apply.

It never seems to be doubted that a purchaser of land acquires his interest subject to the rights of statutory tenants but surprisingly enough the precise basis upon which statutory tenancies are binding has never been clearly established. However, it does seem that a statutory tenant's status of irremovability is effective against "all the world" by reason of the clear words of s.98 of the Rent Act 1977 which states that an order for possession shall not be made against the tenant unless the conditions referred to in the section are satisfied (see *Jessamine Investment Co v Schwartz* [1978] 1 Q.B. 264 and the discussion in the report by the Law Commission,, *Property Law: Third Report on Land Registration* (London: HMSO, 1987), Law Com. No.158, para.2.15, note 71 upon which this paragraph is based). See further para.4.002.

But note that a statutory tenancy that arises following upon the termination of a protected tenancy granted after the execution of a mortgage, in breach of the terms of the mortgage, is not binding on the mortgagee (*Britannia Building Society v Earl* [1990] 2 All E.R. 469, where the tenant unsuccessfully argued that the mortgagee was bound by the statutory tenancy on the basis that it was effective against "all the world"; see further para.32.074.

Assignment of protected tenancies

8.033 The ordinary rules relating to the assignment of contractual tenancies dealt with in Ch.4 apply to protected tenancies. The assignment will therefore be effective whether lawful or unlawful but in either case, if the tenant did not obtain the landlord's consent to the assignment and the landlord is not prepared to accept the assignee as his tenant, he may be able to recover possession. If the assignment was unlawful he should establish the breach (see para.2.013) and then serve a notice under s.146 of the Law of Property Act 1925 upon the assignee and commence proceedings based on forfeiture and Case 1 or 6 of Sch.15 to the Rent Act 1977. If there was no covenant against assigning in the tenancy agreement the landlord should (if the tenancy is for a periodic term) serve a notice to quit and then commence proceedings based upon Case 6. Both Cases 1 and 6 are discretionary grounds and the landlord will have to show that it is reasonable to make the order for possession. In deciding whether it is reasonable to make an order for possession the court is entitled to take into account the fact that by assigning the tenancy in breach of covenant a person has been put into possession who is able to qualify for a statutory tenancy at the end of the term. The fact of assignment in breach of covenant is a significant factor (*Pazgate Ltd v McGrath* (1984) 272 E.G. 1069).

The proper defendant will be the assignee as he is the person in possession (see para.25.009) although it is often worth making the original tenant a defendant as well, as the fact of the assignment may be disputed.

For transfer of the tenancy by order of the court in matrimonial cases see Ch.21.

Assignment of statutory tenancies

A statutory tenancy cannot be assigned except pursuant to Sch.1, para.13 of the **8.034** Rent Act 1977, which provides for the transfer of statutory tenancies by agreement. The agreement must be in writing and must be made between the outgoing tenant, the ingoing tenant and the landlord. If under the previous contractual tenancy the consent of a superior landlord was required for an assignment he must also be a party to the agreement (para.13(1) and (2)).

Any purported assignment of a statutory tenancy other than a transfer under para.13 of Sch.1 is wholly ineffective (see *Oak Property Co v Chapman* [1947] K.B. 886; *Roe v Russell* [1928] 2 K.B. 117 at 126; *Atyeo v Fardoe* (1978) 37 P. & C.R. 494). If the statutory tenant, without any intention of returning, ceases to occupy the dwelling-house he loses his statutory tenancy and the purported assignees will be trespassers. If the tenant intends to return he may well continue to be the statutory tenant and the landlord will not be able to regain possession from either the tenant or those in occupation (see *Atyeo v Fardoe*, and further at para.8.020).

For transfer of the tenancy by order of the court in matrimonial cases see Ch.21.

Sub-letting

Position of tenant

There is nothing to prevent a protected or statutory tenant from sub-letting the **8.035** whole or part of the dwelling-house and creating a valid sub-tenancy as between himself and the sub-tenant. If, however, the tenant has sub-let without the landlord's permission the landlord may be able to obtain an order for possession, at least as against the tenant.

Where the tenancy agreement contains a covenant forbidding sub-letting and a right of re-entry, the landlord may forfeit. He will first have to establish the breach (see para.2.013) and then serve a notice under s.146 of the Law of Property Act 1925 and then commence proceedings for possession based upon the forfeiture (see Ch.2). If the tenancy is a periodic tenancy the landlord may bring the term to an end by serving the appropriate notice to quit.

There are two cases in Sch.15 to the Rent Act 1977 upon which the landlord may then rely in order to try to obtain possession. These are Cases 1 and 6. Case 1 may be relied upon if the sub-letting was in breach of a term in the lease. Case 6 may be relied upon whenever a tenant sub-lets the whole of the dwelling-house, or first part and then the remainder, without the landlord's consent whether or not the sub-letting was forbidden by the terms of the tenancy. Both cases are, however, discretionary grounds for possession and the court will not make an order unless it also considers it reasonable to do so (s.98(1) of the Rent Act 1977). If, for example, the covenant was "not to sublet without the landlord's consent" the court will not make an order for possession if the tenant sub-let after the landlord had been asked for but unreasonably withheld his consent.

8.036   Where a tenant who has sub-let the whole of the dwelling-house has ceased to occupy the premises as his residence the landlord will also be entitled to possession as against him on the ground that the tenant has ceased to be a statutory tenant (*Haskins v Lewis* [1931] 2 K.B. 1). In these circumstances, of course, the landlord will not have to show that it is reasonable to make the order. However, this rule is not absolute. If the tenant has only sub-let for a certain period and has done so with the intention of returning he remains the statutory tenant of the whole. As the landlord is invariably unaware of the full facts of these situations until the evidence actually comes out in court it is always worth pleading his case in the alternative, i.e. on the basis that the tenant is not a statutory tenant but that if he is the landlord is entitled to possession under Case 1 or 6.

If the tenant sub-lets a part of the premises which he has never occupied and never intends to occupy the tenant loses his right to be a statutory tenant of that part (*Crowhurst v Maidment* [1953] 1 Q.B. 23). If the tenant is not sure whether he wishes to reoccupy that part at the termination of the sub-tenancy he remains a statutory tenant of the whole. It is only when he makes a final decision never to reoccupy the part that he has sub-let that he loses his right to be a statutory tenant of it (*Berkeley v Papadoyannis* [1954] 2 Q.B. 149). If the tenant does cease to be a statutory tenant of a part of the premises he nevertheless continues to be a statutory tenant of the rest (*Regalian Securities Ltd v Ramsden* [1981] 2 All E.R. 65 at 75).

Position of sub-tenant

8.037   The sub-tenant, who at common law would lose his right to remain in possession as against the landlord at the determination of the tenant's interest, is not, if he is a lawful sub-tenant, affected by any order for possession made against the tenant upon one of the discretionary grounds pursuant to s.98(1) (s.137(1) of the Rent Act 1977). Furthermore, s.137(2) of the Rent Act 1977 provides that the sub-tenant is deemed to become the tenant of the landlord on the same terms as if the head tenant's protected or statutory tenancy had continued if the following conditions are satisfied:

(a) the sub-tenancy must be lawful at the date of termination of the head tenancy (or if the head tenant is a statutory tenant, at the date proceedings were issued: *Oak Property Co Ltd v Chapman* [1947] K.B. 886); and

(b) the head tenancy must be protected or statutory at the determination of the head tenant's tenancy; and

(c) the sub-tenancy must be protected or statutory at the determination of the head tenant's tenancy.

The sub-tenancy will be unlawful if it was granted contrary to the terms of the head lease (see para.4.015); and will also be unlawful if the sub-tenancy was created after the protected tenancy has been determined, as statutory tenants are bound by s.3(1) of the Rent Act 1977 to observe all the terms and conditions of the original contractual tenancy. A demand for rent from a statutory tenant after knowledge of the unlawful act does not amount to an election to treat the sub-tenant as lawful. This is because the landlord is entitled to demand rent so long as the statutory tenancy continues. However, a demand for rent from a contractual tenant will usually waive the unlawfulness (*Henry Smith's Charity v Willson* [1983] 1 All E.R. 73).

The effect of s.137(2) is that if the sub-tenant was a statutory tenant of the **8.038** former tenant he becomes a statutory tenant of the landlord and if he was a protected tenant of the former tenant he becomes a protected tenant of the land-lord; in the latter case preserving what might be a valuable asset in the form of a long lease (*John Lyon School v Jordan* [1995] 3 W.L.R. 908 CA).

Requirements (a) and (b) above appear from the wording of s.137(2); although see example (3) below. Requirement (c) is not so clear from the wording of s.137 but appears to be generally agreed upon by the leading authors. Any other inter-pretation of s.137 would mean that the sub-tenant would be in a better position as against the head landlord than he is in as against his own landlord, i.e. the tenant. (For authority for the proposition that it is the date of the determination of the head tenant's tenancy that is relevant when considering requirements (b) and (c) see *Jessamine Investment Co v Schwartz* [1978] Q.B. 264 at 273e.)

Listed below are a number of situations that may arise and the consequences that flow from an application of the three requirements referred to above:

(1) The head tenant is a protected or statutory tenant. If he sub-lets part of the **8.039** dwelling-house he is a resident or sharing landlord (see Ch.14) as against the sub-tenant and condition (c) is not satisfied (*Stanley v Compton* [1951] 1 All E.R. 859; *Solomon v Orwell* [1954] 1 W.L.R. 629).

(2) The head tenant is a protected tenant. If the tenant sub-lets the whole conditions (b) and (c) are satisfied, and if the sub-tenancy is lawful s.137(2) will apply. But if the tenant created the sub-tenancy without the landlord's consent the court may order that the sub-tenant deliver up possession where it considers that it would be reasonable to make the order (see Case 6 and *Leith Properties Ltd v Springer* [1983] Q.B. 433).

(3) The head tenant is a statutory tenant. If he sub-lets the whole he will cease to be a statutory tenant because of his failure to occupy the dwelling-house as his residence as required by s.2 of the Rent Act 1977 and so condition (b) will not be satisfied. (See, however, the case of *Henry Smith's Charity v Willson*, particularly Ormrod L.J., which suggests that the sub-tenant does become the tenant even if condition (b) is not satisfied.)

(4) The head tenant is a statutory tenant. If he dies and is not survived by any person entitled to become a statutory tenant by succession pursuant to Sch.1 to the Rent Act 1977 the tenancy will determine immediately on death. If at that time he is a resident or sharing landlord (see Ch.14) condi-tion (c) is not satisfied.

(5) The head tenant is a protected tenant as against the landlord and a resident landlord as against the sub-tenant. The tenancy will not determine at his death but will vest in his personal representatives (see para.4.021). If the sub-tenancy then ceases to be a resident landlord tenancy for one of the reasons set out at para.14.011, the sub-tenant becomes protected, and if the sub-tenancy is lawful, s.137(2) will apply. But if the person entitled to the head tenancy becomes a "resident landlord" again within two years from the date of the original head tenant's death the sub-tenant once again becomes unprotected and s.137(2) will no longer apply.

Prima facie subss.(1) and (2) of s.137 afford no protection to the sub-tenant where the head tenant was not protected, perhaps because the rateable value of the premises which are subject to the head tenancy exceeds the rateable values set out in s.4 of the 1977 Act (*Cow v Casey* [1949] 1 K.B. 474) or because the head tenancy was a tenancy at a low rent (*Knightsbridge Estates Trust Ltd v Deeley* [1950] 2 K.B. 228). However, s.137(3) may provide assistance in such circumstances. The subsection applies where a dwelling-house:

(a) forms part of premises which have been let as a whole on a superior tenancy but do not constitute a dwelling-house let on a statutorily protected tenancy (defined in subss.(4) and (5)); and

(b) is itself subject to a protected or statutory tenancy.

8.040   The "premises" (of which the dwelling-house forms part) must itself be "a dwelling-house" (or in certain circumstances an agricultural holding: see the final paragraph of subs.(3)) within the meaning of the 1977 Act. A shop with residential accommodation above it will invariably be a dwelling-house within the meaning of the Act: *Church Commissioners for England v Baines* [1998] CA: overruling *Pittalis v Grant* [1989] 2 All E.R. 622—see also para.17.015. For further discussion on this subsection see *Laimond Properties Ltd v Al-Shakarchi* (1998) 30 H.L.R. 1099 at 1109).

If subs.(3) does apply, the Rent Act 1977 (including, of course, subss.(1) and (2) of s.137) applies, from the coming to an end of the superior tenancy,

"in relation to the dwelling house as if, in lieu of the superior tenancy, there had been separate tenancies of the dwelling house and of the remainder of the premises, for the like purposes as under the superior tenancy and at rents equal to the just proportion of the rent under the superior tenancy".

The notional "separate tenancies" referred to in the subsection are notional separate tenancies to the head tenant, not the sub-tenant (*Cadogan v Henthorne* [1956] 3 All E.R. 851). This means that in order to decide whether s.137(2) affords the sub-tenant any protection where the head tenancy is not statutorily protected it is necessary to look at the head tenancy and its terms. The part occupied by the sub-tenant must be taken and a proportion of the rent payable by the head tenant must be attributed to the part occupied by the sub-tenant. For example, if the sub-tenant occupies one quarter of the premises let on the superior tenancy it is necessary to divide the rent payable by the head tenant by four. If the effect of this is that rent payable in respect of the quarter is, as thus calculated, a low rent within s.5 of the 1977 Act, the head tenancy will still not be regarded as being protected and the sub-tenancy will not be protected; but if the rent as calculated in this way is not a low rent the sub-tenancy will be protected. A similar calculation can be applied to the rateable value on the appropriate day in respect of the premises that are subject to the superior tenancy and s.4 of the 1977 Act (see Appendix 1). Thus the rateable value on the appropriate day in respect of the whole of the premises may be too high to afford protection to the head tenant but once the figure is divided in four it may be within the limits. If so the head tenant will be regarded as protected for these purposes and the sub-tenant will be able to rely upon s.137(2).

8.041   The fact that the sub-tenant is entitled to the protection of s.137(3) does not prevent him from applying for a vesting order (para.2.112) under s.146(4) of the Law of Property Act 1925—*Factors (Sundries) Ltd v Miller* [1952] 2 All E.R. 630 CA.

Note that s.137 is not comprehensive. There may be circumstances where it does not apply but where (by reason of s.98 of the 1977 Act) the head landlord is precluded from recovering possession from a sub-tenant (see *Jessamine Investment Co v Schwartz* [1978] 1 Q.B. 264 at 273F—statutory sub-tenancy ceasing to exist as against immediate landlord by operation of the Limitation Act, thus making s.137(2) inapplicable, but nevertheless binding on the head landlord upon expiry of head lease). See also the reference to *Woolwich Building Society v Dickman* at para.32.079.

If the head tenancy is a protected tenancy and is brought to an end by the tenant surrendering his lease the sub-tenant will become the tenant of the landlord even if the sub-tenancy was unlawful (see para.4.016); but where a statutory tenant has granted a sub-tenancy this rule will not apply (*Solomon v Orwell* [1954] 1 W.L.R. 629).

Where by prolonged absence the statutory tenant had been taken to have abandoned the property, any sub-letting by that tenant will be ineffective (*Moreland Properties v Dhokia* [2004] L. & T.R. 20 CA).

Bankruptcy: protected tenants

Section 283(3A) of the Insolvency Act 1986 (as introduced by s.117 of the **8.042** Housing Act 1988) provides that a protected tenancy within the meaning of the Rent Act 1977, in respect of which, by virtue of Pt IX of that Act, no premium can lawfully be required as a condition of assignment, does not form part of a bankrupt tenant's estate. Thus, the protected tenancy does not automatically vest in the trustee in bankruptcy under s.306 of the Insolvency Act 1986 on the bankruptcy of the tenant (see generally para.4.018). However, s.308A of the Insolvency Act 1986 (as introduced by s.117 of the 1988 Act) provides that where the trustee serves a notice in writing upon the bankrupt under s.308A the protected tenancy

"vests in the trustee as part of the bankrupt's estate; and except against a purchaser in good faith, for value and without notice of the bankruptcy, the trustee's title to that tenancy has relation back to the commencement of the bankruptcy".

It is unlikely that a trustee in bankruptcy will ever serve a notice under s.308A but where he does serve such a notice so that the tenancy becomes vested in him a former tenant who remains in occupation of the dwelling-house does so as a licensee of the trustee (see para.4.019).

If the trustee disclaims the tenancy the former tenant then being a licensee does not become a statutory tenant. He therefore has no right to remain in occupation (*Smalley v Quarrier* [1975] 1 W.L.R. 938) and if after a request from the landlord he refuses to leave the landlord may recover possession against him as a trespasser. If the trustee does not disclaim the landlord can regain possession at the end of the contractual term (*Stafford v Lay* [1948] 2 All E.R. 256).

Bankruptcy: statutory tenants

A statutory tenancy not being property within the meaning of s.283 of the **8.043** Insolvency Act 1986 cannot vest in the trustee in bankruptcy (*Sutton v Dorf*

[1932] 2 K.B. 304). However, where there is a forfeiture clause in the tenancy agreement providing for re-entry in the event of the tenant's bankruptcy, the act of bankruptcy constitutes a breach of "obligation" for the purposes of Case 1 (*Cadogan Estates Ltd v McMahon* [2000] UKHL 52 HL). Thus, the landlord can rely upon this case even if there are no rent arrears (as was the case in *Cadogan*).

Where the statutory tenant is a sub-tenant and the tenant is a company that has gone into liquidation, the statutory tenant may apply for a vesting order under s.181 of the Insolvency Act 1986 if the liquidator serves a notice of disclaimer under s.178, but if he subsequently discontinues the application he does not lose his statutory tenancy (*Re Vedmay Ltd* [1993] E.G.C.S. 167).

Death of the tenant

8.044 Whether or not the landlord will be able to obtain possession of the dwelling-house on the death of the tenant will depend upon whether there is a person who is entitled to succeed to the tenancy. The position is governed by Sch.1 to the Rent Act 1977 (as amended by s.76 of the Housing Act 1980 and s.39 of and Sch.4 to the Housing Act 1988).

The amendments made by the Housing Act 1988 substantially altered the position in relation to deaths occurring on or after January 15, 1989 (the date upon which the Housing Act 1988 came into force). The paragraphs of Sch.1 to the Rent Act 1977 referred to here are as amended.

Death of original tenant: spouse or civil partner to succeed (Schedule 1 paragraphs 1 and 2)

8.045 If on his death the original tenant leaves a spouse or civil partner he or she is the person who is entitled to succeed to the tenancy, if he or she was residing in the dwelling-house immediately before the death of the tenant. He or she will be the "statutory tenant by succession" (i.e. under the Rent Act 1977) if and so long as he or she occupies the dwelling-house as his or her residence.

A person who was living with the original tenant as his or her wife or husband or civil partner is treated as the spouse or civil partner of the original tenant. Under the law prior to amendment by the Housing Act 1988 a "common law wife" was entitled to succeed because she was regarded as a member of the deceased tenant's family. In deciding whether the person hoping to succeed was so entitled the court looked to see whether the relationship had sufficient stability and permanence for an ordinary person to say that the parties were members of one another's family (e.g. see *Watson v Lucas* [1980] 1 W.L.R. 1493 and *Chios Property Investment Co Ltd v Lopez* [1988] 1 E.G.L.R. 98). If, because the tenant was living with someone as his or her husband or wife or civil partner, there is more than one person who would be entitled to succeed to the tenancy as the tenant's "spouse" or "civil partner" (an unlikely occurrence) the person who is in fact to succeed is decided by agreement or, in default of agreement, by decision of the county court.

8.046 Where the original tenant was a protected (but not a statutory) tenant the position at the end of the statutory tenancy by succession can be somewhat confused. This is because on the death of the protected tenant the contractual tenancy devolves according to the ordinary law on his successor in title, who may be a different person to the person who is to become the statutory tenant by succession.

In *Moodie v Hosegood* [1952] A.C. 61 it was held that during the currency of the statutory tenancy by succession the contractual tenancy goes into abeyance and does not arise again until the statutory tenancy by succession has come to an end. It may be that by that time the holder of the contractual tenancy, which may have passed through several hands, is almost impossible to trace. Yet if the landlord is to regain possession he must have an immediate right to possession which he will not have until the contractual tenancy has been determined (see *Wirral Borough Council v Smith* (1982) 43 P. & C.R. 312). If the contractual tenancy was for a fixed term it will probably have come to an end by the time the statutory tenancy by succession has ended, but if it was a periodic tenancy it will be necessary to serve a notice to quit upon the current contractual tenant. To find out who is the contractual tenant the landlord should make a search at the probate registry for the names of the personal representatives of the estate of the original tenant. It should then be possible to trace the contractual tenancy to its present holder. It will usually be held by the personal representatives because they are unlikely to have vested the interest in the beneficiaries. If they have also died it will be necessary to repeat the process. For the argument that after a number of years the contractual tenancy "dies a natural death" thus relieving the confusion see R.E. Megarry, *The Rent Acts*, 11th edn (London: Sweet & Maxwell, 1988), Vol. 1, p.284. It should also be noted that if a notice of increase in rent was ever served on the original tenant during the contractual period under s.49(4) of the Rent Act 1977, that notice would have terminated the contractual tenancy and brought about a statutory tenancy. Thus, when the tenant died there would have been no contractual tenancy left to go into abeyance. Also note s.196(3) of the Law of Property Act 1925 when the contractual tenancy agreement was in writing and provides for termination by notice to quit (see para.3.013). See also *Egerton v Rutter* [1951] 1 K.B. 472 where a notice to quit addressed to "the executors of the late . . ." and served upon the person in possession was held sufficient to determine the tenancy. It was not necessary to find the personal representatives. But quaere whether this case can apply to the circumstances discussed here, i.e. where the person last in possession was not the original deceased tenant but the statutory tenant.

Death of original tenant: member of tenant's family to succeed (Schedule 1 paragraph 3)

Where there is no surviving spouse or civil partner entitled to succeed but a **8.047** member of the original tenant's family was residing with him in the dwelling-house at the time of and for the period of two years immediately before his death then, after his death, that person is entitled to an assured tenancy of the dwelling-house by succession, i.e. an assured tenancy under the Housing Act 1988 (see below para.8.050 and Ch.6). A person may be "residing with" the tenant even though the tenant is temporarily absent from the premises (*Hedgedale Ltd v Hards* [1991] 1 E.G.L.R. 118 CA: tenant living elsewhere while recovering from the effects of an accident).

(If the original tenant died within the period of 18 months beginning on January 15, 1989 then a person who was residing in the dwelling-house with the original tenant at the time of his death and for the period which began six months before January 15, 1989 is taken to have been residing with the original tenant for the period of two years immediately before his death.)

If there is more than one family member entitled to succeed the persons entitled may agree among themselves as to who is to succeed. If they cannot agree the county court may decide between them. The court must look at all the factors including the wishes of the deceased but these are not conclusive (*Williams v Williams* [1970] 1 W.L.R. 1530). The landlord has no say in determining who should be chosen (*General Management v Locke* (1980) 255 E.G. 155).

As to meaning of "family" see below.

Death of statutory tenant by succession: member of original tenant's family and successor's family entitled to succeed (Schedule 1, paragraphs 4, 5 and 6)

8.048   Where the tenant who has died ("the first successor") was a statutory tenant by succession who succeeded as a spouse or civil partner of the original tenant pursuant to para.2 of Sch.1 and there is a person who was:

(a)   a member of the original tenant's family immediately before the tenant's death; and

(b)   was a member of the first successor's family immediately before the first successor's death; and

(c)   was residing in the dwelling-house with the first successor at the time of and for the period of two years immediately before the first successor's death,

then that person (or, if there is more than one person, such one of them as may be decided by agreement or, in default of agreement, by the county court) is entitled to an assured tenancy of the dwelling-house by succession (see below).

(If the first successor died within the period of 18 months beginning on January 15, 1989 then a person who was residing in the dwelling-house with the first successor at the time of his death and for the period which began six months before January 15, 1989 and ended at the time of his death is taken to have been residing with the first successor for the period of two years immediately before his death.)

A situation can occur whereby a person ("the new tenant") remains in occupation after the death of the original tenant in circumstances which give rise to a new tenancy as between the landlord and the new tenant (by estoppel; see para.1.008) so that on the death of the new tenant the person then in occupation will be treated as the first successor to the new tenant's tenancy, even though the original tenant's tenancy was never determined (*Epping Forest District Council v Pomphrett* [1990] 2 E.G.L.R. 46 CA). See also *Daejan Properties Ltd v Mahoney* [1995] 2 E.G.L.R. 75 CA, where the landlord was estopped from denying that the occupier and the deceased were joint tenants.

"Family"

8.049   The word "family" is not used in any technical sense. It is the popular meaning of the word that applies (*Langdon v Horton* [1951] 1 K.B. 666 at 667). Brothers, sisters, mothers, fathers, children (adopted, illegitimate or stepchildren), grand-children, brothers and sisters-in-law, aunts and uncles, nephews and nieces have all been held to be members of the same family. However, the cases should not be seen as binding authorities: the more distant relatives such as grandchildren, nephews and nieces and certainly cousins may not always be held to be members of the same family (see, e.g. *Jones v Whitehill* [1950] 2 K.B. 204 and *Langdon v Horton*).

It is necessary to draw a distinction between being a member of a family and living as a member of a family (*Sefton Holdings Ltd v Cairns* (1988) 20 H.L.R. 124). Thus, a young man and an elderly lady who assumed a nephew and aunt relationship were held not to be members of the same family (*Carega Properties SA (formerly Joram Developments Ltd) v Fox* [1979] 1 W.L.R. 13) and in *Sefton Holdings Ltd v Cairns* a girl taken in and treated as a daughter was held not to be a member of the family.

The "assured tenancy by succession" (sections 39(5), (6), (7), (9))

Where a person becomes entitled to an assured tenancy by succession "that **8.050** tenancy shall be a periodic tenancy arising by virtue of" s.39(5) of the 1988 Act. It takes effect in possession immediately after the death of the tenant. The periods of the tenancy are the same as those for which rent was last payable by the predecessor (see further s.39(6). If before the death of the predecessor the tenancy was one to which the landlord would be entitled to possession pursuant to Case 19 of Sch.15 to the Rent Act 1977 (shortholds) the tenancy is an assured shorthold tenancy (s.39(7)). See s.39(9) in relation to variation of terms under s.6 of the 1988 Act. The terms of the assured tenancy by succession may be varied pursuant to s.13 of the 1988 Act (see s.39(6)(e), (f)).

In addition to the usual assured tenancy grounds the landlord under an assured tenancy by succession may seek to recover possession pursuant to Cases 11, 12, 16, 17, 18 and 20 of Sch.15 to the Rent Act 1977 (Housing Act 1988 s.39(10), Sch.4, Pt III, para.13—and see para.15 in relation to notices). Note that Ground 6 of Sch.2 (demolition or construction of the dwelling-house) does not apply where the tenancy is an assured tenancy by succession (see para.(c) of that ground).

Quaere whether the *Moodie v Hosegood* problem (see para.8.046) arises where the tenancy succeeded to is an assured tenancy (cf. s.17(1) of the Housing Act 1988).

Chapter 9

Restricted Contracts

A tenancy or other contract entered into after the commencement of the Housing **9.001** Act 1988 (January 15, 1989) cannot be a restricted contract for the purposes of the Rent Act 1977 unless it was entered into in pursuance of a contract made before the commencement of the Act (s.36(1) of the 1988 Act). The rest of this chapter must be read with that fact in mind (see s.36(2) and (3) of the 1988 Act where the terms of a restricted contract are varied for the purpose of deciding whether there has been a new letting granted after the commencement of the 1988 Act).

Where an occupier of a house or part of a house is neither a protected nor a statutory tenant he may nevertheless have some protection, albeit very limited, where the rent "includes payment for the use of furniture or for services" (s.19 of the Rent Act 1977). In these circumstances the agreement under which he occupies the premises is termed a restricted contract (see also Ch.14, "Resident landlords"). If the tenant is a protected or statutory tenant the fact that his rent includes payment for the use of furniture or services does not convert his tenancy from a protected tenancy into a restricted contract (s.19(5)(a) of the Rent Act 1977 and *Baldock v Murray* (1980) 257 E.G. 281). Thus such a payment does not lessen a fully protected tenant's protection. Rather, it gives some protection to a lessee or a licensee who may otherwise not have any. The contract will not be a restricted contract unless the tenant has "exclusive occupation" of some part of the premises. The term "exclusive occupation" does not have the same meaning as "exclusive possession". Thus, the fact that the landlord is entitled to enter the room for the purpose of providing services, etc. does not of itself mean that the occupant does not have exclusive occupation (see *Luganda v Service Hotels Ltd* [1969] 2 Ch. 209). But, subject to a limited exception referred to in s.19(6) of the Rent Act 1977, the fact that he has to share any other part of the premises does not of itself prevent the contract from being a restricted contract (s.19(6)). A contract is not prevented from being a restricted contract by reason of the fact that it was created in breach of a covenant not to sub-let (*R. v Islington Rent Tribunal Ex p. Haines* (1962) 181 E.G. 339).

The protection that is afforded is set out in s.106A of the Rent Act 1977 which was introduced by s.69(2) of the Housing Act 1980 and amounts to a power in the court to defer the date upon which possession must be given up for up to three months. (Note, however, that s.106A of the Rent Act 1977 only applies to tenancies and licences created after November 28, 1980. Residential occupiers who entered into restricted contracts before that date may apply to a rent tribunal for a deferment of the requirement to leave: see ss.102A–106 of the Rent Act 1977.)

Definition of restricted contracts

9.002   Section 19(2) of the Rent Act 1977 provides as follows:

> ". . . this section applies to a contract, whether entered into before or after the commencement of this Act [but note the introduction to this chapter in relation to tenancies entered into after January 15, 1989], whereby one person grants to another person, in consideration of a rent which includes payment for the use of furniture or for services, the right to occupy a dwelling as a residence."

A tenant or a licensee may be an occupier of a dwelling house under a restricted contract, but the terms "landlord" and "tenant" are used throughout this chapter for the sake of convenience (see *Luganda v Service Hotels Ltd* [1969] 2 Ch. 209). The term "dwelling" means a house or part of a house (s.19(8)). The meaning of the term "house" is discussed at para.8.003. (Where the tenant occupies part as a residence and the rest for business purposes the contract can still be restricted: *R. v York, Harrogate, Ripon and Northallerton Areas Rent Tribunal Ex p. Ingle* [1954] 1 Q.B. 456.)

A tenant who seeks to rely on the provision of furniture in order to establish that the contract is a restricted contract must show that under the agreement the landlord has provided furniture in addition to the fixtures and fittings that would normally be present in a house. There must therefore be more than such items as a bath, cooker or fitted wardrobes. (For a full discussion of the type of furniture that will turn an agreement into a restricted contract see *Property Holding Co Ltd v Mischeff* [1948] A.C. 291.)

If the tenant is relying upon the provision of services the definition of "services" set out in s.19(8) of the Rent Act 1977 applies:

> "'services' includes attendance, the provision of heating or lighting, the supply of hot water and any other privilege or facility connected with the occupancy of a dwelling, other than a privilege or facility requisite for the purposes of access, cold water supply or sanitary accommodation."

The landlord must be obliged by the agreement to provide the furniture or services before they can be taken into account (*R. v Hampstead and St Pancras Rent Tribunal Ex p. Ascot Lodge* [1947] K.B. 973). But, so long as more than a minimal amount of furniture or services is provided under the agreement the contract will be a restricted contract (*R. v Blackpool Rent Tribunal Ex p. Ashton* [1948] 2 K.B. 277).

Exceptions

9.003   There are exceptions where the tenant will not even have the limited protection afforded by s.106A of the Rent Act 1977 (or ss.103–106 in case of agreements entered into before November 28, 1980), even though the agreement falls within the definition set out in s.19. The exceptions are as follows.

High rateable values (sections 19(3) and (4) of the Rent Act 1977)

9.004   As with the protected tenancy it is first necessary to ascertain the rateable value of the premises on the appropriate day. The method for doing this is set out in

Appendix 1. The contract will not be a restricted contract if the appropriate day in relation to the dwelling falls or fell on or after April 1, 1973 and the dwelling on the appropriate day has or had a rateable value exceeding £1,500 if the dwelling is in Greater London, or £750 if elsewhere. If the appropriate day in relation to the dwelling fell before April 1, 1973 the contract will not be a restricted contract if on the appropriate day the dwelling had a rateable value exceeding £400 in Greater London (£200 elsewhere) and on April 1, 1973 the dwelling had a rateable value exceeding £1,500 in Greater London (£750 elsewhere).

Regulated tenancies (section 19(5)(a) of the Rent Act 1977)

A contract is not a restricted contract if it creates a protected or statutory tenancy; **9.005** see introduction above.

Local authorities and housing associations, etc. (s.19(5)(aa), (e) of the Rent Act 1977)

A contract is not a restricted contract if under the contract the interest of the **9.006** lessor belongs to a body mentioned in s.14 of the Rent Act 1977 or the tenancy is a "housing association" tenancy as defined in s.86 of the 1977 Act. If, however, the tenant of one of these bodies sub-lets, the agreement between the tenant and the sub-tenant is not precluded from being a restricted contract by this exception.

The Crown (section 19(5)(b) of the Rent Act 1977)

A contract is not a restricted contract if the landlord is the Crown or a government **9.007** department, or is held by the Crown for the purposes of a government department, except that it may be so if the property is under the management of the Crown Estate Commissioners. The position of the sub-tenants is the same as where the landlord is the local authority (see above).

Board (section 19(5)(c) of the Rent Act 1977)

If the rent includes payment in respect of board and the value of the board to the **9.008** tenant forms a substantial proportion of the whole rent the contract is not a restricted contract (see Ch.19).

Agricultural premises (section 19(5)(d) of the Rent Act 1977)

A contract is not a restricted contract if it is a protected occupancy as defined in **9.009** the Rent (Agriculture) Act 1976 (see Ch.18).

Holiday lets (section 19(7) of the Rent Act 1977)

No contract under which a person is entitled to occupy a dwelling for the purpose **9.010** of a holiday can be a restricted contract (see Ch.19). But although a temporary occupation in a hotel cannot be occupation "as a residence", a permanent stay where the tenant actually lives in the hotel can be (*Luganda v Service Hotels Ltd* [1969] 2 Ch. 209).

Overcrowded dwelling-houses (section 101 of the Rent Act 1977)

9.011 Section 106A cannot operate to prevent the landlord from obtaining possession of the dwelling-house at any time when it is overcrowded (see further Ch.21).

Termination and recovery of possession

9.012 If the restricted contract is a tenancy it is brought to an end in the normal way, i.e. by notice to quit, effluxion of time, forfeiture or surrender (see Chs 2 and 3). If it is a licence it will be brought to an end according to the terms of the agreement, subject to the provisions of s.5 of the Protection from Eviction Act 1977 if applicable (see para.3.003). Once validly determined, proceedings for possession may be commenced. If it is a forfeiture case the lease is forfeited by service of the proceedings. The court must make an order for possession but if the contract was entered into after November 28, 1980 the court may on the making of the order, or at any time before its execution, stay or suspend execution of the order, or postpone the date of possession, but the giving up of possession cannot be postponed for longer than three months (s.106A(1), (2) and (3) of the Rent Act 1977). Where the court does stay, suspend or postpone the operation of the order the court must, unless it considers that to do so would cause exceptional hardship to the tenant or would otherwise be unreasonable, impose conditions with regard to payment by the tenant of arrears of rent (if any) and rent or payments in respect of occupation after termination of the tenancy and may impose such other conditions as it thinks fit (s.106(4)). The tenant's spouse or former spouse who remains in occupation has the same rights to postponement of the order under s.106A of the Rent Act 1977 as the tenant himself (s.106A(5), (6)).

If the contract was entered into before November 28, 1980 the tenant's security of tenure is governed by ss.103–106 of the Rent Act 1977, i.e. the tenant may apply to the rent tribunal to extend a notice to quit (see s.102A). If the notice to quit has expired no such application may be made (*R. v City of London Rent Tribunal Ex p. Honig* [1951] 1 K.B. 641) and the court will only be able to delay possession for up to 14 days, or six weeks in cases of exceptional hardship (s.89 of the Housing Act 1980; see para.3.034).

Chapter 10

Secure Tenancies

Tenants of dwelling-houses owned by local authorities and a number of other **10.001** public bodies have a code of protection of their own if they fall within the definition of "secure tenants". The code was introduced by the Housing Act 1980 and is now set out in ss.79 to 117 of the Housing Act 1985 ("the 1985 Act"). It came into force on October 3, 1980 and applies to tenancies granted before as well as after that date (s.47 of the Housing Act 1980).

The 1985 Act specifically treats most licensees of these bodies as tenants **10.002** (s.79(3), (4)). Unless the context otherwise requires, the person in occupation of the dwelling-house is referred to as the tenant throughout this chapter whether he is a licensee or a tenant strictly so called.

Definition of secure tenancies

A secure tenancy is defined by s.79(1) of the 1985 Act in the following terms: **10.003**

> "A tenancy under which a dwelling house is let as a separate dwelling is a secure tenancy at any time when the conditions described in sections 80 and 81 as the landlord condition and the tenant condition are satisfied."

Section 79(1) is subject to the exceptions set out in Sch.1 to the 1985 Act (see below s.79(2)(a)).

A dwelling-house is defined in the 1985 Act as a house or part of a house, and land let together with a dwelling-house is treated as part of the dwelling-house unless the land is agricultural land exceeding two acres (s.112). The effect of the word "separate" is dealt with in Ch.14; see also *Tomkins v Basildon District Council* (referred to at para.17.015) in relation to premises that were initially let for business purposes. The words "at any time" in s.79(1) refer to the conditions in ss.80 and 81, not to the requirement that the property be "let as a separate dwelling". Thus, the tenant must establish the conditions of essential living facilities and exclusive possession by reference to the terms of the agreement (*Parkins v Westminster CC* [1998] 1 E.G.L.R. 22 CA).

As stated in the introduction to this chapter, the 1985 Act applies to licences **10.004** (s.79(3)). However, "a licence can only create a secure tenancy if it confers exclusive possession of a dwelling house" (*Westminster City Council v Clarke* [1992] 1 All E.R. 695 HL, per Lord Templeman at 701). In that case a local authority provided homeless persons with temporary accommodation while dealing with their applications for permanent accommodation under the Housing Act 1985. The agreements under which those persons occupied, which negatived exclusive possession, were held to be genuine licences. As the occupiers did not have exclusive possession, s.79(3) did not apply and their licences could not be regarded as secure tenancies. See also *Parkins v Westminster CC* (1997) 30 H.L.R. 894 CA—teacher granted a licence to occupy a flat "the occupancy to be shared with other persons similarly authorised" —held not a secure tenant. However, see *Mansfield DC v Langridge* [2008] EWCA Civ 264 for an example where the licensee was held to be a secure tenant.

Notwithstanding s.79(3), a licensee is not treated as a secure tenant where the licence was granted as a temporary expedient to a person who entered the dwelling-house or any other land as a trespasser (whether or not before the grant of another licence to occupy that or another dwelling-house had been granted to him) (s.79(4)). But practitioners acting for the occupiers should ensure that what was granted was not a true tenancy before they advise their clients that s.79(4) prevents them from being secure tenants.

The fact that the tenant is an illegal immigrant does not make the tenancy void and does not prevent it from being a secure tenancy (*Akinbolu v Hackney LBC* (1996) 29 H.L.R. 259 CA).

The landlord condition (section 80)

10.005 The principle circumstances in which the landlord condition will apply are set out in s.80 (as amended), which can be summarised as follows:

The landlord condition is satisfied when the interest of the landlord belongs to one of the following bodies:

(a) a local authority;

(b) a development corporation;

(c) a housing action trust;

(d) a Mayoral development corporation;

(e) an urban development corporation;

(f) the Homes and Communities Agency or the Welsh Ministers;

(g) the Regulator of Social Housing;

(h) a housing trust which is a charity; or

(i) a housing association (which is a private registered provider of social housing or a registered social landlord, but is not a co-operative housing association) or a housing co-operative (within the meaning of s.27B of the 1985 Act where the dwelling house is comprised in a housing co-operative agreement within the meaning of that section).

(See s.80 of the 1985 Act (as amended) and s.35(4)(a) and (b) of the 1988 Act.)

Where the interest of the landlord belongs to two bodies the landlord condition will not be satisfied unless they are both one of the above bodies (*R. v Plymouth City Council etc Ex p. Freeman* (1987) 19 H.L.R. 328).

Where the tenancy was entered into before January 15, 1989, reference will have to be made to the previous versions of s.80 of the 1985 Act and s.35 of the Housing Act 1988.

The tenant condition (section 81)

The tenant condition is that the tenant is an individual and occupies the dwelling **10.006** house as his only or principal home; or, where the tenancy is a joint tenancy, that each of the joint tenants is an individual and at least one of them occupies the dwelling house as his only or principal home (s.81).

If the tenant ceases to occupy the dwelling-house as his principal home the tenancy will cease to be secure. It will become an ordinary contractual tenancy, determinable by notice to quit, etc. (see Chs 2 and 3).

There are two elements to consider: (1) Has there been occupation? (2) Whether or not the occupation was that of the individual's only or principal home. The relevant date for ascertaining whether they fulfilled the tenant criteria was at the date of the expiry of the notice to quit. These matters were considered in detail in *Islington London Borough Council v Boyle* [2011] EWCA Civ 1450 where Etherton LJ set out some guidance as to how to approach whether the tenant condition was satisfied. Firstly, *did the tenant "occupy"*? Etherton L.J. at para.55:

"I would summarise as follows the relevant principles to be applied in determining whether a tenant continues to occupy a dwelling as his or her home, for the purposes of the 1985 Act, despite living elsewhere. First, absence by the tenant from the dwelling may be sufficiently continuous or lengthy or combined with other circumstances as to compel the inference that, on the face of it, the tenant has ceased to occupy the dwelling as his or her home. In every case, the question is one of fact and degree. Secondly, assuming the circumstances of absence are such as to give rise to that inference: (1) the onus is on the tenant to rebut the presumption that his or her occupation of the dwelling as a home has ceased; (2) in order to rebut the presumption the tenant must have an intention to return; (3) while there is no set limit to the length of absence and no requirement that the intention must be to return by a specific date or within a finite period, the tenant must be able to demonstrate a 'practical possibility' or 'a real possibility' of the fulfilment of the intention to return within a reasonable time; (4) the tenant must also show that his or her inward intention is accompanied by some formal, outward and visible sign of the intention to return, which sign must be sufficiently substantial and permanent and otherwise such that in all the circumstances it is adequate to rebut the presumption that the tenant, by being physically absent from the premises, has ceased to be in occupation of it. Thirdly, two homes cases, that is to say where the tenant has another property in which he or she voluntarily takes up full-time residence, must be viewed with particular care in order to assess whether the tenant has ceased to occupy as a home the place where he or she formerly lived. Fourthly, whether or not a tenant has ceased to occupy premises as his or her home is a question of fact. In the absence of an error of law, the trial Judge's findings of primary fact cannot be overturned on appeal unless they were perverse, in the sense that they exceeded the generous ambit within which reasonable disagreement about the conclusions to be drawn from the evidence is possible; but the appeal court may in an appropriate case substitute its own inferences drawn from those primary facts."

Secondly, if occupation was satisfied, then consideration needed to be given as to whether or not it was the individual's *only or principal home*. Etherton L.J.:

"56. As I have said, it is not enough to satisfy the Tenant Condition that the tenant occupies the dwelling as his or her home. The dwelling must be occupied as the tenant's only or principal home. This is plainly a tightening of the residence requirement under the Rent Act regime and prevents the possibility of the same individual enjoying statutory protection in respect of more than one dwelling. On the other hand, it is notable that the 1985 Act does not restrict protection to a case where the tenant has only one home. The restriction of the protection to the tenant's "only or principal" home envisages that the tenant may be a secure tenant of a dwelling even though it is not his or her only home. In such a case, however, the tenancy must, be a tenancy of the tenant's "principal" home.

65. In the light of the cases, I would summarise as follows the principles ... which apply to the identification of which of two or more homes of the tenant is or was the tenant's principal home. First, the length or other circumstances of the tenant's absence may raise the inference that the dwelling which is the subject of the proceedings ceased to be the tenant's principal home so as to cast on the tenant the burden of proving the contrary. Secondly, in order to rebut that presumption, it is not sufficient for the tenant to prove that at the material time it was his or her subjective intention and belief that the dwelling remained the principal home. The objective facts must bear out the reality of that belief and intention both in the sense that the intention and belief are or were genuinely held and also that the intention and belief themselves reflect reality. The reason for the absence, the length and other circumstances of the absence and (where relevant) the anticipated future duration of the absence, as well as statements and conduct of the tenant, will all be relevant to that objective assessment. Thirdly, the court's focus is on the enduring intention of the tenant, which, depending on the circumstances, may not be displaced by fleeting changes of mind. Fourthly, the issue is one of fact to be determined in the light of the evidence as a whole, and in respect of which the trial judge's findings of primary fact can only be overturned on appeal if they were perverse in the sense that I have mentioned earlier; but the appeal court may in an appropriate case substitute its own inferences drawn from those primary facts."

As to licences see para.10.004. A person in occupation under a tenancy at will is not in occupation as a secure tenant (*Banjo v Brent LBC* [2005] EWCA Civ 292).

The exceptions (section 79(2)(a) and Schedule 1)

10.007 The exceptions are to be found in Sch.1 to the 1985 Act (as amended), the full text of which is to be found in Appendix 2. They may be summarised as follows:

(1) long leases, i.e. of more than 21 years (see also Ch.16);

(1A) introductory tenancies and certain tenancies which have ceased to be introductory tenancies (see Ch.12);

(2) premises occupied now or in the past three years in connection with employment by employees of certain public bodies, policemen and firemen (see Ch.17);

(3) land acquired for development: the landlord does not have to be the person who has acquired the land for development; it only needs to be the person who is using the land pending the development as temporary housing accommodation (*Hyde Housing Association Ltd v Harrison* [1991] 1 E.G.L.R. 51 CA: land acquired for development by the Department of Transport but used pending the development by the landlord);

(4) homeless persons' accommodation;

(5) temporary accommodation for persons taking up employment;

(6) property leased (or licensed: *Tower Hamlets LBC v Miah* [1992] 2 All E.R. 667 CA) to the landlord for use as temporary housing accommodation;

(7) temporary accommodation during works;

(8) agricultural holdings;

(9) licensed premises (on-licences);

(10) student lettings (see also Ch.19);

(11) business tenancies to which Pt II of the 1954 Act applies (see Ch.17);

(12) almshouses.

Where one of the exceptions applies the tenancy is an ordinary contractual tenancy to which the common law rules relating to termination apply. For example, see *Hackney LBC v Lambourne* [1993] E.G.C.S. 151 where the local authority relying upon exception (6) (short-term arrangements) determined the tenancy by a notice to quit.

Termination and recovery of possession

The termination procedure in respect of secure tenancies is governed by ss.82 and **10.008** 85 of and Sch.2 to the Housing Act 1985. Except in cases where the landlord is seeking to rely upon a forfeiture clause in a lease for a fixed term (see para.10.014) termination and recovery of possession are dealt with together. The order for possession operates to terminate the tenancy from the date upon which the order is executed (s.82(2) of the Housing Act 1985). The court may discharge or rescind the order if it thinks it appropriate (s.85(4)).

Housing Act 1985 sections 82(1), (2)

(1) A secure tenancy which is either—   **10.009**

    (a) a weekly or other periodic tenancy; or
    (b) a tenancy for a term certain but subject to termination by the landlord,

cannot be brought to an end by the landlord except as mentioned in subsection (1A).
(1A) The tenancy may be brought to an end by the landlord—

    (a) obtaining—

        (i) an order of the court for the possession of the dwelling-house; and
        (ii) the execution of the order;

    (b) obtaining an order under subsection (3); or
    (c) obtaining a demotion order under section 82A.

(2) In the case mentioned in subsection (1A)(a), the tenancy ends when the order is executed.

A fixed term comes to an end at the end of the term without the necessity of a court order but thereafter a periodic tenancy automatically arises under s.86 of the

1985 Act which will have to be terminated in court proceedings if the landlord is to recover possession. (An automatic periodic tenancy does not in fact arise under s.86 if the tenant is granted a new secure tenancy, whether for a fixed or periodic term, to begin at the end of the first tenancy.) The periods of the tenancy that arise pursuant to s.86 are the same as those for which rent was last payable under the first tenancy. The terms are the same save in so far as they are incompatible with a periodic tenancy, and they do not include a forfeiture clause (s.86(1), (2)).

The above provisions only relate to termination by the landlord. The tenant may terminate by giving a notice to quit of appropriate length (see *London Borough of Greenwich v McGrady* (1982) 6 H.L.R. 36) or by surrender (*R. v London Borough of Croydon Ex p. Toth* (1988) 20 H.L.R. 576).

Termination notices (s.83)

Housing Act 1985 section 83

10.010   **83.**—(1) The court shall not entertain proceedings for the possession of a dwelling house let under a secure tenancy or proceedings for the termination of a secure tenancy unless—

    (a)   the landlord has served a notice on the tenant complying with the provisions of this section; or

    (b)   the court considers it just and equitable to dispense with the requirement of such a notice.

  (2) A notice under this section shall—

    (a)   be in a form prescribed by regulations made by the Secretary of State;

    (b)   specify the ground on which the court will be asked to make an order for the possession of the dwelling house or for the termination of the tenancy; and

    (c)   give particulars of that ground.

  (3) Where the tenancy is a periodic tenancy and the ground or one of the grounds specified in the notice is Ground 2 in Schedule 2 (nuisance or other anti-social behaviour), the notice—

    (a)   shall also—

       (i)   state that proceedings for the possession of the dwelling house may be begun immediately; and

      (ii) specify the date sought by the landlord as the date on which the tenant is to give up possession of the dwelling house; and

    (b)   ceases to be in force 12 months after the date so specified.

  (4) Where the tenancy is a periodic tenancy and Ground 2 in Schedule 2 is not specified in the notice, the notice—

    (a)   shall also specify the date after which proceedings for the possession of the dwelling house may be begun; and

    (b)   ceases to be in force 12 months after the date so specified.

  (5) The date specified in accordance with subsection (3) or (4) must not be earlier than the date on which the tenancy could, apart from this Part, be brought to an

end by notice to quit given by the landlord on the same date as the notice under this section.

(6) Where a notice under this section is served with respect to a secure tenancy for a term certain, it has effect also with respect to any periodic tenancy arising on the termination of that tenancy by virtue of section 86; and subsection (3) to (5) of this section do not apply to the notice.

(7) Regulations under this section shall be made by statutory instrument and may make different provision with respect to different cases or descriptions of case, including different provision for different areas.

Section 83 of the 1985 Act as amended provides that the court may not entertain **10.011** proceedings for termination of a secure tenancy or possession of a dwelling-house let on a secure tenancy unless the landlord serves on the tenant a notice in a form prescribed by regulations. The regulations in force at the present time are the Secure Tenancies (Notices) Regulations 1987 (SI 1987/755) (as amended). They contain two forms (Forms 20 and 21 of this book; pp.199 and 203) and state that the notice must be in the form of one of those notices "or in a form substantially to the same effect" (reg.2).

In *Dudley Metropolitan BC v Bailey* [1991] 1 E.G.L.R. 53 CA, it was held that a notice which contained the words "The reasons for taking this action are" instead of "Particulars of each ground are as follows" was in a form substantially to the same effect. (An argument to the effect that the regulations, in permitting "a form substantially to the same effect" was ultra vires s.83, was rejected.)

The notice must specify the ground upon which the court will be asked to make the order and must give particulars of that ground (s.83(2)(b), (c); compare the position in respect of assured tenancies, para.6.016). The particulars must be sufficiently informative to tell the tenant what he has to do to put matters right before proceedings are commenced (*Torridge DC v Jones* [1985] 2 E.G.L.R. 54 CA). In that case the landlord served a notice which gave the following particulars: "The reasons for taking this action are non-payment of rent" but failed to give any particulars of the rent alleged. It was held that the notice did not comply with the statutory requirement to give particulars and the landlord's claim was struck out. Compare *Dudley Metropolitan BC v Bailey* where the figure stated as arrears of rent in fact included amounts for rates and water rates. It was held that the notice was not invalidated by this error although it might affect the action which the judge should take on the merits of the case:

"The question is whether, at the date of the notice, the landlord has in good faith stated the ground and given particulars of that ground. The requirement of particulars is satisfied, in my judgment, if the landlord has stated in summary form the facts which he then intends to prove in support of the stated ground for possession. Error in the particulars does not, in my judgment, invalidate the notice although it may well affect the decision of the court on the merits" per Ralph Gibson L.J. at 55J.

In *Marath v MacGillivray* (1996) 28 H.L.R. 484 CA, it was held, in relation to an **10.012** assured tenancy and a s.8 notice under the Housing Act 1988 (where the provisions are similar), that the notice was valid if the information given was sufficient to enable the tenant to ascertain the amount of rent due. However, a wise landlord will state the precise amount and attach a schedule.

Note also the ability, with the leave of the court given under s.84(3), to alter or add to the grounds specified in the notice (see further para.10.017).

There are two types of notice: one appropriate to periodic tenancies and the other appropriate to cases where the landlord is seeking to rely upon a forfeiture clause in a fixed term.

Periodic tenancies (see Form 20)

10.013 Where the tenancy is a periodic tenancy the notice must specify a date after which proceedings for possession of the dwelling-house may be begun (s.83(4)). The date specified must not be earlier than the date on which the tenancy could have been brought to an end by a notice to quit given on the same day as the notice which is to be given under s.83 of the 1985 Act (s.83(5)). Therefore, if the tenancy is a weekly tenancy 28 days' notice is required and if it is a monthly tenancy one calendar month's notice is required (see further para.3.004).

Where the ground or one of the grounds for possession is Ground 2 (nuisance or other anti-social behaviour) the landlord must (i) state that proceedings for possession may be begun immediately and (ii) specify a date sought by the land-lord on which the tenant is to give up possession (s.83(3)). The latter date must not be earlier than the date on which the tenancy could have been brought to an end if the tenancy had been a common law tenancy (s.83(5)). Thus, the landlord may commence proceedings immediately but may not actually have possession until that latter date (s.84(4): para.10.017).

The termination notice served in respect of a fixed term also operates in respect of the subsequent periodic tenancy that arises by virtue of s.82(3) and s.86 and no further notice is required (s.83(5)). Where a notice has not been served during the currency of the fixed term it will be necessary to serve a notice appropriate to periodic tenancies.

(The periodic term that follows a fixed term by virtue of s.82(3) is secure: it would not be necessary to excuse service of a notice under s.83(5) if the periodic tenancy was not secure as one would not be needed in any event. Section 83(6) also clearly implies that a s.86 periodic tenancy is secure.

Fixed terms forfeiture cases (see Form 20)

10.014 Where the landlord is seeking to rely upon a forfeiture clause in a fixed term the position is slightly different from the usual case. The court may not make an order for possession in pursuance of that clause, but it may make an order terminating the fixed term on a date specified in the order (s.82(3) of the Housing Act 1985). Thus, the tenant may find himself without the benefit of a fixed term but still in possession under a s.86 periodic tenancy. The court may, however, go on to make an order for possession if one of the grounds for possession (see below) applies.

Although the court may not make an order for possession in pursuance of the forfeiture clause, s.146 of the Law of Property Act 1925 and any other enact-ments or rules of law that apply to forfeiture cases apply to the proceedings to terminate the tenancy as if they were proceedings to forfeit a lease (s.82(4) of the Housing Act 1985). Thus, the provisions as to s.146 notices and to relief against forfeiture apply. See also the restrictions on forfeiting long leases in Ch. 2. However, s.146(4) which gives underlessees the right to claim relief does not apply.

Form 20: Section 83 notice—possession

**This Notice is the first step towards requiring you to give up possession of your dwelling.
You should read it very carefully.**
HOUSING ACT 1985
Section 83

Notice of Seeking Possession

(1) Name(s) of
Secure Tenant(s) s1.

To (^{1})

If you need advice about this Notice, and what you should do about it, take it as quickly as possible to a Citizens' Advice Bureau, a Housing Aid Centre, or a Law Centre, or to a solicitor. You may be able to receive Legal Aid but this will depend on your personal circumstances.

(2) Insert name

2. The Landlord (^{2})   intends
to apply to the Court for an Order requiring you to give up possession of:

(3) Address of
property

(^{3})

If you are a secure tenant under the Housing Act 1985, you can only be required to leave your dwelling if your landlord obtains an order for possession from the Court. The order must be based on one of the Grounds which are set out in the 1985 Act (see paragraphs 3 and 4 below).

If you are willing to give up possession without a Court order, you should notify the person who signed this Notice as soon as possible and say when you would leave.

(4) Give the text in
full of each Ground
which is being relied
on

3. Possession will be sought on Ground(s) of Schedule 2 to the Housing Act 1985 which read(s)(^{4}):

Whatever Grounds for possession are set out in paragraph 3 of this Notice, the Court may allow any of the other Grounds to be added at a later stage. If this is done, you will be told about it so you can argue at the hearing in Court about the new Ground, as well as the Grounds set out in paragraph 3. if you want to.

(5) Give a full explan-
ation of why each
Ground is being relied
upon. Before complet-
ing the answer (to this
questions please read
the notes overleaf.

4. Particulars of each ground are as follows(^{5});

Before the Court will grant an order on any of the Grounds 1 to 8 or 12 to 16, it must be satisfied that it is reasonable to require you to leave. This means that, if one of these Grounds is set out in paragraph 3 of this Notice, you will be able to argue at the hearing in Court that it is not reasonable that you should have to leave, even if you accept that the Ground applies.

Before the Court grants an order on any of the Grounds 9 to 16, it must be satisfied that there will be suitable alternative accommodation for you when you have to leave. This means that the Court will have to decide that, in its opinion, there will be other accommodation which is reasonably suitable for the needs of you and your family, taking into particular account various factors such as the nearness of your place of work, and the sort of housing that other people with similar needs are offered. Your new home will have to be let to you on another secure tenancy or a private tenancy under the Rent Act of a kind that will give you similar security. **There is no requirement for suitable alternative accommodation where Grounds 1 to 8 apply.** If your landlord is not a local authority, and the local authority gives a certificate that it will provide you with suitable accommodation, the Court has to accept the certificate.

One of the requirements of Ground 10A is that the landlord must have approval for the redevelopment scheme from the Secretary of State (or, in the case of a housing association landlord, the Housing Corporation). The landlord must have consulted all secure tenants affected by the proposed redevelopment scheme.

Cross out this para-
graph if possession *is*
being sought on
Ground 2 of Schedule
2 to the Housing Act
1985 (whether or not
possession is also
sought on another
Ground)

5. The Court proceedings for possession will not he begun until after

. . . .

[give the date after which Court proceedings can be brought]

- Court proceedings cannot be began until after this date, which cannot be earlier than the date when your tenancy or licence could have been brought to an end. This means that if you have a weekly or fortnightly tenancy, there should be at least four weeks between the date this Notice is given and the date in this paragraph.

contd

<table>
<tr><td>

contd

Cross out this para-
graph if possession *not*
being sought on
Ground 2 of Schedule
2 to the Housing Act
1985

</td><td>

- After this date. Court proceedings may be begun at once or at any time during the following 12 months. Once the 12 months are up this Notice will lapse and a new Notice must be served before possession can be sought.

5. Court proceedings for possession of the dwelling house can be begun immediately. The date by which the tenant is to give up possession of the dwelling house is ....

[give the date by which the tenant is to give up possession of the dwelling house]

- Court proceedings may be begun at once or at any time during the following 12 months. Once the 12 months are up this Notice will lapse and a new notice must be served before possession can be sought.

- Possession of your dwelling house cannot be obtained until after this date, which cannot be earlier than the date when your tenancy or licence could have been brought to an end. This means that if you have a weekly or fortnightly tenancy, there should be at least four weeks between the date this Notice is given and the date possession is ordered.

Signed

On behalf of

Address

Tel No.

Date

</td></tr>
</table>

Commencing proceedings

10.015 Where the tenancy is a periodic tenancy, the landlord must commence proceedings after the date specified in the notice (which may be immediately in a Ground 2 case; see para.10.013), but before 12 months from the date specified have elapsed. If he does not do so, the court may not entertain proceedings for possession and the landlord will have to serve a fresh notice (s.83A of the Housing Act 1985). Where the landlord relies upon Ground 2A (domestic violence) the provisions relating to service on the partner who has left, set out in s.83A, apply. Where the tenancy is a fixed-term tenancy the proceedings may not be commenced until after the expiration of the term unless the landlord is seeking to rely upon a forfeiture clause and is bringing proceedings under s.82(3).

Housing Act 1985 section 83A

10.016 (1) Where a notice under section83 has been served on a tenant containing the information mentioned in subsection(3)(a) of that section, the court shall not entertain proceedings for the possession of the dwelling house unless they are begun at a time when the notice is still in force.

(2) Where—

(a) a notice under section 83 has been served on a tenant; and
(b) a date after which proceedings may be begun has been specified in the notice in accordance with subsection (4)(a) of that section,

the court shall not entertain proceedings for the possession of the dwelling house unless they are begun after the date so specified and at a time when the notice is still in force.

(3) Where—

(a) the ground or one of the grounds specified in a notice under section 83 is Ground 2A in Schedule 2 (domestic violence); and

(b)   the partner who has left the dwelling house as mentioned in that ground is not a tenant of the dwelling house,

the court shall not entertain proceedings for the possession of the dwelling house unless it is satisfied that the landlord has served a copy of the notice on the partner who has left or has taken all reasonable steps to serve a copy of the notice on that partner.

This subsection has effect subject to subsection (5).

(4)   Where—

(a)   Ground 2A in Schedule 2 is added to a notice under section 83 with the leave of the court after proceedings for possession are begun; and

(b)   the partner who has left the dwelling house as mentioned in that ground is not a party to the proceedings,

the court shall not continue to entertain the proceedings unless it is satisfied that the landlord has served a notice under subsection (6) on the partner who has left or has taken all reasonable steps to serve such a notice on that partner.

This subsection has effect subject to subsection (5).

(5)   Where subsection (3) or (4) applies and Ground 2 in Schedule 2 (nuisance or other anti-social behaviour) is also specified in the notice under section 83, the court may dispense with the requirements as to service in relation to the partner who has left the dwelling house if it considers it just and equitable to do so.

(6)   A notice under this subsection shall—

(a)   state that proceedings for the possession of the dwelling house have begun;

(b)   specify the ground or grounds on which possession is being sought; and

(c)   give particulars of the ground or grounds.

The grounds for possession

The court is not allowed to make an order for possession of a dwelling-house let **10.017** under a secure tenancy except on one or more of the 18 grounds for possession set out in Sch.2 to the 1985 Act. (See Appendix 2 for the full text of the Schedule.) The ground relied upon must be specified in the termination notice. If it is not, the court may not make an order for possession on that ground (see also reference to s.83).

Housing Act 1985 section 84(3), (4)

(3)   Where a notice under section 83 has been served on the tenant, the court shall not make such an order on any of those grounds above unless the ground is specified in the notice; but the grounds so specified may be altered or added to with the leave of the court.

(4)   Where a date is specified in a notice under section 83 in accordance with sub-section (3) of that section, the court shall not make an order which requires the tenant to give up possession of the dwelling house in question before the date so specified.

Although the grounds in the notice may be altered or added to with the permission of the court (s.84(3); *Camden LBC v Oppong* (1996) 28 H.L.R. 701 CA), it is unlikely that extensive amendments to the notice will be permitted (see e.g. *South Buckinghamshire County Council v Francis* [1985] C.L.Y. 1900 where the notice was invalid because it did not specify the breaches of covenant said to be broken— the county court judge refused to allow the landlord permission to amend the notice to include a schedule of dilapidations and particulars of nuisance; cf. the position in relation to assured tenancies at para.6.024).

In addition to proving that one of the grounds has been made out, the landlord must satisfy the court that the condition(s) appropriate to that ground is (are) satisfied (s.84). The grounds and the appropriate conditions in summary are as follows (for the full text see Appendix 2):

Form 21: Section 83 notice—termination of tenancy and recovery of possession

Secure Tenancies (Notices) Regulations 1987
Schedule, Part II as amended
Notice of seeking termination of tenancy and recovery of possession

Housing Act 1985. section 83

This Notice may lead to your being required to leave your dwelling. You should read it very carefully.

(1) To .... (name(s) of secure tenant(s))

- If you need advice about this Notice, and what you should do about it, take it as quickly as possible to a Citizens' Advice Bureau, a Housing Aid Centre, or a Law Centre, or to a Solicitor. You may be able to receive Legal Aid but this will depend on your personal circumstances.

(2) The [name of landlord] intends to apply to the Court for an order terminating your tenancy and requiring you to give up possession of: .... (address of property) ....

- This Notice applies to you if you are a secure tenant under the Housing Act 1985 and if your tenancy is for a fixed term, containing a provision which allows your landlord to bring it to an end before the fixed term expires. This may be because you have got into arrears with your rent or have broken some other condition of the tenancy. This is known as a provision for re-entry or forfeiture. The Act does not remove the need for your landlord to bring an action under such a provision, nor does it affect your right to seek relief against re-entry or forfeiture, in order words to ask the Court not to bring the tenancy to an end. The Act gives additional rights to tenants, as described below.

- If you are a secure tenant and have a fixed term tenancy, it can only be terminated and you can only be evicted if your landlord obtains an order for possession from the Court. The order must be based on one of the Grounds which are set out in the 1985 Act (see paragraphs 3 and 4 below).

- If you are willing to give up possession without a Court order, you should notify the person who signed this Notice as soon as possible and say when you would leave.

(3) Termination of your tenancy and possession will be sought on Ground(s) .... of Schedule 2 to the Housing Act 1985, which reads: [give the text in full of each Ground which is being relied on]

- Whatever Grounds for possession are set out in paragraph 3 of this Notice, the Court may allow any of the other Grounds to be added at a later stage. If this is done, you will be told about it so you can argue at the hearing in Court about the new Ground, as well as the Grounds set out in paragraph 3, if you want to.

contd

contd

(4) Particulars of each Ground are as follows:— [give a full explanation of why each Ground is being relied upon]

- Before the Court will grant an order on any of the Grounds 1 to 8 or 12 to 16, it must be satisfied that it is reasonable to require you to leave. This means that, if one of these Grounds is set out in paragraph 3 of this Notice, you will be able to argue at the hearing in Court that it is not reasonable that you should have to leave, even if you accept that the Ground applies.

- Before the Court grants an order on any of the Grounds 9 to 16, it must be satisfied that there will be suitable alternative accommodation for you when you have to leave. This means that the Court will have to decide that, in its opinion, there will be other accommodation which is reasonably suitable for the needs of you and your family, taking into particular account various factors such as the nearness of your place of work, and the sort of housing that other people with similar needs are offered. Your new home will have to be let to you on another secure tenancy or a private tenancy under the Rent Act of a kind that will give you similar security. *There is no requirement for suitable alternative accommodation where Grounds 1 to 8 apply.*

- If your landlord is not a local authority, and the local authority gives a certificate that it will provide you with suitable accommodation, the Court has to accept the certificate.

- One of the requirements of Ground 10A is that the landlord must have approval for the redevelopment scheme from the Secretary of State (or, in the case of a housing association landlord, the Housing Corporation). The landlord must have consulted all secure tenants affected by the proposed redevelopment scheme.

Signed ....

On behalf of ....

Address ....

Tel No ....

Date ....

Grounds 1–8: the court must consider it reasonable to make the order for possession

(1) Rent arrears and breach of obligation (see Ch.28). **10.018**

(2) Nuisance and illegal purposes (see Chs 29 and 30).

(2A) Domestic violence.

(3) Deterioration of the premises (see Ch.30).

(4) Deterioration of furniture (see Ch.30).

(5) Tenancy obtained by false statement by tenant or person acting at tenant's instigation (see *Waltham Forest LBC v Roberts* [2004] EWCA Civ 940— on materiality of the statement; *London Borough of Merton v Richards* [2005] EWCA Civ 639—false statements made by interfering mother of the tenant not at tenant's instigation; *London Borough of Islington v Uckac* [2006] EWCA Civ 340—not possible to rely upon Ground 5 against an assignee of the tenancy, even where that person was party to the original fraud—nor is it possible to obtain rescission of a secure tenancy.

(6) Premium paid on an exchange.

(7) Tenant or person residing with him guilty of conduct such that it would not be right for him to continue occupation—tenancy resulting from employment by landlord.

(8) Dwelling-house occupied while improvement works being carried out to previous home which are now completed.

*Grounds 9–11: the court must be satisfied that suitable alternative
accommodation is available*

10.019   (9)   Overcrowding within the meaning of Pt X of the Housing Act 1985
(see Ch.21).

(10)   Demolition or reconstruction (see *Wansbeck DC v Marley* [1988] 20
H.L.R. 247).

(10A) Dwelling-house in redevelopment area.

(11)   Charity cases.

*Grounds 12–16: the court must be satisfied that suitable alternative
accommodation will be available and that it is reasonable to make the
order for possession*

10.020   (12)   Dwelling-house required for employee.

(13)   Dwelling-house designed for the physically handicapped (see *Freeman v
Wansbeck DC* [1984] 2 All E.R. 746).

(14)   Landlord a housing association or housing trust and dwelling-house let
to a person with special needs.

(15)   Social service or special facility in close proximity.

(15A) (England) 16 (Wales) Under occupation following death of the tenant
and s.83 notice served more than six months but less than 12 months
after the date of the previous tenant's death (see further para.10.035).

Suitable alternative accommodation

10.021 Part IV of Sch.2 to the 1985 Act provides that accommodation is suitable if it
consists of premises which are to be let under:

(a) a secure tenancy; or

(b) a protected tenancy (other than one under which the landlord would be
able to recover possession by relying on one of the mandatory grounds in
Sch.15 to the Rent Act 1977); or

(c) an assured tenancy (which is neither an assured shorthold tenancy nor a
tenancy under which the landlord might recover possession under any of
Grounds 1 to 5 in Sch.2 to that Act);

and, in the opinion of the court, the accommodation is reasonably suitable for the
needs of the tenant and his family (Sch.2, Pt IV, para.1 as amended by Sch.17,
para.65 of the Housing Act 1988).
    In determining whether it is reasonably suitable for those needs, the court must
have regard to the factors set out in para.2 of Pt IV (see Appendix 2). The needs
of the tenant's family should not be overlooked even where husband and wife
have separated (*Wandsworth London Borough Council v Fadayomi* [1987] 3 All
E.R. 474). In the context of Ground 16 it has been held that the composition of the

family is to be determined as at the date of the hearing (*London Borough of Wandsworth v Randall* [2007] EWCA Civ 1126—see para.10.031).

Sometimes the landlord may rely upon a certificate of suitability which will be conclusive evidence that the alternative accommodation is suitable (see para.4 of Pt IV).

When considering cases under Pt IV of Sch.2, care should be taken in comparing Rent Act cases because of the exclusion of the words "and character" that appear in para.5(b) of Pt IV of Sch.15 to the Rent Act 1977 and because of the inclusion in Sch.2 to the 1985 Act of a reference to "the nature of the accommodation which it is the practice of the landlord to allocate to persons with similar needs" which permits the court to take into account the needs of other homeless persons in the borough (para.2(a)), see *Enfield London Borough Council v French* (1984) 49 P. & C.R. 223.

The list in para.2 of Pt IV is not exhaustive and the court may take into account needs not specified therein such as the need of the tenant for a garden or to carry on a particular hobby or other activity, but such needs can be outweighed by the fact that all other needs are satisfied by the alternative accommodation (*Enfield v French*).

The order for possession

Where the landlord is relying upon any of the Grounds 1 to 8 or 12 to 16 of **10.022** Sch.2 to the Housing Act 1985 the court may stay or suspend the execution of the order, or postpone the date for possession "at any time before execution of the order" (s.85 of the Housing Act 1985). The tenancy comes to an end on the execution of the order (s.82(2)). If any such stay, suspension or postponement is ordered the court must, unless it considers that to do so would cause exceptional hardship or would otherwise be unreasonable, impose conditions with regard to payment by the tenant of arrears of rent (if any) and rent and may impose such other conditions as it thinks fit. The court may, if it thinks appropriate, discharge or rescind the order for possession (s.85(4)). Where the landlord wishes there to be a condition that is not directly related to the ground for possession (e.g. a condition not to cause a nuisance where the claim is based on arrears of rent) see *Sheffield City Council v Hopkins* [2001] 26 E.G. 163 (CS) CA, dealt with at para.34.009.

Housing Act 1985 section 85

(1) Where proceedings are brought for possession of a dwelling house let under a secure tenancy on any of the grounds set out in Part I or Part III of Schedule 2 (grounds 1 to 8 and 12 to 16: cases in which the court must be satisfied that it is reasonable to make a possession order), the court may adjourn the proceedings for such period or periods as it thinks fit.

(2) On the making of an order for possession of such a dwelling house on any of those grounds, or at any time before the execution of the order, the court may–

  (a) stay or suspend the execution of the order, or
  (b) postpone the date of possession,

  for such period or periods as the court thinks fit.

(3) On such an adjournment, stay, suspension or postponement the court–

  (a) shall impose conditions with respect to the payment by the tenant of arrears of rent (if any) and rent, unless it considers that to do so would cause exceptional hardship to the tenant or would otherwise be unreasonable, and
  (b) may impose such other conditions as it thinks fit.

(4) The court may discharge or rescind the order for possession if it thinks it appropriate to do so having had regard to–

(a) any conditions imposed under subsection (3), and

(b) the conduct of the tenant in connection with those conditions.

The court has no discretion under s.85 where the ground for possession is one of Grounds 9 (overcrowding), 10 (demolition or reconstruction), 10A (dwelling-house in development area) or 11 (charity cases). In these cases the court may not suspend the order for possession for more than 14 days (six weeks in cases of exceptional hardship): s.89 of the Housing Act 1980 (para.3.034).

Relationship with the right to buy

10.023 A tenant cannot exercise the right to buy where there is an order for possession of the property (s.121 of the 1985 Act). Where the tenant is seeking a declaration that he has a right to buy and the landlord is claiming possession, both matters should be heard together and the court should carry out a balancing exercise by considering the overall merits of the parties' positions (see *Basildon District Council v Wahlen* [2006] EWCA Civ 326 and also *Manchester City Council v Benjamin* [2008] EWCA Civ 189).

Assignment, sub-letting and death

Assignment

10.024 Some secure tenancies may not be assigned. Others may be, but in certain circumstances they cease to be secure. Certain tenancies which are not secure, but would be if the tenant condition were satisfied, lose the opportunity of becoming secure if they are assigned.

It is not possible to assign a secure tenancy (or a tenancy which would be secure if the tenant condition were satisfied) which is a periodic tenancy or is for a fixed term that was created on or after November 5, 1982, unless:

(a) the assignment is by way of an exchange with another secure tenant or with an assured tenant who satisfies certain conditions pursuant to the provisions of s.92 of the Housing Act 1985 (as amended by s.163 of the Local Government and Housing Act 1989) (see s.91(1),(3)); or

(b) the assignment is made in pursuance of an order under s.24 of the Matrimonial Causes Act 1973 (see also Sch.7 to the Family Law Act 1996); or

(c) the assignment is to a person who could be a successor on death (see para.10.028).

A deed of release is equivalent to an assignment. One joint tenant cannot therefore release his interest to the other and so make the other the sole tenant unless the circumstances of s.91 apply (*Burton v Camden LBC* [2000] L. & T.R. 235 HL).

A secure tenancy which is for a fixed term and was granted before November 5, 1982 may be assigned but it ceases to be secure, unless one of the circumstances in (a), (b) or (c) above applies (s.91(2) of the Housing Act 1985). Where such a tenancy ceases to be secure it cannot become a secure tenancy again.

A tenant of a social landlord has, under s.158 of the Localism Act 2011, additional rights in certain circumstances to a transfer of their tenancy.

A tenancy that remains secure despite an assignment does not lose its status as **10.025** a secure tenancy by reason of the fact that it was an unlawful assignment, i.e. in breach of a covenant in the tenancy agreement (*Governors of the Peabody Donation Fund v Higgins* [1983] 1 W.L.R. 1091); but it does give the landlord a ground upon which it can claim possession (Ground 1).

A tenancy that loses its security by reason of an assignment does not cease to exist, even if the assignment was unlawful. It continues to exist as a common law tenancy in the hands of the assignee (*Governors of the Peabody Donation Fund v Higgins*). If the landlord wishes to recover possession by reason of the assignment it must therefore determine the tenancy according to common law principles. Where there is a covenant against assigning and a forfeiture clause in the agreement the landlord should serve a notice under s.146 of the Law of Property Act 1925 and then commence forfeiture proceedings. Or, if it is able to do so, the landlord may serve a notice to quit.

(Note that s.91 of the Housing Act 1985 does not apply if the landlord is a co-operative housing association: s.109.)

Sub-letting, parting with possession and lodgers

Section 93(1)(b) of the Housing Act 1985 provides that it is a term of every secure **10.026** tenancy that the tenant will not, without the written consent of the landlord, sub-let or part with possession of part of the dwelling-house. If he does so and there is a forfeiture clause in the lease the landlord may terminate under s.82(3): see para.10.014. Alternatively, if the tenancy is a periodic tenancy he may terminate the tenancy by serving a notice equivalent to at least the period of the tenancy. In each instance the landlord will have to commence proceedings for possession, in which he will be able to rely upon Ground 1. If the tenant seeks the landlord's consent, that consent must not be unreasonably withheld (s.94(2)). Section 94(3) which governs the question of whether the landlord is being unreasonable in withholding his consent provides that the burden is on the landlord to show that its refusal is reasonable. Section 94(3) sets out two matters that are among those that may be taken into account when deciding whether the landlord's refusal is unreasonable. These are (a) that the consent would lead to overcrowding as defined by Pt X of the Housing Act 1985 (see Ch.21) and (b) that the landlord proposes to carry out building works and that these works will affect the accommodation likely to be used by the proposed sub-tenant. If the landlord does withhold his consent unreasonably the consent is treated as having been given (s.94(2)) and it will obviously not be possible for it to recover possession under Ground 1.

The situation is rather different where the tenant parts with possession or sub-lets the whole of the dwelling-house (or sub-lets first part of it and then the remainder). In these circumstances the tenancy ceases to be secure and can never again become secure (s.93(2) e.g. *see Brent LBC v Cranin* (1997) 30 H.L.R. 43 CA). The tenancy will, however, continue as a common law tenancy and if the landlord wishes to recover possession it will have to determine it first according to common law principles, i.e. forfeiture or notice to quit. If a tenancy ceases to be secure because the tenant ceases to reside in the dwelling house (see s.81) the restrictions on parting with possession or sub-letting the whole contained in s.93(2) continue to apply to the tenancy (s.95).

There is no equivalent in the Housing Act 1985 to s.137 of the Rent Act 1977 **10.027** which gives some sub-tenants security of tenure when the landlord obtains possession as against the tenant. The position of sub-tenants at common law is dealt with in Ch.4.

In *Basingstoke and Dean BC v Paice* [1995] 2 E.G.L.R. 9 CA, a mesne landlord who sub-let a garage as a flat in breach of covenant saddled the head landlord (a local authority) with a secure tenancy. On surrender of the mesne tenancy the sub-tenant of the flat became the direct tenant of the council according to normal principles (see para.4.016). The landlord and tenant conditions were satisfied (s.81) and therefore the tenancy was a secure tenancy.

The relationship between the tenant and the sub-tenant is governed by the rules that apply in the private sector. This is because the sub-tenant's immediate landlord, i.e. the tenant, does not fulfil the landlord condition set out in s.80 of the Housing Act 1985. Where the tenant has sub-let part of the dwelling-house he will be a resident or sharing landlord in relation to the sub-tenant who will not therefore be an assured or a protected tenant under s.1 of the Housing Act 1988 or the Rent Act 1977: but (where the tenancy was entered into before January 15, 1989) he will almost certainly hold under a restricted contract. In practice there is unlikely to be a sub-letting and the person sharing accommodation with the tenant will invariably be a lodger (*Monmouth Borough Council v Marlog* [1994] 2 E.G.L.R. 68 CA; see further para.14.007).

Section 93 of the Housing Act 1985 provides that it is a term of every secure tenancy that the tenant may allow any persons to reside as lodgers in the dwelling-house. Taking in lodgers will not therefore provide a basis upon which the landlord may obtain possession but if it is entitled to possession as against the tenant on some other ground it will also be entitled to possession as against the lodger. A lodger is a licensee but if he pays rent he will (if he entered into occupation prior to January 15, 1989) almost certainly be entitled to some degree of protection as against the tenant by reason of the provisions relating to restricted contracts (see Ch.9). As to whether a person is a licensee or sub-tenant see Ch.5.

(Note that ss.93, 94 and 95 of the Housing Act 1985 do not apply to a tenancy when the interest of the landlord belongs to a co-operative housing association: s.109.)

Death (sections 87–90)

Periodic tenancies (section 89)

10.028 Where there are two or more tenants and one dies the remaining tenant or tenants become the sole tenant or remaining joint tenants under the laws relating to the right of survivorship. He (or they) continue to be secure in his (or their) own right. Where a secure tenant is a sole tenant and there is a person qualified under the rules set out in the Housing Act 1985 to succeed him the tenancy vests in that person. If there is more than one such person who is entitled to succeed him the tenancy vests in the person who is to be preferred according to the criteria set out in the Act (see s.89).

10.028A ***Tenancies granted before April 1, 2012 and Wales*** A person is qualified to succeed to the tenancy if he occupied the dwelling-house as his only or principal home at the time of the tenant's death and either:

(a)   he is the tenant's spouse or civil partner; or

(b)   he is another member of the tenant's family and has resided with the tenant throughout the period of 12 months ending with the tenant's death.

(Section 87 of the 1985 Act in its original form as preserved by s.160(6) of the Localism Act 2011).

Where there is more than one person qualified to succeed the tenant, the tenant's spouse or civil partner is to be preferred to any other member of the tenant's family. Where there is no spouse or civil partner who is qualified to succeed but there are two other members of the tenant's family who are qualified they may agree between them who is to succeed, but if they cannot agree the landlord may select a successor (s.89(2)(b)).

Tenancies granted on or after April 1, 2012 in England In relation to tenancies granted on or after April 1, 2012, succession rights under the 1985 Act are limited to a tenant's spouse or civil partner (or a person residing with them as a spouse or civil partner) who have occupied the property as their only or principal home at the time of the tenants death (s.86A as introduced by s.160 of the Localism Act 2011).

However, the landlord can make it an express provision of the tenancy that another person may be entitled to succeed (s.86A(2)) and even permit a succession where the tenant was themselves a successor (s.86A(4)).

Section 89 (1A) provides:

(1A) Where there is a person qualified to succeed the tenant under section 86A, the tenancy vests by virtue of this section—

(a)   in that person, or
(b)   if there is more than one such person, in such one of them as may be agreed between them or as may, where there is no agreement, be selected by the landlord.

General points on succession to periodic secure tenancies It is important to note that it is the relationship between the person who is claiming to succeed and "the tenant" which is important. The tenant must be a "secure tenant". In *Solihull Metropolitan Borough Council v Hickin* [2010] EWCA Civ 868 H and W had a joint weekly secure tenancy. They lived in the house with their daughter. H and W separated and H left. W and the daughter remained in the house. W died six years later. L then served a notice to quit on H and issued proceedings for possession against the daughter. She unsuccessfully claimed a right to succeed to the tenancy. When W died, H as the sole survivor of the joint tenancy, became the sole tenant. As he was not living there the tenancy was not secure. The notice to quit operated to determine his common law tenancy and L was entitled to possession. Section 89 of the Housing Act 1985 did not override that rule. See in particular paras 18 and 22.

Mere physical presence is not enough to amount to "residing with" the tenant. There must be, to a significant degree, an intention that can be characterised as making a home with the tenant – not just staying there. Moreover the nature of the occupation must have the necessary qualities of "residing with" for the whole year before the death. (*Freeman v London Borough of Islington* [2009] EWCA Civ 536—daughter who had lived at the property with her father for seven days a week in the year prior to his death did not satisfy the test for succession. She had initially stayed at the property in order to nurse her father but had also maintained her own property. During that period her father's dwelling was not her home and therefore, she had not "resided with" him).

The family member is not required to have lived with the tenant at the property in question throughout that period. It is sufficient if they resided somewhere together for a 12-month period and in that property together at the date of the tenant's death (*Waltham Forest London Borough Council v Thomas* [1992] 3 All E.R. 245 HL).

10.029   A person is a member of another's family if he is his spouse or civil partner, parent, grandparent, child, grandchild, brother, sister, uncle, aunt, nephew or niece. Relationships by marriage are treated as relationships by blood, half blood and whole blood, and a stepchild is treated as a child of the stepparent. An illegitimate child is treated as the legitimate child of his mother and reputed father. A person is also a member of another's family if they live together as man and wife (s.113 of the 1985 Act). A person is only a member of the family for these purposes if he can bring him or herself within this statutory list. Thus, a distant family member who fell outside the statutory list of family members was not entitled to succeed even though he was close to the tenant and addressed him as "uncle". The tenant was the brother-in-law of the defendant's first cousin once removed (*Wandsworth v Michalak* [2003] 1 W.L.R. 617 CA). And a foster child is not a member of the tenant's family for the purposes of s.113 (*Sheffield City Council v Wall (Personal Representatives of)* [2010] EWCA Civ 922—foster son not entitled to succeed to his foster mother's secure tenancy. Although though he had lived with her for many years and there was a loving mother and son relationship he had never been formally adopted by her).

A temporary move to other accommodation together with an expression of a conditional intention to cease living in the dwelling does not deprive a person of the right to succeed to the tenancy under s.87 (*Camden LBC v Goldenberg* (1996) The Times, April 1 CA—grandson moving out for two months while looking for somewhere else to live did not debar him from his rights to succeed to the tenancy).

10.030   A secure periodic tenancy may only be transferred once (ss.86A (3), 87, 88(1) (a)); that is unless the tenancy was granted in England after April 6, 2012 and there is an express provision in the agreement permitting further succession rights (s.86A(4)). Furthermore, a secure tenancy may not be transferred on the tenant's death in any of the following circumstances:

  (a) where the tenant was originally a joint tenant and at some stage before his death he became a sole tenant (s.88(1)(b)) under the original tenancy. In *Bassetlaw District Council v Renshaw* [1992] 1 All E.R. 925 CA the tenant was originally a joint tenant under a tenancy with her husband who served a notice on the landlord terminating the tenancy and left. The tenant then entered into a new tenancy of the property as a sole tenant. Held: she was not a person who had been a joint tenant under the original tenancy and who had become a sole tenant. Her son was not, therefore, precluded from succeeding to the second tenancy. In *Birmingham City Council v Walker* [2007] UKHL 22 the defendant's mother had been a joint tenant of a local authority, and had become a sole tenant, prior to the introduction of the secure tenancy regime created by the Housing Act 1980. As she had become a sole tenant prior to that date (in fact long before, in 1969) she was not a successor within the meaning of s.88(1)(b) of the 1985 Act. This meant that the defendant was entitled to succeed to the tenancy; or

(b)   where a fixed term was granted to another person or jointly with the deceased tenant and another person and the tenancy has (by virtue of s.86) become a periodic tenancy at the end of the fixed term or by virtue of an order of the court under s.82(3); or

(c)   where the deceased tenant became the tenant on the tenancy being assigned to him (except in dissolution proceedings of a marriage or civil partnership, or where the assignment was by virtue of s.92 of the Housing Act 1985); or

(d)   where the tenancy became vested in him on the death of the previous tenant (ss.87, 88(1)); or

(e)   where the tenancy was previously an introductory tenancy (Ch.12) and he was a successor to the introductory tenancy (s.88(1)(f)).

A situation can occur whereby a person ("the new tenant") remains in occupation **10.031** after the death of the original tenant in circumstances which give rise to a new tenancy as between the landlord and the new tenant (by estoppel) so that on the death of the new tenant the person then in occupation will be treated as the first successor to the new tenant's tenancy, even though the original tenant's tenancy was never determined (*Epping Forest District Council v Pomphrett* [1990] 2 E.G.L.R. 46 CA). No succession rights accrue on the death of a tolerated trespasser (*Hawkins v Newham* LBC [2005] EWCA Civ 451).

Where there is no person qualified to become a secure tenant by succession the tenancy does not cease to exist. Instead it will devolve according to the common law rules set out in Ch.4. If the landlord wishes to recover possession on the death of the tenant where there is no person entitled to succeed as a secure tenant the landlord should determine the tenancy in the usual way, i.e. by notice to quit.

Where there is a person qualified to succeed as a secure tenant the landlord may nevertheless be able to regain possession by relying upon Ground 15A (in England) or 16 (in Wales) (see paras 10.020 and A2.047) if the accommodation afforded by the dwelling-house is more extensive than is reasonably required by the successor. The ground does not apply if the successor was the tenant's spouse. In deciding whether it is reasonable to make an order on Ground 15A or 16 the court must take into account the age of the successor, the period during which he occupied the dwelling-house as his only or principal home and any financial or other support that he gave to the previous tenant.

In order to succeed under Ground 15A or 16 the landlord must also establish that suitable alternative accommodation will be available which is reasonably suitable for the needs of the tenant and his family (see further para.10.021). The composition of the family is to be determined as at the date of the hearing; not the date of succession (*London Borough of Wandsworth v Randall* [2007] EWCA Civ 1126—the local authority landlord sought possession of a four-bedroom house on the ground that the accommodation was more extensive than reasonably required by the successor, a man initially on his own. However, before the hearing his mother and half-sister moved into the property. The landlord offered the tenant a one-bedroom flat as alternative accommodation. As the relevant date was the date of the hearing the alternative accommodation was insufficient). A tenant who concealed his mother's death for three years in order to avoid being moved to a different property on Ground 16 could not be evicted on that ground because the time limit for doing so had expired before the local authority found out about her death. They were not able to rely upon an estoppel (*Newport City Council v Charles* [2008] EWCA Civ 893).

A minor who satisfies the s.87 requirements may succeed to a secure tenancy albeit that he can only hold the equitable interest until he attains a majority: *Kingston upon Thames v Prince* (1999) 31 H.L.R. 794 CA. See also *Newham v Ria* [2004] EWCA Civ 41, applying the Trusts of Land and Appointment of Trustees Act 1996 to the principles set out in *Kingston v Prince*.

Fixed terms (section 90)

10.032 Where a secure tenancy is for a fixed term it will devolve according to the rules set out in Ch.4. Thus, if there are joint tenants the remaining tenants continue as secure tenants. In all other cases the tenancy will remain secure until either (a) the tenancy is vested or otherwise disposed of in the course of the administration of the deceased's estate, or (b) it is known that when the tenancy has been so vested or disposed of it will not be a secure tenancy (s.90(2) of the Housing Act 1985). Once the tenancy has been vested or otherwise disposed of it will only continue to be secure if (a) the vesting or other disposal is in pursuance of an order made either under either s.24 of the Matrimonial Causes Act 1973, s.17 of the Matrimonial and Family Proceedings Act 1984, Sch.1 to the Children Act 1989 or Schs 5 or 7 of the Civil Partnership Act 2004; or (b) the person in whom the tenancy vests would have been entitled to be a secure tenant of the dwelling-house by virtue of s.87 had the tenancy been a periodic tenancy (s.90(3)). If the tenancy remains secure, but the property is more extensive than reasonably required by the new secure tenant, the landlord may be able to obtain possession pursuant to Ground 15A (in England) or 16 (in Wales) (see para 10.031). If the tenancy ceases to be secure it cannot become a secure tenancy (s.90(4)) and thus the landlord will be able to regain possession of the premises at the end of the term without having to rely upon one of the grounds set out in Sch.2. Where the tenancy was granted of a dwelling house in England, the landlord can obtain possession prior to the end of the fixed term by relying on the provisions of s.90 (5) to (10) as introduced by the Localism Act 2011.

Localism Act 2011 section 90

(5)   The following provisions apply where a tenancy that was a secure tenancy of a dwelling-house in England—

(a)   has been vested or otherwise disposed of in the course of the administration of the secure tenant's estate, and

(b)   has ceased to be a secure tenancy by virtue of this section.

(6)   Subject as follows, the landlord may apply to the court for an order for possession of the dwelling-house let under the tenancy.

(7)   The court may not entertain proceedings for an order for possession under this section unless—

(a)   the landlord has served notice in writing on the tenant—

(i)   stating that the landlord requires possession of the dwelling-house, and

      (ii) specifying a date after which proceedings for an order for possession may be begun, and

    (b) that date has passed without the tenant giving up possession of the dwelling-house.

(8) The date mentioned in subsection (7)(a)(ii) must fall after the end of the period of four weeks beginning with the date on which the notice is served on the tenant.

(9) On an application to the court for an order for possession under this section, the court must make such an order if it is satisfied that subsection (5) applies to the tenancy.

(10) The tenancy ends when the order is executed.

Chapter 11

Flexible Tenancies

A flexible tenancy is a species of secure tenancy which has been brought into **11.001** existence by amendments made to the Housing Act 1985 by the Localism Act 2011. Unlike the usual secure tenancy, it is not for an indefinite duration, but is granted for a fixed term of not less than two years. It is an attempt to enable local housing authorities to exert greater control over their increasingly over demanded housing stock.

Prior to granting flexible tenancies each local housing authority must set out their policy on such grants, including their policy on the duration of term.

The authorities in relation to the human rights aspects of introductory tenancies and demoted tenancies are likely to be equally applicable to the use of flexible tenancies, both as to the limiting of security of tenure and the internal review procedures (see Chs 12 and 13).

As at the date of writing, the flexible tenancy provisions had not yet come into force and so readers should check for updates at *www.propertylawuk.net*.

Prerequisites for granting a flexible tenancy

A local housing authority can grant a flexible tenancy either when taking on a new **11.002** tenant or at the end of a Family Intervention tenancy, an introductory tenancy or a demoted tenancy (see s.107A of the 1985 Act). In order to do so, they must first serve a notice on the person who is to become the tenant stating that on the coming to an end of their current tenancy, they will obtain a secure tenancy that would be a flexible tenancy (see para.4ZA(2) of Sch.1 of the 1985 Act (Family Intervention tenancy), s.137A of the 1996 Act (introductory tenancy) and s.143MA of the 1996 Act (demoted tenancy). It is clear then that the notice needs to be served before any tenancy is entered into, not just before the flexible tenancy is granted. It also follows that those who are currently secure tenants (or introductory or demoted) will not be susceptible to becoming a flexible tenant. Further, a tenant who was a secure tenant, but had that tenancy demoted, cannot then be made a flexible tenant on the coming to an end of the demoted tenancy (s.143 MA(1) of the 1996 Act).

Housing Act 1985 section 107A

107A (1) For the purposes of this Act, a flexible tenancy is a secure tenancy to which any **11.003** of the following subsections applies.

(2) This subsection applies to a secure tenancy if—

    (a) it is granted by a landlord in England for a term certain of not less than two years, and

    (b) before it was granted the person who became the landlord under the tenancy served a written notice on the person who became the tenant under the tenancy stating that the tenancy would be a flexible tenancy.

(3) This subsection applies to a secure tenancy if—

    (a) it becomes a secure tenancy by virtue of a notice under paragraph 4ZA(2) of Schedule 1 (family intervention tenancies becoming secure tenancies),

    (b) the landlord under the family intervention tenancy in question was a local housing authority in England,

    (c) the family intervention tenancy was granted to a person on the coming to an end of a flexible tenancy under which the person was a tenant,

    (d) the notice states that the tenancy is to become a secure tenancy that is a flexible tenancy for a term certain of the length specified in the notice, and sets out the other express terms of the tenancy, and

    (e) the length of the term specified in the notice is at least two years.

(4) The length of the term of a flexible tenancy that becomes such a tenancy by virtue of subsection (3) is that specified in the notice under paragraph 4ZA(2) of Schedule 1.

(5) The other express terms of the flexible tenancy are those set out in the notice, so far as those terms are compatible with the statutory provisions relating to flexible tenancies; and in this subsection "statutory provision" means any provision made by or under an Act.

(6) This subsection applies to a secure tenancy if—

    (a) it is created by virtue of section 137A of the Housing Act 1996 (introductory tenancies becoming flexible tenancies), or

    (b) it arises by virtue of section 143MA of that Act (demoted tenancies becoming flexible tenancies).

Terms of the tenancy

11.004 The notice must set out not only the duration of the tenancy but also any other express terms that are to be included.

The duration must not be for less than two years. There is a procedure for the prospective flexible tenant to seek an internal review of that decision (s.107B(2) to (6)) only if the term proposed does not accord with that landlord's policy on the length of term to be granted. Subject to the landlord giving more time, the prospective tenant must seek a review within 21 days of receiving the notice if they are not satisfied with the length of term.

The review procedure is set out in the Flexible Tenancies (Review Procedures) Regulations 2012 (2012/695) and permits an applicant to seek an oral or paper review upon providing reasons why the term proposed does not accord with the landlord's policy on length of term. The prospective tenant must be notified in writing of the outcome and if adverse, reasons must be provided.

Termination of the tenancy

By Tenant

A tenant can end the tenancy on giving not less than four weeks' notice to the **11.005** landlord. That requirement can be waived by the landlord as long as there are no arrears or other material breach of the tenancy (s.107C).

By Landlord—at the end of the fixed term

On the coming to an end of the fixed term, a periodic tenancy will arise by virtue of s.86 of the 1985 Act. Therefore the right to occupy will not determine automatically. The landlord needs to obtain and execute a possession order in order to bring the tenancy to an end. The landlord will be entitled to an order if they comply with three conditions set out in s.107D.

(1) The fixed term must have come to an end and no other tenancy (other than a periodic under s.86) is in existence.

(2) The landlord must have given at least six months notice to the tenant that at the end of the fixed term they do not propose to grant any further tenancy (a Condition 2 notice). This notice must also specify their reasons and alert the tenant to the fact that they have the right to request a review of that decision and the timeframe within which they must do so.

(3) The landlord must serve a further notice stating that they require possession (a Condition 3 notice). At least two months notice must be given for this last notice. In practice therefore possession proceedings should not be started before the two months are up (see similar provision in the Housing Act 1988 at para.7.017). As with the provisions for notices under the Housing Act 1988, the statute specifically provides that this last notice can be given "before or on the day on which the tenancy comes to an end" (s.107D (5)).

It is not clear then whether a condition 3 notice can be served after the expiry of the fixed term. Following the general consensus in relation to notices under s.21 of the Housing Act 1988, it would seem not (although see the arguments the other way at para.7.025). If not, then a landlord will lose the right to possession on a mandatory basis if it failed to serve the condition 3 notice by the end of the fixed term. This is because unlike s.21 of the 1988 Act, there is only one notice that can be served. Section 21 provides for two types of notices. On the general view, one notice for before the fixed term, another for service after the fixed term has come to an end.

If the three conditions are met then, bar one further obstacle, the court must order possession. The further obstacle is that if the tenant has requested a review of the decision not to grant a further tenancy, then if the court is satisfied that that review has not been carried out correctly, it can refuse to make the order and (in a quasi judicial review manner) make directions as to the holding of a review. The court does not have to refuse to make an order in these circumstances, it is given a discretion as s.107D (6) states that the court "may refuse to grant an order for possession".

Housing Act 1985 section 107D

107D Recovery of possession on expiry of flexible tenancy

11.006

(1) Subject as follows, on or after the coming to an end of a flexible tenancy a court must make an order for possession of the dwelling-house let on the tenancy if it is satisfied that the following conditions are met.

(2) Condition 1 is that the flexible tenancy has come to an end and no further secure tenancy (whether or not a flexible tenancy) is for the time being in existence, other than a secure tenancy that is a periodic tenancy (whether or not arising by virtue of section 86).

(3) Condition 2 is that the landlord has given the tenant not less than six months' notice in writing—

    (a) stating that the landlord does not propose to grant another tenancy on the expiry of the flexible tenancy,

    (b) setting out the landlord's reasons for not proposing to grant another tenancy, and

    (c) informing the tenant of the tenant's right to request a review of the landlord's proposal and of the time within which such a request must be made.

(4) Condition 3 is that the landlord has given the tenant not less than two months' notice in writing stating that the landlord requires possession of the dwelling-house.

(5) A notice under subsection (4) may be given before or on the day on which the tenancy comes to an end.

(6) The court may refuse to grant an order for possession under this section if—

    (a) the tenant has in accordance with section 107E requested a review of the landlord's proposal not to grant another tenancy on the expiry of the flexible tenancy, and

    (b) the court is satisfied that the landlord has failed to carry out the review in accordance with provision made by or under that section or that the decision on the review is otherwise wrong in law.

(7) If a court refuses to grant an order for possession by virtue of subsection (6) it may make such directions as to the holding of a review or further review under section 107E as it thinks fit.

(8) This section has effect notwithstanding that, on the coming to an end of the flexible tenancy, a periodic tenancy arises by virtue of section 86.

(9) Where a court makes an order for possession of a dwelling-house by virtue of this section, any periodic tenancy arising by virtue of section 86 on the coming to an end of the flexible tenancy comes to an end (without further notice and regardless of the period) in accordance with section 82(2).

(10) This section is without prejudice to any right of the landlord under a flexible tenancy to recover possession of the dwelling-house let on the tenancy in accordance with this Part.

By Landlord—Grounds

11.007 The last sub section of s.107D clarifies that this is not the only way in which possession can be granted. It remains possible for a landlord to obtain possession at any time (including during the fixed term) if certain grounds are made out (see Ch.10; paras 10.015 and 10.018). This is likely to be used if the landlord has not yet served a condition 3 notice, has grounds for possession and does not wish to wait the requisite two months before issuing proceedings for possession.

Review

The tenant has 21 days from receiving the condition 2 notice to seek a review. **11.008** The review should be conducted in accordance with the Flexible Tenancies (Review Procedures) Regulations 2012 (2012/695). This permits an applicant to seek an oral or paper review of the decision upon providing grounds. The tenant must be notified in writing of the outcome and if adverse, reasons must be provided.

Chapter 12

Introductory Tenancies

Every local housing authority and housing action trust may elect to operate an **12.001**
"introductory tenancy regime" (Housing Act 1996 ss.124–143). If they do so the
general rule is that their periodic tenancies will be "introductory tenancies" rather
than secure tenancies. The election may be revoked at any time, without prejudice
to the making of a further election at some time in the future (Housing Act 1996
s.124(5)).

Bodies which let dwelling-houses under introductory tenancies are under a
duty to publish information about their introductory tenancies; and their introductory tenants must be supplied with a copy of that information and a written statement of the terms of the tenancy, so far as they are neither expressed in the lease
or written tenancy agreement (if any) nor implied by law (s.136).

The rules apply to licences (whether or not granted for a consideration) as well
as tenancies; unless the licence was granted as a temporary expedient to a person
who entered as a trespasser (s.126).

In *McLellan v Bracknell Forest Borough Council* [2001] EWCA Civ 1510 it
was held that the scheme of introductory tenancies did not breach art.6 of the
European Convention on Human Rights (fair trial) because the scope of judicial
review was sufficient. It did interfere with art.8 (respect for family life) but the
evidence revealed that the interference corresponded to a pressing social need.
(See also *R. (On the application of Gilboy) v Liverpool City Council* [2008]
EWCA Civ 751 at [36] and [44] where it was stated that the decision in *McLellan*
had received the seal of approval of the House of Lords in *Kay*—see Ch.23).

Definition

When an election by a housing authority or housing action trust is in force every **12.002**
periodic tenancy of a dwelling-house entered into or adopted by the authority or
trust is, if it would otherwise be a secure tenancy, an introductory tenancy
(s.124(2)).

Exceptions

However, the tenancy is not an introductory tenancy if immediately before the **12.003**
tenancy was entered into or "adopted" the tenant or, in the case of joint tenants,
one or more of them was—

    (a) a secure tenant of the same or another dwelling-house; or

    (b) an assured tenant of a registered social landlord (otherwise than under an assured shorthold tenancy) in respect of the same or another dwelling-house (s.124(2)).

Furthermore, the tenancy will not be an introductory tenancy if the tenancy was entered into or adopted in pursuance of a contract made before the election was made (s.124(3)).

A periodic tenancy is said to be "adopted" for the purpose of these provisions whether the landlord becomes landlord as a result of a disposal or a surrender (s.124(4)).

Duration of the trial period

12.004 The general rule is that the tenancy remains an introductory tenancy for a period of one year from the date on which the tenancy was entered into (s.125(1)(2)(a)—however, see further subss.(2) to (4) when calculating the period; and see *Salford CC v Garner* [2004] H.L.R. 572 CA for guidance on calculating the period of the tenancy and the date by which proceedings must be issued).

Amendments to the Housing Act 1996 by the Housing Act 2004 allow for the period of one year to be extended by six months (see para.12.006 below).

Housing Act 1996 sections 125, 125A–B

12.005 **125.**—(1) A tenancy remains an introductory tenancy until the end of the trial period, unless one of the events mentioned in subsection (5) occurs before the end of that period.

(2) The "trial period" is the period of one year beginning with—

    (a) in the case of a tenancy which was entered into by a local housing authority or housing action trust—

        (i) the date on which the tenancy was entered into; or
        (ii) if later, the date on which a tenant was first entitled to possession under the tenancy; or

    (b) in the case of a tenancy which was adopted by a local housing authority or housing action trust, the date of adoption;

but this is subject to subsections (3) and (4) and to section 125A (extension of trial period by 6 months).

(3) Where the tenant under an introductory tenancy was formerly a tenant under another introductory tenancy, or held an assured shorthold tenancy from a registered social landlord, any period or periods during which he was such a tenant shall count towards the trial period, provided—

    (a) if there was one such period, it ended immediately before the date specified in subsection (2); and

    (b) if there was more than one such period, the most recent period ended immediately before that date and each period succeeded the other without interruption.

(4) Where there are joint tenants under an introductory tenancy, the reference in subsection (3) to the tenant shall be construed as referring to the joint tenant in

whose case the application of that subsection produces the earliest starting date for the trial period.

(5) A tenancy ceases to be an introductory tenancy if, before the end of the trial period—

    (a) the circumstances are such that the tenancy would not otherwise be a secure tenancy;

    (b) a person or body other than a local housing authority or housing action trust becomes the landlord under the tenancy;

    (c) the election in force when the tenancy was entered into or adopted is revoked; or

    (d) the tenancy ceases to be an introductory tenancy by virtue of section 133(3) (succession).

(6) A tenancy does not come to an end merely because it ceases to be an introductory tenancy, but a tenancy which has once ceased to be an introductory tenancy cannot subsequently become an introductory tenancy.

(7) This section has effect subject to section 130 (effect of beginning proceedings for possession).

Extension of trial period by six months

125A—(1) If both of the following conditions are met in relation to an introductory **12.006** tenancy, the trial period is extended by 6 months.

(2) The first condition is that the landlord has served a notice of extension on the tenant at least eight weeks before the original expiry date.

(3) The second condition is that either—

    (a) the tenant has not requested a review under section 125B in accordance with subsection (1) of that section; or

    (b) if he has, the decision on the review was to confirm the landlord's decision to extend the trial period.

(4) A notice of extension is a notice—

    (a) stating that the landlord has decided that the period for which the tenancy is to be an introductory tenancy should be extended by six months; and

    (b) complying with subsection (5).

(5) A notice of extension must—

    (a) set out the reasons for the landlord's decision; and

    (b) inform the tenant of his right to request a review of the landlord's decision and of the time within which such a request must be made.

(6) In this section and section 125B "the original expiry date" means the last day of the period of one year that would apply as the trial period apart from this section.

Review of decision to extend trial period

125B—(1) A request for review of the landlord's decision that the trial period for an **12.007** introductory tenancy should be extended under section 125A must be made before the end of the period of 14 days beginning with the day on which the notice of extension is served.

(2) On a request being duly made to it, the landlord shall review its decision.

(3) The Secretary of State may make provision by regulations as to the procedure to be followed in connection with a review under this section.

Nothing in the following provisions affects the generality of this power.

(4) Provision may be made by regulations—

(a) requiring the decision on review to be made by a person of appropriate seniority who was not involved in the original decision; and

(b) as to the circumstances in which the person concerned is entitled to an oral hearing, and whether and by whom he may be represented at such a hearing.

(5) The landlord shall notify the tenant of the decision on the review.

If the decision is to confirm the original decision, the landlord shall also notify him of the reasons for the decision.

(6) The review shall be carried out and the tenant notified before the original expiry date.

The amendments made by this section do not apply in relation to any tenancy entered into before, or in pursuance of an agreement made before, the day on which this section came into force on June 6, 2005 (s.179(4) of the Housing Act 2004).

Exceptions

12.008 There are exceptions to the rule that the tenancy remains an introductory tenancy for a year (s.125(5)). The tenancy ceases to be an introductory tenancy if, before the end of the trial period:

(a) the circumstances are such that the tenancy would not otherwise be secure (see para.10.003);

(b) a person or body other than a local housing authority or housing action trust becomes the landlord under the tenancy;

(c) the election in force when the tenancy was entered into or adopted is revoked; or

(d) the tenancy ceases to be an introductory tenancy by virtue of s.133(3) (see below, succession on death—para.12.018).

A tenancy does not come to an end merely because it ceases to be an introductory tenancy. Its status will thereafter depend upon the particular reason for it ceasing to be secure; but a tenancy which has once ceased to be an introductory tenancy cannot subsequently become an introductory tenancy (s.125(6)).

An introductory tenancy may, subject to the procedures mentioned below, be terminated during that year. Where the landlord has begun proceedings for possession and the trial period ends the tenancy remains an introductory tenancy until the execution of the order for possession or until the proceedings are otherwise determined (s.130(1)(2)). See also s.130 where the landlord has begun proceedings for possession and one of the events specified above, on which a tenancy ceases to be an introductory tenancy, occurs.

Housing Act 1996 section 130

12.009 (1) This section applies where the landlord has begun proceedings for the possession of a dwelling house let under an introductory tenancy and—

(a) the trial period ends; or

(b) any of the events specified in s.125(5) occurs (events on which a tenancy ceases to be an introductory tenancy).

(2) Subject to the following provisions, the tenancy remains an introductory tenancy until—

(a) the tenancy comes to an end in accordance with s.127(1A); or

(b) the proceedings are otherwise finally determined.

(3) If any of the events specified in s.125(5)(b) to (d) occurs, the tenancy shall there upon cease to be an introductory tenancy but—

(a) the landlord (or, as the case may be, the new landlord) may continue the proceedings; and

(b) if he does so, s.127(1A) and (2) (termination by landlord) apply as if the tenancy had remained an introductory tenancy.

(4) Where in accordance with subs.(3) a tenancy ceases to be an introductory tenancy and becomes a secure tenancy, the tenant is not entitled to exercise the right to buy under Pt V of the Housing Act 1985 unless and until the proceedings are finally determined on terms such that he is not required to give up possession of the dwelling house.

(5) For the purposes of this section proceedings shall be treated as finally determined if they are withdrawn or any appeal is abandoned or the time for appealing expires without an appeal being brought.

Extension of trial period

Where the tenancy was entered into (in England) on or after June 6, 2005 the **12.010** tenancy may, if two conditions are satisfied, be extended for a period of six months (s.125A of the Housing Act 1996 as introduced by s.179 of the Housing Act 2004; the Housing Act 2004 (Commencement No.3) (England) Order 2005 (SI 2005/1451). The first condition relates to service of an extension notice. The second relates to a review of the decision to extend the tenancy. If the tenancy is extended it is so extended for the full period of six months. There is no power to extend the tenancy for a shorter period (s.125A(1) of the Housing Act 1996 as introduced by s.179 of the 2004 Act).

(The tenancy may not be extended if it was entered into pursuant to an agreement made before June 6, 2005: s.179(4) of the 2004 Act).

Notice of extension

A landlord that wants to extend the trial period by six months must serve a notice **12.011** of extension on the tenant. The notice must:

• be served at least eight weeks before "the original expiry date", i.e. "the last day of the period of one year that would apply as the trial period" if it were not being extended;

• state that the landlord has decided that the period for which the tenancy is to be an introductory tenancy should be extended by six months;

• set out the reasons for the landlord's decision;

- inform the tenant of his right to request a review of the landlord's decision;

- inform the tenant that the request for a review must be made before the end of the period of 14 days beginning with the day on which the notice of extension is served (s.125A (2), (4), (5); s.125B(1)).

The power to extend the introductory tenancy was introduced by the Housing Act 2004 as part of a packet of measures to deal with anti-social behaviour. However, there is nothing in the statutory requirements stating that the reasons for serving the notice need have anything to do with anti-social behaviour. Presumably, therefore, any reasons can be given so long as they are not unreasonable.

Review

12.012 A tenant who wishes to review the decision to extend the trial period must make the request for the review "before the end of the period of 14 days beginning with the day on which the notice of extension is served" (s.125B(1)).

There is no special form that the request need take.

If a request for review of the decision is made the landlord must review its decision (s.125B(3)). The procedure for review is set out in regulations—see the Introductory Tenancies (Review of Decisions to Extend a Trial Period) (England) Regulations 2006 (SI 2006/1077); the Introductory Tenancies (Review of Decisions to Extend a Trial Period) (Wales) Regulations 2006 (SI 2006/2983 (W.274)).

The extension

12.013 The trial period is extended if either:

- the tenant does not request a review; or

- if he has, the decision on the review is to confirm the landlord's decision to extend the trial period (s.125A(3)).

As stated above the introductory tenancy is extended for six months.

Termination

Notice of proceedings

12.014 A landlord may not terminate an introductory tenancy unless it has first served a notice of proceedings complying with s.128. If it does not do so the court may "not entertain proceedings" for possession (s.128(1)). The notice must:

(1) state that the court will be asked to make an order for possession of the dwelling-house;
(2) set out the reasons for the landlord's decision to apply for such an order;
(3) specify a date after which proceedings for the possession of the dwelling-house may be begun. The date must not be earlier than the date on which the tenancy could, if the tenancy were an ordinary

common law tenancy, be brought to an end by notice to quit given on the same date;

(4) inform the tenant of his right to request a review of the landlord's decision to seek an order for possession and of the time within which such a request must be made (i.e. 14 days; s.129(1)—see below);

(5) inform the tenant that, if he needs help or advice about the notice, and what to do about it, he should take it immediately to a Citizens' Advice Bureau, a housing aid centre, a law centre or a solicitor.

For the position where a local authority withdraws a notice and then later attempts to proceed on that notice see R. (Forbes) v Lambeth LBC [2003] EWHC 222 QBD (notice invalid); and compare the situation where the authority decided to suspend acting on the notice on agreed terms and then later proceeded when the tenant breached the agreement (R. (Stone) v Cardiff [2003] EWCA Civ 298 (notice valid)).

Review of decision to seek possession

The tenant may request the landlord to review his decision to seek an order for possession but must do so before the end of the period of 14 days beginning with the day on which the notice of proceedings is served (s.129(1)). If the tenant does make such a request the landlord is then under a statutory duty to review its decision (s.129(2)). The procedure for review is contained in the Introductory Tenants (Review) Regulations 1997 which came into force on February 12, 1997 (see below). The landlord must notify the person concerned of the decision on the review; and if the decision is to confirm the original decision he must be notified of the reasons for the decision (s.129(5)). The review should be carried out and the tenant must be notified of the decision before the date specified in the notice of proceedings as the date after which proceedings for possession may be begun (s.129(6)). Notwithstanding the wording of that section reviews carried out after the time period can be valid. Whether or not it is right to quash a local authority's decision to bring proceedings is a matter of discretion depending upon all the circumstances:

"Since Section 129(6) is silent as to the consequences of a failure to comply with the time limit, whether a delay in carrying out a review will or will not be fatal to a decision to commence proceedings will turn upon the facts of the particular case. If the failure has been due to a genuine oversight which is capable of being remedied, there would seem to be no good reason to prevent a landlord from remedying the omission. The underlying purpose of the provision is to ensure that before commencing proceedings, the landlord will have all the information that the tenant wishes to place before him to hand, and be able to review the appropriateness of commencing proceedings in the light of the most recent information from the tenant. It seems to me that those objectives are capable of being achieved, even though a review is carried out, as in the present case, after the expiration of the time limit" (R (on the application of Chelfat) v London Borough of Tower Hamlets [2006] EWHC 313 (Admin, Sullivan J. at [27]).

If on review the local authority decide to suspend their action and later decide to commence action again on different grounds, they must set out those grounds to the tenant in order that he can request a review of the new grounds (R. (Forbes) v Lambeth LBC [2003] EWHC 222).

A challenge to the authority's decision on a review under s.129 can be raised in a possession claim as well as being the subject of judicial review (see further Ch.23).

The Introductory Tenants (Review) Regulations 1997

Citation, commencement and interpretation

12.015   **1.**—(1) These Regulations may be cited as the Introductory Tenants (Review) Regulations 1997 and shall come into force on February 12, 1997.

(2) In these Regulations references to—

(a)   a tenant are to an introductory tenant; and

(b)   a landlord are to a local authority or housing action trust which has elected to operate an introductory tenancy regime.

Right to a hearing

2.   The review under section 129 of the Housing Act 1996 of the decision to seek an order for possession of a dwelling house let under an introductory tenancy shall not be by way of an oral hearing unless the tenant informs the landlord that he wishes to have such a hearing before the end of the time permitted under subsection (1) of that section to request a review of that decision.

Who is to carry out the review

3.—(1) The review shall be carried out by a person who was not involved in the decision to apply for an order for possession.

(2) Where the review of a decision made by an officer is also to be made by an officer, that officer shall be someone who is senior to the officer who made the original decision.

Review without a hearing

4.   If there is not to be a hearing the tenant may make representations in writing in connection with the review and such representations shall be considered by the landlord who shall inform the tenant of the date by which such representations must be received, which shall not be earlier than five clear days after receipt of this information by the tenant.

Review by way of a hearing

5.—(1) Subject to the provisions of this regulation, the procedure in connection with a review by way of hearing shall be such as the person hearing the review shall determine.

(2) A tenant who has requested a hearing has the right to–

(a)   be heard and to be accompanied and may be represented by another person whether that person is professionally qualified or not, and for the purposes of the proceedings any representative shall have the rights and powers which the tenant has under these Regulations;

(b)   call persons to give evidence;

(c)   put questions to any person who gives evidence at the hearing; and

(d)   make representations in writing.

Notice of hearing

6.   The landlord shall give the tenant notice of the date, time and place of the hearing, which shall be not less than five days after receipt of the request for a hearing and if the tenant has not been given such notice, the hearing may only proceed with the consent of the tenant or his representative.

Absence of tenant at hearing

7.   If any person shall fail to appear at the hearing, notice having been given to him in accordance with regulation 6, the person conducting the review may, having regard to all the circumstances including any explanation offered for the absence, proceed with the hearing notwithstanding his absence, or give such directions with a view to the conduct of the further review as that person may think proper.

Postponement of hearing

8.   A tenant may apply to the landlord requesting a postponement of the hearing and the landlord may grant or refuse the application as they see fit.

Adjournment of hearing

9.   A hearing may be adjourned by the person hearing the review at any time during the hearing on the application of the tenant, his representative, or at the motion of the person hearing the review and, if a hearing is adjourned part heard and after the adjournment the person or persons hearing the review differ from those at the first hearing, otherwise than through the operation of paragraph 7, proceedings shall be by way of a complete rehearing of the case.

Absence of person hearing the review

10.   Where more than one person is conducting the review, any hearing may, with the consent of the tenant or his representative but not otherwise, be proceeded with in the absence of one of the persons who is to determine the review.

Proceedings for possession

Housing Act 1996 section 127

(1) The landlord may only bring an introductory tenancy to an end by obtaining—   **12.016**

    (a) an order of the court for the possession of the dwelling-house; and
    (b) the execution of the order.

(1A) In such a case, the tenancy ends when the order is executed.
(2) The court shall make an order of the kind mentioned in subsection (1)(a) unless the provisions of section 128 apply.

The proceedings must not be commenced until after the date specified in the notice of proceedings for possession (s.128(5)).

Section 127(2) states that the court "shall make such an order unless the provisions of section 128 apply". Presumably that means:

(1) The court must make an order for possession if a notice under s.128 has been served and the tenant has failed to ask for a review; or

(2) A review has taken place in accordance with s.129 but the landlord has confirmed its original decision.

When carrying out the review the landlord may need to consider issues of fact. The essence of the landlord's role is to balance the needs of others against those of a tenant where allegation and counter-allegation are being made (*McLellan v Bracknell Forest Borough Council* and *R. (On the application of Gilboy) v Liverpool City Council* [2008] EWCA Civ 751, at [24]).

Where there has been a review the landlord should normally provide evidence to the court showing

"how the [review] procedure was operated in the individual case dealing with the degree of independence of the tribunal from the persons who took the original decision, the way the hearing was conducted and the reason for taking the decision to continue with the proceedings. In that the way the judge will have the information on which he can take an informed view as to whether the matter should be adjourned to allow for an application to be made for judicial review" (*R. (on the application of McLellan) v Bracknell Forest BC* [2001] EWCA Civ 1510, Waller L.J. at [103]).

However, it is not necessary to provide the evidence suggested in *McLellan* where the tenant does not attend the review hearing and the reviewing officer has no new material before him. Such evidence is most appropriate to contested review hearings (*Merton LBC v Williams* [2002] EWCA Civ 980 per Mance L.J., at [35] and [36]).

As stated above a challenge to the review can also be raised in a possession claim (see further Ch.23).

Where the court makes an order for possession the tenancy comes to an end on the execution of the order (s.127(1A)). The order must not take effect later than 14 days after the making of the order

"unless it appears to the court that exceptional hardship would be caused by requiring possession to be given up by that date; and shall not in any event be postponed to a date later than six weeks after the making of the order" (s.89 of the Housing Act 1980; para.3.034).

Assignment and death

Housing Act 1996 section 134

12.017
(1) An introductory tenancy is not capable of being assigned except in the cases mentioned in subsection (2).
(2) The exceptions are—

(a) an assignment in pursuance of an order made under—

(i) section 24 of the Matrimonial Causes Act 1973 (property adjustment orders in connection with matrimonial proceedings);

     (ii)   section 17(1) of the Matrimonial and Family Proceedings Act 1984 (property adjustment orders after overseas divorce, etc.); or

     (iii) paragraph 1 of Sch.1 to the Children Act 1989 (orders for financial relief against parents);

  (b) an assignment to a person who would be qualified to succeed the tenant if the tenant died immediately before the assignment.

(3) Subsection (1) also applies to a tenancy which is not an introductory tenancy but would be if the tenant, or where the tenancy is a joint tenancy, at least one of the tenants, were occupying or continuing to occupy the dwelling house as his only or principal home.

However, also note Sch.7 to the Family Law Act 1996 and the "transfer" of tenancies; see para.21.006.

Death

The provisions in relation to succession on death are set out in ss.131 to 133 and **12.018** s.140.

Housing Act 1996 sections 131–133, 140

131. A person is qualified to succeed the tenant under an introductory tenancy if he occupies the dwelling house as his only or principal home at the time of the tenant's death and either—

(a) he is the tenant's spouse or civil partner; or

(b) he is another member of the tenant's family and has resided with the tenant throughout the period of twelve months ending with the tenant's death;

unless, in either case, the tenant was himself a successor, as defined in section 32.

132.—(1) The tenant is himself a successor if—

(a) the tenancy vested in him by virtue of section 133 (succession to introductory tenancy);

(b) he was a joint tenant and has become the sole tenant;

(c) he became the tenant on the tenancy being assigned to him (but subject to subsection (2) and (3)); or

(d) he became the tenant on the tenancy being vested in him on the death of the previous tenant.

(2) A tenant to whom the tenancy was assigned in pursuance of an order under section 24 of the Matrimonial Causes Act 1973 (property adjustment orders in connection with matrimonial proceedings) or section 17(1) of the Matrimonial and Family Proceedings Act 1984 (property adjustment orders after overseas divorce, etc.) is a successor only if the other party to the marriage was a successor.

(2A) A tenant to whom the tenancy was assigned in pursuance of an order under Part 2 of Schedule 5, or paragraph 9(2) or (3) of Schedule 7, to the Civil Partnership Act 2004 (property adjustment orders in connection with civil partnership proceedings or after overseas dissolution of civil partnership, etc.) is a successor only if the other civil partner was a successor.

(3) Where within six months of the coming to an end of an introductory tenancy ("the former tenancy") the tenant becomes a tenant under another introductory tenancy, and—

(a) the tenant was a successor in relation to the former tenancy; and

(b) under the other tenancy either the dwelling house or the landlord, or both, are the same as under the former tenancy,

the tenant is also a successor in relation to the other tenancy unless the agreement creating that tenancy otherwise provides.

133.—(1) This section applies where a tenant under an introductory tenancy dies.

(2) Where there is a person qualified to succeed the tenant, the tenancy vests by virtue of this section in that person, or if there is more than one such person in the one to be preferred in accordance with the following rules—

(a) the tenant's spouse or civil partner is to be preferred to another member of the tenant's family;

(b) of two or more other members of the tenant's family such of them is to be preferred as may be agreed between them or as may, where there is no such agreement, be selected by the landlord.

(3) Where there is no person qualified to succeed the tenant, the tenancy ceases to be an introductory tenancy—

(a) when it is vested or otherwise disposed of in the course of the administration of the tenant's estate, unless the vesting or other disposal is in pursuance of an order made under—

(i) section 24 of the Matrimonial Causes Act 1973 (property adjustment orders made in connection with matrimonial proceedings);

. . .

(iv) Part 2 of Schedule 5, or paragraph 9(2) or (3) of Schedule 7, to the Civil Partnership Act 2004 (property adjustment orders in connection with civil partnership proceedings or after overseas dissolution of civil partnership, etc.);

140.—(1) A person is a member of another's family within the meaning of this Chapter if—

(a) he is the spouse or civil partner of that person, or he and that person live together as husband and wife or as if they were civil partners; or

(b) he is that person's parent, grandparent, child, grandchild, brother, sister, uncle, aunt, nephew or niece.

(2) For the purpose of subsection (1)(b)—

(a) a relationship by marriage or civil partnership shall be treated as a relationship by blood;

(b) a relationship of the half-blood shall be treated as a relationship of the whole blood; and

(c) the stepchild of a person shall be treated as his child.

Chapter 13

Demoted Tenancies

This chapter deals with demoted tenancies (tenancies that were previously **13.001** secure) and demoted assured shorthold tenancies (tenancies that were previously assured).

Demoted secure tenancies

A tenancy that was previously secure and which has been demoted due to anti- **13.002** social behaviour (see Ch.29) is known as a "demoted tenancy" (s.143A(5)(a) as introduced by s.14 and Sch.1 of the Anti-social Behaviour Act 2003). Most of the provisions that relate to demoted tenancies are contained in ss.143A to 143P of the 1996 Act. However, some of the detail is also contained in the Housing Act 1985 as amended by the 1996 Act.

Definition

The full definition of a demoted tenancy is set out in s.143A of the 1996 Act.   **13.003**

Housing Act 1996 section 143A

143A—(1) This section applies to a periodic tenancy of a dwelling house if each of the following conditions is satisfied.
(2) The first condition is that the landlord is either a local housing authority or a housing action trust.
(3) The second condition is that the tenant condition in section 81 of the Housing Act 1985 is satisfied. [See para.10.007.]
(4) The third condition is that the tenancy is created by virtue of a demotion order under section 82A of that Act.
(5) In this Chapter—

(a) a tenancy to which this section applies is referred to as a demoted tenancy;
(b) references to demoted tenants must be construed accordingly.

Rent

It is a term of the demoted tenancy that any arrears of rent payable at the termina- **13.004** tion of the secure tenancy become payable under the demoted tenancy. It is also a term of the demoted tenancy that any rent paid in advance or overpaid at the termination of the secure tenancy is credited to the tenant's liability to pay rent under the demoted tenancy (s.82A(3)(c)(d) of the Housing Act 1985).

Other terms

13.005 The terms of the secure tenancy in relation to the name of the parties, the period of the tenancy, the amount of the rent and the date on which the rent is payable continue into the demoted tenancy (s.82A(5)). If the secure tenancy was for a fixed term the demoted tenancy becomes a weekly periodic tenancy (s.82(A)(6)).

If the landlord of the demoted tenancy serves on the tenant a statement of any other express terms of the secure tenancy which are to apply to the demoted tenancy such terms are also terms of the demoted tenancy (s.82(A)(7)).

There is also an obligation on landlords of demoted tenancies to publish and supply the tenant with a copy of information relating to the tenancy on the grant of the tenancy or as soon as practicable afterwards (see s.143M of the 1996 Act).

Duration

Standard period—12 months

13.006 The demoted tenancy does not last forever. It will generally continue for a year and if nothing untoward happens it will once again become a secure tenancy (s.143B(1)). Presumably the express terms of the secure tenancy are the same as those as under the demoted tenancy; or do they revert back to the terms under the original secure tenancy? The position is not clear but as most of the important terms are implied by statute it may not make much difference in practise.

Ceasing to be a demoted tenancy

13.007 Section 143B sets out a number of other sets of circumstances in which the tenancy ceases to be a demoted tenancy. It makes it clear that if it ceases to be demoted it does not cease to exist altogether. The continuing status of the tenancy will depend upon the circumstances. In some cases it will become secure again. In others it might simply become a common law tenancy determinable by notice to quit.

> (1) The tenancy will cease to be a demoted tenancy if either of the first or second conditions in s.143A ceases to be satisfied, i.e. the landlord ceases to be a local housing authority or a housing action trust or the tenant condition ceases to be satisfied (s.143B(2)(a)). The sort of tenancy it will become will depend upon the particular circumstances.
>
> (2) The tenancy will cease to be a demoted tenancy if the demotion order is quashed (s.143B(2)(a)—in which case it presumably becomes secure again) or if the tenant dies and no one is entitled to succeed to the tenancy (s.143B(2)(c)—in which case it presumably becomes an ordinary common law tenancy terminable by notice to quit—see para.3.002).

Extension of 12-month period

If the landlord serves a notice of proceedings for possession (see para.13.009) the **13.008** tenancy continues as a demoted tenancy until the end of the one year demotion period or (if later) until any of the following occurs:

- The notice of proceedings is withdrawn by the landlord.

- The proceedings are determined in favour of the tenant.

- The period of six months beginning with the date on which the notice is served ends and no proceedings for possession have been brought s.143B(3)(4)).

Housing Act 1996 section 143B

143B—(1) A demoted tenancy becomes a secure tenancy at the end of the period of one year (the demotion period) starting with the day the demotion order takes effect; but this is subject to subsections (2) to (5).

(2) A tenancy ceases to be a demoted tenancy if any of the following paragraphs applies—

    (a) either of the first or second conditions in section 143A ceases to be satisfied;

    (b) the demotion order is quashed;

    (c) the tenant dies and no one is entitled to succeed to the tenancy.

(3) If at any time before the end of the demotion period the landlord serves a notice of proceedings for possession of the dwelling house subsection (4) applies.

(4) The tenancy continues as a demoted tenancy until the end of the demotion period or (if later) until any of the following occurs—

    (a) the notice of proceedings is withdrawn by the landlord;

    (b) the proceedings are determined in favour of the tenant;

    (c) the period of six months beginning with the date on which the notice is served ends and no proceedings for possession have been brought.

(5) A tenancy does not come to an end merely because it ceases to be a demoted tenancy.

Notice of proceedings for possession

If the landlord wishes to bring a demoted tenancy to an end it must first serve a **13.009** notice of proceedings under s.143E of the 1996 Act (s.143E(1)). The notice must:

- state that the court will be asked to make an order for the possession of the dwelling-house;

- set out the reasons for the landlord's decision to apply for the order (see further below);

- specify the date after which proceedings for the possession of the dwelling-house may be begun. The date must not be earlier than the date on which the tenancy could be brought to an end by notice to quit (if it were a common law tenancy) given by the landlord on the same date as the notice of proceedings (the proceedings must not be begun before the date specified);

- inform the tenant of this right to request a review of the landlord's decision and that any such request must be made before the end of the period of 14 days beginning with the date of service of the notice for possession. The notice should also inform the tenant that if he wants the review to take place by oral hearing he should tell the landlord within the same period of 14 days. This is not a statutory requirement. However, under the regulations that relate to review (see below) any request for an oral review must be made within the same period of 14 days. Not to give notice of the time-limit might constitute a breach of art.6 of the ECHR;

- inform the tenant that if he needs help or advice about the notice or what to do about the notice "he must take the notice immediately to a Citizen's Advice Bureau, a housing aid centre, a law centre or a solicitor".

The demoted tenancy will have been created because of anti-social behaviour (see para.29.058). However, there is nothing in the statutory requirements stating that the reasons for serving the notice of proceedings for possession need have anything to do with anti-social behaviour. For example, the landlord may decide to terminate the demoted tenancy because rent arrears have started to accrue. Presumably any reasons can be given so long as they are not so unreasonable as to be susceptible to judicial review, or disproportionate to be a breach of art.8 (see Ch.23).

Review of decision to seek possession

Request for review

13.010   A tenant who wishes to review the decision to seek possession must make the request for the review before the end of the period of 14 days beginning with the date of service of the notice of possession (s.143F(1)). There is no special form that the request need take. There is no specific provision defining service, which therefore presumably means that service takes place at the time at which the notice is received by the tenant.

If a request for review of the decision is made the landlord must review its decision (s.143F(2)). The procedure for review is set out in the Demoted Tenancies (Review of Decisions) (England) Regulations (SI 2004/1679) and the Demoted Tenancies (Review of Decisions) (Wales) Regulations 2005 (SI 2005/1228 W.86)). These regulations are not contrary to art.6 of the European Convention on Human Rights (*R. (On the application of Gilboy) v Liverpool City Council* [2008] EWCA Civ 751).

Person who may carry out the review

13.011   The review must be carried out by a person who was not involved in that decision. Where the decision to seek possession was made by an officer of the landlord and the review is to be carried out by another officer the latter must "occupy a more senior position within the organisation of the landlord" (reg.2). It is implicit in the rules (although not expressly stated) that more than one person can be involved in the review (see reg.9(2)).

Notice of the review

The landlord must give the tenant not less than five clear days' notice of the **13.012** review (reg.3). If there is to be an oral hearing that notice must also inform the tenant of the time and place at which the review will be heard (reg.4(3)).

Right to an oral hearing

The tenant has the right to an oral hearing. Any request for an oral hearing must **13.013** be made by the tenant to the landlord within the same period of 14 days for serving the request for a review of the decision (reg.4(1)(2)).

Tenant's representations

Whether or not the review is to be by way of an oral hearing the tenant is entitled **13.014** to make written representations to the landlord in connection with the review. They must be received by the landlord not less than two clear days before the date of the review. The landlord must consider any such representations which are received by that date (reg.5).

Oral hearing

Where the review does take place by way of an oral hearing the tenant has a right **13.015** to be heard and to be accompanied or represented by another person (whether or not that person is professionally qualified). The tenant or the representative may call persons to give evidence and put questions to any person who gives evidence at the hearing (reg.6).

Subject to the express requirements of the regulations, the person carrying out the review may determine the procedure to be adopted at the hearing (reg.6(3)).

If proper notice of the oral hearing has been given in accordance with the regulations and neither the tenant nor his representative appears at the hearing the person carrying out the review "may, having regard to all the circumstances" (a) proceed with the hearing or (b) give such directions with a view to the conduct of the review as he considers appropriate (reg.7(2)).

Postponement of hearing

The tenant may request the landlord to postpone a hearing of which notice has **13.016** been given in accordance with the regulations and the landlord may grant or refuse the request. If the hearing is postponed the landlord must give the tenant reasonable notice of the date, time and place of the postponed hearing (reg.8).

Adjournment of the hearing

A hearing may be adjourned by the person carrying out the review at any time, **13.017** either on that person's own initiative or at the request of the tenant, his representative or the landlord.

Where more than one person is carrying out the review by way of an oral hearing, the hearing must be adjourned on each occasion on which any of those persons is absent, unless the tenant or his representative agrees otherwise.

The landlord must give the tenant reasonable notice of the date, time and place of the adjourned hearing.

If the person carrying out the review at the adjourned hearing is not the same person as the person who was carrying out the review at the earlier hearing the review must proceed by way of a complete rehearing of the case unless the tenant, or his representative, agrees otherwise (reg.9).

Proceedings for possession

Order of the court required

13.018 The landlord may only bring a demoted tenancy to an end by obtaining an order of the court for possession of the dwelling-house (s.143D(1)). The proceedings for possession must be brought under the procedure in Pt 55—see Ch.25 (CPR PD 65 para.10.1).

Date for commencement of the proceedings

13.019 The court must "not entertain proceedings begun on or before the date specified in the notice as the date after which proceedings for possession may be begun" (s.143E(4)).

Tenancy ceases to be a demoted tenancy during proceedings

13.020 If the landlord begins proceedings for possession but before those proceedings have been completed the tenancy ceases to be a demoted tenancy by reason of one of the grounds set out in paras (a) to (c) of s.143B(2), the tenancy seemingly becomes a secure tenancy again (s.143G(3)) but the landlord (or the new landlord as the case may be) may nonetheless continue the proceedings (s.143G(2)(3)).

(It would seem that the same position applies if the demotion period ends (see s.143G(1)(a)—i.e. that the landlord can continue with the proceedings—but it is not expressly spelt out in s.143G. Are there some words missing from sub-para.(2) that should have referred to s.143G(1)(a))?).

If the tenancy does cease to be a demoted tenancy and becomes a secure tenancy (s.143G(3)) the tenant is nonetheless not entitled to exercise the right to buy unless the proceedings are finally determined and he is not required to give up possession of the dwelling-house. The proceedings are treated as finally determined if (a) they are withdrawn, (b) any appeal is abandoned or (c) the time for appealing expires within an appeal being brought (s.143G(4)(5)).

The court's decision

13.021 The court must make an order for possession "unless it thinks that the procedure [for notice and review contained in] sections 143E and 143F has not been followed" (s.143D(2)). Presumably if the court is not sure it will require further evidence on the point.

The order

Where the court makes an order for possession the tenancy comes to an end when **13.022** the order is executed (s.143D(1A)). The order must not take effect later than 14 days after the making of the order

> "unless it appears to the court that exceptional hardship would be caused by requiring possession to be given up by that date; and shall not in any event be postponed to a date later than six weeks after the making of the order" (s.89 of the Housing Act 1980; para.3.034).

Assignment and death

Assignment by landlord

The position of the tenancy in the event of a transfer of the landlord's interest is **13.023** dealt with in s.143C of the 1996 Act. The type of tenancy it becomes depends upon the type of landlord to whom the property is transferred.

(1) The tenancy will continue to be a demoted tenancy for the duration of the demotion period if:

    a. at the time the demoted tenancy is created the interest of the landlord belongs to a local housing authority or a housing action trust; and

    b. during the demotion period the interest of the landlord transfers to another person who is a local housing authority or a housing action trust.

(2) The tenancy becomes an assured tenancy if:

    a. at the time the demoted tenancy is created the interest of the landlord belongs to a local housing authority or a housing action trust; and

    b. during the demotion period the interest of the landlord transfers to a person who is a registered social landlord or a person who does not satisfy the landlord condition as defined in s.80 of the Housing Act 1985 (see para.10.005).

(3) The tenancy becomes a secure tenancy if:

    a. at the time the demoted tenancy is created the interest of the landlord belongs to a local housing authority or a housing action trust; and

    b. during the demotion period the interest of the landlord transfers to a person who is not a registered social landlord or a person who does satisfy the landlord condition as defined in s.80 of the Housing Act 1985 (see para.10.005).

Assignment by tenant

A demoted tenancy is not capable of being assigned except in pursuance of an **13.024** order made under:

- s.24 of the Matrimonial Causes Act 1973 (property adjustment orders in connection with matrimonial proceedings);

- s.17(1) of the Matrimonial and Family Proceedings Act 1984 (property adjustment orders after overseas divorce etc.);

- para.1 of Sch.1 to the Children Act 1989 (orders for financial relief against parents). (Section 143K of the 1996 Act.)

Death of tenant

13.025 The provisions in relation to succession on death are set out in ss.143H to 143J and s.143P of the 1996 Act.

Succession to demoted tenancy

13.026   **143H**—(1) This section applies if the tenant under a demoted tenancy dies.
(2) If the tenant was a successor, the tenancy—

    (a) ceases to be a demoted tenancy; but
    (b) does not become a secure tenancy.

(3) In any other case a person is qualified to succeed the tenant if—

    (a) he occupies the dwelling house as his only or principal home at the time of the tenant's death;
    (b) he is a member of the tenants family; and
    (c) he has resided with the tenant throughout the period of 12 months ending with the tenant's death.

(4) If only one person is qualified to succeed under subsection (3) the tenancy vests in him by virtue of this section.
(5) If there is more than one such person the tenancy vests by virtue of this section in the person preferred in accordance with the following rules—

    (a) the tenant's spouse or civil partner or (if the tenant has neither spouse nor civil partner) the person mentioned in section 143P(1)(b) is to be preferred to another member of the tenant's family;
    (b) if there are two or more other members of the tenant's family the person preferred may be agreed between them or (if there is no such agreement) selected by the landlord.

No successor tenant: termination

13.027   **143I**—(1) This section applies if the demoted tenant dies and no person is qualified to succeed to the tenancy as mentioned in section 143H(3).
(2) The tenancy ceases to be a demoted tenancy if either subsection (3) or (4) applies.
(3) This subsection applies if the tenancy is vested or otherwise disposed of in the course of the administration of the tenant's estate unless the vesting or other disposal is in pursuance of an order under—

    (a) section 23A or 24 of the Matrimonial Causes Act 1973 (property adjustment orders in connection with matrimonial proceedings);
    (b) section 17(1) of the Matrimonial and Family Proceedings Act 1984 (property adjustment orders after overseas divorce, etc.);

(c) paragraph 1 of Schedule 1 to the Children Act 1989 (orders for financial relief against parents);

(d) Part 2 of Schedule 5, or paragraph 9(2) or (3) of Schedule 7, to the Civil Partnership Act 2004 (property adjustment orders in connection with civil partnership proceedings or after overseas dissolution of civil partnership, etc.).

(4) This subsection applies if it is known that when the tenancy is vested or otherwise disposed of in the course of the administration of the tenant's estate it will not be in pursuance of an order mentioned in subsection (3).

(5) A tenancy which ceases to be a demoted tenancy by virtue of this section cannot subsequently become a secure tenancy.

Successor tenants

143J—(1) This section applies for the purpose of sections 143H and 143I.   **13.028**

(2) A person is a successor to a secure tenancy which is terminated by a demotion order if any of subsections (3) to (6) applies to him.

(3) The tenancy vested in him—

(a) by virtue of section 89 of the Housing Act 1985 or section 133 of this Act;

(b) under the will or intestacy of the preceding tenant.

(4) The tenancy arose by virtue of section 86 of the Housing Act 1985 and the original fixed term was granted—

(a) to another person; or

(b) to him jointly with another person.

(5) He became the tenant on the tenancy being assigned to him unless—

(a) the tenancy was assigned—

(i) in proceedings under section 24 of the Matrimonial Causes Act 1973 (property adjustment orders in connection with matrimonial proceedings) or section 17(1) of the Matrimonial and Family Proceedings Act 1984 (property adjustment orders after overseas divorce, etc.); or

(ii) in proceedings under Part 2 of Schedule 5, or paragraph 9(2) or (3) of Schedule 7, to the Civil Partnership Act 2004 (property adjustment orders in connection with civil partnership proceedings or after overseas dissolution of civil partnership, etc.).

(b) where the tenancy was assigned as mentioned in paragraph (a)(i), neither he nor the other party to the marriage was a successor; and

(c) where the tenancy was assigned as mentioned in paragraph (a)(ii), neither he nor the other civil partner was a successor.

(6) He became the tenant on assignment under section 92 of the Housing Act 1985 if he himself was a successor to the tenancy which he assigned in exchange.

(7) A person is the successor to a demoted tenancy if the tenancy vested in him by virtue of section 143H(4) or (5).

(8) A person is the successor to a joint tenancy if he has become the sole tenant.

Members of a person's family

143P—(1) For the purposes of this Chapter a person is a member of another's family if— **13.029**

(a) he is the spouse or civil partner of that person;

(b) he and that person live together as a couple in an enduring family relationship, but he does not fall within paragraph (c);

(c) he is that person's parent, grandparent, child, grandchild, brother, sister, uncle, aunt, nephew or niece.

(2) For the purposes of subsgraph (1)(b) it is immaterial that two persons living together in an enduring family relationship are of the same sex.

(3) For the purposes of subsgraph (1)(c)—

(a) a relationship by marriage or civil partnership must be treated as a relationship by blood;

(b) a relationship of the half-blood must be treated as a relationship of the whole blood;

(c) a stepchild of a person must be treated as his child.

Demoted assured shorthold tenancies

13.030 A tenancy that was previously assured and which has been demoted due to anti-social behaviour (see Ch.29) is known as a "demoted assured shorthold tenancy" (s.20B of the Housing Act 1988 as introduced by s.15 of the Anti-social Behaviour Act 2003).

The advantage to the landlord is that during the demotion period the tenant can be removed using the s.21 procedure at any time that the landlord wants. The usual six-month rule that an order for possession cannot take effect during the first six months of the tenancy does not even apply. Nor is the landlord required to go through any review procedure such as applies where the tenancy is a demoted secure tenancy (see above).

Landlords

13.031 Only a private registered provider of social housing or a registered social landlord can be a landlord of a demoted assured shorthold tenancy (s.20B(1)(b)) of the 1988 Act). Registered social landlord has the same meaning as in Pt 1 of the Housing Act 1996 (s.20B(5)).

Terms

Rent

13.032 It is a term of the demoted tenancy that any arrears of rent payable at the termination of the assured tenancy become payable under the demoted tenancy. It is also a term that any rent paid in advance or overpaid at the termination of the assured tenancy is credited to the tenant's liability to pay under the demoted tenancy.

Other terms

13.033 The terms of the assured tenancy in relation to the name of the parties, the period of the tenancy, the amount of the rent and the date on which the rent is payable continue into the demoted tenancy (s.82A(5)). If the assured tenancy was for a fixed term the demoted tenancy becomes a weekly periodic tenancy (s.82(A)(6)).

If the landlord of the demoted tenancy serves on the tenant a statement of any other express terms of the assured tenancy which are to apply to the demoted tenancy such terms are also terms of the demoted tenancy (s.82(A)(7)).

Duration of demoted tenancy

The tenancy continues to be demoted for a period of one year starting with the day **13.034** when the demotion order takes effect. After that period has expired the tenancy ceases to be an assured shorthold tenancy and once again becomes an ordinary assured tenancy (s.20B(2) and para.5A of Sch.2A to the 1988 Act as inserted by s.15(3) of the 2003 Act) unless before that period of one year has expired the landlord gives notice of proceedings for possession of the dwelling-house under s.21 (as to which see para.7.013).

If the landlord does serve a s.21 notice the tenancy continues to be a demoted assured shorthold tenancy until the one-year period has passed or (if later) until one of the following occurs:

- the notice of proceedings for possession is withdrawn;

- the proceedings are determined in favour of the tenant;

- the period of six months beginning with the date on which the notice is given ends and no proceedings for possession have been brought.

If one of the above occurs the tenancy once again reverts to being an ordinary assured tenancy (see s.20B(4)) and para.5A of Sch.2A to the 1988 Act as introduced by s.15(3) of the 2003 Act). It is not clear whether the express terms of the assured tenancy (other than rent and duration) are those that applied under the original assured tenancy or those that applied under the demoted tenancy. This is because, as stated above (para.13.005) the landlord during the period of the demoted tenancy may serve a statement of express terms that is more limited than those in the original tenancy.

If proceedings for possession are brought and proceeded with the normal six-month rule in s.21(5), i.e. that the order may not take effect earlier than six months after the beginning of the tenancy (see para.7.013) does not apply (s.21(5A) as introduced by s.15(2) of the 2003 Act).

Chapter 14

Shared Accommodation and Resident Landlords

Shared accommodation

The tenant may share all or part of his accommodation with his landlord, with **14.001**
other tenants or with his own tenants or lodgers. The effect of the sharing on the
relationship between the different parties and their respective rights to terminate
and claim possession are dealt with in this chapter.

Introduction: sharing "essential living accommodation"

As seen in Chs 6, 8 and 10 it is a requirement of assured, protected and secure **14.002**
tenancies that the dwelling-house is let as a separate dwelling. This does not mean
that the rooms that are subject to the tenancy must be physically partitioned off
from the other accommodation, but that there must be a distinct unit which the
tenant is not obliged, by the agreement, to share with any other person. Thus, part
of a house may be a separate dwelling without being self-contained and even
though the rooms which the tenant is entitled to occupy are spread throughout the
house, provided that all the facilities that make it possible for a person to live there
are present (*Wimbush v Cibulia* [1949] 2 K.B. 564).

Sometimes, however, a tenant may be obliged by the tenancy agreement
to share part of his accommodation with others. If so the dwelling-house is not
being let as a separate dwelling and prima facie the tenancy is not assured,
protected or secure. However, in order to prevent the accommodation from
being assured, protected or secure the tenant must be obliged to share "essential
living accommodation". Sharing the use of a toilet or bathroom is not regarded as
the sharing of essential living accommodation for these purposes. Furthermore,
the courts have tended to ignore minor amounts of sharing, for example where
there is only a very small amount of use of the tenant's kitchen by persons
other than the tenant. (See *Goodrich v Paisner* [1957] A.C. 65; *Marsh v Cooper*
[1969] 1 W.L.R. 803.) Compare the situation where the room let to the tenant
has no cooking facilities and the tenant genuinely shares a kitchen with others
(*Central YMCA Housing Association Ltd v Saunders* (1990) 23 H.L.R. 212 CA;
Central YMCA Housing Association Ltd v Goodman (1991) 24 H.L.R. 109 CA;
see also *Uratemp Ventures Ltd v Collins* [2001] 3 W.L.R. 806 HL, dealt with
above at para.6.004).

"Tenant" sharing with the "landlord" (see Form 22)

14.003 Where a person shares accommodation with the person who has permitted him to enter into occupation he will often be a lodger in occupation under a licence (see *Street v Mountford* [1985] 2 W.L.R. 877 discussed in Ch.5; e.g. see *Huwyler v Riddy* [1996] E.G.C.S. 8 CA). Once the licence has been determined the licensor will be entitled to an order for possession which may not be suspended for more than 14 days (six weeks in cases of exceptional hardship): s.89 of the Housing Act 1980 (para.3.034).

If the occupier is a tenant, he will nonetheless not be an assured or, as the case may be, a protected tenant if he shares "essential living accommodation" with the landlord (see above). A landlord cannot move into the property after it has been let to a tenant without a clear and express term to that effect in the tenancy agreement (see *Miller v Eyo* (1998) 31 M.L.R. 315). However, in any case where the Rent Act 1977 continues to apply, if the rent includes payment for the use of furniture or services, which will usually be the case, the tenant will be an occupier under a restricted contract and the rules as to termination and postponement of orders for possession that apply to restricted contracts (see Ch.9) will apply (s.21 of the Rent Act 1977).

Tenant sharing part with other persons given the right to occupy by the landlord

14.004 Where a "tenant" is required to share with other "tenants" it is possible that they will be regarded as licensees (see para.5.004). However, where the "tenant" is truly a tenant his right to remain in occupation is regulated by statutory provisions.

Where a tenant, whose status is governed by the Housing Act 1988, shares part of his "essential living accommodation" with any person other than his landlord the part that he does not share is deemed to be a dwelling-house let on an assured tenancy (Housing Act 1988 s.3(1)) e.g. *Miller v Eyo*. The landlord cannot therefore obtain possession of that part without proving a Housing Act ground for possession. There are also provisions to protect him in his use of the shared accommodation while he is in occupation of the part that he does not share. If the landlord wishes to terminate or vary the tenant's right to use the shared accommodation he must make an application to the county court (Housing Act 1988 s.10(3)).

Similar rules apply to tenancies governed by the Rent Act 1977 (see s.22).

Form 22: Particulars to be inserted on Form N119—shared accommodation with landlord

1. By an oral agreement made on or about the [*insert date*] the Claimant agreed to allow the Defendant to share occupation of the dwelling house with the Claimant for the sum of £ [*state amount*] per week payable in [*advance/arrears*] each [*state which day of the week*] day. Under the terms of the said agreement the Defendant had the use of one bedroom and the shared use of the bathroom and kitchen facilities.

2. In the premises, the Defendant was a licensee of the Claimant in the dwelling house. In the alternative, the Defendant was a tenant of the Claimant but by reason of the said sharing with the Plaintiff the said tenancy is not an assured tenancy.

3. The said licence (or, in the alternative) tenancy was determined by a notice to quit served on the Defendant on or about [*insert date*], which said notice expired on the day on which a complete period of the said tenancy expired next after the end of four weeks from service of the said notice.

4. Despite the said revocation and despite service of the said notice the Defendant remains in occupation of the dwelling house, without the licence or consent of the Claimant.

5. The Defendant has failed to make any payments to the Claimant since the [*insert date*] AND the Claimant claims:

Housing Act 1988 sections 3 and 10

3.—(1) Where a tenant has the exclusive occupation of any accommodation (in this **14.005**
section referred to as "the separate accommodation") and—

    (a) the terms as between the tenant and his landlord on which he holds
the separate accommodation include the use of other accommodation
(in this section referred to as "the shared accommodation") in common with
another person or other persons, not being or including the landlord; and

    (b) by reason only of the circumstances mentioned in para.(a) above, the sepa-
rate accommodation would not, apart from this section, be a dwelling house
let on an assured tenancy,

    the separate accommodation shall be deemed to be a dwelling house let
on an assured tenancy and the following provisions of this section shall have
effect.

  (2) For the avoidance of doubt it is hereby declared that where, for the purpose of
determining the rateable value of the separate accommodation, it is necessary to
make an apportionment under Part II of Schedule 1 to this Act, regard is to be had
to the circumstances mentioned in subsection (1)(a) above.

  (3) While the tenant is in possession of the separate accommodation, any term of the
tenancy terminating or modifying, or providing for the termination or modification
of, his right to the use of any of the shared accommodation which is living accommodation shall be of no effect.

  (4) Where the terms of the tenancy are such that, at any time during the tenancy, the
persons in common with whom the tenant is entitled to the use of the shared
accommodation could be varied or their number could be increased, nothing in
subs.(3) above shall prevent those terms from having effect so far as they relate to
any such variation or increase.

  (5) In this section "living accommodation" means accommodation of such a nature
that the fact that it constitutes or is included in the shared accommodation is sufficient, apart from this section, to prevent the tenancy from constituting an assured
tenancy of a dwelling house.

    . . .

10.—(1) This section applies in a case falling within subsection (1) of section 3 above
and expressions used in this section have the same meaning as in that section.

  (2) Without prejudice to the enforcement of any order made under subsection (3)
below, while the tenant is in possession of the separate accommodation, no order
shall be made for possession of any of the shared accommodation, whether on the
application of the immediate landlord of the tenant or on the application of any
person under whom that landlord derives title, unless a like order has been made,
or is made at the same time, in respect of the separate accommodation; and the
provisions of s.6 above shall have effect accordingly.

  (3) On the application of the landlord, the court may make such order as it thinks just
either—

    (a) terminating the right of the tenant to use the whole or any part of the shared
accommodation other than living accommodation; or

    (b) modifying his right to use the whole or any part of the shared accommoda-
tion, whether on the application of the immediate landlord of number of
persons entitled to the use of that accommodation or otherwise.

  (4) No order shall be made under subsection (3) above so as to effect any termination
or modification of the rights of the tenant which, apart from section 3(3) above,
could not be effected by or under the terms of the tenancy.

Joint tenants

14.006 Where the tenant shares the whole of the dwelling-house with a joint tenant neither may evict the other save in matrimonial and quasimatrimonial proceedings pursuant to the provisions of the Family Law Act 1996 (see further para.21.001).

Tenant sharing with sub-tenants or licensees

14.007 Where an assured tenant or a protected or statutory tenant sub-lets part of the accommodation he does not lose his protection under the Housing Act or Rent Act (s.4 of the Housing Act 1988; s.23 of the Rent Act 1977; see also *Baker v Turner* [1950] A.C. 401). However, the landlord may be able to obtain possession under Ground 12 of Sch.2 to the Housing Act 1988 or, as the case may be, Case 1 of Sch.15 to the Rent Act 1977 if the tenancy agreement contains a covenant against sub-letting of part of the premises.

For the position of secure tenants who sub-let, part with possession or take in lodgers, see para.10.026.

Where a tenant (of any type) shares occupation of his accommodation with another, that other person will invariably be a licensee. For an example see *Monmouth Borough Council v Marlog* [1994] 2 E.G.L.R. 68 CA where the tenant went into occupation and used one bedroom, accompanied by the defendant and her two children who used two bedrooms. The kitchen, bathroom and living accommodation were shared:

> "Where two persons move into residential premises together under a tenancy granted to one but not the other of them, each occupying a bedroom or bedrooms and the remainder of the premises being shared between them, the court will be slow to infer a common intention that the one who is not the tenant shall be the sub-tenant of the one who is. The natural inference is that what is intended is a contractual house-sharing arrangement under the tenancy of one of them. The inference is greatly strengthened where, as in the present case, there is a written agreement between the landlord and tenant and none between the tenant and the other occupant" (per Nourse L.J. at 70D).

14.008 However, even where the person sharing accommodation with the tenant can be construed as a sub-tenant, the tenant will, as against the sub-tenant, be a sharing landlord (see above) or a resident landlord (see below). Where the arrangement was entered into prior to the commencement of the 1988 Act (i.e. January 15, 1989) or pursuant to a contract entered into before commencement of the Act the lodger or sub-tenant will be in occupation under a restricted contract whether or not the rent includes payment for use of furniture or for services (ss.20 and 21 of the Rent Act 1977) but only so long as the tenant is in "exclusive occupation" of some part of the property (s.19(6)). However, except in the limited case where the person has entered into occupation pursuant to an agreement made before the commencement of the 1988 Act no right of occupation thereafter can be a restricted contract (s.36 of the Housing Act 1988).

Resident landlords

14.009 Where the landlord of a dwelling-house is a "resident landlord" the tenant is not an assured tenant under the Housing Act 1988 or, as the case may be, a protected tenant as defined in s.1 of the Rent Act 1977. The situation discussed here is one step removed from the situation discussed under the heading: "Tenant" sharing with the "Landlord". The landlord and the tenant live in the same building but they each have their own "separate dwelling". In some cases they may live in the same flat, in a purpose-built block of flats, which is big enough to be divided into two separate dwelling-houses. In these circumstances the resident landlord rules will also apply.

In so far as the Housing Act 1988 is concerned the provisions for determining whether the tenancy is precluded from being assured on the resident landlord ground are found in para.10 and Pt III of Sch.1 to the 1988 Act. In Rent Act cases the position is governed by s.12 and Sch.1 of the Rent Act 1977.

This chapter deals with the resident landlord exception under both the Housing Act 1988 and the Rent Act 1977. The main difference to note is that in a Rent Act case a tenant who is not protected by reason of this exception will be a person occupying under a restricted contract (s.20 of the Rent Act 1977); in a Housing Act case it is not possible for there to be a restricted contract (s.36 of the Housing Act 1988; see para.9.001). In a Housing Act case, note also that the landlord is required to occupy the residence as his "only or principal home" (at [10(1)(b)]).

Definition of resident landlord—Housing Act 1988

The landlord will only be a resident landlord and the tenant will only thereby be **14.010** excluded from protection under the Housing Act 1988 if the following conditions are satisfied:

(1) Dwelling-house only part of a building (Sch.10 para.10(1)(a)). The dwelling-house must form part only of a building and that building must not be a purpose-built block of flats. A building is a purpose-built block of flats if, as constructed, it contained, and it still contains, two or more flats; "flat" means a dwelling-house which (a) forms part only of a building and (b) is separated horizontally from another dwelling-house which forms part of the same building. A "conversion" is not a purpose-built block of flats (*Barnes v Gorsuch* (1981) 43 P. & C.R. 294).

(2) Landlord resident in another dwelling in the building. The tenancy must have been granted by a person who, at the time that he granted it and at all times since, has occupied, as his only or principal home, another dwelling-house which also forms part of the same building (or flat). Where the landlord's interest is owned by trustees under a trust for sale the case is deemed to be a resident landlord case if the proceeds of sale are held on trust for any person who occupies another dwelling-house in the building (or flat) (Sch.1 para.18). Where the tenancy was granted by joint owners, only one of whom was residing on the premises, the tenant is not protected (Sch.1 para.17(2)).

Definition of resident landlord—Rent Act 1977

The landlord will only be a resident landlord and the tenant will only thereby be **14.011** excluded from protection under s.1 of the Rent Act 1977 if the following three conditions are satisfied:

(1) Date of grant (s.12(1) of the Rent Act 1977). The tenancy must have been granted on or after August 14, 1974. Where the tenancy was granted prior to that date and it was already protected under the law existing at that time (i.e. because the premises were unfurnished) it remained protected even though the landlord was resident at the date of the grant and has been ever since. If the tenancy was furnished and therefore unprotected prior to August 14, 1974 it remained unprotected thereafter if the landlord was resident but became protected if the landlord was not. (See Sch.24 paras 6, 7 of the Rent Act 1977.) As to whether the tenancy was furnished or not see *Woodward v Docherly* [1974] 1 W.L.R. 966.

(2) Dwelling-house only part of a building (s.12(1)(a) and Sch.2 para.4) (see above). Where the tenancy was granted on or after November 28, 1980 and the landlord and the tenant both live in the same flat which is divided into two or more separate dwelling-houses, with the landlord living in one dwelling-house and the tenant living in another, the landlord will be a "resident landlord" even if the building in which the flat is situated is a purpose-built block of flats.

(3) Landlord resident in another dwelling in the building. The tenancy must have been granted by a person who, at the time that he granted it and at all times since, has occupied, as his residence, another dwelling-house which also forms part of the same building (or flat). (In *Barnatt v O'Sullivan* [1994] 1 W.L.R. 1667 CA, the tenant moved into the flat one week before the landlord took up residence in the same house. It was however part of a planned move from another nearby property where both parties resided and it was held that the landlord qualified as a resident landlord.) Where the landlord's interest is owned by trustees under a trust for sale the case is deemed to be a resident landlord case if the proceeds of sale are held on trust for any person who occupies another dwelling-house in the building (or flat): Sch.2 para.2. Where the tenancy was granted by joint owners, only one of whom was residing on the premises, s.12 applies and the tenant is not protected (*Cooper v Tait* (1984) 48 P. & C.R. 460). Paragraph 5 of Sch.2 provides that a person is to be treated as occupying a dwelling-house as his residence for the purposes of s.12 if, so far as the nature of the case allows, he fulfils the same conditions as are required to be fulfilled by a person who claims to be a statutory tenant. A resident landlord may therefore have two homes or he may remain a resident landlord despite temporary absences; but the dwelling-house must be a home for him to be able to rely upon the resident landlord exception. This subject is discussed in detail in relation to statutory tenants in Ch.8, see para.8.022.

For a case in which the principles were applied to a resident landlord see *Palmer v McNamara* [1991] 1 E.G.L.R. 121 CA: room retained by landlord did not contain a cooker. He either bought food he did not need to cook, or take-away meals. He spent his days in the room and kept all his belongings there. He slept elsewhere because for health reasons he needed help dressing and undressing. The Court of Appeal refused to interfere with the judge's finding of fact that the landlord occupied the premises as a home.

General

Whether or not the landlord's dwelling-house and the tenant's dwelling-house **14.012**
form part of the same building is a question of fact, but in deciding this question
the court will pay regard to the intention of the exclusions which is to allow the
landlord to remove a tenant who lives in close proximity to him.

> "The English word 'building' covers an immense range of all sorts of structures. It is an
> ordinary English word, and its meaning must therefore be a question of fact, always
> assuming that the court directs itself correctly as to the intention and meaning of the
> statute which uses it. As a matter of law, to give a defined or precise meaning to the word
> 'building' is an impossibility. It is beyond the capacity of even the most consummate
> master of the English language to do so. This itself is, in my judgment, an indication that
> Parliament is leaving the question of fact to the judge . . .
>
> I have no doubt that the intention of Parliament in enacting [s.12] was to relieve land-
> lords where it was reasonable to do so . . . [T]he mischief at which the section was aimed
> was the mischief of that sort of social embarrassment arising out of close proximity—
> close proximity which the landlord had accepted in the belief that he could bring it to an
> end at any time allowed by the contract of tenancy" (per Scarman L.J. in *Bardrick v
> Haycock* (1976) 31 P. & C.R. 420 at 424).

Thus, in a case where the landlord lived in a self-contained unit attached to the
end of a building with no interconnecting door it was held that the exception did
not apply (*Bardrick v Haycock* (1976) 31 P. & C.R. 420). Compare *Griffiths v
English* (1982) 261 E.G. 257 where the landlord was the owner of a house with an
extension built on each side. The landlord lived in one extension and the tenant in
the other. It was held that s.12 applied.

In *Lewis-Graham v Conacher* [1992] 1 E.G.L.R. 112 CA an extension which
was originally a granny flat and garage had been added to a semi-detached house.
It had interconnecting doors between the house and the extension which were
locked. There was a common gas supply, electricity supply and water supply. At
that stage there was clearly one building. The landlord started carrying out works,
to separate the two dwellings into two separate "buildings", after service of the
notice to quit but had not completed them by the time the notice to quit had
expired. The Court of Appeal refused to interfere with the judge's finding of fact
that at that date there was still one building, and in any event may not have constituted two buildings after the works had been finished:

> "For my part I am not entirely convinced that, even when the building work was finished,
> this would have amounted to two buildings rather than one. Where something has been
> built as an extension to an existing house, where the other walls are continuous and the
> roofs are contiguous, it may be that it still remains as one building, notwithstanding that
> it was intended to be two separate dwellings. Be that as it may, for my part I would not
> interfere with the learned judge's finding of fact" (per Stuart-Smith L.J. at 112K).

Exclusions

The exclusion does not apply in Housing Act cases where the tenancy was granted **14.013**
to a person who immediately before it was granted was an assured tenant of that
dwelling-house or of any other dwelling-house in the same building (or flat) of the
same landlord (Sch.1 para.10(3)). This prevents landlords avoiding the effect of the
Housing Act 1988 by entering into occupation of a dwelling-house in the building

(or flat) and then granting to the tenant a new tenancy of his dwelling-house or of another dwelling-house in the building (or flat). Similar provisions apply to the Rent Act 1977. (See s.12(2) as amended by s.69(4) of the Housing Act 1980.)

Prior to November 28, 1980 (when s.12 of the Rent Act 1977 was amended by the Housing Act 1980) a landlord who granted a fixed-term tenancy in succession to another fixed term of the same dwelling-house or of any other dwelling-house in the same building could not take advantage of the resident landlord exception. This rule has now been repealed but any tenancy that was protected by reason of it prior to November 28, 1980 continues to be protected (s.69(4) and Sch.25 para.67 of the Housing Act 1980).

Termination and recovery (see Form 22)

14.014 The tenancy is brought to an end in one of the normal ways, i.e. by notice to quit, forfeiture, effluxion of time or surrender. Thereafter the tenant's right to remain in possession is very limited. In a Rent Act situation, he will not have been a protected tenant and so no statutory tenancy arises. At the hearing of the possession claim the landlord need only prove that he is a resident landlord and that the tenancy has been determined.

In Rent Act case, s.20 does, however, provide that if and so long as a tenancy is, by virtue of the resident landlord exception, precluded from being a protected tenancy it is to be treated as a restricted contract notwithstanding that the rent may not include payments for the use of furniture or for services. Thus, where the tenancy was created after November 28, 1980 the court will be able to stay or suspend execution of the order or postpone the date of possession for up to three months. As with other restricted contracts the court will have to impose conditions as to the payment of rent, etc. unless to do so would cause exceptional hardship or would otherwise be unreasonable (s.106A of the Rent Act 1977). Where the tenancy was created before November 28, 1980 the tenant will be able to apply to the rent tribunal pursuant to ss.103–106 of the Rent Act 1977 for a suspension of operation of the notice to quit. If the notice to quit has expired it is not possible to make an application to the rent tribunal (*R. v City of London Rent Tribunal Ex p. Honig* [1951] 1 K.B. 641) and the court will only be able to postpone the order for possession for up to 14 days, or six weeks in cases of exceptional hardship (s.89 of the Housing Act 1980; see para.3.034).

Assignment, bankruptcy and death

14.015 There are no special rules that apply if the tenant assigns, sub-lets, goes bankrupt or dies. The law set out in Ch.4 will generally apply although if the landlord terminates the tenancy following one of these events, perhaps by forfeiting, the court will, because the tenancy is a restricted contract, be able to suspend the order for possession for up to three months. The statutory provisions that do apply in resident landlord cases are concerned with the tenant's position on the assignment of the landlord's interest following a voluntary transfer, his bankruptcy or his death. The tenant's position is not adversely affected by these events. Indeed it may be improved, for in certain circumstances he can become a fully protected tenant.

Assignment

14.016 Where the landlord assigns his successor in title must also live in the dwelling-house throughout his period of ownership; so must any further assignee. If they do not the tenant will become a protected assured tenant (s.12(1)(c) Rent Act 1977/ Sch.1, para.10(1) of the Housing Act 1988). There are, however, periods where the failure to occupy another dwelling-house in the same building is disregarded for the purpose of deciding whether the landlord is to be regarded as resident within s.12(1)(c) of the 1977 Act/Sch.1 para.10 of the 1988 Act. These periods are set out in Sch.2 to the Rent Act 1977/Sch.1 para.17 of the 1988 Act). First, any period of not more than 28 days beginning with the date on which the interest of the landlord became vested in law and equity in the successor is disregarded. Second, if during that 28-day period the assignee notifies the tenant in writing of his intention to occupy another dwelling-house in the building (or flat) the period beginning with the date upon which the assignee became the legal and equitable owner until the earlier of any of the following three periods: (a) the expiry of six months from that date, or (b) the date upon which the assignee ceases to be the owner, or (c) the date upon which the assignee occupies a dwelling-house in the building (or flat), is disregarded.

The court is not allowed throughout any of these periods of disregard to make an order for possession unless it could make an order if the tenancy were a protected or statutory tenancy (Sch.2 para.3 of the 1977 Act) or assured tenancy (Sch.1 para.21 of the 1988 Act).

Where the tenancy is not determined in the period of disregard the tenant will become a protected assured tenant unless the assignee brings that period to an end by moving into one of the dwelling-houses in the building (or flat) before six months have elapsed since he became the owner. But if the absent landlord does bring the tenancy to an end during the period of disregard he will be able to obtain an order for possession at the end of that period without proving a ground even if he never moves in. The reason for this is that because the tenancy was determined during the period of disregard it never became a protected assured tenancy and thus upon determination it was not capable of obtaining statutory protection (see *Landau v Sloane* [1981] 2 W.L.R. 349). But in a Rent Act tenancy if the notice to quit expired after the period of disregard came to an end the tenant will have become fully protected (*Williams v Mate* (1982) 263 E.G. 883).

Form 23: Particulars to be inserted Form N119—resident landlord

---

1. By an oral agreement made on or about the [. . .] the Claimant agreed to let to the Defendant, on a weekly tenancy, the . . . floor flat at the said premises, at a rent of £ . . . per week payable in advance each . . .

2. The said premises are not a purpose-built block of flats.

3. At the time of and at all times since the date of the said agreement the Claimant has occupied as his residence the flat on the . . . floor of the said premises.

4. The said tenancy was determined by a notice to quit served on the . . . which said notice expired on the . . .

5. By reason of the matters set out in paragraphs 4 and 5 above and, by virtue of paragraph 10 of Schedule 1 to the Housing Act 1988, the Defendant's tenancy is not an assured tenancy.

Bankruptcy

In determining whether the condition set out in s.12(1)(c) of the 1977 Act, Sch.1 **14.017** or para.10 of the 1988 Act has been complied with (i.e. that at all material times since the tenancy was granted the interest of the landlord has belonged to a person who at the time that he owned the interest occupied as his residence another dwelling-house in the building (or flat), any period of not more than two years during which the tenancy is vested in trustees as trustees is to be disregarded. A trustee in bankruptcy of the landlord therefore has two years in which to determine the tenancy or sell the property to an intending resident landlord before the tenant will become a protected tenant. No order for possession may be made during that period unless one of the grounds applies (Sch.2 para.3 of the 1977 Act, Sch.1 para.21 of the 1988 Act); but if the trustee determines the tenancy within the period of disregard the person to whom he has sold the property (or the trustee, if he has kept it and two years have expired) will be able to obtain possession without relying upon one of those grounds (*Landau v Sloane* [1981] 2 W.L.R. 349). The trustee must make sure that the notice to quit expires before the period of disregard (*Williams v Mate* (1982) 263 E.G. 883).

Death

14.018   Paragraph 2A of Sch.2 to the Rent Act 1977 provides that where the landlord died on or after November 28, 1980 the condition that the landlord must be resident throughout the tenancy is deemed to be fulfilled for any period beginning with the date on which the landlord's interest becomes vested in his personal representatives and ending when it ceases to be so vested or when two years have expired, whichever is the earlier. The personal representatives may therefore obtain possession pursuant to the resident landlord provisions and sell the property to a non-resident landlord during the administration of the estate. Personal representatives, like assignees and trustees in bankruptcy, must make sure that the tenancy actually comes to an end before the period of two years has expired if they are to ensure that the tenant is not to become fully protected (*Williams v Mate* (1982) 263 E.G. 883).

Where the landlord dies intestate and the tenancy vests in the Probate Judge or the Public Trustee by virtue of s.9 of the Administration of Estates Act 1925 there is, in determining whether there is a landlord who is resident, disregarded a period of up to two years during which it is so vested (Sch.2 para.1(c)). Once it becomes vested in personal representatives para.2A will apply.

For the equivalent Housing Act 1988 provisions see Sch.1 paras 18 and 19.

Chapter 15

Protected Shortholds

Protected shorthold tenancies were created by the Housing Act 1980 with the **15.001** purpose of enabling a landlord to let his property with the knowledge that he would be able to recover possession at the end of the contractual term or thereafter without having to rely upon the usual Rent Act grounds. A shorthold tenancy is a protected tenancy and so the rules relating to protected tenancies explained in Ch.8 apply to shorthold tenancies unless they conflict with the shorthold provisions explained in this chapter.

Effect of the Housing Act 1988

The concept of the "protected shorthold tenancy" was replaced by that of an **15.002** "assured shorthold tenancy" which was introduced by the Housing Act 1988 (see Ch.6). The regime set out in this chapter will continue to apply to protected shorthold tenancies created prior to the commencement of the 1988 Act. However, since January 15, 1989 it has not (except in one limited circumstance) been possible to create a protected shorthold tenancy; and ex-shorthold tenants who are granted new tenancies receive assured shortholds (see details at para.7.005) and saving provisions in Sch.18 para.2 of the Housing Act 1988.

Definition of shorthold

A tenancy will only be a shorthold if it is a protected tenancy within the meaning **15.003** of s.1 of the Rent Act 1977 (s.52(1) of the 1980 Act), and if the conditions set out in s.52 of the 1980 Act are satisfied. The conditions are:

(1) That the tenancy was granted after November 28, 1980.

(2) That the tenancy was granted for a fixed term of not less than one year and not more than five years. If the tenancy contains an option clause allowing the tenant to renew, or provides that at the end of the fixed term the tenancy shall continue as a periodic tenancy, it is nevertheless a shorthold (s.52(5)).

(3) That there must be no clause in the tenancy agreement allowing the land-lord to determine prior to the end of the fixed term except in pursuance of a provision for re-entry or forfeiture for non-payment of rent or breach of any other obligation of the tenancy. (A proviso for re-entry on the bank-ruptcy of the tenant does not prevent the tenancy from being a shorthold: *Paterson v Aggio* [1987] 2 E.G.L.R. 127.)

(4) That the tenancy of the dwelling-house was granted to a new tenant of the landlord, i.e. not an existing protected or statutory tenant of that dwelling-house (but see *Dibbs v Campbell* [1988] 2 E.G.L.R. 122 and *Bolnore Properties Ltd v Cobb* (1996) 29 H.L.R. 202 CA, referred to at para.7.004). However, if an existing protected or statutory tenant enters into a shorthold tenancy of other accommodation he may be a shorthold tenant (s.52(2)).

(5) That the landlord gave the tenant a notice in the prescribed form before the tenancy was granted (s.52(1)(b) and s.52(3)); Protected Shorthold Tenancies (Notice to Tenant) Regulations 1987 (SI 1987/267); see Form 24, p.256 for a specimen form of notice). The wise landlord will have served the notice on the tenant on a date prior to the date of the commencement of the tenancy and have required him to sign, date and return a copy of the notice before the agreement was actually entered into.

15.004 (6) That if the property is in Greater London and the shorthold commenced before May 4, 1987 or if the property is outside Greater London and the shorthold tenancy commenced before December 1, 1981:

   (a) a rent was registered in respect of the dwelling-house at the time the tenancy was granted; or

   (b) the landlord obtained a certificate of fair rent from the rent officer pursuant to s.69 of the Rent Act 1977, and the rent payable under the tenancy for any period before the rent was registered did not exceed the rent specified in the certificate, and an application for the registra-tion of a fair rent was made to the rent officer within 28 days of the commencement (Protected Shorthold Tenancies (Rent Registration) Order 1987 (SI 1987/265).

Generally, if the above conditions have not been complied with the tenancy will not be a shorthold tenancy but a fully protected Rent Act tenancy. However, in proceedings for possession the court may overlook requirements (5) and (6) if it considers it just and equitable to make the order for possession (s.55(2)). For a similar provision in relation to Case 11 of Sch.15 to the Rent Act 1977, see para.6.023.

Termination

15.005 At the end of the fixed term the tenancy is no longer called a shorthold tenancy. If the tenant remains in occupation he will do so either as a tenant under a new fixed term granted pursuant to an option clause, or under a periodic protected tenancy pursuant to a term of the shorthold (s.52(5)), or if there is no such term as a statutory tenant (s.52(1)). However, if there has been no further grant of a fixed term, Case 19 will be available to the landlord if the notice procedure set out below is followed (e.g. see *Gent v de la Mare* [1988] 1 E.G.L.R. 104). It may also be possible for the landlord to terminate the tenancy before or after the expiry of the fixed term if the tenant is in breach of covenant. These matters are dealt with below. The tenant's rights to terminate are also dealt with in this section.

Before the fixed term has expired

The landlord can only seek an order for possession before the end of the fixed **15.006** term in pursuance of a provision for re-entry on forfeiture for non-payment of rent or breach of any other obligation of the tenancy (s.52(1) of the Housing Act 1980).

The tenant may bring the shorthold tenancy to an end before the final term has expired by giving written notice to the landlord. The length of notice is one month for shortholds with a fixed term of two years or less, and for shortholds of over two years notice of not less than three months must be given. The right to terminate before the expiry of the fixed term cannot be excluded by any agreement to the contrary (s.53 of the Housing Act 1980). If, having given notice to the landlord, the tenant refuses to leave and the landlord has contracted to sell or let the dwelling-house or has otherwise been seriously prejudiced the landlord should commence proceedings for possession based upon Case 5 of Sch.15 to the Rent Act 1977.

After the fixed term has expired

Case 19 notice

If the landlord wishes the tenant to leave at the end of the term he must during the **15.007** last three months thereof give the tenant at least three months' written notice of his intention to apply to the court for possession after expiry of the notice pursuant to Case 19 of Sch.15 to the Rent Act 1977; see Form 25, p.257.

If the landlord omits to serve the notice within the last three months of the term, the tenant can stay for a further year either as a statutory tenant or if the terms of the shorthold so provide as a protected periodic tenant and the landlord cannot serve another notice until the last three months of the further year.

It is not possible to serve a notice within the period of three months following the expiry of an earlier notice (Case 19(iv)).

If the landlord does not serve a notice so as to obtain possession at the end of the fixed term and the tenancy continues as a periodic tenancy pursuant to a term in the agreement the landlord must ensure that the length of notice given is at least the same as would be required for a notice to quit. The landlord must also serve a notice to quit in prescribed form (see Form 14 on p.76) so as to terminate the periodic tenancy.

Form 24: Notice of a protected shorthold tenancy

NOTICE OF A PROTECTED SHORTHOLD TENANCY—SECOND REVISION

(The landlord must give this to the tenant *before* a protected shorthold tenancy is granted. It does not commit the tenant to take the tenancy.)

To ....
(Name of proposed tenant)

> IMPORTANT—PLEASE READ THIS NOTICE CAREFULLY, IF THERE IS ANYTHING YOU DO NOT UNDERSTAND YOU SHOULD GET ADVICE (FOR EXAMPLE, FROM A SOLICITOR OR A CITIZENS' ADVICE BUREAU) BEFORE YOU AGREE TO TAKE A SHORTHOLD TENANCY.
>
> N.B. This document is important: keep it in a safe place.

1. You are proposing to take a tenancy of the dwelling known as ....
from .... 20 .... to .... 20........
(day)   (month)   (year)   (day) (month) (year)

2. This notice is to tell you that your tenancy is to be a *protected shorthold tenancy*. Under shorthold, provided you keep the terms of the tenancy, you are entitled to remain in the dwelling for the fixed period agreed at the start of the tenancy. At the end of this period the landlord has the right to repossession if he wants. Full details about shorthold are given in the Department of the Environment and Welsh Office booklet 'Shorthold Tenancies, Second Revision' obtainable free from Rent Officers, council offices and housing aid centres. You are advised to read this booklet before you agree to take a shorthold tenancy.

> *The landlord must cross out the version of paragraph 3 below which does not apply.

*3. A fair rent of   per   is already registered for the dwelling under the Rent Act 1977.

This is the most you can be required to pay as rent until such time as a higher rent is registered. If I apply for a higher rent to be registered you will be told about my application and you will have the opportunity of a consultation with the Rent Officer.

*3 The rent for this tenancy is the rent that we have agreed, and has not been registered by the Rent Officer. But this does not affect your right as tenant or my right as landlord to apply at any time to the Rent Officer for the registration of a fair rent. This is fully explained in the booklet Shorthold Tenancies. Second Revision.'

4. This notice is given to you on .... 20........

Signed ....

(on behalf of) ....

....

(Name and address of landlord)

> *SPECIAL NOTE FOR EXISTING TENANTS*
> IF YOU ARE ALREADY A PROTECTED OR STATUTORY TENANT UNDER THE RENT ACT 1977 YOUR PRESENT TENANCY CANNOT LAWFULLY BE CONVERTED INTO A SHORTHOLD. BUT SHOULD YOU GIVE IT UP AND TAKE A SHORTHOLD TENANCY IN SOME OTHER ACCOMMODATION, INCLUDING ANOTHER FLAT IN THE SAME BUILDING YOU WILL ALMOST CERTAINLY HAVE LESS SECURITY UNDER SHORTHOLD THAN UNDER YOUR EXISTING TENANCY

Reproduced for illustrative purposes only by kind permission of The Solicitors' Law Stationery Society Limited. The Housing Acts 1988 and 1996 abolished the need to serve these notices when creating a new protected shorthold tenancy after January 15, 1989

Form 25: Case 19 notice

Re:

To: A Tenant of [*state address*]

We, [*Landlord Estates Limited*] hereby give you notice that if you do not leave the above premises on the [date that your tenancy of the same expires, namely]   20   proceedings for possession may be commenced under Case 19 of Schedule 15 to the Rent Act 1977 after the expiry of this notice.

This notice expires on   . 20   .

[*Landlord Estates Limited*]

....

DATED

*Do not include words in brackets where tenant held over at end of fixed term as a statutory tenant.
*Note that it may also be necessary to serve a notice to quit in addition to the notice; see text below.

There would appear to be a potential trap for landlords where the shorthold **15.008** contains a provision for the tenancy to be continued on a periodic basis, even where the landlord serves his Case 19 notice on the very first day of the three-month period. This is because if the tenant remains in occupation for a period after the end of the term certain, he presumably does so as a periodic tenant, i.e. as a protected contractual tenant whose contractual tenancy must be determined before proceedings can be commenced (see para.8.024). It is, therefore, suggested that a notice to quit is served together with the Case 19 notice in all cases where the shorthold is one that contains a clause continuing the tenancy as a periodic tenancy.

Tenant's notice

If after expiry of the shorthold the tenancy continues as a periodic tenancy under **15.009** a term in the agreement and the tenant wishes to leave, he must give such notice as is required by the agreement. If there is no such term, the tenant will become a statutory tenant and he must give notice in accordance with s.3 of the Rent Act 1977, which will be the same period as was required when the shorthold was in existence—see para.8.018.

After fixed term has expired: forfeiture

If after the end of the fixed term the tenancy continues as a periodic contractual **15.010** tenancy the forfeiture clause will continue to be a term of the tenancy and if appropriate the landlord may seek to forfeit the lease for breach of a covenant.

Proceedings for possession

Pursuant to a Case 19 notice (see Form 25)

If the notice requirements have been complied with the landlord may recover **15.011** possession pursuant to Case 19 of Sch.15 to the Rent Act 1977 which was added by s.55 of the Housing Act 1980. Proceedings must not be commenced before expiry of the notice, nor more than three months after expiry. The requirement is not merely procedural but is a condition in Case 19 going to jurisdiction and cannot be waived (*Ridehalgh v Horsefield* (1992) 24 H.L.R. 453 CA).

The proceedings should be commenced in accordance with CPR r.55 (see Ch.25). The court must make an order for possession and has no power to postpone the effect of the order for more than 14 days or, if exceptional hardship would be caused by such a short order, six weeks (s.89 of the Housing Act 1980; para.3.034).

Forfeiture

15.012 If the landlord is seeking to rely upon a right to forfeit the tenancy either during the fixed term or during any subsequent periodic tenancy he may do so by bringing an action for possession. The usual rules as to relief against forfeiture apply and possession should be claimed pursuant to Case I of Sch.15 to the Rent Act 1977. The landlord will have to show that it is reasonable to make the order (s.98(1) of the Rent Act 1977). The court will have the usual powers under s.100 of the Rent Act 1977 to stay or suspend execution of the order or postpone the date for possession (see para.8.030).

Assignments, sub-lettings and death

Assignments

15.013 Section 54(2) of the Housing Act 1980 provides that a shorthold tenancy (and any subsequent protected or statutory tenancy held by the original shorthold tenant of a dwelling-house) cannot be assigned except in proceedings pursuant to a court order for a transfer of property under of the Matrimonial Causes Act 1973, Sch.1 of the Children Act 1989 or Schs 5 or 7 of the Civil Partnership Act 2004. A purported assignee will thus have no tenancy, but this section alone will not assist the landlord to obtain possession during the currency of the shorthold term. If during the fixed term the tenant does purport to assign, the landlord should, if there is a clause in the lease prohibiting the tenant from parting with possession, forfeit the lease by serving a notice under s.146 of the Law of Property Act 1925 and then commencing proceedings for possession based upon forfeiture provisions (subject to the restrictions on forfeiture explained in Ch.2) and Case 1 of Sch.15 to the Rent Act 1977 for breach of an obligation.

Form 26: Protected Shorthold—periodic tenancy after fixed term. Particulars of claim to be adapted to Form N119

1. By a agreement in writing dated the [*5th April*] 19[*87*] the Claimant let said premises to the Defendant for a term of one year commencing on the [5th April 19[*87*] and expiring on the [*4th April*] 19[*88*] at a rent of £ [*state amount*] per month payable in advance on the [*5th*] day of every month. The Defendant did not, at the time of the said grant, have a protected or statutory tenancy of the said premises.

2. Prior to granting the said tenancy the claimant gave notice in writing to the Defendant that the said tenancy was to be a protected shorthold tenancy within the meaning of the Housing Act 1980.

3. At the time of the said agreement a rent was registered in respect of the said premises.

[*not necessary outside Greater London if tenancy commenced on or after 1.12.80 or inside London if tenancy commenced on or after 4 May 1987*]

4. The said tenancy expired by effluxion of time on the [*4th April*] 20[88] and thereafter the Defendant remained in occupation of the said premises as a monthly tenant pursuant to the terms of the said agreement.

5. The said periodic tenancy was determined by a notice to quit served on the [*4th January*] 20 which said notice expired on the [*4th April*] 20.

6. By a notice in writing served on the Defendant on the [*4th January*] 20 and expiring on [*4th April*] 20 the Claimant informed the Defendant that proceedings under Case 19 of Schedule 15 to the Rent Act 1977 might be brought after expiry of the said notice.

7. The said premises are residential premises to which the Rent Act 1977 applies and possession is claimed pursuant to the provisions of Case 19 of Schedule 15 to the Rent Act 1977.

Sub-tenancies

A sub-tenant of a shorthold tenant (or ex-shorthold tenant who has now become a **15.014** protected or statutory tenant) has no protection against the head landlord, whether or not he is a lawful sub-tenant. Thus if a landlord is entitled to possession of the premises he is entitled to possession as against the tenant and the sub-tenant (s.54(1) of the Housing Act 1980).

Death

As the shorthold tenancy is a protected tenancy the Rent Act statutory succession **15.015** rules apply (see Ch.8) save that the tenancy to which the successor becomes entitled is an assured shorthold tenancy (s.39(7) of the Housing Act 1988).

Chapter 16

Long Tenancies at Low Rent

This chapter applies to long residential tenancies that fall outside of the Housing **16.001** Act 1988 or the Rent Act 1977. These are likely to be long residential tenancies for which a premium is paid and only a peppercorn or nominal annual rent is payable. Since January 15, 1999, a qualifying long residential tenancy will not expire at the end of its term but will be continued by the provisions of the Local Government and Housing Act 1989 (prior to this date the lease was continued by reason of Pt I of the Landlord and Tenant Act 1954.

For these purposes a long residential tenancy is a tenancy for 21 years or more at a low rent. A low rent for tenancies entered into on or after April 1, 1990 is either no rent or £1,000 or less per year in Greater London or £250 or less per year elsewhere. For tenancies entered into before April 1, 1990 it is a rent of less than two thirds of the rateable value on March 31, 1990 (Sch.10 para.2).

For a long residential tenancy to be a qualifying tenancy under the Act, it must satisfy the conditions for an assured tenancy under the Housing Act 1988 (see chapter 6). However, Sch.1 para.1 of that Act and the exclusion of low rent tenancies are deemed not to apply (Sch.10 paras 1 and 2).

On the termination of the fixed term the tenancy will, if the 1989 Act applies, **16.002** continue as a contractual tenancy at the same rent and on the same terms as before until it is determined by a 1989 Act notice (Sch.10 para.3). There are two types of notices a landlord can serve: a landlord's notice to resume possession; and a landlord's notice proposing an assured tenancy.

A landlord seeking to recover the property will have to serve a notice to resume possession and then issue proceedings. The proceedings are brought after service but before expiry of the notice. If in the proceedings the landlord is unable to show that one of a number of specified grounds has been established he will not be entitled to possession and the tenant will continue as a contractual tenant unless the landlord chooses to convert it into an assured tenancy.

If as a result of the assessment, or any later assessment, the rent becomes greater than the high rent limit (currently £100,000—see para.6.005) the tenant loses their security of tenure (*Hughes v Borodex Limited* [2010] EWCA Civ 425).

Instead of seeking possession the landlord may accept that the tenant will continue in possession at the end of the fixed term either under a contractual tenancy or as an assured tenant. To convert it to an assured tenancy the landlord serves a notice proposing an assured tenancy. The advantage to the landlord is that the rent can be increased and repairs can be dealt with. If the terms of the assured tenancy cannot be agreed the landlord may apply to the rent assessment committee to determine them (Sch.10 para.10).

The parties may not exclude the provisions of the 1989 Act (s.186(4)), but where it appears that the qualifying condition is not satisfied (e.g. because the tenant is not in occupation) and is not likely to be satisfied at the end of the lease the landlord may apply to the court, within 12 months of the end of the fixed term, for a declaration that the 1989 Act does not apply (Sch.10 para.1(3)). The application is commenced by Pt 8 procedure (CPR r.56).

Termination

By landlord: notice to resume possession

16.003 The landlord is defined by s.21 of the Landlord and Tenant Act 1954 as being that person who has an interest in the reversion expectant on the termination of the tenancy and is either the freehold owner, or has a tenancy which is at least five years longer than the tenancy in question ("the competent landlord"); Sch.10 para.19(1) of the 1989 Act which refers to the 1954 Act. If the immediate landlord does not satisfy these conditions, the next one up the chain who falls within this definition will qualify as landlord for the purpose of the Act.

In order to terminate the tenancy the landlord must serve notice in Form 2 of the Long Residential Tenancies (Principal Forms) Regulations 1997 (SI 1997/3008) (as amended) termed a "Landlord's notice to resume possession" (Sch.10 para.4; Form 27, p.264). A notice may be given at any time within the 12 months prior to the end of the fixed term or at any time thereafter (Sch.10 para.4). The notice must specify:

16.004
(1) the termination date which will be more than six but less than 12 months after the date of service of the notice and will be the termination date of the fixed term or later (Sch.10 para.4(1));
(2) the premises;
(3) that if the tenant does not vacate the premises on the termination date the landlord will apply to the court for possession on one of the following grounds specified by Sch.10 para.5(1):

   (a) Ground 6 in, and those in Pt II of, Sch.2 to the Housing Act 1988 (see para.6.024), other than Ground 16; (Ground 6 in Sch.2 to the 1988 Act may not be specified in a landlord's notice to resume possession if the tenancy is a former 1954 Act tenancy);
   (b) the ground that, for the purposes of redevelopment after the termination of the tenancy, the landlord proposes to demolish or reconstruct the whole or a substantial part of the premises; and
   (c) the ground that the premises or part of them are reasonably required by the landlord for occupation as a residence for himself or any son or daughter of his over 18 years of age, his father or mother or the father or mother of his spouse or civil partner and, if the landlord is not the immediate landlord, that he will be at the specified date of termination.

(4) that the tenant must notify the landlord in writing, within two months of service of the landlord's notice, whether the tenant is willing to vacate the premises on the termination date;
(5) if a tenant has a right to acquire the freehold or extend the lease pursuant to either the Leasehold Reform Act 1967 or the Leasehold Reform, Housing and Urban Development Act 1993 the notice must state that the tenant

must notify the landlord of his desire to exercise this right within two months after service of the notice (or four months in the case of collective enfranchisement) and contain consequences which follow if he does so;

(6) the names and addresses of any other persons known or believed by the landlord to have an interest superior to the tenancy.

By landlord: notice proposing an assured tenancy

If the landlord does not require possession (or accepts that he is not entitled to **16.005** possession) but wishes to bring the continuation tenancy to an end and to replace it with an assured tenancy he may serve a landlord's notice proposing an assured tenancy (Sch.10 para.4(5)(a)). The notice must be in Form 1 of the Long Residential Tenancies (Principal Forms) Regulations 1997 (as amended). The notice must include details of various matters including the landlord's proposals in relation to rent and terms (Sch.10 para.4(6)).

The tenant has two months to serve a notice (in prescribed form) setting out different proposals as to rent and/or terms ("a tenant's notice"). If they do not they take the assured tenancy on the terms and at the rent proposed by the landlord. If they serve a tenant's notice then the landlord has two months to respond by making an application to the rent assessment committee for a determination of rent and/or terms. If no such application is made then the tenant will take the tenancy on the terms that he proposed (Sch.10 para.10).

Termination by tenant

The tenant must give not less than one month's written notice to the immediate **16.006** landlord to terminate the tenancy on the termination date or later (Sch.10 para.8).

Enfranchisement/Lease extension

The tenant may have the right during or before the service of a landlord's notice **16.007** (either of them) to make a claim for an extension of their lease or to enfranchise (under either the Leasehold Reform Act 1967 or the Leasehold Reform, Housing and Urban Development Act 1993). In broad terms, if such a claim is made it negates the application of the 1989 Act for the time being. However, there are provisions for the payment of compensation to the landlord for loss of rent for the period of what was an ultimately ineffective claim to extend or enfranchise (see *Hague on Enfranchisement* for further details).

Possession proceedings following service of a notice to resume possession

Where the tenant fails to notify the landlord within two months of the landlord's **16.008** notice to resume possession that he is unwilling to give up possession and at the end of two months from service of the landlord's notice the qualifying condition is not fulfilled (for example because the tenant is not in occupation) the tenancy comes to an end on the date specified in the notice and the landlord is entitled to possession (Sch.10 para.9(3)).

Where the tenant has notified the landlord that he wishes to retain possession or if, at the end of the period of two months after service of the landlord's notice the qualifying condition is fulfilled, the landlord may apply to the county court for an order for possession under the Act (Sch.10 para.13(1)). The application must be made not later than two months after the tenant elects to retain possession. If he has not made such an election, the application must be made not later than four months after service of the landlord's notice (Sch.10 para.13(2)). The application is made by CPR Pt 8 procedure (CPR r.56; Sch.10, para.20).

16.009   At the hearing the landlord will have to prove the ground upon which he relies. Except in redevelopment cases the court must be satisfied that it is reasonable to make the order for possession. If an order is made the court has no power to suspend or postpone the date for possession (except in redevelopment cases) but the order will only take effect on termination of the tenancy, i.e. on the date specified in the landlord's notice as the termination date (Sch.10 para.4(4)). Where the landlord's application for possession fails he may offer the tenant an assured tenancy within one month of the end of the court proceedings to take effect three months from service of the notice (Sch.10 para.15(4)). As above the tenant has an opportunity to serve a counter-notice if he objects to the terms in which case the landlord may by application in prescribed form refer the matter to a rent assessment committee (see para.16.005 above).

If the landlord does not serve a notice proposing an assured tenancy the original notice to resume possession ceases to operate and the original contractual tenancy continues.

Form 27: Landlord's notice to resume possession

LANDLORD'S NOTICE TO RESUME POSSESISON

Paragraph 4(1) of Schedule 10 to the Local Government and Housing Act 1989

The landlord **must** *cross out any text in square brackets which does not apply.*

- This notice will end your existing long residential tenancy and states that, if you are not willing to give up possession, the landlord proposes to apply to court for possession.

- Please read this notice carefully. **There are time limits which you must keep to**. If you need help or advice about this notice, you should take it immediately to any of the following:

  — a Citizens' Advice Bureau
  — a housing aid centre
  — a law centre
  — a solicitor.

- You may be able to get legal aid but this will depend on your personal circumstances.

- Please read the notes at the end of the form.

1. To:

Insert name[s] of tenant[s].

2. From:
of:

Insert name[s] and address of landlord[s].

(see note 1)

3. [I][We] give you notice ending your long residential tenancy of:

Insert address of property to which the notice relates.

on:

Insert the date at which the tenancy is to come to an end.

(see notes 2 to 4)

4. I believe that you are entitled to the protection of Schedule 10 to the Local Government and Housing Act 1989 in respect of

contd

contd

[the whole of the property]

[the following part of the property, namely:

If you consider only part of the property is protected, describe that part.]

(see note 5)

5. You are requested **WITHIN 2 MONTHS**, beginning on the date on which this notice was served, to notify [me] [us] in writing whether or not you wish to remain in possession.

(see notes 6 and 7)

Consequences of this notice if tenant claims the freehold or an extended lease or a new lease

6. If you are the tenant of a house, you may have the right to acquire the freehold or an extended lease of that house under Part I of the Leasehold Reform Act 1967. If you are the tenant of a flat, you may have the right to acquire a new lease of your flat under Part I of the Leasehold Reform, Housing and Urban Development Act 1993 and you may also have the right, collectively with the other tenants of flats in the same buildings, to acquire the freehold of that building under Part I of that Act.

(see note 8)

7. If you want to acquire the freehold under the 1967 Act or a lease under that Act or the 1993 Act, you must serve the appropriate notice for that **WITHIN 2 MONTHS** of the service of this notice. If you and other tenants of flats in the same buildings want to acquire the freehold of that building under the 1993 Act, you and other tenants must serve the notice for that **WITHIN 4 MONTHS** of the service of this notice. If you serve one of those notices, then this notice will not operate.

(see note 9)

8. If you serve one of those notices, then [I][we] [will][will not] be entitled to apply to the county court for possession of the property under:

[section 17 of the 1967 Act] [section 18 of the 1967 Act]

[section 23 of the 1993 Act] [section 47 of the 1993 Act]

[and [propose] [do not propose] to do so].

(see note 10)

9. The following are the names and addresses of other persons known or believed by [me] [us] to have an interest superior to your tenancy or to be the agent concerned with the property on behalf of a person having such an interest:

Insert the names and addresses of any such persons.

Consequences of this notice if tenant does not claim the freehold or an extended lease or a new lease

10. If you are not willing to give up possession of the property let under your long residential tenancy at the date of termination, I propose to apply to the county court for possession of the property on the following ground[s]—
Insert each ground on which you propose to apply to the court for possession and give the full text of each ground. Continue on a separate sheet if necessary.

(see notes 11 to 15)

11. This notice is give under the provisions of paragraph 4(1) of Schedule 10 to the Local Government and Housing Act 1989.

(see note 16)

Signed

Date

To be signed and dated by the landlord or the landlord's agent. If there are joint landlords, each landlord or the agent for that landlord must sign (but one can sign on behalf of another with his consent).

[The name and address of the agent is:

Insert name and address of agent, if signed by an agent.]

NOTES

Note 1: The landlord referred to in this notice is not necessarily the landlord to whom you pay the rent. It is the person who is your landlord for the purposes of Schedule 10 to the Local Government and Housing Act 1989. That, broadly, will be your immediate landlord if he has a lease which is at least five years longer than your tenancy or, if not, the first superior landlord who has such a lease. If there is no landlord with such a lease, it will be the freeholder.

contd

contd

Note 2: Schedule 10 to the Local Government and Housing Act 1989 provides that a tenant of residential property under a long residential tenancy has a right, at the end of the original term of the tenancy, to continue as a tenant on the same terms as before unless the landlord ends the tenancy in accordance with the provisions of that Act. But see also Note 3.

Note 3: In certain circumstances, Schedule 10 does not apply and the landlord can end your tenancy by giving notice in accordance with the ordinary requirements of the law. These circumstances include cases where:

    (a) you pay more than a low rent (see paragraph 2(4) and (5) of Schedule 10) **unless** the property is a house and the tenancy has been extended under section 14 of the Leasehold Reform Act 1967, in which case Schedule 10 applies regardless of whether a low rent is being paid;

    (b) the property has a high rateable value (see paragraph 2 of Schedule 1 to the Housing Act 1988, unless the long tenancy was granted after 31st March 1990, in which case paragraph 1(2A) of Schedule 10 applies);

    (c) the tenancy does not meet certain requirements for the existence of an assured tenancy set out in Part 1 of Schedule 1 to the Housing Act 1988—for instance because the landlord is the Crown, a local authority or another exempt landlord;

    (d) the property is a flat whose lease was extended under Chapter 2 of Part 1 of the Leasehold Reform Housing and Urban Development Act 1993, by virtue of section 59 of that Act.

The above is not intended to give a full account of all the circumstances in which Schedule 10 does not apply. Legal advice should be sought if there is any doubt as to whether Schedule 10 applies in a particular case.

Note 4: The landlord can end the tenancy by notice which, as a general rule, must be served not more than 12 and not less than 6 months before the date of termination specified in the notice. This date must not normally be before the date on which the long residential tenancy expires.

Note 5: Your right to remain in occupation is limited to parts of the property which you occupy at the end of the tenancy.

Note 6: If you wish to give up possession of the property, you should let the landlord know (in writing) **WITHIN 2 MONTHS** of the date this notice was served. Failing to notify the landlord may lead to an unnecessary application to the county court and consequent expense, which you may have to bear.

Note 7: If you do not wish to give up possession of the property, you should let the landlord know (in writing) **WITHIN 2 MONTHS** of the date this notice was served. If you fail to notify the landlord and are not in occupation of the property 2 months after this notice was served, you may lose the protection of the 1989 Act. However, if you fail to notify the landlord, but are in occupation (as your only or principal home) 2 months after this notice was served, you will not lose that protection.

Note 8: Your rights under the 1989 Act are in addition to any right you may have under the Leasehold Reform Act 1967 or the Leasehold Reform, Housing and Urban Development Act 1993.

Note 9: A landlord may, but does not have to, consent in writing to the deadline being extended.

Note 10: Sections 17 and 18 of the Leasehold Reform Act 1967 and sections 23 and 47 of the Leasehold Reform, Housing and Urban Development Act 1993 relate to cases where the landlord can apply to court for repossession if certain conditions are fulfilled (involving redeveloping the property or, under the 1967 Act, the landlord or a member of his family wanting to live in the property).

Note 11: The date of termination (referred to in paragraph 10 of this notice) is the date specified in paragraph 3 of this notice. Where the landlord applies to the county court for an order for possession of the property, the date of termination is the last day of the period of three months starting with the date when the application is finally disposed of.

Note 12: The landlord must state the ground or grounds on which he proposes to apply to court for possession. Only grounds specified in Schedule 10 to the Local Government and Housing Act 1989 may be included. Schedule 10 sets out some of the grounds in full and provides for some of the grounds set out in Schedule 2 to the Housing Act 1988 to apply (with some modifications). An outline of the grounds follows (but **not** the full text):

Schedule 2 to the Housing Act 1988

    Ground 6: landlord intends to demolish or reconstruct a substantial part of the property or needs possession to carry out substantial works to the property; and the long residential tenancy was not formerly a tenancy under Part I of the Landlord and Tenant Act 1954.

    Ground 9: suitable alternative accommodation available for tenant

    Ground 10: some rent in arrears on date possession proceedings begun and on date this notice was served

    Ground 11: tenant persistently delayed paying rent

    Ground 12: obligation under tenancy, other than one related to the payment of rent, not complied with

    Ground 13: condition of the property or common parts has deteriorated because of neglect or default by tenant or other person living at the property

    Ground 14: nuisance or annoyance by tenant or other person living in or visiting the property or conviction for using the property for immoral or illegal purposes or an arrestable offence committed in, or in the locality of, the property

    Ground 14A: landlord is a registered social landlord or housing action trust and there has been domestic violence or threat of violence

    Ground 15: condition of furniture provided for use under the long residential tenancy deteriorated because of the ill-treatment by tenant or other person living at the property

contd

Schedule 10 to the Local Government and Housing Act 1989

Paragraph 5(1)(b): landlord is a public body intending to demolish or reconstruct a substantial part of the property for purposes relevant to its functions
Paragraph 5(1)(c): landlord reasonably requires property to live in himself or for specified relations and landlord's interest in the property purchased or created before 19th February 1966.

Note 13: The landlord may apply to the county court for an order for possession on any of the grounds specified in paragraph 10 of this notice. In order for the application to succeed, the landlord must establish that ground. The landlord will also have to satisfy the court that it is reasonable to grant him possession (except for ground 6 in the 1988 Act and the ground in paragraph 5(1)(c) of Schedule 10 to the 1989 Act. However, if you are not occupying the property (as your only or principal home) at the date of the court hearing, the court will order possession. If the application succeeds, your long residential tenancy will end on the date of termination (see note 11).

Note 14: If you notify the landlord that you want to remain in possession of your property (see note 6), the landlord must apply to the court **WITHIN 2 MONTHS** of the date of service of that notification. If you do not notify the landlord that you want to remain in possession, then the application to the court must be **WITHIN FOUR MONTHS** of the date of service of this notice.

Note 15: If the landlord fails in his application for possession, this notice will lapse.

Note 16: You may decide that you want your long residential tenancy to end at or after the date it would have ended under the terms of the tenancy. If so, you will need to give your immediate landlord not less than one month's notice in writing. Your immediate landlord will be the person to whom you pay your rent and may not be the landlord who has served this notice. It does not make any difference that you have notified the landlord that you wished to remain in possession.

Forfeiture proceedings

In addition to his usual right to claim relief against forfeiture the tenant may also **16.010** rely upon Sch.10 para.20. Where the tenant has made an application in the forfeiture proceedings for relief and the court makes an order for possession at any time up to seven months before the end of the fixed term the order is automatically suspended for 14 days. Within that period the tenant may give the landlord and the court a notice in writing that he desires that the order for possession should have no effect except if and in so far as it provides for the payment of costs and that he desires the tenancy thereafter to have effect as if it had been granted for a fixed term expiring at the end of seven months from the making of the order. The effect of serving the notice is that at the end of the seven months the tenant will no longer have a fixed term but will continue in possession under a continuation tenancy (Sch.10 para.3). If the landlord wishes to obtain possession he will have to serve a notice to resume possession and show that one of the 1989 Act grounds applies (Sch.10 para.4(5)(6)). These provisions will not apply where the landlord is forfeiting on the basis that the tenant is in breach of any term of the lease relating to the payment of rent or rates, insurance of the premises, or use of the premises for immoral or illegal purposes (s.16(4) of the 1954 Act—as applied by Sch.10 para.20 of the 1989 Act).

If the tenant has applied for relief, the court may not make any order for possession in the last seven months of the fixed term unless the landlord is forfeiting for breach of one of the terms referred to in s.16(4) (s.16(3); Sch.10 para.20 of the 1989 Act).

Special provisions apply where proceedings are brought by a superior landlord (Sch.5 para.9 to the Landlord and Tenant Act 1954—see Sch.10 para.19(3) of the 1989 Act).

Possession proceedings in respect of assured and statutory tenancies

16.011 Where a landlord wishes to claim possession of any long tenancy at a low rent which has been converted to an assured tenancy he may do so by relying on any of the grounds in the Housing Act 1988.

For tenancies converted to statutory tenancies prior to January 15, 1999, where a landlord wishes to claim possession of any long tenancy at a low rent that has been converted to a statutory tenancy he may do so by relying on any of the grounds for possession in the Rent Act 1977 save that the landlord cannot proceed on the basis of non-payment of rent, breach of any obligation of the tenancy and nuisance or user for illegal or immoral purposes which occurred prior to the termination of the contractual tenancy (s.10(2) of the Landlord and Tenant Act 1954). However, two additional grounds are available, namely the failure of the tenant to pay any sums due to the landlord for repairs carried out by the landlord necessitated by the tenant's previous failure to comply with his repairing obligations (Sch.1 para.17 to the Landlord and Tenant Act 1954) and failure by the tenant to carry out repairs which he has agreed or the court has ordered him to do (Sch.2 para.4 to the Landlord and Tenant Act 1954).

Local authority landlords

16.012 Where the landlord of a long residential lease is a local authority, on expiry of the fixed term the tenant would not become a qualifying tenant as local authorities fall into the exclusion in Sch.1 of the Housing Act 1988 (para.12—local authority tenancies, etc.). Therefore the 1989 Act will not continue that tenancy on expiration and the common law applies (*Banjo v Brent LBC* [2005] EWCA Civ 292).

Chapter 17

Employees, Premises with a Business Use and Company Lets

Employees

Where an employer allows an employee to occupy residential premises it will **17.001** usually be very inconvenient for the employer's business if at the end of the period of employment he is unable to recover possession of the dwelling-house. The consequence is that many such employees are licensees who have no interest in the property. Even where the employee is a tenant the tenancy will often not be assured under the Housing Act 1988 or, as the case may be, regulated under the Rent Act 1977 because no rent is payable or because the rent payable is too low. Certain employees of local authorities and other public sector bodies are not secure tenants. Where the premises are licensed the employee who lives on the premises will not be a protected, assured or secure tenant. Even where the employee is an assured or regulated tenant there is a special ground for regaining possession. All these situations are discussed in this chapter.

The position of workers in the agricultural sector is discussed in Ch.18.

Licensees

In Ch.5 we saw how the House of Lords in *Street v Mountford* [1985] 2 All E.R. **17.002** 289 reaffirmed the traditional view that, save for certain limited exceptions, an occupier of residential premises for a term at a rent is to be regarded as a tenant if he has been granted exclusive possession of the accommodation. One of the exceptions occurs where the occupier is a "service occupier". It was said in *Street v Mountford* at 294b:

> "A service occupier is a servant who occupies his master's premises in order to perform his duties as a servant. In those circumstances the possession and occupation of the servant is treated as the possession and occupation of the master and the relationship of landlord and tenant is not created. . . . The test is whether the servant requires the premises he occupies in order to better perform his duties as a servant."

For example, in *Thompsons (Funeral Furnishers) Ltd v Phillips* [1945] 2 All E.R. 49 the plaintiffs employed the defendant as a chauffeur. It was a term of the contract of employment that the defendant would live on the premises owned by the plaintiffs. The contract contained the following clause:

"Either I or someone else will be on the premises at all times to take orders, answer messages, or answer enquiries for you. I will vacate the premises immediately I cease to be in your employment".

Fifteen shillings was deducted from the defendant's wages in respect of his use and occupation of the premises. It was held that

"the substance of the agreement with the [plaintiffs] was that he was to occupy those premises as their servant or agent, in order to perform his services in part of those premises, and that it was, therefore, a service occupancy and not a service tenancy" (per Lawrence L.J.).

Where the employee, by an express term, is genuinely required to occupy the premises for the better performance of his duties he will be a licensee, even though his occupation is not necessary for the purposes of the employment (*Norris v Checksfield* [1991] 4 All E.R. 327 CA).

17.003   Where there is no express term requiring the employee to occupy the premises for the better performance of his duties the court will not imply such a term unless there are compelling reasons for so doing (*Hughes v Greenwich London BC* [1993] 4 All E.R. 577 HL; no such term implied in the contract of a headmaster living on premises in the school grounds because it was not essential that he should live in the house in order to do his job).

"In my opinion, the only way in which the term which the appellant council need to imply here could be implied into the contact would be to show that, unless he lived in the Cedars, Mr Hughes could not perform his duties as headmaster. . . . In order that a term may be implied, there has to be a compelling reason for deeming that term to form part of the contract, and that compelling reason is missing in this case, unless it was essential that Mr Hughes should live in the house in order to do his job, but the facts found contradict that proposition. Once the principle . . . is accepted, it becomes pointless for the appellant council to argue that a requirement must be implied in a contract just because in fact for Mr Hughes to live in Cedars may have promoted (or even did promote) the better perform-ance of his duties." (*Hughes v Greenwich LBC*, per Lord Lowry at 583e and 584a).

However, it is much easier to imply such a term where the employee is a school caretaker (*Surrey County Council v Lamond* (1998) 31 H.L.R. 1051 CA and see *Godsmark v Greenwich* [2004] H.L.R. (Case 53) 1029 Ch D: where an express term in a school employee's initial contract of employment was implied into subsequent contract of employments).

If the employee is not required to live on the premises for the better perform-ance of his duties he will be a tenant and if the agreement as properly construed is a tenancy it will be held to be such, whatever the label the parties put on it (see *Facchini v Bryson* [1952] 1 T.L.R. 1386; a case where the employee was "permitted" to occupy the premises rather than required to do so for the purpose of the employment; and *Street v Mountford* at 296d).

See Ch.5 for the termination of licences and Ch.9 for the protection afforded to the licensee if the licence is a restricted contract.

Relationship with the contract of employment

17.004   A right of occupation expressed to be granted for a period of employment creates a contractual licence which is ancillary to the contract of employment and, being ancillary, comes to an end when the contract of employment is terminated even if the employee is wrongfully dismissed, i.e. in breach of contract (*Ivory v Palmer* [1975] I.C.R. 340). It is not, therefore, necessary to serve a notice to quit in accordance with s.5(1A) of the Protection from Eviction Act 1977 which only applies to periodic licences (*Norris v Checksfield* [1991] 4 All E.R. 327; see para.5.014 above). (Note that the employee is not deemed to be a tenant for these purposes by virtue of s.8(2) of the 1977 Act because s.5 is not within Pt I of that Act.) Care must be taken to ensure that the contract of employment is actually at an end. In *Beazer Investment Ltd v Soares* [2004] All E.R. (D) 186 CA, a possession order was set aside on the basis that the tenant/employee had not accepted the repudiatory breach but usually had continued working. The contract subsisted and the landlord/employer was not entitled to possession.

An employee may, however, have a right to claim reinstatement under the Employment Rights Act 1996 where the dismissal was unfair. The court may adjourn the possession action where the employee has made a claim for unfair dismissal to an industrial tribunal in order to see the outcome of that application but not if substantial delay would result (*Elias v King* [1981] CAT 541).

However, in *Whitbread West Pennines Ltd v Reedy* (1988) 20 H.L.R. 642 the **17.005** employer stated that it would not reinstate the employee even if he were to succeed in his claim for unfair dismissal and that it would rather pay an additional amount of compensation under the Employment Protection (Consolidation) Act 1978 (now the Employment Rights Act 1996). The Court of Appeal held that the action for possession should not be adjourned and that the employer was entitled to an order for possession.

The licence is not brought to an end by change in employer by reason of a transfer of the employer's business to which the Transfer of Undertakings (Protection of Employment) Regulations 2006 (as amended) apply. In those circumstances the contract of employment continues to have effect as if originally made between the employee and the new employer and "all the transferor's rights, powers, duties and liabilities under or in connection with any such contract" are transferred to the new employer (reg.4(2)(a)).

Tenancies where the employee pays no rent or a low rent: see Appendix 1

Quite often employees who are provided with accommodation by their employers **17.006** either pay a low rent or even no rent at all. If no rent is payable or the rent payable is less than two-thirds of the rateable value of the premises on "the appropriate day" the employee although he may be a tenant will not be protected under the Rent Act 1977 (see s.5). To constitute rent the payments made by the employee to the employer must be monetary. Money's worth is usually insufficient (*Barnes v Barratt* [1970] 2 Q.B. 657; *Heslop v Burns* [1974] 1 W.L.R. 1241). Where, however, the rent is paid by the provision of a service the value of which is quantified in terms of money by agreement between the parties the sum so quantified is the "rent" and if that sum is greater than two-thirds of the rateable value of the premises the tenancy will be protected. (See *Montagu v Browning* [1954] 1 W.L.R. 1039; the wages of the tenant, who was a caretaker, were deducted from the rent payable. It was held that the amount deducted was rent.) Note that even if the tenancy was at a low rent it may nevertheless be a restricted contract (see Ch.9).

Where the tenancy was granted before April 1, 1990 the tenancy will not be assured if under the tenancy either no rent is payable or the rent payable is less than two-thirds of the rateable value for the time being (Sch.1 para.3B, para.14 to the 1988 Act).

Where the tenancy was granted on or after April 1, 1990 (otherwise than pursuant to a contract made before that date) the tenancy is not assured if the property is in Greater London and the rent is £1,000 or less per year or the property is elsewhere and the rent is £250 or less per year (para.3A).

Local authority and other public sector employees

17.007 The fact that an employee of a local authority was a licensee would not of itself prevent him from being a secure tenant of a dwelling-house provided by his employer (s.79(3) of the Housing Act 1985; see para.10.002). However, a tenancy is not a secure tenancy if the tenant is an employee of the landlord or, if not such an employee, is an employee of a local authority, a development corporation, an urban development corporation, a Mayoral development corporation or the governors of an aided school and his contract of employment requires him to occupy the dwelling-house for the better performance of his duties (Sch.1 para.2 to the Housing Act 1985; see para.A2.037). See also para.2 in relation to policemen and firemen.

This exception contains two distinct conditions in relation to the employee. First that "his contract of employment requires him to occupy the dwelling-house"; second, that the requirement is "for the better performance of his duties". The first condition looks only to the terms of the contract: the question is simply whether the contract contains such a requirement or not. The second condition, however, raises an issue of fact outside the contract: the question is not whether the contract states that the requirement is for the better performance of his duties, but whether the requirement is in fact for the better performance of his duties (*Wragg v Surrey County Council* [2008] EWCA Civ 19).

Where an employee who has a secure tenancy (because his contract of employment does not require him to occupy the dwelling for the better performance of his duties) agrees new terms under which he is required to occupy the dwelling for the better performance of his duties his tenancy will cease to be secure (*Elvidge v Coventry City Council* [1993] 4 All E.R. 903 CA; water bailiff promoted to assistant ranger with additional duties requiring him to live in the park at the accommodation already provided—see also *Greenfield v Berkshire CC* (1996) 28 H.L.R. 691 CA).

Licensed premises

17.008 A tenancy of a dwelling-house which consists of or comprises premises licensed for the sale of intoxicating liquor for consumption on the premises cannot be protected or statutory (s.11 of the Rent Act 1977) or assured (Sch.1 para.5 to the Housing Act 1988).

The landlord, therefore, need only determine the tenancy by the common law rules (see Chs 2 and 3) and he will then be able to obtain an order for possession. It will usually be employees who will be affected by this exception but it will obviously also apply to any tenant of a dwelling-house on licensed premises who is not an employee of the landlord. Note that the exception applies to all "non-licences" and therefore will include restaurants and wine bars but not "off-licences".

If the landlord is a local authority or other public sector body within s.80 of the Housing Act 1985 (see para.10.005) the tenancy will not be a secure tenancy (Sch.1 para.9 to the Housing Act 1985).

Rent Act tenancies: premises required for a new employee (Case 8)

Where a tenant protected under the Rent Act 1977 was in the employment of the **17.009** landlord (or a former landlord) and the dwelling-house was let to him in consequence of that employment and he has ceased to be in that employment the landlord may obtain possession of the dwelling-house after the tenancy has been determined if he can show that the dwelling-house is reasonably required at the date of the hearing either:

(1) for occupation as a residence for some person engaged in the landlord's whole time employment or in the whole time employment of one of the landlord's tenants; or

(2) as a residence for some person with whom, conditional on housing being provided, a contract for employment as a whole time employee has been entered into.

The landlord must also satisfy the court that it is reasonable to make the order for possession (s.98(1) of the Rent Act 1977).

The following points should be noted:

(1) It does not matter that the tenant did not know that the premises were being **17.010** let to him in consequence of his employment. It is the landlord's intention at the date of the letting which is relevant (*Braithwaite & Co Ltd v Elliot* [1946] 2 All E.R. 537 CA).

(2) The landlord and the employer must be the same person at the grant of the tenancy for Case 8 to apply. If the landlord changes and the tenant remains in the employment of the original landlord the present landlord may not rely upon Case 8, even if the nature of his work has completely changed (*Duncan v Hay* [1956] 1 W.L.R. 1329—tenant was originally a farm foreman but became a laundry machine operator when his employer gave up the land).

(3) Case 8 will not apply where the tenant was employed by the landlord and one or more other persons jointly and severally. Thus if the tenant is employed by two partners, but only one of the partners is the landlord, Case 8 will not apply; or where the landlord is a director of the company employing the tenant (see *Evans v Engelson* (1979) 253 E.G. 577).

(4) If the tenant remains in possession after he ceases to be an employee the landlord does not lose his right to claim under Case 8. The landlord may not, for example, immediately require the premises for another employee and the continued acceptance of rent does not prejudice his position; nor necessarily does an increase in rent (*Lever Bros v Caton* (1921) 37

T.L.R. 664). Even if the employee dies the landlord may rely upon this Case against any person who has succeeded him as a statutory tenant (*Bolsover Colliery Co v Abbott*) [1946] K.B. 8; *Railway Executive v Botley* (1950) 155 E.G. 110). If, however, the landlord and tenant either expressly or by implication enter into a new tenancy agreement the landlord will not be able to rely upon Case 8 because the new tenancy will not have been entered into "in consequence" of the earlier employment (*J & F Stone Lighting & Radio Ltd v Levitt* [1945] 2 All E.R. 268).

(5) It is not necessary for the new employee to have actually commenced work at the date of the hearing. It is sufficient that the date for commencement contained in his contract of employment has arrived (*Fuggle (RF) Ltd v Gadsden* [1948] 2 K.B. 236). Thus if the new employee has not been able to start on time because he has been ill or because he has been on holiday the landlord will still be able to obtain an order evicting the old tenant if all the other requirements are satisfied.

Case 8 does not apply to agricultural workers (s.99 of the Rent Act 1977).

Assured tenancies: dwelling let in consequence of employment

17.011 Where the tenancy is an assured tenancy under the Housing Act 1988 and the dwelling-house was let to the tenant in consequence of his employment by the landlord seeking possession or by a previous landlord under the tenancy and the tenant has ceased to be in that employment the landlord may rely upon Ground 16 of Sch.2 to the 1988 Act as a ground for possession. This is a discretionary ground and so the court must be satisfied that it is reasonable to make the order (s.7(4)). The procedure for determining assured tenancies is dealt with in Ch.6.

Note that it is not necessary for the landlord to show that he requires the dwelling-house for a new employee before the ground for possession applies. However, the court may decide not to exercise its discretion in favour of making an order if the dwelling is not so required.

Premises with a business use

17.012 This part of the chapter is concerned with the position of the tenant of a dwelling-house which is used partly for residential and partly for business purposes. A number of different situations may arise. A shop with a flat above may be let together, a doctor may use his front room as a surgery, or a businessman may run his business from home. In each case the tenant may either be a "business tenant" in which case his security of tenure will be governed by the Landlord and Tenant Act 1954 Pt II, or, depending upon the date the tenancy was granted, a regulated tenant under the Rent Act 1977 or an assured tenant under the Housing Act 1988 (or in the public sector a secure tenant protected under the Housing Act 1985).

The private sector—is the tenant an assured/Rent Act tenant?

17.013 Subject to a few transitional cases, a tenancy of a dwelling-house let prior to the commencement of the Housing Act 1988 (January 15, 1989) is capable of being a regulated tenancy under the Rent Act 1977 and a tenancy of a dwelling-house created on or after that date is capable of being an assured tenancy under the 1988 Act (see paras 6.008 and 8.007). The rules for governing whether or not the tenancy is a "residential" tenancy (i.e. regulated or assured) or a "business" tenancy are the same whether the tenancy was granted before or after that date. There are two stages in deciding whether the tenant is a residential tenant or a business tenant. First, it is necessary to look at the purpose of the letting and, second, it is necessary to look at the purpose of the tenant's occupation.

The purpose of the letting

Unless the dwelling-house was let as a separate dwelling it cannot be the subject **17.014** of an (assured) tenancy as it will not fall within the definition of such a tenancy as set out in s.1 of the Housing Act 1988 (or of a protected tenancy as set out in s.1 of the Rent Act 1977). Hence, a dwelling-house which is let so that the tenant may carry on a business from the premises is not "let as a dwelling" even if the tenant in fact lives there. It is the purpose of the letting that is paramount. The relevant time for ascertaining the purpose is the date of the letting unless there is a subsequent agreement (*Russell v Booker* (1982) 263 E.G. 513).

In the leading case of *Wolfe v Hogan* [1949] 2 K.B. 194 at 204 Denning L.J. explained how one goes about ascertaining the purpose of the letting.

> "In determining whether a house or part of a house is 'let as a dwelling' within the meaning of the Rent Restriction Acts, it is necessary to look at the purpose of the letting. If the lease contains an express provision as to the purpose of the letting, it is not necessary to look further. But if there is no express provision, it is open to the court to look at the circumstances of the letting. If the house is constructed for use as a dwelling house, it is reasonable to infer that the purpose was to let it as a dwelling, but if, on the other hand, it is constructed for use as a lock-up shop, the reasonable inference is that it was let for business purposes. If the position were neutral, then it would be proper to look at the actual user. It is not a question of implied terms. It is a question of the purpose for which the premises were let."

Note that if the lease contains covenants against use as a dwelling house it could **17.015** not have been let as a dwelling, but the fact that there are covenants that simply preclude use of the premises for any trade other than those specified in the lease does not necessarily mean that the premises are solely let for the purpose of a business.

Where premises were let (after the Rent Act 1965 came into force) for mixed business and residential use the premises are not "let as a separate dwelling" within s.1 of the 1977 Act unless the business purpose was merely incidental to the residential purpose so that s.23(1) of the 1954 Act would not apply—see below (*Cheryl Investments Ltd v Saldanha* [1978] 1 W.L.R. 1329; *Webb and Barrett v London Borough of Barnet* (1989) 21 H.L.R. 228). If the tenancy was so let for mixed and residential purposes it was not therefore protected. The tenant cannot, simply by unilaterally ceasing the business use, arrogate to himself protection under the Rent Act 1977 (*Tan v Sitkowski* [2007] EWCA Civ 30). (Prior to the 1965 Act, a mixed use tenancy was protected.)

Where the premises are let for a business purpose but the tenant subsequently gives up the business use and merely lives there, the letting does not become regulated/assured. This is because the premises were not originally "let as a dwelling" (*Pulleng v Curran* (1982) 44 P. & C.R. 58; *Trustees of Henry Smith's Charity v Wagle* (1989) 21 H.L.R. 177). Where property is initially let for business purposes or mixed business and residential purposes it is necessary to have a surrender of the business lease and a grant of a new residential lease for the property to be regarded as "let as a separate dwelling" (*Tomkins v Basildon District Council* [2002] EWCA Civ 876).

The purpose of the tenant's occupation

17.016 Once it has been established that the purpose of the letting was residential and that any business purpose was merely incidental, it is then necessary to look at the purpose of the actual occupation. This is because s.24 of the Rent Act 1977 provides that the tenancy is not a regulated tenancy where Pt II of the Landlord and Tenant Act 1954 applies. Similarly, para.4 of Sch.1 to the 1988 Act provides that a tenancy cannot be assured if Pt II of the 1954 Act applies. Section 23(1) of the 1954 Act provides that Pt II applies:

> . . . to any tenancy where the property comprised in the tenancy is or includes premises which are occupied by the tenant and are so occupied for the purpose of a business carried on by him or for those and other purposes.

Thus, even if the premises were let wholly for residential purposes the tenancy will not be regulated/assured if the purpose of the tenant's occupation is a business one. In *Cheryl Investments Ltd v Saldanha* [1978] 1 W.L.R. 1329, however, it was held that it is only where the business purpose is a significant purpose that the 1954 Act will apply. If the business purpose is merely incidental to the residential purpose (e.g. if a person works at home in the evenings: see *Saldanha*, Lord Denning's first example at 1333) the Rent Act 1977 or the Housing Act 1988 will continue to be applicable. The purpose of the tenant's occupation is a question of fact to be decided by the judge on the evidence. The term "business" includes "a trade profession or employment" (s.23(2) of the Landlord and Tenant Act 1954) and whether any particular activity is a business is also a question of fact to be decided in the light of all the circumstances (see *Lewis v Weldcrest* [1978] 1 W.L.R. 1107 where it was held that a tenant who took in five lodgers at very low rents that provided very little profit was not carrying on a trade). (See further *Graysim Ltd v P & O Property Holdings Ltd* [1995] 4 All E.R. 831 at 838j HL—where there are sub-lettings the 1954 Act will not apply to the head tenancy.)

17.017 A tenancy is not within the 1954 Act if it is a fixed term of six months or less unless there is a clause in the lease providing for an extension or renewal or unless the tenant (or any predecessor in the business) has been in occupation for more than 12 months (s.43(3)). Periodic tenancies where the period is less than six months are, however, within the 1954 Act. There are also other exceptions (see s.43).

The time for deciding whether the premises are being occupied for a business purpose is the date that the contractual tenancy would have come to an end. Furthermore, it would appear that if the dwelling-house was let as a separate dwelling but ceased to be regulated at some stage because it was used for a business purpose the tenancy will once again become regulated if the business occupation ceases unless in the meantime a new tenancy has been granted under the 1954 Act (see *Pulleng v Curran* (1982) 44 P. & C.R. 58; *Webb and Barrett v London Borough of Barnet* (1989) 21 H.L.R. 228).

Where the premises were originally let for purely residential purposes, and the tenant subsequently uses them wholly or partly for business purposes Pt II of the 1954 Act applies so that they are no longer protected by the Rent Act 1977. However, if he ceases to use them for business purposes the premises do once again become subject to the protection of the 1977 Act (*Tan v Sitkowski* [2007] EWCA Civ 30).

It should also be noted that if the tenancy is not within the 1954 Act (perhaps because it was originally granted for a term of less than six months) the tenancy nonetheless cannot be a statutory tenancy within the meaning of s.2 of the Rent Act 1977 after the protected tenancy has been determined if the tenant occupies the premises wholly for the purpose of a business (see para.8.013). (See s.64(2) of the Housing Act 1980 for any tenancy that was a controlled tenancy on November 22, 1980.) Nor can such a tenancy be assured because the tenant will not be occupying the property as his only or principal home (s.1(1)(b) of the Housing Act 1988).

The public sector—is the tenant a secure tenant?

As with the private sector it is necessary to go through a two-stage process. **17.018** This is because s.97 of the Housing Act 1985 provides that a tenancy is not capable of being a secure tenancy unless the dwelling-house was let as a dwelling. Second, para.11 of Sch.1 to the 1985 Act provides that a tenancy is not a secure tenancy if it is one to which Pt II of the 1954 Act applies. For an example in the public sector, see *Webb and Barrett v London Borough of Barnet* (1989) 21 H.L.R. 228 and *Tomkins v Basildon DC* [2002] EWCA Civ 876.

Business premises within the 1954 Act

If the tenancy does fall within the 1954 Act rather than the Rent Act 1977, Housing **17.019** Act 1988, or the Housing Act 1985 the tenant may be entitled to a new tenancy under Pt II of the 1954 Act (see Gary Webber, *Business Premises: Possession and Lease Renewal*, 4th edn (London: Sweet & Maxwell, 2009).

Business premises outside the 1954 Act

Where the premises are not protected by the Rent Act 1977, the Housing Act **17.020** 1988, the Housing Act 1985 or the 1954 Act the ordinary common law rules will apply (see Chs 2 and 3).

Company lets

General

A tenancy of a dwelling-house let to a company (prior to the commencement of **17.021** the Housing Act 1988) will be a protected tenancy provided that the conditions of s.1 of the Rent Act 1977 are fulfilled. Upon the termination of the protected tenancy, however, the company tenant will not become a statutory tenant entitled to security of tenure as there can be no personal occupation of the premises by a company as required by s.2 of the Rent Act 1977 (*Firstcross Ltd v East West (Export/Import) Ltd* (1980) 255 E.G. 355). A director or manager of the company tenant who was occupying the premises as his residence does not become a statutory tenant because he was not the protected tenant immediately prior to the termination of the protected tenancy (*Hiller v United Dairies (London) Ltd* [1934] 1 K.B. 57).

Section 1(1)(a) of the Housing Act 1988 provides that a tenancy will not be an assured tenancy unless the tenant, or where there are joint tenants each of them, is an individual. A tenancy granted to a company may not therefore be an assured tenancy.

Where a company permits its employees to occupy the premises, Pt II of the Landlord and Tenant Act 1954 will not apply to the company's tenancy unless it is necessary for the employees to live there in order to carry out their duties properly (see *Chapman v Freeman* [1978] 3 All E.R. 878).

If a company tenant sub-lets to an individual, the sub-tenant may be able to remain in possession pursuant to s.137(2) of the Rent Act 1977 at the end of the company's tenancy (see para.8.038) or, as the case may be, pursuant to s.18(1) of the Housing Act 1988 (para.6.034).

"Sham" company lets

17.022   In many cases tenancies have been granted to companies for the sole purpose of avoiding the Rent Acts. In *Hilton v Plustitle Ltd* [1988] 3 All E.R. 1051 the landlord's advertisement for a tenant made it clear that the letting was to be a company let. At the landlord's suggestion the intending occupier, a Miss Rose, purchased a company "off the shelf" for the specific purpose of taking the tenancy. The tenancy was then granted to the company. The judge found as a fact

> "that it was both parties' clear intention with all knowledge of what this involved that the flat should be let to a company and not to Miss Rose personally".

The Court of Appeal held that the tenancy was not a "sham" and that the company was truly the tenant. (For a similar case see *Estavest Investments v Commercial Express Travel Ltd* (1989) 21 H.L.R. 106.)

However, *Hilton v Plustitle* was decided before the decision of the House of Lords in *Antoniades v Villiers* [1988] 3 All E.R. 1058 in which "shams" in relation to licences were discussed (see para.5.008). In *Antoniades v Villiers* (see Lord Templeman at 1067j) and in *Aslan v Murphy* (*Nos 1 and 2*) [1989] 3 All E.R. 130 it was held that it is not necessary for the court to come to the conclusion that an agreement is a "sham" before disregarding its terms. Even where the agreement is not a "sham" the court will consider whether in the light of the factual situation its provisions were part of the true bargain between the parties or were a pretence intended to evade the Rent Acts.

Subsequently, in *Kaye v Massbetter Ltd* [1991] 2 E.G.L.R. 97 CA Lord Donaldson said that there was nothing to stop the parties agreeing a company let provided it was a genuine one and that

> "[t]he test is: was the letting genuine? If you look at the facts and find that there are indicia that the company was never intended to be the tenant, then you may conclude that it was not genuine. But the issue is simply one of genuineness" (at 98K).

He emphasised that it "is in the end entirely a question of fact". In his judgment Nicholls L.J. said:

"[Counsel for the defendant] submitted that, if the only purpose for which a company **17.023**
was introduced onto the scene and into a residential letting arrangement such as that
involved here was to avoid the Rent Acts, the resultant tenancy agreement is not a
genuine letting to the company.

I cannot accept that proposition as an accurate statement of the law. The issue in every
case involves seeing what, in law, was the agreement between the parties. This involves
identifying who in law were the parties to the agreement. In this regard the terms of a
document signed by the parties or the form of words used by them in an oral agreement
are, of course, not conclusive. Parties cannot contract out of the Rent Acts and the court
will be astute in detecting and frustrating shams or pretences, namely, agreements
expressed in a form which do not truly reflect the parties' intention. Thus, the purpose
for which and the circumstances in which the company is introduced onto the scene are
very important background facts. But it by no means follows that, a company having
been introduced, the parties did not intend in law that the company should be the tenant
and liable as such to the landlord."

The conclusion to be drawn from the cases would therefore seem to be that it
is not necessary for the defendant to show that the agreement, in naming the
company as a tenant, is a sham (whatever precisely that means). It will be sufficient for the defendant to show that it is a pretence. However, if the court is satisfied that the company is genuinely the tenant the "company let" will stand even
though the intention was to avoid letting to an individual who would have had
statutory protection.

See also *Eaton Square Properties Ltd v O'Higgins* [2000] E.G.C.S. 118 CA—
lease taken in company name so that the company could apply to the Inland
Revenue to allow expenses incurred in refurbishment to be set against corporation
tax. Held: genuine company let.

Chapter 18

Agricultural Accommodation

There are six different situations that may arise when one is dealing with what **18.001** might be called "agricultural accommodation". These are as follows:

(1) premises on agricultural land leased to a farmer—Agricultural Holdings Act 1986 and the Agricultural Tenancies Act 1995;

(2) premises occupied by farmworkers who are not protected tenants but who are protected under the Rent (Agriculture) Act 1976;

(3) assured agricultural occupancies under the Housing Act 1988;

(4) premises occupied by farmworkers under protected tenancies—s.99 and Sch.16 of the Rent Act 1977;

(5) a residual category of farmworkers who have protection under s.4 of the Protection from Eviction Act 1977;

(6) premises occupied by ordinary protected tenants that were once occupied by farmworkers—Sch.15, Cases 16, 17 and 18 of the Rent Act 1977.

Agricultural holdings

A tenancy is not a protected, assured or secure tenancy if the dwelling-house is **18.002** comprised in:

(a) an agricultural holding (within the meaning of the Agricultural Holdings Act 1986) and is occupied by the person responsible for the control (whether as tenant or as servant or agent of the tenant) of the farming of the holding; or

(b) (subject to limited transitional exceptions, where the tenancy was granted on or after September 1, 1995) a holding held under a farm business tenancy and is occupied by the person responsible for the control (whether as tenant or as servant or agent of the tenant) of the management of the holding.

(Section 10 of the Rent Act 1977; Sch.1 para.7 of the Housing Act 1988; Sch.1 para.8 of the Housing Act 1985.)

The expression "agricultural holding" is defined in s.1 of the Agricultural Holdings Act 1986. It means the aggregate of the land (whether agricultural land or not) comprised in a contract of tenancy (as defined in s.1(5)) which is a contract for an agricultural tenancy. A contract of tenancy relating to land is "a contract for an agricultural tenancy" if having regard to:

(1) the terms of the tenancy;

(2) the actual or contemplated use of the land at the time of the conclusion of the contract and subsequently; and

(3) any other relevant circumstances;

the whole of the land comprised in the contract, subject to such exceptions only as do not substantially affect the character of the tenancy, is let for use as agricultural land (s.1 of the Agricultural Holdings Act 1986). "Agricultural land" means:

(1) land used for agriculture which is so used for the purposes of a trade or business; and

(2) any other land which, by virtue of a designation under s.109(1) of the Agriculture Act 1947, is agricultural land within the meaning of that Act.

18.003 "Agriculture" is defined as including horticulture, fruit growing, seed growing, dairy farming and livestock breeding and keeping, the use of the land as grazing land, meadow land, osier land, market gardens and nursery grounds, and the use of land for woodlands where that use is ancillary to the farming of land for other agricultural purposes; and "livestock" includes any creature kept for the production of food, wool, skins or fur or for the purpose of its use in the farming of land or the carrying on in relation to land of any agricultural activity (s.96(1) of the Agricultural Holdings Act 1986).

The expressions "farm business tenancy" and "holding" in relation to such a tenancy are defined in the Agricultural Tenancies Act 1995.

Where the dwelling house is comprised in an agricultural holding the tenant of the holding will enjoy the security of tenure provided by the Agricultural Holdings Act 1986. A discussion of the protection that is afforded to tenants who farm agricultural holdings is beyond the scope of this book. Putting it very briefly the landlord will usually only be able to regain possession of the land, in the face of the tenant's objection, if he can prove one of a number of grounds set out in the Agricultural Holdings Act 1986. Most of these grounds relate to agricultural issues. Where the tenancy was granted on or after September 1, 1995 and is a farm business tenancy the rights of the tenant are governed by the Agricultural Tenancies Act 1995 and are much more restricted than those enjoyed by tenants of agricultural holdings.

If the tenant of the holding has himself let a dwelling house comprised in the holding to a farmer who is responsible for the control of the farming the farmer will not be a protected, assured or secure tenant either. He may, however, be protected under the Rent (Agriculture) Act 1976, Ch.III of the Housing Act 1988 or the Protection from Eviction Act 1977 (see below).

Rent (Agriculture) Act 1976

Application of the Act: protected occupiers

The purpose of the Rent (Agriculture) Act 1976 is to provide protection to **18.004** farmworkers living in tied accommodation who are not protected under the Rent Act 1977.

The provisions governing whether a person is protected are s.2 and Schs 2 and 3 to the 1976 Act. They are detailed and complicated and should be referred to in every case. The following is an attempt to give a simplified definition which should cover the situation in most cases. The 1976 Act applies where a person occupies a dwelling-house and the following three conditions are satisfied:

(1) the agreement under which he occupies is a "relevant licence or tenancy". A "relevant licence" is one which, if it were a tenancy, would be a protected tenancy under the Rent Act 1977 if it were not for the fact that it would be a tenancy at a low rent or a tenancy comprised in an agricultural holding. A "relevant tenancy" is a tenancy which would be protected under the Rent Act 1977 if it were not for one of those facts. (See also Sch.2 para.3(3) for cases where board or attendance is provided);

(2) the landlord is the occupier's employer (or ex-employer) or someone with whom his employer (or ex-employer) has made arrangements for the dwelling-house to be used by persons employed in agriculture;

(3) the occupier is or has been employed whole time in agriculture for a period of 91 weeks out of any period of 104 weeks during the subsistence of his licence or tenancy.

Where the above conditions are satisfied the occupier is termed a "protected occupier in his own right" (s.2(4)).

The above conditions cannot generally be satisfied where the tenancy was created on or after January 15, 1989 (commencement of the Housing Act 1988). Since that date it has not been possible (except in a few limited transitional cases: see s.34 of the 1988 Act, para.8.007) to create protected tenancies. See para.18.010 "Assured agricultural occupancies".

Statutory tenants

On determination of the protected occupancy, by whatever means, the protected **18.005** occupier becomes a "statutory tenant in his own right", and remains so as long as he occupies the dwelling-house as his residence (s.4(1) of the Rent (Agriculture) Act 1976). A statutory tenancy may arise by the payment and acceptance of rent following upon the determination of a rent for the tenancy by the rent officer (*Durman v Bell* (1988) 20 H.L.R. 340). Use by the tenant of the property for significant business use (in addition to residential use) does not result in an automatic termination of the statutory tenancy, although it may give rise to a ground for possession if the tenant is acting in breach of a term of the tenancy (*Durman v Bell*). For the terms of the statutory tenancy see s.10 and Sch.5. Where the protected occupancy was a licence the statutory tenancy will be a weekly tenancy (Sch.5 para.3).

Where a person is a licensee because he was required to occupy the dwelling for the better performance of his duties he becomes a statutory tenant on the termination of his employment if thereafter he remains in possession paying rent (*Burgoyne v Griffiths* [1991] 1 E.G.L.R. 14 CA).

A person cannot, however, be a statutory tenant at any time when his landlord is the Crown Estate (unless the dwelling-house is under the management of the Crown Estate Commissioners), one of a number of public bodies referred to in s.5(2), (3) or a housing association registered under the Housing Associations Act 1985 or is a housing co-operative association within the meaning of that Act (s.5).

Termination and recovery of possession

18.006 The procedure for termination and recovery of possession of the dwelling-house is very similar to the procedure that applies where the tenancy is a protected or statutory tenancy under the Rent Act 1977. If the agreement under which the protected occupier occupies is a licence it is determined in accordance with the terms of the agreement by a notice in prescribed form. If it is a tenancy it is determined by notice to quit, forfeiture, etc. It may also be converted to a statutory tenancy by service of a notice of increase in rent under s.16 of the Rent (Agriculture) Act 1976. As with 1977 Act statutory tenancies it is not necessary to serve a notice to quit to determine a statutory tenancy that arises under the 1976 Act after termination of a protected occupancy (s.6(2)). Hence, once the protected occupancy has been brought to an end the landlord should simply commence proceedings for possession. The court will not make an order for possession except in the cases mentioned in Sch.4 to the 1976 Act. There are 13 cases. Cases I–X are discretionary grounds for possession and the court may not make an order for possession unless it considers it reasonable to do so (s.7(1),(2)). Cases XI, XII and XIII are mandatory grounds for possession and if the landlord proves that one of these cases applies the court must make an order for possession (s.6(6)).

The discretionary grounds—Cases I–X

18.007

    I Alternative accommodation provided by a person or body other than the local authority.

    II Alternative accommodation provided or arranged by local authority. (Note the local authority's duty to rehouse under s.27.)

    III Arrears of rent or breach of other obligation of the tenant.

    IV Nuisance, annoyance, immoral or illegal user.

    V Deterioration of the dwelling-house.

    VI Deterioration of the furniture.

    VII Tenant's notice to quit.

    VIII Assigning, sub-letting or parting with possession without consent.

    IX Dwelling-house reasonably required by landlord.

    X Overcharging sub-tenants.

The mandatory grounds

XI   Owner-occupiers.   **18.008**

XII Retirement homes.

XIII Overcrowded dwelling-houses.

Where the court makes an order for possession under one of the discretionary grounds the court may stay or suspend execution of the order, or postpone the date for possession for such period or periods as the court thinks fit (s.7(3)). On any such stay, suspension or postponement the court must, unless it considers that to do so would cause exceptional hardship to the tenant or would otherwise be unreasonable, impose conditions with regard to the payment of arrears of rent (if any) and rent or payments in respect of occupation after termination of the tenancy (mesne profits) and may impose such other conditions as it thinks fit (s.7(4)). If the conditions imposed are complied with, the court may if it thinks fit discharge or rescind the order for possession (s.7(5)).

Where the order for possession is made under one of the mandatory grounds the court may only postpone the date for possession for a maximum of 14 days unless exceptional hardship would be caused by such a short order in which case the court may postpone the effect of the order for up to six weeks (s.89 of the Housing Act 1980; para.3.034).

Sub-letting, bankruptcy and death

See s.9 of the 1976 Act and s.137 of the Rent Act 1977 for the effect upon a sub-   **18.009**
tenant of an order for possession against the tenant and for the position on the determination of a head tenancy either as a result of such an order or otherwise. (Compare the position of protected or statutory sub-tenants: para.8.037.)

For the position on the bankruptcy of the tenant see s.283(3A) and s.308A of the Insolvency Act 1986 (as introduced by s.117 of the Housing Act 1988) (see generally para.4.018).

Section 3 and s.4(3), (4) relate to succession on death of the protected occupier or statutory tenant but note that these provisions have been amended by s.39 and Sch.4 of Pt II of the Housing Act 1988. In particular, the tenancy becomes an assured agricultural occupancy on succession (s.39(8) of the Housing Act 1988).

Assured agricultural occupancies: Housing Act 1988

We are here concerned with tenancies and licences created on or after January 15,   **18.010**
1989 (the date of the commencement of the Housing Act 1988). Since that date it has not been possible (except in some limited cases—see para.8.007) to create protected tenancies and therefore it has not been possible to become a protected occupier under the 1976 Act (see above). Instead persons who would have been protected occupiers under the 1976 Act now become "assured agricultural occupiers" under the 1988 Act.

Assured agricultural occupancies are treated as if they are assured tenancies for the purposes of applying Ch.I of the Housing Act 1988. The provisions relating to notices and recovery of possession that apply to assured tenancies (see Ch.6) therefore apply (subject to some modification) in relation to an assured agricultural occupancy whether the occupant is a tenant or licensee and if he is a tenant whether or not he is an assured tenant (s.24(3) of the 1988 Act).

Definition of assured agricultural occupancies

18.011   In order for a tenancy or licence to be an assured agricultural occupancy two conditions must be fulfilled: (1) the tenancy/licence condition; and (2) the agricultural worker condition (s.24(1)). Where a statutory periodic tenancy arises on the coming to an end of an assured agricultural occupancy it remains an assured agricultural occupancy as long as the agricultural worker condition continues to be satisfied (s.25(1)(a)), and, if no rent was payable under the fixed term, as a monthly occupancy (s.25(1)(b)).

(1) The tenancy/licence condition: s.24(2). This condition is fulfilled if the tenancy or licence is:

(a) an assured tenancy (see para.6.003) which is not an assured shorthold tenancy (para.7.002);

(b) a tenancy which would be an assured tenancy (other than a shorthold) but is not an assured tenancy by reason only of para.3, 3A or 3B (tenancies at a low rent) and/or para.7 (tenancy of agricultural holding) of Sch.1 to the 1988 Act (i.e. the list of exceptions: see para.A2.052 and Appendix 1); or

(c) a licence under which a person has exclusive possession of a dwelling-house as a separate dwelling and which if it were a tenancy would be a tenancy falling within (a) or (b) above.

(2) The agricultural worker condition: s.24(1) and Sch.3 to the 1988 Act. The "agricultural worker condition" is fulfilled with respect to a relevant tenancy or licence if:

(a) the dwelling-house is or has been in "qualifying ownership" at any time during the subsistence of the tenancy or licence (whether or not it was at that time a relevant tenancy or licence); and

(b) the occupier or, where there are joint occupiers, at least one of them:

(i) is a qualifying worker or has been a qualifying worker at any time during the subsistence of the tenancy or licence (whether or not it was at that time a relevant tenancy or licence); or

(ii) is incapable of "whole time work" in agriculture or work in agriculture as a permit worker in consequence of a qualifying injury or disease (Sch.3 para.2).

(The various terms used here have the same meanings that they have in Sch.3 to the Rent (Agriculture) Act 1976, and para.1 of Sch.3 to the 1988 Act.)

Where a tenancy/licence is granted to a person in consideration of his giving up possession of a dwelling-house in respect of which the agricultural worker condition was fulfilled the agricultural worker condition is deemed to be fulfilled in respect of the second property (Sch.3 para.4).

Termination and recovery of possession: section 25

As stated in the introduction to this section, the provisions relating to assured **18.012** tenancies for termination and recovery of possession (see Ch.6) apply (subject to modification) to assured agricultural occupancies. The modifications are as follows:

(1) Ground 16 (dwelling-house let in consequence of employment) is omitted from Sch.2 (the grounds for possession).

(2) Part III of Sch.2 (suitable alternative accommodation) is amended so that the reference in para.2 of that Part to an assured tenancy includes a reference to an assured agricultural occupancy.

Note that a notice by a tenant under an assured agricultural occupancy to terminate his employment cannot constitute a notice to quit as respects the occupancy. Only an actual notice to quit in proper form (see para.3.018) will be sufficient (s.25(4), (5)).

The provisions of s.27 of the Rent (Agriculture) Act 1976 relating to rehousing by local authorities apply to assured occupants (s.26 of the 1988 Act).

Bankruptcy and death

Bankruptcy as with assured tenancies s.283(3A) of the Insolvency Act 1986 (as **18.013** introduced by s.117 of the Housing Act 1988) applies; see further para.4.018.

Death

Schedule 3 to the 1988 Act contains provisions providing for the "agricultural **18.014** worker condition" (see above) to be satisfied on the death of the original occupier thus providing for succession of the agricultural occupancy. The persons who may be entitled to succeed are the occupier's widow, widower, civil partner or a member of his family. There can only be one succession (Sch.3 para.3).

Farmworkers who are protected or statutory tenants

Section 99 and Sch.16 of the Rent Act 1977 ensure that farmworkers who are **18.015** protected or statutory tenants have the same protection as protected occupants or statutory tenants as defined by the Rent (Agriculture) Act 1976. If it were not for these provisions the alternative accommodation grounds would not apply.

For s.99 to apply the following conditions must be satisfied:

(a) the tenancy must be a protected or statutory tenancy within the meaning of ss.1 and 2 of the Rent Act 1977; and

(b) the tenancy must be such that, if it were a tenancy at a low rent and if (where relevant) any earlier tenancy granted to the tenant or to a member of his family had been a tenancy at a low rent, it would be a protected occupancy or statutory tenancy as defined in the Rent (Agriculture) Act 1976.

If the tenancy does fall within the s.99 jurisdiction the court may not make an order for possession unless the court considers it reasonable to make such an order, and the circumstances are as specified in Cases 1–6, 9 and 10 of Sch.15 to the Rent Act 1977 (i.e. all the discretionary grounds except Case 8), or either of the two cases in Sch.16 (see below). In these circumstances the court may stay or suspend execution of the order or postpone the date for possession for such period or periods as the court thinks fit (s.100 of the Rent Act 1977). Proceedings are commenced by action. The landlord can also apply for possession if the circumstances are as specified in Cases 11–15, 19 and 20 of Sch.15 (i.e. all the mandatory grounds except 16, 17 and 18). In these circumstances the court must make an order for possession which can only be suspended for 14 days (or six weeks in cases of exceptional hardship); s.89 of the Housing Act 1980, see para.3.034.

Schedule 16 is concerned with the circumstances in which suitable alternative accommodation is available. Case 1 is where the accommodation is not to be provided or arranged by a housing authority and Case 2 is where it is. Schedule 16 is in the same form as Cases I and II of Sch.4 to the Rent (Agriculture) Act 1976 which is dealt with above.

Protection from Eviction Act 1977 section 4

18.016   Where a farmworker is not a regulated tenant under s.1 of the Rent Act 1977 nor an assured agricultural occupant under Ch.III of the Housing Act 1988 nor a protected occupant or statutory tenant under the Rent (Agriculture) Act 1976 he will probably be entitled to the fairly limited protection of s.4 of the Protection from Eviction Act 1977. To qualify for this protection the farmworker must show that he occupied the premises under the terms of his employment as a person employed in agriculture as defined in s.1 of the Rent (Agriculture) Act 1976 (s.4 of the Protection from Eviction Act 1977). Both tenants and licensees fall within this definition (s.38(2) of the Rent (Agriculture) Act 1976; and see s.4(2A) of the 1977 Act). The farmworker's widow (or widower) is also entitled to rely upon s.4 if that person was residing with him at his death. If the farmworker leaves no widow or widower any member of his family residing with him at his death may rely upon s.1 (s.4(2)).

Section 4(3) gives the courts a discretionary power to suspend the execution of an order for possession, if it is made within the period of six months beginning with the date when the former tenancy or licence came to an end, for the remainder of the six months unless:

(1)   the court is satisfied either:

   (a)   that suitable accommodation is or will be made available within that period;

   (b)   the efficient management of any agricultural land or the efficient carrying on of any agricultural operations will be seriously prejudiced unless the premises are available for another person employed or to be employed by the owner;

   (c)   that greater hardship would be caused by the suspension of the order than by its execution;

   (d)   that the occupier or any person residing with him has caused damage to the premises or has been a nuisance or annoyance to persons occupying other premises; and

(2) the court considers that it would be reasonable not to suspend the execution of the order.

Where the court suspends the order for possession it must do so on such terms and **18.017** conditions including conditions as to payment of arrears of rent, mesne profits and otherwise as the court thinks reasonable (s.4(5)).

In considering whether or how to exercise its powers to suspend execution of the order the court must have regard to all the circumstances of the case and in particular whether the efficient management of any agricultural land or the efficient carrying on of any agricultural operations would be seriously prejudiced unless the premises were available for someone employed by the owner, whether suitable alternative accommodation is available, and whether greater hardship would be caused by a suspension than an immediate order (s.4(8)). An order for costs should not be made where the order for possession is suspended unless, having regard to the conduct of the parties, there are special reasons for making such an order (s.4(8)).

Agricultural accommodation presently occupied by non-agricultural protected tenants (Sch.15, Cases 16, 17 and 18 of the Rent Act 1977).

This part of the chapter is concerned with the situation where the tenant is an **18.018** ordinary protected or statutory tenant who would not be a protected occupant or statutory tenant under the Rent (Agriculture) Act 1976 even if the tenancy were a tenancy at low rent (i.e. a tenant who is not a farmworker). The landlord may, of course, rely upon any of the discretionary or mandatory grounds set out in Sch.15 to the Rent Act 1977, but Pt II of that Schedule includes three grounds for possession that are of particular relevance in the agriculture sector (Cases 16, 17 and 18).

These three cases apply where the dwelling-house has in the past been occupied by a person engaged in agriculture and where the landlord wishes to regain possession from the present tenant so that it can once again be occupied by a person engaged in agriculture. None of these three cases will apply unless the landlord gave the tenant notice in writing stating that possession might be recovered under the relevant case not later than the "relevant date" (usually the date the tenancy commenced; see Sch.15 Pt III para.2). The notice does not have to be in any particular form (*Springfield Investments Ltd v Bell* [1991] 1 E.G.L.R. 115 CA; a certificate of fair rent which stated that it was proposed to let the dwelling

"on a regulated tenancy basis subject to the provisions of Case 16 . . . (whereby repossession could be obtained to house an agricultural worker, employed or to be employed by the Landlord)" was held to be sufficient).

There is no power to dispense with the notice even if it is just and equitable to do so. Each ground is a mandatory ground and so if a notice was given and the case applies the court must make an order for possession which may not be suspended for more than 14 days (or six weeks in case of exceptional hardship) (s.89 of the Housing Act 1980; see para.3.034).

Chapter 19

Student Accommodation, Holiday Accommodation, Board and Attendance

Student accommodation

Lettings to students

A student may, like anyone else, occupy premises under an assured or regulated **19.001** tenancy, a secure tenancy, a restricted contract or a completely unprotected tenancy or licence. If he does so he will usually have the same protection, or lack of it, as all other tenants or licensees in a similar position.

Where, however, a tenancy is granted to a person who is pursuing, or intends to pursue, a course of study provided by a "specified educational institution" and it is granted either by that institution or by another specified institution or body of persons the tenancy cannot be assured or protected even though it would normally fall within the definition of an assured or a protected tenancy (Sch.1 para.8 to the Housing Act 1988; s.8 of the Rent Act 1977). The institutions and bodies specified are the universities and their colleges, and the colleges of further education. A number of other institutions and bodies are also specified. (See the Assured and Protected Tenancies (Lettings to Students) Regulations 1998 (SI 1998/1967) (as amended).)

Thus, once the tenancy has come to an end the educational institution will be **19.002** able to regain possession without having to show one of the usual Rent Act/ Housing Act 1988 grounds.

It is not usually necessary for the educational institution to own the freehold of the premises in question for the exception to apply. It may take a lease of private premises and then sub-let those premises to the student. The student's landlord will thus be a specified educational institution and the tenancy will not be assured/ protected. Once the lease has been determined the college will be able to obtain an order for possession but the owner will not be able to do so without first determining the college's lease (see *St Catherine's College v Dorling* [1980] 1 W.L.R. 66).

Vacation lettings of student accommodation

If a college or other specified educational institution wishes to let a dwelling- **19.003** house which is usually let to students to someone else on an assured tenancy during the vacation period, without losing its right to recover possession at the end of the tenancy, it may do so by complying with Ground 4 of Sch.2 to the Housing Act 1988. In order to comply with the requirements of this case the dwelling-house must be let for a fixed term of 12 months or less, and:

(1) not later than the date the tenancy is entered into the landlord must give notice in writing to the tenant that possession might be recovered under Ground 4 (see Pt IV of Sch.2 in relation to notices); and

(2) at some time within the period of 12 months ending with the beginning of the tenancy (see s.45(2)) the dwelling-house must have been the subject of a tenancy falling within para.8 of Sch.1 to the 1988 Act, i.e. granted to a student by a specified educational institution.

Although the tenancy must be for a fixed term it may contain a forfeiture clause and a clause allowing the tenant to serve a notice to quit.

If the dwelling-house is in fact privately owned but let to the college during the term time (pursuant to an agreement between the owner and the college) the owner will be able to rely on this ground himself, and thus will be able to let out the premises during the vacation without the fear of becoming saddled with an assured tenant. This follows from the wording of Ground 4 which requires that "the landlord" give the appropriate notice which may therefore be either a college or a private owner.

If the landlord, whether it be a college or private owner, satisfies the court that the conditions in Ground 4 have been complied with, the court must make an order for possession as this ground is one of the mandatory possession grounds (s.7(3) of the Housing Act 1988). The court may only suspend the order for possession for up to 14 days, or in the case of exceptional hardship, six weeks (s.89 of the Housing Act 1980, see para.3.034).

Lettings to students by local authorities, housing associations and other public sector bodies (Schedule 1 paragraph 10 to the Housing Act 1985)

19.004 If the landlord is a local authority, or other public sector body mentioned in s.80 of the Housing Act 1985 and s.35(4) of the Housing Act 1988, the tenant will usually be a secure tenant like any other tenant of that body (see Ch.10). A tenancy of a dwelling-house is not a secure tenancy, however, if:

(1) the tenancy was granted for the purpose of enabling the tenant to attend a "designated course" (see the Secure Tenancies (Designated Courses) Regulations 1980 (SI 1980/1407) at a university or other establishment for further education; and

(2) before the grant of the tenancy the landlord notified the student in writing about this exception and the fact that it would apply. The notice must specify the relevant educational establishment.

The tenancy continues to be "unsecure" from the date of its grant until six months after the end of the course; but if the tenant fails to take a designated course at the educational establishment specified in the notice the exception only applies for six months. If the tenancy is not brought to an end within either of these periods the tenant will become a secure tenant. The tenancy will also become secure before the expiry of either six-month period if the landlord notifies the tenant that it is to be regarded as a secure tenancy.

Holiday accommodation

The Housing Act 1988 contains two sets of provisions dealing with the question **19.005** of holiday accommodation. First, it provides that a dwelling-house let for the purpose of a holiday will not be subject to an assured tenancy. Second, it contains a provision permitting the landlord of a dwelling-house used for the purpose of a holiday during the holiday season to let it out on an assured tenancy in between holiday periods and yet recover possession at the end of the term.

Holiday lets

A tenancy will not be an assured tenancy if the purpose of the tenancy is to confer **19.006** on the tenant the right to occupy the dwelling-house for a holiday (Sch.1 para.9 to the Housing Act 1988). Whether that is the purpose is a question of fact which, in the absence of anything in the tenancy agreement regarding the purpose of the tenancy, is determined according to the evidence given in court. Where there is a written agreement containing a term expressly stating that the dwelling-house was let for the purpose of a holiday that term is evidence of the parties' intention, and unless the tenant can show that the statement is in the nature of a sham or a pretence the court will hold that the tenancy is not an assured tenancy (*Buchmann v May* [1978] 2 All E.R. 993; cf. licence cases: see para.5.008 and company lets: para.17.022). On the other hand, a landlord who grants successive "holiday lets" to tenants who he knows are clearly not going to use the premises for the purpose of a holiday is likely to find that the tenants will be assured tenants.

Once the holiday let has come to an end the landlord will be entitled to an order for possession the effect of which the court will not be able to postpone for more than 14 days, or six weeks in cases of exceptional hardship (s.89 of the Housing Act 1980; see para.3.034). As the tenancy is an "excluded tenancy" he need not even take proceedings for possession and may resort to self-help so long as he does not use any violence (see para.22.008).

Out of season lettings

Ground 3 of Sch.2 to the Housing Act 1988 is the provision that gives the owner **19.007** of holiday accommodation the opportunity to let the dwelling-house on an assured tenancy out of season without the danger of the tenant being able to remain in possession at the end of the term. Ground 3 provides that at the end of the tenancy the landlord will be entitled to possession of the dwelling-house if:

(1) the dwelling-house was let for a fixed term of eight months or less; and

(2) not later than the day on which the tenancy is entered into the landlord gave the tenant notice in writing that possession might be recovered on this ground (see Sch.2 Pt IV for rules relating to notices, in particular para.2); and

(3) the dwelling-house was at some time within the period of 12 months ending with the "beginning of the tenancy" (see s.45(2)) occupied under a right to occupy it for a holiday.

The tenancy is for a fixed term notwithstanding that it contains a right of re-entry or a term allowing it to be determined upon the happening of any event (for example, service of a notice to quit by the tenant) other than the giving of notice by the landlord to determine the term.

If Ground 3 applies the court must make an order for possession (s.7(3) of the 1988 Act). The effect of the order may not be postponed for more than 14 days, or six weeks in cases of exceptional hardship (s.89 of the Housing Act 1980; see para.3.034).

Board or attendance

19.008 Where the landlord provides attendance or services which require him or his servants to exercise unrestricted access to and use of the premises the occupier will be a lodger, i.e. a licensee, and not a tenant (see *Street v Mountford* [1985] 2 All E.R. 289, discussed at para.5.001). However, even if the occupier is a tenant his tenancy cannot be protected under s.1 of the Rent Act 1977 if under the tenancy the dwelling-house is bona fide let at a rent which includes payments in respect of board or attendance (s.7(1) of the Rent Act 1977). There is no equivalent provision in the Housing Act 1988 relating to tenancies granted on or after the commencement date of that Act (January 15, 1989).

Form 28: Particulars to be inserted on Form N119—

---

1. By an agreement in writing dated . . . the Claimant let the dwelling house to the Defendant for a term of . . . months commencing on the . . . at a rent of [£] per month.

2. The said tenancy expired on the . . . but the Defendant has failed to give up possession of the said dwelling house to the Claimant and continues in occupation without the licence or consent.

3. The purpose of the said tenancy was to confer on the Defendant the right to occupy the said dwelling house for a holiday. In the premises the Defendant is not entitled to the protection afforded by the Housing Act 1988.

Board

19.009 "Board" is not defined but it is commonly understood to mean the provision of meals. The board provided must be more than minimal if the tenancy is to escape protection but it need be no more than that (*Otter v Norman* [1988] 2 All E.R. 897 HL; a "continental breakfast" consisting of two bread rolls with butter, jam and marmalade, and unlimited tea or coffee with sugar and milk, held to constitute "board"). Where the board is more than minimal the tenancy will be a restricted contract unless one of the exceptions set out in s.19(5) of the Rent Act 1977 applies. One of those exceptions is that the value of the board to the tenant forms a substantial proportion of the whole rent (s.19(5)(c) of the Rent Act 1977; see para.9.009).

Attendance

19.010 Where the rent includes payments in respect of attendance the tenancy will only be excluded from protection if "the amount of rent which is fairly attributable to attendance, having regard to the value of the attendance to the tenant, forms a substantial part of the whole rent" (s.7(2) of the Rent Act 1977).

"Attendance" is a service personal to the tenant performed by an attendant provided by the landlord in accordance with his covenant for the benefit or convenience of the individual tenant in his use or enjoyment of the dwelling-house. Any service that is common to the other tenants in a building, such as the heating of a communal water supply or the provision of a porter, is not personal to the tenant and so, although it is a service, it is not "attendance" (*Palser v Grinling* [1948] A.C. 291).

The provision of clean bed linen and towels is attendance (*Nelson Developments Ltd v Taboada* [1992] 2 E.G.L.R. 107 at 108G).

To be "substantial" the attendance provided must be more than that which is just sufficient to avoid the de minimis principle, but whether the amount of the rent that is attributable to attendance is substantial is a question of fact to be decided by the judge according to the circumstances of each case (*Palser v Grinling*; see also *Marchant v Charters* [1977] 1 W.L.R. 1181). The date at which one assesses the situation is the date of the commencement of the tenancy (*Nelson Developments Ltd*: rent subsequently reduced by rent officer, but the issue was determined on the basis of the rent paid at the commencement of the tenancy).

If, because of the attendance provided, the tenancy is not a protected tenancy it will be a restricted contract unless one of the exceptions set out in s.19(5) of the Rent Act 1977 applies (see Ch.9).

Chapter 20

Mobile Homes

Security of tenure for the owner of a mobile home situated on land belonging to **20.001** another person is governed by the Mobile Homes Act 1983 and the Caravan Sites Act 1968. The Mobile Homes Act 1983 governs the terms of the agreement whereby the mobile home owner is allowed to station his home on that land. If it were not for this Act the mobile home owner would normally only be a licensee of the part of the site upon which the home is situated (see *Taylor v Calvert* [1978] 1 W.L.R. 899). The Caravan Sites Act 1968 protects the owner of the mobile home from eviction without a court order, and from harassment. It also provides for suspension of court orders.

The term "mobile home" means:

"any structure designed or adapted for human habitation which is capable of being moved from one place to another (whether by being towed, or by being transported on a motor vehicle or trailer) and any motor vehicle so designed or adapted but does not include (a) any railway rolling stock which is for the time being on rails forming part of a railway system, or (b) any tent" (s.5(1) of the 1983 Act and s.29(1) of the Caravan Sites and Control of Development Act 1960).

A houseboat on a river moored to a verge of a caravan site does not fall within the definition (*Roy Crimble Ltd v Edgecombe* (1981) 131 N.L.J. 928). A chalet which is capable of being moved from one place to another does fall within the definition (*Wyre Forest District Council v Secretary of State for Environment* [1990] 1 All E.R. 780 and cf. position with assured tenancies at para.6.004).

The Mobile Homes Act 1983 applies to those entitled by agreement to station **20.002** mobile homes which they intend to be their only or main residence on land forming part of a "protected site" (s.1 of the 1983 Act). Land forms part of a protected site when it is licensed for the purpose (or it is land which would be licensed if it were not owned by a local authority) under Pt I of the Caravan Sites and Control of Development Act 1960 (see s.5(1) of the 1983 Act, s.1 of the Caravan Sites Act 1968 and *Balthasar v Mullane* (1985) 17 H.L.R. 561). For guidance on the extent of a "protected site" see *Berkeley Leisure Group v Hampton* [2001] EWCA Civ 1474.

In some circumstances land cannot be a protected site. Those circumstances are as follows (s.5(1) of the 1983 Act and s.1(2) of the 1968 Act):

(1) land for which planning permission or a site licence is granted for holiday use only; and

(2) land for which permission or a licence is granted subject to conditions that there are times of the year when no caravan may be stationed there for human habitation (e.g. *Weeks v Bradshaw* [1993] E.G.C.S. 65; residential occupation forbidden in February of each year).

The residents of the mobile home are referred to in the 1983 Act as "occupiers" and the mobile home site owner as "the owner" (s.1(1)). The Act applies regardless of when the agreement to occupy was made (s.1(3)), whether it is a lease or licence, and whether or not it is for a fixed or a periodic term (see the words "any agreement" in s.1(1)); but the Act probably does not apply to agreements entered into otherwise than for valuable consideration (*Balthasar v Mullane* (1985) 17 H.L.R. 561).

For cases where the "home" is not mobile see paras 6.004 and 8.003. See also *Howard v Charlton* [2002] EWCA Civ 1086 for some guidance on the definition of mobile home.

The agreement

20.003 The Mobile Homes Act 1983 affords the occupier some security by implying into the agreement a number of important terms, for example terms relating to termination, and by requiring the owner to provide the occupier with a written statement of the agreement. The implied terms have effect notwithstanding any express term of the agreement and whether or not a written statement has been given as required (s.2(1) and Pt I of the Schedule to the Act; *Barton v Care* [1992] 2 E.G.L.R. 174 at 175G CA).

The owner is required to give the occupier the written statement 28 days before the making of the agreement to occupy the site (s.1(2) of the 1983 Act). The statement must set out various items, including the implied terms, and must be in prescribed form (s.1(3); Mobile Homes 1983 (Written Statement) (England) Regulations 2011 (SI 2011/1006) and Mobile Homes 1983 (Written Statement) (Wales) Regulations 2007 (SI 2007/3164)). If the owner fails to comply with this requirement the occupier may apply to the appropriate judicial body for an order requiring the owner to provide the statement (s.1(6) and s.4 for determining which judicial body is appropriate). While a shorter period can be agreed in writing for service of the written terms, failure to serve them in time or at all means that the site owner cannot enforce any of the express terms of the agreement unless he applies to the appropriate judicial body. The occupier can rely on and enforce any of the express terms in their favour.

20.004 In addition to the terms which are statutorily implied, the court may, on application by either party within six months of either the date of agreement or the date when the written statement was given (whichever is later) order certain other terms to be implied; that is, terms relating to quiet enjoyment, rent, services provided, maintenance and repair of the mobile home and site, preservation of amenity of the site and access by the owner to the land on which the mobile home is sited (s.2(2) and Pt II of the Schedule). Either party may also apply within the period of six months from the giving of the written statement for any express term to be varied or deleted (s.2(3)). On any application to imply terms or to vary express terms the appropriate judicial body will make such provision as it considers "just and equitable in the circumstances" (s.2(4)).

Duration of the agreement

The right to station a mobile home on land forming part of a protected site **20.005** subsists until the agreement is determined in accordance with the rules for termination set out below (Ch.2, para.1). However, where the owner's estate or interest is insufficient to enable him to grant the right for an indefinite period the period for which the right subsists cannot extend beyond the date when the owner's estate or interest determines (para.2(1)). If planning permission for the use of the site for mobile homes expires at the end of a specified period the period for which the right subsists cannot extend beyond the date when the planning permission expires (para.2(2)). Where in either case there is a change in circumstances which allows a longer period account is taken of that change (para.2(3)).

Termination

Termination by owner

The owner must apply to the judicial body (see s.4 for determining which judicial **20.006** body is appropriate) for an order terminating the agreement on one or more of the three grounds specified by paras 4, 5, 5A and 6 of Ch.2 to the Mobile Homes Act 1983:

(1) Breach of a term of the agreement—The owner shall be entitled to terminate the agreement forthwith if, on the application of the owner, the appropriate judicial body: (a) is satisfied that the occupier has breached a term of the agreement and, after service of a notice to remedy the breach, has not complied with the notice within a reasonable time; and (b) considers it reasonable for the agreement to be terminated. (See *Howard v Charlton* [2002] EWCA Civ 1086, where the owner sought to terminate the agreement on the basis that the occupier had extended the mobile home to such an extent that it was no longer within the definition of a mobile home. The court found that the alterations (a porch) were within the terms of the agreement and so refused to terminate the agreement.)

(2) The appropriate judicial body: (a) is satisfied that the occupier is not occupying the mobile home as his only or main residence; and (b) considers it reasonable for the agreement to be terminated. The relevant date for determining whether the occupier is or is not occupying the mobile home as his only or main residence is the date on which the application to terminate is heard and not the date when the site owner applies to the court for the termination of the agreement (*Omar Parks Ltd v Elkington* [1993] 1 All E.R. 282 CA).

(3) The mobile home is having a detrimental effect on the amenity of the site —for full details see paras 5A and 6 of Ch.2 of the 1983 Act.

If an agreement is terminated under one of these three grounds the occupier may recover any rent paid for the period after termination. If the owner applies for termination to the county court, he must apply to the court which has jurisdiction for the area in which the mobile home is situated (s.5(1)); but if he applies in the wrong court the proceedings are not regarded as a nullity and CPR r.30.2(2) will apply so that the court may either transfer the proceedings, leave them where they are or strike them out (*Faulkner v Love* [1977] Q.B. 937). Application should be made under Pt 7 as there is likely to be a dispute of fact (see Form 29, p.302) or, if it is brought jointly with a claim for possession, should be made under CPR 55 (CPR 55 PD 55A para.1.8). Where approved an order may be made for termination of the agreement forthwith.

Termination by occupier

20.007 The occupier is entitled to terminate the agreement by giving at least four weeks' notice in writing (para.3, Ch.2 of the Mobile Homes Act 1983).

Proceedings for possession

20.008 If the occupier refuses to remove his mobile home after the agreement has come to an end an order excluding the occupier from the land upon which it is situated will then be required and the court has power to suspend the order for up to 12 months (ss.3(1)(b) and 4 of the Caravan Sites Act 1968). The CPR r.55 procedure should be followed as it is a claim for possession against trespassers. It is possible to deal with termination of the agreement and possession in the same proceedings (CPR PD 55.3 para.1.8)

Where the order for possession is suspended, the court may impose such terms and conditions as it thinks reasonable (s.4(2) of the Caravan Sites Act 1968). The court may on the application of either party extend, reduce or terminate the suspension (s.4(3) of the Caravan Sites Act 1968) and in deciding whether to do so will have regard to all the circumstances and in particular will consider whether the occupier has failed to observe any terms or conditions of the agreement, whether the occupier has unreasonably refused an offer by the owner to renew the agreement or to make another agreement for a reasonable period and on reasonable terms, and also whether the occupier has failed to make reasonable efforts to obtain elsewhere other suitable accommodation (s.4(4) of the Caravan Sites Act 1968). If the court suspends any order excluding the occupier from the site there will be no order for costs unless the court considers that there are special reasons having regard to the conduct of either party (s.4(5) of the Caravan Sites Act 1968).

Caravans Site Act 1968

4(1) If in proceedings by the owner of a protected site the court makes an order for enforcing in relation thereto any such right as is mentioned in paragraph (b) of subsection (1) of section 3 of this Act, the court may (without prejudice to any power apart from this section to postpone the operation or suspend the execution of an order, and subject to the following provisions of this section) suspend the enforcement of the order for such period not exceeding twelve months from the date of the order as the court thinks reasonable.

(2) Where the court by virtue of this section suspends the enforcement of an order, it may impose such terms and conditions, including conditions as to the payment of rent or other periodical payments or of arrears of such rent or payments, as the court thinks reasonable.

(3) The court may from time to time, on the application of either party, extend, reduce or terminate the period of suspension ordered by virtue of this section, or vary any terms or conditions imposed thereunder, but shall not extend the period of suspension for more than twelve months at a time.

(4) In considering whether or how to exercise its powers under this section, the court shall have regard to all the circumstances, and in particular to the questions—

(a) whether the occupier of the caravan has failed, whether before or after the expiration or determination of the relevant residential contract, to observe any terms or conditions of that contract, any conditions of the site licence, or any reasonable rules made by the owner for the management and conduct of the site or the maintenance of caravans thereon;

(b) whether the occupier has unreasonably refused an offer by the owner to renew the residential contract or make another such contract for a reasonable period and on reasonable terms;

(c) whether the occupier has failed to make reasonable efforts to obtain elsewhere other suitable accommodation for his caravan (or, as the case may be, another suitable caravan and accommodation for it).

Assignment and death

The occupier may sell his mobile home and assign his agreement to a person **20.009** approved by the owner and the owner must not unreasonably withhold his approval (para.8 Ch.2 of the Mobile Homes Act 1983). He may also give the mobile home, and assign the agreement, to a member of his family approved by the owner, whose approval shall not be unreasonably withheld (para.9).

Consent should be requested before assignment and the occupier should wait a reasonable time for approval to be given. If the approval is refused or simply not given within a reasonable time the occupier can make an application to the court for a declaration that the refusal is unreasonable or the purchaser can take a risk and accept the assignment without consent. If an assignment takes place without the owner's consent it will be effective unless the court subsequently finds that the owner's refusal was reasonable or, in the case of the assignment taking place before the owner's response to the request, that the owner was not given a reasonable period of time to respond to the request for consent (s.3(2); *Ron Grundy (Melbourne) Ltd v Bonehevo* [1993] 1 All E.R. 282 at 287h). A transfer fee not exceeding 10 per cent of the sale price is payable to the owner: the Mobile Homes (Commission) Order 1983 (SI 1983/748).

If the owner dies the agreement is binding on any successor in title (s.3(1) of **20.010** the Mobile Homes Act 1983).

On the death of the occupier, if the occupier's widow, widower or civil partner is residing with the occupier at the time of death, the benefit and burden of the agreement will pass to him or her. If there is no widow, widower or civil partner, the agreement will pass to any member of the deceased's family who was so resident. The successor need not occupy the mobile home and may assign but the owner must approve any assignee, such approval not to be unreasonably withheld. The owner may charge a transfer fee which cannot exceed 10 per cent of the sale price. If there is no member of the family the agreement will pass to the person entitled to the mobile home under the deceased's will or intestacy but the beneficiary will not be able to live in the mobile home unless the owner is willing to enter into a new agreement. He may, however, assign on the same terms as above (s.3(4) of the Mobile Homes Act 1983).

Form 29: Claim for termination of mobile homes agreement

Claim form

1. The Claimant is the owner of [*state name and address of site*] ("the site").

2. The Defendant is the occupier of the mobile home situated on of the site. The Defendant commenced his residence at the site on [*insert date*] under a written agreement dated [*insert date*].

3. It was an express term of the said agreement that a rent of [*state rent*] per week be paid in advance on Monday of each week, and that the mobile home be kept in good repair.

4. In breach of the said express terms the rent is now £ [ ] in arrear and the Defendant has failed to keep the mobile home in good repair in that

(a) the windows are broken

(b) the door is covered with graffiti

(c) . . .

5. By a notice served on [*insert date*] the Claimant required the Defendant to remedy the said breaches within [insert a reasonable time for remedying the breach] but the Defendant has failed to comply with the notice.

7. Furthermore, the Defendant is not occupying the mobile home as his only or main residence. In that he resides permanently at [*state address*].

AND THE Claimant claims:

[1] An order that the agreement dated [insert date] and made between the Claimant and the Defendant be terminated forthwith.

Illegal eviction

20.011 If a person unlawfully deprives the occupier or the occupier's successor on death of his occupation or after termination enforces otherwise than by proceedings any right to exclude the occupier from the site, that person commits an offence (s.3 of the Caravan Sites Act 1968).

Mobile homes owned by site owner

20.012 The Mobile Homes Act 1983 and its provisions relating to agreements and their determination do not apply where the mobile home is owned by the site owner, but the Caravan Sites Act 1968 does. The owner of the caravan will have to give at least four weeks' notice to terminate (s.2 of the 1968 Act; more if the agreement so provides) and will have to obtain a court order before obtaining possession of the home (s.3) and that order may be suspended (s.4). For the possibility that the occupier of the caravan may be an assured tenant or a Rent Act tenant where there is a sufficient degree of permanence, see paras 6.004 and 8.003.

Chapter 21

Miscellaneous

The family home

Where one spouse or civil partner occupies a dwelling-house by virtue of a **21.001** tenancy or licence or by virtue of any enactment giving him or her the right to remain in occupation, and the other spouse or civil partner is not so entitled, s.30 of the Family Law Act 1996 provides that the spouse or civil partner not so entitled has certain "home rights", i.e. a right not to be evicted or excluded from the dwelling-house by the other spouse or civil partner and if not in occupation a right, with the leave of the court, to enter and occupy the dwelling-house. Throughout the rest of this part of this chapter the spouse or civil partner with rights of occupation under the Act is, for the sake of convenience, referred to as the wife and the other spouse or civil partner is referred to as the husband.

Landlord v spouse or civil partner

A wife with matrimonial home rights under the 1996 Act also has certain rights as **21.002** against the "landlord". Any payment or tender of rent or licence fees that she makes is as good as if it were made by the husband (s.30(3)). The "landlord" may not therefore use non-payment of rent or licence fees by the husband as an excuse for obtaining possession where a wife, who has rights of occupation under the Act, is prepared to pay them.

Furthermore, by virtue of s.30(4), the wife's occupation is treated as possession or occupation by the husband for the following purposes, namely:

(1) the Rent Act 1977, in relation to protected and statutory tenancies, and restricted contracts created after November 28, 1980;

(2) the Housing Act 1985, in relation to secure tenancies and the Housing Act 1996 in relation to introductory tenancies;

(3) the Rent (Agriculture) Act 1976, in relation to protected occupancies and statutory tenancies; and

(4) Part I of the Housing Act 1988 in relation to assured tenancies and assured agricultural occupancies.

Thus, so long as a wife with rights of occupation under the Act remains in occupation the landlord may not obtain possession by reason of her husband's absence (e.g. see *Griffiths v Renfree* [1989] 2 E.G.L.R. 46; tenant/husband served a notice to quit; wife remained in occupation; tenancy continued and therefore husband continued to be liable for the rent). It also means that in any possession action against the husband the wife should be joined as a defendant.

Where in any such proceedings the tenancy or contract, under which the husband is entitled to occupy the dwelling-house, is determined the wife's rights of occupation as such also come to an end (s.30(8)(b) of the 1996 Act); but if the court adjourns the hearing or makes an order staying or suspending execution of the order for possession or postpones the date for possession the wife is entitled to the benefit of that adjournment, stay, suspension or postponement. She will continue to be so entitled as long as she remains in occupation of the dwelling-house and may make the application for any such adjournment, stay, suspension or postponement herself (see s.100(4A), (4B) of the Rent Act 1977; s.9(5) of the Housing Act 1988; s.85(5), (6) of the Housing Act 1985; s.7(5A), (5B) of the Rent (Agriculture) Act 1976).

Section 30 only regulates the rights of spouses or civil partners between themselves. It does not restrict the right of an entitled spouse or civil partner to determine his or her contractual relationship with a landlord by serving a notice to quit or effecting a valid surrender, while the non-entitled spouse or civil partner remained in occupation. Further, it does not provide the non-entitled spouse or civil partner with indefinite rights of occupation of the former matrimonial or civil partnership home terminable only by an order of the court (see *Sanctuary Housing Association v Campbell* (2000) 32 H.L.R. 100 CA, a case on s.1 of the Matrimonial Homes Act 1983, the predecessor to s.30 Family Law Act 1996, *Hackney LBC v Snowden* [2001] L. & T.R. 6 CA and *Ealing Family Housing Association Ltd v McKenzie* [2004] H.L.R. (Case 21) 313).

21.003   It is important to note that the rights of occupation under the Family Law Act 1996 only last as long as the marriage or civil partnership is in existence (s.30(8)(a) unless an order to the contrary is made during the marriage or civil partnership (s.33(5)). If he or she wishes to remain in occupation after decree absolute or dissolution of the civil partnership an application must be made for the tenancy to be transferred into his or her name in proceedings under s.24 of the Matrimonial Causes Act 1973, Sch.7 to the 1996 Act, the Children Act 1989 or the Civil Partnership Act 2004 Sch.5 para.7 (see below). For a case where the wife failed to make such an application and thus lost her right to remain in occupation see *Metropolitan Properties Co Ltd v Cronan* (1982) 44 P. & C.R. 1. The court may also make orders under Sch.7 where cohabitees who have lived together as husband and wife have separated (see below).

The above rules do not apply to a dwelling-house which has at no time been and which was at no time intended to be a matrimonial or civil partnership home of the spouses or civil partners in question (s.30(7) of the 1996 Act). For example, see *Hall v King* [1987] 2 E.G.L.R. 121, where the husband took the tenancy for the wife. He never resided there himself and so it was never a matrimonial home.

When deciding whether to serve a notice to quit, a local authority should take into account the occupier's right to apply under Sch.1 of the Children Act 1989 (see para.21.007 below) for a transfer of the tenancy from an ex-cohabitee (*R. v Hammersmith & Fulham LBC Ex p. Quigley* (2000) 32 H.L.R. 379 QBD DC, the local authority's failure to take this into account led to an order of certiorari quashing the service of the notice and a direction that they reconsider the position of the occupier).

Family Law Act 1996 section 30

30.— Rights concerning home where one spouse or civil partner has no estate, etc.   **21.004**

(1) This section applies if—

    (a) one spouse or civil partner ("A") is entitled to occupy a dwelling-house by virtue of—

        (i) a beneficial estate or interest or contract; or
        (ii) any enactment giving A the right to remain in occupation; and

    (b) the other spouse or civil partner ("B") is not so entitled.

(2) Subject to the provisions of this Part, B has the following rights ("home rights")—

    (a) if in occupation, a right not to be evicted or excluded from the dwelling-house or any part of it by A except with the leave of the court given by an order under section 33;
    (b) if not in occupation, a right with the leave of the court so given to enter into and occupy the dwelling-house.

(3) If B is entitled under this section to occupy a dwelling-house or any part of a dwelling-house, any payment or tender made or other thing done by B in or towards satisfaction of any liability of A in respect of rent, mortgage payments or other outgoings affecting the dwelling-house is, whether or not it is made or done in pursuance of an order under section 40, as good as if made or done by A.

(4) B's occupation by virtue of this section—

    (a) is to be treated, for the purposes of the Rent (Agriculture) Act 1976 and the Rent Act 1977 (other than Part V and sections 103 to 106 of that Act), as occupation by A as A's residence; and
    (b) if B occupies the dwelling-house as B's only or principal home, is to be treated, for the purposes of the Housing Act 1985, Part I of the Housing Act 1988 and Chapter I of Part V of the Housing Act 1996, as occupation by A as A's only or principal home.

(5) If B—

    (a) is entitled under this section to occupy a dwelling-house or any part of a dwelling-house; and
    (b) makes any payment in or towards satisfaction of any liability of A in respect of mortgage payments affecting the dwelling-house,

the person to whom the payment is made may treat it as having been made by A, but the fact that that person has treated any such payment as having been so made does not affect any claim of B against A to an interest in the dwelling-house by virtue of the payment.

(6) If B is entitled under this section to occupy a dwelling-house or part of a dwelling-house by reason of an interest of A under a trust, all the provisions of subsections (3) to (5) apply in relation to the trustees as they apply in relation to A.

(7) This section does not apply to a dwelling-house which—

    (a) in the case of spouses, has at no time been, and was at no time intended by them to be, a matrimonial home of theirs; and
    (b) in the case of civil partners, has at no time been, and was at no time intended by them to be, a civil partnership home of theirs.

(8) B's home rights continue—

    (a) only so long as the marriage or civil partnership subsists, except to the extent that an order under section 33(5) otherwise provides; and

(b) only so long as A is entitled as mentioned in subsection (1) to occupy the dwelling-house, except where provision is made by section 31 for those rights to be a charge on an estate or interest in the dwelling-house.

(9) It is hereby declared that [a person]—

(a) who has an equitable interest in a dwelling-house or in its proceeds of sale; but

(b) is not [a person] in whom there is vested (whether solely or as joint tenant) a legal estate in fee simple or a legal term of years absolute in the dwelling-house,

is to be treated, only for the purpose of determining whether he has home rights, as not being entitled to occupy the dwelling-house by virtue of that interest.

Spouse v spouse; civil partner v civil partner

21.005 While the marriage or civil partnership exists it does not matter which spouse or civil partner is the tenant. Neither one of them may be excluded from the matrimonial or civil partnership home by the other save by order of the court made pursuant to the provisions of Pt IV of the Family Law Act 1996 to which reference should be made.

After divorce or dissolution of the civil partnership the parties' relationship to each other in respect of the property is governed by the general law. They are (unless an order was made during the marriage or civil partnership under s.33(5) of the 1996 Act) treated as independent adults. Thus, where the former husband is the tenant the former wife remains in occupation as the husband's licensee under a licence which may be revoked at any time (*O'Malley v O'Malley* [1982] 1 W.L.R. 244); although the former wife must be given a reasonable amount of time to leave (*Vaughan v Vaughan* [1953] 1 Q.B. 762; see also para.5.014). The rights of occupation under the Family Law Act 1996 will have come to an end when the decree was made absolute or civil partnership is dissolved (except where, during the subsistence of the marriage or civil partnership, the court directed otherwise (s.30(8)(a) and s.33(5)).

Transfer of tenancy

21.006 The non-tenant spouse or civil partner may, however, apply for a transfer of a contractual tenancy in proceedings for ancillary relief under s.24 of the Matrimonial Causes Act 1973 (*Hale v Hale* [1975] 1 W.L.R. 931; *Thompson v Thompson* [1976] Fam 25) or Civil Partnership Act 2004 Sch.5 para.7. A Rent Act statutory tenancy may not be transferred under because it is not "property" within the meaning of these provisions. The non-tenant spouse or civil partner may, however, also apply for a transfer of the tenancy into his or her sole name under Sch.7 to the Family Law Act 1996 where the tenancy is a protected or statutory tenancy within the meaning of the Rent Act 1977, a secure tenancy within the meaning of the Housing Act 1985, a statutory tenancy within the meaning of the Rent (Agriculture) Act 1976 or an assured tenancy or assured agricultural occupancy under the Housing Act 1988. Schedule 7 applies to cohabiting couples who have separated.

A transfer under Sch.7 of the 1996 Act is preferable when there are covenants against assignment in the tenancy. A transfer under the 1973 Act or 2004 Act is likely to be breach of covenant, whereas Sch.7 acts to vest the interest in the applicant as it existed immediately before the date of the transfer so that no assignment has actually taken place (Sch.7 para.7(a)). The other advantage of Sch.7 is that it is the order itself which vests the interest in the applicant.

The court can only transfer a statutory tenancy if it was in existence at the date of the application for the transfer (*Lewis v Lewis* [1985] 2 W.L.R. 962). It will not be in existence if a decree absolute of divorce has been made or civil partnership dissolved and the tenant has ceased to occupy because the presence of the ex-spouse or civil partner will no longer be deemed to be on behalf of the tenant (s.30(8)(a), see above). The same rule applies in relation to secure tenancies (*Thompson v Elmbridge Borough Council* (1989) 19 H.L.R. 526; suspended order for possession; tenancy came to an end when condition of the suspension was broken). Further, no order may be made for the transfer of a tenancy if the spouse or civil partner applying has remarried or entered into a new civil partnership unless she applied prior to the remarriage or new civil partnership (s.28(3) of the 1973 Act; Sch.7 para.13 to the 1996 Act; Civil Partnership Act 2004 Sch.5 para.6; *Jackson v Jackson* [1973] 2 All E.R. 395). An application made in the petition for a property transfer order would appear to be sufficient (*Jenkins v Hargood* [1978] 3 All E.R. 1001).

Unlike the position where it is only the non-entitled spouse or civil partner who remains in the property, occupation by a non-entitled cohabitee, will not fulfil the tenant condition under s.81 of the Housing Act 1985. In those circumstances, the secure tenancy will come to an end and will not be available for transfer. This position may be circumvented by first obtaining an occupation order under s.36 of the Family Law Act 1996 (*Gay v Enfield LBC* (1999) 31 H.L.R. 1126 CA. Note that the question of the date at which the secure tenancy conditions needed to be satisfied was left open).

Any application for the transfer of a tenancy under the Family Law Act 1996 must be served on the landlord who is entitled to be heard on the application (Rule 3.8(12) of the Family Proceedings Rules 1991, as amended). It has been suggested that it might not be proper to transfer the tenancy (in the face of opposition from the landlord) where there is a covenant against assignment (*Hale v Hale* [1975] 2 All E.R. 1090 at 1094). In such a case the landlord would have the right to forfeit. See also *Hutchings v Hutchings* (1975) 237 E.G. 571 and *Regan v Regan* [1977] 1 W.L.R. 84.

Where a husband and wife or civil partners are joint tenants the tenancy is a **21.007** joint asset which the court can order to be transferred into the sole name of one of them under the 1973 or 2004 Acts. An action by the landlord for possession of the dwelling should be adjourned to await the outcome of any application by one of the parties for such a transfer where the application has a good prospect of success. If the application has not yet been made at the date of the claim for possession the claim should be adjourned on the undertaking of the relevant spouse or civil partner to apply for a transfer (*Newlon Housing Trust v Al Sulaimen* [1999] 1 A.C. 315).

A notice to quit served by one of two (or more) joint tenants is not a disposition of property for the purposes of s.37 of the Matrimonial Causes Act 1973 and is effective to determine a tenancy (*Newlon Housing Trust v Alsulaimen*; but note the potential Human Rights Act points where the landlord is a public authority, see Ch.23) and is likely to be the same under 2004 Act Sch.5 paras 74 and 75. If this is done prior to a hearing for an application to transfer under s.24 of the Matrimonial Causes Act 1973 (or Sch.5 of the 2004 Act or under Sch.7 to the

Family Law Act 1996), it will defeat the application, as there will no longer be a tenancy to transfer and the court will have no power to reinstate the tenancy. Practitioners should be aware of the comments made by Thorpe L.J. in *Bater v Greenwich LBC* (2000) 32 H.L.R. 127 CA at 136 in the context of the need to guard against a unilateral termination of a joint tenancy between the date of the parties' separation and the date of the determination of an application for the transfer of a tenancy. This can be done by seeking an appropriate written undertaking from the other joint tenant and serving it on the landlord or, if necessary, by application to the court for an injunction pursuant to s.37 of the Matrimonial Causes Act 1973.

Where an order is made for the transfer of a tenancy under the 1973 or 2004 Act the tenancy should be assigned by deed in order to ensure that it is effective against the landlord (*Crago v Julian* [1992] 1 All E.R. 744), see para.4.010. However, under the 1996 Act the order itself transfers the tenancy (para.7(1) and para.8(1)). Where a statutory tenancy that is transferred is subject to an order for possession as against the tenant spouse or civil partner the other spouse or civil partner takes it subject to any terms of the order relating to rent and arrears of rent. However, the landlord is not entitled to enforce the pre-existing possession order against the spouse or civil partner to whom the tenancy has been transferred. He must bring fresh proceedings and the court will consider afresh whether it would be reasonable to grant such an order and upon what terms (*Church Commissioners for England v Al-Emarah* [1996] 3 W.L.R. 633. CA).

Once the tenancy has been transferred to a spouse or civil partner a landlord is not entitled to a possession order based on arrears of rent, accrued by the other spouse or civil partner, (*Notting Hill Housing Trust v Rakey Jones* [1999] L. & T.R. 397 CA).

An order requiring either or both parents of a child to transfer to the applicant, for the benefit of the child "property" (which presumably does not therefore include a statutory tenancy) to which the parent is, or the parents are, entitled may also be made pursuant to para.1(2)(e)(i) of Sch.1 to the Children Act 1989 (and see *K v K* [1992] 1 W.L.R. 530). The power may be exercised at any time (para.1(3)).

Once the tenancy has been transferred the spouse or civil partner who is then the tenant may commence proceedings to evict the other spouse or civil partner if he or she refuses to leave.

Family Law Act 1996 Schedule 7

21.008   PART 1

                                         GENERAL

1. In this Schedule—
    "cohabitant" except in paragraph 3 includes (where the context requires) former cohabitant;
    "civil partner", except in paragraph 2, includes (where the context requires) former civil partner;
    "the court" does not include a magistrates' court,
    "landlord" includes—

    (a) any person from time to time deriving title under the original landlord; and

(b) in relation to any dwelling-house, any person other than the tenant who is, or (but for Part VII of the Rent Act 1977 or Part II of the Rent (Agriculture) Act 1976 would be, entitled to possession of the dwelling-house;

"Part II order" means an order under Part II of this Schedule;
"a relevant tenancy" means—

(a) a protected tenancy or statutory tenancy within the meaning of the Rent Act 1977;
(b) a statutory tenancy within the meaning of the Rent (Agriculture) Act 1976;
(c) a secure tenancy within the meaning of section 79 of the Housing Act 1985;
(d) an assured tenancy or assured agricultural occupancy within the meaning of Part I of the Housing Act 1988; or
(e) an introductory tenancy within the meaning of Chapter I of Part V of the Housing Act 1996;

"spouse", except in paragraph 2, includes (where the context requires) former spouse; and
"tenancy" includes sub-tenancy.

Cases in which the court may make an order   **21.009**

2.—(1) This paragraph applies if one spouse or civil partner is entitled, either in his own right or jointly with the other spouse or civil partner, to occupy a dwelling-house by virtue of a relevant tenancy.
(2) The court may make a Part II order—

(a) on granting a decree of divorce, a decree of nullity of marriage or a decree of judicial separation or at any time thereafter (whether, in the case of a decree of divorce or nullity of marriage, before or after the decree is made absolute), or
(b) at any time when it has power to make a property adjustment order under Part 2 of Schedule 5 to the Civil Partnership Act 2004 with respect to the civil partnership.

3.—(1) This paragraph applies if one cohabitant is entitled, either in his own right or jointly with the other cohabitant, to occupy a dwelling-house by virtue of a relevant tenancy.
(2) If the cohabitants cease to cohabit, the court may make a Part II order.

4.   The court shall not make a Part II order unless the dwelling-house is or was—

(a)   in the case of spouses, a matrimonial home;
(aa) in the case of civil partners, a civil partnership home; or
(b)   in the case of cohabitants, a home in which they cohabited.

Matters to which the court must have regard

5.   In determining whether to exercise its powers under Part II of this Schedule and, if so, in what manner, the court shall have regard to all the circumstances of the case including—

(a) the circumstances in which the tenancy was granted to either or both of the spouses, civil partners or cohabitants or, as the case requires, the circumstances in which either or both of them became tenant under the tenancy;
(b) the matters mentioned in section 33(6)(a), (b) and (c) and, where the parties are cohabitants and only one of them is entitled to occupy the

dwelling-house by virtue of the relevant tenancy, the further matters mentioned in section 36(6)(e), (f), (g) and (h); and

(c) the suitability of the parties as tenants.

PART II

ORDERS THAT MAY BE MADE

References to entitlement to occupy

21.010   **6.**   References in this Part of this Schedule to a spouse, a civil partner or a cohabitant being entitled to occupy a dwelling-house by virtue of a relevant tenancy apply whether that entitlement is in his own right or jointly with the other spouse, civil partner or cohabitant.

Protected, secure or assured tenancy or assured agricultural occupancy

7.—(1) If a spouse, civil partner or cohabitant is entitled to occupy the dwelling-house by virtue of a protected tenancy within the meaning of the Rent Act 1977, a secure tenancy within the meaning of the Housing Act 1985, an assured tenancy or assured agricultural occupancy within the meaning of Part I of the Housing Act 1988 or an introductory tenancy within the meaning of Chapter I of Part V of the Housing Act 1996, the court may by order direct that, as from such date as may be specified in the order, there shall, by virtue of the order and without further assurance, be transferred to, and vested in, the other spouse, civil partner or cohabitant—

(a) the estate or interest which the spouse, civil partner or cohabitant so entitled had in the dwelling-house immediately before that date by virtue of the lease or agreement creating the tenancy and any assignment of that lease or agreement, with all rights, privileges and appurtenances attaching to that estate or interest but subject to all covenants, obligations, liabilities and incumbrances to which it is subject; and

(b) where the spouse, civil partner or cohabitant so entitled is an assignee of such lease or agreement, the liability of that spouse, civil partner or cohabitant under any covenant of indemnity by the assignee express or implied in the assignment of the lease or agreement to that spouse, civil partner or cohabitant.

(2) If an order is made under this paragraph, any liability or obligation to which the spouse, civil partner or cohabitant so entitled is subject under any covenant having reference to the dwelling-house in the lease or agreement, being a liability or obligation falling due to be discharged or performed on or after the date so specified, shall not be enforceable against that spouse, civil partner or cohabitant.

(3) If the spouse, civil partner or cohabitant so entitled is a successor within the meaning of Part 4 of the Housing Act 1985—

(a) his former spouse (or, in the case of judicial separation, his spouse),

(b) his former civil partner (or, if a separation order is in force, his civil partner), or

(c) his former cohabitant,

is to be deemed also to be a successor within the meaning of that Part.

(3A) If the spouse, civil partner or cohabitant so entitled is a successor within the meaning of section 132 of the Housing Act 1996—

(a) his former spouse (or, in the case of judicial separation, his spouse),

(b) his former civil partner (or, if a separation order is in force, his civil partner), or

(c) his former cohabitant,

is to be deemed also to be a successor within the meaning of that section.

(4) If the spouse, civil partner or cohabitant so entitled is for the purposes of section 17 of the Housing Act 1988 a successor in relation to the tenancy or occupancy—

(a) his former spouse (or, in the case of judicial separation, his spouse),
(b) his former civil partner (or, if a separation order is in force, his civil partner), or
(c) his former cohabitant,

is to be deemed to be a successor in relation to the tenancy or occupancy for the purposes of that section.

(5) If the transfer under sub-paragraph (1) is of an assured agricultural occupancy, then, for the purposes of Chapter III of Part I of the Housing Act 1988—

(a) the agricultural worker condition is fulfilled with respect to the dwelling-house while the spouse, civil partner or cohabitant to whom the assured agricultural occupancy is transferred continues to be the occupier under that occupancy, and
(b) that condition is to be treated as so fulfilled by virtue of the same paragraph of Schedule 3 to the Housing Act 1988 as was applicable before the transfer.

Statutory tenancy within the meaning of the Rent Act 1977

8.—(1) This paragraph applies if the spouse, civil partner or cohabitant is entitled to **21.011** occupy the dwelling-house by virtue of a statutory tenancy within the meaning of the Rent Act 1977.

(2) The court may by order direct that, as from the date specified in the order—

(a) that spouse, civil partner or cohabitant is to cease to be entitled to occupy the dwelling-house; and
(b) the other spouse, civil partner or cohabitant is to be deemed to be the tenant or, as the case may be, the sole tenant under that statutory tenancy.

(3) The question whether the provisions of paragraphs 1 to 3, or (as the case may be) paragraphs 5 to 7 of Schedule 1 to the Rent Act 1977, as to the succession by the surviving spouse or surviving civil partner of a deceased tenant, or by a member of the deceased tenant's family, to the right to retain possession are capable of having effect in the event of the death of the person deemed by an order under this paragraph to be the tenant or sole tenant under the statutory tenancy is to be determined according as those provisions have or have not already had effect in relation to the statutory tenancy.

Statutory tenancy within the meaning of the Rent (Agriculture) Act 1976

9.—(1) This paragraph applies if the spouse, civil partner or cohabitant is entitled to **21.012** occupy the dwelling-house by virtue of a statutory tenancy within the meaning of the Rent (Agriculture) Act 1976.

(2) The court may by order direct that, as from such date as may be specified in the order—

(a) that spouse, civil partner or cohabitant is to cease to be entitled to occupy the dwelling-house; and
(b) the other spouse, civil partner or cohabitant is to be deemed to be the tenant or, as the case may be, the sole tenant under that statutory tenancy.

(3) A spouse, civil partner or cohabitant who is deemed under this paragraph to be the tenant under a statutory tenancy is (within the meaning of that Act) a statutory tenant in his own right, or a statutory tenant by succession, according as the other spouse, civil partner or cohabitant was a statutory tenant in his own right or a statutory tenant by succession.

PART III

SUPPLEMENTARY PROVISIONS

Compensation

21.013   **10.**—(1) If the court makes a Part II order, it may by the order direct the making of a payment by the spouse, civil partner or cohabitant to whom the tenancy is transferred ("the transferee") to the other spouse, civil partner or cohabitant ("the transferor").

(2) Without prejudice to that, the court may, on making an order by virtue of sub-paragraph (1) for the payment of a sum—

(a) direct that payment of that sum or any part of it is to be deferred until a specified date or until the occurrence of a specified event, or

(b) direct that that sum or any part of it is to be paid by instalments.

(3) Where an order has been made by virtue of sub-paragraph (1) the court may, on the application of the transferee or the transferor—

(a) exercise its powers under sub-paragraph (2), or

(b) vary any direction previously given under that sub-paragraph,

at any time before the sum whose payment is required by the order is paid in full.

(4) In deciding whether to exercise its powers under this paragraph and, if so, in what manner, the court shall have regard to all the circumstances including—

(a) the financial loss that would otherwise be suffered by the transferor as a result of the order;

(b) the financial needs and financial resources of the parties; and

(c) the financial obligations which the parties have, or are likely to have in the foreseeable future, including financial obligations to each other and to any relevant child.

(5) The court shall not give any direction under sub-paragraph (2) unless it appears to it that immediate payment of the sum required by the order would cause the transferee financial hardship which is greater than any financial hardship that would be caused to the transferor if the direction were given.

Liabilities and obligations in respect of the dwelling-house

21.014   **11.**—(1) If the court makes a Part II order, it may by the order direct that both spouses, civil partners or cohabitants are to be jointly and severally liable to discharge or perform any or all of the liabilities and obligations in respect of the dwelling-house (whether arising under the tenancy or otherwise) which—

(a) have at the date of the order fallen due to be discharged or performed by one only of them; or

(b) but for the direction, would before the date specified as the date on which the order is to take effect fall due to be discharged or performed by one only of them.

(2) If the court gives such a direction, it may further direct that either spouse, civil partner or cohabitant is to be liable to indemnify the other in whole or in part against any payment made or expenses incurred by the other in discharging or performing any such liability or obligation.

12.   The date specified in a Part II order as the date on which the order is to take effect must not be earlier than—

(a) in the case of a marriage in respect of which a decree of divorce or nullity has been granted, the date on which the decree is made absolute;

(b) in the case of a civil partnership in respect of which a dissolution or nullity order has been made, the date on which the order is made final.

Effect of remarriage or subsequent civil partnership

13. Effect of remarriage or subsequent civil partnership

(1) If after the grant of a decree dissolving or annulling a marriage either spouse remarries or forms a civil partnership, that spouse is not entitled to apply, by reference to the grant of that decree, for a Part II order.

(2) If after the making of a dissolution or nullity order either civil partner forms a subsequent civil partnership or marries, that civil partner is not entitled to apply, by reference to the making of that order, for a Part II order.

(3) In sub-paragraphs (1) and (2)—

(a) the references to remarrying and marrying include references to cases where the marriage is by law void or voidable, and

(b) the references to forming a civil partnership include references to cases where the civil partnership is by law void or voidable.

Rules of court

14.—(1) Rules of court shall be made requiring the court, before it makes an order **21.015** under this Schedule to give the landlord of the dwelling-house to which the order will relate an opportunity of being heard.

(2) Rules of court may provide that an application for a Part II order by reference to an order or decree may not, without the leave of the court by which that order was made or decree was granted, be made after the expiration of such period from the order or grant as may be prescribed by the rules.

Saving for other provisions of Act

15.—(1) If a spouse or civil partner is entitled to occupy a dwelling-house by virtue of a tenancy, this Schedule does not affect the operation of section 30 and 31 in relation to the other spouse's or civil partner's home rights.

(2) If a spouse, civil partner or cohabitant is entitled to occupy a dwelling-house by virtue of a tenancy, the court's powers to make orders under this Schedule are additional to those conferred by sections 33, 35 and 36.

Vendor and purchaser

Where the vendor of land permits the purchaser to go into occupation prior to **21.016** completion of the contract, he normally permits him to do so as licensee, notwithstanding that the purchaser enjoys exclusive possession. The circumstances are such that the prima facie intention to create a tenancy, normally construed from the granting of the right to exclusive possession, is negatived (see *Street v Mountford* [1985] 2 All E.R. 289 at 295j and see *Sandhu v Farooqui* (2003) H.L.R. 817 CA for guidance on the terms likely to be implied into that licence). The situation is dealt with in the Standard Conditions of Sale. Condition 5 is, so far as is relevant, in the following terms:

5.2.1 If the buyer is not already lawfully in the property, and the seller agrees to let him into occupation, the buyer occupies on the following terms.

> 5.2.2 The buyer is a licensee and not a tenant. The terms of the licence are that the buyer:
>
> (a) cannot transfer it
> (b) may permit members of his household to occupy the property
> (c) is to pay or indemnify the seller against the outgoings and other expenses in respect of the property
> (d) is to pay the seller a fee calculated at the contract rate on a sum equal to the purchase price and the chattels price (less any deposit paid) for the period of the licence
> (e) is entitled to any rents and profits from any part of the property which he does not occupy
> (f) is to keep the property in as good a state of repair as it was when he went into occupation (except for fair wear and tear) and is not to alter it
> (g) if the property is leasehold, is not to do anything which puts the seller in breach of his obligations in the lease, and
> (h) is to quit the property when the licence ends.
>
> 5.2.4 The buyer's licence ends on the earliest of: completion date, rescission of the contract or when five working days' notice given by one party to the other takes effect.

However, agreements between vendor and purchaser sometimes provide that the Conditions are incorporated into the agreement "so far as the same are not inconsistent herewith". This was the situation in *Joel v Montgomery and Taylor Ltd* [1966] 3 All E.R. 763, where the plaintiff agreed to grant an underlease to the defendant at a premium. The defendant paid the deposit and went into possession prior to completion, paying rent in accordance with the terms of the agreement and the underlease. It was held that the relationship between the parties was not that of vendor and purchaser but of landlord and tenant. The relevant condition was inconsistent with the agreement and thus did not make the defendant a licensee.

21.017   Where a person is granted exclusive possession of premises for a term at a rent and no contract has actually been entered into, he will be held to be a tenant even though he entered into possession with the intention of purchasing the premises and even though neither party intended that a tenancy should be created (*Bretherton v Paton* [1986] 1 E.G.L.R. 172).

Where a person enters into possession of a property during negotiations for the grant of a lease he will usually be held to be a tenant at will (*Javad v Aqil* [1991] 1 All E.R. 243) but the Rent Acts apply to tenancies at will where a sufficient rent is paid (*Chamberlain v Farr* [1942] 2 All E.R. 567; *Francis Jackson Developments Ltd v Stemp* [1943] 2 All E.R. 601).

Purchasing property with "sitting tenant"

21.018 For the dangers inherent in purchasing a property subject to a tenancy see *Appleton v Aspin and Plane* [1988] 1 E.G.L.R. 95. The vendor's tenant was a party to the contract of sale which contained a term whereby the tenant agreed that on completion she would not enforce her right to possession. The court held that the agreement infringed s.98 of the Rent Act 1977 and the purchaser was unable to recover possession from the tenant.

Overcrowding and prohibition orders

Section 101 of the Rent Act 1977 provides that at any time when a dwelling house **21.019**
to which that section applies is overcrowded within the meaning of Pt X of the
Housing Act 1985, in such circumstances as to render the occupier guilty of an
offence, nothing in Pt VII of the Rent Act (i.e. the part relating to security of
tenure) shall prevent the immediate landlord of the occupier from obtaining
possession of the dwelling house. Regulated tenants and occupiers under restricted
contracts will not therefore be able to rely upon ss.98–106A as a means of
preventing orders for possession or as a means of obtaining postponements and
suspensions of such orders in circumstances where s.101 applies. But note that the
tenancy/licence must first be determined in the normal way before proceedings
for possession can be commenced (cf. *Aslan v Murphy (Nos 1 and 2)* [1989] 3 All
E.R. 130; a case in fact relating to closing orders).

For the landlord to be able to rely upon s.101 the circumstances that amount to
the offence must exist at the date of the hearing (*Zbytniewski v Broughton* [1956]
2 Q.B. 673).

Where the premises are subject to a secure tenancy within the meaning of s.79
of the Housing Act 1985 the landlord may seek to obtain possession under Ground
9 of Sch.2 to the Act if the dwelling house is overcrowded within the meaning of
Pt X of the Act, in such circumstances as to render the occupier guilty of an
offence. The court may only make an order for possession if suitable alternative
accommodation is available.

Where the premises are subject to the provisions of the Rent (Agriculture) Act
1976 the landlord may seek to obtain possession under Case XIII of Sch.4 to the
said Act if the dwelling house is overcrowded within the meaning of Pt X of the
1985 Act, in such circumstances as to render the occupier guilty of an offence.
Case XIII is a mandatory ground.

See s.270 and *Beaney v Branchett* (1987) 19 H.L.R. 471 for "demolition **21.020**
orders".

The local authority may be able to obtain possession under s.338 of the 1985
Act where a dwelling is overcrowded. Note that evicted occupiers may have a
right to compensation under ss.29–39 of the Land Compensation Act 1973.

The provisions of the Housing Act 1985 that are relevant to overcrowding are
set out below. (Section 216 of the Housing Act 2004 makes provision for the
amendment of these sections; no amendments have been made as at the date of
publication.) See also s.33 of the Housing Act 2004 in relation to "prohibition
orders" under that Act.

Definition of overcrowding

324.—A dwelling is overcrowded for the purposes of this Part when the number of **21.021**
persons sleeping in the dwelling is such as to contravene—

    (a) the standard specified in section 325 (the room standard), or
    (b) the standard specified in section 326 (the space standard).

325.—(1) The room standard is contravened when the number of persons sleeping in a
dwelling and the number of rooms available as sleeping accommodation is such
that two persons of opposite sexes who are not living together as husband and wife
must sleep in the same room.
(2) For this purpose—

(a)   children under the age of ten shall be left out of account, and

(b)   a room is available as sleeping accommodation if it is of a type normally used in the locality either as a bedroom or as a living room.

326.—(1) The space standard is contravened when the number of persons sleeping in a dwelling is in excess of the permitted number, having regard to the number and floor area of the rooms of the dwelling available as sleeping accommodation.

(2) For this purpose—

(a)   no account shall be taken of a child under the age of one and a child aged one or over but under ten shall be reckoned as one-half of a unit, and

(b)   a room is available as sleeping accommodation if it is of a type normally used in the locality either as a living room or as a bedroom.

(3) The permitted number of persons in relation to a dwelling is whichever is the less of—

(a)   the number specified in Table I in relation to the number of rooms in the dwelling available as sleeping accommodation, and

(b)   the aggregate for all such rooms in the dwelling of the numbers specified in column 2 of Table II in relation to each room of the floor area specified in column 1.

No account shall be taken for the purposes of either Table of a room having a floor area of less than 50 square feet.

Table I

Number of rooms	Number of persons
1	2
2	3
3	5
4	7½
5 or more	2 for each room

Table II

Floor area of room	Number of persons
110 sq ft or more	2
90 sq ft or more but less than 110 sq ft	1½
70 sq ft or more but less than 90 sq ft	1
50 sq ft or more but less than 70 sq ft	½

(4) The Secretary of State may by regulations prescribe the manner in which the floor area of a room is to be ascertained for the purposes of this section; and the regulations may provide for the exclusion from computation, or the bringing into computation at a reduced figure, of floor space in a part of the room which is of less than a specified height not exceeding eight feet.

(5) Regulations under subsection (4) shall be made by statutory instrument which shall be subject to annulment in pursuance of a resolution of either House of Parliament.

(6) A certificate of the local housing authority stating the number and floor areas of the rooms in a dwelling, and that the floor areas have been ascertained in the prescribed manner, is prima facie evidence for the purposes of legal proceedings of the facts stated in it.

Responsibility of occupier

327.—(1) The occupier of a dwelling who causes or permits it to be overcrowded **21.022** commits a summary offence, subject to subsection (2).

(2) The occupier is not guilty of an offence—

    (a) if the overcrowding is within the exceptions specified in section 328 or 329 (children attaining the age of 10 or visiting relatives), or

    (b) by reason of anything done under the authority of, and in accordance with any conditions specified in, a licence granted by the local housing authority under section 330.

328.—(1) Where a dwelling which would not otherwise be overcrowded becomes over crowded by reason of a child attaining the age of one or ten, then if the occupier—

    (a) applies to the local housing authority for suitable alternative accommodation, or

    (b) has so applied before the date when the child attained the age in question,

he does not commit an offence under section 327 (occupier causing or permitting overcrowding), so long as the condition in subsection (2) is met and the occupier does not fail to take action in the circumstances specified in subsection (3).

(2) The condition is that all the persons sleeping in the dwelling are persons who were living there when the child attained that age and thereafter continuously live there, or children born after that date of any of those persons.

(3) The exception provided by this section ceases to apply if—

    (a) suitable alternative accommodation is offered to the occupier on or after the date on which the child attains that age, or, if he has applied before that date, is offered at any time after the application, and he fails to accept it, or

    (b) the removal from the dwelling of some person not a member of the occupier's family is on that date or thereafter becomes reasonably practicable having regard to all the circumstances (including the availability of suitable alternative accommodation for that person), and the occupier fails to require his removal.

329.—Where the persons sleeping in an overcrowded dwelling include a member of the **21.023** occupier's family who does not live there but is sleeping there temporarily, the occupier is not guilty of an offence under section 327 (occupier causing or permitting overcrowding) unless the circumstances are such that he would be so guilty if that member of his family were not sleeping there.

330.—(1) The occupier or intending occupier of a dwelling may apply to the local housing authority for a licence authorising him to permit a number of persons in excess of the permitted number to sleep in the dwelling.

(2) The authority may grant such a licence if it appears to them that there are exceptional circumstances (which may include a seasonal increase of population) and that it is expedient to do so; and they shall specify in the licence the number of persons authorised in excess of the permitted number.

(3) The licence shall be in the prescribed form and may be granted either unconditionally or subject to conditions specified in it.

(4) The local housing authority may revoke the licence at their discretion by notice in writing served on the occupier and specifying a period (at least one

month from the date of service) at the end of which the licence will cease to be in force.

(5) Unless previously revoked, the licence continues in force for such period not exceeding twelve months as may be specified in it.

(6) A copy of the licence and of any notice of revocation shall, within seven days of the issue of the licence or the service of the notice on the occupier, be served by the local housing authority on the landlord (if any) of the dwelling.

. . .

338.—(1) Where a dwelling is overcrowded in circumstances such as to render the occupier guilty of an offence, the local housing authority may serve on the occupier notice in writing requiring him to abate the overcrowding within 14 days from the date of service of the notice.

(2) If at any time within three months from the end of that period—

(a) the dwelling is in the occupation of the person on whom the notice was served or of a member of his family, and

(b) it is overcrowded in circumstances such as to render the occupier guilty of an offence,

the local housing authority may apply to the county court which shall order vacant possession of the dwelling to be given lo the landlord within such period, not less than 14 or more than 28 days, as the court may determine.

(3) Expenses incurred by the local housing authority under this section in securing the giving of possession of a dwelling to the landlord may be recovered by them from him by action.

Ministers of religion

21.024 The protection that is afforded to ministers of the Church of England who have Church livings is governed by the Pluralities Act 1838 (see *Bishop of Gloucester v Cunnington* [1943] K.B. 101; *Worcester Diocesan Trust v Taylor* (1947) 177 L.T. 581).

Other ministers of religion, like anyone else, may be assured, regulated or secure tenants but where the dwelling-house is let on an assured or regulated tenancy a special ground for possession exists. Where the tenancy is an assured tenancy the ground is Ground 5 (of Sch.2 to the Housing Act 1988). Where the tenancy is a regulated tenancy the ground for possession is Case 15 (of Sch.15 to the Rent Act 1977).

The landlord is entitled to possession in either case where the dwelling-house is held for the purpose of being available for occupation by a minister of religion as a residence from which to perform the duties of his office and:

(1) not later than "the beginning of the tenancy" (i.e. not later than the day on which the tenancy is entered into) if the tenancy is assured, or "the relevant date" (usually the date the tenancy commenced) if the tenancy is regulated, the landlord gave notice in writing to the tenant that possession might be recovered on Ground 5 or, as the case may be, Case 15 (for rules governing notices in assured tenancy cases see Pt IV of Sch.2 to the 1988 Act); and

(2) the court is satisfied that the dwelling-house is required for occupation by
a minister of religion as such a residence.

Ground 5 or Case 15 may be relied upon whatever the religion involved
(*Re Watson* [1973] 1 W.L.R. 1472).

The notice requirement may not be dispensed with but if the ground is made
out the court must make an order for possession without considering whether or
not it is reasonable to make such an order (s.7(3) of the 1988 Act; s.98(2) of
the 1977 Act). For the procedure to be used when terminating assured tenancies,
see Ch.6.

The court may not postpone or suspend the order for possession for more than
14 days or six weeks in cases of exceptional hardship (s.89 of the Housing Act
1980; see para.3.034).

Rental purchase

A "rental purchase agreement" is an agreement for the purchase of a dwelling- **21.025**
house under which the whole or part of the purchase price is paid in three or more
instalments and completion of the purchase is deferred until the whole or a specified part of the purchase price has been paid (s.88(4) of the Housing Act 1980).
This definition thus excludes the normal house purchase whereby the purchase
price is paid in two instalments—the deposit on exchange of contracts and the
balance of the purchase price on completion. The normal purchaser who enters
into possession of the property before completion is a licensee and as such has no
security of tenure. However, the Housing Act 1980 extends the benefit of the
Protection from Eviction Act 1977 to a rental purchaser as if the premises had
been let to him under a tenancy which is not statutorily protected and his tenancy
had come to an end with the termination of his agreement or with his right to
possession under it (Sch.25 para.61 to the Housing Act 1980). Thus a court order
is required for a "vendor" under a rental purchase agreement to gain possession.
Further protection is given to a rental purchaser by s.88 of the Housing Act 1980
whereby if possession proceedings are taken, the court has the power to adjourn
the proceedings or stay or suspend execution of the order or postpone the date
for possession for such period or periods as the court thinks fit (s.88(1)). The
usual restrictions on the court's discretion to postpone the date for possession
imposed by s.89 of the Housing Act 1980 do not apply (s.89(2)(e)). The court may
impose any conditions (in particular as to payments in respect of his continued
occupation) as it thinks fit (s.88(2)) and these conditions may be revoked or varied
(s.88(3)).

Those advising the rental purchaser should carefully examine the circumstances
surrounding the creation of the agreement so as to see whether it truly reflects the
intention of the parties at that time. If the agreement does not reflect their true
intentions the court may hold that it is a "sham" or a "pretence" and that the rental
purchaser is a regulated or assured tenant (cf. licence agreements (para.5.008),
and holiday lets (para.19.006) and company lets (para.17.021)). See also *Martin v
Davies* (1952) 159 E.G. 191.

Beneficiaries

21.026   The law relating to land and trusts was radically altered by the Trusts of Land and Appointment of Trustees Act 1996. Any trust property which consists of or includes land is now a "trust of land" (ss.1, 5 and Sch.2). The doctrine of conversion no longer exists; the land is not to be regarded as personal property (s.3). In the case of every trust for sale a term is implied, despite any contrary provision, that the trustees may postpone the sale of land, whether the trust is created before or after the commencement of the 1996 Act; i.e. January 1, 1997 (s.4).

Beneficiaries under a trust of land are given the right to occupy the land if the purposes of the trust include making the land available for their occupation. These rights are regulated by ss.12 and 13 (below and Chapter 33).

Applications for an order for sale, previously made under s.30 of the Law of Property Act 1925, are now made under ss.14 and 15 (below). Section 15 has changed the law and the earlier authorities on s.30 will only give limited assistance in deciding how the court's discretion should be exercised (*Mortgage Corporation v Shaire* [2000] 3 E.G.L.R. 132, Neuberger J.). It should be noted that s.15 expressly states that regard should be had, among other factors, to the welfare of children and the interests of secured creditors of the beneficiaries.

Trusts of Land and Appointment of Trustees Act 1996

21.027   1 Meaning of "trust of land"

(1) In this Act—

(a) "trust of land" means (subject to subsection (3)) any trust of property which consists of or includes land, and
(b) "trustees of land" means trustees of a trust of land.

(2) The reference in subsection (1)(a) to a trust—

(a) is to any description of trust (whether express, implied, resulting or constructive), including a trust for sale and a bare trust, and
(b) includes a trust created, or arising, before the commencement of this Act.

. . .

3 Abolition of doctrine of conversion

(1) Where land is held by trustees subject to a trust for sale, the land is not to be regarded as personal property; and where personal property is subject to a trust for sale in order that the trustees may acquire land, the personal property is not to be regarded as land.
(2) Subsection (1) does not apply to a trust created by a will if the testator died before the commencement of this Act.
(3) Subject to that, subsection (1) applies to a trust whether it is created, or arises, before or after that commencement.

4 Express trusts for sale as trusts of land

(1) In the case of every trust for sale of land created by a disposition there is to be implied, despite any provision to the contrary made by the disposition, a power for the trustees to postpone sale of the land; and the trustees are not liable in any way for postponing sale of the land, in the exercise of their discretion, for an indefinite period.
(2) Subsection (1) applies to a trust whether it is created, or arises, before or after the commencement of this Act.

(3) Subsection (1) does not affect any liability incurred by trustees before that commencement.

5 Implied trusts for sale as trusts of land

(1) Schedule 2 has effect in relation to statutory provisions which impose a trust for sale of land in certain circumstances so that in those circumstances there is instead a trust of the land (without a duty to sell).

(2) Section 1 of the Settled Land Act 1925 does not apply to land held on any trust arising by virtue of that Schedule (so that any such land is subject to a trust of land).

6 General powers of trustees

(1) For the purpose of exercising their functions as trustees, the trustees of land have in relation to the land subject to the trust all the powers of an absolute owner.

. . .

12 The right to occupy

(1) A beneficiary who is beneficially entitled to an interest in possession in land **21.028** subject to a trust of land is entitled by reason of his interest to occupy the land at any time if at that time—

    (a) the purposes of the trust include making the land available for his occupation (or for the occupation of beneficiaries of a class of which he is a member or of beneficiaries in general), or

    (b) the land is held by the trustees so as to be so available.

(2) Subsection (1) does not confer on a beneficiary a right to occupy land if it is either unavailable or unsuitable for occupation by him.

(3) This section is subject to section 13.

13 Exclusion and restriction of right to occupy

(1) Where two or more beneficiaries are (or apart from this subsection would be) entitled under section 12 to occupy land, the trustees of land may exclude or restrict the entitlement of any one or more (but not all) of them.

(2) Trustees may not under subsection (1)—

    (a) unreasonably exclude any beneficiary's entitlement to occupy land, or

    (b) restrict any such entitlement to an unreasonable extent.

(3) The trustees of land may from time to time impose reasonable conditions on any beneficiary in relation to his occupation of land by reason of his entitlement under section 12.

(4) The matters to which trustees are to have regard in exercising the powers conferred by this section include—

    (a) the intentions of the person or persons (if any) who created the trust,

    (b) the purposes for which the land is held, and

    (c) the circumstances and wishes of each of the beneficiaries who is (or apart from any previous exercise by the trustees of those powers would be) entitled to occupy the land under section 12.

(5) The conditions which may be imposed on a beneficiary under subsection (3) include, in particular, conditions requiring him—

    (a) to pay any outgoings or expenses in respect of the land, or

    (b) to assume any other obligation in relation to the land or to any activity which is or is proposed to be conducted there.

(6) Where the entitlement of any beneficiary to occupy land under section 12 has been excluded or restricted, the conditions which may be imposed on any other beneficiary under subsection (3) include, in particular, conditions requiring him to—

    (a) make payments by way of compensation to the beneficiary whose entitlement has been excluded or restricted, or

    (b) forgo any payment or other benefit to which he would otherwise be entitled under the trust so as to benefit that beneficiary.

(7) The powers conferred on trustees by this section may not be exercised—

    (a) so as prevent any person who is in occupation of land (whether or not by reason of an entitlement under section 12) from continuing to occupy the land, or

    (b) in a manner likely to result in any such person ceasing to occupy the land,

unless he consents or the court has given approval.

(8) The matters to which the court is to have regard in determining whether to give approval under subsection (7) include the matters mentioned in subsection (4) (a) to (c).

14 Applications for order

21.029

(1) Any person who is a trustee of land or has an interest in property subject to a trust of land may make an application to the court for an order under this section.

(2) On an application for an order under this section the court may make any such order—

    (a) relating to the exercise by the trustees of any of their functions (including an order relieving them of any obligation to obtain the consent of, or to consult, any person in connection with the exercise of any of their functions), or

    (b) declaring the nature or extent of a person's interest in property subject to the trust,

as the court thinks fit.

(3) The court may not under this section make any order as to the appointment or removal of trustees.

(4) The powers conferred on the court by this section are exercisable on an application whether it is made before or after the commencement of this Act.

15 Matters relevant in determining applications

(1) The matters to which the court is to have regard in determining an application for an order under section 14 include—

    (a) the intentions of the person or persons (if any) who created the trust,

    (b) the purposes for which the property subject to the trust is held,

    (c) the welfare of any minor who occupies or might reasonably be expected to occupy any land subject to the trust as his home, and

    (d) the interests of any secured creditor of any beneficiary.

(2) In the case of an application relating to the exercise in relation to any land of the powers conferred on the trustees by section 13, the matters to which the court is to have regard also include the circumstances and wishes of each of the beneficiaries who is (or apart from any previous exercise by the trustees of those powers would be) entitled to occupy the land under section 12.

(3) In the case of any other application, other than one relating to the exercise of the power mentioned in section 6(2), the matters to which the court is to have

regard also include the circumstances and wishes of any beneficiaries of full age and entitled to an interest in possession in property subject to the trust or (in case of dispute) of the majority (according to the value of their combined interests).

(4) This section does not apply to an application if section 335A of the Insolvency Act 1986 (which is inserted by Schedule 3 and relates to applications by a trustee of a bankrupt) applies to it.

. . .

18 Application of Part to personal representatives

(1) The provisions of this Part relating to trustees, other than sections 10, 11 and **21.030** 14, apply to personal representatives, but with appropriate modifications and without prejudice to the functions of personal representatives for the purposes of administration.

(2) The appropriate modifications include—

(a) the substitution of references to persons interested in the due administration of the estate for references to beneficiaries, and

(b) the substitution of references to the will for references to the disposition creating the trust.

(3) Section 3(1) does not apply to personal representatives if the death occurs before the commencement of this Act.

Minors

No one under the age of 18 can hold an estate in land. Any attempt to grant a **21.031** tenancy to a minor will result in the grantor holding that tenancy on trust for the minor. That gives rise to the unsatisfactory and problematic situation of the landlord also being the paper title tenant. The minor takes the beneficial interest and may also or alternatively have a right to occupy as a licensee under the terms of the tenancy.

By s.2 and Sch.1 of the Trust of Land and Appointment of Trustees Act 1996 ("the 1996 Act") an attempt to convey a legal estate in land to a minor will take effect as a declaration of trust. The effect will be that the grantor will be a trustee in respect of any interest of land purported to be granted to the minor. The minor will be the beneficiary under that trust. So that in *Alexander-David v London Borough of Hammersmith & Fulham* [2009] EWCA Civ 259 the attempt by a local authority to grant a non-secure tenancy lease to a minor meant that they were unable to obtain possession as to do so they needed to serve a notice to quit on themselves as trustee for the minor, but service of such a notice would put them in breach of trust! "[F]or so long as the [the council] held the premises in trust for the Appellant, it could not lawfully destroy the subject matter of the trust by serving notice to quit. . . . service of notice to quit only on the minor beneficiary of the trust was not sufficient to terminate the tenancy that was being held by the [the council] as trustee on her [A's] behalf." (See further below, para.21.033).

Contractual effect of the tenancy agreement

While the tenancy agreement could not grant an interest in land to a minor as a **21.032** contract there is the possibility that it may be binding. Contracts with minors may only be enforceable if they are "necessities" i.e. that they confer a necessary benefit on the minor. The provision of accommodation is very likely to be a necessity. Further, it must not contain harsh and onerous terms. It has been held in *Lowe v Griffith* (1835) 4 L.J.C.P. 94 that a lessee who is under age is liable for rent only if the subject-matter of the lease is a necessity.

It follows that if he has no interest in land because of his minority, and the only basis upon which the minor occupies the property is pursuant to a tenancy agreement, then if it is not pursuant to a tenancy then it must be pursuant to a licence. The tenancy creates a licence to occupy. Further, it also provides the situations in which the licence to occupy can be determined.

As a licensee of residential premises, in order to determine his licence not only will the terms of the tenancy need to be adhered to but also the Protection from Eviction Act 1977 will have to be followed.

Determining the tenancy/trust

21.033 In addition to determining the licence to occupy, the tenancy held on trust should also be determined. To that end, the landlord would need to serve a notice to quit on itself, but as said in *Alexander-David v London Borough of Hammersmith & Fulham* [2009] EWCA Civ 259 that would put them in breach of trust. The court in that case suggested that the solution is probably to appoint someone else as trustee and then serve a notice on that trustee (para.33). This should be a notice to quit a common law tenancy. As this matter involves a trust in any claim for possession, then a claim under the 1996 Act for a declaration that the trust has come to an end by service of the notice to quit on the landlord (s.14 of the 1996 Act) should be pleaded.

It is also a possibility that rather than (or in addition to) occupying pursuant to a licence, the minor will occupy pursuant to an equitable tenancy which is regulated by the 1996 Act and gives them a right of possession as a beneficiary (s.12 of the 1996 Act). If that is right then the equitable tenancy may need to be determined in accordance with the Housing Act 1988 (i.e. service of the s.21 notice (already served) and then possession proceedings). It is unclear whether the Housing Act 1988 applies to equitable tenancies, but there does not seem to be anything in the wording of the Act which would exclude its application.

Equitable agreements

21.034 One way of attempting to avoid the situation above is to create an equitable agreement whereby there is no actual grant of a tenancy to a minor, just an agreement to grant one. A copy of the proposed tenancy agreement should be attached to the contract for the grant of a tenancy agreement.

In *Alexander-David v London Borough of Hammersmith & Fulham* (see para.21.031) it was not possible to construe an equitable tenancy out of the circumstances, particularly where that was not what was intended by the parties and was not expressed on the face of the agreement. The Court of Appeal recognised the difficulty this decision may cause many local authorities and whilst stating that it was not for the court to advise them as to what to do in these situations it did suggest the following for future cases:

- The grant of a licence could be achieved, particularly if ancillary services or monitoring were part of the occupational licence; or

- An agreement to grant a lease (but not the grant of an actual lease) for the period until the applicant turns 18 could be granted (thus creating an equitable tenancy).

In either case, the inability to grant a legal estate should be expressly recognised. Sullivan L.J. at 39: "The problem has arisen in this case because the Respondent's standard form tenancy agreement does not expressly address the Appellant's inability to hold a legal estate, and in consequence does not purport to do anything other than grant her such an estate".

As the Housing Act applies to an agreement to enter into a tenancy, possession can be sought on the usual grounds. Section 45 of that Act interprets "tenancy" as, among other things, an agreement for a tenancy.

However, another twist is that if the legal tenant is the landlord or a third party trustee (see above para.21.031) they will not be in residence and so the tenancy may not fall within the Housing Act 1988. That eventuality can be covered by service of a notice to quit on the landlord or the third party trustee.

Proceedings

Minors need to be represented by a "litigation friend" and if there is no one who is nominated by them then an application to the court can be made to either appoint a next friend on their behalf or to dispense with the necessity of him being represented by a next friend (CPR Pt 21). **21.035**

While possession proceedings can be commenced without the appointment of a litigation friend, no other steps can be taken until one is appointed or until the court makes an order dispensing with the need for one. An application for the appointment or dispensation of a litigation friend should be made at the same time that possession proceedings are commenced.

Part 3

The Proceedings for Possession

Chapter 22

The Necessity for Possession Proceedings

The circumstances in which a landlord or licensor is required to bring proceedings **22.001** for possession are dealt with in part by the statutory provisions relating to security of tenure and in part by the Protection from Eviction Act 1977.

Statutorily protected tenants

Where the tenant of a dwelling-house has been served with a notice terminating **22.002** the tenancy, or requiring possession, the landlord in most cases may only recover possession by bringing proceedings for possession. In the cases listed below this is because the relevant statutory provisions give the tenant a right to remain in occupation until the court orders otherwise. Any attempt to evict him without a court order would therefore be unlawful. The cases referred to are as follows:

(1) an assured tenant (including an assured shorthold tenant) under the Housing Act 1988;

(2) a Rent Act tenant under the Rent Act 1977;

(3) a secure tenant, family intervention tenant and flexible tenant under the Housing Act 1985;

(4) an introductory tenancy under the Housing Act 1996;

(5) a demoted tenancy under the Housing Act 1996;

(6) a tenant of a long lease at a low rent under Pt I of the Landlord and Tenant Act 1954 or under Sch.10 to the Local Government and Housing Act 1989;

(7) an assured agricultural occupant under the Housing Act 1988;

(8) a protected occupant or statutory tenant as defined in the Rent (Agriculture) Act 1976; and

(9) a tenant of an agricultural holding within the meaning of the Agricultural Holdings Act 1986 or a farm business tenancy within the Agricultural Tenancies Act 1995.

Occupiers who are not statutorily protected tenants

22.003   Where there is no statutory protection under one of the above Acts it is nevertheless unlawful to evict the tenant (or any other person who was a lawful resident at the termination of the tenancy) without obtaining a court order after the tenancy has come to an end unless the tenancy was an "excluded tenancy" (ss.3 and 8 of the Protection from Eviction Act 1977). (There is an overlap in protection in relation to statutory tenants in that they are treated as not being statutorily protected for the purposes of s.3 so that s.3 also makes it unlawful to evict a statutory tenant without a court order (s.8(1)(a)), cf. *Haniff v Robinson* [1993] 1 All E.R. 185.)

Occupiers (a) under licences entered into after November 28, 1980 that are restricted contracts within the meaning of the Rent Act 1977 (s.3(2A)) and (b) where the landlord is entitled to recover possession following the death of the tenant under a statutory tenancy within the meaning of the Rent Act 1977 or the Rent (Agriculture) Act 1976, are entitled to the same protection (s.3(3)). Section 3 also applies in relation to all other premises occupied as a dwelling under a licence (whenever entered into), other than an "excluded licence" (see below); s.3(2B).

Section 3 of the 1977 Act is compatible with Article 8 of the ECHR (*Coombes v Waltham Forest London Borough Council* [2010] EWHC 666 (Admin)). Cranston J. at para.54:

> "Section 3 does nothing more than prohibit a property owner, like the council, from re-possessing property without first seeking a possession order from the court. The requirement to seek a possession order, rather than to recover possession without any supervision by the court, cannot be incompatible with Article 8."

Protection from Eviction Act 1977 sections 3 and 8

22.004   **3.**—(1) Where any premises have been let as a dwelling under a tenancy which is neither a statutorily protected tenancy nor an excluded tenancy and—

> (a)   the tenancy (in this section referred to as the former tenancy) has come to an end, but
>
> (b)   the occupier continues to reside in the premises or part of them,
>
> it shall not be lawful for the owner to enforce against the occupier, otherwise than by proceedings in the court, his right to recover possession of the premises.

(2)   In this section "the occupier", in relation to any premises, means any person lawfully residing in the premises or part of them at the termination of the former tenancy.

(2A)   Subsections (1) and (2) above apply in relation to any restricted contract (within the meaning of the Rent Act 1977) which–

> (a)   creates a licence; and
>
> (b)   is entered into after the commencement of section 69 of the Housing Act 1980;
>
> as they apply in relation to a restricted contract which creates a tenancy.

(2B)   Subsections (1) and (2) above apply in relation to any premises occupied as a dwelling under a licence, other than an excluded licence, as they apply in relation to premises let as a dwelling under a tenancy, and in those subsections the expressions "let" and "tenancy" shall be construed accordingly.

(2C) References in the preceding provisions of this section and section 4(2A) below to an excluded tenancy do not apply to—

    (a) a tenancy entered into before the date on which the Housing Act 1988 came into force, or

    (b) a tenancy entered into on or after that date but pursuant to a contract made before that date,

    but, subject to that, excluded tenancy" and "excluded licence" shall be construed in accordance with section 3A below.

(3) This section shall, with the necessary modifications, apply where the owner's right to recover possession arises on the death of the tenant under a statutory tenancy within the meaning of the Rent Act 1977 or the Rent (Agriculture) Act 1976.

8.—(1) In this Act "statutorily protected tenancy" means—   **22.005**

    (a) a protected tenancy within the meaning of the Rent Act 1977 or a tenancy to which Part I of the Landlord and Tenant Act 1954 applies;

    (b) a protected occupancy or statutory tenancy as defined in the Rent (Agriculture) Act 1976;

    (c) a tenancy to which Part II of the Landlord and Tenant Act 1954 applies;

    (d) a tenancy of an agricultural holding within the meaning of the Agricultural Holdings Act 1986 which is a tenancy in relation to which that Act applies;

    (e) an assured tenancy or assured agricultural occupancy under Part I of the Housing Act 1988;

    (f) a tenancy to which Schedule 10 to the Local Government and Housing Act 1989 applies;

    (g) a farm business tenancy within the meaning of the Agricultural Tenancies Act 1995.

(2) For the purposes of Part I of this Act a person who, under the terms of his employment, had exclusive possession of any premises other than as a tenant shall be deemed to have been a tenant and the expressions "let" and "tenancy" shall be construed accordingly.

(3) In Part I of this Act "the owner", in relation to any premises, means the person who, as against the occupier, is entitled to possession thereof.

Forfeiture

Section 2 of the Protection from Eviction Act 1977 provides that it is not lawful to   **22.006** enforce a right of re-entry or forfeiture in any lease where the premises are let as a dwelling otherwise than by proceedings in court while any person is lawfully residing in the premises or part of them (see para.2.072). This section is not affected by the provisions relating to "excluded tenancies". Thus, even where the tenancy is an "excluded tenancy" the landlord must take proceedings if he wishes to recover possession by relying upon a right of re-entry or forfeiture.

Enforcement of possession orders

Where the landlord has an order for possession he may not (if ss.2 or 3 of the 1977   **22.007** Act applies) "enforce" that order otherwise than by the issue and execution of a writ or, as the case may be, warrant for possession. If he does so he will be liable to pay the tenant damages for unlawful eviction (*Borzak v Ahmed* [1965] 2 Q.B. 320; *Haniff v Robinson* [1993] 1 All E.R. 15; see also para.35.001).

Excluded tenancies and licences

22.008 There are six categories of excluded tenancy and licence. They are as follows:

(1) occupier sharing accommodation with the landlord or licensor which the latter occupied immediately before and at the end of the licence or tenancy (see *Sumeghova v McMahon* [2002] EWCA Civ 1581—landlord spent a lot of time in the neighbouring property, which he also owned, but he did not sleep there. He slept in the accommodation that he shared with the tenant. Where a person sleeps is of the most enormous importance in determining whether that was his only or principal home. The accommodation where he slept was his only or principal home, the tenancy was therefore an excluded tenancy—see also *Uratemp Ventures Ltd v Collins* [2001] UKHL 43 at para.6.004);

(2) sharing accommodation with a member of the family of the landlord or licensor;

(3) tenancy or licence granted as a temporary expedient to a trespasser;

(4) holiday accommodation;

(5) tenancy or licence granted otherwise than for money or money's worth;

(6) accommodation in a hostel within the meaning of the Housing Act 1985 provided by local authorities and other specified public bodies (*Rogerson v Wigan Metropolitan Borough Council* [2004] EWHC 1677).

In all of these cases the landlord or licensor may obtain possession without taking proceedings at the end of the tenancy or licence (although he must not use or threaten to use force: see below "Offences"). Full details of these excluded categories are set out in s.3A of the Protection from Eviction Act 1977; see below. (These provisions do not affect s.2 of the 1977 Act which provides that it is not lawful to enforce a right of re-entry otherwise than by proceedings; see above.)

22.009   Note that s.3A of the 1977 Act does not apply to a tenancy entered into before the date on which the Housing Act 1988 came into force (January 15, 1989) or to a tenancy entered into on or after that date but pursuant to a contract made before that date (s.3(2C)). Any such tenancy cannot be an "excluded tenancy" and it will be necessary to take proceedings in order to obtain possession of premises subject to such a tenancy. See further s.8(5), (6) of the 1977 Act where the terms of a tenancy or licence are varied on or after the date on which the Housing Act 1988 came into force.

Protection from Eviction Act 1977 section 3A

3A.—(1) Any reference in this Act to an excluded tenancy or an excluded licence is a reference to a tenancy or licence which is excluded by virtue of any of the following provisions of this section.

(2) A tenancy or licence is excluded if—

    (a)   under its terms the occupier shares any accommodation with the landlord or licensor; and

    (b)   immediately before the tenancy or licence was granted and also at the time it comes to an end, the landlord or licensor occupied as his only or principal home premises of which the whole or part of the shared accommodation formed part.

(3) A tenancy or licence is also excluded if—

    (a)   under its terms the occupier shares any accommodation with a member of the family of the landlord or licensor;

    (b)   immediately before the tenancy or licence was granted and also at the time it comes to an end, the member of the family of the landlord or licensor occupied as his only or principal home premises of which the whole or part of the shared accommodation formed part; and

    (c)   immediately before the tenancy or licence was granted and also at the time it comes to an end, the landlord or licensor occupied as his only or principal home premises in the same building as the shared accommodation and that building is not a purpose-built block of flats.

(4) For the purposes of subsections (2) and (3) above, an occupier shares accommodation with another person if he has the use of it in common with that person (whether or not also in common with others) and any reference in those subsections to shared accommodation shall be construed accordingly, and if, in relation to any tenancy or licence, there is at any time more than one person who is the landlord or licensor, any reference in those subsections to the landlord or licensor shall be construed as a reference to any one of those persons.

(5) In subsections (2) to (4) above—

    (a)   "accommodation" includes neither an area used for storage nor a staircase, passage, corridor or other means of access;

    (b)   "occupier" means, in relation to a tenancy, the tenant and, in relation to a licence, the licensee; and

    (c)   "purpose-built block of flats" has the same meaning as in Part III of Schedule 1 of the Housing Act 1988,

and section 113 of the Housing Act 1985 shall apply to determine whether a person is for the purpose of subsection (3) above a member of another's family as it applies for the purposes of Part IV of that Act.

(6) A tenancy or licence is excluded if it was granted as a temporary expedient to **22.010** a person who entered the premises in question or any other premises as a trespasser (whether or not, before the beginning of that tenancy or licence, another tenancy or licence to occupy the premises or any other premises had been granted to him).

(7) A tenancy or licence is excluded if—

    (a)   it confers on the tenant or licensee the right to occupy the premises for a holiday only; or

    (b)   it is granted otherwise than for money or money's worth.

(8) A licence is excluded if it confers rights of occupation in a hostel, within the meaning of the Housing Act 1985, which is provided by—

    (a)   the council of a county, district or London Borough, the Common Council of the City of London, the Council of the Isles of Scilly, the Inner London Education Authority, a joint authority within the meaning of the Local Government Act 1985 or a residuary body within the meaning of that Act;

    (b)   a development corporation within the meaning of the New Towns Act 1981;

(c) the Commission for the New Towns;

(d) an urban development corporation established by an order under section 135 of the Local Government, Planning and Land Act 1980;

(e) a housing action trust established under Part III of the Housing Act 1988;

(f) the Development Board for Rural Wales;

(g) the Housing Corporation or Housing for Wales;

(h) a housing trust which is a charity or a registered housing association, within the meaning of the Housing Associations Act 1985; or

(i) any other person who is, or who belongs to a class of person which is, specified in an order made by the Secretary of State.

(9) The power to make an order under subsection (8)(i) above shall be exercisable by statutory instrument which shall be subject to annulment in pursuance of a resolution of either House of Parliament.

Offences

22.011 Where a person unlawfully deprives or attempts to deprive a "residential occupier" (i.e. a person occupying premises as a residence under a contract or by virtue of any enactment or rule of law giving him the right to remain in occupation or restricting the right of any other person to recover possession of the premises) of his occupation he commits an offence unless he can prove that he believed, and had reasonable cause to believe, that the residential occupier had ceased to reside in the premises (s.1(2) of the Protection from Eviction Act 1977). In *West Wiltshire District Council v Snelgrove* (1997) 30 H.L.R. 57 DC, friends of the family who were let into occupation on a short-term basis with an arrangement for payment of food and electricity were not residential occupiers as there was no intention to create any interest in land. Alternatively, any licence of occupation was not for money or money's worth, as any money paid was for services and not occupation, and therefore fell outside of s.3A(7)(b)—see above.

It is also an offence for any person to do any act likely to interfere with the peace or comfort of the residential occupier or members of his household or to withdraw persistently or withhold services reasonably required for occupation of the premises (e.g. by turning off gas, electricity or water supplies) if such acts are carried out with the intent to cause the residential occupier to give up occupation of the premises or to refrain from exercising any right or pursuing any remedy in respect of the premises (s.1(3) of the Protection from Eviction Act 1977). Furthermore, the landlord (see wide definition in subs.3(c)) of a residential occupier or an agent of the landlord is guilty of an offence if he engages in such conduct if he knows or has reasonable cause to believe that that conduct is likely to cause the residential occupier to give up occupation of the whole or part of the premises or to refrain from exercising any right or remedy in respect of the whole or part of the premises (s.1(3)(a)) unless the landlord or agent proves that he had reasonable grounds for doing the acts or withdrawing or withholding the services in question (s.1(3)(b)).

22.012 It is only an offence to withhold or withdraw services that the landlord is required to provide by the terms of the tenancy agreement, the licence or the statute under which the tenant occupies (*McCall v Abelesz* [1976] Q.B. 585).

Finally, it is an offence for any person to use or threaten to use violence (to persons or property) to gain entry into premises where there is someone present on the premises who is opposed to the entry and the person using or threatening to use violence knows this (s.6 of the Criminal Law Act 1977). A property owner wishing to evict trespassers should therefore seek possession in proceedings unless re-entry can be effected peaceably. The civil remedy of a person unlawfully evicted by his landlord is to seek an injunction and/or damages (see Ch.35).

There is a defence to the offence under s.6 to any person who is a "displaced residential occupier" such as a person who returns home from a holiday to find squatters in occupation (s.6(3), (7) and s.12). See also s.7 and ss.12 and 12A for the offence committed by the trespasser who fails to leave if required to do so by or on behalf of a displaced residential occupier. For new offences committed by trespassers on residential premises see Ch.31.

Criminal Law Act 1977 section 6

6.—(1) Subject to the following provisions of this section, any person who, without **22.013** lawful authority, uses or threatens violence for the purpose of securing entry into any premises for himself or for any other person is guilty of an offence, provided that—

    (a) there is someone present on those premises at the time who is opposed to the entry which the violence is intended to secure; and

    (b) the person using or threatening the violence knows that that is the case.

(2) The fact that a person has any interest in or right to possession or occupation of any premises shall not for the purposes of subsection (1) above constitute lawful authority for the use or threat of violence by him or anyone else for the purpose of securing his entry into those premises . . . .

   . . .

(4) It is immaterial for the purposes of this section—

    (a) whether the violence in question is directed against the person or against property; and

    (b) whether the entry which the violence is intended to secure is for the purpose of acquiring possession of the premises in question or for any other purpose.

Chapter 23

Human Rights Defences

As a result of the Human Rights Act 1988 the European Convention on Human **23.001** Rights is part of the law of the country. Human Rights points can come up in a number of contexts and are dealt with throughout the book. However, this section of the book is only concerned with the effect of the Convention (if any) on a claim to possession where the owner of the land clearly has a right to possession as a matter of English property law. The question will be whether, not withstanding that right, the owner of the land is prevented from obtaining possession, and if so for how long?

In *Manchester City Council v Pinnock* [2010] UKSC 45 the Supreme Court (consisting of nine judges) unanimously held that where a defendant raises a human rights defence to a claim for possession brought by a public body the question for the judge to determine "is always whether the eviction is a proportionate means of achieving a legitimate aim" (Lord Neuberger at para.52). In coming to this decision the Supreme Court overturned earlier decisions of the House of Lords and instead followed the jurisprudence of the European Court of Human Rights ("ECtHR"). The judgment of the court was given by Lord Neuberger. Unless stated otherwise, all quotations are from that judgment. As will be seen *Pinnock* was confirmed in *London Borough of Hounslow v Powell* [2011] UKSC 8.

European Convention on Human Rights, Article 8

So far as is relevant art.8 of the European Convention on Human Rights provides **23.002** as follows:

"1. Everyone has the right to respect for . . . his home. . . .
2. There shall be no interference by a public authority with the exercise of this right except such as is in accordance with the law and is necessary in a democratic society in the interests of . . . the economic well-being of the country, for the prevention of disorder or crime, . . . or for the protection of the rights . . . of others."

The ECtHR has interpreted art.8 as requiring the court considering the claim to determine whether or not the eviction is proportionate:

"Any person at risk of being dispossessed of his home at the suit of a local authority should in principle have the right to raise the question of the proportionality of the measure, and to have it determined by an independent tribunal in the light of article 8, even if his right of occupation under domestic law has come to an end. . . " (see para.45, where Lord Neuberger distils various decisions of the ECtHR).

As noted in the case at para.61:

"it is only where a person's 'home' is under threat that article 8 comes into play, and there may be cases where it is open to argument whether the premises involved are the defendant's home (e g where very short-term accommodation has been provided)."

What changed as a result of Pinnock?

23.003 Until this decision, the House of Lords had said that the domestic courts should only determine that a defendant had an art.8 defence if he or she could get through one of two "gateways" set out by Lord Hope in *Kay v Lambeth* [2006] 2 A.C. 465 at para.110. It was gateway (b) that was most pertinent:

"(b) if the defendant wishes to challenge the decision of a public authority to recover possession as an improper exercise of its powers at common law on the ground that it was a decision that no reasonable person would consider justifiable, he should be permitted to do this provided ... that the point is seriously arguable. . . "

Those gateways, and the reliance on principles of judicial review, embodied in that statement are now gone. Instead, in all public sector cases (see para.23.004) the court must, when faced with an art.8 defence, consider whether or not it is proportionate to make the order for possession:

"A judicial procedure which is limited to addressing the proportionality of the measure through the medium of traditional judicial review (i e, one which does not permit the court to make its own assessment of the facts in an appropriate case) is inadequate as it is not appropriate for resolving sensitive factual issues." (para.45(b)).

In earlier cases there was debate about whether or not art.8 and proportionality should be considered in all cases or only in highly exceptional cases. In *Pinnock* Lord Neuberger made it clear that the principle applies to all cases (para.51).

"It is necessary to address the proposition that it will only be in 'very highly exceptional cases' that it will be appropriate for the court to consider a proportionality argument. Such a proposition undoubtedly derives support from the views expressed by Lord Bingham, and has been referred to with apparent approval by the EurCtHR in more than one case. Nevertheless, it seems to us to be both unsafe and unhelpful to invoke exceptionality as a guide. It is unhelpful because, as Lady Hale pointed out in argument, exceptionality is an outcome and not a guide. It is unsafe because, as Lord Walker observed in *Doherty v Birmingham* [2009] 1 AC 367, para 122, there may be more cases than the EurCtHR or Lord Bingham supposed where article 8 could reasonably be invoked by a residential tenant."

The position was made clear by Lord Neuberger at para.52:

"The question is always whether the eviction is a proportionate means of achieving a legitimate aim."

To which landlords do the principles apply?

Pinnock was about a local authority seeking possession of premises that were **23.004** subject to a demoted tenancy. It is clear that the decision therefore applies to local authorities. However, the observations in the "judgment apply equally to other social landlords to the extent that they are public authorities under the Human Rights Act 1988". The leading decision on whether or not a social landlord is a public authority for these purposes is *London & Quadrant Housing Trust v Weaver* [2009] EWCA Civ 587 where it was held that one must look at the actual act being carried out and decide whether or not it was a public act. (It is worth noting that at first instance the judge in *Joseph v Nettleton* [2010] EWCA Civ 228 held that a housing co-operative was not a public body for the purposes of the Human Rights Act. The argument was not pursued on appeal.)

However, *Pinnock* does not apply to the private sector. Lord Neuberger made this clear where he said that "nothing in this judgment is intended to bear on cases where the person seeking the order for possession is a private landowner". However, it is possible that in some future case the courts may come to a different conclusion (see paras 4 and 50). The point was just not considered in this case.

Proportionality and the facts

In determining whether or not it is proportionate to make an order for possession **23.005** it is necessary to look at the facts of the case. As stated above, the court is not confined to principles of judicial review. If appropriate the court hearing the possession claim must hear evidence and make necessary findings:

"if our law is to be compatible with article 8, where a court is asked to make an order for possession of a person's home at the suit of a local authority, the court must have the power to assess the proportionality of making the order, and, in making that assessment, to resolve any relevant dispute of fact."

Where there is more than one stage to the process it is the proceedings as a whole that need to be considered to see if art.8 has been complied with (para.45(c)). This would clearly apply to a demoted tenancy but no doubt applies to all cases, in the sense that there is a process which invariably consists of (i) a decision to evict, (ii) the service of a notice, (iii) the taking of proceedings, (iv) the continuation of the proceedings and (v) the eviction itself.

Proportionality and reasonableness

Where the tenancy is a secure tenancy, there is no difficulty. The court invariably **23.006** has to consider whether or not it is reasonable to make the order for possession. In doing so it is also effectively considering the question of proportionality. Paragraphs 55 and 56:

"The conclusion that, before making an order for possession, the court must be able to decide not only that the order would be justified under domestic law, but also that it would be proportionate under article 8(2) to make the order, presents no difficulties of principle or practice in relation to secure tenancies. . . . no order for possession can be made against a secure tenant unless, inter alia, it is reasonable to make the order. Any factor which has to be taken into account, or any dispute of fact which has to be resolved, for the purpose of assessing proportionality under article 8(2), would have to be taken into account or resolved for the purpose of assessing reasonableness under section 84 of the 1985 Act. Reasonableness under that section, like proportionality under article 8(2), requires the court to consider whether to order possession at all, and, if so, whether to make an outright order rather than a suspended order, and, if so, whether to direct that the outright order should not take effect for a significant time.

Moreover, reasonableness involves the trial judge 'tak[ing] into account all the relevant circumstances . . . in . . . a broad common-sense way . . . It therefore seems highly unlikely, as a practical matter, that it could be reasonable for a court to make an order for possession in circumstances in which it would be disproportionate to do so under article 8.'"

The same reasoning would clearly apply to an assured tenancy granted by a registered provider of social housing, where the ground for possession is a discretionary ground such as Ground 10 or 11 (rent) or Ground 14 (nuisance etc.).

Where under the domestic law the land owner has an absolute right to possession—other factors landlord may wish to rely on

23.007 Although the order for possession must always be proportionate, if a local authority has an absolute right to possession as a matter of domestic law that fact will be highly relevant. Paragraph 52:

"Where a person has no right in domestic law to remain in occupation of his home, the proportionality of making an order for possession at the suit of the local authority will be supported not merely by the fact that it would serve to vindicate the authority's ownership rights."

There may also be other factors that will be relevant in the local authority's favour. Lord Neuberger continued at para.52:

"It will also, at least normally, be supported by the fact that it would enable the authority to comply with its duties in relation to the distribution and management of its housing stock, including, for example, the fair allocation of its housing, the redevelopment of the site, the refurbishing of sub-standard accommodation, the need to move people who are in accommodation that now exceeds their needs, and the need to move vulnerable people into sheltered or warden-assisted housing. Furthermore, in many cases (such as this appeal) other cogent reasons, such as the need to remove a source of nuisance to neighbours, may support the proportionality of dispossessing the occupiers."

And at para.54:

"Unencumbered property rights, even where they are enjoyed by a public body such as a local authority, are of real weight when it comes to proportionality. So, too, is the right – indeed the obligation – of a local authority to decide who should occupy its residential property. As Lord Bingham said in *Harrow v Qazi* para 25:

> 'The administration of public housing under various statutory schemes is entrusted to local housing authorities. It is not for the court to second-guess allocation decisions. The Strasbourg authorities have adopted a very pragmatic and realistic approach to the issue of justification.'

> Therefore, in virtually every case where a residential occupier has no contractual or statutory protection, and the local authority is entitled to possession as a matter of domestic law, there will be a very strong case for saying that making an order for possession would be proportionate. However, in some cases there may be factors which would tell the other way."

Personal circumstances

It is the personal circumstances of the defendant that are most likely to be relevant **23.008** when determining whether or not it is proportionate to make the order for possession. Thus, the claimant is not obliged in any particular case to plead and put forward facts about itself that would support the argument that it is proportionate to make the order but it may do so if it wishes. Paragraph 53:

> "the Secretary of State . . . submitted that a local authority's aim in wanting possession should be a 'given', which does not have to be explained or justified in court, so that the court will only be concerned with the occupiers' personal circumstances. In our view, there is indeed force in the point . . . that to require the local authority routinely, from the outset, to plead and prove that the possession order sought is justified would, in the overwhelming majority of cases, be burdensome and futile. In other words, the fact that the authority is entitled to possession and should, in the absence of cogent evidence to the contrary, be assumed to be acting in accordance with its duties, will be a strong factor in support of the proportionality of making an order for possession. But, in a particular case, the authority may have what it believes to be particularly strong or unusual reasons for wanting possession – for example, that the property is the only occupied part of a site intended for immediate development for community housing. The authority could rely on that factor, but would have to plead it and adduce evidence to support it."

When is proportionality most likely to be relevant?

The domestic decisions in which art.8 has so far had most relevance have usually **23.009** concerned vulnerable persons. It is also in these situations where the arguments on proportionality are most likely to have some effect:

> ". . . the suggestions put forward on behalf of the Equality and Human Rights Commission, that proportionality is more likely to be a relevant issue 'in respect of occupants who are vulnerable as a result of mental illness, physical or learning disability, poor health or frailty', and that 'the issue may also require the local authority to explain why they are not securing alternative accommodation in such cases' seem to us well made."

In which situations is Pinnock most likely to have an impact?

23.010 It is really in cases where as a matter of domestic law there is no defence to the claim that *Pinnock* is relevant. Paragraph 57:

> "The implications of article 8 being potentially in play are much more significant where a local authority is seeking possession of a person's home in circumstances in which domestic law imposes no requirement of reasonableness and gives an unqualified right to an order for possession. In such a case the court's obligation under article 8(2), to consider the proportionality of making the order sought, does represent a potential new obstacle to the making of an order for possession. *The wide implications of this obligation will have to be worked out.* As in many situations, that is best left to the good sense and experience of judges sitting in the County Court" (author's emphasis).

The highlighted sentence is important. There are a number of circumstances in which this decision might be relevant:

- Demoted tenancies.

- Introductory tenancies (under Ch.1 of Pt V of the 1996 Act).

- Flexible tenancies.

- Family intervention tenancies.

- Tenancies granted on a temporary basis to the homeless (under Pt VII of the 1996 Act).

- Other non-secure tenancies (HA 1985, Sch.1).

- "Starter tenancies", ie assured shorthold tenancies granted by registered providers of social housing (see para.7.001).

- Assured tenancies granted by registered providers of social housing where the landlord is relying upon a mandatory ground, typically Ground 8 (mandatory ground for possession where there is at least 8 weeks etc. arrears of rent).

- Where one of two joint tenants has served a notice to quit.

- Occupiers who were once licensees who have had their licences determined.

- Even perhaps some trespassers—particularly gypsies.

There may be others.

Demoted tenancies

23.011 *Pinnock* was about a demoted tenancy. The Supreme Court came to the conclusion that the demoted tenancy regime was Human Rights Act compliant because it was possible to read into it the ability of the county court judge hearing the possession claim to determine proportionality and any relevant issues of fact relevant to that issue. See in particular para.104:

> "We are, accordingly, of the view that a County Court judge who is invited to make an order for possession against a demoted tenant pursuant to section 143D(2) can consider whether it is proportionate to make the order sought, and can investigate and determine any issues of fact relevant for the purpose of that exercise. It follows that the demoted tenancy regime in the 1996 Act is compatible with article 8."

However, the fact that the secure tenancy had been demoted made it easier to come to the conclusion that the decision to evict was proportionate (see in particular para.58).

Introductory tenancies and temporary housing for the homeless

Since *Pinnock* the Supreme Court has confirmed that the principles set out in **23.012** *Pinnock* (which related to demoted tenancies) apply equally to homelessness cases and introductory tenancies. (*London Borough of Hounslow v Powell* [2011] UKSC 8—see in particular paras 34 and 92).

Ground 8 cases

Where the tenancy is assured and there are at least eight weeks / two months etc. **23.013** rent in arrears the court must order possession if the landlord relies upon Ground 8 of Schedule to the Housing Act 1988. Sometimes those arrears accrue as a result of problems with housing benefit delays that are not the fault of the tenant. In those circumstances, the tenant may wish to have an adjournment to sort out the problems. In *North British Housing Association Ltd v Matthews* [2004] EWCA Civ 1736 the CA held that the power to adjourn the hearing date for the purpose of enabling the tenant to reduce the arrears to below the Ground 8 threshold may only be exercised in exceptional circumstances; and the fact that the arrears are attributable to maladministration on the part of the housing benefit authority is not an exceptional circumstance. It happens a lot! (See para.28.025). However, this decision may require reconsideration in the light of *Pinnock*. It is not difficult to envisage cases where the court will consider that it is not proportionate to order possession because the arrears are the result of circumstances outside the immediate control of the tenant.

"Starter tenancies"

Starter tenancies are in fact assured shorthold tenancies granted by registered **23.014** providers of social housing for a limited period, usually a year, to give the tenant the opportunity of showing that he or she will be a "good" tenant (para.7.081). They are the housing association equivalent to introductory tenancies. On the face of the legislation a landlord in respect of a starter tenancy can simply serve notice under s.21 and then seek possession at the end of the fixed term. However, *Pinnock* is bound to lead to defence claims that the decision to serve the notice and pursue the possession claim is not proportionate, perhaps where there were only minor infringements of the starter tenancy. This was already occurring under the "gateway (b)" regime set out in Kay. For example, see *West Kent Housing Association v Scott* [2012] EWCA Civ 276, in particular at paras 32 and 33 and *Riverside Group v Thomas* [2012] EWHC 169 (QB)).

Joint tenants—notice to quit by one of them

Unless the tenancy provides otherwise, a "notice to quit" (an odd name in this **23.015** context) served by one of two joint tenants in respect of a periodic tenancy brings the tenancy to an end, even if given without the agreement of the other (*Hammersmith and Fulham LBC v Monk* [1992] 1 A.C. 478, see para.3.018). The landlord is then entitled to possession. In *Sims v Dacorum BC* [2013] EWCA Civ 12, it was held that a claim for possession in these circumstances was not a breach of art.8. Therefore a joint tenant left in the home after the other joint tenant has served a notice on the landlord terminating the tenancy cannot now argue that it is not proportionate to make the order for possession.

At what point in the proceedings should the court consider proportionality?—summary disposal

23.016 Generally speaking proportionately need only be considered when the defendant raises it. Paragraph 61:

> "... as a general rule, article 8 need only be considered by the court if it is raised in the proceedings by or on behalf of the residential occupier."

Further, it should normally be dealt with on a summary basis in the first instance.

> "... if an article 8 point is raised, the court should initially consider it summarily, and if, as will no doubt often be the case, the court is satisfied that, even if the facts relied on are made out, the point would not succeed, it should be dismissed. Only if the court is satisfied that it could affect the order that the court might make should the point be further entertained."

And see *London Borough of Hounslow v Powell* [2011] UKSC 8, Lord Hope at para.35:

> "35. Mr Luba QC accepted that the threshold for raising an arguable case on proportionality was a *high one which would succeed in only a small proportion of cases*. I think that he was right to do so ... Practical considerations indicate that it would be demanding far too much of the judge in the county court, faced with a heavy list of individual cases, to require him to weigh up the personal circumstances of each individual occupier against the landlord's public responsibilities.
>
> If the threshold is crossed, the next question is what legitimate aims within the scope of article 8(2) may the claimant authority rely on for the purposes of the determination of proportionality and what types of factual issues will be relevant to its determination. The aims were identified in Pinnock, para 52. The proportionality of making the order for possession at the suit of the local authority will be supported by the fact that making the order would (a) serve to vindicate the authority's ownership rights; and (b) enable the authority to comply with its public duties in relation to the allocation and management of its housing stock. Various examples were given of the scope of the duties that the second legitimate aim encompasses – the fair allocation of its housing, the redevelopment of the site, the refurbishing of sub-standard accommodation, the need to move people who are in accommodation that now exceeds their needs and the need to move vulnerable people into sheltered or warden-assisted housing."

In *Holmes v Westminster City Council* [2011] EWHC 2857 it was held that a first instance judge was entitled to make an order for possession on a summary basis pursuant to CPR 55, even though there was a dispute of fact as to an alleged assault.

In *West Kent Housing Association v Scott* [2012] EWCA Civ 276 Lord Neuberger, very much encouraged the early and summary disposal of cases (at paras 36 and 39):

". . . we were told that there was no consistency of approach in different County Courts as to how to proceed when a tenant raises an Article 8 proportionality point in possession proceedings. In some courts, the case is automatically listed for a hearing on the merits of the point; in other courts, the case remains in the usual housing possession list, and is then (depending on the court) (i) adjourned for fuller consideration, (ii) automatically re-listed for a hearing, or (iii) briefly considered and then either rejected or adjourned as under (i) or re-listed as under (ii). . .

The only specific point I would make is to emphasise the desirability of a judge considering at an early stage (normally on the basis of the tenant's pleaded case on the issue) whether the tenant has an arguable case on Article 8 proportionality, before the issue is ordered to be heard. If it is a case which cannot succeed, then it should not be allowed to take up further court time and expense to the parties, and should not be allowed to delay the landlord's right to possession. I accept, however, that it may well be that even that cannot be an absolute rule. Apart from that, questions of procedure in this area should perhaps be considered by the CPR Committee, and, meanwhile, Designated Civil Judges may think it worth considering such procedures in the courts for which they have responsibility."

And in *Thurrock Borough Council v West* [2012] EWCA Civ 1435 Etherton L.J. emphasised that where apart from art.8 the defendant would otherwise have no legal right to remain "it is difficult to imagine circumstances in which the defence would operate to give the defendant an unlimited and unconditional right to remain".

What should a court do if it is not proportionate to evict?

If the court considers that it is not proportionate to make the order for possession **23.017** then the usual position will no doubt simply be that no order should be made, at least at that time. Lord Neuberger in *Pinnock* at para.45(d):

"If the court concludes that it would be disproportionate to evict a person from his home notwithstanding the fact that he has no domestic right to remain there, it would be unlawful to evict him so long as the conclusion obtains – for example, for a specified period, or until a specified event occurs, or a particular condition is satisfied."

However, at para.62 Lord Neuberger in *Pinnock* indicated that there might be other sorts of order in other cases:

". . . if domestic law justifies an outright order for possession, the effect of article 8 may, albeit in exceptional cases, justify (in ascending order of effect) granting an extended period for possession, suspending the order for possession on the happening of an event, or even refusing an order altogether."

Perhaps use of the phrase "exceptional cases" in relation to "refusing an order altogether" may be a slip because it would seem to be inconsistent with what Lord Neuberger said in paras 51 and 52 of his judgment (see above).

Lord Neuberger recognised that the court's conclusion may be inconsistent with s.89 of the Housing Act 1980 and some other court rules. Paragraph 63:

". . . the conclusion that the court must have the ability to assess the article 8 proportionality of making a possession order in respect of a person's home may require certain statutory and procedural provisions to be revisited. For example, section 89 of the 1980

Act limits the period for which a possession order can be postponed to 14 days, or, in cases of "exceptional hardship", 42 days. And some of the provisions of CPR 55, which appear to mandate a summary procedure in some types of possession claim, may present difficulties in relation to cases where article 8 claims are raised. Again, we say no more on the point, since these aspects were not canvassed on the present appeal to any significant extent, save in relation to the legislation on demoted tenancies which we are about to discuss under the third issue."

In *London Borough of Hounslow v Powell* [2011] UKSC 8 the Supreme Court gave further consideration to s.89. It was held that whilst the wording of the statute was so clear that it could not be interpreted more liberally to allow for greater periods, it was possible to utilise case management powers to delay the date for possession. However, this was limited to cases involving an appeal or where further information was needed. Lord Hope went on to state clearly at para.63:

"what the court cannot do, if it decides to proceed to make the order, is play for more time by suspending or staying its effect so as to extend the time limit beyond the statutory maximum".

See also Lord Phillips at para.103:

"In any situation where the judge dealing with an application for a possession order has power to refuse to make the order on the ground that it would infringe article 8, no question of incompatibility can arise in relation to section 89. That section merely increases the options open to the judge. He can (i) make an immediate order for possession; (ii) make an order the operation of which is postponed up to the limit permitted by section 89; (iii) refuse to make the order on the ground that it would infringe article 8. The clear limit on the judge's discretion to postpone the operation of the order may thus, in rare cases, have the consequence that the order is refused, whereas it would otherwise have been granted, subject to postponement of its operation for a greater period than section 89 permits. This is not a consequence that Parliament can have envisaged."

Thus, the court may refuse possession altogether if it comes to the conclusion that to make the order would be disproportionate. Further, if the court is of the view that proportionality requires a greater period than six weeks is needed before possession is to be given up, because s.89 will not permit such an order, the court may in rare cases also find itself making no order for possession at all.

Status after refusal to order possession

23.018 What will be the status of the occupier if, in a case where the landlord has an absolute right to possession as a matter of domestic law, the court refuses to order possession because it is not proportionate? This it seems will depend upon the previous status of the tenant. For example, if the tenant had a "Starter tenancy" i.e. an Assured Shorthold Tenancy the refusal to order possession will mean that he or she simply remains as an assured shorthold tenant. This is because the tenancy will not come to an end until executed (*Knowsley v White* [2008] UKHL 70; Sch.11 of the Housing and Regeneration Act 2008). The same would be true, e.g., in any Ground 8 case where the court considers that it it not proportionate to order possession.

But what about a licensee whose licence has been brought to an end? What is that person's status? Is any licence fee payable? Are there any other obligations?

Perhaps we have the making of a new breed of "tolerated trespasser", tolerated by the court if not the landlord!

Summary

- Where a public body brings a possession claim and the defendant chal- **23.019** lenges the claim on the basis of art.8 of the European Convention on Human Rights the question is always whether or not the eviction is a proportionate means of achieving a legitimate aim.
- This decision applies to local authorities, and to registered providers of social housing which are considered to be public bodies. It does not apply to private land owners, who were not considered in the case.
- Where it is necessary to establish that it is reasonable to make an order for possession, e.g. in the case of a secure tenancy, a finding that the order is reasonable will inevitably mean that the order is proportionate.
- It will usually be personal factors relating to the tenant, rather than specific factors relating to the landlord, which will be relevant in determining proportionality.
- Proportionality is most likely to be relevant where the tenant is a vulnerable person in some way.
- The court need normally only consider proportionality if it is raised by the defendant. If the defendant does so the court should do so at an early stage and should initially consider the matter on a summary basis. The threshold for establishing an arguable that the landlord is acting disproportionately is a high one and will be met in only a small proportion of cases.
- It is the court hearing the claim for possession which determines proportionality and any facts that are relevant to that issue.
- If it is not proportionate at the time of the hearing to make the order for possession no order will be made. In some rare cases postponed or suspended possession orders might be appropriate.

Conclusion

For practical purposes, perhaps the most important section in the whole judgment **23.020** of Lord Neuberger in *Pinnock* is at para.54 where he states:

> ". . . in virtually every case where a residential occupier has no contractual or statutory protection, and the local authority is entitled to possession as a matter of domestic law, there will be a very strong case for saying that making an order for possession would be proportionate. However, in some cases there may be factors which would tell the other way."

Chapter 24

Discrimination

The Equality Act 2010 ("the 2010 Act") brought the various strands of discrimina- **24.001** tion law under one Act. The Act deals with discrimination on the grounds of age, disability, gender reassignment, marriage and civil partnership, pregnancy and maternity, race, religion or belief, sex and sexual orientation (referred to as protected characteristics). Part 4 of the Act specifically deals with premises and does not apply to the protected characteristics of age or marriage and civil partnership (s.32). This chapter considers the circumstances in which allegations of discrimination may have an effect on claims for possession.

Key provisions

Section 13 defines discrimination in the following terms **24.002**

"13 (1) A person (A) discriminates against another (B) if, because of a protected characteristic, A treats B less favourably than A treats or would treat others.

(2) If the protected characteristic is age, A does not discriminate against B if A can show A's treatment of B to be a proportionate means of achieving a legitimate aim."

Further, s.35 of Pt 4 provides that

"35 (1) A person (A) who manages premises must not discriminate against a person (B) who occupies the premises . . . (b) by evicting B (or taking steps for the purpose of securing B's eviction). . .

(3) A person (A) who manages premises must not victimise a person (B) who occupies the premises . . . (b) by evicting B (or taking steps for the purpose of securing B's eviction)".

Evicting or taking steps for the purpose of securing eviction will cover possession proceedings.

As noted above in the introduction, s.35 containing the provisions prohibiting discrimination in relation to premises and eviction does not apply to discrimination on the grounds of age, marriage and civil partnership.

Disability

24.003 The most common issue in relation to discrimination in possession claims is disability where it can arise in relation to rent arrears, anti-social behaviour and sub letting. The impact on possession proceedings of the Disability Discrimination Act 1995 (the predecessor in part to the 2010 Act) had been significantly lessened by the House of Lords in *Lewisham v Malcolm* [2008] UKHL 43. They determined that a landlord had not been discriminatory in evicting a tenant who had sublet the property. The tenant had argued that he had only sublet because of his disability. The House of Lords did not consider that this was discriminatory as the landlord would have claimed possession from a tenant, without his disability, who sublet. This was widely seen as undermining the purpose of the 1995 Act and Parliament responded by changing the law on disability discrimination in the Equality Act 2010. In particular, the definition of discrimination for disability has been widened, uncoupled from the need for a comparator and for the first time, there can be indirect discrimination in disability cases.

A person has a disability if they have a physical or mental impairment, and the impairment has a substantial and long-term adverse effect on their ability to carry out normal day-to-day activities (s.6).

For disability, in addition to s.13 above, the definition of discrimination includes the situation where:

"15 (1) A person (A) discriminates against a disabled person (B) if—

(a) A treats B unfavourably because of something arising in consequence of B's disability and

(b) A cannot show that the treatment is a proportionate means of achieving a legitimate aim.

(2) Subsection (1) does not apply if A shows that A did not know, and could not have reasonably have been expected to know, that B had the disability."

As well as direct discrimination under s.13 or s.15, the Act also prohibits indirect discrimination (s.19). For the first time this concept has been introduced into the field of disability discrimination and may have an effect in residential possession cases.

Section 19 states

"19 (1) A person (A) discriminates against another (B) if A applies to B a provision, criterion or practice which is discriminatory in relation to a relevant protected characteristic of B's.

(2) For the purposes of subsection (1), a provision, criterion or practice is discriminatory in relation to a relevant protected characteristic of B's if

(a) A applies, or would apply, it to persons with whom B does not share the characteristic,

(b) it puts, or would put, persons with whom B shares the characteristic at a particular disadvantage when compared with persons with whom B does not share it,

(c) it puts, or would put, B at that disadvantage, and

(d) A cannot show it to be a proportionate means of achieving a legitimate aim."

The significant change in the new legislation is the use of the word "unfavourably" in s.15 rather than "less favourable" in s.13 and the old s.24(1) of the 1995 Act. Section 13 and the old 1995 Act test require the tenant to establish that they had been less favourably treated than someone else without their disability; the comparator. In *Malcolm*, the defence to the possession claim failed because it was held that a person without the disability would also have been evicted if they had sublet. Section 15 does away with the need for a comparator because the test it not whether there has been less favourable treatment when compared to another, but whether the tenant has been treated unfavourably because of something arising as a consequence of their disability. It therefore will not matter if another tenant without the disability would also have been treated in the same way. Therefore, on the facts in *Malcolm*, if his disability had caused him to sublet, there might have been discrimination.

This is not to say that s.13 cannot be relied upon as well, however, *Malcolm* is still likely to apply to that section and therefore cause difficulties in establishing a defence.

Knowledge

For direct discrimination under s.15, a landlord can only be liable if he knows of **24.004** the disability. Whilst a landlord may not know of the disability before proceedings are started, they may have sufficient knowledge if it continues to pursue possession proceedings once the defence has been raised.

Legitimate Aim

Even if there has been discrimination, it is still possible to justify it under s.15 if **24.005** the landlord can show its actions were a proportionate means of achieving a legitimate aim. See *Manchester City Council v Romano* [2004] EWCA Civ 834, under the 1995 Act but likely to be relevant to the 2010 Act and see para.28.029. A policy of not allowing sub letting in order to keep control on the persons occupying premises or wishing to keep rent arrears to a minimum are likely to be legitimate aims. In those cases, it is likely to be a question of proportionality as to whether a landlord would be able to obtain possession.

Small Premises

There is an exemption from the Act (save for Race Discrimination) for small **24.006** premises where accommodation is shared with the landlord (s.38(9) and Sch.5).

Mandatory grounds

Where the ground for possession is a mandatory one, or where the landlord has a **24.007** common law right to possession untrammelled by statutory protection, it will not be possible to obtain an order for possession against a disabled person if obtaining an order would be discriminatory within the meaning of the 2010 Act, unless it is possible to justify possession either under s.15 or s.19. This is the continuing effect of *Malcolm*, where it was said:

"The courts cannot be required to give legal effect to acts proscribed as unlawful" (Lord Bingham, para.19).

"If the service of the notice to quit in the present case was unlawful under s22(3)(c) [now s.35(1)(B)], then the court could not give effect to it. If by seeking an order for possession, a landlord is acting in a way the legislature has held to be unlawful, then, again, the court cannot make such an order" (Lord Neuberger, para.160).

Discretionary grounds

24.008 As in mandatory cases, where a landlord treats a tenant less favourably or unfavourably because of his disability it will be unlawful and no order for possession will be made unless the landlord can bring themselves within one of the exceptions dealt with above (cf. *Manchester City Council v Romano* [2004] EWCA Civ 834 under the 1995 Act).

However, even where there is no discrimination the tenant's disability can be important to the question of whether or not it is reasonable to make an order for possession and whether or not such an order should be suspended or postponed. This has been particularly relevant in anti-social behaviour cases where the tenant's disability has led him or her to commit or tolerate acts of nuisance (see further para.29.018).

Chapter 25

Standard Procedure

Part 55 of the Civil Procedure Rules and the Practice Direction made under that **25.001** Part largely govern claims for possession. This chapter deals with the "standard possession claim" (the authors' term) where the defendant is or was a tenant or licensee. "Possession Claims Online", the online method for claiming possession in rent and mortgage cases, is also dealt with in this chapter.

The accelerated procedure, which may be used in some assured shorthold cases is dealt with in Ch.26. Part 55 also applies to claims against trespassers and where the claim is brought by a mortgagee but subject to certain variations. Trespassers and mortgage claims are dealt with in Chs 31 and 32 respectively.

Introduction

Part 55 must be used where the claim includes a "possession claim" brought by a: **25.002**

- landlord (or former landlord); or
- licensor (or former licensor).

A "possession claim" means a claim for recovery of possession of land (including buildings or parts of buildings) (CPR r.55.1(a)). When the court issues the claim form it will fix a date for the hearing (see further below).

Parties

Claimant

In most claims the position will be straightforward. The claimant will be the **25.003** owner of the property and the landlord or licensor of the defendant. However, the claimant is not necessarily the absolute owner of the property. He need only show that he has a better right to possession than the defendant. Whenever the claimant has let the defendant into possession as a tenant or licensee the tenant/licensee is estopped from denying the claimant's title (see para.1.008). He is also estopped from denying his title where the claimant is an assignee of the original landlord (see *Cuthbertson v Irving* (1859) 4 H. & N. 742).

Where a person has a licence to enter premises for certain purposes (e.g. to carry out building works) he may have sufficient interest to permit him to bring a possession claim against trespassers. Whether or not he has such a right will depend upon the agreement between the owner and the licensee (*Dutton v Manchester Airport* [2000] 1 Q.B. 133; *Countryside Residential (North Thames) Ltd v A Child* (2001) 81 P. & C.R. 10; *Alamo Housing Co-operative Ltd v Meredith* [2003] EWCA Civ 495); see further para.31.004.

Somewhat surprisingly, the Court of Appeal in *Dearman v Simpletest* [1999] All E.R. (D) 1365 even upheld a possession order where the claimant held only one half of the equitable interest in the property at the date of the hearing. However, it should be noted that the legal owners were in court, one of them gave evidence on behalf of the claimant and they agreed to be bound by the order of the court. The defendants also had no defence on the merits and were merely taking the technical point.

Joint owners

25.004 Where there are two or more persons who are jointly entitled to possession as against the defendant(s), e.g. two joint landlords, they should generally both be joined as claimants (CPR r.19.2):

> "**19.2** (1) Where a claimant claims a remedy to which some other person is jointly entitled with him, all persons jointly entitled to the remedy must be parties unless the court orders otherwise.
>
> (2) If any person does not agree to be a claimant, he must be made a defendant, unless the court otherwise orders."

However, following the principal stated above (estoppel), where only one or some of the owners of the property are actually in the position of the landlord only that (those) person(s) need bring the claim.

Example If a husband and wife own a property that was let to tenants but only in the name of the husband, only he needs to be named as the claimant.

The position of particular landlords is now considered before turning to the question of who should be made a defendant to the action.

Companies, partners and sole traders

25.005 A limited liability company may commence proceedings and be represented at trial by any duly authorised employee if the court gives permission (CPR r.39.6 and PD 39A para.5). Partners may sue in the name of their firm but the defendant may compel the claimant to disclose the names of the partners (CCR Ord.5 r.9; RSC Ord.81). Sole traders may only sue in their own name and not in their trading name.

Executors and administrators

25.006 If the landlord dies leaving a will the property vests in his executors from the date of his death. The executors may therefore commence proceedings for possession prior to the grant of probate. Their title, however, is proved by the grant and so if their title is in dispute the executors will not be able to proceed with the possession claim until the grant of probate. The position of an administrator, however, is rather different. He derives title entirely from the grant of letters of administration and the deceased's estate does not vest in him until that time. An administrator may thus only commence and continue proceedings for possession once he has obtained the grant. As to the right of the personal representative to costs out of estate where they are not fully recovered from the defendant, see CPR r.48.4.

LPA receivers

A receiver appointed under the powers conferred by the Law of Property Act 1925 **25.007** is deemed to be the agent of the mortgagor (s.109(2)). A receiver wishing to obtain possession should therefore do so in the name of the mortgagor. However, in some cases it may be more advantageous for the mortgagor to take mortgage possession proceedings, for example where the tenancy was created after the mortgage and is not binding on the mortgagee (see para.32.074), unless the mortgagee does not wish to be a mortgagee in possession with all the responsibilities that that entails.

Change of landlord by reason of assignment, bankruptcy or death

Where the landlord assigns or dies during the court of the proceedings, the claim **25.008** does not come to an end. The assignee or personal representative may apply without notice for an order to carry on the proceedings (CPR rr.19.2 and 19.4).

In the case of assignment where the land is registered the assignment takes effect (so it was held under the Land Registration Act 1925) on the date that the transfer is signed, not the date of registration (*Brown & Root Technology v Sun Alliance and London Assurance Co* [1995] 3 W.L.R. 558). An application for an order to carry on can therefore be made at any time after the transfer.

If the landlord dies and there are no personal representatives, the court may proceed in his absence or appoint someone to represent the estate (CPR r.19.8). If one of two or more claimants who are suing jointly in respect of a joint cause of action dies the other(s) continue the claim without appointing a personal representative. Service of a statement of case in the name of the deceased after he has in fact died is an irregularity but it does not render the proceedings a nullity. The irregularity can be rectified by an amendment (*Fielding v Rigby* [1993] 4 All E.R. 294).

As to bankruptcy see s.49 of the County Courts Act 1984.

Defendant

The defendant will be the person in possession against whom the landlord has an **25.009** immediate right to possession, i.e. the claimant's immediate tenant or licensee whose contractual tenancy or licence has been determined. The phrase "in possession" includes persons who are in receipt of rents. A tenant who has sub-let the whole of the premises should therefore be made a defendant even though he may not be in actual occupation. If any person in possession has not been joined as a defendant he may apply, without notice, to be joined in the proceedings. The application may be made at any stage, even after judgment and execution of the order for possession and should be made pursuant to CPR r.19.4(2). The order for possession operates against any person on the land (*R. v Wandsworth County Court Ex p. Wandsworth London Borough Council* [1975] 1 W.L.R. 1314) so it is not strictly necessary to join any of the tenant's licensees or sub-tenants (but for forfeiture cases see para.25.016). However, it is suggested that if the names of any such persons are known or can be ascertained, it is usually advisable to join them so as to avoid any possible application by such persons for the order for possession to be set aside. Alternatively, the landlord might serve a copy of the claim on persons in occupation together with a letter informing them of their right to be joined in the proceedings. For safe measure, a further copy can be put through the letter box or affixed to the front door in an envelope addressed to "the occupiers".

For service on sub-tenants and mortgagees in a forfeiture claim see para.25.053.

25.010   A foreign state is not immune from proceedings for possession of a dwelling house in respect of which it has a tenancy unless the premises are used for the purposes of a diplomatic mission (ss.6(1)(a) and 16(1)(b) of the State Immunity Act 1978; *Intpro Properties (UK) Ltd v Sauvel* [1983] Q.B. 1019).

The making of a bankruptcy order or a debt relief order against a tenant does not prevent the making of an order for possession of a dwelling let on an assured tenancy on the ground of rent arrears (see para.28.010A).

The court

County court

25.011 All claims for possession must be:

- in the county court;
- for the district in which the land is situated (CPR r.55.3(1)).

If the claimant starts in the wrong county court the proceedings will not be a nullity and the judge will order that the claim:

- be transferred to the county court in which it ought to have been started; or
- continue in the county court in which it has been started; or
- be struck out (CPR r.30.2(3)).

An application for such an order will have to be made in the county court where the claim is proceeding (CPR r.30.2(3)).

A court officer has no power to refuse to issue a claim on the basis that the claimant is seeking to start in the wrong court. He should issue the claim and leave it to the judge to determine whether or not an order should be made under CPR r.30.2 (*Gwynedd County Council v Grunshaw* [1999] 4 All E.R. 304 CA—a case decided under the old rules but which would seemingly also apply under the CPR).

High Court

25.012 It will sometimes be possible to issue in the High Court but only in "exceptional circumstances" (CPR PD 55 para.1.1). Circumstances that may provide justification for starting in the High Court will be if there are:

- complicated disputes of fact; or
- points of law of general importance (CPR PD 55 para.1.3).

The value of the property and the amount of any financial claim may be relevant circumstances but "these factors alone will not normally justify starting the claim in the High Court" (CPR PD 1.4).

The PD also provides that the claim may be begun in the High Court if the county court does not have jurisdiction. However, s.21 of the County Courts Act 1984 states: "A county court shall have jurisdiction to hear and determine any action for the recovery of land".

If the claimant does start in the High Court he will have to file, with his claim form, a certificate stating the reasons for doing so. The certificate will need to be verified with a statement of truth under r.22.1(d) (CPR r.55.3(2)).

A claim wrongly started in the High Court will normally be struck out or transferred to the county court by the court on its own initiative. This is likely to result in delay and the court will normally disallow the costs of starting the claim in the High Court and of any transfer (CPR PD 55 para.1.2).

Quite apart from the restrictions, under CPR Pt 55 there are some statutory **25.013** limitations on bringing claims in the High Court:

- Where the owner is prevented from obtaining possession by virtue of s.3 of the Protection from Eviction Act 1977 (see para.22.003) the proceedings must be commenced in the county court (s.9(1)(a) of the 1977 Act) unless the claim is for forfeiture (s.9(3)).

- Claims for possession under the Local Government and Housing Act 1989 Sch.10 (long tenancies at low rents) may only be commenced in the county court (s.63(1) of the Landlord and Tenant Act 1954 para.20(3) of Sch.10 of the 1989 Act).

There are also statutory limitations on costs. In certain cases if proceedings for possession are taken in the High Court that could have been taken in the county court the landlord will not be entitled to his costs:

- The Housing Act 1988 (s.40).

- The Rent Act 1977, except where the landlord is relying on one of the mandatory grounds referred to in s.98(2) or s.101 in respect of an overcrowded dwelling-house (s.141).

- The Housing Act 1985 (s.110(3)).

- The Rent (Agriculture) Act 1976, except where the landlord is relying upon one of the mandatory grounds in Pt II of Sch.4 to the said Act (s.26).

The practical effect of all the above is that all claims for residential property should be started in the county court. In the extremely rare case that the High Court is the appropriate court an order for transfer can be made.

Starting the claim

Documents required

Two forms are required to issue the claim: **25.014**

1) A claim form—to be used in all possession claims (other than accelerated possession): Form N5 (Form 30 of this book, p.359).

2) Particulars of claim (see below)—which must be filed and served with the claim form (CPR r.55.4).

The various forms used in the proceedings can also be found at *http:// hmctsformfinder.justice.gov.uk/HMCTS/FormFinder.do.*

Claim form

25.015 The claim form (N5) is a simple document and, after completion and issue, will tell the court immediately whether or not the property is residential and the basic ground for the claim. It refers to the particulars of claim that need to be served with it and contains a statement of truth. It must be used in all possession claims, whatever the nature of the property (CPR r.55.3(5); PD 55A para.1.5)). However, the claim is not a nullity simply because the wrong form has been used (CPR r.3.10).

Names

"The claim form must be headed with the title of the proceedings, including the full name of each party. The full name means, in each case where it is known in the case of an individual, his full unabbreviated name and title by which he is known" (CPR PD 16 para.2.6)

Addresses

- The claim form must identify the land to which the claim relates (CPR PD 55A para.2.1).

- Addresses of claimants and defendants must include postcodes unless the court orders otherwise (CPR PD 16 para.2.4).

Particulars of claim

All cases

25.016 Wherever the particulars of claim for possession relate to "rented residential premises" Form N119 must be used (CPR PD 55 para.1.5, Pt 4, Table 1 (forms)). That form can be used in cases where the claim is based upon non-payment of rent and/or other grounds. (See Form 31, p.361 of this book.) (For trespassers and mortgagees see Chs 30 and 31 respectively.)

CPR PD 55A para.2.1 provides that the particulars of claim in possession claims must:

- Identify the land to which the claim relates.

- State whether the claim relates to residential property.

Form 30: Claim form for possession of property

In the	
Claim No.	

Claimant
(name(s) and address(es))

SEAL

Defendant(s)
(name(s) and address(es))

The claimant is claiming possession of

which (includes) (docs not include) residential property. Full particulars of the claim are attached.
(The claimant is also making a claim for money).

This claim will be heard on   20   at   am/pm

at

At the hearing
• The court will consider whether or not you must leave the property and, if so, when.
• It will take into account information the claimant provides and any you provide.

What you should do
• Get help and advice immediately from a solicitor or an advice agency.
• Help yourself and the court by **filling in the defence form and coming to the hearing** to make sure the court knows all the facts

Defendant's
name and
address for
service

Court fee	£
Solicitor's costs	£
Total amount	£

Issue date	

N5 Claim Form for possession of property (06.04)

Claim No.	

Grounds for possession

The claim for possession is made on the following ground(s):

☐ rent arrears

☐ other breach of tenancy

☐ forfeiture of the lease

☐ mortgage arrears

☐ other breach of the mortgage

☐ trespass

☐ Other *(please specify)* ....

Anti-social behaviour

The claimant is alleging:

☐ actual or threatened anti-social behaviour

☐ actual or threatened use of the property for unlawful purposes

Is the claimant claiming demotion of tenancy   ☐ Yes ☐ No

See full details in the attached particulars of claim

Does, or will, the claim include any issues under the Human Rights Act 1998?   ☐ Yes ☐ No

Statement of Truth
*(I believe)(The claimant believes) that the facts stated in this claim form are true.
*I am duly authorised by the claimant to sign this statement.

signed _____ date _____
(Claimant)(Litigation friend)*(where the claimant is a child or a patient)*(Claimant's solicitor)
delete as appropriate

Full name _____

Name of claimant's solicitor's firm _____

position or office held _____
    (if signing on behalf of firm or company)

Claimant's or claimant's solicitor's address to which documents or payments should be sent if different from overleaf

if applicable

Ref. no.	
fax no.	
DX no.	
e-mail	
Tel. no.	

Postcode

Form 31: Particulars of claim for possession

Particulars of claim
for possession
(rented residential premises)

Name of court	Claim No.
Name of Claimant	
Name of Defendant	

1. The claimant has a right to possession of:

2. To the best of the claimant's knowledge the following persons are in possession of the property:

About the tenancy

3. (a) The premises are let to the defendant(s) under a(n)   tenancy
    which began on   .

    (b) The current rent is £   and is payable each (week) (fortnight) (month).
    (*other*   )

    (c) Any unpaid rent or charge for use and occupation should be calculated at £   per day.

4. The reason the claimant is asking for possession is:
    (a) because the defendant has not paid the rent due under the terms of the tenancy agreement.
    (Details are set out below)(Details are shown on the attached rent statement)

    (b) because the defendant has failed to comply with other terms of the tenancy.
    Details are set out below.

    (c) because: (including any (other) statutory grounds)

N119 Particulars of claim for possession (rented residential premises) (08.05)   HMCS

5.   The following steps have already been taken to recover any arrears:

6.   The appropriate (notice to quit) (notice of breach of lease) (notice seeking possession) (notice seeking a demotion order) (*other* _____) was served on the defendant on   20   .

About the defendant

7.   The following information is known about the defendant's circumstances:

About the claimant

8.   The claimant is asking the court to take the following financial or other information into account when making its decision whether or not to grant an order for possession:

Forfeiture

9.   (a) There is no underlessee or mortgagee entitled to claim relief against forfeiture.

or   (b)   of

is entitled to claim relief against forfeiture as underlessee or mortgagee.

What the court is being asked to do:

10. The claimant asks the court to order that the defendant(s):

    (a) give the claimant possession of the premises;

    (b) pay the unpaid rent and any charge for use and occupation up to the date an order is made;

    (c) pay rent and any charge for use and occupation from the date of the order until the claimant recovers possession of the property;

    (d) pay the claimant's costs of making this claim.

11. In the alternative to possession, is the claimant asking the court to make a demotion order or an order suspending the right to buy?

    ☐ Yes   ☐ No

Demotion/Suspension claim
This section must be completed if the claim includes a claim for demotion of tenancy or suspension order in the alternative to possession

12. The (demotion) (suspension) claim is made under:

    ☐ section 82A(2) of the Housing Act 1985

    ☐ section 6A(2) of the Housing Act 1988

    ☐ section 121A of the Housing Act 1985

13. The claimant is a:

    ☐ local authority   ☐ housing action trust

    ☐ registered social landlord   ☐ other please specify (suspension claims only)

    [   ]

(Demotion claims only)
14. Has the claimant served on the tenant a statement of express terms of the tenancy which are to apply to the demoted tenancy?

    ☐ Yes   ☐ No

    If Yes, please give details:

15. The claimant is claiming delete as appropriate (demotion of tenancy) (and) (an order suspending the right to buy) because: *State details of the conduct alleged and **any** other matters relied upon.*

Statement of Truth

*(I believe)(The claimant believes) that the facts stated in these particulars of claim are true.
* I am duly authorised by the claimant to sign this statement.

signed _____ date _____

(Claimant)(Litigation friend(where claimant is a child or a patient)*)(Claimant's solicitor)
delete as appropriate

Full name _____

Name of claimant's solicitor's firm _____

position or office held _____
                     (if signing on behalf of firm or company)

- Give full details about any tenancy agreement (see note below).

- State the ground on which possession is claimed.

- Give details of every person who, to the best of the claimant's knowledge, is "in possession" of the property (see note below).

- Give the name of any person known to be entitled to apply for relief from forfeiture—a copy of the particulars of claim must be filed for service upon the named persons (CPR PD 55 para.2.4).

- Give details of interest claimed (CPR r.16.4).

Notes/suggestions

When giving details of the tenancy the claimant should state the nature of the **25.017** tenancy, e.g. that it is an assured tenancy. If no statutory protection applies, the reason should be stated.

Example

If the tenancy was created on or after April 1, 1990, but the rent is higher than £100,000 per year the particulars of claim should include a paragraph along the following lines:

> "The Housing Act 1988 applies but by virtue of the fact that the rent is higher than £100,000 per annum the tenancy is not an assured tenancy (1988 Act, Schedule 1, para.2(1))".

The term "possession" usually has a technical meaning, referring only to the tenant. However, it is probably wise to give details of all persons who, to the knowledge of the claimant, are in "occupation" including minors. The person "in possession" will be the defendant. See also para.25.009.

A person with a charging order is entitled to claim relief "indirectly" (*Bland v Ingram's Estates Ltd* [2001] 24 E.G. 163 (see para.2.104). His name and address if known should therefore also be given and he should be served.

CPR PD 16 states that particulars of claim should contain a concise statement of the facts upon which the claimant intends to rely (16.2). However, as will be seen below CPR PD 55A also permits and encourages claimants to put all their intended evidence into the particulars of claim. It is necessary to achieve a sensible balance. In simple claims it will normally be appropriate to include all the relevant information in the particulars of claim.

Residential rent cases

Where the claim "relates to residential property let on a tenancy" and the claim **25.018** includes a claim for non-payment of rent it is also necessary (CPR PD 55A para.2.3) to set out:

- The amount due at the start of the proceedings.

- In schedule form, the dates and amounts of all payments due and payments made under the tenancy agreement for a period of two years immediately preceding the date of issue, or if the first date of default occurred less than two years before the date of issue from the first date of default and a running total of the arrears; if the claimant wishes to rely on a history of arrears which is longer than two years, he should state this in his particulars and exhibit a full (or longer) schedule to a witness statement.

- The daily rate of any rent and interest.

- Any previous steps taken to recover the arrears of rent with full details of any court proceedings.

- Any relevant information about the defendant's circumstances, in particular:

  — whether the defendant is in receipt of social security benefits; and
  — whether any payments are made on his behalf directly to the claimant under the Social Security Contributions and Benefits Act 1992.

Notes

25.019
- Form N119 allows for rent details in a simple case to be inserted on the form (para.4)—i.e. otherwise than by way of schedule. Practitioners should make sure that a proper schedule is attached to the Form N119. It should be brought fully up to date at the hearing (see para.25.031).

- Form N119 does not include a paragraph relating to interest. If the claimant wishes to recover interest the necessary details will need to be written in or inserted on a separate sheet.

Documents to attach

25.020 The Practice Direction relating to statements of case states that where a claim is based upon a written agreement

"a copy of the contract . . . should be attached to or served with the particulars of claim and the original should be available at the hearing" (CPR PD 16 para.7.3(1)).

It also states that a party may

"attach to or serve with this statement of case a copy of any document which he considers to be necessary to his claim or defence" (CPR PD 16 para.13.3)).

It should also be noted that CPR PD 55 permits and encourages all the evidence in the case to be in the particulars of claim (see below).

The authors suggest that the practice of attaching documents to particulars of claim should be adopted in possession claims. However, the documentation should be kept to a minimum. If the tenancy agreement is more than, say, three or four pages only the relevant parts should be attached. Perhaps, the front page showing the term and the rent, etc. any page containing a relevant clause and the final page showing the signatures. The notice seeking possession or other similar notice should also be attached, as should any other key document. Careful annexation of the relevant documents should obviate the need for further oral evidence at the hearing in very many cases.

Statement of truth

The particulars of claim (as well as the claim form) must be verified by a statement of truth (CPR rr.22.1(a) and 2.3(1)—"definition of statement of case"). If the statement is in a separate document it must clearly identify the document that it is verifying (CPR r.22.1(7)). The format of the statement should be as described in CPR PD22 para.2.3. Form N119 has a statement of truth section set out on it.

If the claimant fails to verify his statement of case by a statement of truth he may not rely upon it as evidence of any of the matters set out in it; and the court may even strike out the statement of case (CPR r.22.2).

Possession claims online

It is possible to make a claim for possession, based on arrears of rent or mortgage **25.021** arrears, online (*www.possessionclaim.gov.uk/pcol*). The procedure is generally known as "PCOL" and has become standard for claims based on arrears.

In order to use PCOL the property needs to be in England or Wales and the claimant needs to be able to provide the postcode for the property (which they should do anyway). The system uses the postcode to issue in the correct court. There are a number of advantages to using the online service rather than using the traditional method of claiming possession:

- It operates 24 hours per day, seven days per week.
- It is easy to use.
- It avoids filing a paper claim.
- Court fees are paid electronically either by credit or debit card or by direct debit.
- The issue fee is lower.
- The claim is issued immediately and a court hearing date is allocated— usually to take place in about five weeks.
- It is possible to track the claim online.
- Applications can be made online.
- Warrants for possession—and applications to suspend—can be made online.

The procedure is governed by Practice Direction 55B—which can be found at para.25.056. The following points are particularly worth noting:

- PCOL may only be used where the claim is for possession of a residential property based on arrears of rent (not including forfeiture claims) or where it is brought by a mortgagee based on mortgage arrears. No other remedy may be sought.

- PCOL may not be used if a defendant is known to be a child or protected person.

- It is not necessary to file a copy of the tenancy agreement or mortgage deed with the particulars of claim (but of course should be filed and served later).

- Where a full rent statement has been sent to the defendant prior to issue it is possible to insert only a summary in the particulars of claim. (For precise details see CPR PD 55B paras 6.3 to 6.3C—see also para.6.4).

- A defence form or counterclaim can be completed online.

- Statements of truth are signed "by that person entering his name on an online form".

The hearing date

General rule

25.022 As stated above the court will give the claimant a hearing date when the claim is issued. In most cases:

- The hearing date will be not less than 28 days from the date of issue of the claim form—although it may be possible to have this period varied under r.3.l(2)(a)(b) (see below—urgent cases).

- The standard period between the issue of the claim form and the hearing will be not more than eight weeks (CPR r.55.5 (3)).

Urgent cases

25.023 The Practice Direction (CPR PD 55A para.3.2) states that particular consideration should be given to the exercise of the power to shorten time periods if:

- The defendant, or a person for whom the defendant is responsible, has assaulted or threatened to assault:
  — the claimant;
  — a member of the claimant's staff; or
  — another resident in the locality.

- There are reasonable grounds for fearing such an assault; or

- The defendant or a person, for whom the defendant is responsible, has caused serious damage or threatened to cause serious damage to the property or to the home or property of another resident in the locality.

The claim form has a section relating to "anti-social behaviour" in which the claimant can indicate that he is relying upon "actual or threatened anti-social behaviour" or "actual or threatened use of the property for unlawful purposes". If the claimant does wish to rely upon such behaviour and wishes the court to deal with the claim quickly the authors suggest that a CPR Pt 23 application setting out any necessary additional material not shown on the particulars of claim be filed and served with the claim form.

Service

The defendant must be served with the claim form and the particulars of claim not **25.024** less than 21 days before the hearing date (CPR r.55.5(3)). However, the court may extend or shorten the time for compliance under CPR r.3.1(2)(a)(b)). An application to abridge time should be made formally with reasons using Form N244 under Pt 23.

The normal rules of service in Pt 6 will generally apply to standard claims. In *Akram v Adam* [2004] EWCA Civ 1601 a possession claim was served by first-class post to the tenant at his regular address in accordance with CPR r.6.5(6)— service where defendant has no solicitor (now CPR r.6.9). The claim did not come to the tenant's attention and the landlord obtained judgment without the tenant's knowledge. When the tenant found out about the order he applied to set it aside. The district judge found that it was well known that the tenant had been having difficulties with his post, that at the time of service the tenant was at his sister's address and that the landlord knew of his absence. It was held nonetheless that the service was in accordance with the rules and was good. The tenant could only have the order for possession set aside as a matter of discretion under CPR r.13.3. As on the facts he had no real prospect of defending the claim—the landlord had offered suitable alternative accommodation—the order would not be set aside. These rules do not breach art.6 of the ECHR. The situation might have been different if it had been found that the claimant deliberately suppressed the claim form when it arrived by post in his house. Since that case there have been amendments to CPR part 6, in particular, while service at the usual or last known address is still good service, CPR 6.9 (3) provides that where the Claimant has reason to believe that the address is an address where the Defendant no longer resides, the Claimant must take steps to ascertain the address of the Defendant's current residence. Where the claimant serves the claim form and particulars of claim, he must produce a certificate of service of those documents at the hearing and r.6.17(2)(a), which provides for filing of a certificate within 21 days, does not apply: (CPR r.55.8(6)).

For applications to set aside orders for possession in cases of non service see para.34.010.

Action by the defendant

Defence and evidence

There is no requirement on the defendant to file an acknowledgement of service. **25.025** However, he must file a defence. If he fails to do so within 14 days of service of the particulars of claim he may take part in the hearing but his failure to do so may be taken into account when deciding what order to make about costs (CPR r.55.7(3)). It is not possible for the claimant to obtain judgment in default (CPR r.55.7(4)).

The defence filed must be in the form set out in the relevant practice direction (CPR r.55.3(5)), i.e. revised Form N11R. This has a statement of truth on it. The provisions, which allow and encourage all parties to rely upon written evidence verified by a statement of truth, in particular in the statements of case (para.25.020), apply to defendants as much as to claimants. Completion of Form N11R is therefore an important matter.

If the defendant wishes to put in written evidence in addition to matters set out in his defence (N11R) he must serve the witness statements at least two days prior to the hearing.

None of the above prevents the defendant from giving oral evidence at the hearing.

Rent claims

25.026   In rent claims the defendant should (if relevant) give evidence of the amount of any outstanding or housing benefit payments relevant to the rent arrears and the status of:

- Any claims for social security or housing benefit about which a decision has not yet been made.

- Any applications to appeal or review a social security or housing benefit decision where that appeal or review has not yet concluded (CPR PD 55A para.5.3).

The hearing

The judge

25.027   In the county court, the claim may be heard by a judge or a district judge even if allocated to the multi-track (CPR r.2.4; PD 2B para.11.1(b)); but will usually be heard by a district judge in a long possession list with five to 10 minutes set aside for each case.

Open court?

25.028   CPR r.39.2(3)(c) provides that a hearing may be in private if "it involves confidential information (including relating to personal financial matters) and publicity would damage that confidentiality". The Practice Direction relating to this rule states that:

> "A claim by a landlord against one or more tenants or former tenants for the repossession of a dwelling house based on the nonpayment of rent . . . shall in the first instance be listed by the court . . . in private under rule 39.2(3)(c)" (CPR PD 39 para.1.5(2)).

Urgent cases

25.029   Where the claim is an appropriate one for shortening the time between issue and the hearing of the claim but the case cannot be determined at the first hearing "the court will consider what steps are needed to finally determine the case as quickly as reasonably practicable" (CPR PD 55A para.3.3).

Case management

At the initial hearing, or at any adjournment of that hearing, the court may decide **25.030**
the claim or give case management directions (CPR r.55.8(1)). Where the claim is
"genuinely disputed on grounds which appear to be substantial" case management
directions will include the allocation of the claim to a track or directions to enable
it to be allocated (CPR r.55.8(1)(2))—see further below. It should be noted that
the court may give case management directions in relation to a claim without
allocating to a specific track.

Example: A defendant may turn up at the first hearing claiming that there has
been a problem with housing benefit. The judge may consider it appropriate to
adjourn the claim to allow him to bring along relevant documents. To allocate the
case to a track would be pointless but the judge might make a direction listing the
documents that should be produced at the next hearing.

Evidence

If the case is allocated to the fast track or the multi-track or if the court so orders **25.031**
the normal rules about evidence in Pt 32 will apply (CPR r.55.8(1)). However, in
any other case it will be possible to prove the case by written evidence. Rule
55.8(3) expressly provides that any fact that needs to be proved by the evidence
of witnesses at a hearing (or adjourned hearing) may be proved by evidence in
writing. Indeed, evidence in written form is encouraged:

> "Each party should wherever possible include all the evidence he wishes to present in
> his statement of case, verified by a statement of truth" (CPR PD 55A para.5.1).

Where a party wishes to rely upon further written evidence, the witness statements must be filed and served at least two days before the hearing (CPR r.55.8(4)).
As to production of certificates of service where the claim was served by the
claimant see para.25.024.

Rent cases

In a rent case the details contained in the particulars of claim or any witness state- **25.032**
ment that has been served may be out of date by the date of the hearing, even if
served only two days beforehand. If so, the claimant may give evidence orally or
in writing on the day of the hearing if necessary (CPR PD 5.2). See also para.28.017.

Disputing written evidence

Although written evidence is encouraged, if material evidence is disputed and the **25.033**
witness is not at court the court will normally adjourn the hearing so that oral
evidence can be given (CPR PD 5.4).

Track allocation

Generally

As stated above, where the claim is "genuinely disputed on grounds which appear **25.034**
to be substantial" case management directions will include the allocation of the

claim to a track or directions to enable it to be allocated. The general criteria for allocation set out in CPR r.26.8 are not generally appropriate to possession claims. Rule 55.9 therefore provides that the matters to which regard should be had include the matters set out in r.26.8 as modified by the relevant practice direction, i.e.:

- The amount of the arrears in a rent case.

- The importance to the defendant of retaining possession.

- The importance of vacant possession to the claimant.

- If applicable the alleged conduct of the defendant.

In most instances the case will probably be allocated to the fast track. Under the CPR there are various strategies that can be used by the court to shorten cases—including limiting the evidence and cross-examination (CPR r.32.1)—and it should be possible to hear the bulk of defended claims within one day. Obviously, however, the track will be dependent on all the relevant factors and in some cases the multi-track will be appropriate. Where the claim is allocated to the multi-track the case management provisions relating to transfer to a civil trial centre do not apply (CPR PD 26 para.10.1).

Small claims track

25.035 It is only possible to allocate the case to the small claims track if the parties agree (CPR r.55.9(2)). In that case special provisions apply in relation to costs, allowing recovery under a modified form of the fast track rules unless all parties want the small claims costs rules to apply. The claim will be treated, for the purpose of costs, as if it were proceedings on the fast track except that the trial costs "shall be in the discretion of the court and shall not exceed the amount that would be recoverable under r.46.2 (amount of fast track costs) if the value of the claim were up to £3,000" currently £485. If the parties do agree otherwise the court may when it allocates the claim order that r.27.14 (costs on the small claims track) applies.

Summary judgment

25.036 It is possible for a claimant to apply for summary judgment in possession claims but not where the claim is in respect of residential premises

> "against a tenant or person holding over after the end of his tenancy, whose occupancy is protected within the meaning of the Rent Act 1977 or the Housing Act 1988" (CPR r.24.3(2)(a) as amended).

Although permitted in some cases, it is perhaps unlikely that the claimant will apply for summary judgment. This is because the court will only have allocated the case to a track where the claim is "genuinely disputed on grounds which appear to be substantial". However, as the case proceeds it may become apparent that the defendant has no real prospects of success. Defendants may also consider it appropriate to apply in some cases.

The order

Suspending the order

Where the claimant succeeds in obtaining an order for possession the court's **25.037** power to postpone or suspend the execution of that order depends upon the statutory provisions that apply. The position in respect of any particular type of tenancy is dealt with in the appropriate chapter (e.g. see para.6.029 in assured tenancy cases). See also para.28.032 in rent cases and para.34.008: "Suspension of warrant". If in any particular case there is no such statutory power the court may not make any order postponing the date for possession for more than 14 days, or six weeks in cases of exceptional hardship (s.89 of the Housing Act 1980; see para.3.034). The restrictions that limit the power of a court to suspend a possession order in mandatory cases contained in s.89 of the Housing Act 1980 do not apply to a court exercising appellate jurisdiction. A warrant can therefore be stayed by such a court pending an appeal. (*Admiral Taverns (Cygnet) Ltd v Daniel* [2008] EWHC 1688 (QB)).

Where the defendant entered into possession unlawfully the court has no power to postpone the order for possession without the consent of the claimant (*McPhail v Persons Unknown* [1973] Ch. 447; *Boyland and Son Ltd v Rand* [2006] EWCA Civ 1860).

The rules as they affect the county court (unlike the High Court) do not require **25.038** the landlord to serve the tenant with notice of his intention to enforce the order for possession or to obtain the permission of the court (see para.34.001). The tenant should therefore ask the court to make it a term of any suspended order for possession that the order should not be enforced without permission of the court after notice to the tenant of an application for permission (see further para.34.002).

On an application by a tenant for a stay or suspension the landlord may rely upon conduct that did not form part of his claim for possession in order to resist the stay or to form the basis of a condition of the stay or suspension. However, if he wishes to do so he must give notice in clear and specific terms of the conduct upon which he intends to rely (*Sheffield City Council v Hopkins* [2001] EWCA Civ 831—see further para.34.009).

"Consent" orders

Strictly speaking, a consent order cannot be made in a claim for possession of a **25.039** dwelling-house. The court may only make an order for possession without hearing evidence if the tenant admits that:

- no statutory protection applies; or
- the landlord is entitled to possession on a Rent Act, etc. ground; and where the ground is a discretionary one, that it is reasonable to make the order.

If the tenant does so concede, the judge is under no duty to investigate the facts of the case (see *R. v Bloomsbury and Marylebone County Court Ex p. Blackburne* (1984) 14 H.L.R. 56; *Syed Hussain v A M Abdullah Sahib and Co* [1985] 1 W.L.R. 392; *R. v Newcastle-upon-Tyne County Court Ex p. Thompson* [1988] 2 E.G.L.R. 119). An admission can be implied from the terms of the draft consent order. Whether there is such an admission depends on the terms of the order construed in the light of the surrounding circumstances including the issues in the case (*Bruce v Worthing BC* (1994) 26 H.L.R. 223; *Hounslow LBC v McBride* (1998) 31 H.L.R. 143 CA).

25.040   There are many cases where the landlord appreciates that he may have difficulty in obtaining possession and is prepared to compromise the action by paying the tenant a sum to leave. This is often the case where, for example, he is seeking to show that suitable alternative accommodation is available. The inability simply to present the court with an agreed order can be very inconvenient. In the first edition of this book it was suggested that the way to deal with the problem was for the parties to come to an agreement that the landlord will make the payment to the tenant if, and only if, the order for possession is made. Since then Lord Keith of Kinkel in *Syed Hussain* (a Privy Council case) has said:

> "Special considerations might arise if in subsequent proceedings the defendant established by evidence that his agreement was given in pursuance of a compromise which might have involved his being paid a sum of money. Their Lordships prefer to reserve their opinion as to the legal consequences in such a situation".

It is possible, therefore, that the courts will hold that an order for possession made upon an admission by a tenant, induced by a promise of payment, can be set aside. In making any such agreement, the landlord should therefore ensure that it is a term of the agreement that delivery up of possession and payment of the money are concurrent events. It would seem a little difficult for a tenant to challenge an order for possession once he has actually been paid and left the premises even if he can challenge it before then. In these circumstances there will have been a valid surrender.

Where a compromise is reached the parties should write out the terms of the agreement and each sign the document so that there can be no misunderstanding at a later stage. When the case is called on the landlord should inform the judge that an agreement has been reached and the tenant should admit that the Housing Act, etc. does not apply (if that be the case) or that the landlord is entitled to possession under the Act. In the latter case the tenant must make admissions as to the ground for possession (*R. v Newcastle-upon-Tyne County Court Ex p. Thompson* [1988] 2 E.G.L.R. 119).

> "The crucial point is that, in order for the court to have jurisdiction in a case where there is a consent order, the relevant admission, whether express or implied, must be clearly shown. If the true explanation for the consent order may simply be that there was a compromise between the parties, it may well be that it will not be possible to imply the relevant admission. The moral of the story is perhaps that, in all these cases, it is desirable that the consent order should spell out, in express terms, the admission, or, where for some reason that does not happen, the court should ask the tenant what admissions are being made, so that there is no room for confusion or doubt in the future" (*Baygreen Properties Ltd v Gil* [2002] EWCA Civ 1340, Clarke L.J.).

The judge may not readily make the order where the tenant is unrepresented and in those circumstances it may be necessary for the landlord to call the evidence he has in support for his case; but if both parties are represented there will usually be no problem in obtaining the order. Where a "consent order" is made without jurisdiction or without the necessary admissions being made the tenant may apply to quash the decision by means of judicial review (*Ex p. Thompson* (1988)).

For the dangers of using a *Tomlin* order in an assured tenancy case see para.7.007. Further, the parties should ensure that they expressly encompass all the matters that they wish to compromise in an order. In *Henley v Bloom* [2010] EWCA Civ 202 it was held that it was not an abuse of process for a former tenant to commence a disrepair claim some time after compromising previous possession proceedings relying on rent arrears even though he knew at the time that he might make such a claim. The possession claim and the disrepair claim were two separate matters even though they arose out of the same tenancy. As there was no counterclaim in the claim for possession claiming damages for disrepair the compromise terms did not cover the disrepair claim. Lord Neuberger MR at para.33:

" . . .it seems to me that, where an action is brought by a claimant who was simply a defendant in an earlier action involving the same parties, it is more difficult to argue that the later action is an abuse than where the same person was claimant in both actions."

The lesson for landlords is to be very careful when compromising possession claims. Where there is the possibility that the tenant could bring a disrepair claim they should ensure that the tenant's potential claim is covered in the agreement.

Second possession order

The court can make an immediate order for possession on one ground even though **25.041** there is an existing suspended order for possession on another ground. It would be absurd to require a second set of proceedings, which would be unnecessarily wasteful of costs. In making such an order the court should have regard to the guidance in *Sheffield City Council v Hopkins* [2001] EWCA Civ 1023—in particular the requirement that the tenant to be given clear notice of the new allegations being made (*Manchester City Council v Finn* [2002] EWCA Civ 1998—original order for possession related to rent arrears, which was suspended on payment of the current rent plus £2.60 per week off the arrears. The payments were being made so that the suspension remained in force. Subsequently there were breaches of the tenancy agreement relating to use illegal activity at the premises).

Costs

Summary assessment

The county courts have always been in the practice of assessing costs at the end **25.042** of short possession claims but the sums received have been small. Practice Direction 44 para.4.4(1)(b) expressly deals with the position and states: "The general rule is that the court will make a summary assessment of costs . . . at the conclusion of any hearing which has lasted less than one day". The practice therefore continues.

Paragraph 4.5 of PD 44 requires that a written statement of costs should be prepared in Form 1 of the schedule of costs forms. The requirement to provide a detailed statement has had some effect on costs orders made in that higher sums are awarded more frequently than before. In principle, there is no reason why a defeated party to a possession claim should not pay the other party's reasonable costs. The principle of proportionality will of course apply (CPR r.44.4(2) and 44.5(1)) but recovery of possession of a property or the defeat of a claim for possession is very often a matter of great concern to the parties involved.

Indemnity costs; contractual terms

25.043 Where the tenancy agreement provides for costs on an indemnity basis the landlord is invariably entitled to the costs on that basis, whether on a summary or detailed assessment. See further CPR r.48.3 and CPR PD 48 s.50. Regard should also be had to the following statements in *Church Commissioners for England v Ibrahim* [1997] 1 E.G.L.R. 13 CA:

> "... the statements of principle in the *Gomba Holdings* case [see para.32.083] are not confined to mortgage cases and have a wider application. The successful litigant's contractual rights to recover the costs of any proceedings to enforce his primary contractual rights is a highly relevant factor when it comes to making a costs order. He is not, in my view, to be deprived of his contractual rights to costs where he has claimed them unless there is good reason to do so and that applies both to the making of a costs order in his favour and to the extent that costs are to be paid to him" (*Church Commissioners for England v Ibrahim* [1997] 1 E.G.L.R. 13 CA, per Roch L.J. at 14H).

The fact that the case is "a straightforward possession action" is not a good reason for depriving the landlord of his contractual entitlement to indemnity costs. Nor is the landlord's greater bargaining power (*Church Commissioners v Ibrahim*, per Roch L.J. at 14M).

However, too much attention is often paid to the term "indemnity costs". The point is put into perspective by the following passage of Hobhouse L.J. in *Church Commissioners v Ibrahim* at 15J:

> "The difference between the bases of taxation is not a difference between the criterion to be applied. The criterion still remains whether the costs were reasonably incurred and reasonable in amount. The difference between the two bases is that in one any doubt that a taxing master may feel is resolved in favour of the claiming party and in the other in favour of the paying party. The use of the phrase 'indemnity basis' has a historical origin and is misleading. Under both bases the claimant at the end of the day may only recover reasonable costs. The difference relates to the grey area where there is room for doubt on the one side or the other."

It should also be noted that the landlord's right is not absolute. In a forfeiture case (*Forcelux v Binnie* [2009] EWCA Civ 1077), where the tenant had obtained relief from forfeiture and was considered to be substantially the winner of the case, the court made a different order. The court was considering an appeal by the landlord that had failed. Warren J. at paras 12, 13, 15 and 16:

> "As I have said he [counsel for the landlord] accepts the jurisdiction of the court to make a different order notwithstanding the contractual position as he states it, but submits that the general principle is that the discretion should be exercised in line with the contract. He relies on *Gomba Holdings (UK) Ltd v Minories Finance Ltd (No 2)* [1993] CH 171 (a mortgage case) and *Church Commissioners for England v Ibrahim* [1997] 1 EGLR 13 (a lease case) to demonstrate that principle. I do not dissent in any way from the proposition that the general principle is as he states. But the general principle is not a rule of law and it may well be that in a particular case, or even in a class of case, the court's discretion should be used to override the contractual right.

For example, if a lessor loses a piece of litigation at first instance which it was reasonable for him to fight, it might be wrong to deprive him of a contractual right to costs. But if he goes on to appeal the decision against him and loses the appeal, then it is not obvious to me that the general rule should be that the discretion should be exercised in accordance with the contractual right; or if it is the general rule, then the court should be willing to depart from it quite readily.

In my judgment, Mr Binnie has been the substantial winner of the appeal... In choosing to challenge the basis on which relief was given by appealing against the order for HH Judge Hampton upholding the decision to set aside the possession order Forcelux did so at its own risk as to costs."

Fixed costs

The fixed costs rule in relation to possession and demotion claims is now set out **25.044** in CPR Pt 45.1 and 45.4A. Unless the court otherwise orders the amount to be allowed in respect of solicitor's charges is fixed where:

- The claim is for the recovery of land, including a possession claim under Pt 55, whether or not the claim includes a claim for a sum of money and the defendant gives up possession, pays the amount claimed, if any, and the fixed commencement costs stated in the claim form.

- The claim is for the recovery of land, including a possession claim under Pt 55, where one of the grounds for possession is arrears of rent, for which the court gave a fixed date for the hearing when it issued the claim and judgment is given for the possession of land (whether or not the order for possession is suspended on terms) and the defendant:

  — has neither delivered a defence, or counterclaim, nor otherwise denied liability; or
  — has delivered a defence which is limited to specifying his proposals for the payment of arrears of rent.

- The claim is a demotion claim under s.III of Pt 65 or a demotion claim is made in the same claim form in which a claim for possession is made under Pt 55 and that demotion claim is successful.

(See para.26.006 in relation to accelerated possession claims).

Where the claimant obtains judgment the amount to be included in the judgment for the claimant's solicitor's charges is the total of the fixed commencement costs (see table 2) and the sum of £57.25. In addition the claimant is entitled to the court fee (45.1(3)).

The circumstances in which the court might "otherwise order", i.e. award costs greater than fixed costs, is not specified. Examples might include:

- where there has been one or more adjournments at the request of the defendant;

- where there is a complication in the case; or

- where the tenancy agreement makes specific provision as to costs (see para.25.043).

Appeals

25.045 CPR Pt 52 and the Practice Direction to that part, to which readers are referred, govern appeals. However, the main points that are relevant to possession claims are as follows:

- It is necessary to obtain permission to appeal. The application may be made to the lower court at the hearing or to the appeal court in an appeal notice. Where the lower court refuses the application for permission a further application may be made to the appeal court (CPR r.52.3).

- Permission to appeal will only be given where the court considers that the appeal would have "a real prospect of success or there is some other compelling reason why the appeal should be heard" (CPR r.52.3(6)).

- The notice of appeal must be filed "at the appeal court within such period as may be directed by the lower court or where the court makes no such direction" within 21 days of the decision of the lower court (CPR r.52.4). If more time is required it must therefore be expressly requested.

- Unless the appeal court or the lower court orders otherwise an appeal does not operate as a stay of any order or decision of the lower court (CPR r.52.7). It is thus very important for a losing defendant specifically to apply for a stay if he is contemplating an appeal.

- Where the case was heard by a district judge the appeal is made to the circuit judge and an appeal from a circuit judge to a High Court Judge (see CPR PD 52 para.2A.1).

- It is necessary for the advocate to make a note of the judgment. It is no good waiting for a transcript (CPR PD 55 paras 5.12 and 5.14).

- In very limited circumstances the appeal can be referred to the Court of Appeal even though that would not be the usual court to hear the appeal (CPR r.52.14).

25.046 One of the categories of appeal in which the Court of Appeal will consider favourably an application for an expedited hearing of an appeal is cases in which the execution of a possession order is imminent and which appear to have some merit (*Unilever Plc v Chefaro Proprietaries Ltd* [1995] 1 All E.R. 587).

There is no right of appeal on any question of fact if by virtue of any of the following statutory provisions the court can only grant possession on being satisfied that it is reasonable to do so (s.77(6) of the County Courts Act 1984):

- Section 13(4) of the Landlord and Tenant Act 1954.

- Cases III to IX in Sch.4 to the Rent (Agriculture) Act 1976.

- Section 98 of the Rent Act 1977, as it applies to Cases 1 to 6 and 8 and 9 in Sch.15 to that Act, or that section as extended or applied by any other enactment.

- Section 99 of the Rent Act 1977, as it applies to Cases 1 to 6 and 9 in Sch.15 to that Act.

- Section 84(2)(a) of the Housing Act 1985.

- Section 7 of the Housing Act 1988, as it applies to the grounds in Pt II of Sch.2 to that Act.

- Paragraph 13(4) of Sch.10 to the Local Government and Housing Act 1989.

- Any other enactment.

An appeal court can, under CPR r.52.11(1)(b), only hold a re-hearing, as opposed to a review, where

> "the court considers that in the circumstances of an individual appeal it would be in the interests of justice to do so".

London Borough of Ealing v Richardson [2005] EWCA Civ 1798 was a bad case of rent arrears where the district judge nevertheless suspended the warrant for possession—for the ninth time in nine years. The county court judge overturned the suspension. However, on a further appeal to the Court of Appeal the district judge's decision was restored. This was because the circuit judge had tried the hearing before him as a re-hearing. He should not have done so. He should have treated it as a review. Arden L.J.:

> "... the case which the judge had to consider turned on the exercise by the District Judge of her discretion under section 85 of the Housing Act 1985. There is a substantial difference between an appeal by way of a review of the order of the District Judge in these circumstances, and an appeal by way of re-hearing. If it is an appeal by way of review, then the function of the appellate court is limited to seeing whether the exercise of discretion was wrong in principle or went beyond the generous ambit within which disagreement is possible."

Homelessness and the local authority

A tenant who has been evicted and as a result is homeless may be left with no **25.047** alternative other than to apply to the local authority for accommodation under Pt VII of the Housing Act 1996. A person is threatened with homelessness if it is likely that he will become homeless within 28 days (s.175(4)). The housing authority is under a duty to make such inquiries as are necessary to satisfy themselves whether a person applying to it is eligible for assistance and what duty, if any, is owed to him (s.184(1)). If the applicant is homeless and has a priority need the local authority is obliged to find accommodation for him (s.193). Priority need cases are those where the applicant or a person residing with him is pregnant or there are dependent children residing with him, where the applicant is homeless or threatened with homelessness as a result of an emergency or where the applicant or a member of his household is vulnerable as a result of old age, mental illness or physical disability or some other special reason (s.189). There is no duty to house a tenant who has made himself intentionally homeless (s.190).

In *Green v London Borough of Croydon* [2007] EWCA Civ 1367 a local authority in deciding whether or not applicants for housing had been rendered intentionally homeless had relied upon the decision of the district judge in a possession claim that there were rent arrears. There was some scope for arguing that the judge was wrong about that and the applicants argued that the authority should have looked into the matter further before treating them as intentionally homeless. The argument was rejected. The authority was entitled to rely upon the judge's decision and it could not be said that they had failed to make all such enquiries as were necessary (as required by s.184(1)) when coming to its decision on the question of its duty in relation to their homelessness. The case highlights the importance of tenants making sure that if they wish to dispute any suggestion of arrears that they should do so during the possession claim.

A licensee who has no right to remain in possession is homeless (s.175(1)(b); *R. v Kensington and Chelsea RBC Ex p. Minton* (1988) 20 H.L.R. 648) and unless the licence has been revoked as a result of misconduct on his part the fact that he leaves prior to the obtaining of a court order by the licensor does not of itself make him intentionally homeless (*R. v Surrey Heath BC Ex p. Li* (1984) 16 H.L.R. 83). See also the Department for Communities and Local Government, *Homelessness Code of Guidance for Local Authorities* (London: DCLG, July 2006), in particular para.11.27 which indicates that the individual would not be considered to be intentionally homeless where

> ". . . faced with possession proceedings to which there would be no defence, and where the granting of a possession order would be mandatory, [he] surrenders the property to the landlord . . . [A]lthough the housing authority may consider that it would have been reasonable for the tenant to continue to occupy the accommodation, the act should not be regarded as deliberate if the tenant made the decision to leave the accommodation in ignorance of material facts, e.g. the general pressure on the authority for housing assistance."

Compare *R. v LB Croydon Ex p. Jarvis* (1993) 26 H.L.R. 194, where it was held that notwithstanding an earlier similar version, the code it is not necessarily wrong for an authority to require a person to remain in possession until an order is made.

However, once it has been made the person is threatened with homelessness and the duties under s.184 arise. The council should not simply advise the tenants to remain where they are until they are evicted (*R. v Newham LBC Ex p. Khan* (2001) 33 H.L.R. 29 (QBD), Collins J.).

CPR Part 55

Interpretation

25.048 **55.1** In this Part—

(a) "a possession claim" means a claim for the recovery of possession of land (including buildings or parts of buildings);

(b) "a possession claim against trespassers" means a claim for the recovery of land which the claimant alleges is occupied only by a person or persons who entered or remained on the land without the consent of a person entitled to possession of that land but does not include a claim against a tenant or sub-tenant whether his tenancy has been terminated or not;

(c) "mortgage" includes a legal or equitable mortgage and a legal or equitable charge and "mortgagee" is to be interpreted accordingly; and

(d) "the 1985 Act" means the Housing Act 1985;

(e) "the 1988 Act" means the Housing Act 1988;

(f) "a demotion claim" means a claim made by a landlord for an order under section 82A of the 1985 Act or section 6A of the 1988 Act ("a demotion order"); and

(g) "a demoted tenancy" means a tenancy created by virtue of a demotion order;

(h) "a suspension claim" means a claim made by a landlord for an order under section 121A of the 1985 Act.

General Rules

Scope

55.2—(1) The procedure set out in this Section of this Part must be used where the claim includes—

    (a) a possession claim brought by a:

        (i) landlord (or former landlord);
        (ii) mortgagee; or
        (iii) licensor (or former licensor).

    (b) a possession claim against trespassers; or

    (c) a claim by a tenant seeking relief from forfeiture.

(Where a demotion claim or a suspension claim (or both) is made in the same claim form in which a possession claim is started, this Section of this Part applies as modified by rule 65.12. Where the claim is a demotion claim or a suspension claim only, or a suspension claim made in addition to a demotion claim, section III of Part 65 applies).

(2) This section of this Part:

    (a) is subject to any enactment or practice direction which sets out special provisions with regard to any particular category of claim; and

    (b) does not apply where the claimant uses the procedure set out in section II of this Part.

    (c) does not apply where the claimant seeks an interim possession order under section III of this Part except where the court orders otherwise or that Section so provides.

Starting the claim

55.3—(1) The claim must be started in the county court for the district in which the land **25.049** is situated unless paragraph (2) applies or an enactment provides otherwise.

(2) The claim may be started in the High Court if the claimant files with his claim form a certificate stating the reasons for bringing the claim in that court verified by a statement of truth in accordance with rule 22.1(1).

(3) Practice Direction 55A refers to circumstances which may justify starting the claim in the High Court.

(4) Where, in a possession claim against trespassers, the claimant does not know the name of a person in occupation or possession of the land, the claim must be brought against "persons unknown" in addition to any named defendants.

(5) The claim form and form of defence sent with it must be in the forms set out in Practice Direction 55A.

Particulars of claim

55.4 The particulars of claim must be filed and served with the claim form.

(Part 16 Practice Direction 55A provide details about the contents of the particulars of claim).

Hearing date

55.5—(1) The court will fix a date for the hearing when it issues the claim form.

(2) In a possession claim against trespassers the defendant must be served with the claim form, particulars of claim and any witness statements–

   (a) in the case of residential property, not less than 5 days; and

   (b) in the case of other land, not less than 2 days, before the hearing date.

(3) In all other possession claims—

   (a) the hearing date will be not less than 28 days from the date of issue of the claim form;

   (b) the standard period between the issue of the claim form and the hearing will be not more than 8 weeks; and

   (c) the defendant must be served with the claim form and particulars of claim not less than 21 days before the hearing date.

(Rule 3.1(2)(a) provides that the court may extend or shorten the time for compliance with any rule.)

Defendants' response

25.050   **55.7**—(1) An acknowledgment of service is not required and Part 10 does not apply.

(2) In a possession claim against trespassers rule 15.2 does not apply and the defendant need not file a defence.

(3) Where, in any other possession claim, the defendant does not file a defence within the time specified in rule 15.4, he may take part in any hearing but the court may take his failure to do so into account when deciding what order to make about costs.

(4) Part 12 (default judgment) does not apply in a claim to which this Part applies.

The hearing

55.8—(1) At the hearing fixed in accordance with rule 55.5(1) or at any adjournment of that hearing, the court may—

   (a) decide the claim; or

   (b) give case management directions.

(2) Where the claim is genuinely disputed on grounds which appear to be substantial, case management directions given under paragraph (1)(b) will include the allocation of the claim to a track or directions to enable it to be allocated.

(3) Except where–

   (a) the claim is allocated to the fast track or the multi-track; or

   (b) the court orders otherwise,

any fact that needs to be proved by the evidence of witnesses at a hearing referred to in para.(1) may be proved by evidence in writing.

(Rule 32.2(1) sets out the general rule about evidence. Rule 32.2(2) provides that rule 32.2(1) is subject to any provision to the contrary.)

(4) Subject to para.(5), all witness statements must be filed and served at least 2 days before the hearing.

(5) In a possession claim against trespassers all witness statements on which the claimant intends to rely must be filed and served with the claim form.

(6) Where the claimant serves the claim form and particulars of claim, the claimant must produce at the hearing a certificate of service of those documents and rule 6.17(2)(a) does not apply.

Allocation

55.9—(1) When the court decides the track for a possession claim, the matters to which **25.051** it shall have regard include—

(a) the matters set out in rule 26.8 as modified by the relevant practice direction;
(b) the amount of any arrears of rent or mortgage instalments;
(c) the importance to the defendant of retaining possession of the land;
(d) the importance of vacant possession to the claimant; and
(e) if applicable, the alleged conduct of the defendant.

(2) The court will only allocate possession claims to the small claims track if all the parties agree.

(3) Where a possession claim has been allocated to the small claims track the claim shall be treated, for the purposes of costs, as if it were proceeding on the fast track except that trial costs shall be in the discretion of the court and shall not exceed the amount that would be recoverable under rule 46.2 (amount of fast track costs) if the value of the claim were up to £3,000.

(4) Where all the parties agree the court may, when it allocates the claim, order that rule 27.14 (costs on the small claims track) applies and, where it does so, paragraph (3) does not apply.

Practice Direction 55A—Possession Claims
Section I—General Rules

Starting the claim

55.3—1.1 Except where the county court does not have jurisdiction, possession claims **25.052** should normally be brought in the county court. Only exceptional circumstances justify starting a claim in the High Court.

1.2 If a claimant starts a claim in the High Court and the court decides that it should have been started in the county court, the court will normally either strike the claim out or transfer it to the county court on its own initiative. This is likely to result in delay and the court will normally disallow the costs of starting the claim in the High Court and of any transfer.

1.3 Circumstances which may, in an appropriate case, justify starting a claim in the High Court are if—
(1) there are complicated disputes of fact;
(2) there are points of law of general importance; or
(3) the claim is against trespassers and there is a substantial risk of public disturbance or of serious harm to persons or property which properly require immediate determination.

1.4 The value of the property and the amount of any financial claim may be relevant circumstances, but these factors alone will not normally justify starting the claim in the High Court.

1.5 The claimant must use the appropriate claim form and particulars of claim form set out in Table 1 to Part 4 Practice Direction. The defence must be in form N11, N11B, N11M or N11R, as appropriate.

1.6   High Court claims for the possession of land subject to a mortgage will be assigned to the Chancery Division.

1.7   A claim which is not a possession claim may be brought under the procedure set out in section I of Part 55 if it is started in the same claim form as a possession claim which, by virtue of rule 55.2(1) must be brought in accordance with that Section. (Rule 7.3 provides that a claimant may use a single claim form to start all claims which can be conveniently disposed of in the same proceedings)

1.8   For example a claim under paragraphs 4, 5 or 6 of Part I of Schedule 1 to the Mobile Homes Act 1983 may be brought using the procedure set out in section I of Part 55 if the claim is started in the same claim form as a claim enforcing the rights referred to in section 3(1)(b) of the Caravan Sites Act 1968 (which, by virtue of rule 55.2(1) must be brought under section I of Part 55).

1.9   Where the claim form includes a demotion claim, the claim must be started in the county court for the district in which the land is situated.

55.4—Particulars of claim

2.1   In a possession claim the particulars of claim must:
   (1) identify the land to which the claim relates;
   (2) state whether the claim relates to residential property:
   (3) state the ground on which possession is claimed;
   (4) give full details about any mortgage or tenancy agreement; and
   (5) give details of every person who, to the best of the claimant's knowledge, is in possession of the property.

Residential property let on a tenancy

25.053

2.2   Paragraphs 2.3 to 2.4B apply if the claim relates to residential property let on a tenancy.

2.3   If the claim includes a claim for non-payment of rent the particulars of claim must set out:

   (1) the amount due at the start of the proceedings;
   (2) in schedule form, the dates and amounts of all payments due and payments made under the tenancy agreement for a period of two years immediately preceding the date of issue or if the first date of default occurred less than two years before the date of issue from the first date of default and a running total of the arrears;
   (3) the daily rate of any rent and interest;
   (4) any previous steps taken to recover the arrears of rent with full details of any court proceedings; and
   (5) any relevant information about the defendant's circumstances, in particular:

      (a) whether the defendant is in receipt of social security benefits; and
      (b) whether any payments are made on his behalf directly to the claimant under the Social Security Contributions and Benefits Act 1992.

2.3A. If the claimant wishes to rely on a history of arrears which is longer than two years, he should state this in his particulars and exhibit a full (or longer) schedule to a witness statement.

2.4   If the claimant knows of any person (including a mortgagee) entitled to claim relief against forfeiture as underlessee under section 146(4) of the Law of Property Act 1925 (or in accordance with section 38 of the Supreme Court Act 1981, or section 138(9C) of the County Courts Act 1984):

   (1) the particulars of claim must state the name and address of that person; and
   (2) the claimant must file a copy of the particulars of claim for service on him.

2.4A If the claim for possession relates to the conduct of the tenant, the particulars of claim must state details of the conduct alleged.

2.4B If the possession claim relies on a statutory ground or grounds for possession, the particulars of claim must specify the ground or grounds relied on.

55.5—Hearing date

3.1 The court may exercise its powers under rule 3.1(2)(a) and (b) to shorten the time **25.054** periods set out in rule 55.5(2) and (3).

3.2 Particular consideration should be given to the exercise of this power if:

(1) the defendant, or a person for whom the defendant is responsible, has assaulted or threatened to assault:

(a) the claimant;
(b) a member of the claimant's staff; or
(c) another resident in the locality;

(2) there are reasonable grounds for fearing such an assault; or

(3) the defendant, or a person for whom the defendant is responsible, has caused serious damage or threatened to cause serious damage to the property or to the home or property of another resident in the locality.

3.3 Where paragraph 3.2 applies but the case cannot be determined at the first hearing fixed under rule 55.5, the court will consider what steps are needed to finally determine the case as quickly as reasonably practicable.

55.8—The hearing

5.1 Attention is drawn to rule 55.8(3). Each party should wherever possible include all the **25.055** evidence he wishes to present in his statement of case, verified by a statement of truth.

5.2 If relevant the claimant's evidence should include the amount of any rent or mortgage arrears and interest on those arrears. These amounts should, if possible, be up to date to the date of the hearing (if necessary by specifying a daily rate of arrears and interest). However, rule 55.8(4) does not prevent such evidence being brought up to date orally or in writing on the day of the hearing if necessary.

5.3 If relevant the defendant should give evidence of:

(1) the amount of any outstanding social security or housing benefit payments relevant to rent or mortgage arrears; and

(2) the status of:

(a) any claims for social security or housing benefit about which a decision has not yet been made; and

(b) any applications to appeal or review a social security or housing benefit decision where that appeal or review has not yet concluded.

5.4 If:

(1) the maker of a witness statement does not attend a hearing; and

(2) the other party disputes material evidence contained in his statement,

the court will normally adjourn the hearing so that oral evidence can be given.

CPR PD 55B Possession Claims Online

Scope of this Practice Direction

1.1 This practice direction provides for a scheme ("Possession Claims Online") to **25.056** operate in specified county courts—

(1) enabling claimants and their representatives to start certain possession claims under CPR Part 55 by requesting the issue of a claim form electronically via the PCOL website; and

(2) where a claim has been started electronically, enabling the claimant or defendant and their representatives to take further steps in the claim electronically as specified below.

1.2 In this practice direction—

(1) 'PCOL website' means the website which may be accessed via the Business Link website, and through which Possession Claims Online will operate; and

[At the time of writing the service could not be accessed through the Business Link website, but remained accessible through www.possessionclaim.gov.uk/pcol.]

(2) "specified court" means a county court specified on the PCOL website as one in which Possession Claims Online is available.

Information on the PCOL Website

2.1 The PCOL website contains further details and guidance about the operation of Possession Claims Online.

2.2 In particular the PCOL website sets out—

(1) the specified courts; and

(2) the dates from which Possession Claims Online will be available in each specified court.

2.3 The operation of Possession Claims Online in any specified court may be restricted to taking certain of the steps specified in this practice direction, and in such cases the PCOL website will set out the steps which may be taken using Possession Claims Online in that specified court.

Security

3.1 Her Majesty's Courts and Tribunals Service will take such measures as it thinks fit to ensure the security of steps taken or information stored electronically. These may include requiring users of Possession Claims Online—

(1) to enter a customer identification number or password;

(2) to provide personal information for identification purposes; and

(3) to comply with any other security measures,
    before taking any step online.

Fees

4.1 A step may only be taken using Possession Claims Online on payment of the prescribed fee where a fee is payable. Where this practice direction provides for a fee to be paid electronically, it may be paid by—

(1) credit card;

(2) debit card; or

(3) any other method which Her Majesty's Courts and Tribunals Service may permit.

4.2 A defendant who wishes to claim exemption from payment of fees must do so through an organisation approved by Her Majesty's Courts and Tribunals Service before taking any step using PCOL which attracts a fee. If satisfied that the defendant is entitled to fee exemption, the organisation will submit the fee exemption form through the PCOL website to Her Majesty's Courts and Tribunals Service. The defendant may then use PCOL to take such a step.

(Her Majesty's Courts and Tribunals Service website contains guidance as to when the entitlement to claim an exemption from payment of fees arises. The PCOL website will contain a list of organisations through which the defendant may claim an exemption from fees.)

Claims which may be Started using Possession Claims Online

5.1 A claim may be started online if—

(1) it is brought under section I of Part 55;

(2) it includes a possession claim for residential property by—

(a) a landlord against a tenant, solely on the ground of arrears of rent (but not a claim for forfeiture of a lease); or

(b) a mortgagee against a mortgagor, solely on the ground of default in the payment of sums due under a mortgage,

relating to land within the district of a specified court.

(3) it does not include a claim for any other remedy except for payment of arrears of rent or money due under a mortgage, interest and costs;

(4) the defendant has an address for service in England and Wales; and

(5) the claimant is able to provide a postcode for the property.

5.2 A claim must not be started online if a defendant is known to be a child or protected party.

Starting a Claim

6.1 A claimant may request the issue of a claim form by—

(1) completing an online claim form at the PCOL website;

(2) paying the appropriate issue fee electronically at the PCOL website or by some other means approved by Her Majesty's Courts and Tribunals Service.

6.2 The particulars of claim must be included in the online claim form and may not be filed separately. It is not necessary to file a copy of the tenancy agreement, mortgage deed or mortgage agreement with the particulars of claim.

6.2A In the case of a possession claim for residential property that relies on a statutory ground or grounds for possession, the claimant must specify, in section 4(a) of the online claim form, the ground or grounds relied on.

6.3 Subject to paragraphs 6.3A and 6.3B, the particulars of claim must include a history of the rent or mortgage account, in schedule form setting out—

(1) the dates and amounts of all payments due and payments made under the tenancy agreement, mortgage deed or mortgage agreement either from the first date of default if that date occurred less than two years before the date of issue or for a period of two years immediately preceding the date of issue; and

(2) a running total of the arrears.

6.3A Paragraph 6.3B applies where the claimant has, before commencing proceedings, provided the defendant in schedule form with—

(1) details of the dates and amounts of all payments due and payments made under the tenancy agreement, mortgage deed or mortgage account—

(a) for a period of two years immediately preceding the date of commencing proceedings; or

      (b) if the first date of default occurred less than two years before that date, from the first date of default; and

  (2) a running total of the arrears.

6.3B Where this paragraph applies the claimant may, in place of the information required by paragraph 6.3, include in his particulars of claim a summary only of the arrears containing at least the following information—

  (1) The amount of arrears as stated in the notice of seeking possession served under either section 83 of the Housing Act 1985 or section 8 of the Housing Act 1988, or at the date of the claimant's letter before action, as appropriate;

  (2) the dates and amounts of the last three payments in cleared funds made by the defendant or, if less than three payments have been made, the dates and amounts of all payments made;

  (3) the arrears at the date of issue, assuming that no further payments are made by the defendant.

6.3C Where the particulars of claim include a summary only of the arrears the claimant must—

  (1) serve on the defendant not more than seven days after the date of issue, a full, up-to-date arrears history containing at least the information required by paragraph 6.3; and

  (2) either—

    (a) make a witness statement confirming that he has complied with sub-paragraph (1) or (2) of paragraph 6.3A as appropriate, and including or exhibiting the full arrears history; or

    (b) verify by way of oral evidence at the hearing that he has complied with sub-paragraph (1) or (2) of paragraph 6.3A as appropriate and also produce and verify the full arrears history.

    (Rule 55.8(4) requires all witness statements to be filed and served at least two days before the hearing.)

6.4   If the claimant wishes to rely on a history of arrears which is longer than two years, he should state this in his particulars and exhibit a full (or longer) schedule to a witness statement.

6.5   When an online claim form is received, an acknowledgment of receipt will automatically be sent to the claimant. The acknowledgment does not constitute notice that the claim form has been issued or served.

6.6   When the court issues a claim form following the submission of an online claim form, the claim is "brought" for the purposes of the Limitation Act 1980 and any other enactment on the date on which the online claim form is received by the court's computer system. The court will keep a record, by electronic or other means, of when online claim forms are received.

6.7   When the court issues a claim form it will—

  (1) serve a printed version of the claim form and a defence form on the defendant; and

  (2) send the claimant notice of issue by post or, where the claimant has supplied an email address, by electronic means.

6.8   The claim shall be deemed to be served on the fifth day after the claim was issued irrespective of whether that day is a business day or not.

6.9   Where the period of time within which a defence must be filed ends on a day when the court is closed, the defendant may file his defence on the next day that the court is open.

6.10 The claim form shall have printed on it a unique customer identification number or a password by which the defendant may access the claim on the PCOL website.

6.11 PCOL will issue the proceedings in the appropriate county court by reference to the post code provided by the claimant and that court shall have jurisdiction to hear and determine the claim and to carry out enforcement of any judgment irrespective of whether the property is within or outside the jurisdiction of that court. (CPR rule 30.2(1) authorises proceedings to be transferred from one county court to another.)

Defence

7.1 A defendant wishing to file—

(1) a defence; or
(2) a counterclaim (to be filed together with a defence) to a claim which has been issued through the PCOL system, may, instead of filing a written form, do so by—

(a) completing the relevant online form at the PCOL website; and
(b) if the defendant is making a counterclaim, paying the appropriate fee electronically at the PCOL website or by some other means approved by Her Majesty's Courts and Tribunals Service.

7.2 Where a defendant files a defence by completing the relevant online form, he must not send the court a hard copy.

7.3 When an online defence form is received, an acknowledgment of receipt will automatically be sent to the defendant. The acknowledgment does not constitute notice that the defence has been served.

7.4 The online defence form will be treated as being filed—

(1) on the day the court receives it, if it receives it before 16.00 on a working day; and
(2) otherwise, on the next working day after the court receives the online defence form.

7.5 A defence is filed when the online defence form is received by the court's computer system. The court will keep a record, by electronic or other means, of when online defence forms are received.

Statement of Truth

8.1 CPR Part 22 requires any statement of case to be verified by a statement of truth. This applies to any online claims and defences and application notices.

8.2 CPR Part 22 also requires that if an applicant wishes to rely on matters set out in his application notice as evidence, the application notice must be verified by a statement of truth. This applies to any application notice completed online that contains matters on which the applicant wishes to rely as evidence.

8.3 Attention is drawn to—

(1) paragraph 2 of the practice direction supplementing CPR Part 22, which stipulates the form of the statement of truth; and
(2) paragraph 3 of the practice direction supplementing CPR Part 22, which provides who may sign a statement of truth; and
(3) CPR 32.14, which sets out the consequences of making, or causing to be made, a false statement in a document verified by a statement of truth, without an honest belief in its truth.

Signature

9.1 Any provision of the CPR which requires a document to be signed by any person is satisfied by that person entering his name on an online form.

Communication with the Court Electronically by the Messaging Service

10.1 If the PCOL website specifies that a court accepts electronic communications relating to claims brought using Possession Claims Online the parties may communicate with the court using the messaging service facility, available on the PCOL website ("the messaging service").

10.2 The messaging service is for brief and straightforward communications only. The PCOL website contains a list of examples of when it will not be appropriate to use the messaging service.

10.3 Parties must not send to the court forms or attachments via the messaging service.

10.4 The court shall treat any forms or attachments sent via the messaging service as not having been filed or received.

10.5 The court will normally reply via the messaging service where—

(1) the response is to a message transmitted via the messaging service; and

(2) the sender has provided an email address.

Electronic Applications

11.1 Certain applications in relation to a possession claim started online may be made electronically ("online applications"). An online application may be made if a form for that application is published on the PCOL website ("online application form") and the application is made at least five clear days before the hearing.

11.2 If a claim for possession has been started online and a party wishes to make an online application, he may do so by—

(1) completing the appropriate online application form at the PCOL website; and

(2) paying the appropriate fee electronically at the PCOL website or by some other means approved by Her Majesty's Courts and Tribunals Service.

11.3 When an online application form is received, an acknowledgment of receipt will automatically be sent to the applicant. The acknowledgment does not constitute a notice that the online application form has been issued or served.

11.4 Where an application must be made within a specified time, it is so made if the online application form is received by the court's computer system within that time. The court will keep a record, by electronic or other means, of when online application forms are received.

11.5 When the court receives an online application form it shall—

(1) serve a copy of the online application endorsed with the date of the hearing by post on the claimant at least two clear days before the hearing; and

(2) send the defendant notice of service and confirmation of the date of the hearing by post; provided that

(3) where either party has provided the court with an email address for service, service of the application and/or the notice of service and confirmation of the hearing date may be effected by electronic means.

Request for Issue of Warrant

12.1 Where—

(1) the court has made an order for possession in a claim started online; and

(2) the claimant is entitled to the issue of a warrant of possession without requiring the permission of the court

the claimant may request the issue of a warrant by completing an online request form at the PCOL website and paying the appropriate fee electronically at the PCOL website or by some other means approved by Her Majesty's Courts and Tribunals Service.

12.2 A request under paragraph 12.1 will be treated as being filed—

(1) on the day the court receives the request, if it receives it before 16.00 on a working day; and

(2) otherwise, on the next working day after the court receives the request.

(CCR Order 26 rule 5 sets out certain circumstances in which a warrant of execution may not be issued without the permission of the court. CCR Order 26 rule 17(6) applies rule 5 of that Order with necessary modifications to a warrant of possession.)

Application to Suspend Warrant of Possession

13.1 Where the court has issued a warrant of possession, the defendant may apply electronically for the suspension of the warrant, provided that:

(1) the application is made at least five clear days before the appointment for possession; and

(2) the defendant is not prevented from making such an application without the permission of the court.

13.2 The defendant may apply electronically for the suspension of the warrant, by—

(1) completing an online application for suspension at the PCOL website; and

(2) paying the appropriate fee electronically at the PCOL website or by some other means approved by Her Majesty's Courts and Tribunals Service.

13.3 When an online application for suspension is received, an acknowledgment of receipt will automatically be sent to the defendant. The acknowledgment does not constitute a notice that the online application for suspension has been served.

13.4 Where an application must be made within a specified time, it is so made if the online application for suspension is received by the court's computer system within that time. The court will keep a record, by electronic or other means, of when online applications for suspension are received.

13.5 When the court receives an online application for suspension it shall—

(1) serve a copy of the online application for suspension endorsed with the date of the hearing by post on the claimant at least two clear days before the hearing; and

(2) send the defendant notice of service and confirmation of the date of the hearing by post; provided that

(3) where either party has provided the court with an email address for service, service of the application and/or the notice of service and confirmation of the hearing date may be effected by electronic means.

Viewing the Case Record

14.1 A facility will be provided on the PCOL website for parties or their representatives to view—

(1) an electronic record of the status of claims started online, which will be reviewed and, if necessary, updated at least once each day; and

(2) all information relating to the case that has been filed by the parties electronically.

14.2 In addition, where the PCOL website specifies that the court has the facility to provide viewing of such information by electronic means, the parties or their representatives may view the following information electronically—

(1) court orders made in relation to the case; and

(2) details of progress on enforcement and subsequent orders made.

Chapter 26

Accelerated Procedure

CPR Pt 55, Pt II provides for an accelerated possession procedure in certain **26.001**
assured shorthold tenancy cases. Where various conditions are satisfied this
procedure may be used instead of the standard procedure in Ch.25. The main
features of the procedure are that:

- There are prescribed forms for the claim and defence
- It only applies to assured shorthold cases. (It also used to apply in some
  other assured tenancy cases but this is no longer the position.)
- If the court is satisfied that the landlord is entitled to an order for possession no hearing takes place.

The full text of the rules is set out at paras 26.008 to 26.012.

The conditions

The conditions that apply are set out in CPR r.55.12 (see para.26.008). Except **26.002**
where the tenancy is a demoted shorthold all the conditions must be satisfied but
the main conditions to note are that:

- The only purpose of the claim can be to recover possession of the property
  and no other claim, such as a claim for rent, may be made.
- The tenancy must:
  - be the subject of a written agreement;
  - arise by virtue of s.5 of the 1988 Act but follow a tenancy that was the
    subject of a written agreement; or
  - relate to the same or substantially the same property let to the same
    tenant and on the same terms (though not necessarily as to rent or
    duration) as a tenancy which was the subject of a written agreement.

It is important to note that this last set of requirements means that the accelerated
procedure will not apply to "new shortholds" entered into *orally* on or after
February 28, 1997 (see para.7.006).
  Where the landlord is a social landlord and the tenancy is a demoted shorthold
the only conditions to be satisfied are that the only purpose of the claim to recover

possession of the property and no other claim is made and that an appropriate s.21 notice was served. Although the practice direction does not presently provide for it, it seems that there will be a further requirement for a social landlord, in that an additional notice under s.21(1B) will need to be served before the court can make an order for possession (see para.7.013).

Claim form, service and defence

26.003 The claim must be started in the county court for the district in which the property is situated (CPR r.55.11). If it is started in the wrong court see CPR r.30.2(3)—para.26.011. The claim form must be in the form set out in the relevant practice direction (Form N5B—Form 32 of this book—p.399) and must contain information and be accompanied by the documents required by the form. All relevant sections must be completed (CPR r.55.13).

The form is served by the court by first class post (CPR r.55.13(3)).

A defendant who wishes to oppose the claim must file a defence within 14 days after service. This must also be in the form prescribed by practice direction (Form N11B—Form 33 of this book—p.403). If the defendant wishes to oppose the order for possession it is very important that the form be completed otherwise the court will undoubtedly make the order.

If the tenant accepts that an order for possession will be made but wishes to obtain more than the usual 14-day order he must also use the prescribed form. He should set out such matters that may assist in Box 10 of the Defence form. The court may only give an extension of time of up to six weeks and even then only in exceptional circumstances so it is important to set out full details of the matters relied upon (see further para.26.007 below).

Subsequent procedure—reference to a judge

26.004 The procedure after the claim has been issued and the defence served on the defendant is set out in rr.15 and 16 of CPR r.55—see para.26.010. Essentially, the position is as follows:

- If the defendant does not serve his defence within 14 days of service the claimant may file a request for an order for possession and the court will refer the request to a judge.

- If the defendant serves a defence within the 14-day period the defence will be sent to the claimant and the claim and defence will be referred to a judge.

- Where a defence is filed outside the 14-day period but before the claimant files a request the defence will be sent to the claimant and the claim and defence will be referred to a judge.

- Where a defence is served but the claimant does not file a request for an order for possession within three months after expiry of the 14-day period for service of the defence the claim will be stayed.

If the claim is referred to a judge he or she will decide whether:

- to make an order for possession without requiring attendance of the parties; or

- where the judge is not satisfied that the claim form was served or that the claimant is not entitled to possession under s.21 of the 1988 Act direct a date to be fixed for a hearing and give appropriate case management directions; or

- if the claim form discloses no reasonable grounds for bringing the claim, strike out the claim.

If the judge is satisfied that the claim form was served on the defendant and that the requirements of s.21 have been satisfied the order for possession must be made, normally to take effect within not more than 14 days, even if the defendant has asked for a longer postponement on the grounds of exceptional hardship (CPR PD 55A para.8.1—see further below).

As a "working rule", where the Defence form, on its face, raises a case that, if **26.005** true, would constitute an arguable defence to the claim, the judge must fix a date for the hearing (*Manel v Memon* [2000] 33 E.G. 74). If the judge does fix a hearing date the parties will be given not less than 14 days' notice of it. Where the claim is struck out the court will give reasons when serving the order and the claimant has 28 days to apply to restore the claim after the order was served upon him.

Fixed costs

Where a possession order is made where the defendant has neither delivered a **26.006** defence, or counterclaim, nor otherwise denied liability the fixed amount recoverable for the claimant's solicitors charges for preparing and filing (a) the claim form, (b) the documents that accompany the claim form, and (c) the request for possession is £79.50 (CPR r.45.4A(2)). The claimant is entitled to this sum in addition to the issue fee (CPR r.45.1(3)).

Postponement of possession order (Practice Direction 55A, paragraphs 8.1 to 8.4)

The usual order for possession is 14 days. The maximum amount of time that can **26.007** be given is six weeks and even then more than 14 days can only be given in exceptional circumstances (s.89 of the Housing Act 1980; para.3.034).

Where the defendant seeks postponement on the ground of exceptional hardship and the judge on the basis of the defence form, is satisfied that the defendant has shown exceptional hardship he may postpone possession without a hearing but only if:

- he considers that possession should be given up six weeks after the date of the order or, if the defendant has requested postponement to an earlier date, on that date; and

- the claimant indicated on his claim form that he would be content for the court to make such an order without a hearing (para.8 of the form—claimants should note that the paragraph is already printed on the form and will need to be deleted if not acceptable).

In any other case, if the defendant seeks a postponement for longer than 14 days, the judge will direct a hearing of that issue (PD 55A para.8.3). If at the hearing the judge is satisfied that an extended order should be granted on the grounds of exceptional hardship he may vary the order to provide for possession to be given up at a later date. However, that later date may be no later than six weeks after the making of the order for possession on the papers (CPR PD 55A para.8.4).

Part 55, Section II—Accelerated Possession Claims of Property Let on an Assured Shorthold Tenancy
When this Section May Be Used

26.008   55.11 (1) The claimant may bring a possession claim under this Section of this Part where—

- (a)   the claim is brought under section 21 of the 1988 Act to recover possession of residential property let under an assured shorthold tenancy; and
- (b)   subject to rule 55.12(2) all the conditions listed in rule 55.12(1) are satisfied.

(2) The claim must be started in the county court for the district in which the property is situated.

(3) In this Section of this Part, a "demoted assured shorthold tenancy; means a demoted tenancy where the landlord is a registered social landlord.

(By virtue of section 20B of the 1988 Act, a demoted assured shorthold tenancy is an assured shorthold tenancy.)

Conditions

55.12 The conditions referred to in rule 55.11(1)(b) are that—

- (a)   the tenancy and any agreement for the tenancy were entered into on or after January 15, 1989;
- (b)   the only purpose of the claim is to recover possession of the property and no other claim is made;
- (c)   the tenancy did not immediately follow an assured tenancy which was not an assured shorthold tenancy;
- (d)   the tenancy fulfilled the conditions provided by sections 19A or 20(1)(a) to (c) of the 1988 Act;
- (e)   the tenancy—

  - (i)   was the subject of a written agreement;

  - (ii)   arises by virtue of section 5 of the 1988 Act but follows a tenancy that was the subject of a written agreement; or

  - (iii) relates to the same or substantially the same property let to the same tenant and on the same terms (though not necessarily as to rent or duration) as a tenancy which was the subject of a written agreement; and

- (f)   a notice in accordance with sections 21(1) or 21(4) of the 1988 Act was given to the tenant in writing.

(2) If the tenancy is a demoted shorthold tenancy, only the conditions in paragraph (1)(b) and (f) need be satisfied.

Claim Form

55.13 (1) The claim form must—

(a) be in the form set out in Practice Direction 55A; and
(b) (i) contain such information; and
     (ii) be accompanied by such documents, as are required by that form.

(2) All relevant sections of the form must be completed.
(3) The court will serve the claim form by first class post (or an alternative service which provides for delivery on the next working day).

Defence

55.14 (1) A defendant who wishes to—   **26.009**

(a) oppose the claim; or
(b) seek a postponement of possession in accordance with rule 55.18,

must file his defence within 14 days after service of the claim form.
(2) The defence should be in the form set out in Practice Direction 55A.

Claim Referred to Judge

55.15 (1) On receipt of the defence the court will—

(a) send a copy to the claimant; and
(b) refer the claim and defence to a judge.

(2) Where the period set out in rule 55.14 has expired without the defendant filing a defence—

(a) the claimant may file a written request for an order for possession; and
(b) the court will refer that request to a judge.

(3) Where the defence is received after the period set out in rule 55.14 has expired but before a request is filed in accordance with paragraph (2), paragraph (1) will still apply.
(4) Where—

(a) the period set out in rule 55.14 has expired without the defendant filing a defence; and
(b) the claimant has not made a request for an order for possession under para.(2) within three months after the expiry of the period set out in rule 55.14,

the claim will be stayed.

Consideration of the Claim

55.16 (1) After considering the claim and any defence, the judge will—   **26.010**

(a) make an order for possession under rule 55.17;
(b) where he is not satisfied as to any of the matters set out in paragraph (2)—

(i) direct that a date be fixed for a hearing; and

  (ii) give any appropriate case management directions; or

 (c) strike out the claim if the claim form discloses no reasonable grounds for bringing the claim.

(2) The matters referred to in paragraph (1)(b) are that—

 (a) the claim form was served; and

 (b) the claimant has established that he is entitled to recover possession under section 21 of the 1988 Act against the defendant.

(3) The court will give all parties not less than 14 days' notice of a hearing fixed under paragraph (1)(b)(i).

(4) Where a claim is struck out under paragraph (1)(c)—

 (a) the court will serve its reasons for striking out the claim with the order; and

 (b) the claimant may apply to restore the claim within 28 days after the date the order was served on him.

Possession Order

55.17 Except where rules 55.16(1)(b) or (c) apply, the judge will make an order for possession without requiring the attendance of the parties.

Postponement of Possession

26.011 55.18 (1) Where the defendant seeks postponement of possession on the ground of exceptional hardship under section 89 of the Housing Act 1980, the judge may direct a hearing of that issue.

(2) Where the judge directs a hearing under paragraph (1)—

 (a) the hearing must be held before the date on which possession is to be given up; and

 (b) the judge will direct how many days' notice the parties must be given of that hearing.

(3) Where the judge is satisfied, on a hearing directed under paragraph (1), that exceptional hardship would be caused by requiring possession to be given up by the date in the order of possession, he may vary the date on which possession must be given up.

Application to Set Aside or Vary

55.19 The court may

 (a) on application by a party within 14 days of service of the order; or

 (b) of its own initiative,

set aside or vary any order made under rule 55.17.

Practice Direction 55A, Section II—Accelerated possession claims of property let on an assured shorthold tenancy—CPR r.55.18 Postponement of possession

26.012 8.1 If the judge is satisfied as to the matters set out in rule 55.16(2), he will make an order for possession in accordance with rule 55.17, whether or not the defendant seeks a postponement of possession on the ground of exceptional hardship under section 89 of the Housing Act 1980.

8.2 In a claim in which the judge is satisfied that the defendant has shown exceptional hardship, he will only postpone possession without directing a hearing under rule 55.18(1) if—

(1) he considers that possession should be given up six weeks after the date of the order or, if the defendant has requested postponement to an earlier date, on that date; and

(2) the claimant indicated on his claim form that he would be content for the court to make such an order without a hearing.

8.3 In all other cases if the defendant seeks a postponement of possession under section 89 of the Housing Act 1980, the judge will direct a hearing under rule 55.18(1).

8.4 If, at that hearing, the judge is satisfied that exceptional hardship would be caused by requiring possession to be given up by the date in the order of possession, he may vary that order under rule 55.18(3) so that possession is to be given up at a later date. That later date may be no later than six weeks after the making of the order for possession on the papers (see section 89 of the Housing Act 1980).

Form 32: N5B Claim form for possession of property (accelerated procedure)

If you are a registered social landlord or a private registered provider of social housing claiming possession of premises let under a demoted assured shorthold tenancy, you should complete **only** sections 1 and 5 to 9.

1. The claimant seeks an order that the defendant(s) give possession of:
(If the premises of which you seek possession are part of a building identify the part eg. Flat 3, Rooms 6 and 7)

Postcode

('the premises') which is ☐ a dwelling house ☐ part of a dwellinghouse

Is it a demoted tenancy? ☐ Yes ☐ No

If Yes, complete the following:

On the ☐☐/☐☐/☐☐☐☐ , the _____ County Court

made a demotion order. A copy of the most recent (assured) (secure) tenancy agreement marked 'A' and a copy of the demotion order marked 'B' is attached to this claim form. The defendant was previously (an assured) (a secure) tenant.

2. On the ☐☐/☐☐/☐☐☐☐ , the claimant entered into a written tenancy agreement with the defendant(s).

A copy of it, marked 'A' is attached to this claim form. The tenancy did not immediately follow an assured tenancy which was not an assured shorthold tenancy.

[One or more subsequent written tenancy agreements have been entered into. A copy of the most recent one, made on ☐☐/☐☐/☐☐☐☐ , marked 'A1', is also attached to this claim form.]

3. Both the [first] tenancy and the agreement for it were made on or after 28 February 1997.
   a) No notice was served on the defendant stating that the tenancy would not be, or continue to be, an assured shorthold tenancy.
   b) There is no provision in the tenancy agreement which states that it is not an assured shorthold tenancy.
   c) The 'agricultural worker condition' defined in Schedule 3 to the Housing Act 1988 is not fulfilled with respect to the property.

   (or)

   Both the [first] tenancy and the agreement for it were made on or after 15 January 1989.

   a) The [first] tenancy agreement was for a fixed term of not less than six months.

   b) There was no power for the landlord to end the tenancy earlier than six months after it began.

   c) On the ☐☐/☐☐/☐☐☐☐ (before the tenancy began) a notice in writing, stating that the tenancy was to be an assured shorthold tenancy, was served on the defendant(s). It was served by:

   d) Attached to this claim form is a copy of that notice marked 'B' [and proof of service marked 'B1'].

4. Whenever a new tenancy agreement has replaced the first tenancy agreement or has replaced a replacement tenancy agreement,
   a) has it been of the same, or substantially the same, premises? ☐ Yes ☐ No ☐ N/A
   b) was the landlord and tenant the same people at the start of the replacement tenancy as the landlord and tenant at the end of the tenancy which it replaced? ☐ Yes ☐ No ☐ N/A

5. On the ☐☐/☐☐/☐☐☐☐ , a notice in writing, saying that possession of the premises was required, was served upon the defendant(s). It was served by:

The notice expired on the ☐☐/☐☐/☐☐☐☐

Attached to this claim form is a copy of that notice marked 'C' [and proof of service marked 'C1'].

6. Is the property part of a house in multiple occupation? ☐ Yes ☐ No

If Yes, complete the following:

(a) The property is part of a house in multiple occupation and is required to be licensed under part 2 of the Housing Act 2004 and has a valid licence.

The licence was issued by [   ] on ☐☐/☐☐/☐☐☐☐
(name of authority)

If the licence application is outstanding with the local housing authority, evidence of the application should be attached to this claim form marked 'D'.

Is the property required to be licensed under Part 3 of the Housing Act 2004? ☐ Yes ☐ No

If Yes, complete the following:

(b) The property is licensed under part 3 of the Housing Act.

The licence was issued by [   ] on ☐☐/☐☐/☐☐☐☐
(name of authority)

If the licence application is outstanding with the local housing authority, evidence of the application should be attached to this claim form marked 'E'.

7. The following section must be completed in all cases

(a) was a money deposit received on or after 6 April 2007? ☐ Yes ☐ No

If Yes, at the date of service of the Section 21 Notice:

(i) The deposit was held under a Tenancy Deposit Scheme (TDS) authorised under

Part 6 of the Housing Act 2004. My reference number is [   ]

(ii) The initial requirements of the TDS had been complied with in relation to the deposit.

(iii)The claimant had given the defendant and anyone who paid the deposit on behalf of the defendant the prescribed information in relation to the deposit and the operation of the TDS.

(b) Did the claimant received a deposit in the form of property on or after 6 April 2007? ☐ Yes ☐ No

If Yes, at the date of service of the section 21 Notice that property had been returned to the person from whom it was received.

8. If the defendant(s) seek(s) postponement of possession on the grounds of exceptional hardship, is the claimant content that the request be considered without a hearing? ☐ Yes ☐ No

9. The claimant asks the court to order that the defendant(s)

☐ deliver up possession of the property.

☐ to pay the costs of this claim.

Proceedings for contempt of court may be brought against a person who makes or causes to be made, a false statement in a document verified by a statement of truth.

Statement of Truth

*(I believe)(The claimant believes) that the facts stated in this claim form (and any attached sheets) are true.

* I am duly authorised by the claimant to sign this statement.

Signed

Date

(Claimant)(Litigation friend(where claimant is a child or a protected party)*)(Claimant's solicitor)

*delete as appropriate

Full name

Name of claimant's solicitor's firm

Position or office held
(if signing on behalf of firm or company)

Claimant's or claimant's solicitor's address to which documents should be sent if different from that on the front page.

Postcode

If applicable	
Ref. no	
Fax no.	
DX no.	
e-mail	
Tel. no.	

CERTIFICATE OF SERVICE (completed on court copy only)

I certify that the claim form of which this is a true copy was served by me on

by posting it to the defendant(s) on

at the address stated on the first page of the claim form.

OR

The claim form has not been served for the following reasons:

Officer of the Court

You may qualify for assistance from Community Legal Service Fund (CLSF) to meet some or all of your legal costs. Ask about the CLSF at any county court office or any information or help point which displays this logo.

Community Legal Service

Returning the forms

Send your completed form and other documents to the court office at

Telephone:

Fax:

Please address all correspondence to 'The Court Manager'.

Form 33: Defence form (accelerated procedure)

Click here to reset form	Click here to print form

Defence form
(accelerated possession procedure)
(assured shorthold tenancy)

Name of court	Claim No.
Name of Claimant	
Name of Defendant(s)	

To the Defendant

Please read the claim form and all papers delivered with it before completing this form.

Some of the questions in this form refer to numbered sections in the claim form. You will find it helpful to have that open as you answer them.

Please note that if section 1 of the claim form has been completed because you are a tenant of premises let under a demoted assured shorthold tenancy, you need only answer questions 1 and 6 to 11.

If you cannot give exact dates, make it clear that the dates given are approximate.

In all cases you **must** complete and sign the statement of truth.

Please write clearly and in black ink. If there is not enough room for an answer, continue on the last page.

1. Are you the tenant(s) named in the tenancy agreement, marked 'A' (or 'A1'), attached to the claim form? ☐ Yes ☐ No

   Does that tenancy agreement (or do both) set out the present terms of your tenancy (except for any changes in the rent or the length of the tenancy)? ☐ Yes ☐ No

   If No, say what terms have changed and what the changes are:

2. Do you agree the date, in section 2 of the claim form, when the claimant says the tenancy began? ☐ Yes ☐ No

   If No, on what date did it begin? [D D / M M / Y Y Y Y]

3. If the claimant has completed section 3 of the claim form, do you agree with what is said there? ☐ Yes ☐ No

   If No, what do you disagree with and why?

4. If the claimant has completed section 3 of the claim form, did you receive the notice (a copy of which is attached to the claim form and marked 'B') and, if so, when? ☐ Yes ☐ No

If Yes, please give date [D][D]/[M][M]/[Y][Y][Y][Y]

Do you agree with the rest of what is said in section 3? ☐ Yes ☐ No

If No, what do you disagree with and why?

5. If the claimant has not deleted section 4 of the claim form, do you agree that what is said there is correct? ☐ Yes ☐ No

If No, what do you disagree with and why?

6. Did you receive the notice referred to in section 5 of the claim form, (a copy of which is attached to the claim form and marked 'C')? ☐ Yes ☐ No

If Yes, please give date [D][D]/[M][M]/[Y][Y][Y][Y]

7. Do you agree that what is said in section 6 of the claim form is correct? ☐ Yes ☐ No

8. Do you agree that what is said in section 7 of the claim form is correct? ☐ Yes ☐ No

If No, what do you disagree with and why?

9. If there is some other reason, not covered above, why you say the claimant is not entitled to recover possession of the property, please explain it here.

Postponement of possession

10. Are you asking the court, if it makes a possession order, to allow you longer than 14 days to leave the premises because you would suffer exceptional hardship?   ☐ Yes   ☐ No

If Yes, please explain why the hardship you would suffer would be exceptional.

Say how long you wish to be allowed to remain in the premises. up to _____ 20____
(The court cannot allow more than 42 days after the order is made.)

Payment of costs

11. If the court orders you to pay the claimant's costs, do you ask it to allow you more than 14 days to pay?   ☐ Yes   ☐ No

If Yes, give details of your means *(continue onto last page if necessary)*

Statement of Truth

*(I believe)(The defendant(s) believe(s)) that the facts stated in this claim form (and any attached sheets) are true.

* I am duly authorised by the defendant(s) to sign this statement.

Signed _____   Date [D][D]/[M][M]/[Y][Y][Y][Y]

(Defendant)(Litigation friend(where claimant is a child or a protected party)*)(Defendant's solicitor)

*delete as appropriate

Defendant's date of birth [D][D]/[M][M]/[Y][Y][Y][Y]

Full name _____

Name of defendant's solicitor's firm _____

Position or office held
(if signing on behalf of firm or company) _____

Defendant's or defendant's solicitor's address to which documents should be sent.		*If applicable*	
		Ref. no	
		Fax no.	
		DX no.	
		e-mail	
Postcode ☐☐☐☐ ☐☐☐		Tel. no.	

Claim No.

Additional Information

(Include the number of the section which is being continued or to which the information relates)

Signed _____ Date ☐D ☐D / ☐M ☐M / ☐Y ☐Y ☐Y ☐Y

(Continue on a separate sheet if necessary, remembering to sign and date it and heading it with the Claim Number)

Chapter 27

Evidence

Documentary evidence in possession actions

Proof of title

It will rarely be necessary for a landlord or licensor to prove actual title to the land **27.001** as the tenant or licensee will be estopped from denying his title (see paras 1.008 and 5.016). Where the occupiers of the land are alleged to be trespassers (see Ch.31) the claimant will have to prove title. Section 67 of the Land Registration Act 2002 provides that an official copy of a land registration document is admissible in evidence to the same extent as the original. If it is not possible to prove title by means of such a document evidence of prior possession is evidence of a right to possession: *Alan Wibberley v Insley* [1999] 2 All E.R. 897 HL per Lord Hoffmann at 901B.

Production of originals: the lease

The general rule is that a party seeking to rely upon the contents of a document **27.002** such as a lease must produce the original. Although the relationship of landlord and tenant may be proved by evidence other than a lease (for example by evidence of the payment of rent), it is not possible to give evidence of the terms of the lease without producing the actual document (*Augestien v Challis* (1847) 1 Exch 279). If the landlord wishes to rely upon its terms it is the counterpart signed by the lessee which is regarded as the original (even where the lease has been assigned) and which the landlord must produce. If the tenant wishes to rely upon the terms of the lease he must produce the part signed by the landlord (*Roe d. West v Davis* (1806) 7 East 363). As to photocopies see para.27.006.

Once disclosure has taken place, a party is deemed to have admitted the authenticity of the documents disclosed unless a notice requiring the document to be proved at trial is served. The notice must be served by the latest of either the date for serving witness statements or within seven days of disclosure (CPR r.32.19). Further, documents contained in an agreed bundle are admissible at the hearing as evidence of their contents unless the court orders otherwise or a party gives written notice of objection to the admissibility of any particular document (CPR PD 32 para.27.2).

If the other party does deny the authenticity of a document it may be proved by **27.003** evidence of someone who saw the document being signed. If no one saw it being signed the signature may be proved by someone who is familiar with the alleged signatory's writing. A signature may also be proved by comparison in which case an expert will have to be called to give evidence.

Prior to December 1, 2003 most tenancy agreements needed to be stamped. A lease is not admissible in evidence if it is required to be but was not properly stamped (s.14 of the Stamp Act 1891). However, the duty and penalty may be paid to an officer of the court. The document will also be admitted in evidence on a solicitor's undertaking to have the court stamped and to pay the penalty. On December 1, 2003 stamp duty was replaced by Stamp Duty Land Tax which is a tax on the transaction rather than a duty as the paper document so that s.14 of the 1891 Act has no relevance to tenancies granted on or after that date.

Notices to quit and other documents in the hands of another party to the action

27.004   In order to be able to rely upon a notice to quit (or other notice served on the tenant) it is not sufficient merely to produce a copy. The landlord must also prove actual service of the original notice at the proper time. The person who effected service should give evidence to that effect, either orally by statement, in the particulars of claim or otherwise, supported by a statement of truth or in the form of a hearsay statement pursuant to the provisions of the Civil Evidence Act 1995 (see below). The person proving service should produce his copy of the notice. If it bears a memorandum of service signed and dated by the tenant service will have been proved to have taken place on that date. If not, the witness should state where, when and how the notice was served upon the tenant. Where the notice was served by post it is not sufficient simply to produce a recorded delivery slip. Who knows what was in the envelope? Evidence should be given as to how the notice came to be posted. Evidence that the notice was sent by post in a properly stamped addressed envelope will be sufficient evidence of service unless the contrary is shown. (See further paras 3.011 and 3.012.)

If a party wishes to rely upon a document that is held by another party an order for specific disclosure can be sought (CPR r.31.12).

Documents in the hands of a person not a party

27.005   If a relevant document is in the hands of a person who is not a party, the party seeking production of it can make an application under CPR r.31.17. An alternative route for production of documents is by way of witness summons under CPR r.34.2. It should be noted that the general rule is that the non-party will get their costs for the application and for complying with any order for disclosure (CPR r.48.1).

Secondary evidence is admissible where the stranger establishes a claim to privilege (*Mills v Oddy* (1834) 6 C & P 728); where the other party has already managed to obtain possession of the document or where the stranger has lost the document.

Documents lost or destroyed

27.006   The party seeking to rely upon the contents of a document may rely upon secondary evidence of the document, either a copy or oral evidence, if the original has been lost or destroyed. Before being allowed to call secondary evidence it will first be necessary to call direct evidence of its existence at an earlier stage and of its destruction. If it has been lost it is necessary to give evidence of where the document was last seen; that a thorough search has been made at the place; and that the search was unsuccessful. If the court allows secondary evidence to be called production of a copy will be allowed if the copy appears to be genuine.

Evidence of facts

The general rule is that any fact required to be proved at the hearing of a claim **27.007** must be proved by the oral evidence of witnesses given in open court (CPR r.32.2). Witness statements shall stand as evidence in chief unless the court orders otherwise (CPR r.32.5(2)). Where a party wishes to adduce hearsay evidence at trial, in most cases the service of the witness statements themselves will be adequate notice of an intention to rely on hearsay evidence. However, if a party will not be calling a witness whose statement is served, then they must notify the other party that the witness will not be called and explain why not (CPR r.33.2).

Where a possession hearing is taking place which has not been allocated to the fast or multi-track or the court has not ordered otherwise, any fact needed to be proved can be proved by witness statement if those statements were filed and served at least two days before the hearing (CPR r.55.8). Therefore, there is no need to serve hearsay notices in these circumstances. This does not prevent the witness statements being updated on matters such as rent arrears either orally or in writing on the day of the hearing (CPR PD 55 para.5.2). However, if the evidence in the witness statement is disputed and the maker does not attend the hearing the court will normally adjourn to allow for cross-examination (CPR PD 55 para.5.4). See also para.25.031.

Nothing in the above rules affects the weight to be attached to any statement contained in any witness statement or the power of the court to refuse to admit the statement in evidence if in the interest of justice the court thinks fit to do so.

Hearsay: Civil Evidence Act 1995

The law in relation to hearsay evidence was substantially altered by the Civil **27.008** Evidence Act 1995. All hearsay evidence is admissible. For the relevant rules see CPR r.33.

As to the proof of statements contained in records of a business and public authority see para.28.020.

Civil Evidence Act 1995 sections 1 to 7, 13

Admissibility of hearsay evidence

1.—(1) In civil proceedings evidence shall not be excluded on the ground that it is **27.009** hearsay.
(2) In this Act—

(a) "hearsay" means a statement made otherwise than by a person while giving oral evidence in the proceedings which is tendered as evidence of the matters stated; and
(b) references to hearsay include hearsay of whatever degree.

(3) Nothing in this Act affects the admissibility of evidence admissible apart from this section.

(4) The provisions of sections 2 to 6 (safeguards and supplementary provisions relating to hearsay evidence) do not apply in relation to hearsay evidence admissible apart from this section, notwithstanding that it may also be admissible by virtue of this section.

Safeguards in relation to hearsay evidence

2.—(1) A party proposing to adduce hearsay evidence in civil proceedings shall, subject to the following provisions of this section, give to the other party or parties to the proceedings—

    (a)   such notice (if any) of that fact; and

    (b)   on request, such particulars of or relating to the evidence,

as is reasonable and practicable in the circumstances for the purpose of enabling him or them to deal with any matters arising from its being hearsay.

(2) Provision may be made by rules of court—

    (a)   specifying classes of proceedings or evidence in relation to which subsection (1) does not apply; and

    (b)   as to the manner in which (including the time within which) the duties imposed by that subsection are to be complied with in the cases where it does apply.

(3) Subsection (1) may also be excluded by agreement of the parties; and compliance with the duty to give notice may in any case be waived by the person to whom notice is required to be given.

(4) A failure to comply with subsection (1), or with rules under subsection (2)(b), does not affect the admissibility of the evidence but may be taken into account by the court—

    (a)   in considering the exercise of its powers with respect to the course of proceedings and costs; and

    (b)   as a matter adversely affecting the weight to be given to the evidence in accordance with section 4.

3. Rules of court may provide that where a party to civil proceedings adduces hearsay evidence of a statement made by a person and does not call that person as a witness, any other party to the proceedings may, with the leave of the court, call that person as a witness and cross-examine him on the statement as if he had been called by the first-mentioned party and as if the hearsay statement were his evidence in chief.

4.—(1) In estimating the weight (if any) to be given to hearsay evidence in civil proceedings the court shall have regard to any circumstances from which any inference can reasonably be drawn as to the reliability or otherwise of the evidence.

(2) Regard may be had, in particular, to the following—

    (a)   whether it would have been reasonable and practicable for the party by whom the evidence was adduced to have produced the maker of the original statement as a witness;

    (b)   whether the original statement was made contemporaneously with the occurrence or existence of the matters stated;

    (c)   whether the evidence involves multiple hearsay;

    (d)   whether any person involved had any motive to conceal or misrepresent matters;

    (e)   whether the original statement was an edited account, or was made in collaboration with another or for a particular purpose;

    (f)   whether the circumstances in which the evidence is adduced as hearsay are such as to suggest an attempt to prevent proper evaluation of its weight.

Supplementary provisions as to hearsay evidence

5.—(1) Hearsay evidence shall not be admitted in civil proceedings if or to the extent **27.010** that it is shown to consist of, or to be proved by means of, a statement made by a person who at the time he made the statement was not competent as a witness.

For this purpose "not competent as a witness" means suffering from such mental or physical infirmity, or lack of understanding, as would render a person incompetent as a witness in civil proceedings; but a child shall be treated as competent as a witness if he satisfies the requirements of section 96(2)(a) and (b) of the Children Act 1989 (conditions for reception of unsworn evidence of child).

(2) Where in civil proceedings hearsay evidence is adduced and the maker of the original statement, or of any statement relied upon to prove another statement, is not called as a witness—

(a) evidence which if he had been so called would be admissible for the purpose of attacking or supporting his credibility as a witness is admissible for that purpose in the proceedings; and

(b) evidence tending to prove that, whether before or after he made the statement, he made any other statement inconsistent with it is admissible for the purpose of showing that he had contradicted himself.

Provided that evidence may not be given of any matter of which, if he had been called as a witness and had denied that matter in cross-examination, evidence could not have been adduced by the cross-examining party.

6.—(1) Subject as follows, the provisions of this Act as to hearsay evidence in civil proceedings apply equally (but with any necessary modifications) in relation to a previous statement made by a person called as a witness in the proceedings.

(2) A party who has called or intends to call a person as a witness in civil proceedings may not in those proceedings adduce evidence of a previous statement made by that person, except—

(a) with the leave of the court; or

(b) for the purpose of rebutting a suggestion that his evidence has been fabricated.

This shall not be construed as preventing a witness statement (that is, a written statement of oral evidence which a party to the proceedings intends to lead) from being adopted by a witness in giving evidence or treated as his evidence.

(3) Where in the case of civil proceedings sections 3, 4 or 5 of the Criminal Procedure Act 1865 applies, which make provision as to—

(a) how far a witness may be discredited by the party producing him;

(b) the proof of contradictory statements made by a witness; and

(c) cross-examination as to previous statements in writing, this Act does not authorise the adducing of evidence of a previous inconsistent or contradictory statement otherwise than in accordance with those sections.

This is without prejudice to any provision made by rules of court under section 3 above (power to call witness for cross-examination on hearsay statement).

(4) Nothing in this Act affects any of the rules of law as to the circumstances in which, where a person called as a witness in civil proceedings is cross-examined on a document used by him to refresh his memory, that document may be made evidence in the proceedings.

(5) Nothing in this section shall be construed as preventing a statement of any **27.011** description referred to above from being admissible by virtue of section 1 as evidence of the matters stated.

7.—(1) The common law rule effectively preserved by section 9(1) and (2)(a) of the Civil Evidence Act 1968 (admissibility of admissions adverse to a party) is superseded by the provisions of this Act.

(2) The common law rules effectively preserved by section 9(1) and (2)(b) to (d) of the Civil Evidence Act 1968, that is, any rule of law whereby in civil proceedings—

(a) published works dealing with matters of a public nature (for example, histories, scientific works, dictionaries and maps) are admissible as evidence of facts of a public nature stated in them;

(b) public documents (for example, public registers, and returns made under public authority with respect to matters of public interest) are admissible as evidence of facts stated in them; or

(c) records (for example, the records of certain courts, treaties, Crown grants, pardons and commissions) are admissible as evidence of facts stated in them,

shall continue to have effect.

(3) The common law rules effectively preserved by section 9(3) and (4) of the Civil Evidence Act 1968, that is, any rule of law whereby in civil proceedings—

(a) evidence of a person's reputation is admissible for the purpose of proving his good or bad character; or

(b) evidence of reputation or family tradition is admissible—

(i) for the purpose of proving or disproving pedigree or the existence of a marriage; or

(ii) for the purpose of proving or disproving the existence of any public or general right or of identifying any person or thing;

shall continue to have effect in so far as they authorise the court to treat such evidence as proving or disproving that matter.

Where any such rule applies, reputation or family tradition shall be treated for the purposes of this Act as a fact and not as a statement or multiplicity of statements about the matter in question.

(4) The words in which a rule of law mentioned in this section is described are intended only to identify the rule and shall not be construed as altering it in any way.

8.—(1) Where a statement contained in a document is admissible as evidence in civil proceedings, it may be proved—

(a) by the production of that document; or

(b) whether or not that document is still in existence, by the production of a copy of that document or of the material part of it, authenticated in such manner as the court may approve.

(2) It is immaterial for this purpose how many removes there are between a copy and the original.

. . .

13. In this Act–

27.012   "civil proceedings" has the meaning given by section 11 and "court" and "rules of court" shall be construed in accordance with that section;

"document" means anything in which information of any description is recorded, and "copy", in relation to a document, means anything onto which information recorded in the document has been copied, by whatever means and whether directly or indirectly;

"hearsay" shall be construed in accordance with section 1(2);

"oral evidence" includes evidence which, by reason of a defect of speech or hearing, a person called as a witness gives in writing or by signs;

"the original statement", in relation to hearsay evidence, means the underlying statement (if any) by—

(a) in the case of evidence of fact, a person having personal knowledge of that fact; or

(b) in the case of evidence of opinion, the person whose opinion it is; and

"statement" means any representation of fact or opinion, however made.

Chapter 28

Rent Cases

The most common ground for possession is that the tenant is in arrears with his **28.001** rent. It is a ground under the Housing Act 1988 (Grounds 8, 10 and 11), the Rent Act 1977 (Case 1), the Housing Act 1985 (Ground 1) and the Rent (Agriculture) Act 1976 (Case III).

Some preliminary considerations

It should be borne in mind that it can take some time between the time a notice is **28.002** served and the time that possession is finally obtained.

Even where an order for possession is made it will (unless Ground 8 of the Housing Act 1988 is relied upon) usually be suspended upon terms that the arrears are paid off by instalments.

It is, of course, better to avoid proceedings altogether. Where the tenant is having difficulty paying the rent, perhaps because he has become unemployed, the landlord could suggest that the tenant apply for housing benefit and that it be paid directly to the landlord (see below). He could also try to reach a compromise:

- the landlord could agree to waive any arrears of rent if the tenant leaves by a specified date;

- the landlord could offer the tenant a sum of money to leave. The tenant will not be bound by any such agreement and so the landlord should ensure that any such payment is made concurrently with the giving up of possession. Where this course is adopted the landlord should attend the premises with a "respectable" witness on the date that the tenant has agreed to give up possession. He should ensure that the tenant clears out all his possessions and that the keys are handed over, at which point the tenant should be paid. It is also suggested that the locks should then be changed (see also "Surrender", Ch.3).

If proceedings need to be taken it is best at an early stage to consider how any money judgment may be enforced. If rent has been paid by cheque details of the tenant's bank account should be noted for potential third party debt orders (CPR r.72). Details of the tenant's employers would enable attachment of earnings proceedings to be taken. This information could be ascertained before the commencement of the tenancy by requiring references.

Rent arrears protocol—social landlords

28.003 Social landlords need to be aware of and follow the "Pre-Action Protocol for Possession Claims Based on Rent Arrears" the full text of which appears below:

Aims and scope of the protocol

   This protocol applies to residential possession claims by social landlords (such as local authorities, Registered Social Landlords and Housing Action Trusts) and private registered providers of social housing which are based solely on claims for rent arrears. The protocol does not apply to claims in respect of long leases or to claims for possession where there is no security of tenure.

   The protocol reflects the guidance on good practice given to social landlords and private registered providers in the collection of rent arrears. It recognises that it is in the interests of both landlords and tenants to ensure that rent is paid promptly and to ensure that difficulties are resolved wherever possible without court proceedings. Its aim is to encourage more pre-action contact between landlords and tenants and to enable court time to be used more effectively.

   Courts should take into account whether this protocol has been followed when considering what orders to make. Registered Social Landlords, private registered providers of social housing and local authorities should also comply with guidance issued from time to time by the Housing Corporation and the Department for Communities and Local Government.

Initial contact

28.004
1. The landlord should contact the tenant as soon as reasonably possible if the tenant falls into arrears to discuss the cause of the arrears, the tenant's financial circumstances, the tenant's entitlement to benefits and repayment of the arrears. Where contact is by letter, the landlord should write separately to each named tenant.

2. The landlord and tenant should try to agree affordable sums for the tenant to pay towards arrears, based upon the tenant's income and expenditure (where such information has been supplied in response to the landlord's enquiries). The landlord should clearly set out in pre-action correspondence any time limits with which the tenant should comply.

3. The landlord should provide, on a quarterly basis, rent statements in a comprehensible format showing rent due and sums received for the past 13 weeks. The landlord should, upon request, provide the tenant with copies of rent statements in a comprehensible format from the date when arrears first arose showing all amounts of rent due, the dates and amounts of all payments made, whether through housing benefit or by the tenant, and a running total of the arrears.

4. (a) If the landlord is aware that the tenant has difficulty in reading or understanding information given, the landlord should take reasonable steps to ensure that the tenant understands any information given. The landlord should be able to demonstrate that reasonable steps have been taken to ensure that the information has been appropriately communicated in ways that the tenant can understand.

   (b) If the landlord is aware that the tenant is under 18 or is particularly vulnerable, the landlord should consider at an early stage—

      (i) whether or not the tenant has the mental capacity to defend possession proceedings and, if not, make an application for the appointment of a litigation friend in accordance with CPR rule 21;

   (ii) whether or not any issues arise under Disability Discrimination Act 1995; and
   (iii) in the case of a local authority landlord, whether or not there is a need for a community care assessment in accordance with National Health Service and Community Care Act 1990.

5. If the tenant meets the appropriate criteria, the landlord should arrange for arrears to be paid by the Department for Work and Pensions from the tenant's benefit.

6. The landlord should offer to assist the tenant in any claim the tenant may have for housing benefit.

7. Possession proceedings for rent arrears should not be started against a tenant who can demonstrate that he has—
   (a) provided the local authority with all the evidence required to process a housing benefit claim;
   (b) a reasonable expectation of eligibility for housing benefit; and
   (c) paid other sums due not covered by housing benefit.

   The landlord should make every effort to establish effective ongoing liaison with housing benefit departments and, with the tenant's consent, make direct contact with the relevant housing benefit department before taking enforcement action.
   The landlord and tenant should work together to resolve any housing benefit problems.

8. Bearing in mind that rent arrears may be part of a general debt problem, the landlord should advise the tenant to seek assistance from CAB, debt advice agencies or other appropriate agencies as soon as possible.

After service of statutory notices

9. After service of a statutory notice but before the issue of proceedings, the landlord should make reasonable attempts to contact the tenant, to discuss the amount of the arrears, the cause of the arrears, repayment of the arrears and the housing benefit position.   **28.005**

10. If the tenant complies with an agreement to pay the current rent and a reasonable amount towards arrears, the landlord should agree to postpone court proceedings so long as the tenant keeps to such agreement. If the tenant ceases to comply with such agreement, the landlord should warn the tenant of the intention to bring proceedings and give the tenant clear time limits within which to comply.

Alternative dispute resolution

11. The parties should consider whether it is possible to resolve the issues between them by discussion and negotiation without recourse to litigation. The parties may be required by the court to provide evidence that alternative means of resolving the dispute were considered. Courts take the view that litigation should be a last resort, and that claims should not be issued prematurely when a settlement is still actively being explored.   **28.006**
   The Legal Services Commission has published a booklet on 'Alternatives to Court', CLS Direct Information Leaflet 23 (http://www.communitylegaladvice. org.uk/en/legalhelp/leaflet23_1.jsp), which lists a number of organisations that provide alternative dispute resolution services.

Court proceedings

12. Not later than ten days before the date set for the hearing, the landlord should—   **28.007**
   (a) provide the tenant with up to date rent statements;

    (b) disclose what knowledge he possesses of the tenant's housing benefit position to the tenant.

13. (a) The landlord should inform the tenant of the date and time of any court hearing and the order applied for. The landlord should advise the tenant to attend the hearing as the tenant's home is at risk. Records of such advice should be kept.

    (b) If the tenant complies with an agreement made after the issue of proceedings to pay the current rent and a reasonable amount towards arrears, the landlord should agree to postpone court proceedings so long as the tenant keeps to such agreement.

    (c) If the tenant ceases to comply with such agreement, the landlord should warn the tenant of the intention to restore the proceedings and give the tenant clear time limits within which to comply.

14. If the landlord unreasonably fails to comply with the terms of the protocol, the court may impose one or more of the following sanctions—

    (a) an order for costs;

    (b) in cases other than those brought solely on mandatory grounds, adjourn, strike out or dismiss claims.

15. If the tenant unreasonably fails to comply with the terms of the protocol, the court may take such failure into account when considering whether it is reasonable to make possession orders.

Landlord and Tenant Act 1987 sections 47 and 48

28.008 The landlord must be careful to ensure that ss.47 and 48 of the Landlord and Tenant Act 1987 have been complied with. (These sections do not apply where a receiver or manager has been appointed by the court to collect the rent/service charges: s.47(3) and s.48(2).) They apply to premises which consist of or include a dwelling and which are not held under a tenancy to which Pt II of the Landlord and Tenant Act 1954 applies. The word "premises" refers to the subject-matter of the letting, so that an agricultural holding which includes a dwelling comes within the ambit of the Act (*Dallhold Estates (UK) Property Ltd v Lindsey Trading Properties Ltd* [1993] E.G.C.S. 195 CA). These sections apply to tenancies created prior to the date upon which they came into force (*Hussain v Singh* [1993] 2 E.G.L.R. 700A).

    Section 47 requires the landlord to state his name and address on any written demand given to the tenant. If that address is not in England and Wales an address in England and Wales at which notices (including notices in proceedings) may be served on the landlord by the tenant must also be stated. "Demand" means "a demand for rent or other sums payable to the landlord under the terms of the tenancy". If the written demand does not contain the required information any part of the amount demanded which consists of a service charge or administration charge is

> "treated for all purposes as not being due from the tenant to the landlord at any time before that information is furnished by the landlord by notice given to the tenant."

The landlord should ensure that the information is given before proceedings are commenced. If he does not do so he will have no cause of action in respect of the service charge or administration charge at that date and will not be able to recover them in the proceedings.

Section 48 of the 1987 Act requires the landlord "by notice" to furnish the **28.009**
tenant with an address in England and Wales at which notices (including notices
in proceedings) may be served on him by the tenant. Where a landlord fails to
comply with this provision

> "any rent service charge or administration charge otherwise due from the tenant to the
> landlord shall . . . be treated for all purposes as not being due from the tenant to the
> landlord at any time before the landlord does not comply"

with this requirement. Once again therefore the landlord must ensure that the
address is given to the tenant before proceedings are commenced in order to
ensure that at that date the landlord has a cause of action (see *Eshelby v Federated
European Bank Ltd* [1932] 1 K.B. 244 for the general principle that it is necessary
to have a cause of action before the commencement of proceedings). However,
note that in *Rogan v Woodfield Building Services Ltd* [1995] 1 E.G.L.R. 72 CA,
where the landlord was a defendant claiming possession by counterclaim in relation to an assured tenancy and the tenant had suffered no injustice because he
clearly knew the name and address of the landlord, the court held that the landlord
could serve a notice after proceedings had commenced and amend his case.

The wording of the notice should follow precisely the wording of the section if
the landlord wishes to avoid any challenges to the validity of the notice. However,
provided that the address given is in England or Wales it will be assumed that this
is the address for service unless the address is stated to be for some other limited
purpose (*Rogan*—the landlord satisfied the requirements of the section where its
name and only address (which was in England) was included in the tenancy agreement without any specific statement that it was an address for service of notices).
Further, an error in completing the notice which could not reasonably have misled
the tenant might be held in appropriate cases not to invalidate the notice (compare
Official Solicitor v Thomas [1986] 2 E.G.L.R. 1 at 6H-H; see also *Marath v
MacGillivray* (1996) 28 H.L.R. 486 CA—information is an invalid notice under
s.20 of the 1988 Act). In *Drew-Morgan v Hamid-Zadeh* (1999) 32 H.L.R. 316 a
document served in compliance with s.21 of the Housing Act 1988 (see para.7.013)
gave the tenant the required information without limitation or qualification and so
was held to be sufficient for the purposes of s.48. However, a name and address in
a possession summons was not sufficient because the information was given
solely for the purposes of those proceedings.

Another consequence of a failure to comply with ss.47 and 48 is that interest **28.010**
will not begin to accrue upon the arrears until the sections have been complied
with. Until they have been complied with there are no arrears.

A statement as to a landlord's name and address in a notice under s.8 of the
Housing Act 1988 in relation to an assured tenancy is not sufficient to validate that
s.8 notice. The s.48 notice must be served prior to the s.8 notice (*Marath v
MacGillivray* (1996) 28 H.L.R. 486 at 493 CA).

The notice must be in writing (*Rogan*).

Landlord and Tenant Act 1987 sections 46, 47 and 48

46.—(1) This part applies to premises which consist of or include a dwelling and are not
held under a tenancy to which Part II of the Landlord and Tenant Act 1954 apply.
(2) In this Part "service charge" has the meaning given by section 18(1) of the
1985 Act.

(3) In this Part "administration charge" has the meaning given by paragraph (1) of Schedule 11 to the Commonhold and Leasehold Reform Act 2002.

47.—(1) Where any written demand is given to a tenant of premises to which this Part applies, the demand must contain the following information, namely—

    (a) the name and address of the landlord; and

    (b) if that address is not in England and Wales, an address in England and Wales at which notices (including notices in proceedings) may be served on the landlord by the tenant.

(2) Where—

    (a) a tenant of any such premises is given such a demand; but

    (b) it does not contain any information required to be contained in it by virtue of subsection (1),

then (subject to subs.(3)) any part of the amount demanded which consists of a service or an administration charge ("the relevant amount") shall be treated for all purposes as not being due from the tenant to the landlord at any time before that information is furnished by the landlord by notice given to the tenant . . . .

(4) In this section "demand" means a demand for rent or other sums payable to the landlord under the terms of the tenancy.

    . . .

48.—(1) A landlord to which this part applies shall by notice furnish the tenant with an address in England and Wales at which notices (including notices in proceedings) may be served on him by the tenant.

(2) Where a landlord to any such premises fails to comply with subsection (1), any rent, service charge or administration charge otherwise due from the tenant to the landlord shall (subject to subsection (3)) be treated for all purposes as not being due from the tenant to the landlord at any time before the landlord shall comply with the subsection.

    . . .

54.—(1) Any notice required or authorised to be served under this Act (a) shall be in writing; and (b) may be sent by post.

    . . .

60.—(1) In this Act—

"landlord" . . . means the immediate landlord or, in relation to a statutory tenant, the person who, apart from the statutory tenancy, would be entitled to possession of the premises subject to the tenancy.

"notices in proceedings" means notices or other documents served in, or in connection with, any legal proceedings.

Insolvency of the tenant

28.010A The making of a bankruptcy order or a debt relief order against a tenant does not prevent the making of an order for possession of a dwelling on the ground of rent arrears. The claim for possession is not a "remedy . . . in respect of that debt" within the meaning of s.285(3)(a) of the Insolvency Act 1986: *Sharples v Places for People Homes Ltd* [2011] EWCA Civ 813. Etherton L.J. at para.63:

"Those cases [discussed in the judgment] seem to me entirely consistent with, and indeed to support, the following general principles applicable to any consideration of the meaning of IA s.285(3)(a). First, the grant of a tenancy, including an assured tenancy, creates a property interest in the tenant which is an encumbrance on the landlord's title. An order for possession is a remedy which restores to the landlord full proprietary rights, including rights of occupation and letting, in respect the property. Secondly, the failure to pay rent is a breach of a contractual obligation. Neither forfeiture, nor a court order for possession, nor recovery of possession by the landlord, nor an order for bankruptcy, eliminates the personal indebtedness constituted by the rent arrears. Thirdly, it follows, as a matter of general principle, that an order for possession of property, whether let under an ordinary contractual tenancy or a secure tenancy or an assured tenancy, is not a remedy "in respect of" the debt represented by the rent arrears which gave the landlord an entitlement to the order for possession. Fourthly, for those reasons, for the purposes of IA s.285(3)(a) there is no analogy of any kind with the test to be applied in respect of the Limitation Acts, as expounded in Ackbar."

(As to suspended orders for possession upon condition as to payment of the rent see para.28.032.)

Terminating the tenancy and commencing proceedings

The methods of determining tenancies and the stage at which proceedings for **28.011** possession should be commenced are dealt with in Pts 1 and 2 of this book. In a Rent Act case where there is a choice between forfeiture and service of a notice to quit it is usually preferable to serve a notice to quit. This avoids the awkward relief provisions in s.138(1) of the County Courts Act 1984. Where the landlord does not really want possession but simply requires the rent to be paid forfeiture is, however, preferable because it avoids having to wait until a notice to quit has expired before proceedings for possession can be commenced.

Proceedings should be commenced by claim form using the procedure under CPR r.55—see generally Ch.25.

Where possession is claimed on the basis of non-payment of rent it is also possible to use the online service known as PCOL—see para.25.021.

Claim form: particulars of claim

See Form 31 on p.361 and paras 25.015 and 25.016.   **28.012**

The tenant's actions on receipt of the claim form

Advice to tenants

The first thing that an advisor to a tenant should do is to check that the landlord **28.013** has complied with the provisions of ss.47 and 48 of the Landlord and Tenant Act 1987 (see above). If he has not done so the tenant will have a complete defence (at least until those provisions have been complied with) to an action for rent and/or service charges.

Where it would appear that the tenant has fallen into arrears because of financial difficulties advise him to make an immediate application for housing benefit unless he has already done so (see para.28.015).

The Court will have sent the tenant a standard form of defence (Form N11R) and this should be completed.

Where the tenant may have some sort of defence or counterclaim his representative should consider whether it is an appropriate case for track allocation, directions, Pt 18 requests (para.25.034) etc. A proper defence and if, appropriate, a counterclaim should be drafted and served (see para.25.025).

Some possible counterclaims are as follows:

(1) that the landlord is in breach of his obligations to repair (see s.11 of the Landlord and Tenant Act 1985 for the statutorily implied obligations where the lease is for a term of less than seven years and *Barrett v Lounova* [1989] 1 All E.R. 351 CA for common law implied terms. For the general principles governing assessment of damages see *Calabar Properties v Stitcher* [1983] 3 All E.R. 759 CA; *Wallace v Manchester City Council* [1998] 3 E.G.L.R. 38 and *Earle v Charalambous* [2006] EWCA Civ 1090—see further under "Set-off", para.28.066);

(2) that the landlord has been harassing the tenant and is therefore liable to pay the tenant damages for breach of covenant for quiet enjoyment (see Ch.35);

(3) recovery of overpaid rent (see s.57(3) of the Rent Act 1977);

(4) recovery of unlawful premiums (see s.125 of the Rent Act 1977) (as to a counterclaim operating as a set-off see para.28.066);

(5) tenancy deposit claims (para.28.063A).

The tenant will not be able to avoid a possession order by making himself bankrupt (or by having a debt relief order made—see further paras 28.010A and 34.006). As the time given for the hearing is usually only about 10 minutes, if the tenant either files a defence and/or counterclaim and/or notifies the court that he has witnesses and/or wishes to cross-examine the landlord it is likely that the matter will be adjourned to a day when the court has sufficient time to hear the case and that directions will be given or the case may be allocated to a track (see para.25.034). However, it should be noted that it is only where the claim is "genuinely disputed on grounds which appear to be substantial" that the case will be allocated (see further para.25.034).

28.014   If the tenant alleges that rent has been paid which the landlord claims has not been paid he should bring evidence to the court to show this, e.g. cheque stubs, bank statements and rent book. Those acting for the tenant should also check that any requisite notice is in the correct form and that proceedings have not been issued before the proper date.

Where the landlord suggests that agreement be reached upon the lines set out in the first part of this chapter (para.28.002) the tenant should bear in mind that any voluntary departure from the dwelling-house will make him "intentionally homeless" and thus ineligible for rehousing by the local authority under Pt VII of the Housing Act 1996. If he is a person with a "priority need" and so eligible for housing he should only agree to such a course of action if he already has other secure accommodation (see further para.25.047).

Housing benefit

28.015   At the time of writing the housing benefit scheme enables those entitled to receive such benefits to have their rent, licence fees or mesne profits, etc. paid by the local authority. The rules governing housing benefit are contained in the Housing Benefit

Regulations 2006 (SI 2006/213). A useful book dealing with the subject is the *Welfare Benefits and Tax Credits Handbook* (London: CPAG (published annually)). Where it is a private sector tenancy the benefit payable is called local housing allowance.

Licensees as well as tenants may apply for housing benefit. Housing benefit is intended to pay for current rent but in exceptional cases the local authority has a discretion to backdate the benefit payments for up to 12 months (reg.83(12)). For example, it may agree to do so where the tenant is in substantial arrears due to illness and/or where the tenant was unaware of his eligibility to receive benefits. A tenant who thinks that he may be entitled to housing benefit must apply directly to the local authority, which is responsible for paying the benefit. Where the tenant is entitled to both income support and housing benefit a claim for both may be made at the same time by completing the necessary forms and sending them to the local DWP office; although he may make the application for housing benefit direct to the local authority if he wishes to do so.

Where the landlord is a local council the benefit takes the form of a rent rebate. In all other cases a payment (known as a rent allowance) is made. Housing benefit/ local housing allowance is usually paid to the tenant (reg.94(1)). However, it must be paid directly to the landlord:

(1) where the tenant is eight weeks or more in arrears with his rent (except where it is in the overriding interest of the tenant not to make direct payments to the landlord); or

(2) where the DWP is paying deductions from income support to the landlord in respect of arrears (see below) (reg.95).

If neither (1) or (2) above apply the payments may nevertheless be made direct to the landlord if:

(3) the tenant has requested or consented to such a payment;

(4) payment to the landlord is in the interest of the claimant and his family; or

(5) the tenant has abandoned the property owing rent arrears (reg.96).

Where the tenant is in receipt of housing benefit (or, in the private sector, local housing allowance) but is not paying it to the landlord, the court may, in order to protect the landlord and to prevent abuse of the housing benefit system, grant an ex parte injunction requiring the tenant to pay the benefit which he is receiving into court pending determination of the landlord's claim for possession (*Berg v Markhill, The Times*, May 10, 1985).

Government plans to introduce a universal credit mean that most of what is written in these paragraphs and below is likely to change during the life of this edition.

Income support

Where a tenant is in arrears for at least eight weeks and the arrears equal or exceed **28.016** four times the weekly rent, the landlord may ask the DWP to deduct a sum from the tenant's entitlement to income support to be paid directly to the landlord. Deductions may also be made if the arrears are for less than eight weeks if the DWP adjudication officer considers that it is in the overriding interests of the tenant or his family for payments to be made directly to the landlord (see para.5(1) of Sch.9 to the Social Security (Claims and Payments) Regulations 1987

(SI 1987/1968)). If, in a claim for possession on the basis of non-payment of rent where the tenant is in receipt of income support, the court makes a postponed order for possession the amount which the tenant is usually ordered to pay towards the arrears of rent is the amount deducted by the DWP and paid to the landlord. This sum is very small. In the year ending April 2012 it was £3.40.

The hearing

28.017 The tenant is usually unrepresented in rent possession claims. In most cases he will not be disputing the fact of the arrears or their amount but will simply be seeking an opportunity to pay them off by instalments and to avoid eviction. The fact that the tenant is unrepresented should not prevent the landlord's representative from talking to him and asking him for his proposals for payment. If the tenant makes an offer to pay off the arrears at a reasonable rate plus the current rent this should be accepted as it is likely that the judge will find such an offer to be reasonable and make a suspended order in any event (unless of course, you have a mandatory ground for possession). Once in court indicate to the judge that the offer has been made and accepted and ask him to make an order for possession suspended upon condition that the payments are made. The agreement will not be binding on the court but the order sought will usually be made after some brief inquiry as to the facts of the case. As to service of evidence prior to the hearing see para.25.031.

As stated above most cases are in the first instance listed for only five or ten minutes in a long possession list. The priority of the judge is to get through that list and he or she will want the key bits of information immediately. So if you are acting for the landlord be prepared to state the following:

- The amount of the arrears at that date. You should have a copy of an up-to-date rent schedule to hand.
- Whether or not an agreement has been reached.
- If there has been an agreement, the terms of the agreement.
- If there is no agreement, the precise terms of the order you are seeking; i.e. an outright order, a suspended order including the amount to be repaid each week or other period.
- A copy of the relevant notice and evidence of service.

Title

28.018 The landlord will not have to prove his title to the land as the tenant will be estopped from denying it (see para.1.008).

Proving the arrears

28.019 Two issues may arise. First, the tenant may deny that the rent is as claimed by the landlord and, second, he may deny the failure to pay. The landlord must satisfy the court on both matters. The basis upon which the amount of rent due is calculated is dealt with in "Calculating the exact amount of rent due" below (para.28.049). Here we are concerned with proof of non-payment. (Note that the landlord must also comply with the provisions of ss.47 and 48 of the Landlord and Tenant Act 1987; see para.28.008.)

Business records

Rent arrears are often proved by the production of business records. These docu- **28.020**
ments are admissible in evidence by virtue of s.9 of the Civil Evidence Act 1995.
The claimant can prove that the document is part of the business records by
producing a certificate to that effect in accordance with s.9(2); although this is
rarely done in practice.

Civil Evidence Act 1995 section 9

(1) A document which is shown to form part of the records of a business or public **28.021**
authority may be received in evidence in civil proceedings without further
proof.

(2) A document shall be taken to form part of the records of a business or public
authority if there is produced to the court a certificate to that effect signed by
an officer of the business or authority to which the records belong.
For this purpose—

    (a) a document purporting to be a certificate signed by an officer of a busi-
ness or public authority shall be deemed to have been duly given by such
an officer and signed by him; and

    (b) a certificate shall be treated as signed by a person if it purports to bear a
facsimile of his signature.

(3) The absence of any entry in the records of a business or public authority may
be proved in civil proceedings by affidavit of an officer of the business or
authority to which the records belong.

(4) In this section—

    "records" means records in whatever form;

    "business" includes any activity regularly carried on over a period of
time, whether for profit or not, by any body (whether corporate or not) or by
an individual;

    "officer" includes any person occupying a responsible position in relation to
the relevant activities of the business or public authority or in relation to its
records; and

    "public authority" includes any public or statutory undertaking, any govern-
ment department and any person holding office under Her Majesty.

(5) The court may, having regard to the circumstances of the case, direct that all
or any of the above provisions of this section do not apply in relation to a
particular document or record, or description of documents or records.

Rent books

The signature of the landlord or his agent in the rent book is evidence of payment **28.022**
by the tenant, but lack of a signature is not of itself evidence of the tenant's failure
to pay. The landlord may have refused to sign.

Some Ground 8 issues

Ground 8 is a mandatory ground for possession of assured tenancies (para.6.025). **28.023**
If the tenant owes at least eight weeks, etc. rent the court must make an order for
possession. A number of issues have arisen in relation to this ground.

Ground 8 of Schedule 2 to the Housing Act 1988

Both at the date of the service of the notice under section 8 of this Act relating to the proceedings for possession and at the date of the hearing—

(a) if rent is payable weekly or fortnightly at least eight weeks rent is unpaid;

(b) if rent is payable monthly, at least two months' rent is unpaid;

(c) if rent is payable quarterly, at least one-quarter's rent is more than three months in arrears; and

(d) if rent is payable yearly, at least three months' rent is more than three months in arrears;

and for the purpose of this ground "rent" means lawfully due from the tenant.

Use of Ground 8 by Social Landlords

28.024 There is sometimes an issue as to whether or not social landlords can use Ground 8 when seeking possession, particularly as Housing Corporation guidance tends to discourage it. This issue is dealt with at para.14.004.

Adjourning Ground 8 claims

28.025 Where the landlord is relying upon Ground 8 and at the date of the hearing there are still at least eight weeks' arrears, the power to adjourn the hearing date for the purpose of enabling the tenant to reduce the arrears to below the Ground 8 threshold may only be exercised in exceptional circumstances. The fact that the arrears are attributable to maladministration on the part of the housing benefit authority is not an exceptional circumstance (*North British Housing Association Ltd v Matthews; London and Quadrant Housing Ltd v Morgan* [2004] EWCA Civ 1736). Dyson L.J.:

"31. Does it follow that it can never be a proper exercise of the court's discretion to grant an adjournment for the purpose of enabling a tenant to reduce the arrears to a figure below the 8 weeks' threshold before the adjourned hearing date? During the course of argument, a number of extreme examples were considered. Suppose the tenant is on his way to court on the hearing date carrying all the arrears of rent in cash in his pocket, and he is robbed and all his money is stolen. Or suppose the tenant is in receipt of housing benefit, and the housing benefit authority has promised to pay all the arrears of housing benefit, but a computer failure prevents it from being able to do so until the day after the hearing date. Examples of this kind can be multiplied.

32. On behalf of the respondents it is submitted that, even in such cases, there is no power to grant an adjournment: the principle that an adjournment may not be granted for the purpose of enabling a tenant to pay off sufficient arrears to defeat the claim for possession is absolute. But the power to adjourn before the court is satisfied that the landlord is entitled to possession has not been abrogated by the Housing Act. Parliament could have insisted that the power to adjourn should never be exercised if the sole reason for the adjournment is to enable the tenant to reduce arrears of rent below the Ground 8 threshold and thereby defeat the claim for possession. It chose not to do so. Subject to the effect of section 9(6), therefore, the jurisdiction to grant adjournments remains. We acknowledge therefore, that, although there are powerful arguments in favour of the absolute principle contended for by the respondents, there may occasionally be circumstances where the refusal of an adjournment would be

considered to be outrageously unjust by any fair-minded person. We hold that the power to adjourn a hearing date for the purpose of enabling a tenant to reduce the arrears to below the Ground 8 threshold may only be exercised in exceptional circumstances. Cases such as those to which we have referred in para.31 above might fall into this category. But the fact that the arrears are attributable to maladministration on the part of the housing benefit authority is not an exceptional circumstance. It is a sad feature of contemporary life that housing benefit problems are widespread. To a substantial extent, these are no doubt the product of lack of resources. But we do not consider that the non-receipt of housing benefit can, of itself, amount to exceptional circumstances which would justify the exercise of the power to adjourn so as to enable the tenant to defeat the claim.

33. We acknowledge that this conclusion will lead to tenants who are in receipt of housing benefit having no defence to a claim for possession in circumstances where they are not at fault. The statutory scheme is, therefore, potentially draconian in its application."

Query where the landlord is a social landlord, whether such an approach would still be correct in light of subsequent decisions in relation to the Human Rights Act 1998 and the European Convention on Human Rights (see further para.23.013).

Payment at the hearing by cheque

What happens if the tenant turns up at court with a cheque for the arrears? Can the judge adjourn the claim to see if the cheque will clear? The basic rule (as with any other debt) is that a landlord is entitled to have the rent paid in cash unless he has expressly or impliedly agreed to accept rent by some other method, such as by cheque. Where a cheque is accepted it operates as a conditional payment from the time when the cheque was delivered (*Homes v Smith* (2000) Lloyds Law Rep. (Banking) 139). And so in *Coltrane v Day* [2003] EWCA Civ 342, [2003] 1 W.L.R. 1379 it was held that: **28.026**

"An uncleared cheque delivered to the landlord or his agent at or before the hearing and which is accepted by him, or which he is bound by earlier agreement to accept, is to be treated as payment at the date of delivery provided the cheque is subsequently paid on first presentation. At the date of the hearing therefore, the judge has jurisdiction to adjourn the claim to see whether the cheque will be paid on the grounds that he cannot at that time be satisfied that the landlord is entitled to possession, though I do not think he would be bound to do so if he had reason to conclude that the cheque would not be paid. In the ordinary way, the adjournment should only be for, say, seven days to enable the cheque to be cleared—the adjournment of 56 days in this case was obviously excessive. If the cheque is not paid at first presentation then the order for possession must be made, the date of the hearing for the purpose of Ground 8 being the earlier hearing and not the adjourned hearing" (Tuckey L.J. at [11]).

But this does not give tenants carte blanche to turn up at court waiving cheques and think that they will always be able to get the matter adjourned:

". . . the decision whether or not to make a possession order or to adjourn will be a judicial decision, taken in the light of the evidence in the particular case. District judges will be entitled on appropriate evidence to be satisfied that the landlord is entitled to possession on Ground 8, and to reject improbable or unscrupulous last minute offers of payment by cheque. The issue is not a particularly complex one. Any tenant who wishes to persuade a judge or district judge to adjourn a Ground 8 claim for possession on the basis that he has paid by cheque will need, as here, to establish that there are funds to meet the cheque, and that it will be honoured on presentation" (Wall L.J., at [25]).

Money paid into court

28.027   In *Etherington v Burt* [2004] EWHC 95 (QB) the claim for possession was based on rent arrears, including reliance on Ground 8. The judge took into account moneys that the tenant had been ordered to pay into court, which brought the sum outstanding below the Ground 8 level for mandatory possession. The landlord appealed but was unsuccessful. Fulford J. at [11], [12] and [19]:

> "11. .. allowance was made for the respondent's compliance with the order of 18 January 2002 that he should pay the sum of £1,100 into court on account of arrears of rent, reducing the overall figure to £469.50, which was self-evidently below the threshold figure of £880 . . .
>
> 12. The appellants' argument is that the court order expressed the payment in as a payment to abide the event, and they submit this means they were not free to take the money out without accepting it in full and final settlement of the proceedings. It is their contention that the judge should not have treated this sum in the same way as if it had been paid over to the appellants, not least, so it is argued, because the money still belonged in reality to the respondent. They liken this sum to a Part 36 payment (offers to settle and payments into court). Accordingly, the appellants submit that in order for money to operate to reduce rent arrears it must be immediately available to the landlord.
>
> 19. In my judgment the appellants are wrong in their submission that only sums already paid over to the landlords should count towards reducing rent arrears, and that any money that the court has ordered should be paid in on account of rent arrears must be ignored. I accept the submissions of the respondent that in this regard the judge exercised his powers under Part 3 rule 1 of the Civil Procedure Rules 1998, and this money was held as a security, 'to abide the event'. As of the date of hearing the sum of £1,100 was available, therefore, in court 'on account of rent arrears', subject only, in reality, to the determination of the counterclaim. Consistent with that interpretation part of the judge's order on 12 June 2002 was that this sum should be paid to the appellants: '3. The money in Court together with any interest be paid out to the Claimant's solicitors.' Accordingly, in my judgment, at the moment the judge made his order and arrived at the final relevant calculation of the figures, the real position was that only the sum of £469.50 was outstanding by way of arrears of rent, and I consider the submission that he should have ignored the £1,100 that he was simultaneously ordering to be paid out in part satisfaction of the arrears would have led to an artificial and inequitable result. I am satisfied that this approach to monies previously ordered to be paid into court on account of rent arrears to abide the determination of a counterclaim, and which are paid out to the landlord as part of the final order of the court made on the relevant day for these purposes (the date of the hearing), is entirely consistent with the objective and the language of Ground 8, namely there must exist eight weeks unpaid rent as 'at the date of the hearing'. In the absence of any authority to the contrary, the judge was right to treat this sum in the way he did, and accordingly I dismiss this ground of appeal".

Different arrears at the hearing

28.028   In some cases the tenant will have reduced the arrears to less than eight weeks after service of the notice but allowed them to accrue by the date of the hearing once more to a sum of at least eight weeks. A considerable amount of time can elapse between service of the notice and the claim and even more before the hearing. However, the wording of Ground 8 would seem to make it clear that the landlord is entitled to possession on that ground in these circumstances.

Disability discrimination

The fact that the tenant has failed to pay his rent because he has a mental disability **28.029** may give rise to a defence under the Equality Act 2010 (see para.24.003) to a claim for possession based upon Ground 8. However, the tenant will have to show that his disability was related to his failure to pay the rent. The following passage of Mummery L.J. in *S v Floyd* [2008] EWCA Civ 201, although made in relation to the Disability Discrimination Act 1995, is still likely to have relevance for discrimination cases:

> "It is not immediately obvious (a) how the 1995 Act could provide a basis for resisting a claim for possession on a *statutory mandatory ground* or (b) how a landlord would be unlawfully discriminating against a disabled tenant by taking steps to enforce his statutory right to a possession order for admitted non-payment of rent for 132 weeks. The 1995 Act was enacted to provide remedies for disabled people at the receiving end of unlawful discrimination. It was not aimed at protecting them from lawful litigation or at supplying them with a defence to breach of a civil law obligation. Like other anti-discrimination legislation, the 1995 Act created statutory causes of action for unlawful discrimination in many areas, such as employment, the provision of goods, facilities and services and the disposal or management of premises, but it did not create any special disability defence to the lawful claims of others, such as a landlord's claim for possession of premises for arrears of rent. The legislation is not about disability per se: it is about unlawful acts of discrimination on a prohibited ground, ie., unjustified less favourable treatment for a reason which relates to the disabled person's disability" (authors' emphasis).

Even if the tenant makes out discrimination the landlord may still be entitled to possession if he can show that the claim is a proportionate means of achieving a legitimate aim (see further para.24.005).

The fact that a person is disabled will, however, of course be relevant where the landlord is relying upon a discretionary ground for possession.

The order; immediate, suspended or postponed

Where the tenancy is assured and the claim is based upon Ground 8 the court will **28.030** have no option but to make an immediate order for possession (see para.6.025).

Where the order is made on a discretionary ground the court has power to suspend or postpone the order (see para.6.029 assured tenancies: para.8.030 Rent Act tenancies and para.10.022 secure tenancies). There will be two issues; (1) is it reasonable to make any order for possession and (2) if so, is it appropriate to exercise the relevant statutory power to suspend or postpone the order and upon what conditions.

Immediate order

Where the arrears are substantial the court's discretion is somewhat limited. **28.031** "Suspension orders should not be made in cases where it is going to involve the payment of arrears over an almost indefinite period" (*Taj v Ali* [2000] 3 E.G.L.R. 35 CA). In that case the arrears were over £14,500 and the tenant was on income support. The judge suspended the order upon payment of the current rent together with £5 per week off the arrears. It would have taken more than 55 years to discharge the debt. The Court of Appeal allowed the landlord's appeal and ordered the tenant to give possession in 28 days. The statutory powers to suspend confer

". . . a wide discretion, but one that must be exercised judicially . . . suspension for an indefinite period, although within the court's jurisdiction, should be ordered only on extremely rare occasions and when very special circumstances exist . . .

To my mind the facts of this case show that the range of choice is severely limited; either there should be no suspension of the order, or suspension on what are bound to be fairly stringent terms, if such terms could be found, in order to enable the arrears to be cleared off within a period that does not stretch into the mists of time" (per Robert Walker L.J.).

The same principles will apply to postponed orders for possession.

Where the landlord is entitled to a mandatory order for possession on Ground 8 but is contemplating agreement to a suspended order he should appreciate that he will not subsequently be allowed to argue, on a further application to suspend, that there is no power to suspend (*Capital Prime Plus Plc v Wills* (1998) 31 H.L.R. 926 CA).

Suspended orders—N28

28.032 The county court form for a *suspended* possession order is N28. Under that order possession is ordered to be given on a certain date but enforcement of the order is suspended so long as the tenant complies with the conditions of the order. The full wording of the relevant part of Form N28 reads as follows:

". . . and the court orders that

1. The defendant give the claimant possession of [address] on or before [date].
2. The defendant pay the claimant £ for arrears of rent.
3. The defendant pay the claimant's costs of the claim of £ . . .
4. The defendant pay the total of £ . . . to the claimant on or before [date].
5. This order is not to be enforced so long as the defendant pays the claimant the rent arrears and the amount for use and occupation [and costs, totalling] £ . . . by the payments set out below in addition to the current rent.

Payments required
[£ . . . on or before and]
£ . . . per [week/month], the first payment being made on or before [date]."

The effect of this order is that the landlord can issue a warrant or breach without first asking the court's permission (para.34.002).

Postponed orders—N28A

28.033 The county court form for a *postponed* order for possession is N28A. The difference between a suspended and a postponed order is as follows. In the case of a suspended order it is not necessary for the landlord to obtain any further court order if the tenant breaches the conditions of the order before requesting the court to issue a warrant for possession (see above). However, where the order is postponed the landlord needs to apply for an order fixing the date for possession (see para.28.034—fixing the date for possession). The form for postponed orders for possession is N28A and is in the following terms:

1. The defendant is to give up possession of [address] to the claimant.
2. The date on which the defendant is to give up possession of the property to the claimant is postponed to a date to be fixed by the court on an application by the claimant.
3. The defendant must pay the claimant £[] for rent arrears and £[] for costs. The total judgment debt is £[] to be paid by instalments as specified in paragraph 4 below.
4. The claimant shall not be entitled to make an application for a date to be fixed for the giving up of possession and the termination of the defendant's tenancy so long as the defendant pays the claimant the current rent together with instalments of £[] per week towards the judgment debt.
5. The first payment of the current rent and the first instalment must be made on or before [date].
6. Any application to fix the date on which the defendant is to give up possession may be determined on the papers without a hearing (unless the district judge considers that such a hearing is necessary).
7. This order shall cease to be enforceable when the total judgment debt is satisfied.

Fixing the date for possession

If the tenant does not pay the sums stated in accordance with the order the land- **28.034**
lord may apply to have a date fixed for possession. The procedure is set out in CPR PD 55 para.10 (see para.28.038). It applies whether the tenancy is a secure or assured tenancy. The key elements are as follows:

- The landlord must give the tenant 14 days' notice of its intention to apply for a possession date and the application must be made with three months. The notice must contain specified information.

- The landlord's application for a possession date is made by filing an application notice in accordance with CPR r.23, including the issue fee but without serving it on the tenant.

- The application will normally be determined, without a hearing, by the district judge fixing possession for the next working day. However, the district judge has power to fix a date for the application to be heard and to direct service of the application notice and supporting evidence on the tenant.

Which order: suspended or postponed?

The courts therefore have a choice between making a standard N28 suspended **28.035**
order, which will fix a date for possession, and the new N28A postponed order, which will not fix a date for possession.

Under the changes made by Sch.11 to the Housing and Regeneration Act 2008 any periodic tenancy (whether assured or secure) will not now come to an end until execution of the order, whether the order is suspended or postponed.

However, that does not necessarily mean that the N28A postponed order is now redundant. Courts still have a choice between a suspended or postponed order. As stated above, the difference between the two is that in the case of a suspended order it is not necessary for the landlord to make a further application to the court before applying for a warrant; whereas in the case of a postponed order it is necessary for the landlord to apply to the court to fix a date for possession—which, as seen above, requires the landlord to give notice to the tenant of its intention to apply for a date for possession to be fixed.

Ex-tolerated trespassers

The provisions of Sch.11 to the 2008 Act (which mean that the tenancy is not terminated until the order for possession is executed) apply to any order for possession made after the coming into force of those provisions. However, there will be many ex-tenants who remain in occupation in respect of whom suspended orders were made prior to the commencement date and who on the face of it are still tolerated trespassers. However, by virtue of Pt 2 of Sch.11 of the 2008 Act most of those persons cease to be tolerated trespassers. The statutory provisions are horrendously complicated. In essence the position is as follows:

- So long as the property is and has been the person's only or principal home since the coming into force of Sch.11 the ex-tenant gets a new tenancy.

- His new tenancy is, substantially, subject to the same terms and conditions as his original tenancy.

- The new tenancy has the same status as the original tenancy. Thus, for example, if the original tenancy was secure then the new tenancy will be secure.

- However, the new tenancy is subject to the possession order (para.20).

- Thus, if the order is a suspended or postponed order the tenant must comply with the terms of the order if he wants to ensure that he remains in possession.

- If he does not comply with the terms of the possession order the landlord may apply for a warrant. When the warrant is executed the new tenancy will come to an end.

Full regard should be had to Sch.11, the full text of which is set out in Appendix 3 of this book.

Postponed/suspended orders—amount to be paid

28.036 The amount that the tenant will be ordered to pay off the arrears depends upon the circumstances of each case but where the tenant is on income support the court will usually order that only the amount that is deductible from that benefit in respect of arrears be paid, £3.40 at the date of writing (see para.28.016).

In a claim based only upon non-payment of rent the court is not allowed to impose an obligation to pay any sum which is neither arrears of rent, future rent or damages for occupation in relation to the property in question (*Raeuchle v*

Laimond Properties Ltd (2001) 33 H.L.R. 10 CA—the judge wrongly took into account damages he awarded for trespass on another room that had been used for storage when deciding how much should be paid as a condition for suspending the order).

Suspended order conditional on payment of rent: insolvent tenant

We have seen that it possible to bring a possession claim against a tenant where **28.036A** bankruptcy order has been made or where there is debt relief order in force (para.28.010A; *Sharples v Places for Peoples Homes*). In that case the court went on to deal with the extent to which the suspension of the order should be conditional on payment of the arrears and future rent. The order should not be conditional upon payment of the *arrears*:

> "It would be contrary to that policy for the same debt to be recovered by court order, even if the form of the order is by way of a condition for suspension of a possession order" (para.81).

However, it should be conditional upon payment of the *future* rent:

> "A suspended order may, and indeed should, be made conditional on the payment of current rent. That does not in any way interfere with the policy of the insolvency legislation as regards past debt (which is subject to a DRO or provable in the bankruptcy), and enables the social landlord, through court order, to control for the future the management of its housing stock in the case of late payers" (para.83).

No order

If the tenant pays or tenders the arrears after the proceedings are begun but before **28.037** the hearing the court is unlikely to make an order for possession, unless the tenant has persistently delayed in paying the rent in which case an order for possession suspended or postponed on condition that the current rent is paid is likely to be made (see in particular Ground 11 in an assured tenancy case).

Where the only reasons for the arrears are problems caused by the local authority in making payments of housing benefit it may not be reasonable to make any order for possession (e.g. see *Brent LBC v Marks* (1988) 31 H.L.R. 343 at 348 CA).

As to further applications to suspend after the order for possession has been made, see para.34.008.

Practice Direction 55 Section IV—Orders Fixing a Date for Possession

10.1 This paragraph applies where the court has made an order postponing the date for **28.038** possession under section 85(2)(b) of the Housing Act 1985 (secure tenancies) or under section 9(2)(b) of the Housing Act 1988 (assured tenancies).

10.2 If the defendant fails to comply with any of the terms of the order which relate to payment, the claimant, after following the procedure set out in paragraph 10.3, may apply for an order fixing the date upon which the defendant has to give up possession of the property. Unless the court further postpones the date for possession, the defendant will be required to give up possession on that date.

10.3 At least 14 days and not more than three months before applying for an order under paragraph 10.2, the claimant must give written notice to the defendant in accordance with paragraph 10.4.

10.4   The notice referred to in paragraph 10.3 must—

(1)   state that the claimant intends to apply for an order fixing the date upon which the defendant is to give up possession of the property;

(2)   record the current arrears and state how the defendant has failed to comply with the order referred to in paragraph 10.1 (by reference to a statement of the rent account enclosed with the notice);

(3)   request that the defendant reply to the claimant within 7 days, agreeing or disputing the stated arrears; and

(4)   inform the defendant of his right to apply to the court—

(a)   for a further postponement of the date for possession; or

(b)   to stay or suspend enforcement.

10.5   In his reply to the notice, the defendant must—

(1)   where he disputes the stated arrears, provide details of payments or credits made;

(2)   where he agrees the stated arrears, explain why payments have not been made.

10.6   An application for an order under paragraph 10.2 must be made by filing an application notice in accordance with Part 23. The application notice must state whether or not there is any outstanding claim by the defendant for housing benefit.

10.7   The claimant must file the following documents with the application notice—

(1)   a copy of the notice referred to in paragraph 10.3;

(2)   a copy of the defendant's reply, if any, to the notice and any relevant subsequent correspondence between the claimant and the defendant;

(3)   a statement of the rent account showing—

(a)   the arrears that have accrued since the first failure to pay in accordance with the order referred to in paragraph 10.2; or

(b)   the arrears that have accrued during the period of two years immediately preceding the date of the application notice, where the first such failure to pay occurs more than two years before that date.

10.8   Rules 23.2.3, 23.2.4 and 23.2.5 (dealing with applications without a hearing), 23.7 (service of a copy of an application notice), and 23.10 (right to set aside or vary an order made without service of the application notice) do not apply to an application under this section.

10.9   On being filed, the application will be referred to the District Judge who—

(1)   will normally determine the application without a hearing by fixing the date for possession as the next working day; but

(2)   if he considers that a hearing is necessary—

(a)   will fix a date for the application to be heard; and

(b)   direct service of the application notice and supporting evidence on the defendant.

10.10 The court does not have jurisdiction to review a decision that it was reasonable to make an order for possession.

Money judgment and rent deposit

28.039 The landlord will usually wish to ask for a judgment for the rent outstanding as well as an order for possession, particularly where an absolute order has been made.

Where a deposit is held in a rent deposit scheme (see para.7.029) the landlord, if he has obtained a money judgment, should also ask the court to make an order that the money may be taken out of the deposit held in the scheme.

Forfeiture cases

In forfeiture claims where the Rent Act 1977 applies the court has to consider both **28.040** s.138 of the County Courts Act 1984 and s.98 of the 1977 Act (*Wolmer Securities v Corn* [1966] 2 Q.B. 243; *Peachey Property Corporation Ltd v Robinson* [1967] 2 Q.B. 243). Where the court considers that the landlord is entitled to possession it must make an order under both Acts. Special forms have therefore been devised to cope with this situation. Form N27(1) applies where the court does not wish to exercise its jurisdiction to make an order for possession under s.98 and N27(2) applies where the court wishes to make an order for possession upon terms as to payment of arrears and current rent. (For the situation in relation to secure tenants see para.10.014 and assured tenants see para.6.015.)

Rent and mesne profits (damages for use and occupation)

Where the landlord proves that the tenant is in arrears with his rent the court will **28.041** give judgment for the amount of arrears even where no order for possession is made. It will also make an order for mesne profits, i.e. for the sum due to the landlord for the period after the tenancy has come to an end until possession is delivered up. The standard form county court orders referred to above contain provisions relating to the "money judgment" and sums for use and occupation. Strictly speaking a statutory tenant under the Rent Act 1977 or an assured or secure tenant is liable to pay the landlord rent rather than mesne profits as he is not a trespasser but continues in occupation by right under the statutory tenancy. The difference is not of any great importance.

Calculation of mesne profits

In order to claim mesne profits it is not necessary to show that the property would **28.042** have been let to another person had the defendant vacated. The amount awarded is usually the same as the amount of rent (*Swordheath Properties Ltd v Tabet* [1979] 1 All E.R. 240):

"... the plaintiff, when he has established that the defendant has remained on as a trespasser in residential property, is entitled, without bringing evidence that he could or would have let the property to someone else in the absence of the trespassing defendant, to have as damages for the trespass the value of the property as it would fairly be calculated; and, in the absence of anything special in the particular case it would be the ordinary letting value of the property that would determine the amount of damages" (*Swordheath Properties Ltd v Tabet* at 242g).

However, the landlord is entitled to the true value of the property. He may therefore claim such sum as he is able to prove is equivalent to a market rent for the property even if this is higher than the rent originally payable (*Clifton Securities v Huntley* [1948] 2 All E.R. 283). And if the tenant wishes to argue that the market value was less than the rent he previously paid he is probably entitled to do so but the burden will be upon him to prove it (*Halsbury's Statutes of England and*

Wales, 4th edn (London: Butterworths, 1985–1992), Vol.27(1), para.258; cited with approval by Lloyd L.J. in *Ministry of Defence v Ashman* [1993] 2 E.G.L.R. 102 CA).

28.043   But it seems that a landlord has a choice between (a) a restitutionary remedy and (b) a claim for damages, and that where he chooses to pursue his restitutionary remedy the sum awarded is equivalent to the amount of the benefit to the defendant, which may not necessarily be the same as the rent he was paying particularly where that rent was a concessionary one. In such a case the amount of rent that he would have been paying for local authority accommodation suitable to his needs may, for example, be equivalent of the value to him. (See *Ministry of Defence v Ashman* [1993] 2 E.G.L.R. 102 CA and *Ministry of Defence v Thompson* [1993] 2 E.G.L.R. 107 CA; servicemen paying concessionary rent required to pay greater sums in respect of mesne profits):

> "The principles in Ashman may, in my judgment, be summarised as follows: first, an owner of land which is occupied without his consent may elect whether to claim damages for the loss which he has been caused or restitution of the value of the benefit which the defendant has received. Second, the fact that the owner, if he had obtained possession, would have let the premises at a concessionary rent, or even would not have let them at all, is irrelevant to the calculation of the benefit for the purposes of a restitutionary claim. What matters is the benefit which the defendant has received. Third, a benefit may be worth less to an involuntary recipient than to one who has a free choice as to whether to remain in occupation or move elsewhere. Fourth, the value of the right of occupation to a former licensee who has occupied at a concessionary rent and who has remained in possession only because she could not be rehoused by the local authority until a possession order has been made would ordinarily be whichever is the higher of the former concessionary rent and what she would have paid for local authority housing suitable for her needs, if she had been rehoused at the time when the notice expired" (per Hoffman L.J. in *Ministry of Defence v Thompson*; but compare the approach adopted by Kennedy L.J. and Lloyd L.J. in *Ashman*).

28.044   In *Viscount Chelsea v Hutchinson* [1994] 43 E.G. 153 CA, the landlord was held to be entitled to mesne profits from the tenant assessed by reference to the letting value of the property even though the flats were sub-let to a long leaseholder. The tenant had argued that they were not therefore available for letting. However, technically the sub-leases came to an end on the forfeiture and could not be restored until a vesting order had been made and even then only from the date of the order. And in *Inverugie Investments Ltd v Hackett* [1995] 3 All E.R. 841 PC, it was held that the claimant was still entitled to recover a reasonable rent for the wrongful use of his property by the defendants even though the claimant might not have suffered any actual loss by being wrongly deprived of his property and the defendants might not have derived any actual benefit from the use of the property (*Swordheath v Tabet and Stoke-on-Trent City Council v W & J Wass Ltd* [1988] 3 All E.R. 394 applied).

Interest

28.045 By virtue of s.69 of the County Courts Act 1984 the landlord is entitled to claim interest on the rent and (it is submitted) mesne profits outstanding. He may also have a right to claim such interest by reason of the tenancy agreement. However, any claim for interest, whether under the Act or the agreement, must be pleaded

(CPR r.16.4(2)). Although note that the pre-printed wording on Form N119 does not allow for a claim for interest, so such a claim should be written in.

The particulars of claim should show the amount of interest claimed and the rate at which it is claimed. The amount of interest awarded is usually the sum payable on judgment debts in the High Court, currently 8 per cent.

Where the claim for interest is made under s.69 of the 1984 Act the court's power to award interest is discretionary but the burden is upon the tenant to show why interest should not be awarded (*Allied London Investments Ltd v Hambro Life Assurance Ltd* (1985) 50 P. & C.R. 207 at 210 CA). It is submitted that the absence of a clause in a written tenancy agreement entitling the landlord to interest is not a good reason for depriving him of interest under s.69 (there was no such clause in the *Allied London* case).

County Courts Act 1984 section 69

69.—(1) Subject to county court rules, in proceedings (whenever instituted) before a **28.046** county court for the recovery of a debt or damages there may be included in any sum for which judgment is given simple interest, at such rate as the court thinks fit or as may be prescribed, on all or any part of the debt or damages in respect of which judgment is given, or payment is made before judgment for all or any part of the period between the date when the cause of action arose and—

    (a)   in the case of any sum paid before judgment, the date of the payment; and

    (b)   in the case of the sum for which the judgment is given, the date of the judgment.

  (2) ...

  (3) Subject to county court rules, where—

    (a)   there are proceedings (whenever instituted) before a county court for the recovery of a debt; and

    (b)   the defendant pays the whole debt to the plaintiff (otherwise than in pursuance of a judgment in the proceedings),

    the defendant shall be liable to pay the plaintiff simple interest, at such rate as the court thinks fit or as may be prescribed, on all or any part of the debt for all or any part of the period between the date when the cause of action arose and the date of the payment.

  (4) Interest in respect of a debt shall not be awarded under this section for a period during which, for whatever reason, interest on the debt already runs.

  (5) Interest under this section may be calculated at different rates in respect of different periods.

  (6) In this section "plaintiff" means the person seeking the debt or damages and "defendant" means the person from whom the plaintiff seeks the debt or damages.

    ...

  (8) In determining whether the amount of any debt or damages exceeds that prescribed by or under any enactment, no account shall be taken of any interest payable by virtue of this section except where express provision to the contrary is made by or under that or any other enactment.

Interest on judgment debts

Although as a general rule a claimant in the county court may recover interest on **28.047** a judgment debt for a sum of not less than £5,000, such interest is not payable where the relevant judgment grants the landlord of a dwelling-house a suspended order for possession (s.74 of the County Courts Act 1984 and the County Court (Interest on Judgment Debts) Order 1991).

Calculating the exact amount of rent due

Payable in arrears or in advance

28.048 Rent is payable in arrears unless there is an express agreement that it should be payable in advance. Where the rent is payable in arrears the landlord is only entitled to rent up until the date the tenancy is determined. If therefore it is determined in the middle of a rent period, it is necessary to calculate, on a daily basis, the proportion of the rent due from the last rent day until the date of determination. Where the rent is payable in advance the landlord is entitled to the whole of the rent that was due on the last rent day before termination even though the tenancy has come to an end in the middle of the rent period (*Ellis v Rowbotham* [1900] 1 Q.B. 740).

Where the landlord forfeits, the date of termination is the date the proceedings are served. Therefore, if the rent was payable in arrears rent is calculated up to the date of service. The landlord is entitled to mesne profits for the period thereafter (*Canas Property Co Ltd v KL Television Services Ltd* [1970] 2 Q.B. 433).

28.049 It is important therefore to ascertain the rent day and to see whether the termination occurred before or after that date. If the rent was payable quarterly the quarters are calculated from the date of the agreement unless the lease states that the rent is to be paid on the usual quarter days, which are:

Lady Day—March 25

Midsummer—June 24

Michaelmas—September 29

Christmas Day—December 25

If the rent is payable in advance the tenant is not liable for the rent unless the tenancy has continued up until the end of the rent day (*Re Aspinall* [1961] Ch. 526).

Local authority rents are usually payable weekly, in advance, each Monday.

Appropriation of payment to specific debt

28.050 Where several distinct debts are owing by a debtor to his creditor, the debtor has the right when he makes a payment to appropriate the money to any of the debts that he pleases, and the creditor is bound if he takes the money, to apply it in the manner directed by the debtor. If the debtor does not make any appropriation at the time when he makes the payment, the right of appropriation devolves on the creditor (see further para.2.055).

Amount of rent: fair rent

28.051 The amount of rent that is due depends upon the terms of the tenancy. Certain tenancies, however, are subject to a limit. Where the tenancy is a protected or statutory tenancy the rent will probably be registered (see Pts IV and VI of the

1977 Act). A registered rent is the maximum rent that can be charged for the premises. It is registered in respect of the property and not the tenancy; so if a tenant goes into possession of premises subject to a registered rent only the amount that is registered is recoverable, whatever the terms of the tenancy (s.44(1), (2) and s.88(1), (2) of the 1977 Act).

Rents in respect of restricted contracts may also be registered (see Pt V of the 1977 Act). (See also s.13 of the Rent (Agriculture) Act 1976 in relation to statutory tenancies under that Act.)

Local housing authority rents should be "reasonable" (see s.24(1) of the Housing Act 1985; and *Belcher v Reading Corporation* [1950] Ch. 380).

Variation of rents

An application can be made to increase the registered rent in respect of a protected **28.052** or statutory tenancy every two years (s.67(3) of the Rent Act 1977). Phasing of rent increases was abolished in respect of rents for regulated tenancies that were registered on or after May 4, 1987 (Rent (Relief from Phasing) Order 1987 (SI 1987/264)). Once the rent has been registered, the landlord must serve a notice of increase in rent if he wishes to recover the higher rent (s.49 of the Rent Act 1977; Rent Act 1977 (Forms, etc.) Regulations 1980 (SI 1980/1697)). If the tenancy is protected it will also be necessary to determine the contractual tenancy before the rent can be increased. In order to deal with this situation without the necessity of also having to serve a notice to quit, s.49(4) of the 1977 Act provides that where a notice of increase is served during a contractual period and the protected tenancy could, by a notice to quit served by the landlord at the same time, be brought to an end before the date specified in the notice of increase, the notice operates to convert the protected tenancy into a statutory tenancy from that date. At the hearing the landlord should prove service of the notice of increase.

An application for an interim increase in rent on account of council tax may be made under s.67A of the Rent Act 1977 or s.13 of the Rent (Agriculture) Act 1976, pending the next full rent registration.

The Rent Acts (Maximum Fair Rent) Order 1999 (SI 1999/6) limits any increase in the fair rent to no more than the increase in the RPI since the last registration, plus 7.5 per cent on the first application after the date of the order, dropping to 5 per cent on any subsequent application (*R. v Secretary of State for Environment, Transport and Regions Ex p. Spath Holme Ltd* [2000] E.G.C.S. 152 HL).

See ss.102 and 103 of the Housing Act 1985 and *Kilby (Maurice) (R. on the application of) v Basildon District Council* [2007] EWCA Civ 479 in respect of secure tenancies (other than where the interest of the landlord belongs to a co-operative housing association: s.109 of the 1985 Act). See s.25 of the 1985 Act where the landlord is a local housing authority but the tenancy is not secure.

Assured tenancies; market rents

There is no provision for variation of rents agreed by landlords and tenants in **28.053** respect of assured tenancies (unless the tenancy is an assured shorthold: s.22 of the 1988 Act). However, the landlord may apply for an increase in rent where (a) the tenant has remained in occupation at the end of a fixed-term tenancy as a statutory periodic tenant, or (b) in the case of any other periodic tenancy which is an assured tenancy except where there is a rent review clause. This exception applies not simply to cases "where the amount of the increase in the rent is set by the tenancy agreement but also in cases where the tenancy agreement merely provides machinery for increasing the rent" (*Contour Homes Ltd v Rowen* [2007] EWCA Civ 842) (s.13(1)).

The rent may be increased at the end of the fixed term and in all other cases annually (s.13(2)). The increase is brought into operation by a notice served by the landlord under s.13 unless the tenant applies to the rent assessment committee within the time-limit prescribed or the parties come to some other agreement (s.13(4)). As from February 11, 2003 s.13 was amended so that landlords can choose a fixed date for future rent increases. See Regulatory Reform (Assured Periodic Tenancies) (Rent Increases) Order 2003 (SI 2003/259) and Assured Tenancies and Agricultural Occupancies (Forms) (Amendment) (England) Regulations 2003 (SI 2003/260); the Assured Tenancies and Agricultural Occupancies (Forms) (Amendment) (Wales) Regulations 2003 (SI 2003/307 (W.46)).

The rent assessment committee determines the rent in accordance with s.14. The obligation in s.14(2)(c) of the 1988 Act to disregard

"any reduction in the value of the dwelling house attributable to a failure by the tenant to comply with any terms of the tenancy"

refers to the present tenant (*N & D (London) Ltd v Gadson* [1992] 1 E.G.L.R. 112; son who succeeded to father's tenancy not affected by father's failure to keep the property in good repair—rent therefore assessed on basis that the property was in bad repair).

Period of the tenant's liability

28.054 The tenant is liable to pay rent from the commencement of the tenancy until its end. An ordinary contractual tenancy comes to an end when the landlord serves forfeiture proceedings upon the tenant, when a notice to quit served upon the tenant has expired, or when a fixed term has expired. Where the tenant remains in possession after termination of the tenancy he is liable to pay the landlord mesne profits. Statutory tenants are not trespassers and so they remain liable to pay rent until the statutory tenancy is brought to an end by order of the court and pay mesne profits thereafter (see also para.28.042). For the position where the tenant abandons/surrenders see "Rent", para.3.030. In *Griffiths v Renfree* (1989) 21 H.L.R. 338 the tenant husband served a notice to quit on his landlord and left but his wife remained in occupation. Held: the tenant continued to be liable for the rent after expiry of the notice to quit until possession was given up. (See also para.21.002.)

Although a tenant is estopped from disputing his landlord's title he is under no obligation to pay the rent after the landlord's title has been determined, even where there is no third party claiming title. The tenant will only be estopped if he continued to pay rent after having knowledge that the landlord's title had come to an end (*National Westminster Bank Ltd v Hart* [1983] Q.B. 773).

Failure by tenant to remove sub-tenant, etc.

28.055 Where a tenancy comes to an end the tenant must give up complete possession. If a sub-tenant (or, presumably, other person who originally entered into occupation under the tenant) remains in occupation the tenant remains liable to pay the rent until possession is delivered up, unless the landlord accepts that person as a new

tenant (*Harding v Crethorn* (1793) 1 Esp 57); even if the occupier remains
in occupation against the wishes of the tenant (*Ibbs v Richardson* (1839) 9 A
& E 849).

> "When a lease is expired, the tenant's responsibility is not at an end; for if the premises
> are in possession of an under-tenant, the landlord may refuse to accept the possession,
> and hold the original lessee liable; for the lessor is entitled to receive the absolute
> possession at the end of the term. But it may be proved, that the lessor had accepted the
> under-tenant as his tenant, as by his having accepted the key from the original lessee,
> while the under-tenant was in possession, by his acceptance of rent from him, or by
> some act tantamount to it" (*Harding v Crethorn*, per Lord Kenyon).

The tenant will not however be liable if the tenant is entitled to remain in occupation by virtue of some right to do so, e.g. under s.137 of the Rent Act 1977
(para.8.037) or s.18 of the Housing Act 1988 (para.6.034).

Assignment by landlord

Where the new landlord has assigned his interest in the property only the new **28.056**
landlord may recover future rent from the date of the assignment, whether the
tenancy was granted before or after the Landlord and Tenant (Covenants) Act
1995 came into force (see generally para.4.003). However, the tenant is not to be
considered to be in breach of covenant to pay rent by failure to pay rent to the new
landlord before notice of the assignment has been given to him; and payment to
the old landlord before that time is a sufficient discharge of the obligation to pay
rent (s.151 of the Law of Property Act 1925).

Law of Property Act 1925 section 151

(1)   Where land is subject to a lease—   **28.057**

    (a)   the conveyance of a reversion in the land expectant on the determination of the
        lease . . .
    (b)   . . . shall be valid without any attornment of the lessee:

    Nothing in this subsection—

    (i)   affects the validity of any payment of rent by the lessee to the person making
        the conveyance or grant before notice of the conveyance or grant is given to
        him by the person entitled thereunder; or
    (ii) renders the lessee liable for any breach of covenant to pay rent, on account of
        his failure to pay rent to the person entitled under the conveyance or grant
        before such notice is given to the lessee.

If the tenant pays the rent before it is due and before that date the landlord assigns
his interest the tenant remains liable to the new landlord for the rent (*De Nicholls
v Saunders* (1870) L.R. 5 C.P. 589 at 594).

    As for the tenant's ability or otherwise to sue, or counterclaim against, the new
landlord in respect of breaches committed by the previous landlord, see para.4.006.

Irrecoverable rent and reductions in rent

The landlord may not recover rent that is more than six years in arrears (s.22 of **28.058**
the Limitation Act 1980).

The landlord is not entitled to recover any rent paid by the tenant to a managing agent whose instructions have been withdrawn, unless he has already informed the tenant of the same.

A landlord's agreement to allow a reduction in rent must be supported by consideration if the tenant is to be able to rely upon it. A threat by the tenant to terminate and leave unless the landlord agrees to a reduction together with the promise to stay if the landlord agrees to a reduction is sufficient consideration. The courts construe the circumstances as a surrender and the grant of a new lease at a lower rent (*Parker v Briggs* (1893) 37 S.J. 452). No consideration for the landlord's promise to accept a lower rent is required if the tenant acts in reliance upon that promise. The landlord will be estopped from recovering the full rent unless he gives the tenant reasonable notice to pay it (*Central London Property Trust Ltd v High Trees House Ltd* [1947] K.B. 130; see also *Brikom Investments Ltd v Carr* [1979] Q.B. 467).

Lost rent

28.059 Where the tenant sends the rent by post he takes the risk and if it is lost will continue to be liable for that amount of the rent unless the parties have expressly or impliedly agreed that payment should be made by posting (*Beevers v Mason* (1979) 37 P. & C.R. 452).

Payment of rent to the landlord by a third party does not discharge the tenant unless the payer was the tenant's agent (*Smith v Cox* [1940] 2 K.B. 558). If the payer had no authority at the time of the payment the tenant can later ratify.

Rent books

28.060 Where a tenant has a right to occupy premises as a residence in consideration of a rent payable weekly the landlord must provide the tenant with a rent book or other similar document for use in respect of the premises which contains information specified by statutory instrument (s.4(1) of the Landlord and Tenant Act 1985; Rent Book (Forms of Notice) Regulations 1982 (SI 1982/1474)). Failure to provide such a rent book is an offence but the rent does not thereby become irrecoverable (*Shaw v Groom* [1970] 2 Q.B. 504).

Payment by a surety

28.061 Payment by a surety of the tenant's rent discharges the tenant from liability to pay the rent (*Milverton Group Ltd v Warner World Ltd* [1995] 32 E.G. 70 CA).

Service charges

28.062 The amount of service charges recoverable from the tenant in respect of a flat is limited by ss.18–30 of the Landlord and Tenant Act 1985 (as amended). Note also the provisions of ss.47 and 48 of the 1987 Act (see para.28.008). See further para.2.006 onwards in relation to service charges and forfeiture.

Landlord under no duty to mitigate

28.063 A landlord's claim for rent is a debt claim and not a claim for damages; and there is no duty on the landlord to mitigate by seeking to find a new tenant if the tenant has left during the period of the tenancy with accruing rent arrears (*Reichman v Beveridge* [2006] EWCA Civ 1659). It is only where it would be "wholly unreasonable" to allow an innocent party to enforce its full contractual rights that the court might interfere and it

> "would have to be a most extraordinary case for a tenant to show that the landlord's conduct could properly be characterised in this way"(Lloyd L.J. at para.40).

Further the court held that, in order to establish such a claim against the landlord the tenant would also have to show that damages would be an adequate alternative remedy. This would not be the case in a rent arrears matter as should the landlord take back the premises and then be unable to re-let at the full rental level under the old lease, he would not be able to recover damages to compensate for the difference between the two rental levels.

Set-off

Tenancy Deposit Claims

There are two common types of set-off pleaded by tenants in claims for possession based upon arrears of rent. As well as a set-off for breach of the landlord's repairing covenant (dealt with below), assured tenants are increasingly having recourse to the statutory penalties imposed on landlords for their failure to comply with the tenancy deposit requirements.   **28.063A**

Between April 6, 2007 and April 1, 2012, when the requirements were amended, landlords were faced with a mandatory penalty of three times the deposit for failure to register. The strictures of the legislation were initially cut down by the courts and have now been made more flexible by amendments made to the Housing Act 2004 by the Localism Act 2011.

A landlord who fails to register a deposit (or provide prescribed information) may face a claim by a tenant under s.214 of the Housing Act 2004 for a statutory penalty ranging from the amount of the deposit up to three times the amount of the deposit. Initially the sanction applied only if the landlord had not registered the deposit and provided the information by the time of the hearing (see *Tiensia v Vision Enterprises Limited* [2010] EWCA Civ 1224, which meant that landlords could defeat proceedings that had commenced by subsequently registering the deposit and providing the information). However, the amendments provide a strict application of the sanction in cases where the deposit is not registered and the information is not provided within 30 days of receipt. The quid pro quo being that the landlord now has longer to comply and the courts have a discretion as to the amount of penalty. The authors acknowledge that there has been some debate on the application of the amendments in the letters pages of the Landlord and Tenant Review (2012 16(3), 119–123).

Disrepair

This is not the place to consider in any detail claims by tenants for disrepair but it should be noted that a claim by a tenant is most likely to arise under s.11 of the Landlord and Tenant Act 1985. Where the tenant has a claim in respect of disrepair he may wish to try to set off his claim against the landlord's claim for rent and   **28.064** thus defeat or at least make more difficult the landlord's claim for possession based upon arrears.

Where the landlord is in breach of his covenant to repair the dwelling-house and the tenant has carried out the repairs himself, the tenant may have a right at common law to set off the cost of repairs. If he has not actually carried out the repairs the set-off will not arise at common law but equity may allow him to set off any claim for damages that he might have had against the rent. Although most of the cases are concerned with a landlord's failure to repair equity will permit the tenant to set off any other claims for damages that he has against the rent due. If the set-off is equal to or greater than the amount of rent claimed, the landlord will have lost the ground upon which he claims possession (for an example, see *Televantos v McCulloch* [1991] 1 E.G.L.R. 123 CA; tenant successfully resisted a claim for possession based upon non-payment of rent by setting off a counter-claim for damages for failure to repair).

The common law and equitable principles are discussed in *Lee-Parker v Izzet* [1971] 1 W.L.R. 1688 and *British Anzani v International Marine* [1979] 2 All E.R. 1063.

Common law

28.065   "There are at least two sets of circumstances in which at common law there can be a set-off against rent, one where the tenant expends money on repairs to the demised premises which the landlord has covenanted to carry out, but in breach has failed to do so (at any rate where the breach significantly affects the use of the premises), and the other where the tenant has paid the money at the request of the landlord in respect of some obligation of the landlord connected with the land demised. To this proposition must be added two riders. First, that as the landlord's obligation to repair premises demised does not arise until the tenant has notified him of want of repair, such notification must be given before the set-off can arise; and secondly that the set-off must be for a sum which has actually been paid and in addition its quantum has either been acknowledged by the landlord or in some other way can no longer be disputed by him, as, for instance, if it is the subject of an award on a submission to arbitration" (*British Anzani* per Forbes L.J. at 1070).

In *Lee-Parker v Izzet* Goff L.J. had said that he considered that the full amount of expenditure properly incurred could be set off against the rent and that it was a question of fact in each case whether and to what extent the expenditure was proper. Forbes J. takes a slightly narrower view:

"My view is that the right is slightly more restricted, namely that it can only be exercised when the sum is certain and its amount cannot really be disputed by the landlord. . . . It seems the quantum of the sum must have been either unchallenged or unchallengeable before it could be regarded as deductible" (see at 1070f).

Tenants should, therefore, be careful before rushing out and spending large sums of money on repairs, with a view to then withholding rent. They must try to make sure that the amount "cannot really be disputed by the landlord". It will usually be better to seek an order under s.17 of the Landlord and Tenant Act 1985 for specific performance of the repairing covenant.

If the tenant is permitted to deduct the sums expended he may do so from future rent (*Lee Parker v Izzet*) or from arrears of rent (*Asco Developments Ltd v Gordon* (1978) 248 E.G. 683).

Equity

Where the tenant does not actually expend sums on having the repairs carried out **28.066** he cannot set off the sum which it would have cost against the rent and, contrary to popular belief, he cannot simply stop paying rent until the repairs are carried out (*Taylor v Webb* [1937] 2 K.B. 283). He may, however, set off a sum equal to the amount of damages to which he is entitled for breach of the landlord's covenant to repair (*British Anzani v International Marine* [1979] 2 All E.R. 1063 at 1074c) and, if there is a reasonable prospect of the tenant's counterclaim matching or exceeding the landlord's claim, the tenant may be granted a stay of the claim for possession until the hearing of the counterclaim (*Haringey LBC v Stewart* [1991] 2 E.G.L.R. 252 at 253B). As the tenant is not spending the money on repairs the sum awarded will not be the cost of repair. The basis upon which damages for breach of a landlord's repairing covenant are assessed has been explained in *Calabar Properties v Stitcher* [1983] 3 All E.R. 759 CA:

> "The object of awarding damages against a landlord is not to punish the landlord but, so far as money can, to restore the tenant to the position he would have been in had there been no breach. This object will not be achieved by applying one set of rules to all cases regardless of the particular circumstances of the case. The facts of each case must be looked at carefully to see what damage the tenant has suffered and how he may be fairly compensated by a monetary award" (per Griffiths L.J. at 768f).

Where repairs are eventually carried out the tenant is entitled to damages under three heads: (a) the cost of alternative accommodation while the works are being earned out; (b) the cost of redecorating; and (c) "some award for all the unpleasantness of living in the [dwelling] as it deteriorated until it became uninhabitable" (per Griffiths L.J. at 768j). If the tenant has rented the property to let it out and the landlord is aware of this the tenant may be entitled to his loss of rent if he cannot let it because of the breach (per Griffiths L.J. at 770a). See further *Wallace v Manchester City Council* [1998] EWCA Civ 1166; *Shine v English Churches Housing Group* [2004] EWCA Civ 434; *Earle v Charalambous* [2006] EWCA Civ 1090.

As stated above, the right of set-off in equity is not limited to repair cases but may arise whenever the tenant has a claim for damages against the landlord, but only so long as the counterclaim arises out of the tenancy or a transaction closely connected to the tenancy (*British Anzani*).

Notice of want of repair

The landlord's obligation to start carrying out works of repair to the demised **28.067** premises does not arise until he has notice of the work of repair (*O'Brien v Robinson* [1973] 1 All E.R. 583 HL). It is therefore imperative that the tenant give the landlord such notice. However, it is sufficient notice if the landlord actually receives the relevant information from a person other than the tenant (*Dinefwr Borough Council v Jones* [1987] 2 E.G.L.R. 58 CA).

It is not necessary to give notice of repairs required to parts retained by the landlord (*Duke of Westminster v Guild* [1984] 3 All E.R. 144 at 152h; *Loria v Hammer* [1989] 2 E.G.L.R. 249 at 258L).

(For the possibility that the courts may re-appraise the notice requirement in a suitable case see *Earle v Charalambous* [2006] EWCA Civ 1090—"addendum to judgment".)

Excluding the tenant's right to set off

28.068 Many leases seek to prevent the tenant from deducting sums from the rent by stating that it must be paid "without deductions". However, these words will not normally be sufficient to exclude the equitable right to set off. Clear words are required (*Connaught Restaurants Ltd v Indoor Leisure Ltd* [1993] E.G.C.S. 143 CA). In *Edlington Properties Ltd v JH Fenner & Co Ltd* [2006] EWCA Civ 403 Neuberger L.J. said that:

> "... the effect of the decision ... in Connaught was almost this: that at least in the absence of any clear indication to the contrary in the lease, a covenant or other provision relating to the payment of rent will not exclude the tenant's normal right to claim equitable set-off, save where the word 'set-off' is specifically used" (at [75]).

If the words are sufficiently clear the Unfair Contracts Term Act 1977 does not apply (*Electricity Supply Nominees v IAF Group* [1993] 3 All E.R. 372; *Unchained Growth III Plc v Granby* [1999] L. & T.R. 186 CA). However, the Unfair Terms in Consumer Contracts Regulations 1999 will normally apply to residential tenancy agreements (*London Borough of Newham v Khatun* [2004] EWCA Civ 55). Further, see para.1(b) of Sch.2 to the Regulations which deals with set-off provisions in general and the Office of Fair Trading, *Guidance on Unfair Terms in Tenancy Agreements* (The Stationery Office, November 2001).

Failure of tenant's counterclaim

28.069 "In ordinary circumstances it will not be reasonable to make a possession order if the tenant has made arrangements in the event of failure of his counterclaim to clear the arrears by an anticipatory payment into court (to give one example), or by setting aside funds which can be devoted for that purpose (to give another example) or, at the very least, to put forward proposals for an early discharge of the arrears.

If he is able to take those steps towards satisfying the proper demands of the lessor for payment of rent it will, in general, be unreasonable for an order to be made against him. In exceptional cases, however, as for example where the tenant has already a very poor record for persistent late payment of rent, the ordinary benevolent course will not be followed, and the making of an order would be regarded as reasonable upon the ground that the tenant has disqualified himself from the court's sympathy by the persistency of his past defaults ..." (*Haringey LBC v Stewart* [1991] 2 E.G.L.R. 252 CA, per Waite L.J. at 253B).

Chapter 29

Anti-social behaviour

This book is about possession claims but when one is dealing with anti-social **29.001** behaviour it is not possible to consider the remedy of possession in isolation. Where the tenant is causing nuisance or annoyance to neighbours or others, private sector landlords are confined essentially to the traditional remedy of possession and perhaps in a limited number of cases an injunction for breach of a term of the tenancy.

However in the public sector, landlords have a wide range of remedies that they can call upon, possession being only one. The full range of remedies available is set out below—although not all are available to all public sector landlords:

- Possession—full and suspended orders (para.29.011).

- Injunctions under the Housing Act 1996 including anti-social behaviour injunctions (para.29.020), which need to be distinguished from anti-social behaviour orders.

- Demotion orders—reducing secure or assured tenancies to a "demoted" and less secure status generally for a period of one year (para.29.058).

- Extension of introductory tenancy length by six months—see Ch.12.

- Anti-social behaviour orders in the county court as part of other proceedings (para.29.077), which need to be distinguished from the more common anti-social behaviour order granted in the magistrates' court).

- Secure tenancies—withholding of consent to mutual exchange (para.29.086).

- Suspension of right to buy (para.29.087).

- Family intervention tenancy (para.29.088).

The law was changed substantially by the Anti-social Behaviour Act 2003 and the Housing Act 2004. However, the relevant provisions are not to be found directly in these statutes. Rather, they amend earlier legislation, to which one needs to look, in its amended form, i.e.:

- Housing Act 1985;

- Housing Act 1988;

- Housing Act 1996.

(Local authorities also have specific powers under s.222 of the Local Government Act 1972 to obtain injunctions "for the promotion or protection of the interests of the inhabitants in their area" and this can include injunctions to prevent nuisance. However, in most cases a local authority should seek to restrain anti-social behaviour by use of their anti-social behaviour powers under the Crime and Disorder Act 1998 (ASBOs) rather than under s.222(1)(a) of the Local Government Act 1972 (injunctions). The Crime and Disorder Act 1998 had created a complete code to deal with anti-social behaviour and required evidence to be established on the criminal standard of proof. Even if it was appropriate in such cases to use the 1972 Act, the standard applied should be the criminal standard (*Birmingham City Council v Shafi* [2008] EWCA Civ 1186)).

Possession

29.002 When a court is deciding whether or not to make an order for possession in a nuisance case it must consider four issues:

(1) Is the ground made out?

(2) Is it reasonable to make the order?

(3) Should the order be suspended?

(4) If so, on what conditions?

Grounds

29.003 The relevant anti-social behaviour grounds, depending upon the tenancy, are as follows:

- assured tenancies—Ground 14 of Sch.2 to the Housing Act 1988;
- secure tenants—Ground 2 of Sch.2 to the Housing Act 1985;
- regulated tenants—Case X of Sch.15 to the Rent Act 1977;
- agricultural occupancies—Case X of the Rent (Agriculture) Act 1976.

There are however differences. The grounds provided to landlords of assured and secure tenants are stronger than in the other cases; in particular they allow more readily for possession in cases where the conduct has been committed by a third party. The full grounds in each case are set out in Appendix 2 to this book.

The landlord may rely upon events occurring after service of the proceedings (*Kelsey Housing Association v King* (1996) 28 H.L.R. 270 CA; see further para.6.023).

Nuisance and annoyance

29.004 "Nuisance" is an interference with the ordinary comfort of adjoining occupiers. "Annoyance" is wider and covers anything which an ordinary sensible person would deem to be a disturbance. What would annoy an oversensitive person is unlikely to be sufficient (cf. *Tod-Heatly v Benham* (1889) 40 Ch. D. 80).

Where the tenancy is assured or secure the landlord may rely upon the relevant ground where the

"tenant or a person residing in or visiting the dwelling house has been guilty of conduct causing or likely to cause a nuisance or annoyance to a person residing, visiting or otherwise engaging in a lawful activity in the locality".

Where the tenancy is a Rent Act tenancy only nuisance or annoyance caused by someone "residing" in the premises counts and it is only "nuisance or annoyance to adjoining occupiers" which will allow the landlord to rely upon Case 2. Nuisance caused by a third party visiting but not residing on the premises will not allow the landlord to rely on Case 2 unless the tenant should be, but is not, taking reasonable steps to prevent it (*Commercial General Administration Ltd v Thomsett* (1979) 250 E.G. 547). The term "adjoining occupier" refers to any person whose premises are near enough to be affected by the tenant's conduct at the demised premises. They do not need to be immediately adjacent (*Cobstone Investments Ltd v Maxim* [1984] 2 All E.R. 635).

For an example of a case in which the parents lost their assured tenancy because of the conduct of their son who was living in the premises see *West Kent Housing Association v Davies* (1998) 31 H.L.R. 415 CA. They had not approved of or encouraged his bad behaviour but they had failed to control him. Approval of his conduct was not required to prove the ground. (See also *Newcastle upon Tyne City Council v Morrison* [2000] L. & T.R. 333—a secure tenancy.) However, it will be relevant in deciding whether or not it is reasonable to make the order and whether or not to suspend it (*Portsmouth CC v Bryant* (2000) 32 H.L.R. 906 CA).

Criminal offences

When the tenancy is assured or secure and one is concerned with a criminal **29.005** offence the ground applies where "a person residing or visiting" is a person convicted of using the dwelling-house or allowing it to be used for immoral or illegal purposes. The ground also applies where an offence is committed in, or in the locality of, the dwelling-house (e.g. dealing in drugs on the estate).

Conviction of an offence tried on indictment is proved by production of a certified extract of the court record signed by the clerk or other officer of the Crown Court (s.13 of the Evidence Act 1851). Conviction of an offence tried in a magistrates' court is proved by the record of conviction signed by a magistrate or properly authorised officer (s.18 of the Prevention of Crimes Act 1871).

A possession order can be made on this ground even where the offence was committed prior to the commencement of the tenancy (*Raglan Housing Association Ltd v Fairclough* [2007] EWCA Civ 1087—offences committed when tenant was the tenant of one property in the locality but he was convicted after he was transferred to and became the tenant of the neighbouring subject property).

Tenancy agreement restricting use of grounds

It is possible for a landlord to limit itself by the terms of the tenancy agreement to **29.006** a narrower ground than that stated in the statute. Ground 14 of the Housing Act 1988 provides a ground of possession in respect of assured tenancies where "the tenant or a person residing in or visiting the dwelling house has been guilty of conduct causing or likely to cause a nuisance . . . or has been convicted of . . . an arrestable offence committed in, or in the locality of, the dwelling house".

However, in *Pollards Hill Housing Association v Marsh* [2002] EWCA Civ 199 the tenancy agreement stated: "The following are the only grounds and circumstances in which the association will serve notice and seek to recover possession". One of those circumstances was stated in the following terms:

"You or anyone living in or visiting the premises have been guilty of conduct causing or likely to cause a nuisance . . . or you have been convicted of using the premises for immoral or illegal purposes or of an arrestable offence carried out at or in the locality of the premises" (Ground 14).

The tenant's partner was convicted of a drugs offence, committed at the property. The Court of Appeal held that there was a contractual intention to restrict the rights to apply for possession under Ground 14.

"One could see that a party to a contract of this kind might take the view that it was wider than was necessary and be prepared to limit the use that it could make of that ground".

The landlord could not therefore rely upon Ground 14 as set out in the statute.

Evidence; hearsay

29.007 In order to prove nuisance or annoyance those who have complained of the nuisance or annoyance should be brought to court to give evidence. If they will not attend court, perhaps because they are frightened of the tenant, any letters of complaint that they have written or other records of nuisance may be produced to the court pursuant to the Civil Evidence Act 1995 (see Ch.28). Evidence on oath, however, will obviously be of much greater weight.

In *Solon South West Housing Association Ltd v James* [2004] EWCA Civ 1847 the landlord relied on both oral evidence given at court and hearsay evidence. The judge granted an outright order in a serious case where the family had been terrorising the neighbourhood. The criticism, on appeal, that the judge was wrong to admit the hearsay evidence on the ground that no adequate reason was given for non-attendance of the relevant witness at trial and so that its admission constituted a breach of art.6 of the ECHR was roundly rejected. The reason for not adducing live evidence from the hearsay witnesses was their fear of reprisals. That was clearly a reason that the judge had been entitled to put into the balance in deciding what weight to give to the evidence. In any event, the judge had stated that he took the live evidence as a primary concern and that the hearsay evidence had been consistent with or fitted the pattern of the live evidence.

Where there is a history of allegations between the tenant and the complainant with each side accusing the other of causing the nuisance or annoyance, for example by continually making loud and unwarranted noise, it may be worthwhile the landlord employing an investigator to make an assessment of the situation and then using his evidence at the hearing.

It may be possible to prove nuisance or annoyance without adducing evidence of neighbours. For example, where it is proved that the premises are used for prostitution it will be assumed that a nuisance has been caused (*Frederick Platts Co Ltd v Grigor* [1950] 1 All E.R. 941).

Reasonableness

Whatever the tenancy the court may only make an order for possession if it is **29.008** reasonable to do so. In deciding whether or not it is reasonable to make the order the judge must of course have regard to all relevant factors. Where the tenancy is a secure tenancy or an assured tenancy the court is told by statute that it must consider in particular the following factors when deciding whether or not it is reasonable to make an order for possession:

- the effect of the nuisance or annoyance has had on persons other than the person against whom the order is sought;

- any continuing effect the nuisance or annoyance is likely to have on such persons;

- the effect that the nuisance or annoyance would be likely to have on such persons if the conduct is repeated.

(Section 85A of the 1985 Act and s.9A of the 1988 Act—each introduced by s.16 of the 2003 Act.)

These considerations are of course not new. They appear as important factors in many cases prior to these statutory amendments (for example see the cases cited below under suspended orders). However, they give a clear structure from which the court can work. The focus on the effect on others may also strengthen a landlord's claim for possession where, since proceedings were commenced, the conduct has abated. If the neighbours still live in fear because of the extremity of the pre-proceeding conduct, then it may still be reasonable to grant possession despite there being no recent allegations.

There is a tendency in nuisance cases for advocates to cite other county court **29.009** decisions on similar facts. However, these decisions are not in any sense binding and each case must be decided on its own facts. Whether or not it is reasonable to make an order for possession is a matter for the trial judge and the Court of Appeal will rarely interfere in his decision if the requirements of s.85A of the 1985 Act or s.9A of the 1988 Act have been followed.

A judge who failed to make an order for possession where the defendant was guilty of noise and bad language on the basis that in some areas bad language was common could not reasonably have come to his conclusion. The Court of Appeal substituted a suspended order for possession (*Woking EC v Bistram* (1993) 27 H.L.R. 1 CA). See also *Newcastle upon Tyne City Council v Morrison* [2000] L. & T.R. 333 CA, where the judge's decision, in relation to a secure tenancy, that it was not reasonable to make the order was overturned. There had been a catalogue of quite appalling behaviour over a period of years. The fact that there were other possible remedies was held to be irrelevant. The council should not have been obliged to pursue them.

Although the court always continues to have a discretion, an order for possession will usually be made where the landlord has proved illegal or immoral use (*Yates v Morris* [1951] 1 K.B. 77). In *Bristol City Council v Mousah* [1997] EWCA Civ 1081 it was held that where the premises have been used for a serious criminal offence it will be only in exceptional circumstances that court will not make an order for possession (supply of drugs on the premises). However, the fact that it is reasonable for an order for possession does not mean that the order will not be suspended).

Effect of the ASBO

29.010 In *Knowsley Housing Trust v McMullen* [2006] EWCA Civ 539 the claim for possession was against a tenant because of the behaviour of her son (see para.29.014). Among various other measures that had been taken against him, the son was subject to an anti-social behaviour order ("ASBO"). The tenant's counsel argued that the son's behaviour was effectively controlled by the ASBO so that the judge should not have made the order that he did make. The argument was rejected. A landlord can choose between his different remedies and the mere fact that there is an ASBO in force does not of itself prevent an order from being made. However, it can be a relevant matter when the court is deciding whether it is reasonable to make an order for possession, and whether to suspend it.

Suspended and postponed orders

29.011 Deciding that it is reasonable to make an order for possession is not the end of the matter. The judge must then go on to consider whether or not the order should be suspended. The courts very rarely make postponed orders (para.28.033) rather than suspended orders for possession in anti-social behaviour cases.

However, where a postponed order for possession has been made and subsequently there are disputed allegations of nuisance it is not appropriate to fix a date for possession by way of a summary determination on the papers. (*Wandsworth London Borough Council v Whibley* [2008] EWCA Civ 1259). Where there are issues that needed resolving it is the court's obligation to examine them properly. In this case a summary paper determination was not appropriate. Sedley L.J. at para.12:

> ". . . if, on being notified of the impending application and invited to respond, the defendant remains silent or puts in a plainly spurious or irrelevant response, an order may properly be made summarily. But if, as is more probable in nuisance cases, an issue is raised which is capable of affecting the court's decision, justice will require the defendant to be given an opportunity to put his or her case. The court will of course be astute not to let merely fictitious or obstructive responses impede a summary disposal; but, inconvenient though it will be for the lessor and for a time nightmarish for the neighbours, it is not permissible for a tenant who has a possible tenable answer to lose his or her home unheard. How the evidence is to be taken is governed by principles of law on which it is not necessary to embark here, but which permit the use of hearsay and enable most such hearings to be expeditiously conducted. Everything depends, both in arrears cases and in nuisance cases, on a judicial appraisal of how the issues can be fairly and economically determined."

The court instead of making any order for possession can adjourn the claim on conditions as to the conduct of the tenant for such period as it thinks fit (*Hastoe Housing Association Ltd v Ellis* [2007] EWCA 1238). However, this is only likely to occur where the parties agree to such an order.

In *London Borough of Lambeth v Howard* Sedley L.J. stated that in considering whether or not to make an outright or suspended order for possession, the court (having regard to art.8 of the European Convention Human Rights) should approach the matter in a structured way as follows:

"The question, therefore, is whether the interference is necessary in a democratic society for the protection of the rights and freedoms of others. Necessary in a democratic society does not mean indispensable; nor does it mean desirable. Convention jurisprudence has decided that it means:

(a) that the reasons given to justify the interference must be relevant and sufficient;
(b) that the interference must correspond to a pressing social need; and
(c) that the interference must be proportionate to the aim pursued . . ."

In *Sheffield City Council v Shaw* [2007] EWCA Civ 42 Sedley J. reminded the county courts of what he said in that case and continued as follows:

". . . article 8(2) limits legitimate interference to measures which are not only lawful but are 'necessary in a democratic society', a phrase which the European Court of Human Rights interprets as meaning proportionate. This calls up the kind of structured analysis which is . . . in *Howard*. I will not repeat it. I will simply reiterate that it is not a formal exercise. It is a practical and principled way of reaching a self-explanatory decision about reasonableness."

Offences

In *Greenwich LBC v Grogan* (2001) 33 H.L.R. 12 CA, the order was suspended **29.012** on condition that no further offences were committed. The tenant was a young man (17) convicted of receiving stolen goods worth about £1,200 who was "making an attempt to live a life free of crime".

In *Stonebridge Housing Action Trust v Gabbidon* [2002] All E.R. (D) 326, Ch D; T.L.R. 21 the tenant was in breach of a suspended possession order in that further rent arrears had accrued. He had also allowed the premises to be used for taking drugs. These were serious matters that caused a nuisance and as stated above in *Bristol City Council v Mousah* [1997] EWCA Civ 1081 it had been held that where the premises had been used for a serious criminal offence it would be only in exceptional circumstances that court would not make an order for possession. However, the judge refused to make an immediate order for possession because he was satisfied that T had not been involved personally in drug dealing and that she had a young child. The order was suspended. L's appeal was dismissed.

In *Knowsley Housing Trust v Prescott* [2009] EWHC 924 (QB) it was held that where the tenant had been convicted of drug dealing in the area near to the property a postponed possession order was inappropriate because there was no evidence that his behaviour would abate. An outright order should have been made. Although the Court of Appeal recognised that the decision to grant a postponed or an outright order was a matter of discretion for the judge the appeal by the landlord in this case was allowed. Blair J.:

"In my respectful opinion, the learned judge gave too little weight to the scale of Mr. Prescott's drug dealing, gave too much weight to the fact that it was not happening at the house itself (when it was happening in the near locality), and did not direct himself in accordance with the principle that so far as postponement of possession in such cases is concerned, the court is looking to the future, and thereby erred in principle. Before the judge could contemplate postponing the possession order, there had to be cogent evidence that the course of conduct which gave rise to the convictions would not be repeated, and there was none" (para.27).

Mother and son

29.013 In *New Charter Housing (North) Ltd v Ashcroft* [2004] EWCA Civ 310 the tenant was a secure tenancy. The nuisance was caused by her 17-year-old son. The boy was a considerable nuisance to neighbours over a long period of time and an anti-social behaviour order had been made against him. He was in breach of the order and was made subject of a detention and training order. The judge made a suspended order for possession to give the mother an opportunity to curb the son's behaviour on his release. On appeal by the landlord the Court of Appeal lifted the suspension. On the facts undue weight had been given to the mother's interest over that of the neighbours. She herself had threatened the neighbours and there was no reason to suppose she would or could curb her son's behaviour.

In *Manchester City Council v Higgins* [2005] EWCA Civ 1423 the nuisance was caused by the son of the tenant who was completely out of control and who, in particular, had terrorised a neighbour, a widow with three mentally handicapped children. The mother had shown no remorse and seemed to be completely unappreciative of the effect that her son's behaviour was having on her neighbours. The judge thought it reasonable to make the order but suspended it for 18 months on conditions. The Court of Appeal held on the facts that the judge was wrong to suspend the order for possession, even though it meant that the mother and her three children (including a child suffering from a hole in the heart) lost possession. Ward L.J.:

> ". . . the behaviour of the defendant herself and her children, especially James, was quite intolerable. Absent any expression of remorse or any well founded expectation of improvement it was disproportionate not to make an immediate possession order. The defendant had forfeited her right to respect for her home."

29.014 In *Knowsley Housing Trust v McMullen* [2006] EWCA Civ 539 the mother (tenant) had an IQ of 63, could not read or write beyond the standard of a nine-year-old, was an "immature and vulnerable person who lacks assertiveness skills" and was "unable to discipline or control the actions of her son" who was in his late teens and "of tall and large build". She was found to be a "disabled person" within the meaning of s.22(3)(c) of the Disability Discrimination Act 1995. However, the judge found as a fact that the tenant's inability to control the son was not related to her disability. He decided that it was reasonable to make an order for possession and suspended the order on terms that there were no further acts of nuisance on the part of the tenant or her son. The Court of Appeal upheld the order but with one modification (dealt with in para.28.017). In an earlier case (*Newcastle City Council v Morrison* (2000) 32 H.L.R. 891) Sedley J. had said:

> "It may very well be unreasonable to make even a suspended order against somebody who will be powerless to rectify the situation, *and it will almost certainly be unreasonable to make an outright order against such a person*" (authors' emphasis).

Those acting for tenants frequently latched on to the second part of the sentence in seeking to prevent outright orders. However, this part of the sentence was disapproved of by Neuberger L.J. in McMullen at [28]:

> "I regard the second part of the observation as going further than is justified by principle or authority. It appears to me wrong in principle to rule out an outright order for

possession in a case when the 1988 Act clearly contemplates such an order provided that it is reasonable, especially given that reasonableness turns on the particular facts of each case. . .".

Neuberger L.J. went on to state at [32] and [33]:

"In these circumstances, I reject the contention that, in this case, an order for possession, whether outright or suspended, could, or even should, not have been made as a matter of principle, simply because the tenant could not control the activities of the person in her household responsible for the nuisance. . . . It seems to me that the fact that the tenant cannot control the nuisance-maker is a factor which would normally assist the tenant in resisting an order for possession in relation to *past breaches*, especially where she has done her best to stop the nuisance. However, *unless the nuisance-maker has vacated, or will shortly vacate*, the property, it seems to me to be a factor which may often assist the landlord if he is asking the court to make an outright order for possession or to suspend the order for possession on terms which relate to the behaviour of the nuisance-maker" (authors' emphasis).

Suspension or injunction—loss of right to buy

In *Norwich City Council v Famuyiwa* [2004] EWCA Civ 1770 the judge accepted **29.015** the landlord's case that the tenant's conduct was causing nuisance or annoyance to, and constituted harassment of, her neighbours. However, he reached the conclusion that it would not be reasonable to make an order for possession. He therefore dismissed the claim. He thought that a suspended order would not in practice control the tenant's anti-social behaviour. However, he then went on to grant an injunction restraining the tenant from insulting, abusing, threatening or harassing any person in the neighbourhood. On appeal it was held that it is not right in principle to refuse an order for possession on the grounds that such an order, suspended on conditions, would provide no basis, in practice, for the control of the tenant's anti-social behaviour. The judge overlooked the possibility that, by postponing the date for possession upon appropriate conditions, the situation could be controlled by the court.

One of the factors that influenced the judge was the loss of the right to buy if an order were made. However, on appeal Jacob L.J. made the following points:

"The judge was clearly influenced by the consideration that if a possession order were made the tenant would lose her right to buy. He overlooked the fact that it is possible for the possession order to be discharged or rescinded under section 85(4). But if a suspended order was made her right to buy will also go into suspension. If she behaved she would in due course be able to get the possession order removed and proceed with her right to buy."

Tenant's partner, who caused the trouble, had gone—order not suspended

In *London Quadrant Housing Trust v Root* [2005] EWCA Civ 43 the landlord was **29.016** a housing trust. D1 was one of its tenants in a house on a small estate in a quiet residential neighbourhood. D2 was her partner. The landlord received many complaints from neighbours about the behaviour of D2, who ran a business repairing and scrapping cars from the premises in breach of the agreement.

The housing manager was unable to carry out her work on the property for fear of D2. There were also complaints about the state of the outside of the property which was in a terrible mess as a result of D2's activities. The local authority obtained an interim anti-social behaviour order against D2, who then left the property.

The judge made a final order for possession even though D2 was no longer at the property. He said the court had to balance the needs of D1 and her children against the very considerable hardships to which the neighbours had been exposed. However sympathetic he might be to D1 the neighbours and the landlord's employees had suffered enough. There was a long waiting list of those who wanted this desirable house and would look after it, and no doubt integrate with the rest of the community. D1 appealed arguing that the possession order should have been suspended. The appeal was dismissed. Brooke L.J.:

> "In my judgment, this is a case in which it would not be open to this court to say that this very experienced judge had been wrong in forming the view that it was inappropriate to suspend the possession order. This was a very bad case, and although . . . it was [D2] who caused the case to be so very bad and that to some extent [D1] would have been influenced by his character—and indeed the judge found that she had been subjected to violence—there is a limit to which the courts can be willing to tolerate behaviour of this kind out of the kindness of their hearts to a woman and three children when their neighbours have suffered as much as they have on this occasion, and when right up to the very week before the hearing [D1] was still refusing to allow the landlords in, as they were fully entitled to enter, to inspect the inside of the premises."

Order requiring permission to apply for warrant

29.017 Where an order for possession in a nuisance case is suspended upon condition that no further nuisance takes place, arguments can often arise subsequently as to whether or not the condition has been breached. One method of ensuring that any such dispute has been dealt with before the landlord applies for a warrant is to insert a term in the order that the landlord shall not apply for the warrant without first obtaining the permission of the court. However, the Court of Appeal has disapproved of this practice—at least in most cases (*Knowsley Housing Trust v McMullen* [2006] EWCA Civ 539). There is nothing

> "which forbids a suspended order for possession in any case from requiring the claimant to apply for permission from the court before obtaining a warrant of possession. Each case must turn on its own facts" (Neuberger L.J. at [49]).

However, it should not normally happen. Neuberger L.J. at [65]:

> "Normally, a suspended order for possession should not include a term that the landlord should have to apply to the court for permission before applying for a warrant. However, as I have emphasised more than once, the appropriate order in a particular case must depend on the facts of that case, and, accordingly, in some exceptional cases, such a term may be justified."

In *Knowsley* there were exceptional circumstances requiring such a provision, in particular the circumstances surrounding the tenant's disability (see paras 29.014 and below as to effect of disability in anti-social behaviour cases).

Equality Act 2010

Special considerations apply where the defendant is disabled within the meaning **29.018** of the 2010 Act. Under s.35 of the 2010 Act it is unlawful to discriminate against a disabled person by evicting the disabled person or taking steps to evict them. Discrimination occurs if the landlord treats a tenant less favourably than he would treat others because of the disability (s.13) or he treats the tenant unfavourably because of something arising in consequence of the tenant's disability (s.15). If the landlord discriminates because of s.15, then he will be able to overcome that if the treatment was a proportionate means of achieving a legitimate aim (s.15(1) (b)) (see para.24.005).

Two cases decided under the predecessor to the 2010 Act (the Disability **29.019** Discrimination Act 1995) may have some continuing relevance under the 2010 Act, but should be treated with some caution. (*North Devon Homes v Brazier* [2003] EWHC 574 and *Manchester City Council v Romano* [2004] EWCA Civ 834).

Injunctions under the Housing Act 1996

Introduction

In theory any landlord can apply for an injunction to prevent a breach of a term **29.020** of a tenancy agreement. However, this is a remedy that is rarely pursued. For various reasons standard principles for the grant of injunctions do not seem to be sufficient when applied to anti-social behaviour in the residential tenancy context (e.g. see *Medina Housing Association Ltd v Case* [2002] EWCA Civ 2001). However, as will be seen public sector landlords have greatly enhanced rights under the Housing Act 1996 as amended by the Anti-Social Behaviour Act 2003.

What sort of injunctions may be granted?

There are three types of injunction that may be granted under the Housing Act **29.021** 1996 (as amended by the Anti-social Behaviour Act 2003):

1) anti-social behaviour injunctions (s.153A of the 1996 Act);

2) injunctions against unlawful use of premises (s.153C of the 1996 Act);

3) injunctions against breach of tenancy agreement (s.153D of the 1996 Act).

The phrase "anti-social behaviour injunction" or "ASBI" is often used loosely to describe all three of these injunctions and in many ways they overlap. Strictly speaking only the first is an "ASBI". The collective term for all three used in this chapter is "1996 Act injunction".

Anti-social behaviour injunctions (s.153A)

The landlords who may apply

The following bodies may apply for this type of injunction: **29.022**

- a housing action trust;

- a local authority (within the meaning of the Housing Act 1985);

- a non-profit registered provider of social housing;

- a registered social landlord;

- some charitable housing trusts (see s.153E(8)).

The anti-social behaviour

29.023 The section is designed to deal with and applies to conduct:

- which is capable of causing nuisance or annoyance to any person, and

- which directly or indirectly relates to or affects "the housing management functions of a relevant landlord" (s.153A(1)).

In *Swindon v Redpath* [2009] EWCA Civ 943 it was held that (1) a broad interpretation should be given to the phrase housing-related conduct in s.153A; and (2) that it indicates that it is a part of the housing management functions to preserve the peace in the neighbourhood; and (3) that an individual's conduct should be taken as a whole and not piecemeal. In the case there had been no incidents for a year after the defendant's eviction. However, he then returned to the area and further anti-social behaviour ensued and an ASBI was granted against him. There was a sufficient nexus between the defendant, the area and his behaviour to bring him within s.153A(1); even though he was no longer a tenant.

It does not matter where the conduct occurs. Thus, the conduct could for example take place some way from the home occupied by the tenant against whom the order is sought.

The conditions for the grant of anti-social behaviour injunctions

The court on the application of a relevant landlord may grant an anti-social behaviour injunction if two conditions are satisfied. The first relates to the type of conduct. The second relates to the person affected by the conduct. The two conditions are:

(1) That the person against whom the injunction is sought is engaging, has engaged or threatens to engage in conduct to which the section applies (i.e. the anti-social behaviour described above); and

(2) That the conduct is capable of causing nuisance or annoyance to any of the following persons (s.153A(4)):

    (a) a person with a right (of whatever description) to reside in or occupy housing accommodation owned or managed by the relevant landlord—i.e. the landlord's other tenants and licensees;

    (b) a person with a right (of whatever description) to reside in or occupy other housing accommodation in the neighbourhood of housing accommodation mentioned in (a)—i.e. the neighbours;

    (c) a person engaged in lawful activity in or in the neighbourhood of housing accommodation mentioned in (a)—e.g. the postman, milkman, shopkeeper, indeed just about anyone;

(d) a person employed (whether or not by the relevant landlord) in connection with the exercise of the relevant landlord's housing management functions—e.g. the housing officer.

The person against whom the order is made

It can be seen from the above that the person against whom the injunction may be **29.024** made is not necessarily a tenant of the relevant landlord. It could be anyone, so long as each of the two conditions specified above is satisfied. (As to minors—see below.)

Some definitions

"Housing management functions of a relevant landlord" are defined as including **29.025** (a) functions conferred by or under any enactment and (b) the powers and duties of the landlord as the holder of an estate or interest in housing accommodation (s.153E(11)).

"Housing accommodation" has a wide definition and includes—

- flats, lodging-houses and hostels;

- any yard, garden, outhouses and appurtenances belonging to the accommodation or usually enjoyed with it;

- in relation to a neighbourhood, the whole of the housing accommodation owned or managed by a relevant landlord in the neighbourhood and any common areas used in connection with the accommodation (s.153E(9)).

A landlord owns housing accommodation if he is the freehold owner or has a lease granted for a term of three years or more. (For a more precise definition see s.153E(10).)

The standard order

An anti-social behaviour injunction prohibits the person in respect of whom it is **29.026** granted from engaging in conduct which is capable of causing nuisance or annoyance to any person, and which directly or indirectly relates to or affects "the housing management functions of a relevant landlord" (s.153A(1)).

Exclusion orders

In certain circumstances the court may include in the injunction a provision **29.027** prohibiting the person in respect of whom it is granted from entering or being in:

- any premises specified in the injunction; or

- any area specified in the injunction (s.153C(2)).

Such an order may be made even if it has "the effect of excluding a person from his normal place of residence" (s.153E(2)(b)).

The court may grant either of these orders if:

- the conduct consists of or includes the use or threatened use of violence; or

- there is a significant risk of harm to a person mentioned in s.153A(4) (s.153C(1)). "Harm" includes serious ill-treatment or abuse (whether physical or not) (s.153E(12)).

Drafting the order

29.028 The order must be very carefully drafted. The injunction should be:

- readily understandable by those whose conduct they are intended to restrain;

- leave no doubt as to what can and cannot be done;

- appropriate and proportionate to the facts of the case.

Consideration must also be given to art.8 and art.1 of the First Protocol of the European Convention of Human Rights. The injunction will often relate to the defendant's tenancy (and therefore his property) and to his home.

Under the earlier provisions of the 1996 Act (i.e. before the amendments made by the 2003 Act) the following comments were made in *Manchester City Council v Lee* [2003] EWCA Civ 1256.

> "Careful consideration needs to be given by the court in each case to the scope of the injunction which is justified by the evidence. In the exercise of its discretion the court must ensure that the injunction granted is framed in terms appropriate and proportionate to the facts of the case. Thus, if the judge finds that there is a risk of significant harm to a particular person or persons it would usually be appropriate for the injunction to identify that person or those persons, so that the respondent knows the circumstances in which he might be in breach of the injunction, and liable for contempt of court if he caused a nuisance or annoyance to them in the future.

In order to justify granting a wider injunction against the respondent, restraining him from causing a nuisance or annoyance to, 'a person of a similar description', it would normally be necessary for the judge to make a finding that there had been use or threats of violence to persons of a similar description, and that there was a risk of significant harm to persons of a similar description if an injunction was not granted in respect of them" (Mummery L.J. at [38] and [39]).

> "It cannot be sensible or a proper exercise of the statutory power to grant an injunction in terms which are not readily understandable by those whose conduct they are intended to restrain. Further an injunction which leaves doubt as to what can and cannot be done is not a proper basis for committal proceedings" (Chadwick L.J. at [54]).

Duration of the order

29.029 The order may be made for a specified period or until varied or discharged (s.153E).

Injunction against unlawful use of premises (section 153B)

The landlords who may apply

29.030 The following bodies may apply for this type of injunction:

- a housing action trust;

- a local authority (within the meaning of the Housing Act 1985);

- a non-profit registered provider of social housing;

- a registered social landlord;

- some charitable housing trusts (see s.153E(8)).

The conduct

"This section applies to conduct which consists of or involves using or threatening to **29.031**
use housing accommodation owned or managed by a relevant landlord for an unlawful
purpose" (s.153B(1)).

Thus an injunction can be obtained against unlawful use even if that use is not
causing a nuisance or annoyance, e.g. use of the premises for taking drugs would
not necessarily cause a nuisance or annoyance.

The order

The court may grant an injunction under this section prohibiting the person in **29.032**
respect of whom the injunction is granted from engaging in conduct to which the
section applies, i.e. from using or threatening to use housing accommodation
owned or managed by a relevant landlord for an unlawful purpose.

Exclusion orders

The court may also grant an exclusion order where (a) the conduct consists of or **29.033**
includes the use or threatened use of violence or (b) there is a significant risk of
harm to one of the persons mentioned in s.153A(4) (s.153C).
   Such an order may be made even if it has "the effect of excluding a person from
his normal place of residence" (s.153E(2)(b)).

The person against whom the order is made

Note that as with anti-social behaviour injunctions under s.153A (para.29.018) the **29.034**
person against whom the tenancy is granted is not necessarily the tenant of the
property.

Duration of the order

It may be made for a specified period or until varied or discharged (s.153E).   **29.035**

Injunction against breach of tenancy agreement (section 153D).

Who may make the application?

- a housing action trust;   **29.036**
- a local authority (within the meaning of the Housing Act 1985);
- a non-profit registered provider of social housing;

- a registered social landlord;
- a charitable housing trust which is not a registered social landlord.

(Such a body cannot apply for the first two injunctions mentioned above.)

The tenant

29.037 The main difference between this injunction and the two other injunctions dealt with above is that it may only be made against a tenant.

This section applies if a relevant landlord applies for an injunction against a tenant in respect of the breach or anticipated breach of a tenancy agreement on the grounds that the tenant:

(a) is engaging or threatening to engage in conduct that is capable of causing nuisance or annoyance to any person; or

(b) is allowing, inciting or encouraging any other person to engage or threaten to engage in such conduct.

The phrase "tenancy agreement" is widely defined to include "any agreement for the occupation of residential accommodation owned or managed by a relevant landlord" (s.153D(5)—as to ownership by the relevant landlord see s.153E(10)).

Exclusion orders

29.038 The order may include an exclusion order (from any premises or any area) if the conduct includes the use or threatened use of violence, or there is a significant risk of harm to "any person". The reference to "any person" would in theory seem to be wider than the class of persons listed when one is considering an anti-social behaviour injunction (para.29.021). However, as the list is so extensive it would seem unlikely that the distinction will make any difference in practice.

An exclusion order may be made even if it has "the effect of excluding a person from his normal place of residence" (s.153E(2)(a)).

Duration of the order

29.039 The order may be made for a specified period or until varied or discharged (s.153E).

Interim orders without notice—all Housing Act injunctions

29.040 "If the court thinks it just and convenient it may grant or vary an injunction without the respondent having been given such notice as is otherwise required by rules of court" (s.153E(4)).

If the court does make an interim order without notice

"it must give the person against whom the injunction is made an opportunity to make representations in relation to the injunction as soon as it is practicable for him to do so" (s.153E(5)).

The circumstances in which an exclusion order will be made without notice to the respondent will be very rare. The principles were explained in *Moat Housing Group South Ltd v Harris* [2005] EWCA Civ 287:

"62. It is hard to envisage a more intrusive 'without notice' order than one which requires a mother and her four young children to vacate their home immediately. It is clearly necessary to restate certain principles governing the grant of 'without notice' injunctions, and particularly those of an 'intrusive' nature, that will be very familiar to family law practitioners.

63. As a matter of principle no order should be made in civil or family proceedings without notice to the other side unless there is a very good reason for departing from the general rule that notice must be given. Needless to say, the more intrusive the order, the stronger must be the reasons for the departure. It is one thing to restrain a defendant from what would in any event be anti-social behaviour for a short time until a hearing can be arranged at which both sides can be heard. It is quite another thing to make a 'without notice' order directing defendants to leave their home immediately and banning them from re-entering a large part of the area where they live.

71. It needs to be clearly understood, however, that to grant an injunction without notice is to grant an exceptional remedy. There is a useful discussion of the topic in Zuckerman's Civil Procedure (2003), paras 9.133–9.136, although the author for understandable reasons does not concern himself with the kind of issues relating to personal safety which are of most concern in a family law or ASBI context. He says, correctly, at para.9.133, that:

'Notice of an application for an interim injunction must be given to the respondent as a matter of elementary justice.'

He goes on to cite a passage in the judgment of the High Court of Australia in *Thomas A Edison Ltd v Bock* (1912) . . .:

'There is a primary precept governing the administration of justice, that no man is to be condemned unheard; and therefore, as a general rule, no order should be made to the prejudice of a party unless he has the opportunity of being heard on defence.'

72. It would in our judgment be best if judges in the county courts, when deciding whether to exercise their discretion to make an ASBI without notice, followed the guidance given in section 45(2)(a) of the Family Law Act 1996. They should bear in mind:

(1) that to make an order without notice is to depart from the normal rules as to due process and warrants the existence of exceptional circumstances;
(2) that one such exceptional circumstance is that there is a risk of significant harm to some person or persons attributable to conduct of the defendant if the order is not made immediately;
(3) that the order must not be wider than is necessary and proportionate as a means of avoiding the apprehended harm.

84. We have already concluded that the extent of the injunction was much too wide, and that it ought to have been restricted to what was judged necessary to protect prospective witnesses from acts of violence or threats of violence, and to restrain acts of nuisance. Any question of the appropriateness of an ouster order or an exclusion order should have been reserved to the hearing on notice that was to take place the following week.

85. As to the length of the injunction, it was directed to remain in force for six months unless it was varied or discharged before that time. The district judge did not address this issue at all in her oral judgment, so that we do not know what she had in mind. It is well known, however, that many judges now take the view that a 'without notice' restraining injunction should be made in this type of case for an initial period of (say) six months, provided that they know that a full hearing on notice is shortly to take place at which their initial order may be varied or discharged. This practice has the merit, at a time when the arrangements for drawing up county court orders are not as good as they used

to be, of ensuring that the court's protection will remain in place if there is any risk of delay in drawing up the replacement order. It also saves the time and expense involved in drawing up a new order if it is merely a mirror image of one already in place.

86. So long as the 'without notice' order is of a non-intrusive type (such as a typical non-molestation or non-nuisance order) and the 'on notice' hearing takes place timeously, we can see no harm in this practice. On the present occasion, therefore there would have been nothing objectionable in the district judge making on a 'without notice' basis an injunction of the type set out in paras (2), (3) and (5) of her order (see para 3 above) for an initial period of six months, while at the same time fixing the 'on notice' hearing in six days' time."

Minors

29.041 It is a vexed question whether or not a 1996 Act injunction can or should be granted against a minor. *Enfield LBC v B (A Minor)* [2000] 1 W.L.R. 2259 left open the question in relation to the old provisions under the 1996 Act. In *G v Harrow London Borough Council* [2004] EWHC 17 Roderick Evans J. overturned an injunction against a 17-year-old on the basis that he would be too young to go to prison and there was no other realistic way in which an injunction could be enforced. In *Manchester City Council v Lee* [2003] EWCA Civ 1256 the Court of Appeal left the question open.

Where one is concerned with juveniles it may be more appropriate to make an application for an anti-social behaviour order in the magistrates' court; or if there are already existing proceedings in the county court under s.1B of the Crime and Disorder Act 1998 in those proceedings (but see further below para.29.077).

Procedure

29.042 CPR Pt 8 as modified by CPR r.65.3 and CPR PD 65 applies to an application for a 1996 Act injunction.

The court

29.043 The application can be made to the High Court or the county court (s.153E(6)); but will invariably be made in the county court. The claim must be commenced in the county court for the district in which the defendant resides or the conduct complained of occurred (CPR r.65.3(2)(b)). If the claim is commenced in the wrong court it is treated as an error of procedure that may be corrected (CPR r.3.10). The court staff should not refuse to the issue of the claim (*Gwynedd County Court v Grunshaw* [2000] 1 W.L.R. 494 CA). The judge however may order that the claim:

- be transferred to the county court in which it ought to have been started;
- continue in the county court in which it has been started; or
- be struck out (CPR r.30.2(3)).

The judge

29.044 In the county court circuit judges and district judges (including deputy district judges) have jurisdiction to hear applications for 1996 Act injunctions (CPR PD

2B para.8.1). They may also commit for breaches of 1996 Act injunctions (CPR PD 2B para.8.3; s.158 of the 1996 Act).

Starting the claim

The application must be made using Form N16A (i.e. the general form for an **29.045** application for an injunction). This is treated as the Pt 8 claim form (CPR PD 65 para.1.1) and must be supported by a witness statement which must be filed with the claim form (CPR r.65.3(2)(c)).

Under the rules (CPR r.65.3(3) incorporating r.8.2) the claim form must state the following:

- the fact that the claim is being made under the Housing Act 1996—specify the relevant sections of the Act in the space at the top of the form;

- that Pt 8 applies—tick the box at the top of the form;

- the terms of the injunction applied for—careful consideration should be given to the precise wording of the injunction sought—see below;

- the legal basis for the remedy sought—there is in fact no space for further information on N16A. However, the legal basis will be apparent from the section numbers specified and the contents of the witness statement.

Wherever possible the claimant should also file with the application notice a draft of the order sought preferably with a disk containing the draft in a format the court uses (CPR PD 25 para.2.4). If it is not possible to file the draft order with the application it is very bad practice not to have a draft order ready for the court by the time of the hearing. Careful consideration should be given to the precise wording of the injunction sought.

On notice applications; acknowledgement of service

If the application is made on notice it must be served, together with a copy **29.046** of the witness statement, by the claimant on the defendant personally (CPR r.65.3(5)).

The defendant must file an acknowledgement of service not more than 14 days after service of the claim form and serve it on the claimant. The acknowledgement must state whether the defendant contests the claim (CPR r.8.3).

Where the defendant fails to file an acknowledgement of service and the time for doing so has expired the defendant may attend the hearing of the claim but may not take part in the hearing unless the court gives permission (CPR r.8.4). However, it would seem highly unlikely that the court would ever refuse to give permission, especially if the defendant is unrepresented.

Short service

As stated above the defendant under Pt 8 must file the acknowledgement not more **29.047** than 14 days after service of the claim form. However, there will be many cases where the landlord will not want to wait that long before obtaining an injunction under the 1996 Act. The rules therefore provide that an application made on notice can be listed for a hearing before the expiry of the time for the defendant to file an acknowledgement of service has passed. In such a case:

- the claimant must serve the application notice and witness statement on the defendant not less than two days before the hearing; and

- the defendant may take part in the hearing whether or not he has filed an acknowledgement of service (CPR r.65.3(6)).

Without notice

29.048 In some cases the matter will be so urgent that the landlord will wish to apply for an injunction without notice. The circumstances in which such an injunction is likely to be ordered is set out above (para.29.034). If the application is made without notice the witness statement in support of the application must state the reasons why the notice has not been given (CPR r.65.3(4)(a)). Where an application is made without notice Pt 8 is modified so that:

- the defendant does not need to acknowledge service;

- it is not necessary to serve the claimant's evidence on the defendant and the normal rules about serving evidence in CPR r.8.5(2)–(6) and r.8.6(1) do not apply;

- CPR r.8.7, which relates to Pt 20 claims does not apply;

- the defendant cannot object to the use of the Pt 8 procedure under CPR r.8.8.

Variation or discharge

29.049 Either the person in respect of whom the injunction is made or the relevant landlord may apply to vary or discharge the injunction (s.153E(3)). The application should be made under Pt 23.

Power of arrest

Orders made on notice

29.050 The court may attach a power of arrest to an anti-social behaviour injunction (para.29.022) or an unlawful use injunction (para.29.030) if:

- the conduct consists of or includes the use or threatened use of violence; or

- there is a significant risk of harm to a person mentioned in s.153A(4), i.e. other tenants, neighbours, postmen, etc. housing officers, etc. (s.153C(1)— see para.29.023).

A power of arrest may also be attached to a breach of tenancy injunction if:

- the conduct includes the use or threatened use of violence; or

- there is a significant risk of harm to "any person". (The reference to "any person" would in theory seem to be wider than the class of persons listed when one is considering an anti-social behaviour injunction or an injunction against unlawful use of the premises. However, whether in practice this distinction will make any difference is not clear.)

Harm includes serious ill-treatment or abuse (whether physical or not).

The power of arrest may be added to specific clauses. It does not need to be attached to all the restrictions in the order.

Orders made without notice

When deciding whether or not to attach a power of arrest to an application made **29.051** without notice the court must have regard to the following factors:

- whether it is likely that the applicant will be deterred or prevented from seeking the exercise of the power of arrest if the power is not exercised immediately; and

- whether there is reason to believe that the respondent is aware of the proceedings for an injunction but is deliberately evading service and that the applicant or any one of the persons described in s.153A(4) will be seriously prejudiced if the decision as to whether to exercise the power were delayed until substituted service is effected (s.154(1)).

If the court does attach a power of arrest to a without notice injunction it must give the respondent an opportunity to make representations relating to the exercise the power as soon as just and convenient at a hearing of which notice has been given to all the parties in accordance with rules of court (s.154(2)).

Form of order

There is a specific form that is completed where a power of arrest is attached to some **29.052** or all of the provisions of the injunction—Form 110A—so that it can be delivered to the police (see immediately below). This should only contain those provisions—not any other provision of the injunction to which no power of arrest is attached.

Delivery of order to the police

Where the injunction contains one or more provisions to which a power of arrest **29.053** is attached "each relevant provision must be set out in a separate paragraph of the injunction" (which is sensible practice in any injunction) and "the claimant must deliver a copy of the relevant provisions to any police station for the area where the conduct occurred" (CPR r.65.4(2)), i.e. using Form 110A. However, where the injunction has been granted without notice the claimant must not do so before the defendant has been served with the injunction containing the relevant provisions (CPR 65.4(3)).

Where an order is made varying or discharging any injunction to which a power of arrest is attached the claimant must immediately inform the police station to which a copy of the original order was delivered and deliver a copy of the order to any such police station (CPR r.65.4(4)). The rule does not state when the copy of the new order must be delivered to the police station but presumably it should be done as soon as possible.

Arrest

29.054 Where a power of arrest has been attached to certain provisions of an injunction a constable may arrest without warrant any person whom he has reasonable cause for suspecting to be in breach or otherwise in contempt in relation to a breach. If so, he must be brought before the judge within 24 hours, who will deal with the breach or may remand him (see further s.155).

Application for warrant

29.055 If the court has not attached a power of arrest, or has only attached it to certain provisions, but could have done the applicant may apply to the judge for the issue of a warrant for the arrest of the respondent if the applicant considers that the respondent has failed to comply with the injunction (s.155(3)). The application must be on oath and the judge must have "reasonable grounds for believing that the respondent has failed to comply with the injunction" before he can issue a warrant (s.155(5)).

An application for a warrant should be made in accordance with Pt 23 and may be made without notice. The applicant must:

- file an affidavit (a witness statement is not good enough) setting out grounds for the application with the application notice; or

- give oral evidence on oath as to the grounds for the application at the hearing (CPR r.65.5; CPR PD 65 para.2.1).

The warrant may not be issued unless "the judge has reasonable grounds for believing that the defendant has failed to comply with the injunction" (CPR PD 65 para.2.1(2)).

Proceedings following arrest—committal

29.056 Where a person is arrested pursuant to a power of arrest or a warrant the judge before whom the person is brought following his arrest may deal with the matter or adjourn the proceedings. Where the proceedings are adjourned the judge may remand the arrested person in accordance with s.155(2)(b) or (5) or release him (CPR r.65.6(2)(3)).

The procedure for applying for bail is dealt with in CPR PD 65 paras 3.1 and 3.2. If the court fixes the amount of any recognisance see CPR r.65.7(1)).

Where the proceedings are adjourned and the arrested person is released the matter must be dealt with (whether by the same or another judge) within 28 days of the date on which the arrested person appears before the court and the arrested person must be given not less than two days' notice of the hearing (CPR r.65.6(4)).

An application notice seeking committal for contempt of court of the arrested person may be issued even if the arrested person is not dealt with within the period of 28 days of the date on which the arrested person appears in court at the hearing that was adjourned (CPR r.65.6(5)).

Where an application to commit is made in the county court district judges (including deputies) as well as circuit judges may deal with the application (Housing Act 1996 s.158(1)(b); CPR r.65.6(6); CPR PD 2B para.8.3)).

Applications or discharge

In the High Court see RSC Ord.52 r.8. In the county court see CCR Ord.29 r.3.   **29.057**

Demotion orders

A demotion order is an order that replaces an assured or secure tenancy   **29.058**
with a "demoted tenancy" during the period of demotion. A demoted tenant has
virtually no security of tenure. As will be seen, further rights are also affected.
The idea is that a demotion order will give the tenant a serious warning that if his
behaviour does not change he will be out and will provide a positive incentive to
change behaviour.

A demotion order may be sought on its own or as an alternative to a possession
claim. In many ways the demotion tenancy is similar to a suspended
possession order. However, it perhaps has the advantage to the landlord of bringing
the future of the tenant in the property under the landlord's complete control
during the period of demotion. If the landlord decides to terminate the
demotion tenancy he will be able to do so provided that the appropriate steps are
taken (see Ch.13). On the other hand if there is a suspended order for possession
the court will continue to have some control and may for example vary the terms
of the order.

The court cannot make a demotion order in possession proceedings unless an
application has been made for such an order.

This section of the book deals with the circumstances in which a court will make
a demotion order and the procedure for applying for such an order. Demoted tenancies and the procedure for terminating those tenancies are dealt with in Ch.13.

Secure tenancies

If a demotion order is made the secure tenancy is replaced with a "demoted   **29.059**
tenancy". In the normal course of events the period of demotion will last
for a period of one year. As will be seen from the details contained in Ch.13 the
security of tenure available to the tenant is virtually non-existent. Two further
particular consequences of a secure tenancy being demoted are that the right
to mutual exchange of property is suspended during the period of demotion;
and the landlord may apply to suspend the right to buy—see further paras 29.087
and 29.087.

Who may apply?

The landlords who may apply for a demotion order in respect of a secure   **29.060**
tenancy are:

- a local housing authority;
- a housing action trust;
- a private registered provider of social housing;
- a registered social landlord (s.82A)(1)).

Form 34: Notice before proceedings for a demotion order—Housing Act 1985 section 83

This Notice is the first step towards the termination of your secure tenancy and its replacement with a demoted tenancy. You should read it very carefully.

- *If you need advice about this Notice, and what you should do about it, take it as quickly as possible to a Citizen's Advice Bureau, a Housing Aid Centre, or a Law Centre, or to a Solicitor*

1. To ....
.... [Name(s) of secure tenant(s)]
....
....
....
....
.... [address of property]

2. The .... [name of landlord] **intends to apply to the Court for a demotion order, the effect of which will be the termination of your secure tenancy and its replacement with a demoted tenancy.**

- *Demoted tenants have less security and fewer rights than secure tenants.*

- *If your landlord is a registered social landlord then the demoted tenancy would be a demoted assured shorthold tenancy as set out in section 20B of the Housing Act 1988 (inserted by section 15 of the Anti-social Behaviour Act 2003). A demoted assured shorthold tenancy will become an ordinary assured tenancy after one year unless the landlord gives notice of proceedings for possession within that year.*

- *If your landlord is a local authority (LA) or a housing action trust (HAT) the demoted tenancy would be a demoted tenancy as set out in Chapter 1A of Part 5 of the Housing Act 1996 (inserted by section 14 of and Schedule 1 to the Anti-social Behaviour Act 2003). A LA or HAT demoted tenancy will become a secure tenancy after one year unless the landlord gives notice of proceedings for possession within that year.*

3. The grounds for the demotion order are that you or a person residing in or visiting [first line of the address of property] **has engaged or has threatened to engage in conduct to which section 153A or 153B of the Housing Act 1996 (anti-social behaviour or use of premises for unlawful purposes) applied. The court must also be satisfied that it is reasonable to make the order.**

- *Section 153A applies to conduct which is capable of causing nuisance or annoyance to any person and which directly or indirectly relates to or affects the housing management functions of your landlord.*

- *Section 153B applies to conduct which consists of or involves using or threatening to use housing accommodation owned or managed by your landlord for an unlawful purpose.*

4. The particulars of the conduct in respect of which the demotion order is sought are as follows—

> ....
> ....
> ....
> ....
> ....
> ....
> ....
> ....
> [give full details]
>
> - *Even if you accept that the conduct referred to above has occurred, you will still have the right to argue at the hearing that it is not reasonable for a demotion order to be made.*
>
> **5. The Court proceedings for demotion will not be begun until after** .... [give the date after which Court proceedings can be begun]
>
> - *Court proceedings cannot be begun until after this date, which cannot be earlier than the date when, apart from the provisions of the Housing Act 1985, your tenancy or licence could have been brought to an end. This means that if you have a weekly or fortnightly tenancy, there should be at least 4 weeks betweeen the date this Notice is given and the date in this paragraph.*
>
> - *After this date, Court proceedings can be begun at once or at any time during the following twelve months. Once the twelve months are up this Notice will lapse and a new notice must be served before proceedings for a demotion order can be brought".*

Notice

The court cannot entertain proceedings for a demotion order unless (a) the land-   **29.061**
lord has served a notice on the tenant complying with s.83 of the 1985 Act (as amended) or (b) the court considers it just and equitable to dispense with the requirement of such a notice (s.83(1)).

The notice must:

- be in prescribed form;

- specify the ground on which the court will be asked to make the demotion order; and

- give particulars of that ground;

- specify the date after which the proceedings may be begun (the notice will cease to be in force 12 months after the date so specified—s.83(4A) (b));

- the date specified must not be earlier than the date on which the tenancy could (if the 1985 Act did not apply) be brought to an end by notice to quit given by the landlord on the same date as the notice being served under s.83.

(Section 82(3), (4A).)

If the secure tenancy is for a fixed term the notice has effect in respect of any periodic tenancy arising on the termination of that tenancy by virtue of s.86; and it is not necessary to satisfy the further requirements in subs.(3) to (5) of s.86 that would normally apply to periodic tenancies (s.83(6)). The form of notice is prescribed by the Secure Tenancies (Notices) Regulations 1987 as amended in England by the Secure Tenancies (Notices) (Amendment) (England) Regulations 2004 (SI 2004/1627) and in Wales by the Secure Tenancies (Notices) (Amendment) (Wales) Regulations 2005 (SI 2005/1226 (W.84)).

Assured tenancies

29.062 If a demotion order is made the assured tenancy is replaced with a "demoted assured shorthold tenancy"; i.e. the tenancy becomes a shorthold tenancy with the added disadvantage that the assured tenancy can be brought to an end within the first six months of the tenancy. See further above (para.29.058) and Ch.13.

Which landlord may apply?

29.063 The ability to apply for a demotion order in respect of an assured tenancy is only available to a non-profit registered provider of social housing, a profit making registered provider of social housing or a registered social landlord (s.6A of the Housing Act 1988, as introduced by the 2003 Act).

Notice

29.064 The court cannot entertain proceedings for a demotion order unless (a) the landlord has served a notice on the tenant or (b) the court thinks it just and equitable to dispense with the requirement of the notice.

There is no prescribed form for the notice but s.6A(6) does set out certain statutory requirements for the notice. The notice must:

- give particulars of the conduct in respect of which the order is sought;
- state that the proceedings will not begin before the date specified in the notice. The date specified must not be before the end of the period of two weeks beginning with the date of service of the notice;
- state that the proceedings will not begin after the end of the period of 12 months beginning with the date of service of the notice. (Presumably any proceedings begun after that date may not be entertained unless the court dispenses with the requirement of the notice although the section does not state so expressly—compare s.83(4A)(b) of the 1985 Act in relation to secure tenancies.)

Grounds for making the order—both cases

29.065 The court must not make a demotion order in respect of a secure or an assured tenancy unless it is satisfied:

- that the tenant or a person residing in or visiting the dwelling-house has engaged or has threatened to engage in conduct to which s.153A or s.153B of the Housing Act 1996 applied; i.e. conduct which is capable of causing nuisance or annoyance to any person, and which directly or indirectly relates to or affects the housing management functions of a relevant landlord or conduct which consists of or involves using or threatening to use housing accommodation owned or managed by a relevant landlord for an unlawful purpose; and

- that it is reasonable to make the order.

(Section 82A(4) of the 1985 Act in relation to secure tenancies and s.6A(4) of the 1988 Act in relation to assured tenancies.)

Thus the following questions need to be considered before an order can be made:

- What sort of conduct has been engaged in or threatened? Is it conduct:
  - —capable of causing nuisance or annoyance to any person and which directly or indirectly affects housing management functions of a relevant landlord; or
  - —which constitutes unlawful use or threatened unlawful use?
- Has that conduct been carried out or threatened by a tenant, person residing in the dwelling-house, or person visiting the dwelling-house?
- Is it reasonable to make the order?

Effect of the order

Secure tenancy: If the demotion order is made the secure tenancy is terminated **29.066** with effect from "the date specified in the order". If the tenant remains in occupation of the dwelling-house after that date "a demoted tenancy is created with effect from that date" (s.82(A)3(a)(b)). However, the phrase "demoted tenancy" has a different meaning depending upon the nature of the landlord:

- if the landlord is a local housing authority or a housing action trust the demoted tenancy is a demoted secure tenancy to which s.143A of the 1996 Act applies (s.82A(8)(a));
- if the landlord is a private registered provider of social housing or a registered social landlord the demoted tenancy is a demoted assured shorthold tenancy to which s.20B of the Housing Act 1988 Act applies (s.82A(8)(b)). This situation applies to those tenants who had secure tenancies created prior to January 15, 1989. As can be seen from Ch.13 if the period of demotion passes without possession being granted the tenant will not go back to being a secure tenant but will become an assured tenant.

The terms of the demoted tenancy are dealt with in Ch.13.

Assured tenancy

The demotion order terminates the assured tenancy with effect from "the date **29.067** specified in the order". If the tenant remains in occupation of the dwelling-house after that date a demoted tenancy is created with effect from that date (s.6A(3)(a) (b)). It becomes an assured shorthold tenancy known as "a demoted assured shorthold tenancy". (See further Ch.13, para.13.030).

Court procedure—demotion claims

29.068 This section deals with the procedure to be adopted when applying for a demotion order (whether demoting a secure or assured tenancy). The procedure is known as a "demotion claim" and is set out in CPR Pt 65 s.III and CPR PD 65. (Pt 65 also applies to certain other "demotion claims"—see CPR PD 65 para.11.)

Demotion claim and alternative claims for possession

29.069 Where the only claim is for a demotion order the procedure is set out in CPR Pt 65 (Pt III) and CPR PD 65 (CPR r.65.13). However, where a demotion order is claimed in the alternative to a possession order, the claimant must use the Pt 55 procedure (see Ch.22; and CPR PD 65 para.5.1 which requires the particulars of claim to state certain information). The claim must be made in the county court for the district in which the property to which the claim relates. (CPR r.65.12: there are some limited circumstances in which a possession claim can be brought in the High Court. However, this is not available at all where a demotion claim is made in the alternative.)

This chapter is only concerned with the position where the claim is only for a demotion order.

The court

29.070 The application for a demotion order is made to the county court (s.82A(2)). It must be made in the county court for the district in which the property to which the claim relates is situated (CPR r.65.14(1); CPR PD 54 para.6.1). If the claim is begun in the wrong court the proceedings will not be a nullity but the judge may order that the claim (i) be transferred to the correct court, (ii) continue in the county court in which it was started or (iii) be struck out (CPR r.30.2(3); and see para.25.011).

Claim form

29.071 The claim form to be used is N6: see p.476. The particulars of claim form that must be used is N122: see p.478. The information required is as follows:

- whether the demotion claim is a claim under s.82A(2) of the 1985 Act (i.e. in relation to a secure tenancy) or s.6A(2) of the 1988 Act (i.e. an assured tenancy)—there are appropriate boxes to tick on form N122;

- whether the claimant is a local housing authority, a housing action trust or a registered social landlord or a private registered provider of social housing—again there are appropriate boxes to tick on N122;

- identify the property to which the claim relates;

- provide details of the tenancy relating to the parties, the period of the tenancy, the amount of rent, the dates on which the rent is payable;

- details of any statement of express terms of the tenancy served on the tenant (see paras 13.005 and 13.033);

- details of the conduct alleged.

(See Form N122 on p.478 and CPR PD 65 paras 6 and 7).

The particulars of claim should wherever possible include all the evidence the landlord wishes to rely upon, verified by the statement of truth (CPR PD 65 para.9.1). However, there will obviously be many cases where the landlord wishes to rely upon a number of witness statements in addition to the details contained within the particulars of claim. If so, that is obviously acceptable. It really does not need setting out in a practice direction but Pt 65 specifically states that the evidence should include details of the anti-social behaviour relied upon (para.9.2)

The particulars of claim must be filed and served with the claim form (CPR r.65.15).

Form 35: Claim form for demotion or suspended order

In the	
Claim No.	

Claimant
(name(s) and address(es))

SEAL

Defendants)
(name(s) and address(es))

The claimant is claiming a:
☐ demotion order
☐ suspension order

in relation to the tenancy of:

which is a residential property. Full particulars of the claim are attached.

This claim will be heard on: 20   at   am/pm

at

At the hearing the court will consider:
• whether you have or a person residing in or visting the property has, engaged or threatened to engage in anti-social behaviour; or used or threatened to use the property for unlawful purposes; and
• whether it is reasonable to make the order

What you should do
• Get help and advice immediately from a solicitor or an advice agency.
• Help yourself and the court by **filling in the defence form** and **coming to the hearing** to make sure the court knows all the facts.

Defendant's name and address for service

Court fee	£
Solicitor's costs	£
Total amount	£

Issue date	

N6 Claim form for demotion of tenancy/suspension of right to buy (08.05)

Claim No.	

The claimant is alleging:

☐ actual or threatened anti-social behaviour

☐ use or threatened use of the property for unlawful purposes

Does, or will, the claim include any issues under the Human Rights Act 1998?   ☐ Yes ☐ No

---

Statement of Truth
*(I believe)(The claimant believe(s)) that the facts stated in this claim form are true.
*I am duly authorised by the claimant to sign this statement.

signed _____ sign _____ date _____
(Claimant))(Claimant's solicitor)
*delete as appropriate

Full name _____

Name of claimant's solicitor's firm _____

position or office held _____
(if an authorised signatory not acting as a solicitor

Claimant's or
claimant's solicitor's
address to which
documents or payments
should be sent if
different from overleaf.

	if applicable
Ref. no.	
fax no.	
DX no.	
e-mail	
Postcode Tel. no.	

Form 36: Particulars of claim for demotion order

Particulars of claim for demotion order/suspension of right to buy

Name of court	Claim No.
Name of Claimant	
Name of Defendant	

The claimant

1. The claimant is making this claim under:

☐ section 82A(2) of the Housing Act 1985 ☐ section 121A of the Housing Act 1985

☐ section 6A(2) of the Housing Act 1988

In relation to the tenancy of:

2. The claimant is a:

☐ local housing authority ☐ registered social landlord or a private registered provider of social housing

☐ housing action trust ☐ other please specify (suspension claims only)

The tenancy

3. The premises are let under: ☐ a secure tenancy ☐ an assured tenancy

4. The tenancy began on: ☐ / / DD/MM/YY

5. The rent is: £

6. The rent is paid: ☐ weekly ☐ monthly

☐ fortnightly ☐ other (please specify)

7. The claimant is seeking the order because (State details of the conduct alleged and any other matters relied upon.)

Demotion Orders

8. Have you served on the defendant any statement of express terms of the tenancy which are to apply to the demoted tenancy? ☐ Yes ☐ No

If Yes, please give details of the terms

9. (a) Have you served the appropriate notice on the defendant giving particulars of the conduct alleged and of these proceedings? ☐ Yes ☐ No

(b) If Yes, when did you serve this notice? [/ /] DD/MM/YY

Statement of Truth
*(I believe)(The claimant believes) that the facts stated in these particulars of claim are true.
* I am duly authorised by the claimant to sign this statement.

signed _____ date _____
*(Claimant)(Claimant's solicitor)
*delete as appropriate

Full name _____

Name of claimant's solicitor's firm _____

Position or office held _____
            (if an authorised signatory not acting as a solicitor)

Service of claim form

The defendant must generally be served with the claim form and the particulars of **29.072** claim not less than 28 days before the hearing date (see CPR r.65.16(4)).

Where the claimant serves the claim form and particulars of claim he will be required to produce at the hearing a certificate of service of those documents (CPR r.65.18(5)).

The defendant

29.073 No acknowledgement of service is required. The tenant can file a defence and should do so. The defence must be in Form N11D (CPR PD 65 para.6.2) and wherever possible should include all the evidence the tenant wishes to present, verified by a statement of truth (CPR PD 65 para.9.1). If he does not do so within the time specified in r.15.4 (14 days after service of the particulars of claim) he may take part in the hearing but the court may take his failure to do so into account when deciding what order to make about costs. It is not possible to obtain judgment in default of a defence in a demotion claim (CPR r.65.17).

As will be seen below, time can be shortened in which case there may well be cases where the defendant does not initially have the opportunity to serve a defence within the 14-day period specified.

The hearing date

29.074 The court fixes a date for the hearing when it issues the claim form. The hearing date will be not less than 28 days from the date of issue of the claim form. The standard period between issue and the hearing should not be more than eight weeks.

The court may shorten the time period, particularly where there are threats of assault, reasonable grounds for fearing assaults and serious damage or threats of such damage (see further CPR PD 65 para.8.2). In such a case if the case cannot be determined at the first hearing the court will consider what steps are needed to finally determine the case as quickly as reasonably practicable (CPR PD 65 para.8.3).

Form 37: Defence Form—demotion of tenancy

Name of Court	Claim No.
Name of Claiment	
Name of Defendant(s)	
Date of hearing	

Personal details
Please give your:

Forenames

Address *(if different from the address on the claim form)*

Surname

Post code

(Demotion claims only)

Did you receive the notice from the claimant referred to at paragraph 9 of the particulars of claim?

☐ Yes ☐ No

/ / DD/MM/YY

Disputing the claim
Do you agree with what is said about your conduct or use of the property?

☐ Yes ☐ No

If No, set out your reasons below:

(Continued overleaf)

N11D Defence form (demotion of tenancy) (suspension of right to buy) (08.05)

(Use additional sheets if necessary)

Statement of Truth
*(I believe)(The defendant(s) believe(s)) that the facts stated in this defence are true.
*I am duly authorised by the claimant to sign this statement.

signed _____ date _____
(Defendant)(Litigation friend)(*where the defendant is a child or a patient*)(Defendant's solicitor)
*delete as appropriate

Full name _____

Name of claimant's solicitor's firm _____

position or office held _____
(if signing on behalf of firm or company)

The hearing

The hearing may be dealt with by a district judge, including a deputy (CPR PD 2B **29.075** para.11.1(b)).

At the hearing or at any adjournment of the hearing the court may decide the demotion claim or give case management directions. Where

"the demotion claim is genuinely disputed on grounds which appear to be substantial case management directions will include allocation of the claim to a track or directions to enable it to be allocated" (CPR r.65.18(2)).

If the court does decide that it is appropriate to allocate it to a track it will have regard to the normal matters set out in CPR r.26.8 plus "the nature and extent of the conduct alleged" (CPR r.65.19).

Except where the claim is allocated to the fast track or the multi-track or the court directs otherwise any fact that needs to be proved by the evidence of witnesses may be proved by evidence in writing (CPR r.65.18(2)). However, if the court is likely to hear the case at the hearing the parties are obviously best advised to have the witnesses present. All witness statements must be filed and served at least two days before the hearing (CPR r.65.18(4)). If the maker of a witness statement does not attend a hearing and the other party disputes material evidence contained in the statement the court will normally adjourn the hearing so that oral evidence can be given (CPR PD 65 para.9.3).

Fixed costs

Where the landlord succeeds in obtaining a demotion order (whether or not **29.076** brought with a possession claim) fixed costs rules apply (CPR r.45.1(2)(f)) unless the court otherwise orders (CPR r.45.1(1)). The amount recoverable will be the issue fee (CPR r.45.1(3)), the fixed commencement costs and £57.25 (CPR rr.45.2A(1); 45.4A(1)(b)(ii)).

Other remedies

Anti-social behaviour orders—county court

As stated in the introduction to this chapter the power of the county court dealt **29.077** with in this section is not to be confused with anti-social behaviour orders made in the magistrates' courts. It is not possible to apply to the court for a free-standing anti-social behaviour order. We are here concerned with situations where there are already existing proceedings in the county court. In those circumstances the county court has power to make an anti-social behaviour order (ASBO) under s.1B of the Crime and Disorder Act 1998.

Who may apply?

The application may be made by a "relevant authority" who is a party to the **29.078** proceedings (s.1B(2)). The definition of a "relevant authority" includes:

- the council for a local government area;

- in relation to England, a county council;
- any non-profit registered provider of social housing which provides or manages any houses or hostel in a local government area;
- any person registered under s.1 of the Housing Act 1996 as a social landlord who provides or manages any houses or hostel in a local government area; or
- a housing action trust established by order in pursuance of s.62 of the Housing Act 1988.

(Section 1(1A) of the 1998 Act—see the subsection for a full list.)

The relevant authority may make an application for an ASBO under s.1B of the 1998 Act if it

> "considers that a party to those proceedings is a person in relation to whom it would be reasonable for it to make an application under section" (s.1B(2)).

If the relevant authority is not already a party to the proceedings it may apply to be joined (s.1B(3)).

Against whom may the order be made?

29.079 It follows from the above that an order may be made against a person who is a party to the proceedings (s.1B(2)). However, the relevant authority may also apply for a person who is not a party to the proceedings to be joined if that person "has acted in an anti-social manner" and that "the person's anti-social acts are material in relation to the principal proceedings" (s.1B(3A), (3B)). Generally speaking, an application to join someone may only be made against a person aged 18 or over (CPR PD 65 para.13.2). However, a pilot scheme has operated in some courts (until March 31, 2006) in relation to children under 18 (see CPR PD 65 para.13.3).

Conditions

29.080 An ASBO under s.1B may be made if the following two conditions are satisfied:

- the person against whom the complaint is made has acted in "in an anti-social manner, that is to say, in a manner caused or was likely to cause harassment, alarm or distress to one or more persons not of the same household as himself"; and
- that such an order is necessary to protect "relevant persons" as defined by s.1(1B) of the 1998 Act, essentially anyone in the area but see the subsection for a more precise definition.

Section 1B(4)incorporating the definition of anti-social behaviour in section 1(1) of the 1998 Act

29.081 In deciding whether the conditions are satisfied the court must disregard "any act of the defendant which he shows was reasonable in the circumstances" (s.1B(7) incorporating s.1(5)).

Procedure for applying for an order

The procedure is set out in Pt IV of CPR r.65; i.e. CPR rr.65.21 to 65.26.   **29.082**

The order

The court may make an order which prohibits the person against whom the **29.083**
order is made "from doing anything described in the order" (s.1B(4)). The prohi-
bitions that

> "may be imposed . . . are those necessary for the purpose of protecting (whether relevant
> persons or persons elsewhere in England and Wales) from further anti-social acts by the
> defendant" (s.1(6); s.1B(7)).

The order "shall have effect for a period (not less than two years) specified in the
order or until further order" (s.1(7); s.1B(7)).
    Either the applicant to the order or the person against whom the order was made
can apply for it to be varied or discharged (s.1B(5)) but no order can be discharged
before the end of two years beginning with the date of service of the order without
the consent of both parties.

Interim orders

Interim orders may be made if the court considers that it is just to make such an **29.084**
order pending determination of the main application—see s.1D.

Service of the order—effect of the order

The order (whether on notice or interim) must be served personally on the **29.085**
defendant (CPR PD 65 para.13.1).
    Doing something in breach of the order constitutes an offence (s.1B(7)).

Mutual exchange

Section 92 of the Housing Act 1985 provides that it is a term of every secure **29.086**
tenancy that the tenant may, with the written consent of the landlord, assign the
tenancy to another secure tenant or in certain cases assured tenant. Consent can
only be withheld on one of the grounds set out in Sch.3 to the 1985 Act.
    Section 191 of the Housing Act 2004 inserted a new ground, Ground 2A, into
Sch.3 of the 1985 Act for withholding consent. Under this ground consent to the
assignment can be withheld where a "relevant order" or a suspended Ground 2
(in relation to secure tenancies) or Ground 14 (in relation to assured tenancies)
possession order is in force, or an application is pending before any court for
a relevant order, a demotion order or a Ground 2 or 14 possession order in
respect of the tenant or the proposed assignee or a person who is residing with
either of them.
    Ground 2A contains a long list of "relevant orders", essentially one of a number
of injunctions made under the Housing Act 1996, anti-social behaviour order
under s.1 of the 1998 Act or an injunction to which a power of arrest is attached
under s.91 of the Anti-social Behaviour Act 2003, i.e. where local authorities

bring proceedings under s.222 of the Local Government Act 1972 (see para.29.001).

Suspension of the right to buy

29.087 Section 192 of the Housing Act 2004 inserted a new s.121A of the Housing Act 1985 giving landlords of secure tenants the right to apply for an order from the court suspending the right to buy for a specified period on the grounds of anti-social behaviour. The court may only make such an order if it is satisfied that the tenant or a person residing in or visiting the property has engaged or threatened to engage in anti-social behaviour (as defined in ss.153A or 153B of the 1996 Act—see para.29.023), and that it is reasonable to make the order. When deciding if it is reasonable to make the order, the court will consider, in particular, whether it is desirable for the property to be managed by the landlord during the suspension period, and to the effect the behaviour has had, or would have if repeated, on other people.

A suspension order will end any existing applications to exercise the right to buy and prevent any new applications being made during the period specified by the court. The suspension of the right to buy does not have any impact on the accumulation of discount or qualifying period.

The landlord may request, on one or more occasions, an extension to the suspension period. However, the court may not extend the suspension period unless, since the making of the suspension order (or since the last extension) the tenant, or a person residing in or visiting the property, has engaged or threatened to engage in anti-social behaviour, and that it is reasonable to make the further order.

Section 192 allows regulations to be made that will continue the effect of a suspension order where the secure tenant becomes an assured tenant, as he would otherwise be able to exercise the Preserved Right to Buy (ss.171A–171H of the Housing Act 1985), or the Right to Acquire (ss.16–17 of the Housing Act 1996), instead of the Right to Buy.

Section 193 of the 2004 Act also makes amendments to s.138 of the 1985 Act so as to prevent a tenant being able to compel completion of a right to buy sale if an application is pending for a demotion order a suspension order or a possession order sought on the grounds of anti-social behaviour.

The procedure is to be found in CPR Pt 65 and PD 5A, 6 and 7.2.

Family intervention tenancy

29.088 The Housing and Regeneration Act 2008 added yet another tool in the armoury of certain landlords to deal with anti-social behaviour. The Act introduced a new concept—"the family intervention tenancy". It enables local housing authorities and social landlords to offer these tenancies, which will not be secure or assured, to tenants against whom a possession order has been made on anti-social behaviour grounds or against whom such an order could in the opinion of the landlord be made. These tenancies are offered for the purpose of providing "behaviour support services" to the tenant. See s.97 of the 2008 Act which inserts a new para.4ZA to Sch.1 of the Housing Act 1985 (tenancies which are not secure); and a new para.12ZA to Sch.1 of the Housing Act 1988 (tenancies which are not assured). The tenancy can be brought to an end by the service of a notice to quit. Section 298 of the Housing and Regeneration Act 2008 sets out provisions that prevent a local housing authority from serving a notice to quit, in respect of a family intervention tenancy, unless there has first been a review of the decision to terminate the tenancy. The review provisions are contained in the Family Intervention Tenancies (Review of Local Authority Decisions) (England) Regulations 2008 (SI 2008/3111).

Housing and Regeneration Act 2008 section 298

298.—(1) A local housing authority must not serve a notice to quit on the tenant of a family intervention tenancy unless–

(a) the authority has served a notice under subsection (2) on the tenant, and

(b) either–

(i) the tenant has not requested a review of the kind mentioned in subsection (2)(e) within the period of 14 days beginning with the service of the notice,

(ii) any such request has been withdrawn, or

(iii) the authority has served a notice on the tenant under subsection (4) (b).

(2) A notice under this subsection is a notice in writing stating–

(a) that the authority has decided to serve a notice to quit on the tenant,

(b) the effect of serving a notice to quit,

(c) the reasons for the authority's decision,

(d) when the authority is intending to serve the notice to quit, and

(e) that the tenant has the right to request, within the period of 14 days beginning with the service of the notice under this subsection, a review of the authority's decision.

(3) Subsection (4) applies if the tenant requests a review of the kind mentioned in subsection (2)(e) within the period of 14 days beginning with the service of the notice under subsection (2) and the request is not withdrawn.

(4) The local housing authority must–

(a) review its decision to serve a notice to quit on the tenant, and

(b) serve a notice on the tenant informing the tenant of the decision of the authority on the review and the reasons for it.

(5) The appropriate national authority may by regulations make provision about the procedure to be followed in connection with such a review.

...

(7) A notice under subsection (2), and a notice to quit, served by a local housing authority in respect of a family intervention tenancy must contain advice to the tenant as to how the tenant may be able to obtain assistance in relation to the notice.

(8) The appropriate national authority may by regulations make provision about the type of advice to be provided in such notices.

(9) In this section–

"appropriate national authority" means–

(a) in relation to England, the Secretary of State, and

(b) in relation to Wales, the Welsh Ministers,

"family intervention tenancy" has the same meaning as in paragraph 4ZA of Schedule 1 to the Housing Act 1985 (c. 68),

and other expressions used in this section and in para.4ZA of that Schedule have the same meaning as in that paragraph.

(10) This section does not apply to any tenancy granted before the coming into force of this section.

Chapter 30

Other Grounds for Possession

Deterioration of the dwelling-house or furniture

Where the landlord seeks to rely upon Grounds 13 or 15 of Sch.2 to the Housing **30.001**
Act 1988 (or their equivalent) it will have to prove two matters: (a) that there has
been a deterioration in the condition of the dwelling-house or the furniture and (b)
that the deterioration has been caused by the neglect or default of the tenant or one
of the persons referred to in the cases. The landlord must therefore call evidence
to prove the state of the premises or the furniture at some earlier stage and make
a comparison to their present state. It will usually be possible to infer that the
tenant is responsible for any deterioration that has taken place from the fact that
the dwelling-house and the furniture are under his control. In more difficult cases
it may be necessary to call the evidence of a surveyor to prove the cause of the
deterioration.

Any person seeking to rely upon such expert evidence may not simply call the
expert at the trial. He must first seek directions from the district judge as to the
preparation and disclosure of reports so that the other side is not taken by surprise
(see CPR r.55. 8(1)(6) and CPR r.35).

The landlord may rely upon a deterioration in the state of the tenant's garden
(*Holloway v Povey* (1984) 271 E.G. 195).

This ground is a discretionary ground and the court may not make an order
unless it is reasonable to do so.

Domestic violence (Ground 14A)

This ground of Sch.2 to the Housing Act 1988 which only applies where the land- **30.002**
lord is a social landlord (see Appendix A2.064).

The other conditions are as follows:

(a) the dwelling was occupied by a married couple, civil partners or a couple
living together as man and wife or as civil partners;

(b) one or both of the partners is a tenant;

(c) one partner (the victim) has left due to violence towards him/her or a resident family member;

(d) the court is satisfied that the victim is unlikely to return.

It should be noted that the ground applies whether the tenant is the violent partner or the victim. However, the ground can only be relied upon if the victim is unlikely to return. Thus, if the victim would return if the violent partner were to be evicted the ground cannot be relied upon. There is no obligation on the landlord to grant a new tenancy to the victim. Thus, it seems that this ground is not intended to help the victim but to punish the aggressor.

The Ground applies where the violence has occurred after the perpetrator has left the property (*Metropolitan Housing Trust v Hadjazi* [2010] EWCA Civ 750).

There are special service requirements in relation to s.8 notices when this ground is relied upon (see para.6.020).

This ground is a discretionary ground for possession and the court may not make the order unless it considers it reasonable to do so. The court may also suspend the order for possession.

Recovering possession of a home

30.003 Where the landlord of a dwelling-house let on a protected tenancy under the Rent Act 1977 wishes to recover possession of the premises so that he may live there himself he may rely upon any of the normal grounds for possession that may be available to him. He may, for example, be in a position to offer the tenant suitable alternative accommodation or if the tenant has neglected the premises he may be able to rely upon Case 3. There are, however, four grounds for possession that are particularly appropriate to the situation where the landlord wishes to live in the dwelling-house himself. The two most important are Cases 9 and 11. Case 9, which is a discretionary ground, may be used where the landlord reasonably requires possession for himself (or for certain other members of his family). Generally speaking Case 11 is available where the landlord occupied the premises prior to the letting and not later than the commencement of the tenancy served upon the tenant a notice informing him that the landlord would require possession at the end of the term pursuant to Case 11. The landlord will also have to show that he requires possession for himself (or a member of his family) but he will not have to show that his requirement is a reasonable one.

The two other cases are Cases 12 and 20 which relate to premises purchased as a retirement home and premises let by members of the armed services.

Where the tenancy is an assured tenancy see Ground 1 of Sch.2 to the Housing Act 1988 (see para.30.016).

Case 9: premises reasonably required

30.004 A landlord wishing to rely upon Case 9 of the Rent Act 1977 must, once he has determined the contractual tenancy, commence proceedings in the county court for the area in which the property is situated (para.25.011). There will be four matters that the court will have to consider at the hearing of the action:

(1) the landlord's requirement;

(2) whether the landlord is landlord by purchase;

(3) the greater hardship test;

(4) overall reasonableness.

The landlord's requirement

In order to recover possession of the dwelling-house the landlord will have to **30.005** show that he reasonably requires possession of the dwelling-house for occupation as a residence for:

(1) himself; or
(2) any son or daughter of his over 18 years of age; or
(3) his father or mother; or
(4) the father or mother of his spouse.

The burden of proving that he reasonably requires possession rests upon the landlord and so he must produce evidence to that effect. Where he is seeking possession so that one of the listed members of his family can live there that person should, if at all possible, be called to give evidence. The landlord must show that he has a genuine need for possession. He need not show an absolute necessity but he must show something more than a desire. The landlord should adduce evidence to show that he requires possession at the date of the hearing (*Alexander v Mohamadzadeh* (1986) 51 P. & C.R. 41) or at some time in the not too distant future (*Kidder v Birch* (1983) 265 E.G. 773). Whether the landlord requires possession is a question of fact to be decided on the evidence available to the court at the date of the hearing. When drafting the particulars of claim on behalf of the landlord it is better to give some detail as to the reasons for requiring possession rather than simply stating that possession is claimed under Case 9. The judge will then have some idea of the landlord's case before he hears the evidence.

In deciding whether the landlord requires possession for "himself" the court will take into account the requirements of his wife and children who are under 18, even where the landlord is not actually going to live on the premises himself (*Smith v Penny* [1947] K.B. 230; a father separated from his wife and living in a public house where he was the manager wanted possession of the dwelling-house so that his two children and a house-keeper could live there. Held: he required possession for "himself" and was entitled to possession.) In all other cases where the landlord is requiring possession for "himself" he must be part of the household which is to occupy the dwelling-house (see *Richter v Wilson* [1963] 2 Q.B. 426; partially blind 83-year-old landlord living on the ground floor of the building which he owned required the upper floor for friends who were to look after him. Held: that he did not require the upper floor for "himself").

Joint owners may claim possession under Case 9 for occupation by themselves **30.006** but only if the dwelling-house is required for all of them (*McIntyre v Hardcastle* [1948] 2 K.B. 82). If only one of the joint owners requires possession the others should transfer their interest to him. A husband and wife who are joint landlords of a house are entitled to claim possession pursuant to Case 9 if it is required as a residence for a child who is the natural son of the wife but neither the natural nor the adopted son of the husband (*Potsos v Theodotou* [1991] 2 E.G.L.R. 93 CA).

A person who in his capacity as a personal representative or trustee is a landlord of a dwelling-house cannot claim possession for a beneficiary unless the beneficiary is also one of the relatives listed in Case 9. Nor can such a person usually claim possession for himself as to do so would be in breach of trust and therefore unreasonable. In *Patel v Patel* [1981] 1 W.L.R. 1342, however, personal representatives claimed possession so that they could live in the dwelling-house with the children of the deceased, whom they had adopted. The children were beneficiaries of their parents' estate. In these circumstances there was no breach of trust and the personal representatives were entitled to possession.

The landlord may rely upon Case 9 where he needs only part of the premises but in such circumstances it may not be reasonable to make the order (*Kelley v Goodwin* [1947] 1 All E.R. 810).

Landlord by purchase

30.007 The court may not make an order for possession where the landlord purchased the dwelling-house after one of the dates set out in Case 9 (usually March 23, 1965) and in so doing became the tenant's landlord. The intention of this provision is to prevent landlords from buying houses over the heads of sitting tenants and then having them evicted. The tenant will usually know whether the present landlord was the landlord at the commencement of the tenancy but where he is not sure, which is sometimes the case where the property is managed by managing agents, his solicitors should use the power to seek further and better particulars and discovery of documents to ascertain the true position. The relevant date to discover is the date that contracts were exchanged on the purchase and not the date of completion (*Emberson v Robinson* [1953] 1 W.L.R. 1129).

Where the landlord has become the landlord after the commencement of the tenancy in some way other than by purchase he is not precluded from relying on Case 9 by reason of the landlord by purchase provision:

> "the acquisition of the reversion, whether it be a freehold or leasehold, for money or money's worth . . . is plainly a purchase but the acquisition of it under a will is not a purchase" (see *Thomas v Fryer* [1970] 2 All E.R. 1).

In *Mansukhani v Sharkey* [1992] 2 E.G.L.R. 107 CA a transfer by parents to a son of a property "in consideration of mutual love and affection" which was subject to a mortgage and in which the son covenanted to pay money due under the mortgage was held to be a gift rather than a purchase.

Where the landlord claims that he has become the landlord otherwise than by way of purchase the ability to seek discovery should once again be used. The tenant's representative should demand to see any relevant testamentary documents or trust deeds, etc. which should be carefully scrutinised so as to ensure that the landlord really has not given anything by way of money or money's worth in return for his present interest in the property.

The greater hardship test

30.008 Before making an order for possession of the dwelling-house the court must be satisfied that having regard to all the circumstances of the case, including the question of whether other accommodation is available to the landlord or the tenant, greater hardship would be caused by granting the order than by refusing to grant it. This is a question of fact and the judge's decision on the question is final. The burden of proving greater hardship is on the tenant who must therefore adduce evidence to show the hardship that an order for possession would cause him (*Sims v Wilson* [1946] 2 All E.R. 261; *Baker v McIver* [1990] 2 E.G.L.R. 105).

Each party should make investigations as to alternative accommodation that may be available to him, in particular by making enquiries of the local authority. If the tenant is able to give evidence that he sought other accommodation and that none is available he will be in a better position to show that greater hardship would be caused by making the order than refusing it; but if he is not able to give such evidence the court may come to the conclusion that he has not satisfied the burden placed on him (see, e.g. *Alexander v Mohamadzadeh* (1986) 51 P. & C.R. 41 at 49). The effect of a local authority's duty to give priority to certain persons under Pt VII of the Housing Act 1996 should also be borne in mind (see para.25.047). Paradoxically it may mean that a single person who does not have a priority need is better able to show greater hardship than a person with young children who will have a priority need; although it should be borne in mind that the housing shortage is such that in many areas families spend long periods in bed and breakfast accommodation before being housed permanently.

The representative for each party should also cross-examine the other party on his income and capital position as this will obviously be relevant to the ability of either of them to find other accommodation. The tenant may not be able to find anything as cheap as his present accommodation but such a factor is not likely to have much weight if he can afford a higher rent.

Hardship to persons other than the landlord or the tenant may be taken into account (e.g. members of the landlord's or the tenant's family or lodgers who are residing with the tenant) but regard must be had to the proximity of third parties to the landlord or the tenant and the extent to which hardship to the former would constitute hardship to the latter (*Harte v Frampton* [1948] 1 K.B. 73).

Where the court is considering making a possession order to take effect at some time in the future the judge should consider whether greater hardship will be caused at the end of the period of postponement (*Wheeler v Evans* [1948] 1 K.B. 459).

Overall reasonableness

The tenant, in particular, should remember that the court must finally consider the question of overall reasonableness before making the order for possession (s.98 of the Rent Act 1977). Where the judge finds that greater hardship would be caused by refusing the order than by granting it he will nearly always consider it reasonable to make the order but there may be other factors that the tenant is able to draw to the court's attention in an attempt to persuade it that it would not be reasonable to do so. For example, the court may not consider it reasonable to make the order if the tenant has recently redecorated the premises or turned down other accommodation in reliance upon a representation from the landlord that he would not be seeking possession in the near future. Where the court does make an order for possession under Case 9 it may stay or suspend execution of the order or postpone the date for possession for such period or periods as it thinks fit on the usual conditions (s.100 of the Rent Act 1977; see para.8.030). It is usual to postpone possession for a period of longer than the 28 days that is normally granted in rent cases. Three months is not uncommon but obviously every case will turn upon its own facts and if the landlord's requirement for possession is particularly urgent a much shorter order may be made. The fact that the landlord will already have had to wait for some time by the date of the hearing may be drawn to the judge's attention, particularly where the landlord has disclosed full details of his case prior to commencing proceedings.

Unless the case is clear cut, which is not likely, the unsuccessful tenant should try to persuade the judge to use his discretion to make no order as to costs.

30.009

Case 11: premises let by a previous occupier

30.010 Case 11 (as amended by the Rent (Amendment) Act 1985) is available where a person (referred to in the Case as "the owner-occupier") who let the dwelling-house on a regulated tenancy had, at any time before the letting, occupied it as his residence. The owner-occupier need not be the freehold owner. He may be a lease-hold owner or a person who occupied under a more informal tenancy agreement. What is important is that the person who granted the tenancy is a person who occupied the dwelling-house as his residence at some time prior to the letting. (He need not have occupied it immediately prior to the letting but he must not, since certain dates set out in the Case, have let the premises on a protected tenancy without first having given a Case 11 notice; see below.) However, the landlord does not need to show that he occupied the residence "as a home" prior to the letting (cf. the position of statutory tenants; para.8.018). Temporary or intermittent occupation as a residence will be sufficient (*Mistry v Isidore* [1990] 2 E.G.L.R. 97 CA).

Where the landlord seeks to rely upon Case 11 he should determine the contractual tenancy if it has not already been determined (see para.8.024) and then commence proceedings based upon this Case. Where the landlord foresees problems with proving service of the Case 11 notice it is wise to commence proceedings based upon Case 11 and Case 9 in the alternative.

The landlord's requirements for possession

30.011 The owner-occupier may rely upon Case 11 where he requires possession of the dwelling-house as a residence for himself or for any member of his family who resided with him when he last occupied the dwelling-house as a residence (Case 11 (c); Pt V para.2(a)).

Where there were joint owner-occupiers who let the premises any one of them may seek to obtain possession alone (*Tilling v Whiteman* [1980] A.C. 1). Note that it is not necessary for the owner-occupier to show that the dwelling-house is reasonably required for himself as he would have to if he were relying upon Case 9. It is sufficient for him to show that he genuinely intends to occupy the premises at once or within a reasonable time (*Kennealy v Dunne* [1977] Q.B. 837). There is nothing in Case 11 which imports a requirement for permanent residence as a "home", or rules out temporary or intermittent occupation. The landlord will, therefore, be entitled to possession even if he only intends to reside in it at times when he is able to take advantage of it by reason of his presence in England (see *Naish v Curzon* (1985) 273 E.G. 1221; *Davies v Peterson* (1988) 21 H.L.R. 63). (If the landlord is abroad and not in a position to return until possession has been obtained, evidence of his intention to return and live in the house should be given by statement under the Civil Evidence Act 1995 (see para.27.008).) An intention to live in the house until it is sold is sufficient (*Whitworth v Lipton* [1993] E.G.C.S. 172).

The owner-occupier may also recover possession of the dwelling-house if it is not reasonably suitable to his needs, having regard to his place of work, and he requires it for the purpose of disposing of it with vacant possession so that he can use the proceeds to acquire, as his residence, a dwelling-house which is more suitable to those needs (Sch.15, Pt V para.2(f)). See *Bissessar v Ghosn* (1986) 18 H.L.R. 486.

Case 11 requirements

In order to recover possession under Case 11 the landlord must show: **30.012**

(1) that not later than the "relevant date", which is usually the date the tenancy commenced (see Sch.15, Pt III), the landlord gave the tenant a notice in writing that possession might be recovered under Case 11; and

(2) that the dwelling-house has not since the prescribed date (in most cases December 8, 1965 (see the text of Case 11(b)) been let by him on a protected tenancy in regard to which a Case 11 notice has not been served upon the tenant in accordance with the above paragraph.

Thus, if the owner-occupier has let the dwelling-house on a protected tenancy at any time since the prescribed date without first having served a Case 11 notice the owner-occupier will never (subject to the power to dispense with the requirements) be able to rely on Case 11.

Dispensing with the requirements

Under both the Housing Act (Ground 1, see para.30.016) and the Rent Act **30.013** (Case 11) the court may dispense with the requirement for the appropriate notice if the court considers it just and equitable to do so. (Note the slightly different wording between the grounds. Under the Housing Act the reference is merely to the court being of the opinion that it is just and equitable to dispense with the requirement. Under the Rent Act the reference is to the court being of the opinion that it is just and equitable to make an order for possession. However, it would seem that nothing turns on this difference.) The question of when it will be just and equitable to dispense with the above requirements was considered in *Bradshaw v Baldwin-Wiseman* (1985) 49 P. & C.R. 382 where Griffiths L.J. expressed the following view:

> "I would regard the use of those words (just and equitable) as directing the court to look at all the circumstances of the case. Those would embrace the circumstances affecting the landlord, or his successors-in-title, the circumstances of the tenant and, of course, the circumstances in which the failure to given written notice arose. It is only if, having considered all those circumstances, the court considers that it would be just and equitable to give possession that it should do so, because it must be borne in mind that, by failing to give the written notice, the tenant may well have been led into a wholly false position. As I say, in the circumstances of this case, where it is apparent that there never was any intention to create what I might call 'a Case 11 tenancy' it cannot be just and equitable to dispense with written notice" (at 388).

In *Fernandes v Pavardin* (1982) 264 E.G. 49 an oral notice was given but not a written one. It was held that as the oral notice was clearly made and understood no injustice or inequity had flowed from failing to put the notice in writing, and the requirements were waived. See also *Minay v Sentongo* (1983) 45 P. & C.R. 190 where the notice had been sent but the tenant alleged that it had never been received. The court dispensed with the notice requirements because the landlord honestly believed that the tenant had been given proper notice.

However, oral notice will not always suffice. In *White v Jones* (1994) 26 H.L.R. 477 oral notice was given but the court refused to dispense with the requirement for written notice. The oral notice had been treated with minimal significance since neither party believed there was security of tenure. The court also had regard to the length of time the tenants had used the property and the limited requirements of the landlord. It was a pied-à-terre used for only three months in the year.

30.014   Conversely, although oral notice may lead a court to dispense with the requirement for a written notice it is not a prerequisite of such a decision (*Boyle v Verrall* [1997] 1 E.G.L.R. 25 CA):

> "Clearly, if oral notice was given when a tenancy was granted, it may, with or without other circumstances, be an important factor favouring dispensation: see for example, *Fernandes v Parvardin* [above]. However, it does not follow that oral notice is a prerequisite of such a decision" (*Boyle v Verrall*).

Other factors taken into account in *Boyle v Verrall* were that (1) the reason why the landlord did not serve a Ground 1 notice was because she, mistakenly, thought she was granting an assured shorthold, (2) the tenant noticed the mistake made by the landlord in her attempt to create the shorthold (no proper s.20 notice) but failed to draw it to her attention, (3) early written notice of the requirement for the property (seven months) and (4) the tenant's persistent late payment of rent.

See also *Mustafa v Ruddock* [1997] 30 H.L.R. 495 CA where the landlord's estate agent who granted the tenancy on his behalf failed to serve a s.20 notice prior to the grant of the tenancy. He needed the property for his own use and relied on Ground 1 even though no notice under that ground had been served. The Court of Appeal held that the judge should have dispensed with the requirement for notice and should have made an order for possession on Ground 1.

The order

30.015   Where Case 11 is applicable the court must make an order for possession. The landlord does not have to show that it would be reasonable to make the order (s.98(2) of the Rent Act 1977). The order for possession may be postponed for no more than 14 days, or six weeks in cases of exceptional hardship (s.89 of the Housing Act 1980; para.3.034).

Recovering possession of a home: Housing Act 1988

30.016   Where a landlord of an assured tenant wishes to recover possession of a home the appropriate ground of Sch.2 to the Housing Act 1988 is Ground 1. This ground is similar to but much wider in its scope than Case 11 of Sch.15 to the Rent Act 1977. If the landlord wishes to recover possession under Ground 1 he should serve a notice of intention to bring proceedings for possession, pursuant to s.8 of the 1988 Act, and after expiry of the date specified in the notice commence proceedings by summons.

Notice requirement

30.017   The landlord may only recover possession if not later than the beginning of the tenancy the landlord who granted the tenancy gave notice in writing to the tenant that possession might be recovered on Ground 1 or the court is of the opinion that it is just and equitable to dispense with the requirement of notice (see further para.30.013).

Facts to prove

The landlord must also establish one or other of the two following facts: **30.018**

(1) Previous occupation: he may show that at some time before the beginning of the tenancy, he or, in the case of joint landlords seeking possession at least one of them, occupied the dwelling-house as his only or principal home.

(2) Required now for occupation: he may show that he or, in the case of joint landlords seeking possession at least one of them, requires the dwelling-house as his or his spouse's only or principal home.

However, this ground is not available if the landlord seeking possession (or, in the case of joint landlords, any one of them) or any other person who, as landlord, derived title under the landlord who gave the Ground 1 notice acquired the reversion on the tenancy for money or money's worth.

Suitable alternative accommodation

If it considers it reasonable to do so the court may make an order for possession **30.019** of a dwelling-house which has been let on a protected or statutory tenancy if it is satisfied that suitable alternative accommodation is available for the tenant or will be available for him when the order takes effect (see s.98(1)(a), (4) and Sch.15, Pt IV of the Rent Act 1977 as amended). The burden is on the landlord to show that the alternative accommodation is suitable (*Nevile v Hardy* [1921] 1 Ch. 404). He need not provide the accommodation himself. He may persuade either the local housing authority for the district in which the dwelling-house is situated or some other person or body to do so.

Where the tenancy is an assured tenancy see s.7 and Sch.2, Pt II, Ground 9 and Pt III of the Housing Act 1988 which contains similar provisions (para.A2.061).

Local authority certificates

If the accommodation is to be provided by the local housing authority a certificate **30.020** from that body certifying that it will provide suitable alternative accommodation by a date specified in the certificate is conclusive evidence that suitable alternative accommodation will be available for him by that date (Sch.15, Pt IV, para.3 of the Rent Act 1977). Any document purporting to be signed by a proper officer of the local housing authority may be adduced in evidence, and unless the contrary is shown, is deemed to be such a certificate without further proof (Sch.15, Pt IV, para.7 of the Rent Act 1977). In practice it is rare for local authorities to provide such certificates.

Other accommodation

30.021 Where the landlord is unable to rely upon a local housing authority certificate under para.3 the alternative accommodation is deemed to be suitable if it is to be let to the tenant on a protected tenancy (other than one under which the landlord might recover possession under Cases 11–20 of Sch.15, i.e. the mandatory grounds) or on terms which will, in the opinion of the court, afford to the tenant security of tenure reasonably equivalent to that afforded by the Rent Act 1977 to such a protected tenancy. For the status of a person granted a protected tenancy after the commencement of the Housing Act 1988 (January 15, 1989) see s.34(1) (c) of that Act (para.8.011). It would seem that since the passing of the Housing Act 1980 a secure tenancy of a dwelling-house provided by a local housing authority would suffice. So would a tenancy for a reasonably lengthy fixed term (*Fulford v Turpin* [1955] J.P.L. 365).

Paragraphs 4 and 5 of Pt IV of Sch.15 to the Rent Act 1977 provide that where there is no local authority certificate under para.3 the court must also be satisfied that:

(1) the accommodation is reasonably suitable to the needs of the tenant and his family as regards proximity to place of work; and

(2) either:

    (a) similar as regards rental and extent to the accommodation afforded by dwelling-houses provided by the local authority to tenants with similar needs to the tenant in the case (see further paras 5(2) and 7; and *Jones v Cook* [1990] 2 E.G.L.R. 109; the actual extent of accommodation provided by the local housing authority is proved by a certificate of that authority but the judge must still determine whether or not the alternative accommodation proposed is similar to it); or

    (b) reasonably suitable to the means of the tenant and to the needs of the tenant and his family as regards extent and character; and

(3) if any furniture is provided in his present home, the alternative accommodation contains furniture which is either similar to the furniture in the present home or is reasonably suitable to the needs of the tenant and his family.

In considering whether the alternative accommodation is reasonably suitable to the needs of the tenant's family, regard is only had to those members of the family who reside with the tenant on a permanent basis (see *Standingford v Probert* [1950] 1 K.B. 377; *Scrace v Windust* [1955] 1 W.L.R. 475). As to the meaning of "family" see para.8.050. Each member of the family has a right to be heard and should be joined in the proceedings (see *Wandsworth LBC v Fadayomi* [1987] 3 All E.R. 474; husband and wife wanting different things). The place of work to which regard must be had is not necessarily an office or factory. It may be an area (*Yewbright Properties Ltd v Stone* (1980) 40 P. & C.R. 402).

Comparison with the tenant's present accommodation

30.022 A common objection that is raised by the tenant to the proposed alternative accommodation is that it is not suitable as regards character because it does not come up to the same standard as his present home. In *Redspring v Francis* [1973] 1 W.L.R. 134 Buckley L.J. stated that

> "what [the tenant] needs is somewhere where he can live in reasonably comfortable conditions suitable to the style of life to which he leads, and environmental matters must inevitably affect the suitability of offered accommodation to provide him with the sort of conditions in which it is reasonable that he should live".

The standard to be applied, however, is that of the ordinary tenant and not one which will completely satisfy "all the fads and fancies and preferences of the tenant" (*Christie v Macfarlane* (1930) S.L.T. (Sh Ct) 5 at 10). Difference in character will normally only make the accommodation unsuitable if it relates to a difference in kind rather than degree. (See *Redspring v Francis* (1973), per Sachs L.J. at 140.)

A good (but not typical) example of the problems that arise is to be found in the case of *Hill v Rochard* [1983] 1 W.L.R. 478. The dwelling-house was set in one and a half acres of land, consisted of many rooms and had attached to it a stable and a paddock. The landlord offered the tenants a modern detached house in the country on the outskirts of a village. It had a large garden and four bedrooms but no stable and paddock. The judge held that although the alternative accommodation would not enable them to have the same lifestyle as before it would permit them to live in a reasonably comfortable condition in a reasonably similar way, and that therefore the accommodation was suitable. The Court of Appeal refused to interfere with the decision and commented that the Rent Act 1977 was not concerned with incidental advantages but with the provision of housing.

Having failed to persuade the court that the alternative accommodation is **30.023** unsuitable, the tenant will sometimes argue that it is not reasonable to make the order for possession on the basis that the alternative is far below the standard of his present accommodation (see further below). However, such arguments do not tend to find a great deal of favour in the more extreme cases as can be seen from the following comment of Nourse L.J. in *Dame Margaret Hungerford Charity Trustees v Beazley* [1993] 2 E.G.L.R. 143 at 146H CA, a case in which the tenant was being required to move from a 17-bedroom "Warden's House" to a three-bedroom council house:

> "The tragedy of this case from the defendant's point of view, and I well understand that that may not be too strong a word, is that the eccentricities of the Rent Act have accustomed her and her family to accommodation of a quality and character far in excess of anything to which they can be compelled to move as an alternative. It is no great comfort for them now to be told that they have been very fortunate to be there for nearly ten years since the contractual term expired, nor that there are many other families who, for economic reasons, find themselves facing a similar prospect, when they themselves have to face it for quite different reasons."

(Compare *Dawncar Investments Ltd v Plews* and see further on reasonableness para.30.025.)

It is the character of the property that is relevant and so it is not possible to take into account the fact that the tenant will be moved far from friends or his present cultural and religious activities if he has to move to the alternative accommodation (*Siddiqu v Rashid* [1980] 1 W.L.R. 1018; which concerned a Muslim tenant who would not be able to attend his mosque if he moved to the new accommodation).

In deciding whether the alternative accommodation is suitable the judge may visit either dwelling-house. Solicitors acting for tenants should always visit the premises as should any barrister instructed. They should also consider whether to make an application to the judge for a view to take place. The decision to inspect is a matter of judicial discretion and neither party may compel the judge to hold a view or prevent him from doing so (*Salsbury v Woodland* [1970] 1 Q.B. 324). He invariably does do so. Both sides should be present at the view which is part of the evidence. Photographs of both dwelling-houses and the immediate area are always useful.

Other matters

30.024 A part of the accommodation presently occupied by the tenant may be held to be a suitable alternative (*Mykolyshyn v Noah* [1970] 1 W.L.R. 1271), but it may nevertheless still not be reasonable to make the order for possession (*Yoland v Reddington* (1982) 263 E.G. 157; offer of part held to be suitable but not reasonable to make the order as the tenant would lose his small but crucial income from sub-letting). If the court does also consider it reasonable to order possession it should do so upon the condition that the landlord grant a tenancy of the relevant part (*Parmee v Mitchell* [1950] 2 K.B. 199). In deciding whether the accommodation is suitable the court may take into account the provision or otherwise of a garden (*Redspring v Francis* [1973] 1 W.L.R. 134), or of a garage (*Macdonnell v Daly* [1969] 1 W.L.R. 1482). The alternative accommodation will not be unsuitable merely because the tenant will not be able to get all his furniture into it (*McIntyre v Hardcastle* [1948] 2 K.B. 82; see *Selwyn v Hamill* [1948] 1 All E.R. 70 at 72).

Accommodation is not deemed to be suitable to the needs of the tenant and his family if the result of their occupation would be that it would be an overcrowded dwelling-house for the purpose of Pt X of the Housing Act 1985; see Ch.19 (Sch.15, Pt IV para.6 of the Rent Act 1977).

The landlord may himself be a tenant of the accommodation that he is offering as an alternative. If there is a covenant against sub-letting the tenant may then find himself being evicted by the head landlord from the alternative accommodation. It has been suggested therefore that the tenant should insist upon the landlord disclosing his title documents on discovery. If there is a covenant against sub-letting without the landlord's consent the tenant should insist upon the consent being obtained. If it is not the tenant should argue that it is not reasonable to make the order for possession. (See the article by Nic Madge [1983] *LAG Bulletin* 140.)

The alternative accommodation may be a property owned by the tenant but the landlord is not entitled to seek an injunction preventing the tenant from disposing of that property prior to the hearing (*Fennbend Ltd v Millar* (1988) 20 H.L.R. 19).

Form 38: Particulars of claim to be inserted on Form N119—suitable alternative accommodation

Particulars to be inserted at paragraph 4C of Form N119

The said premises are premises to which the Housing Act 1988 applies and possession is claimed pursuant to Ground 9 of Schedule 2 to the said Act.

The ground upon which possession is claimed is that suitable alternative accommodation is available at [*address of accommodation*] for the Defendant and will be available for her if and when an order for possession takes effect. The said suitable alternative accommodation consists of:

(a) [2 rooms. One is 11 feet 3 inches by 9 feet 6 inches and the other is 14 feet 3 inches by 9 feet 6 inches;]

(b) [a kitchenette measuring 4 feet 3 inches by 6 feet 6 inches;]

(c) [a bathroom measuring 5 feet by 8 feet 6 inches;]

(d) [a hall measuring 4 feet by 6 feet 3 inches.]

[Hot water is provided by an immersion heater and the said alternative accommodation is only some few hundred yards from the said premises.]

The Landlord will contend that it is reasonable to make the order because he requires the premises for his elderly mother.

Reasonableness

It is important to remember that the court must also consider the question of **30.025** reasonableness. Many of the factors that may not be taken into account when deciding whether the alternative accommodation is suitable may be relied upon by the tenant when it comes to arguing that it is not reasonable to make the order. In *Battlespring Ltd v Gates* (1983) 268 E.G. 355 the tenant was an elderly lady who had been in occupation for 35 years. The landlord was interested in the property for financial reasons. Although the court considered that the alternative accommodation was suitable it did not consider that it was reasonable to make the order. See also *Dawncar Investments Ltd v Plews* [1993] E.G.C.S. 117 where the court considered that it was not reasonable to expect the tenant, a woman with a young child, to live in the alternative accommodation. The flat the landlord sought to recover was in a pleasant part of Hampstead. The alternative was on a busy commercial road with heavy lorries going by, a railway to the front and back and two public houses nearby.

In *Amrit Holdings Co Ltd v Shahbakhti* [2005] EWCA Civ 339 the accommodation that the landlord said was available to the tenant was owned by the defendant tenant and was occupied by assured shorthold tenants. To get hold of the accommodation it would be necessary to remove these tenants. It would also mean that the defendant would lose his income from the property and would have to rearrange his financial affairs. On all the facts that judge held that it was not reasonable to make an order for possession and the Court of Appeal refused to interfere with that decision.

The landlord must also remember to put forward and plead those facts and matters upon which he relies in support of his contention that it would be reasonable to make the order (*Wint v Monk* (1981) 259 E.G. 45; where the landlord failed to do so and no order was made). The question is not whether it is reasonable for the landlord to make the claim but whether it is reasonable for the court to make the order.

In *Whitehouse v Lee* [2009] EWCA Civ 375 the judge was wrong to find that it was reasonable to make an order for possession where the tenant, with her husband (who died between the hearing and the appeal), had been tenants for 45 years, and were active in the local community having set up a local neighbourhood association. The landlord and the other beneficiaries of the property had retired and wished to sell the property with vacant possession in order to reduce their on-going obligations and to maximise their profit on sale. The Judge was wrong to consider only whether it was reasonable for the landlord to seek possession balanced against the reasonableness of the tenant and her husband wishing to stay in her home. The Judge should have considered reasonableness more widely and should have included an evaluation of the impact on the landlord of not making an order.

Chapter 31

Trespassers

Part 55 and its practice direction must be used where "the claim includes a posses- **31.001**
sion claim against trespassers" (CPR r.55.2). However, there are certain modifications that apply in these cases. The general procedure under Pt 55 is set out in
Ch.25. The modifications that apply to trespasser claims are in this chapter.
Interim Possession Orders are dealt with in Pt 55 s.III (para.31.009). There is also
a new criminal offence where a person knowingly trespasses and then resides or
intends to reside in residential property (s.144 of the Legal Aid, Sentencing and
Punishment of Offenders Act 2012). This does not apply to a tenant or licensee
who holds over.

The term "a possession claim against trespassers" is defined in CPR r.55.1(b).
It means:

> ". . . a claim for the recovery of land which the claimant alleges is occupied only by a
> person or persons who entered or remained on the land without the consent of a person
> entitled to possession of that land but does not include a claim against a tenant or sub-
> tenant whether his tenancy has been terminated or not."

Under this definition the rules that apply to trespassers may not be used against
sub-tenants.

The procedure is most commonly associated with "squatters" but it is clear
from the above wording that it may also be used where bare or contractual licensees have had their licences revoked (see *Greater London Council v Jenkins*
[1975] 1 W.L.R. 155).

Modifications to Part 55A

The modifications of the normal CPR r.55 procedure relate to: **31.002**

- Issue in the High Court.

- Claims against persons whose names are not known.

- The particulars of claim.

- The date of the hearing.

- Service of the claim and other evidence.

- The lack of a requirement on the defendants to file a defence.

High Court: CPR PD 55.3 states:

> "Except where the county court does not have jurisdiction, possession claims should normally be brought in the county court. Only exceptional circumstances justify starting a claim in the High Court."

The county court in fact has jurisdiction in all claims relating to the possession of land (s.21 of the County Courts Act 1984).

The PD specifically states that:

> "circumstances which may, in an appropriate case, justify starting a claim in the High Court are if:
>
> (1) there are complicated disputes of fact;
>
> (2) there are points of law of general importance; or
>
> (3) the claim is against trespassers and there is a substantial risk of public disturbance or of serious harm to persons or property which properly require immediate determination.
>
> If the claim is started in the High Court and the court decides that it should have been started in the county court, the court will normally strike the claim out or transfer it to the county court on its own initiative" (CPR PD 55 para.1.2).

As the PD goes on to state:

> "This is likely to result in delay and the court will normally disallow the costs of starting the claim in the High Court of any transfer".

Thus, only a brave claimant in very serious circumstances will start the claim in the High Court.

Defendants whose names are not known: where the claimant does not know the name of a person in occupation, the claim must be brought against "persons unknown" in addition to any named defendants.

31.003   *Particulars of claim*: as with all possession claims it is necessary to use two documents (i) a claim form (Form N5) and (ii) particulars of claim. The claim form has a specific question, which indicates immediately to the court that the claim is against trespassers. There is a form of Particulars of Claim that relates specifically to trespassers that must be used (Form N121 see Form 39 on p.508). In addition to any other relevant matters the particulars of claim must state:

- The identity of the land to which the claim relates.

- Whether the claim relates to residential property.

- The claimant's interest in the land or the basis of his right to claim possession.

- The circumstances in which it has been occupied without licence or consent (CPR PD 55 para.2.6).

Date of hearing: as with all possession claims the court will fix a date for the hearing when it issues the claim form. There is no specific statement within Pt 55 or the PD to the effect that the case will be listed within a specific period. The rules merely refer to the date of service. However, as a matter of practice the hearing date will be much closer to the issue date in trespasser claims than in other cases.

Time for service: in the case of residential property the defendant must be served with the claim form, particulars of claim and any witness statements not less than five days before the hearing date. In all other cases these documents must be served not less than two days before the hearing date (CPR r.55.5). In a particularly urgent case an application can be made to shorten time under Pt 3.1 (2)(a)). All the witness statements on which the claimant intends to rely must be filed and served with the claim form (CPR r.55.8(5)).

Method of service: where the claim is issued against "persons unknown" there are specific rules for service by attaching the documents to the main door or some other part of the land so that they are clearly visible and if practicable, inserting them in a sealed transparent envelope to the occupiers through the letter box. As an alternative, service may be effected by placing stakes in the land where they are clearly visible with the documents attached (CPR r.55.6). The court will effect service if the claimant wishes but it will be necessary to provide sufficient stakes and transparent envelopes (CPR PD 55 para.4.1).

Response by the defendant: the defendant does not need to respond. There is no requirement to serve an acknowledgment or a defence. He is entitled just to turn up and defend the claim (CPR r.55.8). However, if he has time a defendant with a substantive defence will be well advised to file a defence or witness statement, verified by a statement of truth, setting out his position.

Who has the right to claim possession?

As stated above the claimant must state his "interest in the land or the basis of his **31.004** right to claim possession". Normally, the claimant will be the owner of the land or someone, such as a tenant, with an obvious right to possession. However, a licensee or even a trespasser who has been in actual possession may evict a subsequent trespasser who has subsequently gone into occupation (see para.1.008). In *Dutton v Manchester Airport Plc* [1999] 2 All E.R. 675, it was even held that a person with a right to occupy under a licence could bring a claim against trespassers even though he had never been in occupation:

> ". . . the true principle is that a licensee not in occupation may claim possession against a trespasser if that is a necessary remedy to vindicate and give effect to such rights of occupation as by contract with his licensor he enjoys. This is the same principle as allows a licensee who is in de facto possession to evict a trespasser. There is no respectable distinction, in law or logic, between the two situations. An estate owner may seek an order whether he is in possession or not. So, in my judgment, may a licensee, if other things are equal. In both cases, the plaintiff's remedy is strictly limited to what is required to make good his legal right. The principle applies although the licensee has no right to exclude the licensor himself. Elementarily he cannot exclude any occupier who, by contract or estate, has a claim to possession equal or superior to his own. Obviously, however, that will not avail a bare trespasser" (Laws L.J. at 689a).

However, this principle will not be taken too far. A contractual right to access is not enough. The licence must give the licensee effective control over the land before he can bring a claim to evict a trespasser (*Countryside Residential (North Thames) Ltd v Tugwell* [2000] 34 E.G. 87 CA—licences under option agreement to a developer to carry out investigatory work on the sites which had not yet entered the site).

In *Hall v The Mayor of London* [2010] EWCA Civ 817, although the Mayor of London ("Boris") had no proprietary interest in the area of land over which he sought possession (Parliament Square Gardens), he had sufficient control over it to enable him to claim possession as well as an injunction against trespassers who were protesting there. Boris was not the owner of the square, the Crown was. However, he had statutory powers in relation to the control and maintenance of the land. Reference was made to *Western Australia v Ward* (2002) 213 CLR 1, a decision of the Australian High Court, in which it was said that a person was in possession of land if he can "control access to the [land] by others, and, in general, decide how the land will be used". In the face of argument that no claim for possession could be maintained by a party who had no proprietary interest in the land, as was the case here, Lord Neuberger MR:

> "there is obvious force in the point that the modern law relating to possession claims should not be shackled by the arcane and archaic rules relating to ejectment, and, in particular, that it should develop and adapt to accommodate a claim by anyone entitled to use and control, effectively amounting to possession, of the land in question – along the lines of the view expressed by Laws KJ in *Dutton* [2000] 1 QB 133 and by Lady Hale in *Meier* [2009] 1 WLR 2780." [para.27].

Possession order in respect of neighbouring land

31.005 An order for possession of land not actually occupied by trespassers is too wide. The fact that there is a fear that they might go on to occupy other land also owned by the claimant is not a justification for such an order. The basis of a claim for possession is that the owner had been ousted and should "recover" the land. Where the owner is still in possession there was nothing to recover: *Secretary of State for the Environment Food & Rural Affairs v Meier* [2009] UKSC 11, Lord Neuberger at paras 64 and 65:

> "The notion that an order for possession may be sought by a claimant and made against defendants in respect of land which is wholly detached and separated, possibly by many miles, from that occupied by the defendants, accordingly seems to me to be difficult, indeed impossible, to justify. The defendants do not occupy or possess such land in any conceivable way, and the claimant enjoys uninterrupted possession of it. Equally, the defendants have not ejected the claimant from such land. For the same reasons, it does not make sense to talk about the claimant recovering possession of such land, or to order the defendant to deliver up possession of such land.
>
> This does not mean that, where trespassers are encamped in part of a wood, an order for possession cannot be made against them in respect of the whole of the wood (at least if there are no other occupants of the wood), just as much as an order for possession may extend to a whole house where the defendant is only trespassing in one room (at least if the rest of the house is empty)."

Injunctions in advance of trespass

31.006 An injunction may however be appropriate. Lord Neuberger in *Meier* at para.79:

> "That brings me to the question whether an injunction restraining travellers from trespassing on other land should be granted in circumstances such as the present. Obviously, the decision whether or not to grant an order restraining a person from trespassing will

turn very much on the precise facts of the case. Nonetheless, where a trespass to the claimant's property is threatened, and particularly where a trespass is being committed, and has been committed in the past, by the defendant, an injunction to restrain the threatened trespass would, in the absence of good reasons to the contrary, appear to be appropriate."

The order

Where the defendant has entered into the land unlawfully the court has no power **31.007** to give a trespasser time to vacate when making an order for possession unless the land owner consents. No such power has been introduced by s.89 of the Housing Act 1980; nor pursuant to the European Convention on Human Rights (*Boyland and Son Ltd v Rand* [2006] EWCA Civ 1860—see further into Human Rights Act 1998 considerations Ch.23). Where a contractual licensee occupied under a Rent Act 1977 restricted contract, which had come to an end, the court can suspend the order for possession for up to three months (see Ch.9). In other cases, where an occupier was a tenant or licensee (without any statutory protection) who has remained in occupation as a trespasser, it would seem that the court does have some residual discretion, but this will be limited to 14 days or in exceptional cases, six weeks (s.89 of the Housing Act 1980, para.3.034—and *Boyland*: Neuberger L.J. at paras 5 to 7).

Enforcement

The provisions for enforcement contained in RSC Ord.113 r.7 and CCR Ord.24 **31.008** r.6 relating to writs and warrants for possession respectively, where an order for possession has been obtained against trespassers, remain in force. However, an important point to note is that it is possible to enforce a county court order for possession made in a claim against trespassers in the High Court or the county court (The High Court and County Courts Jurisdiction article 8B of Order 1991 (SI 1991/724)).

A warrant or writ of possession to enforce an order for possession may be issued at any time after the making of the order but not before the date on which possession is ordered to be given (CCR Ord.24 r.6; RSC Ord.113 r.7). No warrant or writ of possession will be issued after the expiry of three months from the date of the order without the leave of the court.

The bailiff enforcing the warrant may evict any person he finds on the premises even though that person was not a party to the proceedings (*R. v Wandsworth County Court Ex p. Wandsworth London Borough Council* [1975] 1 W.L.R. 1314). Where a person who has been evicted returns the applicant may apply for leave to issue a warrant/writ of restitution (see para.34.007).

Interim orders: county court

There is also a procedure whereby a landowner may apply for an "interim possession **31.009** order" under Pt 55 s.III. If made, the interim order requires the defendant to vacate within 24 hours of service of the order. It can also be an offence to be present on the premises as a trespasser at any time during the currency of the order (s.76 of the Criminal Justice and Public Order Act 1994). On the making of the order, the court fixes a hearing date "which will be not less than seven days after the date on which the IPO is made" (CPR r.55.25(4)). There are a number of county court forms to be used from the application to the order; see Forms N130 to 136 (not in this book).

On the face of it the "interim possession order" provides the property owner with a powerful weapon. It enables a property owner to regain possession speedily (in some within a few days) and the police are increasingly aware of the provisions and willing to assist in enforcing the order. However, the conditions to be satisfied before an interim order can be made are stringent. They include a requirement that the claimant has had an immediate right to possession "throughout the period of the unlawful occupation alleged" (CPR r.55.21(1)(b)), and "that the claim is made within 28 days of the date on which the claimant first knew, or ought reasonably to have known, that the Defendant, or any of the Defendants, was in occupation" (CPR r.55.21(1)(c)); and that the application is issued within 24 hours of issue (CPR 55.23(1)).

The procedure and the rules governing it are also complicated and, being of an interim nature, provide no certainty. It would, for example, not help in evicting a person who claims some sort of right to possession, however spurious, just before exchange of contracts for the sale of the premises. The claimant may obtain his interim order and then exchange contracts only to find that the order is not converted into a final order on the hearing date. This procedure is therefore unlikely to be of any use except in the simplest of squatter cases; and even there the extra costs and time likely to be expended in using the procedure will deter many property owners. An obvious example where it might be of some use would be where a family comes home to find the house occupied by squatters. However, even in these circumstances it should not be necessary to rely upon the procedure. It is an offence for a trespasser to refuse to leave if required to do so by a "displaced residential occupier" (s.7 of the Criminal Law Act 1977). See also now the new offence of squatting (para.31.001). A simpler solution therefore may be to call the police.

Form 39: Particulars of claim for possession (trespassers)

Particulars of claim In the		Claim No.
for possession		
(trespassers)		

Claimant

Defendant(s)

1. The claimant has a right to possession of:

   which is occupied by the defendant(s) who entered or (has)(have) remained on the land without the claimant's consent or licence.

2. The defendant(s) (has)(have) never been a tenant or sub-tenant of the land.

3. The land mentioned at paragraph 1 does (not) include residential property.

4. The claimant's interest in the land (or the basis of the claimant's right to claim possession) is
   Give details:

5. The circumstances in which the land has been occupied are
   Give details:

6. The claimant does not know the name(s) of (all) the defendant(s).

7. The claimant asks the court to order that the defendant(s):

    (a) give the claimant possession of the land;

    (b) pay the claimant's costs of making this claim.

Statement of Truth

*(I believe)(The claimant believes) that the facts stated in these particulars of claim are true.
*I am duly authorised by the claimant to sign this statement.

Signed _____ date _____
*(Claimant)(Litigation friend (*where claimant is a child or a patient*)) (Claimant's solicitor)
delete as appropriate

Full name _____

Name of claimant's solicitor's firm _____

position or office held _____
                               (*if signing on behalf of firm or company*)

N121 particulars of claim for possession (trespassers)(10.01)   *Printed on behalf of The Court Service*

CPR Practice Rule 55

Scope

55.2—(1) The procedure set out in this Section of this Part must be used where the **31.010** claim includes—

    (b)   a possession claim against trespassers; or

(2) This Section of this Part

    (a)   is subject to any enactment or practice direction which sets out special provisions with regard to any particular category of claim;

    (b)   does not apply where the claimant uses the procedure set out in Section II of this Part; . . .

Hearing date

55.5—(1) The court will fix a date for the hearing when it issues the claim form.   **31.011**

    (2) In a possession claim against trespassers the defendant must be served with the claim form, particulars of claim and any witness statements—

    (a)   in the case of residential property, not less than five days; and

    (b)   in the case of other land, not less than two days,

    before the hearing date.

(Rule 3.1(2)(a) provides that the court may extend or shorten the time for compliance with any rule.)

Service of claims against trespassers

55.6 Where, in a possession claim against trespassers, the claim has been issued against **31.012** "persons unknown", the claim form, particulars of claim and any witness statements must be served on those persons by—

    (a)

        (i)   attaching copies of the claim form, particulars of claim and any witness statements to the main door or some other part of the land so that they are clearly visible; and

(ii) if practicable, inserting copies of those documents in a sealed transparent envelope addressed to "the occupiers" through the letter box; or

(b) placing stakes in the land in places where they are clearly visible and attaching
to each stake copies of the claim form, particulars of claim and any witness
statements in a sealed transparent envelope addressed to "the occupiers".

Defendant's response

31.013   55.7—(1) An acknowledgment of service is not required and Part 10 does not apply.

(2) In a possession claim against trespassers rule 15.2 does not apply and the
defendant need not file a defence.

55.8 (5) In a possession claim against trespassers all witness statements on which the
claimant intends to rely must be filed and served with the claim form.

Practice Direction 55A

55.3—starting the claim

31.014   1.1 Except where the county court does not have jurisdiction, possession claims
should normally be brought in the county court. Only exceptional circumstances justify starting a claim in the High Court.

1.2 If a claimant starts a claim in the High Court and the court decides that it
should have been started in the county court, the court will normally either
strike the claim out or transfer it to the county court on its own initiative. This
is likely to result in delay and the court will normally disallow the costs of
starting the claim in the High Court and of any transfer.

1.3 Circumstances which may, in an appropriate case, justify starting a claim in
the High Court are if—

(1) there are complicated disputes of fact;

(2) there are points of law of general importance; or

(3) the claim is against trespassers and there is a substantial risk of public
disturbance or of serious harm to persons or property which properly
require immediate determination.

Possession claim against trespassers

31.015   2.6 If the claim is a possession claim against trespassers, the particulars of claim
must state the claimant's interest in the land or the basis of his right to claim
possession and the circumstances in which it has been occupied without
licence or consent.

55.6—Service in claims against trespassers

31.016   4.1 If the claim form is to be served by the court and in accordance with
rule 55.6(b) the claimant must provide sufficient stakes and transparent
envelopes.

Chapter 32

Mortgage Possession Proceedings

This chapter deals with a large number of matters that might arise in mortgage possession claims. The most useful section for practitioners is likely to be that dealing with the courts discretionary powers to adjourn or suspend orders for possession which can be found at para.32.058 onwards.

Introduction: the mortgagee's right to possession

A mortgage operates by way of legal demise (ss.85, 86 and 87 of the Law of **32.001** Property Act 1925) and so in the absence of any contractual or statutory right the mortgagee (the lender) is entitled to possession the moment the mortgage has been executed.

> "[T]he right of the mortgagee to possession in the absence of some specific contract has nothing to do with default on the part of the mortgagor. The mortgagee may go into possession before the ink is dry on the mortgage unless by a term expressed or necessarily implied in the contract he has contracted himself out of that right. He has the right because he has a legal term of years in the property" (*Four-maids Ltd v Dudley Marshall (Properties) Ltd* [1957] 2 All E.R. 35 at 36).

In practice the lender leaves the borrower in possession of the property, the mortgage being security for repayment of the debt. Typically a standard High Street mortgage stipulates that the power of sale becomes exercisable following a number of different events including, usually, two months arrears or breach of some other term of the mortgage. A mortgage entered into to secure a consumer credit debt only becomes enforceable after a default notice has been served in respect of the debt (see further para.32.006). A bank mortgage taken out to secure an overdraft usually becomes enforceable once the bank has made a demand for the sums owed. A mortgage entered into to secure the debts of another or the obligations of another, such as a tenant's covenants under a lease, usually becomes enforceable as soon as the principal debtor is in default.

Losing the right to possession

In exceptional circumstances a bank can lose its right to possession by reason of **32.002** adverse possession. In *National Westminster Bank Plc v Ashe* [2008] EWCA Civ 55 the failure by the bank to enforce its right to possession for more than 12 years, in circumstances where the borrowers made no repayments in that time, meant that its right to claim possession became statute barred and its security extinguished.

Adjourning the order for possession

32.003 At common law the court's power to adjourn an order for possession in a mortgage case is limited to a short period enabling the borrower to redeem the mortgage by paying the loan in full (*Birmingham Citizens Permanent Building Society v Caunt* [1962] 1 All E.R. 163 at 182; *Western Bank Ltd v Schindler* [1976] 2 All E.R. 393. Parliament has, however, given the court extensive discretionary powers in the Administration of Justice Acts 1970 and 1973 to adjourn proceedings, stay or suspend execution of the judgment or postpone the date for possession where a lender is seeking to recover possession of residential premises (see para.32.060). See also the even greater powers in Consumer Credit Act 1974 cases (see para.32.067).

Technically, the lender can avoid the court's discretionary powers by using its power to sell the property, directly or after the appointment of a receiver (see *Ropaigealach v Barclays Bank plc* [1999] 4 All E.R. 235 and *Horsham Properties Group v Clark* [2008] EWHC 2327 (Ch)). These decisions have caused much controversy in recent years on the basis that they provide a gaping hole in the law. There have been a number of attempts by Private Members Bills to overturn them which at the time of writing have not been successful. However, the Council of Mortgage Lenders has produced a Voluntary Statement discouraging members from using this option (*www.cml.org.uk/cml/policy/issues/4707*):

> "In respect of mortgages secured against owner occupied residential properties CML members will not seek to sell a mortgaged property when the borrower is in default without first obtaining a court order for possession. In addition CML members will not appoint a receiver to sell a residential property without first obtaining a court order for possession.
>
> This voluntary agreement only applies to mortgages secured over owner occupied residential properties (the customer's home) and does not apply to commercial transactions (which would include buy-to-let loans, business loans secured against a residential property or bridging loans.) It does not apply to vacant or abandoned properties or to cases of fraud. In addition there may be exceptional cases where the sale takes place with the full informed consent of the borrower and the statement would not apply in such circumstances."

Relationship with sale and leasing

32.004 The lender usually wishes to obtain possession so that it may exercise its statutory power of sale (s.101 of the Law of Property Act 1925). Unless the lender has possession it will not be able to sell the property with vacant possession. However, the lender does not have to sell the property. It may instead exercise its power to grant leases (s.99 of the Law of Property Act 1925). The lender may wait before selling the property but if it does so the borrower may apply to the court for an order for sale. If the borrower makes such an application the court has an unfettered discretion to deal with the property to do what is just and equitable (*Palk v Mortgage Services Funding Plc* [1993] 2 All E.R. 481; the lender wanted to let the property on short-term lettings until the market improved but the court considered that it would be unduly prejudicial to do so because a much greater debt would accrue and ordered a sale; see further para.32.066). The exercise by mortgagees of the power of sale under s.101 of the Law of Property Act 1925 (i.e. without any court order) does not breach Article 1 of the First Protocol to the European Convention on Human Rights (*Horsham Properties Group Ltd v Clark* [2008] EWHC 2327 (Ch)).

Consumer credit cases: preliminary points

Where the loan was made pursuant to a consumer credit agreement that is a **32.005** "regulated agreement" the court's powers to prevent an immediate order for possession will be governed by the Consumer Credit Act 1974 rather than the Administration of Justice Act 1970 (see ss.8, 16 of the 1974 Act and s.38A of the Administration of Justice Act 1970).

The normal purchase of property by way of loan secured by mortgage, will not fall within the Consumer Credit Act 1974 as it is likely to be an exempt agreement (see s.16 and in particular ss.16(1) and 16(6C)). However, second charges secured against property are more likely to be within the 1974 Act. Since April 6, 2008, there has been no limit on the amount covered by a regulated agreement.

It will be apparent from the documentation whether or not the agreement is a regulated agreement.

The main provisions of the Consumer Credit Act 1974 that are likely to be relevant in consumer credit cases are contained in this chapter. See generally *Goode, Consumer Credit: Law and Practice* (London: Butterworths, 1999).

Default notices

Where the 1974 Act does apply the lender must serve a "default notice", in **32.006** prescribed form (Consumer Credit (Enforcement, Default and Termination Notices) Regulations 1983 (SI 1983/1561) as amended) pursuant to ss.87 and 88 of the 1974 Act. If he does not do so he will not be able to enforce his security. Nor will he be able to terminate the agreement or demand earlier payment of any sum (see further s.87). If the borrower complies with the requirements of the default notice he is treated as not being in default (s.89). Service of documents, such as default notices, is dealt with in s.176 of the 1974 Act. (These sections, so far as is relevant, are set out below.)

In many agreements the lender has the right on the default of the borrower to terminate the agreement and to demand immediate repayment of all sums due. If the lender exercises those rights judgment is given for the full amount owed by the borrower without any allowance for the rebate to which he may be entitled on early settlement pursuant to ss.94 and 95 of the 1974 Act. However, when the borrower pays the judgment debt he may deduct the amount of credit for early settlement to which he may be entitled from the sum paid (*Forward Trust Ltd v Whymark* [1989] 3 All E.R. 915).

If the borrower fails to comply with the default notice the lender must take court proceedings if it wishes to enforce the security (s.126 of the Consumer Credit Act 1974). (The normal procedures for commencing a Consumer Credit Act claim do not apply when the claim relates to the recovery of land (CPR PD 7B para.3.2, see below for procedure). The court's powers to protect the borrower are dealt with at para.32.067.

Consumer Credit Act 1974 sections 87, 88, 89, 126, 176, 176A and 189

Need for default notices

32.007 87.—(1) Service of a notice on the debtor or hirer in accordance with section 88 (a "default notice") is necessary before the creditor or owner can become entitled, by reason of any breach by the debtor or hirer of a regulated agreement—

 (a) to terminate the agreement; or
 (b) to demand earlier payment of any sum; or
 (c) to recover possession of any goods or land; or
 (d) to treat any right conferred on the debtor or hirer by the agreement as terminated, restricted or deferred; or
 (e) to enforce any security.

Contents and effect of default notice

32.008 88.—(1) The default notice must be in the prescribed form and specify—

 (a) the nature of the alleged breach;
 (b) if the breach is capable of remedy, what action is required to remedy it and the date before which that action is to be taken;
 (c) if the breach is not capable of remedy, the sum (if any) required to be paid as compensation for the breach and the date before which it is to be paid.

 (2) A date specified under subsection (1) must not be less than 14 days after the date of service of the default notice, and the creditor or owner shall not take action such as is mentioned in section 87(1) before the date so specified or (if no requirement is made under subsection (1)) before those 14 days have elapsed.

 (3) The default notice must not treat as a breach failure to comply with a provision of the agreement which becomes operative only on breach of some other provision, but if the breach of that other provision is not duly remedied or compensation demanded under subs.(1) is not duly paid, or (where no requirement is made under subsection (1)) if the 14 days mentioned in subsection (2) have elapsed, the creditor or owner may treat the failure as a breach and section 87(1) shall not apply to it.

 (4) The default notice must contain information in the prescribed terms about the consequences of failure to comply with it and any other prescribed matters relating to the agreement.

 (4A) The default notice must also include a copy of the current default information sheet under section 86A.

 (5) A default notice making a requirement under subs.(1) may include a provision for the taking of action such as is mentioned in section 87(1) at any time after the restrictions imposed by subsection (2) will cease, together with a statement that the provision will be ineffective if the breach is duly remedied or the compensation duly paid.

Compliance with default notice

32.009 89.—If before the date specified for that purpose in the default notice the debtor or hirer takes the action specified under section 88(1)(b) or (c) the breach shall be treated as not having occurred.

 . . .

126.—A land mortgage securing a regulated agreement is enforceable (so far as provided in relation to the agreement) on an order of the court only.

 . . .

Service of documents

176.—(1) A document to be served under this Act by one person ("the server") on **32.010**
another person ("the subject") is to be treated as properly served on the subject if
dealt with as mentioned in the following subsections.

(2) The document may be delivered or sent by an appropriate method to the subject, or
addressed to him by name and left at his proper address.

(3) For the purposes of this Act, a document sent by post to, or left at, the address last
known to the server as the address of a person shall be treated as sent by post to, or
left at, his proper address.

(4) Where the document is to be served on the subject as being the person having any
interest in land, and it is not practicable after reasonable inquiry to ascertain the
subject's name or address, the document may be served by—

(a) addressing it to the subject by the description of the person having that interest
in the land (naming it); and

(b) delivering the document to some responsible person on the land or affixing it,
or a copy of it, in a conspicuous position on the land.

(5) Where a document to be served on the subject as being a debtor, hirer or surety, or
as having any other capacity relevant for the purposes of this Act, is served at any
time on another person who—

(a) is the person last known to the server as having that capacity; but

(b) before that time has ceased to have it;

the document shall be treated as having been served at that time on the subject.

(6) Anything done to a document in relation to a person who (whether to the knowledge
of the server or not) has died shall be treated for the purposes of subsection (5) as
service of the document on that person if it would have been so treated had he not died.

(7) The following enactments shall not be construed as authorising service on the Public
Trustee (in England and Wales) or the Probate Judge (in Northern Ireland) of any docu-
ment which is to be served under this Act—section 9 of the Administration of Estates
Act 1925; section 3 of the Administration of Estates Act (Northern Ireland) 1955.

(8) References in the preceding subsections to the serving of a document on a person
include the giving of the document to that person.

Electronic transmission of documents

176A.—(1) A document is transmitted in accordance with this subsection if—   **32.011**

(a) the person to whom it is transmitted agrees that it may be delivered to him by
being transmitted to a particular electronic address in a particular electronic
form;

(b) it is transmitted to that address in that form; and

(c) the form in which the document is transmitted is such that any information in
the document which is addressed to the person to whom the document is transmitted is capable of being stored for future reference for an appropriate period
in a way which allows the information to be reproduced without change.

(2) A document transmitted in accordance with subs.(1) shall, unless the contrary is
proved, be treated for the purposes of this Act, except section 69, as having been delivered on the working day immediately following the day on which it is transmitted.

(3) In this section, "electronic address" includes any number or address used for the
purposes of receiving electronic communications.

189–(1) . . .
"appropriate method" means—

    (a) post; or
    (b) transmission in the form of an electronic communication in accordance with
        section 176A(1);

"electronic communication" means an electronic communication within the meaning of the Electronic Communications Act 2000 (c.7).

Family homes

32.012 Unless the defendants are husband and wife or civil partners who are joint mortgagors the claimant must carry out a search at the Land Registry (Land Registry Form HR) to ascertain whether any notice or caution has been registered or, in the case of unregistered land, at the Land Charges Department to ascertain whether any Class F land charge has been registered, to protect the rights under the Matrimonial Homes Act 1967, or s.1 of the Matrimonial Homes Act 1983 or the Family Law Act 1996 or the Civil Partnership Act 2004 Sch.5. If the search reveals any such rights that fact must be alluded to in the particulars of claim (see para.32.024) and the result of the search must be attached to the particulars of claim or exhibited to a witness statement in support (para.32.025). It will also be necessary to serve the particulars of claim on the protected spouse or civil partner s.56(2) of the 1996 Act (CPR PD 55.4 para.2.5).

    The non-owning spouse or civil partner who is able to meet the borrowing spouse or civil partner's liabilities may apply to the court to be made a party before the action is "finally disposed of in the court". The court can refuse to make him or her a party if it is not satisfied that the non-owning spouse or civil partner can satisfy the borrower's liabilities and obligations (s.55). The non-owning spouse has a right to make such payments (s.30(3); see para.21.004). See also s.55(3) where some other "connected person" has obtained an order under s.35 or s.36 of the 1996 Act.

Family Law Act 1996 sections 54 to 56

Dwelling-house subject to mortgage

32.013   **54.**—(1) In determining for the purposes of this Part whether a person is entitled to occupy a dwelling-house by virtue of an estate or interest, any right to possession of the dwelling-house conferred on a mortgagee of the dwelling-house under or by virtue of his mortgage is to be disregarded.

    (2) Subsection (1) applies whether or not the mortgagee is in possession.

    (3) Where a person ("A") is entitled to occupy a dwelling house by virtue of an estate or interest, a connected person does not by virtue of—

        (a) any home rights conferred by section 30; or
        (b) any rights conferred by an order under sections 35 or 36,

    have any larger right against the mortgagee to occupy the dwelling house than A has by virtue of his estate or interest and of any contract with the mortgagee.

    (4) Subsection (3) does not apply, in the case of home rights, if under section 31 those rights are a charge, affecting the mortgagee, on the estate or interest mortgaged.

    (5) In this section "connected person", in relation to any person, means that person's spouse, former spouse, civil partner, former civil partner, cohabitant or former cohabitant.

Actions by mortgagees: joining connected persons as parties

55.—(1) This section applies if a mortgagee of land which consists of or includes a **32.014** dwelling house brings an action in any court for the enforcement of his security.

(2) A connected person who is not already a party to the action is entitled to be made a party in the circumstances mentioned in subsection (3).

(3) The circumstances are that—

    (a) the connected person is enabled by section 30(3) or (6) (or by section 30(3) or (6) as applied by section 35(13) or 36(13)), to meet the mortgagor's liabilities under the mortgage;

    (b) he has applied to the court before the action is finally disposed of in that court; and

    (c) the court sees no special reason against his being made a party to the action and is satisfied—

        (i) that he may be expected to make such payments or do such other things in or towards satisfaction of the mortgagor's liabilities or obligations as might affect the outcome of the proceedings; or

        (ii) that the expectation of it should be considered under section 36 of the Administration of Justice Act 1970.

(4) In this section "connected person" has the same meaning as in section 54.

Actions by mortgagees: service of notice on certain persons

56.—(1) This section applies if a mortgagee of land which consists, or substantially **32.015** consists, of a dwelling house brings an action for the enforcement of his security, and at the relevant time there is—

    (a) in the case of unregistered land, a land charge of Class F registered against the person who is the estate owner at the relevant time or any person who, where the estate owner is a trustee, preceded him as trustee during the subsistence of the mortgage; or

    (b) in the case of registered land, a subsisting registration of—

        (i) a notice under section 31(10);

        (ii) a notice under section 2(8) of the Matrimonial Homes Act 1983; or

        (iii) a notice or caution under section 2(7) of the Matrimonial Homes Act 1967.

(2) If the person on whose behalf—

    (a) the land charge is registered; or

    (b) the notice or caution is entered;

is not a party to the action, the mortgagee must serve notice of the action on him.

(3) If—

    (a) an official search has been made on behalf of the mortgagee which would disclose any land charge of Class F, notice or caution within subsection (1)(a) or (b);

    (b) a certificate of the result of the search has been issued; and

    (c) the action is commenced within the priority period,

the relevant time is the date of the certificate.

(4) In any other case the relevant time is the time when the action is commenced.

(5) The priority period is, for both registered and unregistered land, the period for which, in accordance with section 11(5) and (6) of the Land Charges Act 1972, a certificate on an official search operates in favour of a purchaser.

Jurisdiction

32.016 The county court has jurisdiction to hear all claims for possession (s.21(1) of the County Courts Act 1984). It is important to note that the county court has exclusive jurisdiction in mortgage possession claims where the land consists of or includes a dwelling-house situated outside Greater London (s.21(3)); in the unreported case of *Platform Funding Ltd v Easeman*, Briggs J.—Chancery Division, Liverpool District Registry, February 26, 2012—held that the claim cannot be transferred to the High Court, except where the claim for possession is made in an action for foreclosure or sale (s.21(4)).

County Courts Act 1984 section 21

32.017   **21.**—(1) A county court shall have jurisdiction to hear and determine any action for the recovery of land.
              (2) . . .
              (3) Where a mortgage of land consists of or includes a dwelling house and no part of the land is situated in Greater London then, subject to subsection (4), if a county court has jurisdiction by virtue of this section to hear and determine an action in which the mortgagee under that mortgage claims possession of the mortgaged property, no court other than a county court shall have jurisdiction to hear and determine that action.
              (4) Subsection (3) shall not apply to an action for foreclosure or sale in which a claim for possession of the mortgaged property is also made.
                  . . .
              (7) In this section—

                   "dwelling house" includes any building or part of a building which is used as a dwelling;
                   "mortgage" includes a charge and "mortgagor" and "mortgagee" shall be construed accordingly;
                   "mortgagor" and "mortgagee" includes any person deriving title under the original mortgage or mortgagee.

              (8) The fact that part of the premises comprised in a dwelling house is used as a shop or office or for business, trade or professional purposes shall not prevent the dwelling house from being a dwelling house for the purposes of this section.
              (9) This section does not apply to a mortgage securing an agreement which is a regulated agreement within the meaning of the Consumer Credit Act 1974.

Generally, the lender only claims possession. It does not need to make a money claim because its intention is usually to sell the property and then to take all sums due from the proceeds of sale. However, the lender may wish to make a claim for sums due, in addition to possession, if the value of the property is less than the total of the sums owed. Should it wish to make such a claim it may do so pursuant to the court's unlimited jurisdiction in contract (s.15 of the County Courts Act 1984; para.11 of the prescribed form; p.528).

Consumer credit cases

32.018 Where the agreement secured by the mortgage is a regulated agreement within the meaning of the Consumer Credit Act 1974 the proceedings must be brought in the county court (s.141 of the Consumer Credit Act 1974). If they are commenced in the High Court the claim will not be struck out (*Sovereign Leasing v Ali* (1991) *The Times*, March 21, QBD) but will be transferred to the county court (s.141(1), (2) of the 1974 Act).

Consumer Credit Act 1974 section 141

(1) In England and Wales the county court shall have jurisdiction to hear and determine—

    (a) any action by the creditor or owner to enforce a regulated agreement or any security relating to it;

    (b) any action to enforce any linked transaction against the debtor or hirer or his relative;

and such an action shall not be brought in any other court.

(2) Where an action or application is brought in the High Court which, by virtue of this Act, ought to have been brought in the county court it shall not be treated as improperly brought but shall be transferred to the county court.

Mortgage arrears protocol

Before commencing a claim for possession based on mortgage arrears, the parties **32.018A** (in particular the lender) should comply with the pre-action protocol set out below where applicable.

Pre-Action Protocol for Possession Claims based on Mortgage or Home Purchase Plan Arrears in Respect of Residential Property

I Introduction

1 Preamble

1.1 This Protocol describes the behaviour the court will normally expect of the parties prior to the start of a possession claim within the scope of paragraph 3.1 below.

1.2 This Protocol does not alter the parties' rights and obligations.

1.3 It is in the interests of the parties that mortgage payments or payments under home purchase plans are made promptly and that difficulties are resolved wherever possible without court proceedings. However in some cases an order for possession may be in the interest of both the lender and the borrower.

2 Aims

2.1 The aims of this Protocol are to—

    (1) ensure that a lender or home purchase plan provider (in this Protocol collectively referred to as 'the lender') and a borrower or home purchase plan customer (in this Protocol collectively referred to as 'the borrower') act fairly and reasonably with each other in resolving any matter concerning mortgage or home purchase plan arrears; and

    (2) encourage more pre-action contact between the lender and the borrower in an effort to seek agreement between the parties, and where this cannot be reached, to enable efficient use of the court's time and resources.

2.2 Where either party is required to communicate and provide information to the other, reasonable steps should be taken to do so in a way that is clear, fair and not misleading.

If the lender is aware that the borrower may have difficulties in reading or understanding the information provided, the lender should take reasonable steps to ensure that information is communicated in a way that the borrower can understand.

3 Scope

3.1 This Protocol applies to arrears on—

(1) first charge residential mortgages and home purchase plans regulated by the Financial Services Authority under the Financial Services and Markets Act 2000;

(2) second charge mortgages over residential property and other secured loans regulated under the Consumer Credit Act 1974 on residential property; and

(3) unregulated residential mortgages.

3.2 Where a potential claim includes a money claim and a claim for possession this protocol applies to both.

4 Definitions

4.1 In this Protocol—

(1) 'possession claim' means a claim for the recovery of possession of property under Part 55 of the Civil Procedure Rules 1998;

(2) 'home purchase plan' means a method of purchasing a property by way of a sale and lease arrangement that does not require the payment of interest;

(3) 'bank holiday' means a bank holiday under the Banking and Financial Dealings Act 1971;

(4) 'business day' means any day except Saturday, Sunday, a bank holiday, Good Friday or Christmas day; and

(5) 'Mortgage Rescue Scheme' means the shared equity and mortgage to rent scheme established either—

(a) by the UK Government to help certain categories of vulnerable borrowers avoid repossession of their property in England, announced in September 2008 and opened in January 2009; or

(b) by the Welsh Assembly Government to help certain categories of vulnerable borrowers avoid repossession of their property in Wales, first announced in June 2008.

II Actions Prior to the Start of a Possession Claim

5 Initial contact and provision of information

5.1 Where the borrower falls into arrears the lender must provide the borrower with—

(1) where appropriate, the required regulatory information sheet or the National Homelessness Advice Service booklet on mortgage arrears; and

(2) information concerning the amount of arrears which should include—

(a) the total amount of the arrears;

(b) the total outstanding of the mortgage or the home purchase plan; and

(c) whether interest or charges will be added, and if so and where appropriate, details or an estimate of the interest or charges that may be payable.

5.2 The parties must take all reasonable steps to discuss with each other, or their representatives, the cause of the arrears, the borrower's financial circumstances and proposals for repayment of the arrears (see 7.1). For example, parties should consider whether the causes of the arrears are temporary or long term and whether the borrower may be able to pay the arrears in a reasonable time.

5.3 The lender must advise the borrower to make early contact with the housing department of the borrower's Local Authority and, should, where necessary, refer the borrower to appropriate sources of independent debt advice.

5.4 The lender must consider a reasonable request from the borrower to change the date of regular payment (within the same payment period) or the method by which payment is made. The lender must either agree to such a request or, where it refuses such a request, it must, within a reasonable period of time, give the borrower a written explanation of its reasons for the refusal.

5.5 The lender must respond promptly to any proposal for payment made by the borrower. If the lender does not agree to such a proposal it should give reasons in writing to the borrower within 10 business days of the proposal.

5.6 If the lender submits a proposal for payment, the borrower must be given a reasonable period of time in which to consider such proposals. The lender must set out the proposal in sufficient detail to enable the borrower to understand the implications of the proposal.

5.7 If the borrower fails to comply with an agreement, the lender should warn the borrower, by giving the borrower 15 business days notice in writing, of its intention to start a possession claim unless the borrower remedies the breach in the agreement.

6 Postponing the start of a possession claim

6.1 A lender must consider not starting a possession claim for mortgage arrears where the borrower can demonstrate to the lender that the borrower has—

(1)   submitted a claim to—

(a)   the Department for Works and Pensions (DWP) for Support for Mortgage Interest (SMI); or
(b)   an insurer under a mortgage payment protection policy; or
(c)   a participating local authority for support under a Mortgage Rescue Scheme,

and has provided all the evidence required to process a claim;
(2)   a reasonable expectation of eligibility for payment from the DWP or from the insurer or support from the local authority; and
(3)   an ability to pay a mortgage instalment not covered by a claim to the DWP or the insurer in relation to a claim under paragraph 6.1(1)(a) or (b).

6.2 If a borrower can demonstrate that reasonable steps have been or will be taken to market the property at an appropriate price in accordance with reasonable professional advice, the lender must consider postponing starting a possession claim. The borrower must continue to take all reasonable steps actively to market the property where the lender has agreed to postpone starting a possession claim.

6.3 Where the lender has agreed to postpone starting a possession claim the borrower should provide the lender with a copy of the particulars of sale, the Energy Performance Certificate (EPC) or proof that an EPC has been commissioned and (where relevant) details of purchase offers received within a reasonable period of time specified by the lender. The borrower should give the lender details of the estate agent and the conveyancer instructed to deal with the sale. The borrower should also authorise the estate agent and the conveyancer to communicate with the lender about the progress of the sale and the borrower's conduct during the process.

6.4 Where the lender decides not to postpone the start of a possession claim it must inform the borrower of the reasons for this decision at least 5 business days before starting proceedings.

7 Further matters to consider before starting a possession claim

Starting a possession claim should normally be a last resort and such a claim must not normally be started unless all other reasonable attempts to resolve the position have failed. The parties should consider whether, given the individual circumstances of the borrower and the form of the agreement, it is reasonable and appropriate to do one or more of the following—

(1) extend the term of the mortgage;
(2) change the type of mortgage;
(3) defer payment of interest due under the mortgage;
(4) capitalise the arrears; or
(5) make use of any Government forbearance initiatives in which the lender chooses to participate.

8 Complaints to the Financial Ombudsman Service

8.1 The lender must consider whether to postpone the start of a possession claim where the borrower has made a genuine complaint to the Financial Ombudsman Service (FOS) about the potential possession claim.

8.2 Where a lender does not intend to await the decision of the FOS it must give notice to the borrower with reasons that it intends to start a possession claim at least 5 business days before doing so.

9 Compliance

9.1 Parties must be able, to explain the actions that they have taken to comply with this protocol.

Particular points to note are as follows:

(1) The lender must consider a reasonable request to change the date or method of payment (5.4)

(2) The protocol specifically deals with the situation where the borrower is trying to sell the property and gives the lender some comfort by requiring the borrower to demonstrate the steps they are taking to progress a sale (6.3). See further para.32.064—where these matters would be relevant to the question of whether an order for possession should be made at a hearing.

(3) Failure to comply with the protocol could result in a hearing being adjourned and/or adverse cost orders (see para.4.1 of Practice Direction—Pre Action Conduct and CPR 3.1 (4) and (5), 3.9 (1) (e) and 44.3 (5) (a)).

Procedure

Which court?

32.019 The general rule is that proceedings must be commenced in the county court for the district in which the land is situated (CPR rr.55.2 and 55.3). For the position where the proceedings have been commenced in the wrong court, see CPR r.55 PD 55.3 para.1.2 and CPR r.30.2.

Issuing the proceedings

Proceedings for possession based on mortgage arrears may now be issued online. **32.020** The system is generally known as "PCOL" This is now the normal method used by very many claimants (*www.possessionclaim.gov.uk*). In order to use PCOL the property needs to be in England or Wales and the Claimant needs to be able to provide the postcode for the property. The system uses the code to issue in the correct court. The procedure is governed by Practice Direction 55B—which can be found at para.25.056. See also the notes at para.25.021 where PCOL is discussed in relation to rent possession claims.

To issue proceedings by filing at court, the following must be filed:

(1) A claim for the possession of property (Form N5 see p.359).

(2) The particulars of claim (Form N120 see p.525).

(3) If appropriate, a certificate stating why the claim has been commenced in the High Court.

(4) The court fee.

Copies must be filed for each Defendant (CPR r.6.3) and a further copy if the Claimant's search has shown that there is a person who is required to be served in accordance with s.56(2) of the Family Law Act 1996 (see para.32.015).

The court will fix a date when it issues the claim form at which it will either decide the claim or make case management directions (CPR rr.55.5 and 55.8).

Where there has been a previous order for possession, but the arrears have been paid off, it is not necessary (or indeed permissible) to issue fresh proceedings on more recent arrears, if the original possession order was suspended on condition that current monthly instalments be paid (see para.32.061). The mortgagee can simply proceed to enforce the order (*Zinda v Bank of Scotland Plc* [2011] EWCA Civ 706). As a matter of good practice, they should first notify the borrower of their intentions. Where however, no possession order was made, but the claim was adjourned on terms, the mortgagee needs to apply for a hearing to restore the claim.

Proceedings taken by a second mortgagee

If proceedings are proposed to be taken by a second mortgagee, he should write **32.021** to the first mortgagee asking whether he has already obtained an order for possession and whether he has any observations to make on the proposed application. A copy of the letter and any reply should be produced at the hearing. If there is more than one prior mortgagee letters on the same lines should be sent to them all.

The particulars of claim

The rules relating to the particulars of claim are set out in CPR r.55 PD 55.4 paras **32.022** 2.1 and 2.5 (see below). The main points to note are as follows:

(1) In all mortgage possession claims where the land consists of or includes a dwelling the particulars of claim must be in prescribed form (CPR PD 55.3 para.1.5; Form N120, p.525). The form is to be used where the mortgage secures a regulated consumer credit agreement and in cases where it does not do so (para.4). The particulars of claim must state whether or not the agreement is a regulated consumer credit agreement (CPR PD 55.4 para.2.5(4)).

(2) The particulars of claim will be sent with the Defence Form to Mortgaged Residential Premises (N11M) and Notes for the defendant (Form N7).

(3) The claimant must give details of the defendant's financial and other circumstances so far as they are known to it and must state whether the claimant is paid interest or arrears direct under social security regulations and, if so, how much (CPR PD 55.4 para.2.5(6)). Relevant information might include the defendant's age, marital and family circumstances, his occupation and any physical or mental handicap.

(4) The claimant must state that they will serve notice of the claim on persons on whose behalf a land charge is registered (under Matrimonial Homes Act 1967), or notice is registered or entered (under Matrimonial Homes Act 1983 or Family Law Act 1996) (CPR PD 55.4 para.2.5(1)).

Form 40: Particulars of claim for possession
(mortgaged residential premises)

Particulars of claim   In the   Claim No.
for possession
(mortgaged residential
premises)

Claimant

Defendant

1. The claimant has a right to possession of:

About the mortgage

2. On   the claimant(s) and the defendant(s) entered into a mortgage of the above premises.

3. To the best of the claimant's knowledge the following persons are in possession of the property:

[*Delete (a) or (b) as appropriate*]
4. (a) The agreement for the loan secured by the mortgage (or at least one of them) is a regulated consumer credit
      agreement. Notice of default was given to the defendant(s) on
20 .

    (b) The agreement for the loan secured by the mortgage is not (or none of them is) a regulated consumer credit
      agreement.

5. The claimant is asking for possession on the following ground(s):

    (a) the defendant(s)(has)(have) not paid the agreed repayments of the loan and interest.
    Give details (as required under paragraph 2.5 of Practice Direction accompanying Part 55 of the Civil Procedure Rules):

(b) because:

6. (a) The amount loaned was £
    (b) The current terms of repayment are: (*include any current periodic repayment and any current payment of interest*)

    (c) The total amount required to pay the mortgage in full as at   20   (not more than 14
        days after the claim was issued) would be £   taking into account any adjustment for
        early settlement. This includes £   payable for solicitor's costs and administration charges.

    (d) The following additional payments are also required under the terms of the mortgage:

        £   for   [not] included in 6(c)

        £   for   [not] included in 6(c)

        £   for   [not] included in 6(c)

    (e) Of the payments in paragraph 6(d), the following are in arrears:

                              arrears of £

                              arrears of £

                              arrears of £

    [(f) The total amount outstanding under the regulated loan agreement secured by the mortgage is £   ]

    (g) Interest rates which have been applied to the mortgage:

        (i) at the start of the mortgage   % p.a.

        (ii) immediately before any arrears were accrued   % p.a.

        (iii) at the start of the claim   % p.a.

7. The following steps have already been taken to recover the money secured by the mortgage:

About the defendant(s)

8. The following information is known about the defendant's circumstances:
   (in particular say whether the defendant(s) (is)(are) in receipt of social security benefits and whether any payments are made directly to the claimant)

[Delete either (a) or (b) as appropriate]
9. (a) There is no one who should be given notice of these proceedings because of a registered interest in the property under section 31(10) of the Family Law Act 1996 or section 2(8) or 8(3) of the Matrimonial Homes Act 1983 or section 2(7) of the Matrimonial Homes Act 1967.

   (b) Notice of these proceedings will be given to   who has a registered interest in the property.

Tenancy

[Delete if inappropriate]
10. A tenancy was entered into between the mortgagor and the mortgagee on
    A notice was served on

What the court is being asked to do

11. The claimant asks the court to order that the defendant(s):
    (a) give the claimant possession of the premises:
    (b) pay to the claimant the total amount outstanding under the mortgage.

> Statement of Truth
>
> *(I believe)(The claimant believes) that the facts stated in these particulars of claim are true.
> *I am duly authorised by the claimant to sign this statement.
>
> signed _____ date _____
> *(Claimant)(Litigation friend (*where claimant is a child or a patient*))(Claimant's solicitor)
> *deleted as appropriate
>
> Full name _____
>
> Name of claimant's solicitor's firm _____
>
> position or office held _____
>   (*if signing on behalf of firm or company*)

CPR PD 55.4—particulars of claim

32.023   2.1 In a possession claim the particulars of claim must:

    (1) identify the land to which the claim relates;
    (2) state whether the claim relates to residential property;
    (3) state the ground on which possession is claimed;
    (4) give full details about any mortgage or tenancy agreement; and
    (5) give details of every person who, to the best of the claimant's knowledge, is in possession of the property.

Land subject to a mortgage

32.024   2.5 If the claim is a possession claim by a mortgagee, the particulars of claim must also set out:

    (1) if the claim relates to residential property whether:

        (a) a land charge of Class F has been registered under section 2(7) of the Matrimonial Homes Act 1967;
        (b) a notice registered under section 2(8) or 8(3) of the Matrimonial Homes Act 1983 has been entered and on whose behalf; or
        (c) a notice under section 31(10) of the Family Law Act 1996 has been registered and on whose behalf; and

        if so, that the claimant will serve notice of the claim on the persons on whose behalf the land charge is registered or the notice or caution entered.

    (2) the state of the mortgage account by including:

        (a) the amount of:
            (i) the advance;
            (ii) any periodic repayment; and
            (iii) any payment of interest required to be made.
        (b) the amount which would have to be paid (after taking into account any adjustment for early settlement) in order to redeem the mortgage at a stated date not more than 14 days after the claim started specifying the

amount of solicitor's costs and administration charges which would be payable;

(c) if the loan which is secured by the mortgage is a regulated consumer credit agreement, the total amount outstanding under the terms of the mortgage; and

(d) the rate of interest payable:

  (i) at the commencement of the mortgage;
  (ii) immediately before any arrears referred to in paragraph (3) accrued;
  (iii) at the commencement of the proceedings.

(3) if the claim is brought because of failure to pay the periodic payments when due:

(a) in schedule form, the dates and amounts of all payments due and payments made under the mortgage agreement or mortgage deed for a period of two years immediately preceding the date of issue, or if the first date of default occurred less than two years before the date of issue from the first date of default and a running total of the arrears;

(b) give details of:

  (i) any other payments required to be made as a term of the mortgage (such as for insurance premiums, legal costs, default interest, penalties, administrative or other charges);
  (ii) any other sums claimed and stating the nature and amount of each such charge; and
  (iii) whether any of these payments is in arrears and whether or not it is included in the amount of any periodic payment.

(4) whether or not the loan which is secured by the mortgage is a regulated consumer credit agreement and, if so, specify the date on which any notice required by sections 76 or 87 of the Consumer Credit Act 1974 was given;

(5) if appropriate details that show the property is not one to which section 141 of the Consumer Credit Act 1974 applies;

(6) any relevant information about the defendant's circumstances, in particular:

(a) whether the defendant is in receipt of social security benefits; and

(b) whether any payments are made on his behalf directly to the claimant under the Social Security Contributions and Benefits Act 1992.

(7) give details of any tenancy entered into between the mortgagor and mortgagee (including any notices served); and

(8) state any previous steps which the claimant has taken to recover the money secured by the mortgage or the mortgaged property and, in the case of court proceedings, state:

(a) the dates when the claim started and concluded; and

(b) the dates and terms of any orders made.

2.5A If the claimant wishes to rely on a history of arrears which is longer than two years, he should state this in his particulars of claim and exhibit a full (or longer) schedule to a witness statement.

Evidence in support

Unless the case is allocated to the Fast or Multi Track or the court orders other- **32.025** wise, the claimant will be able to prove his claim by evidence in writing. The claimant could include all their evidence in their statement of case, verified by a statement of truth, and update the amount of arrears and interest either in writing or orally at the hearing (CPR r.55.8 and CPR PD 55.8 para.5.1 and 5.2). Matters and documents which must be included in either the Particulars of Claim or a witness statement in support are:

(1) The official copy of the register with a copy of the charge certificate.

(2) A schedule detailing the accrual of current arrears and interest (see para.31.025).

(3) Service of the notices pursuant to CPR r.55.10 and exhibit copies of them (see para.32.027).

(4) If the mortgage incorporates standard mortgage conditions, those conditions (only the relevant sections need to be attached to the Particulars of Claim, but the full conditions must be available at the hearing).

(5) The "Offer letter" if that document rather than the mortgage contains particulars of the advance, the term of the loan, the rate of interest or the amount of instalments.

(6) Unless the defendants are husband and wife or civil partners who are joint mortgagors, an up-to-date certificate of search from the Land Registry or in the case of unregistered land from the Land Charges Department (see para.32.012).

Relevant documents can be attached to the Particulars of Claim and if verified by a statement of truth will be admissible as evidence (CPR PD 16 para.8.3, originals of the documents should be brought to the hearing).

When the court fixes a date for the hearing a notice of hearing (possession claims) will be sent out notifying the parties of the date of the hearing and reiterating that any evidence must be filed with the court and served on the other parties at least two clear days before the hearing (CPR r.55.8(4)).

It should also be remembered that a Form N123 must be produced at the hearing (two copies—CPR PD 55A para.5.5)

Payment by the borrower after commencement

32.026 Where the borrower pays the arrears after commencement of the claim the lender should not withdraw the proceedings but adjourn the claim generally. If arrears accrue again the claim can be restored without the necessity of commencing fresh proceedings (CPR r.3—under the courts general powers of case management; and see further para.32.020).

Form 41: Witness statement of the claimant-mortgagee

IN THE	COUNTY COURT	Claim No

BETWEEN

Claimant

-AND-

Defendant

WITNESS STATEMENT OF CLAIMANT

I. [JOHN BROWN, of Honeymoon Solicitors [state address] state as follows:

1. I am a Legal Assistant in the employ of Honeymoon Solicitors, solicitors for the claimant. I am the person, under the supervision of my principals, with the conduct of this claim and am authorised to make this witness statement on its behalf. I make this witness statement from information acquired by me during my conduct of the claim, from the documents attached to this statement and from information supplied to me by the arrears office of the Claimant.

2. I have read the Particulars of Claim in this claim dated [state date] and say that the same were true and accurate in all respects at the that date.

3. A true copy of the Legal Charge is annexed hereto and marked "JB 1".

4. A copy of the Official Copy Entries for the property is annexed hereto and marked "JB 2".

5. I sent Copies of the notices sent to:
   a.) the property addressed to the 'tenant or the occupier';
   b.) the housing department of the local authority within which the property is located; and
   c.) the following registered proprietors of a registered charge other than the claimant [*delete if not applicable*]

by first class post on [date] are annexed hereto and marked "JB 3". No-one has responded to these notices and to the best of my knowledge and belief there are no other persons occupying the property other than the Defendant. [*or insert details of any responses received and exhibit the same*].

6. The Defendant has failed to make payments due under the mortgage and arrears have accrued. The current state of the mortgage account is as follows:

Current monthly instalment payable on 3rd of each month	£ . . . . .
Arrears	£ . . . . .
Current balance outstanding	£ . . . . .
Daily rate of interest at today's date	£ . . . . .
The last payment was made on . . . . in the sum of	£ . . . . .

The basis upon which these figures and the figures stated in the Particulars of Claim have been calculated is set out in a schedule which is now produced and shown to me and marked "JB 4".

7. No previous proceedings of any kind in connection with the mortgaged property or the monies secured by mortgage have been taken against the Defendant.

8. There is now produced and shown to me marked "JB 5" a true copy of a certificate of search at H.M. Land Registry showing that no Notice has been registered against the said title.

9. To the best of my knowledge and belief the Defendant is still in physical occupation of the said property.

Service of the proceedings; notice to occupiers

32.027 Service of the proceedings may be affected in the same way as for proceedings against a tenant (see para.25.024). It has been held that service effected on one of two joint borrowers where one borrower was not resident at the mortgaged property and whose whereabouts were unknown was good service to which an order for possession could be obtained (*Alliance Building Society v Yap* [1962] 1 W.L.R. 857).

In addition to the ordinary service of the proceedings on the defendants, notice of the proceedings containing certain details of them is required to be sent to the property addressed to "the tenant or the occupier" as well as to the relevant local authority and any other registered chargees. These need to be sent out within five days of the mortgagee receiving notification of the date of the hearing. A copy of the notices and evidence of service must be produced at the hearing (CPR 55.10 (4)). The rights of tenants are dealt with in para.32.073.

CPR rule 55.10

32.028   (1) This rule applies where a mortgagee seeks possession of land which consists of or includes residential property.

(2) Within 5 days of receiving notification of the date of the hearing by the court, the claimant must send a notice to—

(a) the property, addressed to 'the tenant or the occupier';

(b) the housing department of the local authority within which the property is located; and

(c) any registered proprietor (other than the claimant) of a registered charge over the property.

(3) The notice referred to in paragraph (2)(a) must—

(a) state that a possession claim for the property has started;

(b) show the name and address of the claimant, the defendant and the court which issued the claim form; and

(c) give details of the hearing.

(3A) The notice referred to in paragraph 2(b) must contain the information in paragraph (3) and must state the full address of the property.

(4) The claimant must produce at the hearing—

(a) a copy of the notices; and

(b) evidence that they have been sent.

(4A) An unauthorised tenant of residential property may apply to the court for the order for possession to be suspended.

Defendant's action on receipt of proceedings

32.029 When the defendant receives the particulars of claim he will find that the court has also sent him a form titled "Defence form (Mortgaged residential premises) N11M" and Notes for Defendant N7. It is very important that this form be completed by the defendant. It contains a large number of questions designed to assist the court in determining whether or not to make an order for possession and whether or not to exercise its discretionary powers to suspend orders, etc.

If the defendant wishes to raise any substantive defence to the claim he should file a full defence in addition to or, if appropriate, instead of the reply. Strictly speaking any defence should be filed within 14 days after service of the claim (CPR r.15.4). The defendant may appear on the date fixed for the hearing and dispute the claim notwithstanding that no defence has been served but he will usually place himself in a better position if he serves a defence early and may risk an order for costs being made against him if he does not do so (CPR r.55.7(3)). As to defences that may be raised see below.

CPR rule 55.7

Defendant's response

(1) An acknowledgment of service is not required and Part 10 does not apply. **32.030**

. . .

(3) Where . . . the defendant does not file a defence within the time specified in rule 15.4, he may take part in any hearing but the court may take his failure to do so into account when deciding what order to make about costs.

(4) Part 12 (default judgement) does not apply in a claim to which this Part applies.

The hearing

Mortgage possession claims are invariably heard by the district judge and will, at **32.031** least initially, be heard in private (CPR PD 2B and CPR PD 39A para.1.5). The lender should produce two completed copies of the mortgage pre-action protocol checklist in Form N123 (CPR PD 55A para.5.5).

Once the claim is issued the court will fix a date for hearing at which the court may decide the matter or give case management directions (CPR 55.8(1)). This allows for a quick determination of the claim if it is unopposed, there is no real defence or the defendant merely wishes the court to exercise its powers to suspend orders or, in a consumer credit case, to make a time order. If the matter is not so simple, the court will give case management directions which are likely to deal with allocation, evidence and the filing of a Defence (if not already filed).

However, although, the Claimant may now prove his claim by way of written statements, if the maker of a statement does not attend the hearing, and a party wishes to cross examine on material evidence, the court will adjourn to allow the maker to attend (CPR PD 55.8 para.5.4).

Defences: setting aside the mortgage

Non-borrowing spouse in occupation not asked for consent

In *Williams and Glynns Bank Ltd v Boland* [1980] 2 All E.R. 408 it was held that **32.032** a spouse with a beneficial interest in the matrimonial home registered at the Land Registry who is in actual occupation has an "overriding interest" within the meaning of para.2 of Sch.3 of the Land Registration Act 2002 (see para.32.078) and that if the other spouse enters into a mortgage the lender's interest is subject to the non-borrowing spouse's rights of occupation. It is, therefore incumbent on the lender to obtain the non-borrowing spouse's consent to the mortgage even though he/she is not the legal owner. If the lender does not do so it will not be able to enforce the mortgage against the spouse. Children living in the property with their parents who are the legal owners cannot be said to be in actual occupation so as to have an overriding interest; they are there because their parents are there (*Hypo-Mortgage Services Ltd v Robinson* (1997) *The Times*, January 2).

The relevant date for determining whether or not the non-borrowing spouse has an overriding interest is the date the mortgage was executed, not the date of registration (*Abbey National Building Society v Cann* [1990] 1 All E.R. 1085 HL). In *Link Lending Ltd v Bustard* [2010] EWCA Civ 424 a person with mental health problems who was admitted to a psychiatric hospital and then resided in a care home was held to be in actual occupation. She continued to visit the property because she considered it to be her home and wanted to return. Her furniture was there and arrangements had been made to pay the bills to maintain the property.

If the non-borrowing spouse's consent is obtained the mortgage will be binding upon him or her. In *Bristol and West Building Society v Henning* [1985] 2 All E.R. 606 the husband was the legal owner of the property which had been mortgaged to the building society to raise the money for the purchase with the knowledge and consent of the wife who was not a party to the mortgage. The marriage between the parties broke down and the husband left and stopped paying the mortgage. The wife claimed to have an equitable interest in the property, or alternatively an irrevocable licence, which she argued prevented the lender from obtaining possession. There was no declaration of trust in writing or any express agreement as to her having a beneficial interest or the lesser right of an irrevocable licence. It was, therefore, necessary to determine from the parties' actions what their express or imputed intentions as to her beneficial interest or irrevocable licence were. It was held that as the wife knew of and supported the proposal to raise the purchase money for the house by the mortgage the common intention of the parties must have been that any interest the wife had was subject to the lender's charge which the lender was therefore entitled to enforce by obtaining possession.

32.033 As to whether or not a spouse or other person has an equitable interest based upon a constructive trust see *Stack v Dowden* [2007] UKHL 17 and *Jones v Kernott* [2011] UKSC 53 (see Ch.33).

In *Boland* the money was advanced by the lender to a sole proprietor who held the land as sole trustee. The position is very different where the legal ownership is in the names of two or more persons and the money is advanced to two or more of those persons. In these circumstances the interest of a beneficiary of the trust for sale will be "overreached" and he will not be able to rely on an overriding interest for protection notwithstanding that he may be in actual occupation. The lender will be entitled to possession (see *City of London Building Society v Flegg* [1987] 3 All E.R. 435.) The fact that no capital money is actually advanced at the time of the charge does not assist the occupiers (*State Bank of India v Sood* [1997] 1 All E.R. 169 CA).

In *Equity and Law Home Loans Ltd v Prestridge* [1992] 1 All E.R. 909 CA, the court considered the effect on the equitable interest of a wife who had consented to a first mortgage where her husband had subsequently remortgaged the property without her consent. The court held that it was to be imputed that the wife consented to the second mortgage to the extent to which she consented to the first.

Signature to mortgage a forgery

32.034 There are some cases where one spouse, let us say the husband, who is the joint owner of the property with his wife, forges his wife's signature on the mortgage deed. In these circumstances the mortgage is ineffective as a legal charge but the husband's conduct does have the effect of creating a valid equitable charge in the lender's favour on the husband's share in the proceeds of sale in the house (*Ahmed v Kendrick and Ahmed* [1988] 2 F.L.R. 22 CA).

The equitable charge created by the husband's behaviour is sufficient to permit the lender to apply for an order for sale of the house; see *First National Bank Plc v Achampong* [2003] EWCA Civ 487; *Edwards v Lloyds Bank Plc* [2004] EWHC 1745 (Ch); *Edwards v Bank of Scotland* [2010] EWHC 652 (Ch)—see further

Ch.33. Alternatively, a lender who cannot enforce the mortgage because of the forgery can bring proceedings for the money loaned and interest and costs. Once a judgment has been obtained, a charging order can be applied for in respect of the husband's share in the proceeds of sale with the intention of subsequently applying for an order for sale of the house—see again Ch.33.

Lender misrepresenting the mortgage

"The relationship between banker and customer is not one which ordinarily gives rise to **32.035** a presumption of undue influence; and . . . in the ordinary course of banking business a banker can explain the nature of the proposed transaction without laying himself open to a charge of undue influence" (*National Westminster Bank v Morgan* [1985] 1 All E.R. 821 HL per Lord Scarman at 892j).

A bank is of course under a duty to ensure that it does not negligently misstate the effect of the mortgage. In particular, where the mortgage covers further advances this should be explained to the customer. If the bank is negligent the customer will be entitled to damages for any loss suffered but the mortgage will not be set aside unless the customer can show that the bank has taken unfair advantage of him (*Cornish v Midland Bank Plc* [1985] 3 All E.R. 513).

Misrepresentation or undue influence of a third party

Introduction

It is very common for one person (the surety) to charge his property to the lender **32.036** to secure the debts of the borrower. A company director charges his home to secure the company's debts: a wife agrees to the matrimonial home in which she has an equal share being charged to secure her husband's business debts. In the usual case if the borrower defaults the lender is entitled to possession of the property.

In some cases the surety contends that he (or, more commonly, she) was induced to enter into the mortgage by undue influence or that it is vitiated for some other reason. In the husband and wife context the wife commonly asserts that the husband presented her with the documents and misrepresented their meaning or that he somehow forced her to sign them against her will. Even in the absence of "actual undue influence" the courts will often, but not always, find that the wife has placed trust and confidence in her husband and go on to presume that the husband has unduly influenced the wife to enter into the transaction (see further 32.040). The question then arises as to whether or not the mortgage is invalidated by that misconduct: is the lender to be affected by the borrower's misconduct (see *First National Bank v Walker* [2001] 1 F.L.R. 595 CA at 615)?

Thus, in every case there are two stages to consider:

(1) Has there been a misrepresentation, undue influence or some other legal wrong practised by the debtor on the surety?

(2) Is the creditor affected by that wrong? It will be so affected if it had actual or constructive notice of that wrong, or if the wrongdoer acted as the bank's agent in procuring the surety to sign the charge.

In order to simplify the text in the rest of this chapter the wrongdoer is generally referred to as the husband, the surety as the wife and the lender as the bank. The principles apply to all surety documents but we shall assume that the document is a charge over the matrimonial home. The leading cases on the subject are *Barclays Bank v O'Brien* [1994] 1 A.C. 180 HL and *Royal Bank of Scotland v Etridge (No.2)* [2001] 4 All E.R. 449 HL).

32.037   Where a wife only consents to a mortgage due to the undue influence of her husband, a subsequent affirmation of the charge (made without any undue influence), defeats the effect of the prior undue influence (see *First National Bank v Walker*—where the wife had conducted matrimonial proceedings on the basis that the charge was valid but in possession proceedings brought by the mortgagee she claimed that it ought to be set aside due to undue influence. The Court of Appeal stated that it was not acceptable to conduct these proceedings inconsistently).

Stage One: conduct of the husband or other wrongdoer

32.038 As stated, the first step in any attempt to set aside the transaction is to show misconduct on the part of the husband. The wife must show that the husband has procured the charge by misrepresentation, undue influence or some other legal wrong. It is not enough to show that she "lacked an adequate understanding" or that the she was not properly advised as to the effect of the mortgage.

Misrepresentation can occur in a number of ways. The husband may misrepresent the terms of the mortgage or the purpose or the amount of the loan; or there may be some other misrepresentation which has led the wife to enter into the mortgage.

What is undue influence? It occurs where a person enters into a transaction as a result of threats or victimisation rather than folly or recklessness; i.e. where it is not freely entered into. (See generally *National Westminster Bank v Morgan* [1985] 1 All E.R. at 827-828 HL; Lord Scarman citing *Allcard v Skinner* (1887) 36 Ch. D. 145.)

Undue influence falls into two categories: actual or presumed. In cases of actual undue influence it is necessary for the wife to prove affirmatively that her husband exerted undue influence on her to enter into the charge.

In presumed undue influence cases it is not necessary to prove this. Undue influence will be presumed where there is a relationship of trust and confidence between the complainant and the wrongdoer. Some relationships (such as doctor and patient) automatically give rise to the presumption. However, the relationship of husband and wife is not one of them. Before the presumption is raised the wife must show that she placed trust and confidence in her husband in relation to her financial affairs although the fact that the "sexual and emotional ties between the parties provide a ready weapon for undue influence" makes it easier to raise the presumption in husband and wife cases than in other situations where those ties are absent.

32.039   The position was explained by Lord Nicholls in *Etridge* when he stated that:

"Whether a transaction was brought about by the exercise of undue influence is a question of fact. Here, as elsewhere, the general principle is that he who asserts a wrong has been committed must prove it. The burden of proving an allegation of undue influence rests upon the person who claims to have been wronged. This is the general rule. The evidence required to discharge the burden of proof depends on the nature of the alleged undue influence, the personality of the parties, their relationship, the extent to which the transaction cannot readily be accounted for by the ordinary motives of ordinary persons in that relationship, and all the circumstances of the case.

Proof that the complainant placed trust and confidence in the other party in relation to the management of the complainant's financial affairs, coupled with a transaction which calls for explanation, will normally be sufficient, failing satisfactory evidence to the contrary, to discharge the burden of proof. On proof of these two matters the stage is set for the court to infer that, in the absence of a satisfactory explanation, the transaction can only have been procured by undue influence. In other words, proof of these two facts is prima facie evidence that the defendant abused the influence he acquired in the parties' relationship. He preferred to his own interests. He did not behave fairly to the other. So the evidential burden then shifts to him. It is for him to produce evidence to counter the inference which otherwise should be drawn.

. . .

The availability of this forensic tool in cases founded on abuse of influence arising from the parties' relationship has led to this type of case sometimes being labelled 'presumed undue influence'. This is by way of contrast with cases involving actual pressure of the like, which are labelled 'actual undue influence': see *Bank of Credit and Commerce International SA v Aboody* [1990] 1 Q.B. 923, 953, and *Royal Bank of Scotland Plc v Etridge (No.2)* [1998] 4 All E.R. 705, 711–712, paras 5–7. This usage can be a little confusing. In many cases where a plantiff has claimed that the defendant abused the influence he acquired in a relationship of trust and confidence the plaintiff has succeeded by recourse to the rebuttable evidential presumption. But this need not be so. Such a plaintiff may succeed even where this presumption is not available to him; for instance, where the impugned transaction was not one which called for an explanation.

The evidential presumption discussed above is to be distinguished sharply from a different form of presumption which arises in some cases. The law has adopted a sternly protective attitude towards certain types of relationship in which one party acquires influence over another who is vulnerable and dependent and where, moreover, substantial gifts by the influenced or vulnerable person are not normally to be expected. Examples of relationships within this special class are parent and child, guardian and ward, trustee and beneficiary, solicitor and client, and medical adviser and patient. In these cases the law presumes, irrebuttably, that one party had influence over the other. The complainant need not prove he actually reposed trust and confidence in the other party. It is sufficient for him to prove the existence of the type of relationship.

It is now well established that husband and wife is not one of the relationships to which this latter principle applies. In *Yerkey v Jones* (1939) 63 C.L.R. 649, 675 Dixon J. explained the reason. The Court of Chancery was not blind to the opportunities of obtaining and unfairly using influence over a wife which a husband often possesses. But there is nothing unusual or strange in a wife, from motives of affection or for other reasons, conferring substantial financial benefits on her husband. Although there is no presumption, the court will nevertheless note, as a matter of fact, the opportunities for abuse which flow from a wife's confidence in her husband. The court will take this into account with all the other evidence in the case. Where there is evidence that a husband has taken unfair advantage of his influence over his wife, or her confidence in him, it is not difficult for the wife to establish her title to relief: see *In re Lloyds Bank Ltd, Bomze v Bomze* [1931] 1 Ch. 289, at 302, per Maugham J." (458j to 460e).

The wife will usually seek to establish that she reposed trust and confidence in her husband in relation to their financial affairs by giving evidence to that effect and by producing documents to show that her husband dealt with all the major financial matters, such as mortgages, life policies, bills, etc. Copies of such documents may also be found among the bank's own files, particularly if the husband and wife both had accounts with the bank. They will frequently show that the dealings with the bank were carried out by the husband.

Transaction not readily explicable by the relationship of the parties; manifest disadvantage?

32.040 While the House of Lords in *Etridge* appeared to discard the need for manifest disadvantage in the case of presumed undue influence, they actually appear to have turned this element of a wife's claim into an "in all the circumstances of the case" test. It is necessary to establish that there has been some disadvantage or an inexplicable transaction. This is perhaps better explained in the case of *Barclays Bank v Coleman* (2001) 33 H.L.R. 86 CA, where Nourse L.J. stated:

> "Manifest disadvantage is a necessary ingredient in a case of presumed undue influence . . . 'manifest' . . . means clear and obvious. So there must be disadvantage and it must be clear and obvious. But that does not mean it must be large or even medium-sized. Provided it is clear and obvious and more than de minims, the disadvantage may be small" (at 101).

Lord Nicholls in *Etridge* clearly recognised the difficulty with the phrase manifest disadvantage, particularly when it involved a wife standing surety for her husband's business, which was the main provider for the family. Lord Nicholls stated:

> "So something more is needed before the law reverses the burden of proof, something which calls for an explanation. When that something more is present, the greater the disadvantage to the vulnerable person, the more cogent must be the explanation before the presumption will be regarded as rebutted".

This was the approach adopted by Lord Scarman in *National Westminster Bank Plc v Morgan* [1985] A.C. 686 at 703–707. He cited Lindley L.J.'s observations in *Allcard v Skinner* 36 Ch. D. 145 at 185, which have been set out above. He noted that whatever the legal character of the transaction, it must constitute a disadvantage sufficiently serious to require evidence to rebut the presumption that in the circumstances of the parties' relationship, it was procured by the exercise of undue influence. Lord Scarman concluded, at 704:

> "The Court of Appeal erred in law in holding that the presumption of undue influence can arise from the evidence of the relationship of the parties without also evidence that the transaction itself was wrongful in that it constituted *an advantage taken of the person subjected to the influence which, failing proof to the contrary, was explicable only on the basis that undue influence had been exercised to procure it*" (emphasis added).

Lord Scarman attached the label "manifest disadvantage" to this second ingredient necessary to raise the presumption. This label has been causing difficulty. It may be apt enough when applied to straightforward transactions such as a substantial gift or a sale at an undervalue. But experience has now shown that this expression can give rise to misunderstanding. The label is being understood and applied in a way which does not accord with the meaning intended by Lord Scarman, its originator.

The problem has arisen in the context of wives guaranteeing payment of their husband's business debts. In recent years judge after judge has grappled with the baffling question whether a wife's guarantee of her husband's bank overdraft, together with a charge on her share of the matrimonial home, was a transaction manifestly to her disadvantage.

In a narrow sense, such a transaction plainly ("manifestly") is disadvantageous **32.041** to the wife. She undertakes a serious financial obligation, and in return she personally receives nothing. But that would be to take an unrealistically blinkered view of such a transaction. Unlike the relationship of solicitor and client or medical adviser and patient, in the case of husband and wife there are inherent reasons why such a transaction may well be for her benefit. Ordinarily, the fortunes of husband and wife are bound up together. If the husband's business is the source of the family income, the wife has a lively interest in doing what she can to support the business. A wife's affection and self-interest run hand-in-hand in inclining her to join with her husband in charging the matrimonial home, usually a joint-owned asset, to obtain the financial facilities needed by the business. The finance may be needed to start a new business, or expand a promising business, or rescue an ailing business.

Which, then, is the correct approach to adopt in deciding whether a transaction is disadvantageous to the wife: the narrow approach, or the wider approach? The answer is neither. The answer lies in discarding a label which gives rise to this sort of ambiguity. The better approach is to adhere more directly to the test outlined by Lindley L.J. in *Allcard v Skinner* 36 Ch. D. 145, and adopted by Lord Scarman in *National Westminster Bank Plc v Morgan* [1985] A.C. 686, in the passages cited in this work.

> "I return to husband and wife cases. I do not think that, in the ordinary course, a guarantee of the character I have mentioned is to be regarded as a transaction which, failing proof to the contrary, is explicable only on the basis that it has been procured by the exercise of undue influence by the husband. Wives frequently enter into such transactions. There are good and sufficient reasons why they are willing to do so, despite the risks involved for them and their families. They may be enthusiastic. They may not. They may be less optimistic than their husbands about the prospects of the husbands' businesses. They may be anxious, perhaps exceedingly so. But this is a far cry from saying that such transactions as a class are to be regarded as prima facie evidence of the exercise of undue influence by husbands" (at 461d to 462f).

A claimant who proves actual undue influence, or misrepresentation, is not under **32.042** any further burden of proof. He is entitled as of right to have it set aside as against the person exercising undue influence (*CIBC Mortgages Plc v Pitt* [1993] 4 All E.R. 433):

> "Actual undue influence is a species of fraud. Like any other victim of fraud, a person who has been induced to carry out a transaction which he did not freely and knowingly enter into is entitled to have that transaction set aside as of right. . . . A man guilty of fraud is no more entitled to argue that the transaction was beneficial to the person defrauded than is a man who has procured a transaction by misrepresentation. The effect of the wrongdoer's conduct is to prevent the wronged party from bringing a free will and properly informed mind to bear on the proposed transaction which accordingly must be set aside in equity as a matter of justice.
>
> I therefore hold that a claimant who proves actual undue influence is not under the further burden of proving that the transaction induced by undue influence was manifestly disadvantageous: he is entitled as of right to have it set aside."

Negation of the undue influence

The fact that the wife establishes a presumption of undue influence based upon **32.043** her reposing trust and confidence in her husband in relation to her business affairs does not automatically mean that she passes Stage One. It may be possible for the bank to rebut the presumption; i.e. to prove that notwithstanding the presumption she did in fact enter into the transaction of her own free will. This may be done by establishing that she obtained independent legal advice prior to entering into the transaction but there may well be other factors that establish the position (e.g. see *Banco Exterior Internacional SA v Thomas* [1997] 1 All E.R. 46 CA—where it is clear from the totality of the facts that the surety went ahead with the transaction because she wanted to do so and received a large benefit).

Stage Two: Bank put on enquiry?

32.044 As stated above there are two stages to be dealt with in these cases. The first is to establish misrepresentation, undue influence (actual or presumed) or some other legal wrong on the part of the husband. The second is to establish that the bank is affected by it. The most common way in which a bank is bound by the wrong-doing is by virtue of the fact that it had notice, actual or constructive, of the wrongdoing.

According to Lord Browne-Wilkinson in *O'Brien*, in the case of a husband and wife, a bank is put on inquiry when a wife offers to stand surety for her husband's business debts by the combination of two factors:

(1) The transaction is on its face not to the financial advantage of the wife.

(2) There is a substantial risk that the husband has committed a legal or equi-table wrong entitling her to set the transaction aside.

Lord Hoffmann stated in *Barclays Bank v Boulter* (1999) 32 H.L.R. 170, that:

"in the case of undue influence exercised by a husband over a wife, the burden is prima facie very easily discharged. The wife needs to show only that the bank knew that she was a wife living with her husband and that the transaction was not on its face to her financial advantage. The burden is then upon the bank to show that it took reasonable steps to satisfy itself that her consent was properly obtained" (para.31.036).

Lord Nicholls in *Etridge* interpreted the passage above from Lord Browne-Wilkinson as "to be taken to mean, quite simply, that a bank is put on inquiry whenever a wife offers to stand surety for her husband's debts" (at 465j). He further went on to state:

"The position is likewise if the husband stands surety for his wife's debts. Similarly, in the case of unmarried couples, whether heterosexual or homosexual, where the bank is aware of the relationship: see Lord Browne-Wilkinson in *O'Brien's* case, at p.198. Cohabitation is not essential. The Court of Appeal rightly so decided in *Massey v Midland Bank Plc* [1995] 1 All E.R. 929: see Steyn L.J., at 933.

As to the type of transactions where a bank is put on inquiry, the case where a wife becomes surety for her husband's debts is, in this context, a straightforward case. The bank is put on inquiry. On the other side of the line is the case where money is being advanced, or has been advanced, to husband and wife jointly. In such a case the bank is not put on inquiry, unless the bank is aware the loan is being made for the husband's purposes, as distinct from their joint purposes. That was decided in *CIBC Mortgages Plc v Pitt* [1994] 1 A.C. 200.

Less clear cut is the case where the wife becomes surety for the debts of a company whose shares are held by her and her husband. Her shareholding may be nominal, or she may have a minority shareholding or an equal shareholding with her husband. In my view the bank is put on inquiry in such cases, even when the wife is a director or secretary of the company. Such cases cannot be equated with joint loans. The share-holding interests, and the identity of the directors, are not a reliable guide to the identity of the persons who actually have the conduct of the company's business" (at 466d to h).

Where the bank is put on inquiry it is required to take reasonable steps to satisfy **32.045** itself that the wife's agreement has been properly obtained (*O'Brien* at 196E); or to put it another way, to satisfy itself that the surety has entered into the obligation freely and in knowledge of the true facts (*O'Brien* at 198H). If it does not do so the creditor is fixed with constructive notice of the wife's rights (*O'Brien* at 196).

It should be noted that the bank's obligation is merely to take reasonable steps "to satisfy itself". It does not have to show that the wife's agreement was in fact properly obtained; although if it does so the wife's defence will obviously fail (under Stage One above).

Reasonable steps: what is necessary?

In all transactions the bank should: **32.046**

(1) take steps to bring home to the wife the risks she is running; and

(2) advise her to take independent advice (*O'Brien* at 196G).

Past transactions

In transactions that took place before the House of Lords decision in **32.047** *O'Brien* (October 21, 1993), whether these steps have been taken will be a question of fact. The sort of factors that may be relevant are as follows:

(1) What steps did the bank take to bring home to the wife the risk she was running?

  (a) Was the transaction explained to her?
  (b) Did the bank communicate with the wife directly?
  (c) Was it explained in the absence of her husband?
  (d) Did the bank tell the wife the extent of her liability?
  (e) Was she told of any existing liability; and the amount by which the facility was to increase?
  (f) Was she informed of the increase in the facility?

(2) What steps did the bank take to ensure that the wife had independent advice?

  (a) Did they deal with her through a solicitor?
  (b) Did they arrange for her to see a solicitor?
  (c) Did the bank receive a certificate from a solicitor stating that the contents of the charge had been explained to her? (See further below.)

Future transactions

After *O'Brien* but before *Etridge* (i.e. October 2001), the lender will **32.048** have discharged its obligations if a solicitor who was acting for the wife gave confirmation to the lender that the wife had been advised of the risk she was taking by standing surety.

Following the House of Lords in *Etridge*, in all transactions the lender should:

- communicate directly with the wife and not proceed until it had received an appropriate response directly. In particular, it should enquire as to the name of the solicitor that she wishes to act for her;

- if relying on a solicitor to impart the necessary legal advice, send the solicitor all the relevant financial information;

- not proceed with the transaction without written confirmation from the solicitor that advice has been given.

Further, *Etridge* stated that in acting for the wife, it was a solicitor's duty to:

- meet the wife face to face in the absence of the husband;

- ensure he gets all the relevant financial information from the lender;

- ensure that he was not in any conflict of duty by acting for the wife;

- confirm with the wife that she is happy for him to act for her:

- explain the nature and effect of his written confirmation to the lender;

- explain the nature of the documents and the transaction and the risks attached;

- ensure that she is aware of any previous lending and any future liability under the charge;

- inform the wife that she does not have to enter into the surety;

- ascertain whether she consents to him providing written confirmation to the lender or whether she wishes him to negotiate on her behalf with the lender over terms.

Sureties other than wives

32.049 The principle relating to constructive notice enunciated in *O'Brien* is not only applicable to wives. It applies "in every case where the relationship between the surety and the debtor is non-commercial" (*Etridge* at [87]). Thus, it applies in all cases "where there is an emotional relationship between cohabitees", including homosexual ones (at 431d), if the lender is aware of the relationship (at 431g). It can apply to the relationship between employer and employee (*Credit Lyonnais Bank Nederland NV v Burch* [1997] 1 All E.R. 144 CA). It may also apply where children take advantage of elderly parents (*O'Brien* at 431) but will not apply in a normal family arrangement where parents are willing to assist their children in business ventures (*ASB Bank Ltd v Harlick* [1996] N.Z.L.R. 655).

Summary

32.050 In *O'Brien* Lord Browne-Wilkinson summarised the position as follows:

"Where one cohabitee has entered into an obligation to stand surety for the debts of the other cohabitee and the creditor is aware that they are cohabitees: (1) the surety obligation will be valid and enforceable by the creditor unless the suretyship was procured by the undue influence, misrepresentation or other legal wrong of the principal debtor; (2) if there has been undue influence, misrepresentation or other legal wrong by the principal debtor, unless the creditor has taken reasonable steps to satisfy himself that the surety entered into the obligation freely and in knowledge of the true facts, the creditor will be unable to enforce the surety obligation because he will be fixed with the constructive notice of the surety's right to set aside the transaction; (3) unless there are special exceptional circumstances, a creditor will have taken such reasonable steps to avoid being fixed with constructive notice if the creditor warns the surety (at a meeting not attended by the principal debtor) of the amount of her potential liability and of the risks involved and advises the surety to take independent legal advice.

I should make it clear that in referring to the husband's debts I include the debts of a company in which the husband (but not the wife) has a direct financial interest."

Solicitor's certificate on the charge

There may still be some cases where despite confirmation from a solicitor, the **32.051** charge can be set aside.

In *National Westminster Bank Plc v Breeds* (2001) 151 N.L.J. 170, Collins J. allowed an appeal by a wife and set aside a charge securing sums advanced to the husband's company. The solicitor advising the wife was also the company secretary and was active within the company, furthermore, the husband and his business partner were found to be unreliable. The bank had knowledge of all these matters and it was therefore unreasonable for them to rely on the solicitor's advice.

There is another Court of Appeal case that provides comfort to sureties. It needs to be treated with a certain level of caution because the court was clearly appalled by the particular facts of the case (cf. *Barclays Bank Plc v Goff* (2001) 98(20) L.S.G. 45 CA), they "offended the conscience of the court". In *Credit Lyonnais Bank Nederland NV v Burch* [1997] 1 All E.R. 144 CA, an employee (a young woman), had charged her small flat to secure her employer's business debts. The employer already had a facility of £250,000 (a fact which was not disclosed to Ms Burch) and the charge merely increased the facility to £270,000. The charge not only had the effect of providing security over her flat, it also consisted of a personal guarantee for the whole debt. In those circumstances the court held that a statement voluntarily made to Ms Burch in writing on numerous occasions by a solicitor acting for the bank that the charge was "unlimited both in amount and in time" was insufficient. She could not assess the significance of that statement without being told of the extent of the borrower's current borrowings and current limit. The bank should have told her that the current borrowings were £163,000, that the overdraft limit already stood at £250,000 and that the proposal was to extend it to £270,000. Without being provided with that information she might have thought that the limit was only being extended from £10,000 to £30,000. Nor was it sufficient for the bank to tell her that she should take independent legal advice:

"It was at the least necessary that she should receive such advice. That is because the first thing an independent solicitor would have done . . . was to enquire as to the extent of [the borrower's] current borrowings and the current limit and, on receiving the answers, to advise Miss Burch that she should not on any account enter into a transaction in that form" (per Nourse L.J. at 152b).

32.052 In this context Millett L.J. at 156 considered the principles:

> "Such advice [i.e. independent legal advice] is neither always necessary nor always sufficient. It is not a panacea. The result does not depend mechanically on the presence or absence of legal advice. I think there has been some misunderstanding of the role which the obtaining of independent legal advice plays in these cases . . .
>
> It is next necessary [i.e. after considering whether or not there has been a misrepresentation or undue influence] to consider the position of the third party who has been put on enquiry of the possible existence of some impropriety and who wishes to avoid being fixed with constructive notice. One means of doing so is to ensure that the complainant obtains competent and independent legal advice before entering into the transaction. If she does so, and enters into the transaction nonetheless, the third party will usually escape the consequences of the notice. This is because he is normally entitled to assume that the solicitor has discharged his duty and that the complainant has followed his advice. But he cannot make any such assumption if he knows or ought to know that it is false."

There may also be a difference between undue influence and misrepresentation. The fact that a person has had the effect of a document explained to her by a solicitor does not necessarily mean that the undue influence has been negated; and the bank may be aware of that fact. To take an extreme example, a husband may, in front of the bank manager, hold a gun to his wife's head and say "you must sign the charge". In these circumstances a requirement by the bank to obtain independent legal advice would not (one hopes) be sufficient. There is clearly a risk, known to the bank, that the undue influence will operate.

Solicitors need to be careful about the advice that they give. This is not a mere formality. Merely advising a client not to enter into a transaction falls far short of the duty imposed on the solicitor. The solicitor must establish the relevant facts before advising and if that cannot be done in time, the solicitor should refuse to advise in a short, hurried meeting. The fact that advice is given freely is irrelevant; it must still be given properly (*Padden v Bevan Ashford* [2011] EWCA Civ 1616—judge had been wrong to dismiss a wife's claim of professional negligence against a firm of solicitors who had given inadequate legal advice in two short, free sessions).

Agency—the husband

32.053 A second argument (in addition to constructive notice) which has been relied upon in order to establish that the bank is bound by the husband's wrongdoing is that the husband acted as the bank's agent in procuring the wife to enter into the charge. The argument arises from the following passages in the speech of Lord Browne-Wilkinson in *O'Brien*:

> "Of course, if the wrongdoing husband is acting as agent for the creditor bank in obtaining the surety from the wife, the creditor will be fixed with the wrongdoing of its own agent and the surety contract can be set aside as against the creditor. . . . Similarly, in cases . . . where the wife has been induced to enter into the transaction by the husband's misrepresentation, her equity to set aside the transaction will be enforceable against the creditor if either the husband was acting as the creditor's agent or the creditor had actual or constructive notice (*O'Brien* at 191C) . . .
>
> Under the ordinary principles of equity, her right to set aside that transaction will be enforceable against the third parties (e.g. against a creditor) if either the husband was acting as the third party's agent or the third party had actual or constructive notice of the

facts giving rise to her equity. Although there may be cases where, without artificiality, it can properly be held that the husband was acting as the agent of the creditor in procuring the wife to stand as surety, such cases will be of very rare occurrence" (*O'Brien*).

The point was taken in *Dunbar Bank v Nadeem* [1997] 2 All E.R. 253 where the bank sent the charge to the husband with a letter saying "you will find enclosed the Legal Charge for execution by Mrs Nadeem and yourself together with an additional copy for your own use". However, it did not find much favour with the judge who stated:

"In my view it would be 'artificial' to describe Mr Nadeem as the bank's agent in the present circumstances. He was not acting in the bank's interests in getting Mrs Nadeem to execute the charge, but rather in his own interests. I do not think that merely sending Mr Nadeem the charge for execution by himself and his wife can properly be called appointing him the bank's agent for any purpose. There may however be other cases where it is not artificial to state that the bank has used the husband to procure the wife's signature to the charge."

Agency—the solicitor

A further argument based on the agency principle is that the solicitor, who it is **32.054** alleged has given incompetent advice or is aware, or should be aware, of the misrepresentation or undue influence is the agent of the bank. This argument has met with even less success in the courts.

Lord Nicholls in *Etridge* put an end to such an argument when he stated:

"Confirmation from the solicitor that he has advised the wife is one of the bank's preconditions for completion of the transaction. But it is central to this arrangement that in advising the wife the solicitor is acting for the wife and no one else. The bank does not have, and is intended not to have, any knowledge of or control over the advice the solicitor gives the wife. The solicitor is not accountable to the bank for the advice he gives to the wife. To impute to the bank knowledge of what passed between the solicitor and the wife would contradict this essential feature of the arrangement. The mere fact that, for its own purposes, the bank asked the solicitor to advise the wife does not make the solicitor the bank's agent in giving that advice.

In the ordinary case, therefore, deficiencies in the advice given are a matter between the wife and her solicitor. The bank is entitled to proceed on the assumption that a solicitor advising the wife has done his job properly. I have already mentioned what is the bank's position if it knows this is not so, or if it knows facts from which it ought to have realised this is not so" (at 472).

Effect on the charge of finding of constructive notice

In some cases the wife enters into the charge as a result of a misrepresentation that **32.055** it is limited to a particular sum. The issue has arisen as to whether the charge should take effect up to the limit of the sum she was prepared to guarantee. However, it has been held that a legal charge over a matrimonial home induced by husband's misrepresentation is wholly unenforceable by the bank. Thus if the charge is an "all monies" charge but the husband misrepresents the position and tells his wife that it only secures the debt up to, say, £60,000 the bank cannot enforce the charge to secure payment for that sum even though she was prepared to enter into the charge up to that limit. It is set aside in its entirety (*TSB Bank Plc v Camfield* [1995] 1 All E.R. 951 CA).

In Camfield the wife received no benefit from the loan. It has been distinguished in a case where the wife did obtain some benefit: *Dunbar Bank v Nadeem* [1997] 2 All E.R., Robert Englehart QC. The judge set aside the charge as against Mrs Nadeem on condition that she pay one half of the sum used to purchase the property plus interest. He went on to say:

> "If Ms Nadeem is unwilling or unable to comply with the condition, the charge will stand. I will hear the parties on what is an appropriate time for Mr Nadeem to raise this sum; my present inclination is that it should not be a very lengthy period".

The decision is a harsh one as it is unlikely that a wife in these circumstances will be able to raise the sum required and certainly not within a short period.

Execution

32.056   The court has power to make an order for possession against only one of two joint borrowers. However, it would not generally do so where it would be of no benefit to the lender, such as where the lender is entitled to possession as against a husband but the wife is defending the claim on the basis that she was induced to enter into the transaction by reason of undue influence. In those circumstances the court should adjourn the proceedings against the husband with liberty to restore if the wife left or an order for possession was made against her (*Albany Home Loans Ltd v Massey* [1997] 2 All E.R. 609). In practice the order for possession will be made against both at the hearing of the wife's defence, if she loses.

Counterclaims

32.057   The existence of a counterclaim for a sum of money, however valid, and even if it exceeds the amount of the debt to the lender, will not by itself defeat the lender's claim to possession (*National Westminster Bank Plc v Skelton* [1993] 1 All E.R. 242 CA at 249c). This principle rests on the rule that a lender is entitled to possession at any time after the mortgage is executed (see "Introduction", para.32.001). The principle is applicable both where the counterclaim is a mere counterclaim and where it is a counterclaim for unliquidated damages which if established would give rise to a right by way of equitable set-off (*Skelton* at 249f; whether or not a claim to a liquidated sum discharges the debt is undecided).

The principle is not confined to principal debtors but applies where the mortgage has been executed by a person guaranteeing the debts of a third party (*Ashley Guarantee Plc v Zacaria* [1993] 1 All E.R. 254):

> "I can see no distinction in principle between a case where the mortgagor is the principal debtor of the mortgagee and one where he is only a guarantor. In each case the mortgagee has, as an incident of his estate in the land, a right to possession of the mortgaged property. In each case the cross-claims cannot be unilaterally appropriated in discharge of the mortgage debt. The fact that in the latter case the mortgagor is not primarily liable for payment of the debt is immaterial. When he comes to be made liable his position vis-à-vis the appropriation of the cross-claims is at best no different from, and certainly cannot be better than, that of a mortgagor who is the primary debtor."

Further, it is highly unlikely that the existence of a counterclaim will entitle the court to exercise its powers under the Administration of Justice Act 1970 to adjourn, suspend, etc.

However, in practice, the court might make an order for possession but stay execution pending the trial of a counterclaim, if the claim is likely to be resolved relatively quickly; it has good prospects of success; and the amount in issue is likely to make a material difference to the borrower's overall financial liability to the lender.

Discretionary powers: Administration of Justice Act 1970

If the court is satisfied that the lender is entitled to possession under the terms of **32.058** the mortgage it must (unless the agreement under which the money was lent is a "regulated agreement" within the meaning of the Consumer Credit Act 1974 (see para.32.005)) go on to consider s.36(1)–(4) of the Administration of Justice Act 1970 which is in the following terms:

> **36.**—(1) Where the mortgagee under a mortgage of land which consists of or includes a dwelling house brings an action in which he claims possession of the mortgaged property . . . the court may exercise any of the powers conferred on it by subs.(2) below if it appears to the court that in the event of its exercising the power the mortgagor is likely to be able within a reasonable period to pay any sums due under the mortgage or to remedy a default consisting of a breach of any other obligation arising under or by virtue of the mortgage.
>
> (2) The court—
>
> > (a) may adjourn the proceedings; or
> > (b) on giving judgment, or making an order, for delivery of possession of the mortgaged property, or at any time before the execution of such judgment or order, may—
> >
> > > (i) stay or suspend execution of the judgment or order; or
> > > (ii) postpone the date for delivery of possession, for such period or periods as the court thinks reasonable.
>
> (3) Any such adjuornment, stay, suspension or postponement as is referred to in subs.(2) above may be made subject to such conditions with regard to payment by the mortgagor of any sum secured by the mortgage or the remedying of any default as the court thinks fit.
>
> (4) The court may from time to time vary or revoke any condition imposed by virtue of this section.

Section 39 of the Administration of Justice Act 1970 provides as follows:

> **39.**—(1) In this Part of this Act [i.e. Pt IV, which includes s.36]—"dwelling house" includes any building or part thereof which is used as a dwelling;
> "mortgage" includes a charge and "mortgagor" or "mortgagee" shall be construed accordingly; "mortgagor" and "mortgagee" includes any person deriving title under the original mortgagor or mortgagee.
>
> (2) The fact that part of the premises comprised in a dwelling house is used as a shop or office or for business, trade or professional purposes shall not prevent the dwelling house from being a dwelling house for the purposes of this Part of this Act.

Administration of Justice Act 1973 section 8

32.059 In certain cases s.8(1), (2) and (4) of the Administration of Justice Act 1973 must also be borne in mind:

Administration of Justice Act 1973 section 8

8.—(1) Where by a mortgage of land which consists of or includes a dwelling house, or by any agreement between the mortgagee under such a mortgage and the mortgagor, the mortgagor is entitled or is to be permitted to pay the principal sum secured by instalments or otherwise to defer payment of it in whole or in part. But provision is also made for earlier payment in the event of any default by the mortgagor or of a demand by the mortgagee or otherwise, then for purposes of s.36 of the Administration of Justice Act 1970 (under which a court has power to delay giving a mortgagee possession of the mortgaged property so as to allow the mortgagor a reasonable time to pay any sums due under the mortgage) a court may treat as due under the mortgage on account of the principal sum secured and of interest on it only such amounts as the mortgagor would have expected to be required to pay if there had been no such provision for earlier payment.

(2) A court shall not exercise by virtue of subsection (1) above the powers conferred by section 36 of the Administration of Justice Act 1970 unless it appears to the court not only that the mortgagor is likely to be able within a reasonable period to pay any amounts regarded (in accordance with subsection (1) above) as due on account of the principal sum secured, together with the interest on those amounts, but also that he is likely to be able by the end of that period to pay any further amounts that he would have expected to be required to pay by then on account of that sum and of interest on it if there had been no such provision as is referred to in subsection (1) above for earlier payment.

. . .

(4) For purposes of this section the expressions "dwelling house", "mortgage", "mortgagee" and "mortgagor" shall be construed in the same way as for the purposes of Part IV of the Administration of Justice Act 1970.

Notes:

(1) Example: a borrower borrows £20,000 from a building society which he repays at the rate of £200 per month but is two months in arrears. Under the terms of the mortgage the borrower must now repay the whole of the outstanding principal sum because he has defaulted. However, by virtue of s.8 of the Administration of Justice Act 1973 the court may treat the sum due under the mortgage as being only £400.

(2) Section 8 of the 1973 Act has been held to apply where the interest payable under the mortgage was to be paid regularly but the principal was to be paid as a lump sum at an unspecified date after it had become formally due; i.e. a loan secured by a mortgage to be paid by the proceeds of a collateral insurance policy which will mature after a number of years (*Centrax Trusts Ltd v Ross* [1979] 2 All E.R. 952 and *Bank of Scotland v Grimes* [1985] 2 All E.R. 254).

(3) Section 8 of the 1973 Act does not however apply to a bank overdraft on a borrower's current account secured by a charge on the borrower's house because there is no express term deferring payment of the principal sum after it has become due. Usually the sum simply does not become due until

the bank makes a written demand for it and up until that time there is no due date from which any deferment of payment can be made. If s.8 were to apply in these circumstances the result would be

"to deprive banks who use the usual charge for security for an overdraft of any right of enforcement, as long as the debtor continued to pay interest on the capital lent" (*Habib Bank Ltd v Tailor* [1982] 1 W.L.R. 1218, per Cumming-Bruce L.J.).

Exercise of the discretion

When assessing a "reasonable period" it is appropriate for the court to take **32.060** account of the whole of the remaining part of the original term of the mortgage (*Cheltenham and Gloucester BS v Norgan* [1996] 1 All E.R. 449 CA).

"... it does seem to me that the logic and spirit of the legislation require ... that the court shall take as its starting point the full term of the mortgage and post at the outset the question: would it be possible for the mortgagor to maintain payment-off of the arrears by instalments over that period?" (per Waite L.J. at 458j).

The considerations that are likely to be relevant when a "reasonable period" has to be established for the purposes of s.36 were set out in the judgment of Evans L.J. in *Norgan* (at 463a):

"In conclusion, a practical summary of our judgments may be helpful in future cases. Drawing on the above and on the judgment of Waite L.J. the following considerations are likely to be relevant when a 'reasonable period' has to be established for the purposes of section 36 of the 1970 Act. (a) How much can the borrower reasonably afford to pay, both now and in the future? (b) If the borrower has a temporary difficulty in meeting his obligations, how long is the difficulty likely to last? (c) What was the reason for the arrears which have accumulated? (d) How much remains of the original term? (e) What are relevant contractual terms, and what type of mortgage is it, i.e. when is the principal due to be repaid? (f) Is it a case where the court should exercise its power to disregard accelerated payment provisions (section 8 of the 1973 Act)? (g) Is it reasonable to expect the lender, in the circumstances of the particular case, to recoup the arrears of interest (1) over the whole of the original term, or (2) within a shorter period, or even (3) within a longer period, i.e. by extending the repayment period? Is it reasonable to expect the lender to capitalise the interest, or not? (h) Are there any reasons affecting the security which should influence the length of the period for payment?

In the light of the answers to the above, the court can proceed to exercise its overall discretion, taking account also of any further factors which may arise in the particular case."

The borrower may apply for a stay, etc. under s.36 of the Administration of Justice **32.061** Act 1970 even where the lender is entitled to possession under the mortgage without showing any default on the part of the borrower: *Western Bank v Schindler* [1977] Ch. 1. In that case, however, the court refused to exercise its discretion under s.36 to stay or suspend the order because, although the borrower had not broken any term of the mortgage, he had allowed a collateral insurance policy to lapse and thereby prejudiced the lender's interest. The relevant time for ascertaining whether the land consists of or includes a dwelling in s.36(1) is when the claim for possession is made and not when the mortgage was taken out (*Royal Bank of Scotland v Miller* [2001] 3 W.L.R. 523).

The borrower should adduce evidence, either orally or by way of witness statement, as to his means with the intention of showing that he will be able to pay off the arrears within a reasonable period but the court may act without evidence on the basis of informal material (*Cheltenham & Gloucester BS v Grant* (1994) *Independent*, May 23 CA). Any relevant documents should be produced at the hearing or attached to the witness statement. The borrower should always complete the court reply form. Confirmation of the answers given together with any up-to-date information will provide the court with the necessary evidence to assist the borrower.

The court is also likely to have regard to the requirements and information in the Pre-Action Protocol when exercising its discretion.

The normal order made is for possession to be given within 28 days suspended upon condition that the arrears are paid off at the rate of £x per month plus the current payments as they fall due.

However, provided the court is satisfied that the arrears will be paid off within a reasonable period, it may not be necessary to require the borrower to make the contractual monthly instalment payments. The provisions relating to conditions in s.36(3) give the court a wide discretion.

The existence of a counterclaim does not affect the lender's legal right to possession. It is unlikely that this rule can be circumvented by the provisions of s.36 of the 1970 Act but even if it can do so the borrower will only be able to forestall the order for possession where he can show that the counterclaim means that he is "likely within a reasonable period" to pay off the arrears (an unlikely event in most cases) (see *Citibank Trust Ltd v Ayivor* [1987] 3 All E.R. 241 at 246g).

Adjournment for sale by the borrower

32.062 As seen above, in a standard mortgage possession case, where the property is not going to be sold the starting point for determining how long is a reasonable period for the payment of the arrears is the full term of the mortgage (*C&G Building Society v Norgan*—para.32.062). Where the property is going to be sold such an argument is not really apposite. However, that does not mean that the property must be sold immediately. What is reasonable is still a question of fact and degree for the court to decide. There is no rule of law to the effect that an order for possession of mortgaged property will only be adjourned or suspended if a sale will take place within a short period of time (*National and Provincial BS v Lloyd* [1996] 1 All E.R. 630 CA).

> ". . . it has been said that in the case of the sale of mortgaged property the adjournment or suspension which will be allowed will only be allowed if a sale will take place within a short period of time. Speaking for myself, however, I do not understand that there is any rule of law to this effect. Accordingly, if there were in a hypothetical case, clear evidence that the completion of the sale of a property, perhaps by piecemeal disposal, could take place in six or nine months or even a year, I see no reason why a court could not come to the conclusion in the exercise of its discretion under the two sections that, to use the words of the section, 'the mortgagor [was] likely to be able within reasonable period to pay any sums due under the mortgage'. The question of a 'reasonable period' would be a question for the court in the individual case" (per Neill L.J. at 638a).

In *Bristol & West Building Society v Ellis* [1996] EWCA Civ 1294 it was stated that the period of one year referred to in *Lloyd* was not a maximum period either:

> ". . . as a rule of law or as a matter of general guidance. It all depends on the individual circumstances of each case, though the important factors in most are likely to be the

extent to which the mortgage debt and arrears are secured by the value of the property and the effect of time on that security.

Where the property is already on the market and there is some indication of delay on the part of the mortgagor, it may be that a short period of suspension of only a few months would be reasonable . . .

Where there is likely to be considerable delay in selling the property and/or its value is close to the total of the mortgage debt and arrears so that the mortgagee is at risk as to the adequacy of the security, immediate possession or only a short period of suspension may be reasonable. Where there has already been considerable delay in realising a sale of the property and/or the likely sale proceeds are unlikely to cover the mortgage debt and arrears or there is simply no sufficient evidence as to sale value, the normal order would be for immediate possession . . .'" (Auld J.).

However, if the order is to be suspended so that a sale can take place the court must be satisfied that the proceeds will be sufficient to discharge the entire mortgage debt—not just the arrears.

"One of the matters decided by the important Markham's case was that among the assets which a mortgagor can have taken into account is the mortgaged property itself. But it was also made clear that in such a case one is not concerned only with the arrears but that the court must also consider the total sum which is due under the mortgage. Thus it is plain that, if the mortgaged property is going to be sold, then the security for the mortgage disappears too. So, when one is exercising the discretion under the 1970 and 1973 Acts, the figure to be looked at is not only the arrears, but also the total sum due under the mortgage" (Lloyd, per Neill L.J. at 635g).

Further, the court has no power to suspend an order for possession where the **32.063** borrower is in a position of negative equity unless he is able to make up the shortfall from other sources. In such circumstances the court should not stay possession pending an application by the borrower under s.91(2) for the sale of the property (*Cheltenham and Gloucester Plc v Krausz* [1997] 1 All E.R. 21 CA—see section below).

"It is . . . quite clear that section 36 does not empower the court to suspend possession in order to permit the mortgagor to sell the mortgaged premises where the proceeds of sale will not suffice to discharge the mortgage debt, unless of course other funds will be available to the mortgagor to make up the shortfall" (per Phillips L.J. at 29c).

The unreported decision of the Court of Appeal in *Mortgage Services Funding Plc v Steele* (April 10, 1996) is frequently relied upon by advocates for lenders for the proposition that the court only has power to adjourn where contracts have been exchanged. They do so because of a remark by Nourse L.J. in the case where he said:

"The general approach of the court in cases of this kind, where the mortgagor recognises that the property has got to be sold, is not, on that account, to delay the mortgagee from enforcing his remedies. If the property has to be sold, it can just as well be sold by the mortgagee, whose duty is always to obtain the best price reasonably obtainable at the date of the sale. If there is a potential purchaser at hand, then all the mortgagor has to do is to put the mortgagee in touch with him and the matter can proceed from there. Unless there is firm evidence that a particular sale is about to be completed, it is not the practice of the court to prevent the mortgagee from enforcing his remedy of obtaining possession and exercising his own power of sale over the property."

However, a number of important factors should be noted about the case: **32.064**

- It was an application for permission to appeal made by an unrepresented borrower. It was not a full hearing containing full argument and full case citation. It should not therefore even be cited (see Practice Direction, Citation of Authorities, May 1, 2001, [2001] 1 W.L.R. 1001). Further, the court did not refer to and had no regard to *National and Provincial Building Society v Lloyd* and *Bristol & West Building Society v Ellis*, cases which had looked at all the relevant earlier authorities. The general statement made by Nourse L.J. (quoted above) is clearly inconsistent with those two earlier Court of Appeal decisions.

- The evidence relied upon by the borrower was described as "utterly flimsy" (Ward L.J.) so it is impossible to say that there was a factual situation in the case that could give rise to any legal principle—bearing in mind once again this was only an application for permission to appeal.

- Although it is true to say that the lender is under a duty to obtain the best price reasonably obtainable, it is still well known in the real world that a forced sale can lead to a lower price without the lender being in breach of duty. In fact, leaving the borrower in possession will frequently lead to an earlier sale. Indeed this was recognised in the Court of Appeal in *Target Home Loans Ltd v Clothier* [1994] 1 All E.R. 439 (another case not referred to in *Steele*) where the court made an order for possession to take place in three months time so as to allow the sale to take place by the borrower because the prospects of an early sale were best served by leaving the property with the borrower.

The Pre-Action Protocol contains specific provisions relating to the sale of the property (para.6.2) which the court will normally expect the parties to have complied with (see p.521).

32.065 Thus notwithstanding the comments in *Steele* it is quite clear that the court has a very wide discretion and that each case must be decided on its own facts. An order that is sometimes made is in the following terms:

> "Order for possession suspended for [. . .] for the property to be sold upon condition that the defendant keeps the claimant informed as to the progress of the sale. Permission to the lender to apply to the court to lift the suspension if the claimant is not kept informed or if the claimant becomes concerned that the defendant is not making genuine attempts to sell."

In practical terms, a borrower seeking to persuade the court to suspend the order for possession pending a sale should produce evidence as to the value of the property and the likelihood of its being sold within the reasonable period suggested. Detailed evidence from a qualified valuer is far more persuasive than, say, a simple letter from an estate agent. In order to ensure that the district judge will have regard to it the document containing the evidence should also contain a statement of truth.

Relationship with borrower's right to apply for an order for sale

32.066 As a general rule, it is the lender that wants to obtain possession and the borrower who wants to resist possession while he seeks to sell the property. In some cases however the position is reversed. The lender wants the borrower to hang on while the market revives; yet the borrower wants to sell the property. An application to sell may be made by the borrower pursuant to the Law of Property Act s.91(2):

91.—(2) In any action, whether for foreclosure, or for redemption, or for sale, or for the raising and payment in any manner of mortgage money, the court, on the request of the mortgagee, or of any person interested either in the mortgage money or in the right of redemption, and, notwithstanding that—

(a) any other person dissents; or

(b) the mortgagee or any person so interested does not appear in the action;

and without allowing any time for redemption or for payment of any mortgage money, may direct a sale of the mortgaged property, on such terms as it thinks fit, including the deposit in court of a reasonable sum fixed by the court to meet the expenses of sale and to secure performance of the terms.

The court has an unfettered discretion under s.91 to do what is just and equitable. It may order sale even though the proceeds will not be sufficient to discharge the mortgage debt (*Palk v Mortgage Services Funding Plc* [1993] 2 All E.R. 481 CA—lender wanted to let the property on short-term lettings until market improved—court considered that would prejudice the borrower because a much greater debt would accrue—sale ordered).

See also *Polonski v Lloyds Bank Mortgages Ltd* [1998] 1 F.L.R. 896 where the court made an order for sale under s.91(2) where the applicant wished to move for social reasons, including better schooling, even though there was negative equity. The bank wanted her to stay because it believed that property prices would increase. It wanted her to remain until the value was sufficient to pay off the mortgage.

Discretionary powers: consumer credit act cases

Section 36 of the Administration of Justice Act 1970 (see above) does not apply to a **32.067** mortgage securing an agreement which is a regulated agreement within the meaning of the Consumer Credit Act 1974 (s.38A of the 1970 Act). The court's powers in consumer credit cases are contained in the 1974 Act and are twofold. First, it may make a "time order" in relation to any sum owed, or any other breach of the agreement providing for payment of the arrears by instalments or for the remedying of the breach within a specified period. Second, it may suspend orders for possession and impose conditions in relation to any such order. In addition, the court has power to amend any agreement or security in consequence of a term of any order made. The relevant provisions are ss.129, 130, 135 and 136 of the 1974 Act (see para.32.069).

The test to be applied under these provisions is different to that which applies under the Administration of Justice Acts. The court does not have to be satisfied that the borrower "is likely to be able within a reasonable period" to pay the sums due under the agreement. The court may make a time order under s.129 or suspend an order under s.135(1) if it appears to the court "just to do so".

However, consideration of what is "just" includes consideration of the creditor's position as well as that of the debtor. Further, where as a result of the default the principal sum has become due the court will take into account that the section is directed at rescheduling the whole of the indebtedness under the regulated agreement, as well as the arrears and the current interest and if there is no prospect of the debtor being able to pay any part of the principal the court is unlikely to exercise its discretion in his favour (*First National Bank Plc v Syed* [1991] 2 All E.R. 250 CA). The circumstances of the case were that there had been a fairly long history of default and sporadic payments on the defendants' part. There was no realistic, as opposed to merely speculative, prospect of improvement in the defendants' finances and the instalments that the defendants could afford were too little even to keep down the accruing interest on their account. There was no prospect whatsoever of being able to repay the principal without a sale of the house. The court therefore considered that it would not be just to require the plaintiff to accept the instalments offered by the defendants and upheld the order for possession.

32.068   The reply form sent to defendants when a claim is made for possession, if completed, should give the district judge the information he requires to come to a decision. However, that information should if necessary be updated at the hearing.

It is important to note that where the lender brings possession proceedings the court has the power under ss.129 and 136 to alter the contractual terms of the agreement so as to reduce the monthly payments and the interest payable, in relation to both past and future sums due (*Southern & District Finance v Barnes* [1996] 1 F.C.R. 679 CA). The principles to be applied when exercising the discretion are set out in the judgment of Leggatt L.J. (at 686):

> "(1) When a time order is applied for, or a possession order sought of land to which a regulated agreement applies, the court must first consider whether it is just to make a time order. That will involve consideration of all the circumstances of the case, and of the position of the creditor as well as the debtor.
>
> (2) When a time order is made, it should normally be made for a stipulated period on account of temporary financial difficulty. If, despite the giving of time, the debtor is unlikely to be able to resume repayment of the total indebtedness by at least the amount of the contractual instalments, no time order should be made. In such circumstances it will be more equitable to allow the regulated agreement to be enforced.
>
> (3) When a time order is made relating to the non-payment of money:
>
>> (a) the 'sum owed' means every sum which is due and owing under the agreement, but where possession proceedings have been brought by the creditor that will normally comprise the total indebtedness; and
>>
>> (b) the court must consider what instalments would be reasonable both as to amount and timing, having regard to the debtor's means.
>
> (4) The court may include in a time order any amendment of the agreement, which it considers just to both parties, and which is a consequence of a term of the order. If the rate of interest is amended, it is relevant that smaller instalments will result both in a liability to pay interest on accumulated arrears and, on the other hand, in an extended period of repayment. But to some extent the high rate of interest usually payable under regulated agreements already takes account of the risk that difficulties in repayment may occur.
>
> (5) If a time order is made when the sum owed is the whole of the outstanding balance due under the loan, there will inevitably be consequences for the term of the loan or for the rate of interest or both.
>
> (6) If justice requires the making of a time order, the court should suspend any possession order that it also makes, so long as the terms of the time order are complied with."

The borrower may make an application for a time order pursuant to s.129(1)(b) without waiting for the lender to commence proceedings.

On the application of "any person affected" by a time order or by a provision included under s.135(1) the court may vary or revoke the order (s.130(6); s.135(4)).

Consumer Credit Act 1974

Time orders

32.069   129.—(1) . . . if it appears to the court just to do so—

(a) ...

(b) on an application made by a debtor or hirer under this paragraph after service on him of—

    (i) a default notice; or

    (ii) a notice under section 6(1) or section 98(1); or

(c) in an action brought by a creditor or owner to enforce a regulated agreement or any security, or recover possession of any goods or land to which a regulated agreement relates, the court may make an order under this section (a "time order").

(2) A time order shall provide for one or both of the following, as the court considers just—

(a) the payment by the debtor or hirer or any surety of any sum owed under a regulated agreement or a security by such instalments, payable at such times, as the court, having regard to the means of the debtor or hirer and any surety, considers reasonable;

(b) the remedying by the debtor or hirer of any breach of a regulated agreement (other than non-payment of money) within such period as the court may specify.

Supplemental provisions about time orders

130.—(1) Where in accordance with rules of court an offer to pay any sum by instalments is made by the debtor or hirer and accepted by the creditor or owner, the court may in accordance with rules of court make a time order under section 129(2)(a) giving effect to the offer without hearing evidence of means.   **32.070**

(2) In the case of a hire-purchase or conditional sale agreement only, a time order under section 129(2)(a) may deal with sums which, although not payable by the debtor at the time the order is made, would if the agreement continued in force become payable under it subsequently.

...

(5) Without prejudice to anything done by the creditor or owner before the commencement of the period specified in a time order made under section 129(2)(b) ("the relevant period")—

(a) he shall not while the relevant period subsists take in relation to the agreement any action such as is mentioned in section 87(1):

(b) where—

    (i) a provision of the agreement ("the secondary provision") becomes operative only on breach of another provision of the agreement ("the primary provision"), and

    (ii) the time order provides for the remedying of such a breach of the primary provision within the relevant period;

(c) if while the relevant period subsists the breach to which the order relates is remedied it shall be treated as not having occurred.

(6) On the application of any person affected by a time order, the court may vary or revoke the order.

Power to impose conditions, or suspend operation of order

135.—(1) If it considers it just to do so, the court may in an order made by it in relation to a regulated agreement include provisions—   **32.071**

    (a)   making the operation of any term of the order conditional on the doing of specified acts by any party to the proceedings;

    (b)   suspending the operation of any term of the order either—

        (i)   until such time as the court subsequently directs or;

        (ii)   until the occurrence of a specified act or omission.

. . .

(4) On the application of any person affected by a provision included under subsection (1), the court may vary the provision.

Power to vary agreements and securities

32.072   **136.**—The court may in an order made by it under this Act include such provision as it considers just for amending any agreement or security in consequence of a term of the order.

Relationship between lender and borrower's tenant

32.073   As has been noted (para.32.028) it is a requirement of the Civil Procedure Rules that the claimant send a notice to the occupiers within 5 days of receiving notification of the date of the hearing by the court (CPR 55.10(2)). This should help to prevent cases arising where the occupiers are not aware of the case until bailiffs seek to enforce the order for possession. Any occupier so notified of the hearing who wishes to oppose the claim should apply to be joined as a party pursuant to CPR r.19.

The rights of tenants in occupation are considered below.

Where tenancy granted after the mortgage

32.074   By statute a borrower in possession has the power to grant certain leases so as to bind the lender (s.99 of the Law of Property Act 1925). However, building societies and most other lenders exclude this statutory power. A lease made outside the provisions of s.99 of the 1925 Act or contrary to the provisions of the mortgage deed will be binding on both the borrower and his tenant by estoppel but as between the tenant and the lender the lease is of no effect. Even a protected or statutory tenant under the Rent Act 1977 has no rights as against a lender where the tenancy has been granted without the consent of the lender (*Britannia Building Society v Earl* [1990] 2 All E.R. 469 CA). In any such case the tenant will not be able to resist proceedings for possession brought by the lender once it is entitled to possession against the borrower. Nor is the tenant entitled to ask the court to exercise its powers to suspend, etc. the order for possession under s.36 of the Administration of Justice Act 1970 (*Britannia Building Society v Earl*). It follows that where the power is not excluded (for example in most buy-to-let mortgages), the mortgagee may be entitled to possession as against the mortgagor but not as against the tenant. The mortgagee will have to terminate that tenancy before being able to obtain physical possession of the property. Further, where the land is registered and a tenancy is granted after the mortgage is entered into but before the lender registers the charge the tenancy has priority over the mortgage. Subsequent registration of the charge does not remedy the position. The date of registration is taken to be the date on which application for registration was made. There should not therefore be many cases where the problem may arise (*Barclays Bank Plc v Zaroovabli* [1997] 2 All E.R. 19—the bank for some inexplicable reason failed to register the charge for over six years).

Where the lender's consent in writing is required the onus of proving that **32.075** consent was given is upon the tenant. Mere inaction on the part of the lender after it has become aware of the unlawful tenancy does not amount to consent (*Taylor v Ellis* [1960] 1 All E.R. 549).

A discharge of a mortgage and its replacement with an almost identical charge does not make the tenancy lawful (*Walthamstow Building Society v Davies* (1991) *The Times*, November 11).

However, it is open to the lender to accept the tenant as its own tenant and acceptance of rent by the lender raises an implication of a new tenancy, particularly where the payment is made pursuant to a notice from the lender to pay rent (*Chatsworth Properties Ltd v Effiom* [1971] 1 W.L.R. 144). A new tenancy with the lender destroys the old tenancy (*Taylor v Ellis*).

Lenders should not take summary proceedings pursuant to CPR r.55 to evict tenants of mortgagors. The claim for possession should either be made in the claim against the borrower or by separate claim (*London Goldhawk Building Society v Eminer* (1977) 242 E.G. 462).

Limited protection for unlawful tenants

Introduction

The Mortgage Repossessions (Protection of Tenants) Act 2010 came into force on October 1, 2010. It gives limited statutory protection to unauthorised tenants whose landlords are repossessed by their lender. This Act is designed to give some limited measure of protection to tenants whose tenancies are not binding on mortgagees. In essence the court has power, on the application of the tenant, to postpone the date for delivery of possession for up to two months.

Application of the Act

The Act applies where a mortgagee of land which consists of or includes a dwelling-house brings an action in which it claims possession of the property, and there is an unauthorised tenancy of all or part of the property (s.1(1)). An unauthorised tenancy means either an assured, protected or statutory tenancy to which the mortgagee's interest is not subject to (s.1(8)). As the Act only applies to unauthorised tenancies it does not apply to buy to let mortgages or where the landlord has otherwise obtained consent to let. In those circumstances the tenant has a right to remain in possession as against the lender (see para.32.076).

Court's powers

When making an order for possession, the court may postpone the date for delivery of possession for up to two months (s.1(2) of the Act):

> "(2) When making an order for delivery of possession of the property, the court may, on the application of the tenant, postpone the date for delivery of possession for a period not exceeding two months."

Furthermore, if the court has already made an order for possession, it may in the circumstances set out in s1.(3)(4) subsequently stay or suspend execution of the order for up to two months:

> "(3) Subsection (4) applies where an order for delivery of possession of the property has been made but not executed.
> (4) The court may, on the application of the tenant ("the applicant"), stay or suspend execution of the order for a period not exceeding two months if—
>> (a) the court did not exercise its powers under subsection (2) when making the order or, if it did, the applicant was not the tenant when it exercised those powers,
>> (b) the applicant has asked the mortgagee to give an undertaking in writing not to enforce the order for two months beginning with the date the undertaking is given, and
>> (c) the mortgagee has not given such an undertaking."

In the county court it has been has held that subparagraph (a) is to be read disjunctively from (b) and (c), so that if a tenant (perhaps because he was not aware of the possession proceedings and is not aware of the requirements of (b) and (c)) applies without first having requested an undertaking from the mortgagee the court may hear the application (*Bank of Scotland v Ashraf*, Romford County Court, HH Judge Platt, October 5, 2010).

When considering whether to exercise its powers the court is required to have regard to (a) the circumstances of the tenant, and (b) if there is an outstanding breach by the tenant of a term of the unauthorised tenancy (i) the nature of the breach, and (ii) whether the tenant might reasonably be expected to have avoided breaching the term or to have remedied the breach (subs.(5)).

The court may make any postponement, stay or suspension conditional on the making of payments to the mortgagee in respect of the occupation of the property during the period of the postponement, stay or suspension (subs.(6)).

Execution

32.076 Where an order for possession has been made it will only be possible to execute the order if the lender has given notice at the property and only after the expiry of a prescribed period—see para.32.085.

Where tenancy granted before the mortgage

32.077 If the borrower creates a tenancy before the mortgage, the tenancy will, in most cases, be binding on the lender. If the land is registered, the lender is deemed to have notice of the tenancy. In the case of a lease granted for a term of seven years or less or where the tenant is in occupation unless enquiry has been made of the tenant and the right not disclosed. Further, it will not bind the lender if the interest belongs to a person whose occupation would not have been obvious on a reasonably careful inspection of the land at the time of the disposition and the lender does not have actual knowledge at that time; (see s.29 and Sch.3 of the Land Registration Act 2002 set out below). The relevant date for determining whether or not the tenancy is protected by actual occupation and so has priority over the mortgage is the date when the mortgage is created and not the date when it is registered (*Abbey National Building Society v Cann* [1990] 1 All E.R. 1085).

Where the property is unregistered the tenant will have a similar prior right to the lender (*Universal Permanent Building Society v Cooke* [1951] 2 All E.R. 893 CA).

Land Registration Act 2002 section 29 Schedule 3

29.—(1) If a registrable disposition of a registered estate is made for valuable consideration, completion of the disposition by registration has the effect of postponing to the interest under the disposition any interest affecting the estate immediately before the disposition whose priority is not protected at the time of registration.
  (2) For the purposes of subsection (1), the priority of an interest is protected—

    (a) in any case, if the interest—

        (i) is a registered charge or the subject of a notice in the register;
        (ii) falls within any of the paragraphs of Schedule 3; or

        . . .

32.078

Schedule 3

UNREGISTERED INTERESTS WHICH OVERRIDE REGISTERED DISPOSITIONS

Leasehold estates in land

  1 A leasehold estate in land granted for a term not exceeding seven years from the date of the grant, except for—

    (a) a lease the grant of which falls within section 4(1)(d), (e) or (f);
    (b) a lease the grant of which constitutes a registrable disposition.

Interests of persons in actual occupation

  2 An interest belonging at the time of the disposition to a person in actual occupation, so far as relating to land of which he is in actual occupation, except for—

    (a) an interest under a settlement under the Settled Land Act 1925 (c.18);
    (b) an interest of a person of whom inquiry was made before the disposition and who failed to disclose the right when he could reasonably have been expected to do so;
    (c) an interest—
        (i) which belongs to a person whose occupation would not have been obvious on a reasonably careful inspection of the land at the time of the disposition; and
        (ii) of which the person to whom the disposition is made does not have actual knowledge at that time;
    (d) a leasehold estate in land granted to take effect in possession after the end of the period of three months beginning with the date of the grant and which has not taken effect in possession at the time of the disposition.

A consent form signed by the tenant acknowledging "that any right of occupation I may now or later have is postponed to the rights of the mortgagee" will deprive the tenant of his rights under the tenancy as against the lender. However, in the case of a tenancy with statutory protection the consent will only have effect if it has been noted on the register in accordance with s.29(3) of the Land Registration Act 2002 which states that the overriding interest will not take priority if it has been the subject of a notice in the register at any time since the

32.079

coming into force of this section (*Woolwich Building Society v Dickman* [1996] 3 All E.R. 204 CA—a case under the Law of Property Act 1925). In Housing Act cases, s.5 of that Act prevents an order from being made unless the particular requirements of the Act are satisfied (see para.6.009). In other cases the lender is likely to be able to argue that the tenant is estopped from denying his consent. The position was explained by Morritt L.J. in *Dickman* at 213e:

> "Nothing to 'the contrary was expressed on the register' in relation to the letters of consent, so as to exclude the deeming effect of that section. In my view it must follow that whatever the result of the letters as between the building society and the Todds [the tenants] as persons, they had no effect on the property or charges register in the Land Registry so as to preclude the Todds' tenancy being an overriding interest. Accordingly, the property was subject to that overriding interest at the time of the charge and was an interest subject to which the charge was granted and took effect, for no estoppel between the building society and the Todds could exclude the effect of section 70(1). [Author's note: Does Morritt L.J. mean s.98(1) of the 1977 Act?]
>
> In the case of registered land other than a dwelling house subject to a protected or statutory tenancy it will not matter whether the effect of the estoppel is to remove an overriding interest or merely to set up a bar as between the parties to the estoppel so as to prevent the one relying on that interest as against the other. But in the case of a dwelling house let on a protected tenancy it does" (*Dickman*, per Morritt L.J. at 214e).

32.080 The fact that the tenancy is binding upon the lender does not mean that the lender cannot in any circumstances obtain possession from the tenant. The strict legal position is that the mortgage operates as a concurrent lease. The lender is therefore entitled to possession as against the borrower the moment the mortgage deed is signed (or, where there is a clause in the deed to that effect, when the mortgagor defaults) and is the owner of the reversion immediately expectant on the termination of the tenant's tenancy (ss.85, 86 and 87 of the Law of Property Act 1925; *Woolwich BS v Dickman* at 213e). The tenant in practice pays his rent to the person who granted him the tenancy (the borrower) but this is only because the lender permits it.

If the lender seeks possession he therefore takes the same steps that the original landlord/borrower would take in order to recover possession. If the tenancy is a protected tenancy he serves a notice to quit (if possible) and if the tenancy is an assured tenancy or an assured shorthold he serves an appropriate notice under the Housing Act 1988 (see Chs 6 and 7).

Section 45 of the 1988 Act states that except where the context otherwise requires "landlord" includes any person from time to time deriving title under the original landlord and also includes, in relation to a dwelling-house, any person other than a tenant who is, or but for the existence of an assured tenancy would be, entitled to possession of the dwelling-house. There is a similar provision in s.152 of the Rent Act 1977. The lender is therefore treated as "the landlord" for the purpose of either Act and may rely upon any ground that is available to "the landlord" (see *Dickman* at 213e; see also *Mortgage Corporation Ltd v Ubah* (1996) 29 H.L.R. 399 CA). In each Act there are also particular provisions that apply to mortgagors:

Rent Act 1977

32.081 A lender under a mortgage created by deed before the commencement of the tenancy, who is entitled to exercise a power of sale under the mortgage or s.101 of the Law of Property Act 1925, may (if the Rent Act 1977 applies to the tenancy) rely upon Cases 11, 12 or 20 of Sch.15 to the 1977 Act if possession of the

dwelling-house is required for the purpose of disposing of it with vacant possession in exercise of that power (see Sch.15, Pt V, para.2(f)). The lender must obviously show that the requirements of the Case relied upon have been satisfied.

Housing Act 1988

Where the tenancy is an assured tenancy under the Housing Act 1988 the lender, **32.082**
seeking to obtain possession for the purpose of disposing of it with vacant possession in exercise of the power of sale, may rely upon Ground 2 of Sch.2 to the 1988
Act (para.A2.058) if either:

(1) a Ground 1 notice was given not later than the beginning of the tenancy
(see para.30.016);

(2) or the court is satisfied that it is just and equitable to dispense with the
requirement of notice.

Where the assured tenancy is for a fixed term the lender may recover possession
under this ground during the fixed term if the terms of the tenancy make provision
for it to be brought to an end under Ground 2 (whether that provision takes the
form of a provision for re-entry, for forfeiture, for determination by notice or
otherwise) (s.7(6) of the 1988 Act; see para.6.028).

Costs

A lender who is successful in a claim for possession is almost invariably entitled **32.083**
to add the costs of the claim to his security under the terms of the mortgage. When
making the possession order the district judge will therefore normally say nothing
specific about costs. Some judges sometimes say words such as "costs to be added
to the security" but no order in those terms is required. Thus, it is not usual to ask
for an order for costs.

The fact that an order for costs is not usually made does not mean that a borrower
However, where the lender is under-secured it is sensible to do so in order that
the lender can try to recover the shortfall on costs by some other method. Where
an order for costs is made they are subject to assessment in the normal way but in
exercising its discretion the court has to give effect to the contractual right to add
costs to the security. This will mean that the lender will be entitled to costs on an
indemnity basis, so that it will be for the borrower to show that any particular item
was unreasonably incurred or unreasonable in amount (CPR r.48.3 and PD 48
s.50; *Gomba Holdings (UK) Ltd v Minories Finance Ltd (No.2)* [1992] 4 All E.R.
588 CA—see also para.25.043).

The fact that an order for costs is not usually made does not mean that a borrower
cannot challenge the costs that the lender seeks to add to the security. He can do
so but once again the principle is that the court will give effect to the contractual
terms in the mortgage and it will be for the borrower to show that the individual
items were unreasonably incurred or unreasonable in amount (CPR r.48.3, etc.).
The costs can be challenged on the taking of an account or on an assessment,
either summary or detailed (CPR PD 48 s.50.4). If there is to be an assessment it
will usually be more proportionate to carry out a summary assessment.

Borrowers seeking to challenge the various costs items added to the security
usually have an uphill task. However, lenders do not always follow the contractual stipulations in the mortgage and individual items can sometimes be shown to

be unreasonable. The problem can often be that the cost of challenging the costs so far incurred will, if the borrower is unsuccessful, add to the burden.

If the mortgage deed does not contain a provision providing for costs on an indemnity basis they will be awarded on the standard basis in the normal way (*Helden v Strathmore* [2011] EWCA Civ 542).

Lord Neuberger MR at paras 57 and 58:

> "It is perfectly true that the majority, probably the great majority, of mortgages contractu-
> ally provide that the mortgagee should be entitled to recover its costs of enforcing the
> mortgage on an indemnity basis, and that, in the absence of a good reason to the contrary,
> the court will give effect to that provision when exercising its discretionary power in rela-
> tion to costs. However, in this case, the 2006 Charge did not contain a provision entitling
> Strathmore to recover the costs of enforcing its rights, on an indemnity basis or at all. In
> those circumstances, with due respect to the Judge, who gave an excellent judgment on
> the substantive issues, he went wrong in dealing with costs effectively on the assumption
> that the 2006 Charge did so provide. Where an agreement contains no provision stating
> how the costs of proceedings will be dealt with, then it seems to me that it would be wrong
> in principle for the court to proceed on the basis that there is such a provision, simply
> because the majority of agreements of the type in question do contain such a provision. If
> anything, one would presume that the parties intentionally departed from the norm."

For costs in claims involving third parties, see *Parker-Tweedale v Dunbar Bank Plc (No.2)* [1990] 2 All E.R. 588.

Interest on judgment debts

32.084 Although as a general rule a claimant in the county court may recover interest on a judgment debt for a sum of not less than £5,000 such interest is not payable where the relevant judgment:

(1) is given in proceedings to recover money due under an agreement regulated by the Consumer Credit Act 1974; or

(2) grants the mortgagee under a mortgage of land which consists of or includes a dwelling-house a suspended order for possession. (See s.74 of the County Courts Act 1984 and r.2 of the County Courts (Interest on Judgment Debts) Order 1991.) The lender will of course retain its contractual right to interest.

Execution

32.085 Enforcement of the order may be effected in the same way as possession orders against a tenant (see Ch.34). However, in the High Court, if the possession order has been suspended on conditions leave to issue execution is required (RSC Ord.46 r.2(1)(d)). The application must be supported by an affidavit (for contents see RSC Ord.46 r.4(2)). The borrower must be given the opportunity of being heard (*Fleet Mortgage and Investment Co Ltd v Lower Maisonette, 46 Eaton Place Ltd* [1972] 2 All E.R. 737).

A lender, seeking to enforce an order for possession which has been suspended on the usual terms as to payment of a reasonable sum off the arrears and the current monthly instalment, does not have to start fresh proceedings if the borrower pays off the arrears but subsequently defaults again (*Greyhound*

Guaranty v Caulfield [1981] C.L.Y. 1808; *Bradford & Bingley Plc v Harris* (unrep); and *Halifax Plc v Taffs* [1999] EWCA Civ 698). The same principle applies where the lender has consolidated the arrears. The borrower is still required to comply with any requirement of the suspended order to pay the current monthly instalments, and subject to any application to vary or revoke the conditions under s.36(4), that requirements continues until the end of the mortgage term (*Zinda v Bank of Scotland* [2011] EWCA Civ 706).

Notice to tenants of intention to apply for a warrant

Notice must be given to occupiers at the property before the mortgagee can **32.086** enforce an order for possession (s.2 of the Mortgage Repossessions (Protection of Tenants) Act 2010 (see para.32.075)). The prescribed form of notice is contained in the Schedule to the Dwelling-Houses (Execution of Possession Orders by Mortgagees) Regulations 2010. The mortgagee cannot execute the warrant until fourteen days after giving the notice (reg.3). Regulation 5 also sets out the manner in which the notice may be given:

> "5.—(1) The mortgagee's notice under regulation 4 may be given in any of the following ways—
>
> (a) by sending the notice to the property by first class post or registered post in an envelope addressed—
>
>   (i) to the tenant by name, or
>   (ii) if the tenant's name is not known, to "The Tenant or Occupier";
>
> (b) by leaving the notice at the property—
>
>   (i) in an envelope addressed as described in subparagraph (a), or
>   (ii) affixed to and displayed in a prominent place where its contents can be read by a person entering the property; or
>
> (c) by personal service upon a person who appears to be in residence at the property."

CCR Order 26, rule 17 (Warrant of possession) has been amended by the insertion of the following paragraph:

> "(2A) When applying for a warrant of possession of a dwelling-house subject to a mortgage, the claimant must certify that notice has been given in accordance with the Dwelling Houses (Execution of Possession Orders by Mortgagees) Regulations 2010)."

Form N325 Request for Warrant of Possession of Land requires the mortgagee to certify that notice has been given when it applies for a warrant of possession.

Application to court suspend order

Part 55.10 of the Civil Procedure Rules has been amended, inserting a new rule **32.087** 4A, to enable the unauthorised tenant to make an application to the court to suspend the order for possession.

Chapter 33

Orders for Sale

In this chapter we look at a number of different situations in which a party is **33.001** applying for an order for sale. The situation dealt with in most detail is where one of two joint owners of a residential property is seeking an order against a co-owner or, at least, a person who is a co-occupier who claims an interest in the property.

Who can apply?

Co-ownership cases

Introduction

The situation under discussion in this section is, generally, one where a couple who are not married, or in a civil partnership, have bought a property to live in. The relationship is now at an end. What is to happen to the property? As there was no marriage or civil partnership the court cannot use its powers under the Matrimonial Causes Act 1973 or the Civil Partnership Act 2005 to deal with the situation. What is therefore to happen? There are four key issues that may arise in any co-ownership case:

- Does each party have a beneficial interest in the property?
- If so, what are their respective shares in the property?
- Should the property be sold?
- Having calculated the parties respective shares, is it necessary to make any adjustment having regard to such matters as the fact that one of the parties has remained in occupation and perhaps has continued to pay the mortgage and the other has left?

In this section we deal with the first two questions. The leading cases concerned with the nature and extent of the interests of the parties are *Stack v Dowden* [2007] UKHL 17 and *Jones v Kernott* [2011] UKSC 53.

The last two questions are dealt with below (para.33.009 onwards).

33.002 *Express declaration of trust*

The starting point is to look to see whether or not there is any express declaration as to the ownership of the property.

- Is there a trust deed?

- Is there an express declaration on the transfer document, TR1 (since April 1, 1998)—para.10 of that document?

If there is an express declaration of trust, that will be the end of the matter both as to the existence of a beneficial ownership and as to shares (if stated). The court will only go behind an express declaration of trust if there are grounds to set aside or rectify the instrument on the basis of mistake, fraud or undue influence; or possibly on the basis of subsequent agreement or an estoppels. See Baroness Hale at para.49 in *Stack* and *Pankhania v Chandegra* [2012] EWCA Civ 1438, Mummery L.J.:

"There is no room for inserting a constructive trust in substitution for the express trust. Neither fraud nor mistake are alleged. No claim has been made at any stage for rectification of the transfer . . . In the absence of a vitiating factor, such as fraud or mistake, as a ground for setting aside the express trust or as a ground for rectification of it, the court must give legal effect to the express trust declared in the transfer. In the absence of such claims the court cannot go behind that trust ... Finally, reliance on *Stack v Dowden* and *Jones v Kernott* for inferring or imputing a different trust in this or other similar cases which have already been before this court is misplaced where there is an express declaration of trust of the beneficial title and no valid legal grounds for going behind it".

Severance of a beneficial joint tenancy results in a beneficial tenancy in common in equal shares (Lady Hale at para.49 in *Stack*).

33.003 *No express declaration of trust—the starting point*

In *Stack v Dowden* the House of Lords held that the beneficial interest will generally be the same as the legal ownership. It will be for the party who is asserting something different to establish that the contrary is the case. As can be seen there is a distinction between sole legal ownership and joint legal ownership. Lord Hope at para.4:

"The cases can be broken down into those where there is a *single legal* ownership and those where there is *joint legal ownership*. There must be consistency of approach between these two cases. . . . I think that consistency is to be found by deciding where the onus lies if a party wishes to show that the beneficial ownership is different from the legal ownership. I agree with Baroness Hale that this is achieved by taking *sole beneficial ownership as the starting point in the first case and by taking joint beneficial ownership as the starting point in the other*. In this context joint beneficial ownership means that the shares are presumed to be divided between the beneficial owners equally. So in a case of sole legal ownership the onus is on the party who wishes to show that he has any beneficial interest at all, and if so what that interest is. In a case of joint legal ownership it is on the party who wishes to show that the beneficial interests are divided other than equally." (authors' emphasis).

And Lady Hale at para.56:

> "Just as the starting point where there is sole legal ownership is sole beneficial owner-
> ship, the starting point where there is joint legal ownership is joint beneficial ownership.
> The onus is upon the person seeking to show that the beneficial ownership is different
> from the legal ownership. So in sole ownership cases it is upon the non-owner to show
> that he has any interest at all. In joint ownership cases, it is upon the joint owner who
> claims to have other than a joint beneficial interest."

Thus, in the case of sole legal ownership there are two questions:

- Can the person who is not the legal owner establish that he has a beneficial
  interest?
- If so, what is that interest?

In the case of joint legal ownership the starting point is that each person has an
equal beneficial interest in the property. The burden is on the person who is
asserting otherwise to prove it.

Establishing a different share

As stated by Lady Hale at para.68:   **33.004**

> "The burden will therefore be on the person seeking to show that the parties did intend
> their beneficial interest to be different from their legal interests and in what way. This is
> not a task to be lightly embarked upon. . . . In joint names cases it is also unlikely to lead
> to a different result unless the facts are very unusual."

The question then arises as to how one goes about satisfying that burden? How
does a court determine when the shares are different? In *Stack* the House of Lords
rejected an argument that the principles of resulting trusts should be applied (as
advanced by Lord Neuberger in a dissenting judgment on this point) and held that
a wider look at all the facts should be undertaken in order to ascertain the intention
of the parties when the property was purchased. The factors to be taken into
account were set out by Lady Hale at para.69, which may include:

- Any advice or discussions at the time of the transfer which cast light upon
  their intentions then;
- The reasons why the home was acquired in their joint names;
- The reasons why (if it be the case) the survivor was authorised to give a
  receipt for the capital moneys;
- The purpose for which the home was acquired;
- The nature of the parties' relationship;
- Whether they had children for whom they both had responsibility to
  provide a home;
- How the purchase was financed, both initially and subsequently;
- How the parties arranged their finances, whether separately or together or
  a bit of both;

- How they discharged the outgoings on the property and their other household expenses.

- When a couple are joint owners of the home and jointly liable for the mortgage, the inferences to be drawn from who pays for what may be very different from the inferences to be drawn when only one is owner of the home. The arithmetical calculation of how much was paid by each is also likely to be less important. It will be easier to draw the inference that they intended that each should contribute as much to the household as they reasonably could and that they would share the eventual benefit or burden equally.

- The parties' individual characters and personalities may also be a factor in deciding where their true intentions lay. In the cohabitation context, mercenary considerations may be more to the fore than they would be in marriage, but it should not be assumed that they always take pride of place over natural love and affection.

However, at the end of the day, having taken all this into account, cases in which the joint legal owners are to be taken to have intended that their beneficial interests should be different from their legal interests will, said the House of Lords, be very unusual.

As it happens, in *Stack* the House of Lords held that the case was in fact "a very unusual one" so that the presumption that they should be ***equal joint owners*** was rebutted. The parties were in a relationship for 27 years and had four children together. The particular factors that seem to be have been taken into account in coming to the conclusion that she should have a 65 per cent share and he a 35 per cent share are (Lady Hale at paras 87–92):

- Ms Stack contributed a great deal more than Mr Dowden.

- They maintained separate finances throughout their time together—making separate savings and finances.

- The property was purchased to be a home for themselves and four children but they undertook separate responsibility for different parts of the expenditure.

In fact, the facts in *Stack* are probably not that unusual. There must be many couples whether married or not where one contributes much more than the other and where they keep largely separate finances. It is important to remember that each case will be determined on its own facts and that it is open to other courts to come to a different conclusion on facts that seem very similar (e.g. see Rimer L.J. in the Court of Appeal in *Jones v Kernott* [2010] EWCA Civ 578 at para.75—the case subsequently went to the Supreme Court—see below; *Fowler v Barron* [2008] EWCA Civ 377).

Generally speaking it will be necessary to look at the parties' intentions at the time that they purchased the property. However, there are cases where there has been a ***change in circumstances*** and it is appropriate to look at the parties' intentions at some subsequent time. *Jones v Kernott* [2011] UKSC 53 was a joint ownership case where it was held that a change in circumstances—the man leaving and having nothing more to do with the property for many years—led to a change from 50/50 ownership to 90/10. In this context the Supreme Court took the opportunity to revisit the principles in *Stack v Dowden*. They were not changed in any way but clarified.

Lord Walker and Lady Hale in a joint speech set out to clarify the position by setting out five principles to be applied where a family home is bought in *joint names* of a cohabiting couple who are both responsible for any mortgage, but without any express declaration of their beneficial interests. The five principles are set out at para.51:

> "(1) The starting point is that equity follows the law and they are joint tenants both in law and in equity.
>
> (2) That presumption can be displaced by showing (a) that the parties had a different common intention at the time *when they acquired* the home, or (b) that they *later* formed the common intention that their respective shares would change.
>
> (3) Their common intention is to be deduced *objectively from their conduct*: "the relevant intention of each party is the intention which was reasonably understood by the other party to be manifested by that party's words and conduct notwithstanding that he did not consciously formulate that intention in his own mind or even acted with some different intention which he did not communicate to the other party" (Lord Diplock in *Gissing v Gissing* [1971] AC 886, 906). Examples of the sort of evidence which might be relevant to drawing such inferences are given in *Stack v Dowden*, at para 69.
>
> (4) In those cases where it is clear either (a) that the parties did not intend joint tenancy at the outset, or (b) had changed their original intention, but it is not possible to ascertain by direct evidence or by inference what their actual intention was as to the shares in which they would own the property, "the answer is that each is entitled to that share which the court considers *fair having regard to the whole course of dealing between them in relation to the property*": Chadwick LJ in *Oxley v Hiscock* [2005] Fam 211, para 69. In our judgment, "the whole course of dealing . . . in relation to the property" should be given a broad meaning, enabling a similar range of factors to be taken into account as may be relevant to ascertaining the parties' actual intentions.
>
> (5) Each case will turn on its own facts. Financial contributions are relevant but there are many other factors which may enable the court to decide what shares were either intended (as in case (3)) or fair (as in case (4))."

Sole name cases

Both *Stack v Dowden* and *Jones v Kernott* were cases where the legal ownership **33.005** of the property was in joint names. Where the property was put into one party's sole name the starting point will be different but the subsequent considerations will be the same. *Jones v Kernott* at para.52:

> "This case is not concerned with a family home which is put into the name of one party only. The starting point is different. The first issue is whether it was intended that the other party have any beneficial interest in the property at all. If he does, the second issue is what that interest is. There is no presumption of joint beneficial ownership. But their common intention has once again to be deduced objectively from their conduct. If the evidence shows a common intention to share beneficial ownership but does not show what shares were intended, the court will have to proceed as at para 51(4) and (5) above."

Other cases

As stated above, one will normally be concerned with what should happen to a **33.006** property on the breakdown of a relationship between a cohabiting couple. However, the principles in *Stack v Dowden* have also been held to apply to a domestic sharing arrangement between a mother and son (*Adekunle v Ritchie*

[2007] EW Misc 5 (EWCC), H.H.J. Behrens, Leeds County Court; confirmed by Lord Neuberger in *Laskar v Laskar* [2008] EWCA Civ 347 at para.16); but will probably not apply to an arm's length commercial case of co-ownership where the property is bought for development of letting (Lord Neuberger in *Laskar v Laskar* [2008] EWCA Civ 347 at para.16).

Charging orders

33.007   A person with the benefit of a charging order may apply for an order for sale. CPR Part 73 deals with the procedure and practice in relation to charging orders. The procedure for applying for an order for sale once a charging order has been made is contained in CPR 73.10. The Part 8 procedure is used (73.10(4)). Sample forms of Order for Sale are contained in Appendix A to PD 73. The forms are not prescribed and may be adapted or varied as is appropriate. The court has a discretion as to whether or not to make an order for sale (see further 33.013).

Fraud leading to beneficial interests

33.008   As we have seen in Chapter 32 a lender who has been deprived of a legal mortgage by reason of fraud or forgery will have acquired a beneficial interest in the property. Such a lender may then apply for an order for sale to enforce that interest (see 32.034).

Or in some cases the lender may apply for a judgment for the money loaned and interest and costs and then apply for a charging order. It sometimes occurs at the hearing of the application for an interim charging order to be made final that a wife, who is not unnaturally seeking to divorce her husband, requests the court to adjourn the matter to be heard at the same time as her application for a financial order transferring the property to her. If the application was made after the interim charging order the court will almost certainly refuse the wife's application and make the charging order final. The competing equities between the lender and the wife will be determined on the application for sale made by the lender pursuant to s.13 of the Trusts of Land, etc., Act 1996 (*Mortgage Corporation v Shaire* [2001] 4 All E.R. 364, Neuberger J., and *Alliance & Leicester v Slayford* [2000] E.G.C.S. 113, CA). Where however the wife's application for a financial order is made before the interim charging order, the court is more likely to order the application to be adjourned to be heard with the application for a financial order (*Harman v Glencross* [1986] 1 All E.R. 513, CA; *Austin-Fell v Austin-Fell* [1990] 2 All E.R. 455).

Orders for sale and regulating occupation

Trusts of Land etc. Act 1996

33.009   The rights of the parties in relation to sale and occupation of the property are contained in ss.12–15 of the Trusts of Land and Appointment of Trustees Act 1996.

Trusts of Land and Appointment of Trustees Act 1996

12. *The right to occupy.*

(1) A beneficiary who is beneficially entitled to an interest in possession in land **33.010**
subject to a trust of land is *entitled by reason of his interest to occupy* the land at
any time if at that time—

    (a) the *purposes of the trust* include making the land available for his occupation
(or for the occupation of beneficiaries of a class of which he is a member or
of beneficiaries in general), or

    (b) the land is held by the trustees so as to be so available.

(2) Subsection (1) does not confer on a beneficiary a right to occupy land if it is either
unavailable or unsuitable for occupation by him.

(3) This section is subject to section 13.

13. *Exclusion and restriction of right to occupy.*

(1) Where two or more beneficiaries are (or apart from this subsection would be)
entitled under section 12 to occupy land, *the trustees of land may exclude or
restrict* the entitlement of any one or more (but not all) of them.

(2) Trustees may not under subsection (1)—

    (a) unreasonably exclude any beneficiary's entitlement to occupy land, or

    (b) restrict any such entitlement to an unreasonable extent.

(3) The trustees of land may from time to time *impose reasonable conditions on any
beneficiary* in relation to his occupation of land by reason of his entitlement under
section 12.

(4) The matters to which trustees are to have regard in exercising the powers conferred
by this section include—

    (a) the intentions of the person or persons (if any) who created the trust.

    (b) the purposes for which the land is held, and

    (c) the circumstances and wishes of each of the beneficiaries who is (or apart
from any previous exercise by the trustees of those powers would be) entitled
to occupy the land under section 12.

(5) The conditions which may be imposed on a beneficiary under subsection (3)
include, in particular, conditions requiring him—

    (a) to pay any *outgoings or expenses* in respect of the land, or

    (b) to assume any other obligation in relation to the land or to any activity which
is or is proposed to be conducted there.

(6) Where the entitlement of any beneficiary to occupy land under section 12 has
been excluded or restricted, the conditions which may be imposed on any other
beneficiary under subsection (3) include, in particular, conditions requiring him to—

    (a) make *payments by way of compensation* to the beneficiary whose entitle-
ment has been excluded or restricted, or

    (b) forgo any payment or other benefit to which he would otherwise be entitled
under the trust so as to benefit that beneficiary.

(7) The powers conferred on trustees by this section may not be exercised—

    (a) so as prevent any person who is in occupation of land (whether or not
by reason of an entitlement under section 12 from continuing to occupy the
land, or

    (b) in a manner likely to result in any such person ceasing to occupy the land,

unless he consents or the court has given approval.

(8) The *matters to which the court is to have regard* in determining whether to give approval under subsection (7) include the matters mentioned in subsection (4)(a) to (c).

14. *Applications for order.*

(1) Any person who is a *trustee* of land or *has an interest* in property subject to a trust of land may make an application to the court for an order under this section

(2) On an application for an order under this section the court may make any such order—

   (a) relating to the exercise by the trustees of any of their functions (including an order relieving them of any obligation to obtain the consent of, or to consult, any person in connection with the exercise of any of their functions), or

   (b) declaring the nature or extent of a person's interest in property subject to the trust, as the court thinks fit.

(3) The court may not under this section make any order as to the appointment or removal of trustees.

(4) The powers conferred on the court by this section are exercisable on an application whether it is made before or after the commencement of this Act.

15. *Matters relevant in determining applications.*

(1) The matters to which the court is to have regard in determining an application for an order under section 14 include—

   (a) the *intentions* of the person or persons (if any) who created the trust,

   (b) the *purposes* for which the property subject to the trust is held,

   (c) the *welfare of any minor* who occupies or might reasonably be expected to occupy any land subject to the trust as his home, and

   (d) the interests of any *secured creditor* of any beneficiary.

(2) In the case of an application relating to the exercise in relation to any land of the powers conferred on the trustees by section 13 the matters to which the court is to have regard also include the *circumstances and wishes of each of the beneficiaries* who is (or apart from any previous exercise by the trustees of those powers would be) entitled to occupy the land under section 12.

(3) In the case of any other application, other than one relating to the exercise of the power mentioned in section 6(2), the matters to which the court is to have regard also include the circumstances and wishes of any beneficiaries of full age and entitled to an interest in possession in property subject to the trust or (in case of dispute) of the majority (according to the value of their combined interests).

(4) This section does not apply to an application *if section 335A of the Insolvency Act 1986* (which is inserted by Schedule 3 and relates to applications by a trustee of a bankrupt) applies to it.

Bankruptcy

33.011 In a bankruptcy situation it is also necessary to have regard to s.335A(3) of the Insolvency Act 1986 which in essence provides that where the application is made after one year from the date on which the bankrupt's estate first vests in his trustee, there is a statutory assumption that unless the circumstances are exceptional the interests of the bankrupt's creditors outweigh all other considerations.

Section 335A of the Insolvency Act 1986

(1) Any application by a trustee of a bankrupt's estate under section 14 of the Trusts **33.012** of Land and Appointment of Trustees Act 1996 (powers of court in relation to trusts of land) for an order under that section for the sale of land shall be made to the court having jurisdiction in relation to the bankruptcy.

(2) On such an application the court shall make such order as it thinks just and reasonable having regard to:

    (a) the interests of the bankrupt's creditors;

    (b) where the application is made in respect of land which includes a dwelling house which is or has been the home of the bankrupt or the [bankrupt's spouse or civil partner or former spouse or former civil partner]:

        (i) the conduct of the [spouse, civil partner, former spouse or former civil partner], so far as contributing to the bankruptcy,

        (ii) the needs and financial resources of the [spouse, civil partner, former spouse or former civil partner], and

        (iii) the needs of any children; and

    (c) all the circumstances of the case other than the needs of the bankrupt.

(3) Where such an application is made after the end of the period of *one year beginning with the first vesting* under Chapter IV of this Part of the bankrupt's estate in a trustee, the court shall assume, *unless the circumstances of the case are exceptional*, that the interests of the bankrupt's creditors outweigh all other considerations.

(4) The powers conferred on the court by this section are exercisable on an application whether it is made before or after the commencement of this section.

In *Nicolls v Lan and Nicholls* [2006] EWHC 1255 (Ch) (Paul Morgan QC sitting as a Deputy High Court Judge) the District Judge at first instance held that there were exceptional circumstances based upon on the psychiatric evidence of Mrs N's chronic schizophrenia. Having carried out a balancing exercise by reference to the matters in s.335A(2), he concluded that there should be an order for sale and that the vacant possession should be delivered up within 18 months of the date of the order. The High Court judge held that the district judge was entitled to come to that conclusion.

Charging orders

The primary purpose of a charging order is to provide the creditor with security **33.013** for the debt. However, the existence of the charging order allows the creditor to apply for an order for sale. Whether or not an order will be made is a matter of discretion, the court having regard to all the circumstances of the case. Where the property is the home of the debtor Article 8 of the European Convention of Human Rights will be relevant and the court will have to consider whether it is proportionate to make an order for sale.

Whether or not ss.14 and 15 of the 1996 Act will apply when the debtor/s is/are the sole legal owner/s is not entirely clear (cf *Pickering v Wells* [2002] EWHC 273). Strictly the answer is that they do not, but in the exercise of its discretion under CPR 73.10 the court will have regard to the same factors (*Close Invoice Finance Ltd v Pile* [2008] EWHC 1580 (Ch); *National Westminster Bank Plc v Rushmer* [2010] EWHC 554 (Ch)).

Where the property is jointly owned and the debtor is only one of the joint owners ss.14 and 15 will apply (*Mortgage Corporation v Shaire* [2001] Ch.743).

However, the interests of the creditor are an important factor to be taken into account (*Bank of Ireland Home Mortgages Ltd v Bell* [2001] 2 F.L.R.809).

Size of the debt

33.014 Increasingly, bankers and credit card companies are seeking orders for sale in respect of fairly small debts. How should court approach such a case? In *Packman Lucas Ltd v Mentmore Towers Ltd* [2010] EWHC 1037 (TCC) it was held that an order for sale can be made even if the charging order was only for a small amount relative to the value of the property; it is just one of the considerations to be taken into account, and not an overriding one. Coulson J.:

> "I consider that it is potentially dangerous for a court to identify any hard and fast rules that seek to link the size of the debt with the ability to obtain a charging order or an order for sale. Who is to say when a debt is "small"? A debt of £1,000 will mean very little to a large commercial concern, but for a small trader it might be the difference between bankruptcy and solvency." (para 25)
>
> "Comparing the size of the debt with the value of the asset concerned is equally fraught with difficulty. The present case is a good example of that. CSHL say that an order for sale is inappropriate because they compare the debt of £35,000 odd against the value of the property, which may be more than £15 million, and rely on the disparity between the two. But that argument would not be open to them if the property in question was a modest house in a provincial town worth £250,000. So, if it were right, this disparity submission means that the greater the value of the asset (and therefore the greater the default on the part of the debtor in failing to realise any part of that asset to pay the debt), the greater the chance the debtor would have of avoiding a charging order or an order for sale. That offends against common sense" (para.26).
>
> "In my judgment, the size of the debt, and its value relative to the debt, are matters which should be taken into account in the exercise of the court's discretion under CPR 73.10. But they are only two factors, along with the parties' conduct, the absence of any other enforcement options and the like, for the court to weigh in the balance. Beyond that, I do not consider that there are any rules or presumptions as to the size of the debt, or its comparative value, when dealing with an application for a charging order or an order for sale" (para.27).

The principle would seem to be right, ie that the size of the debt compared to the value of the property is only one circumstance to take into account. However, it is worth noting the commercial nature of this case. Where the court is concerned with, say, a small credit card debt compared to a large equity in a person's home it is perhaps likely that the judge can and should give greater weight to the difference between the two.

"Equitable accounting"

Introduction

33.015 The phrase "equitable accounting" has been commonly used in the past to determine whether or not there should be some re-adjustment of sums payable (after the court has determined whether or not each party has a share in the property; and if so what that share is—see above); normally to take account of the fact that one person has continued to live in the property and possibly continued to pay the expenses on his or her own. There are three different matters that are usually looked at:

- *Occupation rent*: Should the party who has remained in the property pay to the other a contribution having regard to the fact that he or she has had sole occupation of the property?

- *Mortgage instalments*: If one party has continued to pay a greater sum to the mortgage than the other, is he or she entitled to a contribution in respect of those payments?

- *Improvements*: If the party who has remained has improved the property after the other has left should that party receive some contribution in respect of those costs?

Trusts of Land etc. Act 1996

Introduction

Equitable principles used to be adopted to determine whether any adjustments **33.016** should be made. In *Stack v Dowden* the HL held that the situation is now governed by ss.12–15 of the Trusts of Land and Appointment of Trustees Act 1996 (Lady Hale at paras 93 and 94; Lord Neuberger, paras 148 to 157, in particular para.151— see also *Murphy v Gooch*); although the result in any given case is unlikely to be different. Lord Neuberger in *Stack*:

> "I think that it would be a rare case where the statutory principles would produce a different result from that which would have resulted from equitable principles".

Earlier cases may therefore provide good examples of how the court will approach any particular case.

Key points under 1996 Act

The key points arising out of the 1996 Act which will apply when considering **33.017** whether or not there should be some re-allocation of sums to be paid by one party to the other are as follows:

- Section 12(1) gives each beneficiary a right to occupy the land.

- Under s.13 the trustees have the power to exclude or restrict that right but the power must be exercised reasonably.

- Under s.13 the trustees have power to impose conditions upon the occupier, which include the paying of outgoings or expenses or paying compensation to a person whose right to occupy has been excluded or restricted.

- An application can be made to the court under s.14, by the trustees or the beneficiaries, for an order relating to the exercise of these functions.

Factors

The factors that must be taken into account when determining how to are set out **33.018** in s.15 (see Lady Hale in Stack at para.93):

- The intentions of the person or persons who created the trust;

- The purposes for which the property subject to the trust is held;

- The welfare of any minor who occupies or might reasonably be expected to occupy the property as his home; and

- The interests of any secured creditor of any beneficiary.

- The circumstances and wishes of each of the beneficiaries who would otherwise be entitled to occupy the property.

Occupation rent

Entitlement

33.019 At common law one joint owner is not entitled to an occupation rent from the other. However, where one party has excluded the other from the property equity requires that the excluded party receive an occupation rent (see generally *Dennis v McDonald* [1981] 1 W.L.R. 810); and this is now reflected in the statutory provisions contained in the 1996 Act quoted above, which must be applied (*Murphy v Gooch* below).

This has been extended in recent years so that "the presentation of a petition for divorce by the party remaining in occupation of the matrimonial home should normally be taken to signify a refusal to take the other party back into the matrimonial home, and a willingness to pay an occupation rent" (*Re Pavlou* [1993] 1 W.L.R. 1046, per Millet J.). Separating unmarried couples are treated in the same way (*Murphy v Gooch* [2007] EWCA Civ 603). Generally an actual order excluding one party from the property has not been required; and the courts have basically done what is necessary to meet the justice of the situation.

In *Stack v Dowden* Mr Stack had been excluded under a court order but once that had come to an end he had still not gone back. Lord Neuberger thought that Mr Stack had effectively been excluded and was therefore entitled to an occupation rent. However, the majority thought not, which is somewhat inconsistent with some of the earlier cases, and perhaps a bit unrealistic. At the end of the day the courts will treat each case on its own facts. In *Murphy v Gooch* [2007] EWCA Civ 603, the first Court of Appeal case after *Stack*, the Court held (applying the principles in *Stack*) that she did not have to prove ouster before becoming entitled to claim an occupation rent. The end of the relationship and her leaving was enough (para.18). Overall, the test is one of fairness and the court acts in order "to do equity".

How much?

33.020 There is no fixed method for calculating how much should be paid by way of occupation rent but in *Stack* Lord Neuberger stated that the power to award compensation for occupation is now to be derived from ss.12–15 of the 1996 Act—s.13(3) and (6) in particular; that the amount payable should be calculated by reference to the rental value of the property and that the outgoings will be taken into account when assessing rental value (para.154). The cost of the alternative accommodation that Mr Stack had taken was a rational basis on which to calculate the sum (para.157).

Mortgage payments

Although the remaining occupier may be obliged to pay an occupation rent to the **33.021**
party that has left, it is often the situation that the person in occupation continues
to pay the mortgage on his or her own. Where the mortgage involves payment of
capital and interest, the remaining occupier (if he has paid the mortgage) may
often be able to claim credit for half the capital part but not the interest on the
basis that the interest reflects the occupation rent (*Leake v Bruzzi* [1974] 1 W.L.R.
1528). This can often, but not always, be a fair and sensible way of dealing with
the situation. See also now *Murphy v Gooch* above—her entitlement to credit for
occupation rent offset the whole of his credits for mortgage interest and rent. (See
also *Re Richards (A Bankrupt)* [2009] EWHC 1760 (Ch)).

Repairs and improvements

Where one party has spent money on repairs or improvements that have increased **33.022**
(or perhaps even retained) the value of the house the other party will frequently be
required to give credit for a fair share (one half in the case of joint ownership) of
the cost of those works (*Pavlou* [1993] 1 W.L.R. 1046). Where justice requires it
other payments may also be required (*Bernard v Josephs* [1982] Ch. 391).

Timing

The obligation to account arises on separation, when the implied purpose of the **33.023**
trust ends (*Clarke v Harlowe* [2005] EWHC 3062 (Ch); *Wilcox v Tait* [2006]
EWCA Civ 1867).

Trustee in bankruptcy—entitlement to rent from spouse remaining in occupation

Where a co-owner remains in occupation of a property after the bankruptcy of the **33.024**
other joint owner, the trustee in bankruptcy is entitled, on the sale of the property,
to set off a sum in respect that occupation against the co-owner's half share. The
trustee would not have been entitled under the 1996 Act because he was not a
beneficiary. However, the equitable principles continue to apply where the
Act does not (*French v Barcham* [2008] EWHC 1505 (Ch)).

Chapter 34

Enforcement, Suspension and Setting Aside

The rules relating to enforcement are still contained in the old county court and **34.001** High Court rules, which have been preserved in Schs 1 and 2 to the Civil Procedure Rules. In the county court the order for possession is enforced by a "warrant of possession" and in the High Court by a "writ of possession". Except in the case of an "excluded tenancy or licence" (see Ch.22) the landlord must apply for a warrant/writ of possession before he can get the property back (*Borzak v Ahmed* [1965] 2 Q.B. 320). It has also been held that a statutory tenancy continues as such until the order is lawfully executed and so any attempt by the landlord to evict without the assistance of the court gives rise to a claim for unlawful eviction (*Haniff v Robinson* [1993] 1 All E.R. 185).

It is now very unlikely that a claim for possession of residential property will proceed and be enforced in the High Court except possibly in some trespasser claims (see para.31.008). This chapter therefore concentrates on the procedure in the county court although a number of the principles are of general application. Where the claim is in the High Court the enforcement rules are to be found in RSC Ord.45 r.3. The most important difference between the two courts is that a writ of possession will not be issued without permission of the court, except in mortgage cases (RSC Ord.45 r.3(2)), and leave will only be given for breach of a suspended order if the defendant has been given a chance of being heard (*Fleet Mortgage and Investment Co Ltd v Lower Maisonette 46 Eaton Place Ltd* [1972] 1 W.L.R. 765).

Issue of warrant

The relevant rule is CCR Ord.26 r.17, which states that, a "judgment or order for **34.002** the recovery of land shall be enforceable by warrant of possession". A warrant for possession can only be applied for after the date fixed for possession in the order. That is apparent from Ord.26 r.17(2) and is reflected in Form N325 which requires the claimant or his solicitor to sign a statement on the face of the Form certifying "that the defendant has not vacated the land as ordered". It is also clear from the Form of Warrant itself, N49, which, among other things, requires the insertion of the date on which possession has been ordered to be given. (See *Tuohy v Bell* [2002] EWCA Civ 423—although the warrant was a nullity because it was issued prematurely the Court of Appeal upheld a prison sentence against the defendant because he had refused to comply with the possession order and had told the judge that he had no intention of complying with the order. That was a contempt that justified the imprisonment.)

Where the order for possession is suspended on certain terms the suspension terminates automatically if the defendant fails to comply with those terms. There is nothing in the rules requiring the claimant to give notice to the defendant before he applies for a warrant of possession (cf. the High Court). However, the following points should be noted:

- The order for possession may itself require the claimant to apply for permission to execute the order (*Yates v Morris* [1951] 1 K.B. 77 at 81).

- In *Barking & Dagenham LBC v Saint* (1998) 31 H.L.R. 620 CA it was held that a tenant who was arrested after the order for possession was made and who, to the knowledge of the landlord, was in prison at the time the warrant was issued should have been notified in prison of its issue—but note the full facts of the case which included further blameworthy acts on the part of the landlord—see para.34.012).

34.003 In *Barking* the court expressed the view, obiter, that s.76 of the County Courts Act 1984 (general principles of practice in the High Court may be adopted and applied in the county court) might apply to this situation and

"it appears arguable that the general principle of natural justice, that notice of application for a warrant of possession should be given to the tenant (that principle having been expressed in RSC Ord.45 r.3) could be invoked in the county court" (per Gibson L.J. at 629).

However, the argument was expressly rejected in *Jephson Homes Housing Association v Moisejevs* [2001] 2 All E.R. 901 CA:

"in the light of the evident continuing reluctance of the Rules Committee to amend the County Court Rules, to find . . . a requirement in natural justice that the tenant be given notice . . .".

In *St Brice v Southwark LBC* [2001] EWCA Civ 1138 an argument that the procedure for issuing warrants without notice breached the European Convention on Human Rights was also rejected.

In order to obtain the warrant the claimant must file a request certifying that the defendant has not vacated the land as ordered (r.17(2)) (Form N325). Where a money judgment was made in addition to the order for possession the claimant may also apply for execution against the defendant's goods (r.17(3)).

Where the order was suspended on terms as to payment of a sum of money by instalments, the claimant must in his request certify—

(a) the amount of money remaining due under the judgment or order; and

(b) that the whole or part of any instalment due remains unpaid (r.17(3A)).

34.004 Note also CCR Ord.26 r.1(4) which, in the case of a warrant issued to enforce an order for payment of money requires the court officer, unless the district judge responsible for execution of the warrant directs otherwise, to send "a warning notice to the person against whom the warrant is issued and, where such a notice is sent, the warrant shall not be levied until seven days thereafter".

In *Barking & Dagenham LBC v Saint* (1998) 31 H.L.R. 621 at 629, the failure to send such a notice to a tenant in prison where he was incarcerated seems to have contributed to a finding that the issue of the warrant was oppressive—see further below (para.34.012).

A warrant may not be issued without permission of the court more than six years after the order for possession was made (CCR Ord.26 r.17(6) and r.17(5)). Once issued the warrant is valid for 12 months but if not executed within that time may be renewed under r.6(1) (see r.17(6)).

Execution of the warrant

The landlord will be given an appointment when the bailiff will call at the premises   **34.005** to execute the warrant which, where the court has many warrants to issue, may be more than a month from the date of the application. Where a claimant is seeking to enforce an order for possession in the *High Court* there is no requirement in the rules or otherwise to give notice to an occupier of the *date for eviction* (*Pritchard v Teitelbaum* [2011] EWHC 1063). The decision would also seem to apply to the county court as there is also nothing in CCR Ord.26 r.17 requiring notice of the date of eviction to be given to the occupiers. The landlord or his solicitor should be at the premises to meet the bailiff together with a locksmith if the landlord wishes to change the locks. The landlord or his agent will be asked to sign a receipt indorsed on the warrant to acknowledge having received possession. In order to enforce the warrant the bailiff need not remove any goods or chattels from the premises (s.111(1) of the County Courts Act 1984; see further para.34.006A). The bailiff is entitled to evict anyone he finds on the premises even though that person was not a party to the proceedings (*R. v Wandsworth County Court Ex p. Wandsworth London Borough Council* [1975] 1 W.L.R. 1314 and the note in the Green Book to CCR Ord.26 r.17). Where a bailiff is executing a warrant against a person who has entered into or remained in occupation of the premises without the licence or consent of the person claiming possession, and the occupier resists or intentionally obstructs the bailiff, the occupier commits an offence (s.10 of the Criminal Law Act 1977). If a person found on the premises claims to have some right as against the landlord to remain there, he should apply to the court to be joined in the proceedings pursuant to CPR 19.4 and for the order for possession to be set aside (see para.34.010). If he fails to do this after having been given a reasonable opportunity to do so the bailiff may evict him.

Effect of insolvency

Section 285(3)(a) of the Insolvency Act 1986 provides as follows: **34.006**

"After the making of a bankruptcy order no person who is a creditor of the bankrupt in respect of the debt provable in the bankruptcy shall—(a) have any remedy against the property or person of the bankrupt in respect of that debt."

However, this provision will not prevent the enforcement of an order for possession (*Harlow District Council v Hall* [2006] EWCA Civ 156). In that case a secure tenant thought that he might prevent enforcement by making himself bankrupt. However, as the tenancy came to an end on the date for possession he no longer had any "property". Similarly in relation to debt relief orders see *Sharples v Places for People Homes Ltd* [2011] EWCA Civ 813 and para.28.010A.

Goods left on the premises

34.006A   Where goods are left on premises by a former tenant, whether following an eviction or a voluntary departure, the land owner is left with the problem of knowing what to do with them. Very often they will look like unwanted rubbish and the landlord will simply dispose of them. However, the landlord may be wary of such a course and will want to avoid any potential claim from the former tenant in respect of the goods. If practicable, the best solution is often for the landlord simply to store them safely until they are collected by the tenant.

In strict legal terms the landlord (it is submitted) between himself and the tenant is usually entitled at common law to put the goods out on the street (see a combination of *Jones v Foley* [1891] 1 Q.B. 730; *Hemmings v The Stoke Poges Golf Club* [1920] 1 K.B. 721, CA; *Aligonby v Cohen* [1955] 1 Q.B. 559 (QBD). In many cases he will obviously not want or be able to do so; not least because the local authority will not exactly be delighted.

In some cases what should happen to goods left on the premises will be dealt with by a provision in the lease. If not, another option might be to sell the goods in accordance with the procedures set out in ss.12 and 13 of the Torts (Interference with Goods) Act 1977; and see Sch.1. Note that the Act does not allow the landlord to deduct rent arrears from the proceeds of sale—only the costs of sale (s.12(5)). However, if the landlord proceeds under s.12 and the tenant turns up claiming some money, the landlord can no doubt counterclaim/set-off the arrears due. The landlord has no right to sell the goods other than pursuant to the provisions of the 1977 Act; or possibly under the terms of the lease.

Warrant of restitution

34.007   Where the tenant unlawfully re-enters the premises after the warrant for possession has been executed the landlord should apply for a warrant of restitution (CCR Ord.26 r.17(4)). Permission to issue the warrant is required and may be applied for without giving notice. The application should be supported by a witness statement evidencing the wrongful re-entry and of such further facts as would, in the High Court, enable the judgment creditor to have a writ of restitution issued (CCR Ord.26 r.17(5)).

The warrant may be issued in order to evict any persons on the land, whether they were parties to the original possession proceedings or not, provided there is a sufficient nexus between the acts of trespass concerned. The question to ask is, "were the acts or episodes of trespass complained of during the overall period properly to be regarded as essentially one transaction?" (*Wiltshire County Council v Frazer* [1986] 1 All E.R. 65).

In *Anchor Housing Association v Persons Unknown* (H.H. Judge Weekes QC sitting as a High Court judge in Bristol—October 2002, *Legal Action* 29) the landowner obtained an order for possession against squatters. A writ for possession was issued but the squatters vacated so that it was not necessary to execute the order. A few months later a different group of squatters took over the property.

Held: The landowner was not entitled to rely upon the writ to evict this second group of squatters. It was necessary to bring fresh proceedings.

Suspension of warrant

Where the warrant for possession is issued pursuant to an order for possession **34.008** made following proof by the landlord of one of the following grounds for possession, namely Grounds 9–16 of Sch.2 to the Housing Act 1988 (assured), Cases 1–10 of Sch.15 to the Rent Act 1977 (regulated); Grounds 1–8 or 12–16 of Sch.2 to the Housing Act 1985 (secure); or Cases I–X of Sch.4 to the Rent (Agriculture) Act 1976 (agricultural occupancy), the tenant may apply for execution of the order to be stayed or suspended, or the date for possession to be postponed, at any time before execution of the order. The court may stay or suspend execution of the order or postpone the date of possession for such period or periods as it thinks fit.

On any such stay, suspension or postponement the court must, unless it considers that to do so would cause exceptional hardship to the tenant or would otherwise be unreasonable, impose conditions with regard to payment of arrears of rent (if any) and rent or mesne profits in respect of occupation after termination of the tenancy and may impose such other conditions as it thinks fit. (See s.9 of the Housing Act 1988; s.100 of the Rent Act 1977; s.85 of the Housing Act 1985; s.7 of the Rent (Agriculture) Act 1976.)

Where the landlord has brought a claim in respect of an assured tenancy on Grounds 8, 10 and 11 and agrees to a suspended order for possession, even though the rent is such that Ground 8 obviously applies at the date of the hearing, he cannot subsequently argue (on a further application to suspend) that there is no power to suspend (*Capital Prime Plus Plc v Wills* (1998) 31 H.L.R. 926 CA).

Where the court has refused to suspend an order for possession when it was made it is subsequently very unlikely to exercise the power to suspend unless there is an unexpected and significant change of circumstances proved by proper evidence (*Taj v Ali (No.2)* (2001) 33 H.L.R. 27 CA—only after the possession order was made did the tenant make any serious proposals to pay off the arrears—suspension not granted).

On an application for a stay or suspension the court is not restricted to considering **34.009** the ground relied upon by the landlord in the claim for possession (*Sheffield City Council v Hopkins* [2001] EWCA Civ 1023 CA—the landlord wished to rely on allegations of nuisance even though the original order was only made on the ground of rent arrears). In situations where a landlord might rely upon certain conduct if any application for a suspension or stay were to be made, although not being relied upon as a ground for possession, it should give notice to the tenant. Where also at the possession claim the landlord wants a condition relating to other matters to form part of the order that condition should be sufficiently specified and made clear so that the tenant would be in no doubt as to what would constitute a breach (*Hopkins*).

The court has no power to stay execution in any case not covered by one of the statutory provisions above unless the landlord consents (*Moore v Lambeth County Court Registrar* [1969] 1 W.L.R. 141; *West Sussex County Council v Wood* [1982] CLY 1779, county court).

In *R. v Ilkeston County Court Ex p. Kruza* (1985) 17 H.L.R. 539, it was held that an order for possession which was "suspended for seven days or for as long as the tenant paid her rent" was not to be read as an order that enabled the landlord to execute the order as soon as rent was not paid. The court, therefore, had jurisdiction to entertain an application by the tenant for suspension of the warrant for possession which the landlord sought to execute for non-payment of rent. See also para.34.002.

It is not possible to postpone a date for possession under s.85(2) of the Housing Act 1985 (secure tenancies) once the tenant has left the premises voluntarily, whether following upon the issuing of a warrant for possession or not (*Dunn v Bradford Metropolitan DC; Marston v Leeds City Council* [2002] EWCA 1137.

Setting aside

34.010 Although the hearing of a possession claim on the first date is not a trial for the purposes of CPR 39.3, in most cases that part should be used to determine whether or not an order should be set aside for failure to attend that hearing (*London Borough of Hackney v Findlay* [2011] EWCA Civ 8, see *Forcelux v Binnie* [2009] EWCA Civ 854 for an example of an exceptional case where failure to attend a hearing meant that it was appropriate for the court to have recourse to the wider provisions for setting aside an order under CPR 3.1—forfeiture of a long lease).

In some cases the application of the part should be less strictly applied according to Arden L.J. in *Findlay*:

> "Parliament clearly contemplated in s85(2) of the Housing Act 1985 that the tenant should have the chance there described of persuading a court to modify an outright possession order. It follows that *the requirements of CPR 39.3(5) need not be applied in such a case with the same rigour* as in the case of a final order that does not have this characteristic...
>
> Accordingly, the court should not decline to exercise its power to set aside a possession order if in consequence the statutory purpose in s85(2) would be defeated. Moreover, in my judgment the court can have regard to the wider social context in which these cases come before the courts. Accordingly, in deciding whether the tenant has a good reason for non-attendance the court can in my judgment have regard to the provisions of the Rent Arrears Pre-Action Protocol and to best practice among social landlords. It may conclude that, while in the ordinary case a defendant might have had no proper excuse for not attending a court hearing at which the possession order was made, given best practice of social landlords and the provisions of that protocol, a tenant is in fact able to provide an appropriate explanation." (para.24)

Therefore in most cases where a party does not attend a hearing or a trial and the court gives judgment or makes an order against them the party who failed to attend may apply for the judgment or order to be set aside (CPR r.39.3(3)). The court may grant the application only if the applicant:

 (a) acted promptly when he found out that the court had exercised its power to make the order against him;

 (b) had a good reason for not attending the trial; and

 (c) has a reasonable prospect of success at the trial. (CPR r.39.3(5); and see *Bank of Scotland v Pereira* [2011] EWCA Civ 241 where Neuberger MR sets out in detail the considerations to be made on such an application).

Where a party is dissatisfied with judgment at a hearing at which they failed to attend and their main cause for complaint arises out of the failure to adjourn the matter, the proper route is an application to set the judgment aside under CPR 39.3(3) rather than appeal (*Williams v Hinton* [2011] EWCA Civ 1123).

An application to set aside by someone who was not a party to the proceedings should be made (CPR r.40.9) together with an application to be joined in the proceedings (CPR r.19.4(2)(b); e.g. see *Wandsworth LBC v Fadayomi* [1987] 3 All E.R. 474).

After Execution

Once a warrant is executed the court no longer has any power to suspend the order **34.011** for possession. The defendant will only have a remedy if he is entitled to have the ***order for possession set aside*** (*Governors of the Peabody Donation Fund v Hay* (1986) 19 H.L.R. 145) or if the warrant has been obtained by ***fraud, abuse of process or oppression*** (*Hammersmith and Fulham LBC v Hill* [1994] 2 E.G.L.R. 51 at 52H; *Circle 33 Housing Trust Ltd v Ellis* [2005] EWCA Civ 1233—see below).

An application for an order to set aside an order for possession may be made after the order has been executed (*Minet v Johnson* (1890) 63 L.T. 507). It was held under the old CCR that if a judgment or order for possession is set aside, any execution issued on the judgment or order ceases to have effect, even if the order for possession has actually been executed (*Governors of Peabody Donation Fund v Hay* (1987) H.L.R. 145) in which case the landlord should let the tenant back into possession. However, so long as the order is in force the claimant is entitled to enforce it. Execution of the order for possession does not make the landlord liable for breach of the covenant for quiet enjoyment if it is subsequently set aside (*Brent LBC v Botu* (2001) 33 H.L.R. 14 CA).

The fact that the warrant had been executed is a relevant factor in determining whether or not to set aside the possession order. In *Findlay*, Arden L.J. stated:

> "Where there has been execution of a possession order, that factor will clearly also constitute a relevant circumstance that the court should take into account on any application to set aside that possession order. The weight to be given to it will depend on the particular circumstances of the case. However, it is difficult to think of a case in which, in the absence of some compelling factor, execution would not be a highly relevant factor if the landlord had proceeded properly to allocate the property to some other tenant or indeed (in some cases at least) to incur expense in refurbishing the property so that it could be allocated to another tenant." (para.25)

Oppression

As stated above one of the grounds upon which the court might set aside the order **34.012** is "oppression". The court will rarely be willing to find oppression but "the categories of oppression are not closed and the court must have the power to intervene in the interests of justice in an appropriate case to correct the position where its procedures have been used unfairly to the oppression of a party" (*Barking & Dagenham LBC v Saint* (1998) 31 H.L.R. 620 CA per Gibson L.J. at 626).

"Oppression includes oppressive conduct which effectively deprives a tenant of his opportunity to apply for a stay" (*Lambeth LBC v Hughes* (2001) 33 H.L.R. 350 CA per Arden J.; and see *Circle 33 Housing Trust Ltd v Ellis* [2005] EWCA Civ 1233). However "a possession warrant obtained and executed without fault on anyone's part cannot properly be set aside as oppressive" (*Jephson Homes Housing Association v Moisejevs* [2000] EWCA Civ 271, per Simon Brown L.J., at [37]).

A warrant obtained without the court's permission in breach of CCR Ord.26 r.5 where six years or more have elapsed since the date of the order for possession is an abuse of process (*Governors of the Peabody Donation Fund v Hay* (1986)—see above). In *Barking & Dagenham v Saint* execution of a county court warrant was held to be oppressive where the tenant, who to the knowledge of the landlord, was in prison—but note the full facts of the case which included a failure properly to notify him of a right to make a further claim for housing benefit which led to increased arrears.

Oppression can include oppression caused by misleading information given by the court office (*Hammersmith & Fulham LBC v Lemeh*, Unreported, April 3, 2000 CA—tenant wrongly told by member of court staff that there appeared to be no case on the court system—warrant then executed; and *Lambeth LBC v Hughes* (2001) 33 H.L.R. 350—tenant told, inaccurately, that no warrant had been issued and given other inaccurate information. Once he realised the true position he applied immediately to set aside the warrant and it was set aside even though he did not have a strong case for a suspension of the order. He was entitled to be put back into the position he would have been in had there been no oppression.) However, simply being under a genuine misapprehension as to what is required to prevent the eviction, which has not been induced by any other person, is insufficient to set aside the order (*Jephson Homes Housing Association v Moisejevs* [2000] EWCA Civ 271—which discusses the various cases, including the unreported ones referred to above).

34.013   In *Rendham Holdings Ltd v Patel* [2002] All E.R. (D) 132, December 2002 *Legal Action* 21, the tenant applied for a stay of execution of a possession order pending appeal. Due to an error in the court office the application was not put before a judge. A warrant for possession was issued and executed. The tenant successfully applied to have the warrant set aside on the basis of oppression and obtained relief from forfeiture. The landlord's appeal to the High Court was unsuccessful. The tenant was entitled to believe that a warrant would not be issued and enforced before considering the application for the stay.

If a judgment or order for possession is set aside "any execution issued on the judgment or order shall cease to have effect unless the Court otherwise orders" (CCR Ord.37 r.8(3)); even if the order for possession has actually been executed (*Governors of Peabody Donation Fund v Hay* (1986) 19 H.L.R. 145). However, so long as the order is in force the claimant is entitled to enforce it. Execution of the order for possession does not make the landlord liable for breach of the covenant for quiet enjoyment if it is subsequently set aside (*Brent LBC v Botu* (2001) 33 H.L.R. 14 CA).

Chapter 35

Unlawful Eviction and Harassment: The Occupier's Remedies

Introduction

A person who unlawfully evicts or harasses an occupier of residential premises **35.001** commits an offence under s.1 of the Protection from Eviction Act 1977 (see Ch.22). That provision does not give the occupier a civil remedy in respect of any such unlawful action, but neither does it take away any such remedy that he might have (s.1(5); *McCall v Abelesz* [1976] 1 All E.R. 727 CA).

The principal civil remedy of a tenant, or other occupier, who has been unlawfully evicted or who is being harassed is an injunction requiring the landlord to permit the tenant to return to live in the premises and to discontinue the harassment.

An occupier of residential premises who has been unlawfully evicted or harassed may also claim damages. These may be claimed in contract or tort or under ss.27 and 28 of the Housing Act 1988. As will be seen below, damages awarded under the 1988 Act are based upon the profit that the landlord obtains by evicting the tenant and can, depending on the expert evidence, be substantial. They are only awarded where the tenant is not restored to the property before a certain point in time (see notes (5) and (7), para.35.021). As a result there has been an increasing tendency, since the introduction of the 1988 Act, for tenants only to claim damages and not to seek injunctions.

Further, where the landlord pursues a course of conduct which amounts to harassment, it might also be possible for a tenant to bring a claim under the Protection from Harassment Act 1997. That Act gives rise to criminal liability as well as forming the basis for a claim for a civil injunction and for damages. It does not enable the tenant to regain possession of the property but could be used in conjunction with other claims based on the unlawful eviction and conduct of the landlord.

Basis of the claim

A tenant's claim for an injunction or damages is based upon the covenant for quiet **35.002** enjoyment or the covenant not to derogate from the tenant's grant. If not expressed in a tenancy agreement these covenants will be implied as a matter of law. An unlawful eviction also constitutes a trespass giving rise to a claim in tort. Where the tenant is a statutory tenant the covenants in the tenancy are carried over from the protected tenancy into the statutory tenancy by s.3 of the Rent Act 1977. See also s.5 of the Housing Act 1988 in relation to a statutory periodic tenancy.

A licensee may also seek an injunction to prevent the licensor from excluding him from the premises in breach of contract (*Millennium Productions Ltd v Winter Garden Theatre (London) Ltd* [1946] 1 All E.R. 678 per Lord Greene M.R.; *Hounslow London Borough Council v Twickenham Garden Development Ltd* [1971] Ch. 233). Where the eviction is unlawful by virtue of s.3 of the Protection from Eviction Act 1977 (see para.22.003), an actionable tort is committed which gives the occupier a right to claim an injunction (*Warder v Cooper* [1970] 1 Ch. 495; *Love v Herrity* [1991] 2 E.G.L.R. 44).

An occupier of residential premises who has been unlawfully evicted or harassed may also claim damages.

Examples of harassment

35.003 The following are examples where the landlord has not actually evicted the tenant but where he has been found in breach of the covenant for quiet enjoyment: where the landlord removed doors and windows from the premises (*Lavender v Betts* [1942] 2 All E.R. 72); where the gas and electricity were cut off causing the tenant to leave (*Perera v Vandiyar* [1953] 1 W.L.R. 672); where the landlord failed to pay the electricity bill so that it was cut off (*McCall v Abelesz* [1976] Q.B. 585); where the landlord knocked on the tenant's door, shouted threats of physical eviction and wrote letters threatening immediate eviction (*Kenny v Preen* [1963] 1 Q.B. 499); and where there were extensive building works (*Mira v Aylmer Square Investment Ltd* [1990] E.G.L.R. 45) and where the tenant is assured and the landlord goes into occupation of other rooms in the dwelling without a clear and specific term entitling him to do so (*Miller v Eyo* (1998) 31 H.L.R. 315).

Where the harassment reaches such a level that the occupier is forced to leave he will be treated as having been evicted and will be entitled to claim damages accordingly (*Sampson v Floyd* [1989] 2 E.G.L.R. 49; *Dowkes v Athelston* (1993)).

In *Abbott v Bayley* (1999) 32 H.L.R. 72, it was found that the following did not constitute acts done to interfere with the peace and comfort of the tenant: (1) an invalid notice to quit; (2) offensive comments, in letters stating that the tenant was "devious, nasty and dishonourable"; and (3) letting other tenants into the property with exclusive possession of parts and shared use of communal areas. What did constitute such acts were the introduction of other tenants to the property and a threat forcibly to evict.

Injunctions

County court jurisdiction

35.004 An application for an injunction seeking to restrain the landlord from keeping the tenant out or from harassing the tenant may be made in the county court, whatever the rateable value of the premises and notwithstanding there is no other claim (ss.15 and 38 of the County Courts Act 1984). However, if the occupier is relying upon an agreement for a lease so that he needs to seek specific performance (see para.1.009) he may, subject to agreement, only bring proceedings in the county court if the value of the land (i.e. the value of the freehold interest) does not exceed the county court limit, currently £30,000 (ss.23(d), 24 of the County Courts Act 1984).

The application can be made to the Circuit Judge and in some cases to the district judge (CPR PD 2B para.8.1(a) and para.11.1(b)).

Without notice applications

A without notice application is one that is made by one party in the absence of the other and may be made prior to the commencement of the claim. Such an application should only be made in urgent cases. However, applications in unlawful eviction cases (although not necessarily in harassment cases) are invariably urgent, for two reasons: **35.005**

(1) the claimant has been evicted from his home and needs somewhere to live; and

(2) the defendant may re-let the property to someone else unless the claimant takes quick action.

The difficulties that can arise are demonstrated by the case of *Love v Herrity* [1991] 2 E.G.L.R. 44. Between the eviction and the application to the court for an injunction, the landlord re-let the property to someone else. An order requiring the landlord to remove the new tenant would have been unenforceable because the landlord had no right to possession against the new tenant and so it was not made. Instead it made a declaration that the original tenant was entitled to possession as against the landlord and gave liberty to apply to join the new tenant for the purpose of obtaining possession.

The application should be made in the appropriate prescribed form (N16A; Form 42 of this book—p.591) and should state the terms of the injunction applied for. It should be supported by a witness statement (CPR r.25.3(2)—see Form 43 of this book, p.592) which should: **35.006**

- state the grounds upon which the application is made; and

- explain why the application is made without notice (CPR r.25.3(3)).

As stated above, the application may be made before the proceedings are begun (CPR r.25.2(1)(a)). Whenever possible a draft of the order sought (Form N16) should be filed with the application notice and a disc containing the draft should also be available (CPR PD 25A para.2.4).

The PD states that an application should be filed whenever possible two hours before it is heard (CPR PD 25 para.4.3). It is therefore possible to obtain a without notice injunction by turning up at court with an application, short witness statement and draft order although the court should be telephoned in advance to notify the staff of the intention to make the application.

In ignorance of the rules, county court staff sometimes require the applicant to issue proceedings and to pay the necessary fee before the papers will be put before the judge. In order to avoid any difficulty it is therefore worth drafting particulars of claim (Form 44, p.593) and issuing the proceedings if time will allow. If there really has been no opportunity to do so, the legal representative should point out the above rules and politely insist upon the matter being put before the judge. If necessary, ask to speak to the Chief Clerk.

35.007   The application is heard "in public" unless the judge orders that it is to be heard in private (CPR r.39.2). However, the hearing normally takes place in the judge's room and robes are not generally worn.

If the application is granted, it will be on terms providing for the issue of the claim form in the court granting the application (if it has not already been issued) and on such other terms as the court thinks fit (CPR r.25.2(3)). The tenant will always be required to give an undertaking as to damages, the effect of which should be explained to the tenant in advance. As part of his order, the judge will usually fix a return date for an on notice hearing. If not, he will give permission to the defendant to apply for a discharge of the injunction on short notice. Even where he makes no such provision, the defendant is always at liberty to apply, on notice if necessary, although it will be a rare case where an order discharging an injunction will be made without notice to the tenant.

Injunctions on notice

35.008   Where the matter is not so urgent the claimant should issue proceedings by filing with the court a claim form together with:

(1) the particulars of claim;

(2) an application for an interim injunction;

(3) a witness statement in support; and

(4) a draft order (with a copy on disc).

An extra copy of each of the above four documents should be prepared in respect of each defendant (CPR PD 25 paras 2.3 and 2.4). Service should take place not less than three days before the hearing (CPR PD 25A, 2.2). To apply for short notice see CPR r.23.7(4).

When drafting the particulars of claim at this stage, the claimant will be unlikely to be able to give full particulars of the damages claimed. It is, therefore, suggested that a general claim be made and that the particulars be amended subsequently to provide all the details required (see Form 44, p.593; and further the section below on damages).

The application for the interim injunction (whether as an original injunction or the return date following upon a without notice injunction) will be heard by the judge in public unless otherwise directed (CPR r.39.2). The general principles governing the granting of interim injunctions will apply, i.e. can the claimant demonstrate that there is a serious issue to be tried, would damages be an adequate compensation for any loss that he may suffer and where does the balance of convenience lie (*American Cyanamid Co v Ethicon Ltd* [1975] A.C. 396)? In practice, this means that if the claimant can show that he is an occupier of residential premises who has been put out otherwise than by proceedings in court he will almost invariably be granted an order compelling the landlord to allow him to return (*Warder v Cooper* [1970] 1 Ch. 495). But compare the position when the landlord has re-let the property (para.35.005—reference to *Love v Herrity*).

Form 42: Application for Injunction (General Form)

Application for Injunction (General Form)

Name of court	Claim No.
Claimant's Name and Ref.	
Defendant's Name and Ref.	

Notes on completion

Tick which boxes apply and specify the legislation where appropriate

(1) Enter the full name of the person making the application

(2) Enter the full name of the person the injunction is to be directed to

(3) Set out any proposed orders requiring acts to be done. Delete if no mandatory order is sought.

(4) Set out here the proposed terms of the injunction order (if the defendant is a limited company delete the wording in brackets and insert 'whether by its servants, agents, officers or otherwise').

(5) Set out here any further terms asked for including provision for costs

(6) Enter the names of all persons who have sworn affidavits or signed statements in support of this application

(7) Enter the names and addresses of all persons upon whom it is intended to serve this application

(8) Enter the full name and address for service and delete as required

☐ By application in pending proceedings

☐ Under Statutory provision _____

☐ This application is made under Part 8 of the Civil Procedure Rules

Seal

This application raises issues under the Human Rights Act 1998 ☐ Yes ☐ No

The Claimant[1]

applies to the court for an injunction order in the following terms:

The Defendant[2]

must[3]

The Defendant

be forbidden (whether by himself or by instructing or encouraging or permitting any other person)[4]

And that[5]

The grounds of this application are set out in the written evidence

of[6]   sworn (signed) on

This written evidence is served with this application.

This application is to be served upon[7]

This application is filed by[8]

(the Solicitors for) the Claimant (Applicant/Petitioner)

whose address for service is

Signed _____   Dated _____

---

* Name and address of the person application is directed to

To*

of

This section to be completed by the court

This application will be heard by the (District) Judge

at

on   the   day of   20   at   o'clock

If you do not attend at the time shown the court may make an injunction order in your absence

If you do not fully understand this application you should go to a Solicitor, Legal Advice Centre or a Citizens' Advice Bureau

The court office at

is open between 10am and 4pm Mon - Fri. When corresponding with the court, please address all forms and letters to the Court Manager and quote the claim number.

N16A General form of application for injunction (04.07)   HMCS

Form 43: Witness statement in support of application for interim injunction

IN THE COUNTY COURT	Claim No

BETWEEN

Claimant

—AND—

Defendant

I [*state name and address of Claimant*] will say as follows:

1. I make this witness statement in support of my application for an injunction compelling the Defendant to allow me to return to [*state address of premises*] and for an injunction preventing him from excluding me from the said property.

2. [In about February . . . . I became the Defendant's tenant at 2, Scone Street, Bakewell, Derbyshire ("the premises"). It was agreed orally between us that I would pay him a rent of £40 per week, payable on Mondays in advance. The Defendant does not live at the premises.

3. From the time I moved in I paid the rent every Monday. However, in early . . . I lost my job and it has taken some time to sort out payment of housing benefit. I have not therefore been able to pay all the rent due. On 24 May . . . I went away to Dundee for a long weekend to see my parents who live there. I returned to Bakewell on 29th May . . . and on arriving at the premises found that the locks on the front door had been changed. I went around to the back of the property and noticed through a window that there was no sign of my clothes or possessions on the premises. It was too late to go to the Defendant's office but I immediately went to his house. Nobody was there. I had very little money on me and no family in Bakewell with whom I could stay. In the end a friend said I could sleep the night on her sofa.]

4. [I telephoned the Defendant's office this morning, 30 May, and was told by him that as I had not paid the rent he would not let me live at the premises. He told me that I could collect my belongings from his office. As stated above I have no family in Bakewell I can stay with and only a friend's sofa to sleep on.]

5. I therefore require an injunction as a matter of urgency and apply to the court for an order in the following terms:

(1) that the Defendant do forthwith permit me to return to the premises; and

(2) that the Defendant whether by himself his servants or agents or otherwise howsoever be forbidden from excluding me from the premises or interfering with my quiet enjoyment of the premises.

Statement of truth etc.

The procedure after the hearing is that the case will be allocated to a track and directions will be given. The claimant may then continue his claim for a permanent injunction and, if he so wishes, damages.

Service of the order; breach of the order

35.009 The order for an injunction is indorsed with a penal notice indicating that disobedience of the order amounts to contempt punishable by imprisonment (Form N16). The order must be served personally on the party against whom the order has been made. Failure to obey the order can result in that person having to show the court why a committal order should not be made (CCR Ord.29; e.g. see *Saxby v McKinley* (1996) 29 H.L.R. 569 CA—landlord sent to prison for 28 days). In order to save time the claimant can arrange for a process server to attend court to collect the injunction for service. Alternatively the tenant may serve the injunction but if violence is feared he should ask for a police officer to be present.

Form 44: Particulars of claim—changing the locks

IN THE	COUNTY COURT	Claim No

BETWEEN

Claimant

—AND—

Defendant

PARTICULARS OF CLAIM

1. The Defendant is the freehold or leasehold owner of a dwelling-house situate at and known as [insert address of premises] ("the premises").

2. By an oral agreement made on or about [state date] the Defendant agreed to let the premises to the Claimant on a weekly tenancy at a rent of £_____ [State amount of rent] per week payable in advance each and every [state day of week]. In the premises the Claimant granted the Defendant a weekly periodic assured shorthold tenancy pursuant to the Housing Act 1988.

3. It was an implied term of the said agreement that the Defendant would not interfere with the Claimant's quiet enjoyment of the premises.

4. On or about the [insert date] the Defendant, in breach of the said agreement and of the said implied term, changed the locks on the front door of the premises and thereby excluded the Claimant from the same. The Defendant refuses to allow the Claimant to re-enter the premises.

5. By reason of the matters aforesaid the Claimant has suffered loss and damage, inconvenience, frustration, vexation and distress.

AND the Claimant claims:

(1) An order that the Defendant do forthwith permit the Claimant to return to the premises;
(2) An order that the Defendant, whether by himself his servants or agents or otherwise howsoever be restrained from excluding the Claimant from the said premises or interfering with her quiet enjoyment of the said premises; and
(3) Damages including aggravated and exemplary damages and damages pursuant to sections 27 and 28 of the Housing Act 1988. [Note that it will be necessary to amend the particulars after the injunction has been granted in order fully to particularise the claim, see para.32.008].

DATED

Statement of truth etc.

CPR r.25.1 Orders for interim remedies

(1) The court may grant the following interim remedies—   **35.010**

    (a) an interim injunction; . . .

(4) The court may grant an interim remedy whether or not there has been a claim for a final remedy of that kind.

CPR r.25.2 Time when an order for an interim remedy may be made

(1) An order for an interim remedy may be made at any time, including—   **35.011**

    (a) before proceedings are started; and
    (b) after judgment has been given.

    (Rule 7.2 provides that proceedings are started when the court issues a claim form)
(2) However—

(a) paragraph (1) is subject to any rule, practice direction or other enactment which provides otherwise;

(b) the court may grant an interim remedy before a claim has been made only if—

    (i) the matter is urgent; or

    (ii) it is otherwise desirable to do so in the interests of justice; and

(c) unless the court otherwise orders, a defendant may not apply for any of the orders listed in rule 25.1 (1) before he has filed either an acknowledgement of service or a defence.

(Part 10 provides for filing an acknowledgment of service and Part 15 for filing a defence)

(3) Where the court grants an interim remedy before a claim has been commenced, it may give directions requiring a claim to be commenced.

CPR r.25.3 How to apply for an interim remedy

35.012

(1) The court may grant an interim remedy on an application made without notice if it appears to the court that there are good reasons for not giving notice.

(2) An application for an interim remedy must be supported by evidence, unless the court orders otherwise.

(3) If the applicant makes an application without giving notice, the evidence in support of the application must state the reasons why notice has not been given.

CPR PD 25A

Making an application

35.013

2.1 The application notice must state:

    (1) the order sought; and

    (2) the date, time and place of the hearing.

2.2 The application notice and evidence in support must be served as soon as practicable after issue and in any event not less than three days before the court is due to hear the application.

2.3 Where the court is to serve, sufficient copies of the application notice and evidence in support for the court and for each respondent should be filed for issue and service.

2.4 Whenever possible a draft of the order sought should be filed with the application notice and a disk containing the draft should also be available to the court. This will enable the court officer to arrange for any amendments to be incorporated and for the speedy preparation and sealing of the order.

Evidence

35.014

3.1 Applications for search orders and freezing injunctions must be supported by affidavit evidence.

3.2 Applications for other interim injunctions must be supported by evidence set out in either:

    (1) a witness statement; or

(2) a statement of case provided that it is verified by a statement of truth; or

(3) the application provided that it is verified by a statement of truth,

3.2 unless the court, an Act, a rule or a practice direction requires evidence by affidavit.

3.3 The evidence must set out the facts on which the applicant relies for the claim being made against the respondent, including all material facts of which the court should be made aware.

3.4 Where an application is made without notice to the respondent, the evidence must also set out why notice was not given.

(See Part 32 and the practice direction that supplements it for information about evidence.)

Urgent applications and applications without notice

4.1 These fall into two categories: **35.015**

(1) applications where a claim form has already been issued; and

(2) applications where a claim form has not yet been issued,

and, in both cases, where notice of the application has not been given to the respondent.

4.2 The applications are normally dealt with a court hearing but cases of extreme urgency may be dealt with by telephone.

4.3 Applications dealt with at a court hearing after issue of a claim form:

(1) the application notice, evidence in support and a draft order (as in 2.4 above) should be filed with the court two hours before the hearing wherever possible;

(2) if an application is made before the application notice has been issued, a draft order (as in 2.4 above) should be provided at the hearing, and the application notice and evidence in support must be filed with the court on the same or next working day or as ordered by the court; and

(3) except in cases where secrecy is essential, the applicant should take steps to notify the respondent informally of the application.

4.4 Applications made before the issue of a claim form:

(1) in addition to the provisions set out as 4.3 above, unless the court orders otherwise, either the applicant must undertake to the court to issue a claim form immediately or the court will give directions for the commencement of the claim;

(2) where possible the claim form should be served with the order for the injunction;

(3) an order made before the issue of a claim form should state in the title after the names of the applicant and respondent "the Claimant and Defendant in an Intended Action".

4.5 Applications made by telephone: **35.016**

(1) where it is not possible to arrange a hearing, application can be made between 10.00 a.m. and 5.00 p.m. weekdays by telephoning the Royal Courts of Justice on 020 7947 6000 and asking to be put in contact with High Court Judge of the appropriate Division available to deal with an emergency application in a High Court matter. The appropriate district registry may also be contacted by telephone. In county court proceedings, the appropriate county court should be contacted;

(2) where an application is made outside those hours the applicant should either:

    (a) telephone the Royal Courts of Justice on 020 7947 6000 where he will be put in contact with the clerk to the appropriate duty judge in the High Court (or the appropriate Circuit Judge where known); or

    (b) the Urgent Court Business Officer of the appropriate Circuit who will contact the local duty judge.

(3) where the facility is available it is likely that the judge will require a draft order to be faxed to him;

(4) the application notice and evidence in support must be filed with the court on the same or next working day or as ordered, together with two copies of the order for sealing,

(5) injunctions will be heard by telephone only where the applicant is acting by counsel or solicitors.

Orders for injunctions

35.017

5.1 Any order for an injunction, unless the court orders otherwise, must contain:

(1) an undertaking by the applicant to the court to pay any damages which the respondent sustains which the court considers the applicant should pay;

(2) if made without notice to any other party, an undertaking by the applicant to the court to serve on the respondent the application notice, evidence in support and any order made as soon as practicable;

(3) if made without notice to any other party, a return date for a further hearing at which the other party can be present;

(4) if made before filing the application notice, an undertaking to file and pay the appropriate fee on the same or next working day; and

(5) if made before issue of a claim form—

    (a) an undertaking to issue and pay the appropriate fee on the same or next working day; or

    (b) directions for the commencement of the claim.

5.1A When the court makes an order for an injunction, it should consider whether to require an undertaking by the applicant to pay any damages sustained by a person other than the respondent, including another party to the proceedings or any other person who may suffer loss as a consequence of the order.

5.2 An order for an injunction made in the presence of all parties to be bound by it or made at a hearing of which they have had notice, may state that it is effective until trial or further order.

5.3 Any order for an injunction must set out clearly what the respondent must do or not do.

Damages

35.018 The Housing Act 1988 substantially amended the law relating to damages that may be awarded to a residential occupier who has been unlawfully evicted or who has been so harassed by the landlord that he has been forced to leave. Damages are awarded "in respect of his loss of the right to occupy" the dwelling as his residence (s.27(3)). Section 27 sets out the circumstances in which damages are payable. Section 28 explains/directs how the damages are to be assessed.

Where the occupier has remained or returned to the property ss.27 and 28 will not apply (see notes below) but he will be able to claim damages in contract or tort.

Housing Act 1988: entitlements to damages

27.—(1) This section applies if, at any time after 9th June 1988, a landlord (in this **35.019** section referred to as "the landlord in default") or any person acting on behalf of the landlord in default unlawfully deprives the residential occupier of any premises of his occupation of the whole or part of the premises.

(2) This section also applies if, at any time after 9th June 1988, a landlord in this section referred to as ("the landlord in default") or any person acting on behalf of the landlord in default—

    (a) attempts unlawfully to deprive the residential occupier of any premises of his occupation of the whole or part of the premises; or

    (b) knowing or having reasonable cause to believe that the conduct is likely to cause the residential occupier of any premises—

        (i) to give up his occupation of the premises or any part thereof; or

        (ii) to refrain from exercising any right or pursuing any remedy in respect of the premises or any part thereof, does acts likely to interfere with the peace or comfort of the residential occupier or members of his household, or persistently withdraws or withholds services reasonably required for the occupation of the premises as a residence and, as a result, the residential occupier gives up his occupation of the premises as a residence.

(3) Subject to the following provisions of this section, where this section applies, the landlord in default shall, by virtue of this section, be liable to pay to the former residential occupier, in respect of his loss of the right to occupy the premises in question as his residence, damages assessed on the basis set out in section 28 below.

(4) Any liability arising by virtue of subsection (3) above—

    (a) shall be in the nature of a liability in tort; and

    (b) subject to subsection (5) below, shall be in addition to any liability arising apart from this section (whether in tort, contract or otherwise).

(5) Nothing in this section affects the right of a residential occupier to enforce any liability which arises apart from this section in respect of his loss of the right to occupy premises as his residence; but damages shall not be awarded both in respect of such a liability and in respect of a liability arising by virtue of this section on account of the same loss.

(6) No liability shall arise by virtue of subsection (3) above if—

    (a) before the date on which proceedings to enforce the liability are finally disposed of, the former residential occupier is reinstated in the premises in question in such circumstances that he becomes again the residential occupier of them; or

    (b) at the request of the former residential occupier, a court makes an order (whether in the nature of an injunction or otherwise) as a result of which he is reinstated as mentioned in paragraph (a) above;

and, for the purposes of paragraph (a) above, proceedings to enforce a liability are finally disposed of on the earliest date by which the proceedings (including any proceedings on or in consequence of an appeal) have been determined and any time for appealing or further appealing has expired, except that if any appeal is abandoned, the proceedings shall be taken to be disposed of on the date of the abandonment.

35.020   (7) If, in proceedings to enforce a liability arising by virtue of subsection (3) above, it appears to the court—

    (a) that, prior to the event which gave rise to the liability, the conduct of the former residential occupier or any person living with him in the premises concerned was such that it is reasonable to mitigate the damages for which the landlord in default would otherwise be liable; or

    (b) that, before the proceedings were begun, the landlord in default offered to reinstate the former residential occupier in the premises in question and either it was unreasonable of the former residential occupier to refuse that offer or, if he had obtained alternative accommodation before the offer was made, it would have been unreasonable of him to refuse that offer if he had not obtained that accommodation, the court may reduce the amount of damages which would otherwise be payable to such amount as it thinks appropriate.

    (8) In proceedings to enforce a liability arising by virtue of subsection (3) above, it shall be a defence for the defendant to prove that he believed, and had reasonable cause to believe—

    (a) that the residential occupier had ceased to reside in the premises in question at the time when he was deprived of occupation as mentioned in subsection (1) above or as the case may be, when the attempt was made or the acts were done as a result of which he gave up his occupation of those premises; or

    (b) that, where the liability would otherwise arise by virtue only of the doing of acts or the withdrawal or withholding of service, he had reasonable grounds for doing the acts or withdrawing or withholding the services in question.

    (9) In this section—

    (a) "residential occupier", in relation to any premises, has the same meaning as in section 1 of the 1977 Act;

    (b) "the right to occupy", in relation to a residential occupier, includes any restriction on the right of another person to recover possession of the premises in question;

    (c) "landlord", in relation to a residential occupier, means the person who, but for the occupier's right to occupy, would be entitled to occupation of the premises and any superior landlord under whom that person derives title;

    (d) "former residential occupier", in relation to any premises, means the person who was the residential occupier until he was deprived of or gave up his occupation as mentioned in subsection (1) or subsection (2) above (and, in relation to a former residential occupier, "the right to occupy" and "landlord" shall be construed accordingly).

Notes:

35.021   (1) A purchaser of a house who is let into occupation as licensee under the terms of the contract to purchase prior to completion (see para.21.016) is a "landlord" for the purposes of s.27(1). He may be ordered to pay damages under that section if he unlawfully evicts any residential occupier during that period (s.27(9)(c); *Jones v Miah* [1992] 2 E.G.L.R. 50).

(2) A "residential occupier" is defined in s.1 of the Protection from Eviction Act 1977 as

> "a person occupying the premises as a residence, whether under a contract or by virtue of any enactment or rule of law giving him the right to remain in occupation or restricting the right of any other person to recover possession of the premises" (see s.27(9)). See also *West Wiltshire DC v Snelgrove* (1997) 30 H.L.R. 57.

(3) In a harassment case it is not necessary to prove that the landlord intended to deprive the residential occupier of the property (subs.(2)(b)).

(4) The right to damages given by the section is in addition to any other right the residential occupier may have (whether in tort, contract or otherwise; see below para.35.024, but damages may not be awarded twice in respect of the same loss (subss.(4), (5)). The claimant does not have to elect formally under which tranche to seek damages but whatever is awarded the smaller amount must be deducted in reaching the net amount (*Mason v Nworkorie* [1994] 1 E.G.L.R. 59 CA—see below para.35.027). However, aggravated damages relating to the circumstances of the eviction can be awarded in addition to damages for the loss of occupation (*Francis v Brown* (1997) 30 H.L.R. 143 CA, per Sir Iain Glidewell at 150).

(5) No liability arises under the section if the residential occupier is reinstated to the property before the proceedings are finally disposed of (subs. (6)) but the occupier is not obliged to accept reinstatement under this subsection. He may choose between reinstatement and damages under the Act (*Tagro v Cafane* [1991] 2 All E.R. 235 CA). The claimant does not have to elect between statutory damages or reinstatement until trial (*Osei Bonsu v Wandsworth* [1999] 1 All E.R. 265 CA). Damages awarded under ss.27 and 28 can be substantially greater than those awarded in contract and tort. There will, therefore, be many cases where the displaced occupier will prefer not to accept an offer of reinstatement. An interim injunction allowing the tenant back into the room (which was complied with) but which was discharged one week later, was not to be taken as constituting reinstatement for the purpose of s.27(6) (*Mehta v Royal Bank of Scotland* (1999) 32 H.L.R. 45).

(6) The presentation by the landlord to the tenant of a key to a broken door and an invitation to resume occupation in a wrecked room was held not to constitute proper reinstatement (*Tagro v Cafane*).

(7) However, where an offer of reinstatement is made before proceedings are begun, damages may be reduced under s.27(7)(b). The word "proceedings" in that subsection refers to the claim for damages rather than an initial claim for an injunction. Thus, damages awarded will be reduced under s.27(7)(b) if an offer of reinstatement is made at any time before proceedings for damages are commenced, notwithstanding that proceedings to obtain an injunction to force reinstatement have already been commenced (*Tagro v Cafane* (obiter)).

(8) Subsection (7)(a) contains a further basis upon which damages may be reduced and subs.(8) provides a defence in certain circumstances. A failure to pay rent can be "conduct" such that it is reasonable to mitigate the

damages (*Regalgrand Ltd v Dickerson & Wade* (1996) 29 H.L.R. 620 CA). See also Osei Bonsu where the unlawful "eviction was clearly the culmination of an unbroken chain of events starting with the Respondent's conduct" and resulted in a substantial reduction in damages.

(9) Only the landlord can be made liable; not his agent who carries out the unlawful acts (*Sampson v Wilson* (1995) 29 H.L.R. 18 CA). Acts done by a receiver or managing agent appointed by the mortgagee, will be the responsibility of the mortgagor (*Mehta v Royal Bank of Scotland* (1999) 32 H.L.R. 45 at 58 QBD).

(10) A mistake as to the law may amount to a defence under s.27(8)(a), but only as long as there was "reasonable cause" to make such a mistake (*Osei Bonsu*—the council's mistake as to the effect of a notice to quit was a potential defence but in the circumstances was not found to have been a reasonable mistake to make).

(11) There can be no claim for unlawful eviction where the exclusion from the property was pursuant to a possession order which was subsequently set aside. No sustainable cause of action arises out of compliance with a court order, regardless of whether that court order is subsequently set aside or reversed (*London Borough of Brent v Botu* (2001) 33 H.L.R. 151 CA).

Housing Act 1988: measure of damages

35.022   **28.**—(1) The basis for the assessment of damages referred to in section 27(3) above is the difference in value, determined as at the time immediately before the residential occupier ceased to occupy the premises in question as his residence, between—

   (a) the value of the interest of the landlord in default determined on the assumption that the residential occupier continues to have the same right to occupy the premises as before that time; and

   (b) the value of that interest determined on the assumption that the residential occupier has ceased to have the right.

(2) In relation to any premises, any reference to his interest in the interest of the landlord in default is a reference to his interest in the building in which the premises in question are comprised (whether or not that building contains any other premises) together with its curtilage.

(3) For the purposes of the valuations referred to in subsection (1) above, it shall be assumed—

   (a) that the landlord in default is selling his interest on the open market to a willing buyer;

   (b) that neither the residential occupier nor any member of his wishes to buy; and

   (c) that it is unlawful to carry out any substantial development of any of the land in which the landlord's interest subsists or to demolish the whole or part of any building on that land.

(4) In this section "the landlord in default" has the same meaning as in section 27 above and subsection (9) of that section applies in relation to this section as it applies in relation to that.

(5) Section 113 of the Housing Act 1985 (meaning of "members of a person's family") applies for the purposes of subsection (3)(b) above.

(6) The reference in subsection (3)(c) above to substantial development of any of the land in which the landlord's interest subsists is a reference to any development other than—

    (a) development for which planning permission is granted by a general development order for the time being in force and which is carried out so as to comply with any condition or limitation subject to which planning permission is so granted; and

    (b) a change of use resulting in the building referred to in subsection (2) above or any part of it being used as, or as part of, one or more dwelling houses; and in this subsection "general development order" has the same meaning as in section 43(3) of the Town and Country Planning Act 1971 and other expressions have the same meaning as in that Act.

Notes:

(1) The effect of the section is to deprive the landlord of the profit that he will **35.023** make by forcing the tenant out. The measure of damages is the difference between (i) the value of the landlord's interest (in the building containing the premises) with the occupier enjoying a right to occupy and (ii) the value of the landlord's interest without the occupier having a right to occupy. Expert evidence will be required. The valuation must be carried out on a factual not a notional basis. Thus, if other occupiers remain their presence should be taken into account. This may often mean that the landlord's interest has not increased in value by reason of the unlawful eviction (*Melville v Bruton* (1996) 29 H.L.R. 319 CA).

(2) Section 28(1) requires a valuation of the landlord's interest subject to the tenant's right to occupy, without regard to the length of time it would actually take to get a possession order. Therefore, where there was an agreement, which operated as an estoppel, that the occupier would leave in six days time she was only entitled to damages on that basis even though it would have taken longer lawfully to evict (*King v Jackson* (1997) 30 H.L.R. 541 CA).

(3) The interest that is valued is the interest of the landlord in default, not the abstract interest of a notional willing buyer. "Although the concept of a willing buyer helps to fix the respective valuations, one postulates the landlord's continuing ownership in fact" (*Wandsworth LBC v Osei Bonsu* (1999) 1 All E.R. at 265).

(4) The time of the assessment is at the time immediately before the residential occupier ceased to occupy the premises.

(5) For s.113 of the Housing Act 1985 (members of a person's family); see Ch.10.

Damages for breach of contract/tort

As stated above ss.28 and 29 of the Housing Act 1988 do not apply where the **35.024** residential occupier has been reinstated to the property. However, the residential occupier will still be entitled to damages in respect of any tort or breach of contract which occurred prior to the reinstatement. Since the object of a covenant for quiet enjoyment in a lease or tenancy agreement cannot be described as being to provide peace of mind or freedom from distress, damages for injured feelings and mental distress are not recoverable for breach of a covenant for quiet enjoyment. However, such damages may be recoverable in tort as damages for trespass (*Branchett v Beaney* [1992] 3 All E.R. 910 at 914 CA).

Some examples are given under heading "Quantum; common law damages", para.35.027.

Aggravated and exemplary damages

35.025   "Aggravated damages and exemplary damages are not only different in themselves, they are awarded for two different purposes. Aggravated damages are awarded to compensate the plaintiff for injury to his proper feelings of dignity and pride and for aggravation generally, whereas exemplary damages are awarded in order to punish the defendant" (*Ramdath v Oswald Daley* [1993] 1 E.G.L.R. 82 per Nourse L.J. at 84D).

Exemplary damages may be awarded where

"the defendant's conduct has been calculated by him to make a profit for himself which may exceed the compensation payable to the plaintiff", that is:
   "Where a defendant with a cynical disregard for a plaintiff's rights has calculated that the money to be made out of his wrongdoing will probably exceed the damages at risk, it is necessary for the law to show that it cannot be broken with impunity. This category is not confined to money making in the strict sense. It extends to cases in which the defendant is seeking to gain at the expense of the plaintiff some object—perhaps some property which he covets—which he either could not obtain at all or not obtain except at a price greater than he wants to put down. Exemplary damages can properly be awarded whenever it is necessary to teach a wrongdoer that tort does not pay" (*Rookes v Barnard* [1964] A.C. 1129, per Lord Devlin at 1226–1227).

In *Drane v Evangelou* [1978] 1 W.L.R. 455 CA, it was held that this principle applies to cases of unlawful eviction of a tenant ("more accurately an action for trespass to land and goods", Nourse L.J. in *Ramdath v Oswald Daley*):

"To my mind this category includes cases of unlawful eviction of a tenant. The landlord seeks to gain possession at the expense of the tenant—so as to keep or get a rent higher than that awarded by the rent tribunal—or to get possession from a tenant who is protected by the Rent Acts. So he resorts to harassing tactics. Such conduct can be punished now by the criminal law. But it also can be punished by the civil law by an award of exemplary damages" (per Lord Denning, *Drane v Evangelou* at 459F).

35.026   However, it must be shown that the defendant has a sufficient interest in the property to bring him within the category (*Ramdath v Oswald Daley* [1993] 1 E.G.L.R. 82 CA—an award for exemplary damages could not be made against the landlord's managing agent who actually carried out the eviction because he had no interest in the property).

Exemplary damages have also been awarded in cases where the tenant has been forced to leave by harassment (*Guppy's (Bridport) Ltd v Brookling* (1984) 269 E.G. 846—disconnection of electricity, interference with water supply, washing and toilet facilities and demolition of rooms).

In assessing the amount of the exemplary damages awarded the court should have regard to the means of the parties (*Cassell & Cox v Broome* [1972] A.C. 1027). The fact that a person has been fined for an offence under the Protection from Eviction Act 1977 should be taken into account, but does not preclude the court from making an award of exemplary damages (*Ashgar v Ahmed* (1984) 17 H.L.R. 25). Only one sum of exemplary damages can be awarded even when there is more than one tortfeasor. The amount should be the lowest figure for which any of the joint tortfeasors could be held liable (*Francis v Brown* (1997) 30 H.L.R. 143 at 149–150).

A claim for aggravated or exemplary damages must be properly pleaded (CPR r.16.4(1)(c)).

Quantum; common law damages

Care needs to be taken when reading reports of "comparables" in unlawful evic- **35.027**
tion cases. The details given are always brief yet each case very much turns upon its own facts. In particular, the factual basis upon which an award for exemplary damages has been given is not always clear and it often seems that the principles set out above in relation to exemplary damages are not strictly followed. It is also important to note that in many cases the major element of the award is the item of damages given under ss.27 and 28 of the 1988 Act. As the amount of such damages depends on the expert evidence as to the value of the property in the particular case the award in one case under this head will be of no assistance in any other case. Where there is only a limited licence or an assured shorthold tenancy, as opposed to a Rent Act or assured tenancy, damages may not be large because in carrying out the valuation the valuer must have regard to the interest of the landlord subject to the actual rights of the occupier. This can lead to quite a low award (see para.35.023).

The following two cases illustrate the relationship between the 1988 Act and **35.028**
the award of common law damages:

Mason v Nwokorie [1994] 1 E.G.L.R. 59: the claimant occupied a bedsitting room without security of tenure, but he was entitled to 28 days' notice. The defendant gave 14 days' notice to quit and enforced it without taking proceedings. The claimant was awarded £4,500 Housing Act damages, £500 general damages and £1,000 exemplary and aggravated damages. The Court of Appeal held that exemplary damages were not appropriate (see above), but considered that the conduct of the defendant in evicting the claimant was calculated to cause humiliation and shame and that on the evidence an award of £1,000 for aggravated damages was appropriate. However, the award for general and aggravated damages was set off against the sum of £4,500 which was awarded under the Housing Act.

Kaur v Gill (1995) *The Times*, June 15: Orme J. awarded £15,000 for unlawful eviction under the Housing Act and in addition common law damages of £500 for breach of covenant for quiet enjoyment. The landlord appealed, contending that in view of the decision in *Mason* (see above) the common law damages should have been set off against the statutory damages. The Court of Appeal dismissed the appeal and distinguished Mason, on the basis that in this case the award of general damages was not made for any loss of the right to occupy but rather because of the tenant's complaints of harassment by the landlord.

Cases are regularly reported in *Legal Action* and *Current Law*. Details of many **35.029**
cases can be found in Nic Madge and Claire Sephton, *Housing Law Casebook* (London: LAG, 2012). The following are some examples:

Biga v Martin (June 2001) *Legal Action* (Ilford County Court, H.H. Judge Platt, November 16, 2001). The claimant was an assured shorthold tenant. The Defendant landlord had refused to provide documents to enable the claimant to get housing benefit and told the claimant to leave. He ignored a letter from the claimant's solicitor regarding the illegality of his actions and removed the tenant. He changed the locks and ignored an injunction for restatement by breaking in with others. An award of £10,000 general damages (including aggravated damages and personal injury—post traumatic stress disorder at the lower end of the Judicial Studies Board Guidelines); £900 special damages; and £2,500 exemplary damages within second category of *Rookes v Barnard* [1964] A.C. 1129 HL.

Pillai v Amendra (October 2000) *Legal Action* (Central London County Court, H.H. Judge Green QC, July 27, 2000). An assured tenant was locked out and his possessions were placed in the front of the garden. He gained re-entry with help of the police which led to his car window being smashed and a threatening note left. He was then locked out a second time. The judge stated that this was a bad case, but not at the very top end. There was no actual violence and the claimant was not a vulnerable member of the community. £6,000 general damages, £10,000 aggravated and exemplary for trespass, £3,000 aggravated damages for trespass to goods.

Dimoutsikou v Penrose (October 2000) *Legal Action* (Leeds County Court, District Judge Bellamy, May 17, 2000). An assured shorthold tenant was locked out and refused re-entry while on holiday. Damages were awarded at a rate of £125 per day. This sum took into account the fact that the alternative accommodation found was less desirable and more expensive. Aggravated damages of £1,500 and exemplary damages of £1,500.

35.030   *Cooper v Sharma* (May 2004) *Legal Action* (Brentford County Court, District Judge Plaskow, February 23, 2004). An assured shorthold tenant suffered initially from having her utilities disconnected by her landlord who then changed the locks and threw her belongings on the street. The landlord was committed for failing to adhere to an injunction to readmit the tenant. General damages of £23,350 were awarded: comprising £200 a day for disconnection of utilities; £250 a day for having to sleep on a friend's floor; £150 per day for having to stay in bed and breakfast accommodation; £100 per day for staying in non-secure accommodation; £4,000 aggravated damages and £2,500 exemplary damages.

Daley v Mahmood (2005) (Central London County Court, H.H. Judge Medawar QC, August 12, 2005). The landlord acquired a property at auction which was subject to protected tenancies. A campaign of harassment ensued which included breaking into the property, abuse and threatening behaviour. At one point three men entered the property and started to clear out one tenant's possessions. Utilities were cut off and walls demolished. Exemplary damages of £7,500 were awarded to each tenant on the basis of the landlord's anticipated profit on obtaining vacant possession. Aggravated damages were awarded both for harassment (£1,500) and for the eviction (£10,000).

Poku-Awuah v Lenton (February 2005) *Legal Action* 2006 (Lambeth County Court, District Judge Jacey, December 5, 2005). The Claimant, an assured shorthold tenant, was awoken at night by her landlord with four men and two women who packed up her goods and put them in bags, changed the locks and forcibly removed her from the property. She spent one night in her car and was provided with alternative accommodation about two weeks later after an injunction was granted. She was awarded general damages of £5,100 (£300 per day), £1,000 aggravated damages and £2,000 exemplary damages.

35.031   *Evans v Copping* (January 2007) *Legal Action* 2008 (Ashford County Court, Deputy District Judge Cagney, November 14, 2007). The tenant was excluded without warning when she returned to property to find locks changed. On an injunction, the landlord misled the court about the property being relet which led to the tenant's application for an interim injunction to be dismissed. At trial three months later, the landlord's deception was revealed and resulted in exemplary damages of £1,500 in addition to general damages of £2,500, aggravated of £599 and special of £240.

Addison v Croft (June 2008) *Legal Action* (Preston County Court, H.H. Judge Appleton April 17, 2008). An argument between the tenant and his landlord led to the landlord arriving a few weeks later with others, kicking in the front door and throwing the tenant and his girlfriend out on the streets. He was let in after 20 days when he obtained an injunction. £3,000 general damages, £1,000 aggravated and £1,000 exemplary.

Rubio-Manzano v Ace Lettings (June 2008) *Legal Action* (Clerkenwell and Shoreditch County Court, District Judge Sterlini, April 17, 2008). The tenant took issue over longstanding and substantial disrepair at the property and stated that she would withhold rent until it was remedied. The landlord responded by threatening eviction. Three men then went to the property and forced entry, threatened the tenant, ripped the phone off the wall when another tenant tried to call the police and knocked over another. The landlord then sent a letter to the tenant falsely claiming to be from certified bailiffs stating they were going to enter the property and seize her goods. This caused the tenant to leave and store most of her belongings with friends. She returned to find the locks changed and some of her possessions removed. The landlord was prosecuted under the Protection from Eviction Act 1977 and fined £2,200. In the county court, general damages of £6,000 were awarded with exemplary damages of £840.40.

Deelah v Rehman (2011) Legal Action, July 2011 (Clerkenwell and Shoreditch County Court, D.J. Millard, March 10, 2011), the Claimant was an assured shorthold tenant of the Defendant and lived at the property with his wife and two sons. The Defendant assaulted the Claimant and threatened to change the locks and throw his belongings into the street. About a month later, the Claimant's wife and one of his sons returned home to find the locks changed. When the son tried to get back in by climbing over a fence, the Defendant approached him with a metal bar and threatened to kill him. An injunction for reinstatement was eventually complied with. £1,000 was awarded for the four nights that the family had been excluded from the property, £1,500 for the harassment, £1,500 for aggravated damages and £2,500 for exemplary damages (it was claimed that the eviction had been intended to save the landlord the cost of court proceedings; it was suggested that the property was an unlicensed HMO).

Dada v Adeyeye (2012) Legal Action, March 2012 (Central London County Court, H.H.J. Gerald, August 24, 2011), the Claimant had been an assured shorthold tenant and had paid a deposit equal to two weeks rent. He fell into arrears and the landlady began harassing him in order to make him leave; this included threats to kill and ultimately changing the locks. He spent 13 nights on the streets and just over a year in local authority temporary housing accommodation as well as suffering from depression. He was awarded: £600 for a deposit claim (the landlady had not protected the deposit), £1,500 for harassment and trespass, £2,600 for the 13 days on the street and £10,000 for the period in temporary accommodation. £2,000 was also awarded as exemplary damages and £570 special damages.

Part 4

Appendices

Appendix 1

Two Rent/Housing Act Exceptions

Two Rent/Housing Act Exceptions

Dwelling-houses above certain rateable values/high rents

In order to ascertain whether the tenancy is precluded from being protected under **A1.001** the Rent Act 1977 by reason of this exception it is first necessary to discover the "rateable value" of the dwelling-house on the "appropriate day" (ss.4 and 25 of the 1977 Act). The appropriate day is March 23, 1965 unless the property first appeared in the Valuation List on a later day, in which case the appropriate day is the day on which the dwelling's rateable value first appeared in the Valuation List. If the appropriate day fell on or after the March 22, 1973 but before April 1, 1973 it will also be necessary to discover the rateable value of the property on April 1, 1973. If the appropriate day fell before March 22, 1973 it will be necessary to know the rateable value on (a) the appropriate day (b) March 22, 1973 and (c) April 1, 1973. The rates department of the local council will be able to provide this information. (Note that the rateable value of the premises on the appropriate day is not the same as the "net annual value for rating" which needs to be ascertained in order to discover whether the county court has jurisdiction.)

Sometimes the dwelling-house forms part of a larger property in respect of which there is a rateable value in the Valuation List for the whole but not for the part. In these circumstances, an apportionment should be made. If the dwelling-house consists of more than one property, each of which is separately rated, an aggregation is made. If there is any dispute as to the proper apportionment or aggregation to be made the issue is determined by the county court, the decision of which cannot be appealed against. Events which take place after the appropriate day (*Dixon v Allgood* [1987] 3 All E.R. 1082), except where the rateable value is varied after the appropriate day so that the variation takes effect not later than the appropriate day in which case it is the figure as varied which is taken for the purposes of the Rent Act 1977 and not the original figure (s.25(4)).

Once the rateable value on the appropriate day, and if necessary, the rateable **A1.002** values on March 22, 1973 and April 1, 1973, have been discovered it is next necessary to see whether the dwelling-house falls within one of the classes set out below.

If the premises are in Greater London the tenancy is not protected if:

(1) The appropriate day in relation to the dwelling-house falls or fell on or after April 1, 1973 and the dwelling-house on the appropriate day has or had a rateable value exceeding £1,500.

(2) The appropriate day in relation to the dwelling-house fell on or after March 22, 1973, but before April 1, 1973 and the dwelling-house (a) on the appropriate day had a rateable value exceeding £600 and (b) on April 1, 1973 had a rateable value exceeding £1,500.

(3) The appropriate day in relation to the dwelling-house fell before March 22, 1973 and the dwelling-house (a) on the appropriate day had a rateable value exceeding £400 (b) on March 22, 1973 had a rateable value exceeding £600, and (c) on April 1, 1973 had a rateable value exceeding £1,500.

If the premises are outside Greater London the figure set out below should be substituted for the above figures as follows:

(1) £750 for £1,500;

(2) £300 for £600 and £750 for £1,500;

(3) £200 for £400, £300 for £600, and £750 for £1,500.

If in any proceedings there is a dispute as to whether the dwelling-house falls within one of these three categories the court will presume that it does not unless the contrary is shown (Rent Act 1977 s.4(3)).

Where the tenancy was entered into on or after April 1, 1990 see s.4(1) of the 1977 Act as amended and s.4(4)–(7) as introduced by paras 15 and 16 of The References to Rating (Housing) Regulations 1990 (SI 1990/434). Generally, the tenancy will not be protected if the rent payable exceeds £25,000.

For the position in relation to assured tenancies see Housing Act 1988 Sch.1 paras 2, 2A and 14–16.

Tenancies where no rent or a low rent is payable

A1.003 A tenancy which was entered into before April 1, 1990 or (where the dwelling-house under the tenancy had a rateable value on March 31, 1990) is entered into on or after April 1 in pursuance of a contract made before that date is not a protected tenancy if under the tenancy either no rent is payable or, the rent payable is less than·two-thirds of the rateable value which is or was the rateable value of the dwelling-house on the appropriate day (s.5 of the Rent Act 1977).

As to "the rateable value on the appropriate day" see the previous exception relating to high rateable values. But note that, where premises are in Greater London and the appropriate day fell before March 22, 1973 and on the appropriate day the rateable value exceeded £400 the appropriate day for the purposes of this section is deemed to be March 22, 1973. If the premises are outside Greater London read £200 for £400 (Rent Act 1977 s.5(2)).

Where the tenancy is entered into on or after April 1, 1990 (otherwise than where the dwelling-house had a rateable value on March 31, 1990 in pursuance of a contract made before that date) the tenancy is not protected if the rent payable is £1,000 or less (Greater London) or £250 or less (elsewhere). (The Reference to Rating (Housing) Regulations 1990 reg.7.)

To constitute rent within the meaning of the section the payments made by the **A1.004** tenant may be payable in kind, for example by the provision of goods or services, but only if these payments have by agreement been quantified in terms of money. Otherwise the payments must be monetary (see *Montague v Browning* [1954] 1 W.L.R. 1039; *Barnes v Barratt* [1970] 2 Q.B. 657). "Rent" usually includes the amount of any rates and other taxes payable to the landlord (*Sidney Trading Co Ltd v Finsbury Corporation* [1952] 1 All E.R. 460). But, if the tenancy was originally granted for a term exceeding 21 years and it may not be determined before the end of that term by notice given to the tenant, any sums expressed to be payable "in respect of rates, services, repairs, maintenance, or insurance" paid by the tenant to the landlord should be disregarded in calculating the rent for the purposes of this section of the Act (Rent Act 1977 s.5(4) and (5)). For the protection afforded to tenants with long leases at low rents by the Landlord and Tenant Act 1954, see Ch.16). The burden is on the tenant to show that the rent he pays is sufficient (*Ford v Langford* [1949] 1 All E.R. 483).

Where this exception does not apply because the rent is more than two-thirds of the rateable value it does not apply after the protected tenancy is determined if after that date the rent in respect of the statutory tenancy is reduced to less than two-thirds (*McGee v London Borough of Hackney* (1969) 210 E.G. 1431).

Section 5 of the Rent Act 1977 does not apply to any tenancy which, immediately before the repeal of controlled tenancies on November 28, 1980, was a controlled tenancy. Thus, the tenancy will remain protected even if the rent is less than two-thirds of the rateable value on the appropriate day (s.125 and Sch.25 para.75 of the Housing Act 1980).

For the position in relation to assured tenancies, see Housing Act 1988 Sch.I paras 3, 3A, 3B, 3C and 14 to 16.

Appendix 2

Statutory Extracts

Rent (Agriculture) Act 1976 (c.80)

Grounds for Possession of Dwelling-House Subject to Protected
Occupancy or Statutory Tenancy

Part I

Cases where court has a discretion

Case I

Alternative accommodation not provided or arranged by housing authority

1. The court is satisfied that suitable alternative accommodation is available **A2.001** for the tenant, or will be available for him when the order for possession takes effect.

2.—(1) Accommodation shall be deemed suitable in this Case if it consists of—

(a) premises which are to be let as a separate dwelling such that they will then be let on a protected tenancy within the meaning of the Rent Act 1977, or

(b) premises which are to be let as a separate dwelling on terms which will, in the opinion of the court, afford to the tenant security of tenure reasonably equivalent to the security afforded by Part VII of the Rent Act 1977 in the case of a protected tenancy,

and, in the opinion of the court, the accommodation fulfils the conditions in paragraph 3 below.

3.—(1) The accommodation must be reasonably suitable to the needs of the tenant and his family as regards proximity to place of work and either—

(a) similar as regards rental and extent to the accommodation afforded by dwelling-houses provided in the neighbourhood by the housing authority concerned for persons whose needs as regards extent are similar to those of the tenant and his family, or

(b) reasonably suitable to the means of the tenant, and to the needs of the tenant and his family as regards extent and character.

(2) For the purposes of sub-paragraph (1)(a) above, a certificate of the housing authority concerned stating—

    (a) the extent of the accommodation afforded by dwelling-houses provided by the authority to meet the needs of tenants with families of such number as may be specified in the certificate, and

    (b) the amount of the rent charged by the housing authority concerned for dwelling-houses affording accommodation of that extent,

shall be conclusive evidence of the facts so stated.

(3) If any furniture was provided by the landlord for use under the tenancy, furniture must be provided for use in the alternative accommodation which is either similar, or is reasonably suitable to the needs of the tenant and his family.

4. Accommodation shall not be deemed to be suitable to the needs of the tenant and his family if the result of their occupation of the accommodation would be that it would be an overcrowded dwelling-house for the purposes of the Part X of the Housing Act 1985.

5. Any document purporting to be a certificate of the housing authority concerned issued for the purposes of this Case and to be signed by the proper officer of the authority shall be received in evidence and, unless the contrary is shown, shall be deemed to be such a certificate without further proof.

6. In this Case no account shall be taken of accommodation as respects which an offer has been made, or notice has been given, as mentioned in paragraph 1 of Case II below.

Case II

Alternative accommodation provided or arranged by housing authority

A2.002   **1.** The housing authority concerned have made an offer in writing to the tenant of alternative accommodation which appears to them to be suitable, specifying the date when the accommodation will be available and the date (not being less than 14 days from the date of offer) by which the offer must be accepted.

OR

The housing authority concerned have given notice in writing to the tenant that they have received from a person specified in the notice an offer in writing to rehouse the tenant in alternative accommodation which appears to the housing authority concerned to be suitable, and the notice specifies both the date when the accommodation will be available and the date (not being less than 14 days from the date when the notice was given to the tenant) by which the offer must be accepted.

    2. The landlord shows that the tenant accepted the offer (by the housing authority or other person) within the time duly specified in the offer.

OR

The landlord shows that the tenant did not so accept the offer, and the tenant does not satisfy the court that he acted reasonably in failing to accept the offer.

    3.—(1) The accommodation offered must in the opinion of the court fulfil the conditions in this paragraph.

(2) The accommodation must be reasonably suitable to the needs of the tenant and his family as regards proximity to place of work.

(3) The accommodation must be reasonably suitable to the means of the tenant, and to the needs of the tenant and his family as regards extent.

4. If the accommodation offered is available for a limited period only, the housing authority's offer or notice under paragraph 1 above must contain an assurance that other accommodation—

(a) the availability of which is not so limited,

(b) which appears to them to be suitable, and

(c) which fulfils the conditions in paragraph 3 above,

will be offered to the tenant as soon as practicable.

Case III

Rent lawfully due from the tenant has not been paid,   A2.003
    OR
Any other lawful obligation of the tenancy, whether or not it is an obligation created by this Act, has been broken or not performed.

Case IV

The tenant, or any person residing or lodging with him or sub-tenant of his, has   A2.004
been guilty of conduct which is a nuisance or annoyance to adjoining occupiers, or has been convicted of using the dwelling-house, or allowing the dwelling-house to be used, for immoral or illegal purposes.

Case V

1. The condition of the dwelling-house has, in the opinion of the court, dete-   A2.005
    riorated owing to acts of waste by, or the neglect or default of, the tenant or any person residing or lodging with him, or any sub-tenant of his.

2. If the person at fault is not the tenant, the court must be satisfied that the tenant has not, before the making of the order for possession, taken such steps as he ought reasonably to have taken for the removal of the person at fault.

Case VI

1. The condition of any furniture provided by the landlord for use under the   A2.006
    tenancy has, in the opinion of the court, deteriorated owing to ill-treatment by the tenant or any person residing or lodging with him, or any sub-tenant of his.

2. If the person at fault is not the tenant, the court must be satisfied that the tenant has not, before the making of the order for possession, taken such steps as he ought reasonably to have taken for the removal of the person at fault.

Case VII

A2.007 1. The tenant has given notice to quit and in consequence of that notice the landlord has contracted to sell or let the dwelling-house, or has taken any other steps as a result of which he would, in the opinion of the court, be seriously prejudiced if he could not obtain possession.

2. This Case does not apply where the tenant has given notice to terminate his employment and that notice has operated to terminate the tenancy.

Case VIII

A2.008 1. The tenant has, without the consent of the landlord, assigned, sub-let or parted with possession of the dwelling-house, or any part of it.

2. This Case does not apply if the assignment, sub-letting or parting with possession was effected before the operative date.

Case IX

A2.009 1. The dwelling-house is reasonably required by the landlord for occupation as a residence for—

(a) himself, or
(b) any son or daughter of his over 18 years of age, or
(c) his father or mother, or the father or mother of his wife, or husband or civil partner, or
(d) his grandfather or grandmother, or the grandfather or grandmother of his wife, or husband or civil partner,

and the landlord did not become landlord by purchasing the dwelling-house, or any interest in it, after 12th April 1976.

2. The court, having regard to all the circumstances of the case, including the question whether other accommodation is available for the landlord or tenant, is satisfied that no greater hardship would be caused by granting the order than by refusing to grant it.

Case X

A2.010 1. Any part of the dwelling-house is sublet.

2. The court is satisfied that the rent charged by the tenant is or was in excess of the maximum rent recoverable for that part, having regard to the provisions of Part III or Part V of the Rent Act 1977 or Part II of this Act, as the case may require.

3. Paragraph 2 does not apply to a rental period beginning before the operative date.

Part II

Cases in which Court Must Order Possession

Case XI

A2.011 1. The person who granted the tenancy or, as the case may be, the original tenancy ("the original occupier") was, prior to granting it, occupying the dwelling-house as his residence.

2. The court is satisfied that the dwelling-house is required as a residence for the original occupier or any member of his family who resided with the original occupier when he last occupied the dwelling-house as his residence.

3. Not later than the relevant date the original occupier gave notice in writing to that tenant that possession might be recovered under this Case.

4. The dwelling-house has not since the operative date been let by the original occupier to a tenant as respects whom the condition mentioned in paragraph 3 above was not satisfied.

5. The court may dispense with the requirements of either or both of paragraphs 3 and 4 if of opinion that it is just and equitable so to do.

6. In this case and in Case XII below—

> "original tenancy", in relation to a statutory tenancy, means the tenancy on the termination of which the statutory tenancy arose;
> "the relevant date" means the date of the commencement of the tenancy or, as the case may be, the original tenancy, or the expiration of the period of six months beginning with the operative date, whichever is the later.

Case XII

1. The person who granted the tenancy or, as the case may be, the original **A2.012** tenancy ("the owner") acquired the dwelling-house, or any interest in it, with a view to occupying it as his residence at such time as he should retire from regular employment.

2. The court is satisfied—

(a) that the owner has retired from regular employment and requires the dwelling-house as his residence, or

(b) that the owner has died and the dwelling-house is required as a residence for a member of his family who was residing with him at the time of his death.

3. Not later than the relevant date the owner gave notice in writing to the tenant that possession might be recovered under this Case.

4. The dwelling-house has not since the operative date been let by the owner to a tenant as respects whom the condition mentioned in paragraph 3 above was not satisfied.

5. The court may dispense with the requirements of either or both of paragraphs 3 and 4 if of opinion that it is just and equitable so to do.

Case XIII

The dwelling-house is overcrowded, within the meaning of the Part X of the **A2.013** Housing Act 1985, in such circumstances as to render the occupier guilty of an offence.

Rent Act 1977 (c.42)

SCHEDULE 15

GROUNDS FOR POSSESSION OF DWELLING-HOUSES LET ON OR
SUBJECT TO PROTECTED OR STATUTORY TENANCIES

PART I

CASES IN WHICH COURT MAY ORDER POSSESSION

Case 1

A2.014 Where any rent lawfully due from the tenant has not been paid, or any obligation of the protected or statutory tenancy which arises under this Act, or—

    (a) in the case of a protected tenancy, any other obligation of the tenancy, in so far as is consistent with the provisions of Part VII of this Act, or

    (b) in the case of a statutory tenancy, any other obligation of the previous protected tenancy which is applicable to the statutory tenancy

has been broken or not performed.

Case 2

A2.015 Where the tenant or any person residing or lodging with him or any sub-tenant of his has been guilty of conduct which is a nuisance or annoyance to adjoining occupiers, or has been convicted of using the dwelling-house or allowing the dwelling-house to be used for immoral or illegal purposes.

Case 3

A2.016 Where the condition of the dwelling-house has, in the opinion of the court, deteriorated owing to acts of waste by, or the neglect or default of, the tenant or any person residing or lodging with him or any sub-tenant of his and, in the case of any act of waste by, or the neglect or default of, a person lodging with the tenant or a sub-tenant of his, where the court is satisfied that the tenant has not, before the making of the order in question, taken such steps as he ought reasonably to have taken for the removal of the lodger or sub-tenant, as the case may be.

Case 4

A2.017 Where the condition of any furniture provided for use under the tenancy has, in the opinion of the court, deteriorated owing to ill-treatment by the tenant or any person residing or lodging with him or any sub-tenant of his and, in the case of any ill-treatment by a person lodging with the tenant or a sub-tenant of his, where the court is satisfied that the tenant has not, before the making of the order in question, taken such steps as he ought reasonably to have taken for the removal of the lodger or sub-tenant, as the case may be.

Case 5

Where the tenant has given notice to quit and, in consequence of that notice, the landlord has contracted to sell or let the dwelling-house or has taken any other steps as the result of which he would, in the opinion of the court, be seriously prejudiced if he could not obtain possession. **A2.018**

Case 6

Where, without the consent of the landlord, the tenant has, at any time after— **A2.019**

(a) [. . .]
(b) 22nd March 1973, in the case of a tenancy which became a regulated tenancy by virtue of section 14 of the Counter-Inflation Act 1973;
(bb) the commencement of section 73 of the Housing Act 1980, in the case of a tenancy which became a regulated tenancy by virtue of that section.
(c) 14th August 1974, in the case of a regulated furnished tenancy; or
(d) 8th December 1965, in the case of any other tenancy,

assigned or sublet the whole of the dwelling-house or sublet part of the dwelling-house, the remainder being already sublet.

Case 7

[. . .] **A2.020**

Case 8

Where the dwelling-house is reasonably required by the landlord for occupation as a residence for some person engaged in his whole-time employment, or in the whole-time employment of some tenant from him or with whom, conditional on housing being provided, a contract for such employment has been entered into, and the tenant was in the employment of the landlord or a former landlord, and the dwelling-house was let to him in consequence of that employment and he has ceased to be in that employment. **A2.021**

Case 9

Where the dwelling-house is reasonably required by the landlord for occupation as a residence for— **A2.022**

(a) himself, or
(b) any son or daughter of his over 18 years of age, or
(c) his father or mother, or
(d) if the dwelling-house is let on or subject to a regulated tenancy, the father or mother of his spouse or civil partner,

and the landlord did not become landlord by purchasing the dwelling-house or any interest therein after—

    (i)   7th November 1956, in the case of a tenancy which was then a controlled tenancy;

    (ii) 8th March 1973, in the case of a tenancy which became a regulated tenancy by virtue of section 14 of the Counter-Inflation Act 1973;

    (iii) 24th May 1974, in the case of a regulated furnished tenancy; or

    (iv) 23rd March 1965, in the case of any other tenancy.

Case 10

A2.023 Where the court is satisfied that the rent charged by the tenant—

    (a) for any sublet part of the dwelling-house which is a dwelling-house let on a protected tenancy or subject to a statutory tenancy is or was in excess of the maximum rent for the time being recoverable for that part, having regard to Part III of this Act, or

    (b) for any sublet part of the dwelling-house which is subject to a restricted contract is or was in excess of the maximum (if any) which it is lawful for the lessor, within the meaning of Part V of this Act to require or receive having regard to the provisions of that Part.

PART II

CASES IN WHICH COURT MUST ORDER POSSESSION WHERE DWELLING-HOUSE SUBJECT TO REGULATED TENANCY

Case 11

A2.024 Where a person (in this Case referred to as "the owner-occupier") who let the dwelling-house on a regulated tenancy had, at any time before the letting, occupied it as his residence and—

    (a) not later than the relevant date the landlord gave notice in writing to the tenant that possession might be recovered under this Case, and

    (b) the dwelling-house has not, since—

        (i)   22nd March 1973, in the case of a tenancy which became a regulated tenancy by virtue of section 14 of the Counter-Inflation Act 1973;

        (ii) 14th August 1974, in the case of a regulated furnished tenancy; or

        (iii) 8th December 1965, in the case of any other tenancy,

been let by the owner-occupier on a protected tenancy with respect to which the condition mentioned in paragraph (a) above was not satisfied, and

    (c) the court is of the opinion that of the conditions set out in Part V of this Schedule one of those in paragraphs (a) and (c) to (f) is satisfied.

If the court is of the opinion that, notwithstanding that the condition in paragraph (a) or (b) above is not complied with, it is just and equitable to make and the order for possession of the dwelling-house, the court may dispense with the requirements of either or both of those paragraphs, as the case may require.

The giving of a notice before 14th August 1974 under section 79 of the Rent Act 1968 shall be treated, in the case of a regulated furnished tenancy, as compliance with paragraph (a) of this case. [Where the dwelling-house has been let by the owner-occupier on a protected tenancy (in this paragraph referred to as "the earlier tenancy") granted on or after 16th November 1984 but not later than the end of the period of two months beginning with the commencement of the Rent (Amendment) Act 1985 and either—

(i) the earlier tenancy was granted for a term certain (whether or not to be followed by a further term or to continue thereafter from year to year or some other period) and was during that term a protected shorthold tenancy as defined in section 52 of the Housing Act 1980, or

(ii) the conditions mentioned in paragraphs (a) to (c) of Case 20 were satisfied with respect to the dwelling-house and the earlier tenancy,

then for the purposes of paragraph (b) above the condition in paragraph (a) above is to be treated as having been satisfied with respect to the earlier tenancy.

Case 12

Where the landlord (in this Case referred to as "the owner") intends to occupy the **A2.025** dwelling-house as his residence at such time as he might retire from regular employment and has let]1 it on a regulated tenancy before he has so retired and—

(a) not later than the relevant date the landlord gave notice in writing to the tenant that possession might be recovered under this Case; and

(b) the dwelling-house has not, since 14th August 1974, been let by the owner on a protected tenancy with respect to which the condition mentioned in paragraph (a) above was not satisfied; and

(c) the court is of the opinion that of the conditions set out in Part V of this Schedule one of those in paragraphs (b) to (e) is satisfied.

If the court is of the opinion that, notwithstanding that the condition in paragraph (a) or (b) above is not complied with, it is just and equitable to make an order for possession of the dwelling-house, the court may dispense with the requirements of either or both of those paragraphs, as the case may require.

Case 13

Where the dwelling-house is let under a tenancy for a term of years certain not **A2.026** exceeding 8 months and—

(a) not later than the relevant date the landlord gave notice in writing to the tenant that possession might be recovered under this Case; and

(b) the dwelling-house was, at some time within the period of 12 months ending on the relevant date, occupied under a right to occupy it for a holiday.

For the purposes of this Case a tenancy shall be treated as being for a term of years certain notwithstanding that it is liable to determination by re-entry or on the happening of any event other than the giving of notice by the landlord to determine the term.

Case 14

A2.027 Where the dwelling-house is let under a tenancy for a term of years certain not exceeding 12 months and—

(a) not later than the relevant date the landlord gave notice in writing to the tenant that possession might be recovered under this Case; and

(b) at some time within the period of 12 months ending on the relevant date, the dwelling-house was subject to such a tenancy as is referred to in section 8(1) of this Act.

For the purposes of this Case a tenancy shall be treated as being for a term of years certain notwithstanding that it is liable to determination by re-entry or on the happening of any event other than the giving of notice by the landlord to determine the term.

Case 15

A2.028 Where the dwelling-house is held for the purpose of being available for occupation by a minister of religion as a residence from which to perform the duties of his office and—

(a) not later than the relevant date the tenant was given notice in writing that possession might be recovered under this Case, and

(b) the court is satisfied that the dwelling-house is required for occupation by a minister of religion as such a residence.

Case 16

A2.029 Where the dwelling-house was at any time occupied by a person under the terms of his employment as a person employed in agriculture, and

(a) the tenant neither is nor at any time was so employed by the landlord and is not the widow of a person who was so employed, and

(b) not later than the relevant date, the tenant was given notice in writing that possession might be recovered under this Case, and

(c) the court is satisfied that the dwelling-house is required for occupation by a person employed, or to be employed, by the landlord in agriculture.

For the purposes of this Case "employed", "employment" and "agriculture" have the same meanings as in the Agriculture Wages Act 1948.

Case 17

A2.030 Where proposals for amalgamation, approved for the purposes of a scheme under section 26 of the Agriculture Act 1967, have been carried out and, at the time when the proposals were submitted, the dwelling-house was occupied by a person responsible (whether as owner, tenant, or servant or agent of another) for the control of the farming of any part of the land comprised in the amalgamation and

(a) after the carrying out of the proposals, the dwelling-house was let on a regulated tenancy otherwise than to, or to the widow of, either a person ceasing to be so responsible as part of the amalgamation or a person who is, or at any time was, employed by the landlord in agriculture, and

(b) not later than the relevant date the tenant was given notice in writing that possession might be recovered under this Case, and

(c) the court is satisfied that the dwelling-house is required for occupation by a person employed, or to be employed, by the landlord in agriculture, and

(d) the proceedings for possession are commenced by the landlord at any time during the period of 5 years beginning with the date on which the proposals for the amalgamation were approved or, if occupation of the dwelling-house after the amalgamation continued in, or was first taken by, a person ceasing to be responsible as mentioned in paragraph (a) above or his widow, during a period expiring 3 years after the date on which the dwelling-house next became unoccupied.

For the purposes of this Case "employed" and "agriculture" have the same meanings as in the Agricultural Wages Act 1948 and "amalgamation" has the same meaning as in Part II of the Agriculture Act 1967.

Case 18

Where—   **A2.031**

(a) the last occupier of the dwelling-house before the relevant date was a person, or the widow of a person, who was at some time during his occupation responsible (whether as owner, tenant, or servant or agent of another) for the control of the farming of land which formed, together with the dwelling-house, an agricultural unit within the meaning of the Agriculture Act 1947

(b) the tenant is neither—

　　(i) a person, or the widow of a person, who is or has at any time been responsible for the control of the farming of any part of the said land, nor

　　(ii) a person, or the widow of a person, who is or at any time was employed by the landlord in agriculture, and

(c) the creation of the tenancy was not preceded by the carrying out in connection with any of the said land of an amalgamation approved for the purposes of a scheme under section 26 of the Agriculture Act 1967, and

(d) not later than the relevant date the tenant was given notice in writing that possession might be recovered under this Case, and

(e) the court is satisfied that the dwelling-house is required for occupation either by a person responsible or to be responsible (whether as owner, tenant, or servant or agent of another) for the control of the farming of any part of the said land or by a person employed or to be employed by the landlord in agriculture, and

(f) in a case where the relevant date was before 9th August 1972, the proceedings for possession are commenced by the landlord before the expiry of 5 years from the date on which the occupier referred to in paragraph (a) above went out of occupation.

For the purposes of this Case "employed" and "agriculture" have the same meanings as in the Agricultural Wages Act 1948 and "amalgamation" has the same meaning as in Part II of the Agriculture Act 1967.

Case 19

A2.032 Where the dwelling-house was let under a protected shorthold tenancy (or is treated under section 55 of the Housing Act 1980 as having been so let) and—

    (a) there either has been no grant of a further tenancy of the dwelling-house since the end of the protected shorthold tenancy or, if there was such a grant, it was to a person who immediately before the grant was in possession of the dwelling-house as a protected or statutory tenant; and

    (b) the proceedings for possession were commenced after appropriate notice by the landlord to the tenant and not later than 3 months after the expiry of the notice.

A notice is appropriate for this Case if—

    (i) it is in writing and states that proceedings for possession under this Case may be brought after its expiry; and

    (ii) it expires not earlier than 3 months after it is served nor, if, when it is served, the tenancy is a periodic tenancy, before that periodic tenancy could be brought to an end by a notice to quit served by the landlord on the same day;

    (iii) it is served—

        (a) in the period of 3 months immediately preceding the date on which the protected shorthold tenancy comes to an end; or

        (b) if that date has passed, in the period of 3 months immediately preceding any anniversary of that date; and

    (iv) in a case where a previous notice has been served by the landlord on the tenant in respect of the dwelling-house, and that notice was an appropriate notice, it is served not earlier than 3 months after the expiry of the previous notice.

Case 20

A2.033 Where the dwelling-house was let by a person (in this Case referred to as "the owner") at any time after the commencement of section 67 of the Housing Act 1980 and—

    (a) at the time when the owner acquired the dwelling-house he was a member of the regular armed forces of the Crown;

    (b) at the relevant date the owner was a member of the regular armed forces of the Crown;

    (c) not later than the relevant date the owner gave notice in writing to the tenant that possession might be recovered under this Case;

    (d) the dwelling-house has not, since the commencement of section 67 of the Act of 1980 been let by the owner on a protected tenancy with respect to which the condition mentioned in paragraph (c) above was not satisfied; and

    (e) the court is of the opinion that—

        (i) the dwelling-house is required as a residence for the owner; or

        (ii) of the conditions set out in Part V of this Schedule one of those in paragraphs (c) to (f) is satisfied.

If the court is of the opinion that, notwithstanding that the condition in paragraph (c) or (d) above is not complied with, it is just and equitable to make an order for possession of the dwelling-house, the court may dispense with the requirements of either or both of these paragraphs, as the case may require.

For the purposes of this Case "regular armed forces of the Crown" has the same meaning as in section 1 of the House of Commons Disqualification Act 1975.

PART III

PROVISIONS APPLICABLE TO CASE 9 AND PART II OF THIS SCHEDULE

Provision for Case 9

1. A court shall not make an order for possession of a dwelling-house by **A2.034** reason only that the circumstances of the case fall within Case 9 in Part I of this Schedule if the court is satisfied that, having regard to all the circumstances of the case, including the question whether other accommodation is available for the landlord or the tenant, greater hardship would be caused by granting the order than by refusing to grant it.

Provision for Part II

2. Any reference in Part II of this Schedule to the relevant date shall be construed as follows:—

   (a) except in a case falling within paragraph (b) or (c) below, if the protected tenancy, or, in the case of a statutory tenancy, the previous contractual tenancy, was created before 8th December 1965, the relevant date means 7th June 1966; and

   (b) except in a case falling within paragraph (c) below, if the tenancy became a regulated tenancy by virtue of section 14 of the Counter-Inflation Act 1973 and the tenancy or, in the case of a statutory tenancy, the previous contractual tenancy, was created before 22nd March 1973, the relevant date means 22nd September 1973; and

   (c) in the case of a regulated furnished tenancy, if the tenancy or, in the case of a statutory furnished tenancy, the previous contractual tenancy was created before 14th August 1974, the relevant date means 13th February 1975; and

   (d) in any other case, the relevant date means the date of the commencement of the regulated tenancy in question.

3. For the purposes of section 98(1)(a) of this Act, a certificate of the [local housing authority] [1] for the district in which the dwelling-house in question is situated, certifying that the authority will provide suitable alternative accommodation for the tenant by a date specified in the certificate, shall be conclusive evidence that suitable alternative accommodation will be available for him by that date.

A2.035   **4.**—(1) Where no such certificate as is mentioned in paragraph 3 above is produced to the court, accommodation shall be deemed to be suitable for the purposes of section 98(1)(a) of this Act if it consists of either—

(a) premises which are to be let as a separate dwelling such that they will then be let on a protected tenancy (other than one under which the landlord might recover possession of the dwelling-house under one of the Cases in Part II of this Schedule), or

(b) premises to be let as a separate dwelling on terms which will, in the opinion of the court, afford to the tenant security of tenure reasonably equivalent to the security afforded by Part VII of this Act in the case of a protected tenancy of a kind mentioned in paragraph (a) above,

and, in the opinion of the court, the accommodation fulfils the relevant conditions as defined in paragraph 5 below.

5.—(1) For the purposes of paragraph 4 above, the relevant conditions are that the accommodation is reasonably suitable to the needs of the tenant and his family as regards proximity to place of work, and either—

(a) similar as regards rental and extent to the accommodation afforded by dwelling-houses provided in the neighbourhood by any housing authority for persons whose needs as regards extent are, in the opinion of the court, similar to those of the tenant and of his family; or

(b) reasonably suitable to the means of the tenant and to the needs of the tenant and his family as regards extent and character; and

that if any furniture was provided for use under the protected or statutory tenancy in question, furniture is provided for use in the accommodation which is either similar to that so provided or is reasonably suitable to the needs of the tenant and his family.

(2) For the purposes of sub-paragraph (1)(a) above, a certificate of a local housing authority stating—

(a) the extent of the accommodation afforded by dwelling-houses provided by the authority to meet the needs of tenants with families of such number as may be specified in the certificate, and

(b) the amount of the rent charged by the authority for dwelling-houses affording accommodation of that extent,

shall be conclusive evidence of the facts so stated.

6.   Accommodation shall not be deemed to be suitable to the needs of the tenant and his family if the result of their occupation of the accommodation would be that it would be an overcrowded dwelling-house for the purposes of Part X of the Housing Act 1985.

7.   Any document purporting to be a certificate of a [local housing authority]1 named therein issued for the purposes of this Schedule and to be signed by the proper officer of that authority shall be received in evidence and, unless the contrary is shown, shall be deemed to be such a certificate without further proof.

8. In this Part "local housing authority" and "district" in relation to such an authority have the same meaning as in the Housing Act 1985.

PART V

PROVISIONS APPLYING TO CASES 11, 12 AND 20

1.   In this Part of this Schedule—   **A2.036**

"mortgage" includes a charge and "mortgagee" shall be construed accordingly;

"owner" means, in relation to Case 11, the owner-occupier; and

"successor in title" means any person deriving title from the owner, other than a purchaser for value or a person deriving title from a purchaser for value.

2.   The conditions referred to in paragraph (c) in each of Cases 11 and 12 and in paragraph (e)(ii) of Case 20 are that—

(a) the dwelling-house is required as a residence for the owner or any member of his family who resided with the owner when he last occupied the dwelling-house as a residence;

(b) the owner has retired from regular employment and requires the dwelling-house as a residence;

(c) the owner has died and the dwelling-house is required as a residence for a member of his family who was residing with him at the time of his death;

(d) the owner has died and the dwelling-house is required by a successor in title as his residence or for the purposes of disposing of it with vacant possession;

(e) the dwelling-house is subject to a mortgage, made by deed and granted before the tenancy, and the mortgagee—

(i) is entitled to exercise a power of sale conferred on him by the mortgage or by section 101 of the Law of Property Act 1925; and

(ii) requires the dwelling-houses for the purpose of disposing of it with vacant possession in exercise of that power; and

(f) the dwelling-house is not reasonably suitable to the needs of the owner, having regard to his place of work, and he requires it for the purpose of disposing of it with vacant possession and of using the proceeds of that disposal in acquiring, as his residence, a dwelling-house which is more suitable to those needs.

Housing Act 1985 (c.68)

SCHEDULE 1

TENANCIES WHICH ARE NOT SECURE TENANCIES

Long leases

A2.037   **1.**   A tenancy is not a secure tenancy if it is a long tenancy.

Introductory tenancies

1A. A tenancy is not a secure tenancy if it is an introductory tenancy or a tenancy which has ceased to be an introductory tenancy—

    (a) by virtue of section 133(3) of the Housing Act 1996 (disposal on death to non-qualifying person), or

    (b) by virtue of the tenant, or in the case of a joint tenancy every tenant, ceasing to occupy the dwelling-house as his only or principal home.

1B. A tenancy is not a secure tenancy if it is a demoted tenancy within the meaning of section 143A of the Housing Act 1996.

Premises occupied in connection with employment

2.—(1) Subject to sub-paragraph (4B) A tenancy is not a secure tenancy if the tenant is an employee of the landlord or of—

    a local authority,
    a development corporation,
    a housing action trust
    a Mayoral development corporation,
    an urban development corporation, or
    the governors of an aided school,

and his contract of employment requires him to occupy the dwelling-house for the better performance of his duties.

    (2) Subject to sub-paragraph (4B) A tenancy is not a secure tenancy if the tenant is a member of a police force and the dwelling-house is provided for him free of rent and rates in pursuance of regulations made under section 50 of the Police Act 1996 (general regulations as to government, administration and conditions of service of police forces).

    (3) Subject to sub-paragraph (4B) A tenancy is not a secure tenancy if the tenant is an employee of a fire and rescue authority and—

    (a) his contract of employment requires him to live in close proximity to a particular fire station, and

    (b) the dwelling-house was let to him by the authority in consequence of that requirement.

(4) Subject to sub-paragraph (4A) and (4B) A tenancy is not a secure tenancy if—

    (a) within the period of three years immediately preceding the grant the conditions mentioned in sub-paragraph (1), (2) or (3) have been satisfied with respect to a tenancy of the dwelling-house, and

    (b) before the grant the landlord notified the tenant in writing of the circumstances in which this exception applies and that in its opinion the proposed tenancy would fall within this exception,

(4A) Except where the landlord is a local housing authority, a tenancy under sub-paragraph (4) shall become a secure tenancy when the periods during which the conditions mentioned in sub-paragraph (1), (2) or (3) are not satisfied with respect to the tenancy amount in aggregate to more than three years. (4B) Where the landlord is a local housing authority, a tenancy under sub-paragraph (1), (2), (3) or (4) shall become a secure tenancy if the authority notify the tenancy that the tenancy is to be regarded as a secure tenancy.

(5) In this paragraph "contract of employment" means a contract of service or apprenticeship, whether express or implied and (if express) whether oral or in writing.

Land acquired for development

3.—(1) A tenancy is not a secure tenancy if the dwelling-house is on land which has been acquired for development and the dwelling-house is used by the landlord, pending development of the land, as temporary housing accommodation.

(2) In this paragraph "development" has the meaning given by section 55 of the Town and Country Planning Act 1990 (general definition of development for purposes of that Act).

Accommodation for homeless persons

4. A tenancy granted in pursuance of any function under Part VII of the Housing Act 1996 (homelessness) is not a secure tenancy unless the local housing authority concerned have notified the tenant that the tenancy is to be regarded as a secure tenancy. **A2.038**

Accommodation for asylum-seekers

4A.—(1) A tenancy is not a secure tenancy if it is granted in order to provide accommodation under section 4 or Part VI of the Immigration and Asylum Act 1999.

(2) A tenancy mentioned in sub-paragraph (1) becomes a secure tenancy if the landlord notifies the tenant that it is to be regarded as a secure tenancy.

Accommodation for persons with Temporary Protection

4B. A tenancy is not a secure tenancy if it is granted in order to provide accommodation under the Displaced Persons (Temporary Protection) Regulations 2005.

Temporary accommodation for persons taking up employment

A2.039   **5.**—(1) Subject to sub-paragraphs (1A) and (1B), a tenancy is not a secure
tenancy if—

(a) the person to whom the tenancy was granted was not, immediately
before the grant, resident in the district in which the dwelling-
house is situated,

(b) before the grant of the tenancy, he obtained employment, or an
offer of employment, in the district or its surrounding area,

(c) the tenancy was granted to him for the purpose of meeting his
need for temporary accommodation in the district or its
surrounding area in order to work there, and of enabling him to
find permanent accommodation there, and

(d) the landlord notified him in writing of the circumstances in which
this exception applies and that in its opinion the proposed tenancy
would fall within this exception;

(1A) Except where the landlord is a local housing authority, a tenancy
under sub-paragraph (1) shall become a secure tenancy on the expiry
of one year from the grant or on earlier notification by the landlord
to the tenant that the tenancy is to be regarded as a secure tenancy.

(1B) Where the landlord is a local housing authority, a tenancy under sub-
paragraph (1) shall become a secure tenancy if at any time the
authority notify the tenant that the tenancy is to be regarded as a
secure tenancy.

(2) In this paragraph–

"district" means district of a local housing authority; and
"surrounding area", in relation to a district, means the area consisting
of each district that adjoins it.

Short-term arrangements

6.   A tenancy is not a secure tenancy if—

(a) the dwelling-house has been leased to the landlord with vacant
possession for use as temporary housing accommodation,

(b) the terms on which it has been leased include provision for the
lessor to obtain vacant possession from the landlord on the expiry of
a specified period or when required by the lessor,

(c) the lessor is not a body which is capable of granting secure tenancies,
and

(d) the landlord has no interest in the dwelling-house other than under the
lease in question or as a mortgagee.

Temporary accommodation during works

7.   A tenancy is not a secure tenancy if—

(a) the dwelling-house has been made available for occupation by the
tenant (or a predecessor in title of his) while works are carried out on
the dwelling-house which he previously occupied as his home, and

(b) the tenant or predecessor was not a secure tenant of that other dwelling-house at the time when he ceased to occupy it as his home.

Agricultural holdings etc.

8.—(1) A tenancy is not a secure tenancy if—

A2.040

    (a) the dwelling-house is comprised in an agricultural holding and is occupied by the person responsible for the control (whether as tenant or as servant or agent of the tenant) of the farming of the holding, or

    (b) the dwelling-house is comprised in the holding held under a farm business tenancy and is occupied by the person responsible for the control (whether as tenant or as servant or agent of the tenant) of the management of the holding.

(2) In sub-paragraph (1) above—

    "agricultural holding" means any agricultural holding within the meaning of the Agricultural Holdings Act 1986 held under a tenancy in relation to which that Act applies, and

    "farm business tenancy", and "holding" in relation to such a tenancy, have the same meaning as in the Agricultural Tenancies Act 1995.

Licensed premises

9. A tenancy is not a secure tenancy if the dwelling-house consists of or includes premises which, by virtue of a premises licence under the Licensing Act 2003, may be used for the supply of alcohol (within the meaning of section 14 of that Act) for consumption on the premises.

Student lettings

10.—(1) Subject to sub-paragraphs (2A) and (2B), a tenancy of a dwelling-house is not a secure tenancy if—

    (a) it is granted for the purpose of enabling the tenant to attend a designated course at an educational establishment, and

    (b) before the grant of the tenancy the landlord notified him in writing of the circumstances in which this exception applies and that in its opinion the proposed tenancy would fall within this exception;

(2) A landlord's notice under sub-paragraph (1)(b) shall specify the educational establishment which the person concerned proposes to attend.

(2A) Except where the landlord is a local housing authority, a tenancy under sub-paragraph (1) shall become a secure tenancy on the expiry of the period specified in sub-paragraph (3) or on earlier notification by the landlord to the tenant that the tenancy is to be regarded as a secure tenancy.

(2B) Where the landlord is a local housing authority, a tenancy under sub-paragraph (1) shall become a secure tenancy if at any time the authority notify the tenant that the tenancy is to be regarded as a secure tenancy.

(3) The period referred to in sub-paragraph (2A) is—

(a) in a case where the tenant attends a designated course at the educational establishment specified in the landlord's notice, the period ending six months after the tenant ceases to attend that (or any other) designated course at that establishment;

(b) in any other case, the period ending six months after the grant of the tenancy.

(4) In this paragraph—

"designated course" means a course of any kind designated by regulations made by the Secretary of State for the purposes of this paragraph;

"educational establishment" means a university or institution which provides higher education or further education (or both); and for the purposes of this definition "higher education" and "further education" have the same meaning as in the Education Act 1996.

(5) Regulations under sub-paragraph (4) shall be made by statutory instrument and may make different provision with respect to different cases or descriptions of case, including different provision for different areas.

1954 Act tenancies

A2.041   **11.** A tenancy is not a secure tenancy if it is one to which Part II of the Landlord and Tenant Act 1954 applies (tenancies of premises occupied for business purposes).

Almshouses

12. A licence to occupy a dwelling-house is not a secure tenancy if—

(a) the dwelling-house is an almshouse, and

(b) the licence was granted by or on behalf of a charity which—

(i) is authorised under its trusts to maintain the dwelling-house as an almshouse, and

(ii) has no power under its trusts to grant a tenancy of the dwelling-house;

and in this paragraph "almshouse" means any premises maintained as an almshouse, whether they are called an almshouse or not; and "trusts", in relation to a charity, means the provisions establishing it as a charity and regulating its purposes and administration, whether those provisions take effect by way of trust or not.

SCHEDULE 2

GROUNDS FOR POSSESSION OF DWELLING-HOUSES LET
UNDER SECURE TENANCIES

PART I

GROUNDS ON WHICH COURT MAY ORDER POSSESSION IF IT
CONSIDERS IT REASONABLE

Ground 1

Rent lawfully due from the tenant has not been paid or an obligation of the tenancy **A2.042**
has been broken or not performed.

Ground 2

The tenant or a person residing in or visiting the dwelling-house—

(a) has been guilty of conduct causing or likely to cause a nuisance or annoyance to a person residing, visiting or otherwise engaging in a lawful activity
in the locality, or

(b) has been convicted of—

(i) using the dwelling-house or allowing it to be used for immoral or
illegal purposes, or

(ii) an indictable offence committed in, or in the locality of, the
dwelling-house.

Ground 2A

The dwelling-house was occupied (whether alone or with others) by a married
couple, a couple who are civil partners of each other, a couple living together as
husband and wife or a couple living together as if they were civil partners and—

(a) one or both of the partners is a tenant of the dwelling-house,

(b) one partner has left because of violence or threats of violence by the other
towards—

(i) that partner; or

(ii) a member of the family of that partner who was residing with that
partner immediately before the partner left, and

(c) the court is satisfied that the partner who has left is unlikely to return.

Ground 3

The condition of the dwelling-house or of any of the common parts has deterio- **A2.043**
rated owing to acts of waste by, or the neglect or default of, the tenant or a person
residing in the dwelling-house and, in the case of an act of waste by, or the neglect
or default of, a person lodging with the tenant or a sub-tenant of his, the tenant has
not taken such steps as he ought reasonably to have taken for the removal of the
lodger or sub-tenant.

Ground 4

The condition of furniture provided by the landlord for use under the tenancy, or for use in the common parts, has deteriorated owing to ill-treatment by the tenant or a person residing in the dwelling-house and, in the case of ill-treatment by a person lodging with the tenant or a sub-tenant of his, the tenant has not taken such steps as he ought reasonably to have taken for the removal of the lodger or sub-tenant.

Ground 5

The tenant is the person, or one of the persons, to whom the tenancy was granted and the landlord was induced to grant the tenancy by a false statement made knowingly or recklessly by–

    (a) the tenant, or
    (b) a person acting at the tenant's instigation.

Ground 6

A2.044 The tenancy was assigned to the tenant, or to a predecessor in title of his who is a member of his family and is residing in the dwelling-house, by an assignment made by virtue of section 92 (assignments by way of exchange) and a premium was paid either in connection with that assignment or the assignment which the tenant or predecessor himself made by virtue of that section.

    In this paragraph "premium" means any fine or other like sum and any other pecuniary consideration in addition to rent.

Ground 7

The dwelling-house forms part of, or is within the curtilage of, a building which, or so much of it as is held by the landlord, is held mainly for purposes other than housing purposes and consists mainly of accommodation other than housing accommodation, and—

    (a) the dwelling-house was let to the tenant or a predecessor in title of his in consequence of the tenant or predecessor being in the employment of the landlord, or of—

        a local authority,
        a new town corporation,
        a housing action trust
        an urban development corporation, or
        the governors of an aided school, and

    (b) the tenant or a person residing in the dwelling-house has been guilty of conduct such that, having regard to the purpose for which the building is used, it would not be right for him to continue in occupation of the dwelling-house.

Ground 8

The dwelling-house was made available for occupation by the tenant (or a pred-ecessor in title of his) while works were carried out on the dwelling-house which he previously occupied as his only or principal home and—

  (a) the tenant (or predecessor) was a secure tenant of the other dwelling-house at the time when he ceased to occupy it as his home,

  (b) the tenant (or predecessor) accepted the tenancy of the dwelling-house of which possession is sought on the understanding that he would give up occupation when, on completion of the works, the other dwelling-house was again available for occupation by him under a secure tenancy, and

  (c) the works have been completed and the other dwelling-house is so available.

PART II

GROUNDS ON WHICH THE COURT MAY ORDER POSSESSION IF SUITABLE
ALTERNATIVE ACCOMMODATION IS AVAILABLE

Ground 9

The dwelling-house is overcrowded, within the meaning of Part X, in such **A2.045** circumstances as to render the occupier guilty of an offence.

Ground 10

The landlord intends, within a reasonable time of obtaining possession of the dwelling-house—

  (a) to demolish or reconstruct the building or part of the building comprising the dwelling-house, or

  (b) to carry out work on that building or on land let together with, and thus treated as part of, the dwelling-house,

and cannot reasonably do so without obtaining possession of the dwelling-house.

Ground 10A

The dwelling-house is in an area which is the subject of a redevelopment scheme approved by the Secretary of State or the Housing Corporation or Scottish Homes in accordance with Part V of this Schedule and the landlord intends within a reasonable time of obtaining possession to dispose of the dwelling-house in accordance with the scheme.

  or

Part of the dwelling-house is in such an area and the landlord intends within a reasonable time of obtaining possession to dispose of that part in accordance with the scheme and for that purpose reasonably requires possession of the dwelling-house.

Ground 11

The landlord is a charity and the tenant's continued occupation of the dwelling-house would conflict with the objects of the charity.

PART III

GROUNDS ON WHICH THE COURT MAY ORDER POSSESSION IF IT CONSIDERS IT REASONABLE AND SUITABLE ALTERNATIVE ACCOMMODATION IS AVAILABLE

Ground 12

A2.046 The dwelling-house forms part of, or is within the curtilage of, a building which, or so much of it as is held by the landlord, is held mainly for purposes other than housing purposes and consists mainly of accommodation other than housing accommodation, or is situated in a cemetery, and—

(a) the dwelling-house was let to the tenant or a predecessor in title of his in consequence of the tenant or predecessor being in the employment of the landlord or of—

a local authority,
a development corporation,
a housing action trust
a Mayoral development corporation,
an urban development corporation, or
the governors of an aided school,

and that employment has ceased, and

(b) the landlord reasonably requires the dwelling-house for occupation as a residence for some person either engaged in the employment of the landlord, or of such a body, or with whom a contract for such employment has been entered into conditional on housing being provided.

Ground 13

The dwelling-house has features which are substantially different from those of ordinary dwelling-houses and which are designed to make it suitable for occupation by a physically disabled person who requires accommodation of a kind provided by the dwelling-house and—

(a) there is no longer such a person residing in the dwelling-house, and
(b) the landlord requires it for occupation (whether alone or with members of his family) by such a person.

Ground 14

The landlord is a housing association or housing trust which lets dwelling-houses only for occupation (whether alone or with others) by persons whose circumstances (other than merely financial circumstances) make it especially difficult for them to satisfy their need for housing, and—

(a) either there is no longer such a person residing in the dwelling-house or the tenant has received from a local housing authority an offer of accommodation in premises which are to be let as a separate dwelling under a secure tenancy, and

(b) the landlord requires the dwelling-house for occupation (whether alone or with members of his family) by such a person.

Ground 15

The dwelling-house is one of a group of dwelling-houses which it is the practice **A2.047** of the landlord to let for occupation by persons with special needs and—

(a) a social service or special facility is provided in close proximity to the group of dwelling-houses in order to assist persons with those special needs,
(b) there is no longer a person with those special needs residing in the dwelling-house, and
(c) the landlord requires the dwelling-house for occupation (whether alone or with members of his family) by a person who has those special needs.

Ground 15A

The dwelling-house is in England, the accommodation afforded by it is more extensive than is reasonably required by the tenant and—

(a) the tenancy vested in the tenant by virtue of section 89 (succession to periodic tenancy) or 90 (devolution of the term certain) in a case where the tenant was not the previous tenant's spouse or civil partner, and
(b) notice of the proceedings for possession was served under section 83 (or, where no such notice was served, the proceedings for possession were begun) more than six months but less than twelve months after the relevant date.

For this purpose, "the relevant date" is—

(a) the date of the previous tenant's death, or
(b) if the court so directs, the date on which, in the opinion of the court, the landlord (or, in the case of joint landlords, any one of them) became aware of the previous tenant's death).

The matters to be taken into account by the court in determining whether it is reasonable to make an order on this ground include—

(a) the age of the tenant,
(b) the period (if any) during which the tenant has occupied the dwelling-house as the tenant's only or principal home, and
(c) any financial or other support given by the tenant to the previous tenant.

Ground 16

The dwelling-house is in Wales, the accommodation afforded by it is more extensive than is reasonably required by the tenant and—

(a) the tenancy vested in the tenant by virtue of section 89 (succession to periodic tenancy) or 90 (devolution of the term certain) in a case where the tenant was not the previous tenant's spouse or civil partner, and
(b) notice of the proceedings for possession was served under section 83 (or, where no such notice was served, the proceedings for possession were

begun) more than six months but less than twelve months after the relevant date.

For this purpose, "the relevant date" is—

(a) the date of the previous tenant's death, or

(b) if the court so directs, the date on which, in the opinion of the court, the landlord (or, in the case of joint landlords, any one of them) became aware of the previous tenant's death).

The matters to be taken into account by the court in determining whether it is reasonable to make an order on this ground include—

(a) the age of the tenant,

(b) the period (if any) during which the tenant has occupied the dwelling-house as the tenant's only or principal home, and

(c) any financial or other support given by the tenant to the previous tenant.

PART IV

SUITABILITY OF ACCOMMODATION

A2.048   1.   For the purposes of section 84(2)(b) and (c) (case in which court is not to make an order for possession unless satisfied that suitable accommodation will be available) accommodation is suitable if it consists of premises—

(a) which are to be let as a separate dwelling under a secure tenancy, or

(b) which are to be let as a separate dwelling under a protected tenancy, not being a tenancy under which the landlord might recover possession under one of the Cases in Part II of Schedule 15 to the Rent Act 1977 (cases where court must order possession), or

(c) which are to be let as a separate dwelling under an assured tenancy which is neither an assured shorthold tenancy, within the meaning of Part I of the Housing Act 1988, nor a tenancy under which the landlord might recover possession under any of Grounds 1 to 5 in Schedule 2 to that Act.

and, in the opinion of the court, the accommodation is reasonably suitable to the needs of the tenant and his family.

2.   In determining whether the accommodation is reasonably suitable to the needs of the tenant and his family, regard shall be had to–

(a) the nature of the accommodation which it is the practice of the landlord to allocate to persons with similar needs;

(b) the distance of the accommodation available from the place of work or education of the tenant and of any members of his family;

(c) its distance from the home of any member of the tenant's family if proximity to it is essential to that member's or the tenant's well-being;

(d) the needs (as regards extent of accommodation) and means of the tenant and his family;

(e) the terms on which the accommodation is available and the terms of the secure tenancy;

(f) if furniture was provided by the landlord for use under the secure tenancy, whether furniture is to be provided for use in the other accommodation, and if so the nature of the furniture to be provided.

3.   Where possession of a dwelling-house is sought on ground 9 (overcrowding such as to render occupier guilty of offence), other accommodation may be reasonably suitable to the needs of the tenant and his family notwithstanding that the permitted number of persons for that accommodation, as defined in section 326(3) (overcrowding: the space standard), is less than the number of persons living in the dwelling-house of which possession is sought.

4.—(1) A certificate of the appropriate local housing authority that they will provide suitable accommodation for the tenant by a date specified in the certificate is conclusive evidence that suitable accommodation will be available for him by that date.

(2) The appropriate local housing authority is the authority for the district in which the dwelling-house of which possession is sought is situated.

(3) This paragraph does not apply where the landlord is a local housing authority.

PART V

APPROVAL OF REDEVELOPMENT SCHEMES FOR PURPOSES OF GROUND 10A

1.—(1) The Secretary of State may, on the application of the landlord, approve **A2.049** for the purposes of ground 10A in Part II of this Schedule a scheme for the disposal and re-development of an area of land consisting of or including the whole or part of one or more dwelling-houses.

(2) For this purpose—

    (a) "disposal" means a disposal of any interest in the land (including the grant of an option), and

    (b) "redevelopment" means the demolition or reconstruction of buildings or the carrying out of other works to buildings or land;

and it is immaterial whether the disposal is to precede or follow the redevelopment.

(3) The Secretary of State may on the application of the landlord approve a variation of a scheme previously approved by him and may, in particular, approve a variation adding land to the area subject to the scheme.

2.—(1) Where a landlord proposes to apply to the Secretary of State for the approval of a scheme or variation it shall serve a notice in writing on any secure tenant of a dwelling-house affected by the proposal stating—

    (a) the main features of the proposed scheme or, as the case may be, the scheme as proposed to be varied,

    (b) that the landlord proposes to apply to the Secretary of State for approval of the scheme or variation, and

    (c) the effect of such approval, by virtue of section 84 and ground 10A in Part II of this Schedule, in relation to proceedings for possession of the dwelling-house,

and informing the tenant that he may, within such period as the landlord may allow (which shall be at least 28 days from service of the notice), make representations to the landlord about the proposal.

(2) The landlord shall not apply to the Secretary of State until it has considered any representations made to it within that period.

(3) In the case of a landlord to which section 105 applies (consultation on matters of housing management) the provisions of this paragraph apply in place of the provisions of that section in relation to the approval or variation of a redevelopment scheme.

3.—(1) In considering whether to give his approval to a scheme or variation the Secretary of State shall take into account, in particular—

    (a) the effect of the scheme on the extent and character of housing accommodation in the neighbourhood,

    (b) over what period of time it is proposed that the disposal and redevelopment will take place in accordance with the scheme, and

    (c) to what extent the scheme includes provision for housing provided under the scheme to be sold or let to existing tenants or persons nominated by the landlord;

and he shall take into account any representations made to him and, so far as they are brought to his notice, any representations made to the landlord.

(2) The landlord shall give to the Secretary of State such information as to the representations made to it, and other relevant matters, as the Secretary of State may require.

4.   The Secretary of State shall not approve a scheme or variation so as to include in the area subject to the scheme—

    (a) part only of one or more dwelling-houses, or

    (b) one or more dwelling-houses not themselves affected by the works involved in redevelopment but which are proposed to be disposed of along with other land which is so affected,

unless he is satisfied that the inclusion is justified in the circumstances.

5.—(1) Approval may be given subject to conditions and may be expressed to expire after a specified period.

(2) The Secretary of State, on the application of the landlord or otherwise, may vary an approval so as to—

    (a) add, remove or vary conditions to which the approval is subject; or

    (b) extend or restrict the period after which the approval is to expire.

(3) Where approval is given subject to conditions, the landlord may serve a notice under section 83 (notice of proceedings for possession) specifying ground 10A notwithstanding that the conditions are not yet fulfilled but the court shall not make an order for possession on that ground unless satisfied that they are or will be fulfilled.

6.   Where the landlord is a [social landlord registered in the register maintained by the Housing Corporation under section 1 of the Housing Act 1996 or a housing association registered in the register maintained by Scottish Homes under section 3 of the Housing Associations Act 1985, the Housing Corporation, or Scottish Homes, (and not the Secretary of State) has the functions conferred by this Part of this Schedule.

7.   In this Part of this Schedule references to the landlord of a dwelling-house include any authority or body within section 80 (the landlord condition for secure tenancies) having an interest of any description in the dwelling-house."

Housing Act 1988 (c.50)

SCHEDULE 1

TENANCIES WHICH CANNOT BE ASSURED TENANCIES

PART I

THE TENANCIES

Tenancies entered into before commencement

1. A tenancy which is entered into before, or pursuant to a contract made before, **A2.050** the commencement of this Act.

Tenancies of dwelling-houses with high rateable values

2.—(1) A tenancy—

    (a) which is entered into on or after 1st April 1990 (otherwise than, where the dwelling-house had a rateable value on 31st March 1990, in pursuance of a contract made before 1st April 1990), and

    (b) under which the rent payable for the time being is payable at a rate exceeding £100,000 a year. [see para.6.005.]

    (2) In sub-paragraph (1) "rent" does not include any sum payable by the tenant as is expressed (in whatever terms) to be payable in respect of rates, council tax, services, management, repairs, maintenance or insurance, unless it could not have been regarded by the parties to the tenancy as a sum so payable.

2A. A tenancy—

    (a) which was entered into before the 1st April 1990, or on or after that date in pursuance of a contract made before that date, and

    (b) under which the dwelling-house had a rateable value on the 31st March 1990 which, if it is in Greater London, exceeded £1,500 and, if it is elsewhere, exceeded £750.

Tenancies at a low rent

3. A tenancy under which for the time being no rent is payable.
3A. A tenancy—

   (a) which is entered into on or after 1st April 1990 (otherwise than, where the dwelling-house had a rateable value on 31st March 1990, in pursuance of a contract made before 1st April 1990), and

   (b) under which the rent payable for the time being is payable at a rate of, if the dwelling-house is in Greater London, £1,000 or less a year and, if it is elsewhere, £250 or less a year.

3B. A tenancy—

   (a) which was entered into before 1st April 1990 or, where the dwelling-house had a rateable value on the 31st March 1990, on or after 1st April 1990 in pursuance of a contract made before that date, and

   (b) under which the rent for the time being payable is less than two-thirds of the rateable value of the dwelling-house on 31st March 1990.

3C. Paragraph 2(2) above applies for the purposes of paragraphs 3, 3A and 3B as it applies for the purposes of paragraph 2(1).

Business tenancies

A2.051   **4.**   A tenancy to which Part II of the Landlord and Tenant Act 1954 applies (business tenancies).

Licensed premises

5.   A tenancy under which the dwelling-house consists of or comprises premises which, by virtue of a premises licence under the Licensing Act 2003, may be used for the supply of alcohol (within the meaning of section 14 of that Act) for consumption on the premises.

Tenancies of agricultural land

6.—(1) A tenancy under which agricultural land, exceeding two acres, is let together with the dwelling-house.

   (2) In this paragraph "agricultural land" has the meaning set out in section 26(3)(a) of the General Rate Act 1967 (exclusion of agricultural land and premises from liability for rating).

Tenancies of agricultural holdings, etc.

A2.052   **7.**—(1) A tenancy under which the dwelling-house—

   (a) is comprised in an agricultural holding, and

   (b) is occupied by the person responsible for the control (whether as tenant or as servant or agent of the tenant) of the farming of the holding.

   (2) A tenancy under which the dwelling-house—

   (a) is comprised in the holding held under a farm business tenancy, and

(b) is occupied by the person responsible for the control (whether as tenant or as servant or agent of the tenant) of the management of the holding.

(3) In this paragraph—

"agricultural holding" means any agricultural holding within the meaning of the Agricultural Holdings Act 1986 held under a tenancy in relation to which that Act applies, and
"farm business tenancy" and "holding", in relation to such a tenancy, have the same meaning as in the Agricultural Tenancies Act 1995.

Lettings to students

8.—(1) A tenancy which is granted to a person who is pursuing, or intends to pursue, a course of study provided by a specified educational institution and is so granted either by that institution or by another specified institution or body of persons.

(2) In sub-paragraph (1) above "specified" means specified, or of a class specified, for the purposes of this paragraph by regulations made by the Secretary of State by statutory instrument.

(3) A statutory instrument made in the exercise of the power conferred by sub-paragraph (2) above shall be subject to annulment in pursuance of a resolution of either House of Parliament.

Holiday lettings

9. A tenancy the purpose of which is to confer on the tenant the right to occupy the dwelling-house for a holiday.

Resident landlords

10.—(1) A tenancy in respect of which the following conditions are fulfilled— **A2.053**

(a) that the dwelling-house forms part only of a building and, except in a case where the dwelling-house also forms part of a flat, the building is not a purpose-built block of flats; and

(b) that, subject to Part III of this Schedule, the tenancy was granted by an individual who, at the time when the tenancy was granted, occupiedashisonlyorprincipalhomeanotherdwelling-housewhich—

(i) in the case mentioned in paragraph (a) above, also forms part of the flat; or

(ii) in any other case, also forms part of the building; and

(c) that, subject to Part III of this Schedule, at all times since the tenancy was granted the interest of the landlord under the tenancy has belonged to an individual who, at the time he owned that interest, occupied as his only or principal home another dwelling-house which–

(i) in the case mentioned in paragraph (a) above, also formed part of the flat; or

       (ii) in any other case, also formed part of the building; and

    (d) that the tenancy is not one which is excluded from this sub-paragraph by sub-paragraph (3) below.

(2) If a tenancy was granted by two or more persons jointly, the reference in sub-paragraph (1)(b) above to an individual is a reference to any one of those persons and if the interest of the landlord is for the time being held by two or more persons jointly, the reference in sub-paragraph (1)(c) above to an individual is a reference to any one of those persons.

(3) A tenancy (in this sub-paragraph referred to as "the new tenancy") is excluded from sub-paragraph (1) above if—

    (a) it is granted to a person (alone, or jointly with others) who, immediately before it was granted, was a tenant under an assured tenancy (in this sub-paragraph referred to as "the former tenancy") of the same dwelling-house or of another dwelling-house which forms part of the building in question; and

    (b) the landlord under the new tenancy and under the former tenancy is the same person or, if either of those tenancies is or was granted by two or more persons jointly, the same person is the landlord or one of the landlords under each tenancy.

Crown tenancies

A2.054   **11.**—(1) A tenancy under which the interest of the landlord belongs to Her Majesty in right of the Crown or to a government department or is held in trust for Her Majesty for the purposes of a government department.

(2) The reference in sub-paragraph (1) above to the case where the interest of the landlord belongs to Her Majesty in right of the Crown does not include the case where that interest is under the management of the Crown Estate Commissioners or it is held by the Secretary of State as the result of the exercise by him of functions under Part III of the Housing Associations Act 1985.

Local authority tenancies etc.

12.—(1) A tenancy under which the interest of the landlord belongs to—

    (a) a local authority, as defined in sub-paragraph (2) below;

    (b) the Commission for the New Towns;

    (d) an urban development corporation established by an order under section 135 of the Local Government, Planning and Land Act 1980;

    (e) a development corporation, within the meaning of the New Towns Act 1981;

    (ee) the London Fire and Emergency Planning Authority;

    (f) an authority established under section 10 of the Local Government Act 1985 (waste disposal authorities);

    (fa) an authority established for an area in England by an order under section 207 of the Local Government and Public Involvement in Health Act 2007 (joint waste authorities);

(g) a residuary body, within the meaning of the Local Government Act 1985;

(gg) The Residuary Body for Wales (Corff Gweddilliol Cymru);

(h) a fully mutual housing association; or

(i) a housing action trust established under Part III of this Act.

(2) The following are local authorities for the purposes of sub-paragraph (1)(a) above—

(a) the council of a county, county borough, district or London borough;

(b) the Common Council of the City of London;

(c) the Council of the Isles of Scilly;

(d) the Broads Authority;

(da) a National Park authority;

(e) the Inner London Education Authority; and

(f) a joint authority, within the meaning of the Local Government Act 1985 and

(g) a police authority established under section 3 of the Police Act 1996.

Accommodation for asylum-seekers

12A.—(1) A tenancy granted by a private landlord under arrangements for the **A2.055**
provision of support for asylum-seekers or dependants of asylum-seekers made under section 4 or Part VI of the Immigration and Asylum Act 1999.
(2) "Private landlord" means a landlord who is not within section 80(1) of the Housing Act 1985.

Accommodation for persons with Temporary Protection

12B.—(1) A tenancy granted by a private landlord under arrangements for the provision of accommodation for persons with temporary protection made under the Displaced Persons (Temporary Protection) Regulations 2005.
(2) "Private landlord" means a landlord who is not within section 80(1) of the Housing Act 1985.

Transitional cases

13.—(1) A protected tenancy, within the meaning of the Rent Act 1977.
(2) A housing association tenancy, within the meaning of Part VI of that Act.
(3) A secure tenancy.
(4) Where a person is a protected occupier of a dwelling-house, within the meaning of the Rent (Agriculture) Act 1976, the relevant tenancy, within the meaning of that Act, by virtue of which he occupies the dwelling-house.

PART II

RATEABLE VALUES

A2.056   **14.**—(1) The rateable value of a dwelling-house at any time shall be ascertained for the purposes of Part I of this Schedule as follows—

    (a) if the dwelling-house is a hereditament for which a rateable value is then shown in the valuation list, it shall be that rateable value;

    (b) if the dwelling-house forms part only of such a hereditament or consists of or forms part of more than one such hereditament, its rateable value shall be taken to be such value as is found by a proper apportionment or aggregation of the rateable value or values so shown.

(2) Any question arising under this Part of this Schedule as to the proper apportionment or aggregation of any value or values shall be determined by the county court and the decision of that court shall be final.

15. Where, after the time at which the rateable value of a dwelling-house is material for the purposes of any provision of Part I of this Schedule, the valuation list is altered so as to vary the rateable value of the hereditament of which the dwelling-house consists (in whole or in part) or forms part and the alteration has effect from that time or from an earlier time, the rateable value of the dwelling-house at the material time shall be ascertained as if the value shown in the valuation list at the material time had been the value shown in the list as altered.

16. Paragraphs 14 and 15 above apply in relation to any other land which, under section 2 of this Act, is treated as part of a dwelling-house as they apply in relation to the dwelling-house itself.

PART III

PROVISIONS FOR DETERMINING APPLICATION OF PARAGRAPH 10
(RESIDENT LANDLORDS)

A2.057   **17.**—(1) In determining whether the condition in paragraph 10(1)(c) above is at any time fulfilled with respect to a tenancy, there shall be disregarded—

    (a) any period of not more than twenty-eight days, beginning with the date on which the interest of the landlord under the tenancy becomes vested at law and in equity in an individual who, during that period, does not occupy as his only or principal home another dwelling-house which forms part of the building or, as the case may be, flat concerned;

    (b) if, within a period falling within paragraph (a) above, the individual concerned notifies the tenant in writing of his intention to occupy as his only or principal home another dwelling-house in the building or, as the case may be, flat concerned, the period beginning with the date on which the interest of the landlord under the tenancy becomes vested in that individual as mentioned in that paragraph and ending—

(i) at the expiry of the period of six months beginning on that date, or

(ii) on the date on which that interest ceases to be so vested, or

(iii) on the date on which that interest becomes again vested in such an individual as is mentioned in paragraph 10(1)(c) or the condition in that paragraph becomes deemed to be fulfilled by virtue of paragraph 18(1) or paragraph 20 below,

whichever is the earlier; and

(c) any period of not more than two years beginning with the date on which the interest of the landlord under the tenancy becomes, and during which it remains, vested—

(i) in trustees as such; or

(ii) by virtue of section 9 of the Administration of Estates Act 1925, in the Probate Judge or the Public Trustee.

(2) Where the interest of the landlord under a tenancy becomes vested at law and in equity in two or more persons jointly, of whom at least one was an individual, sub-paragraph (1) above shall have effect subject to the following modifications–

(a) in paragraph (a) for the words from "an individual" to "occupy" there shall be substituted "the joint landlords if, during that period none of them occupies"; and

(b) in paragraph (b) for the words "the individual concerned" there shall be substituted "any of the joint landlords who is an individual" and for the words "that individual" there shall be substituted "the joint landlords".

18.—(1) During any period when—

(a) the interest of the landlord under the tenancy referred to in paragraph 10 above is vested in trustees as such, and

(b) that interest is held on trust for any person who or for two or more persons of whom at least one occupies as his only or principal home a dwelling-house which forms part of the building or, as the case may be, flat referred to in paragraph 10(1)(a),

the condition in paragraph 10(1)(c) shall be deemed to be fulfilled and accordingly, no part of that period shall be disregarded by virtue of paragraph 17 above.

(2) If a period during which the condition in paragraph 10(1)(c) is deemed to be fulfilled by virtue of sub-paragraph (1) above comes to an end on the death of a person who was in occupation of a dwelling-house as mentioned in paragraph (b) of that sub-paragraph, then, in determining whether that condition is at any time thereafter fulfilled, there shall be disregarded any period—

(a) which begins on the date of the death;

(b) during which the interest of the landlord remains vested as mentioned in sub-paragraph (1)(a) above; and

(c) which ends at the expiry of the period of two years beginning on the date of the death or on any earlier date on which the condition in paragraph 10(1)(c) becomes again deemed to be fulfilled by virtue of sub-paragraph (1) above.

19. In any case where—

    (a) immediately before a tenancy comes to an end the condition in paragraph 10(1)(c) is deemed to be fulfilled by virtue of paragraph 18(1) above, and

    (b) on the coming to an end of that tenancy the trustees in whom the interest of the landlord is vested grant a new tenancy of the same or substantially the same dwelling-house to a person (alone or jointly with others) who was the tenant or one of the tenants under the previous tenancy,

the condition in paragraph 10(1)(b) above shall be deemed to be fulfilled with respect to the new tenancy.

    20.—(1) The tenancy referred to in paragraph 10 above falls within this paragraph if the interest of the landlord under the tenancy becomes vested in the personal representatives of a deceased person acting in that capacity.

    (2) If the tenancy falls within this paragraph, the condition in paragraph 10(1)(c) shall be deemed to be fulfilled for any period, beginning with the date on which the interest becomes vested in the personal representatives and not exceeding two years, during which the interest of the landlord remains so vested.

    21. Throughout any period which, by virtue of paragraph 17 or paragraph 18(2) above, falls to be disregarded for the purpose of determining whether the condition in paragraph 10(1)(c) is fulfilled with respect to a tenancy, no order shall be made for possession of the dwelling-house subject to that tenancy, other than an order which might be made if that tenancy were or, as the case may be, had been an assured tenancy.

    22. For the purposes of paragraph 10 above, a building is a purpose-built block of flats if as constructed it contained, and it contains, two or more flats; and for this purpose "flat" means a dwelling-house which—

    (a) forms part only of a building; and

    (b) is separated horizontally from another dwelling-house which forms part of the same building.

SCHEDULE 2

GROUNDS FOR POSSESSION OF DWELLING-HOUSES LET ON ASSURED TENANCIES

PART I

GROUNDS ON WHICH COURT MUST ORDER POSSESSION

Ground 1

A2.058 Not later than the beginning of the tenancy the landlord gave notice in writing to the tenant that possession might be recovered on this ground or the court is of the opinion that it is just and equitable to dispense with the requirement of notice and (in either case)—

    (a) at some time before the beginning of the tenancy, the landlord who is seeking possession or, in the case of joint landlords seeking possession, at least one of them occupied the dwelling-house as his only or principal home; or

(b) the landlord who is seeking possession or, in the case of joint landlords seeking possession, at least one of them requires the dwelling-house as his, his spouse's or his civil partner's only or principal home and neither the landlord (or, in the case of joint landlords, any one of them) nor any other person who, as landlord, derived title under the landlord who gave the notice mentioned above acquired the reversion on the tenancy for money or money's worth.

Ground 2

The dwelling-house is subject to a mortgage granted before the beginning of the tenancy and—

(a) the mortgagee is entitled to exercise a power of sale conferred on him by the mortgage or by section 101 of the Law of Property Act 1925; and

(b) the mortgagee requires possession of the dwelling-house for the purpose of disposing of it with vacant possession in exercise of that power; and

(c) either notice was given as mentioned in Ground 1 above or the court is satisfied that it is just and equitable to dispense with the requirement of notice;

and for the purposes of this ground "mortgage" includes a charge and "mortgagee" shall be construed accordingly.

Ground 3

The tenancy is a fixed term tenancy for a term not exceeding eight months and—

(a) not later than the beginning of the tenancy the landlord gave notice in writing to the tenant that possession might be recovered on this ground; and

(b) at some time within the period of twelve months ending with the beginning of the tenancy, the dwelling-house was occupied under a right to occupy it for a holiday.

Ground 4

The tenancy is a fixed term tenancy for a term not exceeding twelve months and— **A2.059**

(a) not later than the beginning of the tenancy the landlord gave notice in writing to the tenant that possession might be recovered on this ground; and

(b) at some time within the period of twelve months ending with the beginning of the tenancy, the dwelling-house was let on a tenancy falling within paragraph 8 of Schedule 1 to this Act.

Ground 5

The dwelling-house is held for the purpose of being available for occupation by a minister of religion as a residence from which to perform the duties of his office and—

(a) not later than the beginning of the tenancy the landlord gave notice in writing to the tenant that possession might be recovered on this ground; and

(b) the court is satisfied that the dwelling-house is required for occupation by a minister of religion as such a residence.

Ground 6

A2.060 The landlord who is seeking possession or, if that landlord is a registered social landlord or charitable housing trust, a superior landlord intends to demolish or reconstruct the whole or a substantial part of the dwelling-house or to carry out substantial works on the dwelling-house or any part thereof or any building of which it forms part and the following conditions are fulfilled—

(a) the intended work cannot reasonably be carried out without the tenant giving up possession of the dwelling-house because—

(i) the tenant is not willing to agree to such a variation of the terms of the tenancy as would give such access and other facilities as would permit the intended work to be carried out, or

(ii) the nature of the intended work is such that no such variation is practicable, or

(iii) the tenant is not willing to accept an assured tenancy of such part only of the dwelling-house (in this sub-paragraph referred to as "the reduced part") as would leave in the possession of his landlord so much of the dwelling-house as would be reasonable to enable the intended work to be carried out and, where appropriate, as would give such access and other facilities over the reduced part as would permit the intended work to be carried out, or

(iv) the nature of the intended work is such that such a tenancy is not practicable; and

(b) either the landlord seeking possession acquired his interest in the dwelling-house before the grant of the tenancy or that interest was in existence at the time of that grant and neither that landlord (or, in the case of joint landlords, any of them) nor any other person who, alone or jointly with others, has acquired that interest since that time acquired it for money or money's worth; and

(c) the assured tenancy on which the dwelling-house is let did not come into being by virtue of any provision of Schedule 1 to the Rent Act 1977, as amended by Part I of Schedule 4 to this Act or, as the case may be, section 4 of the Rent (Agriculture) Act 1976, as amended by Part II of that Schedule.

For the purposes of this ground, if, immediately before the grant of the tenancy, the tenant to whom it was granted or, if it was granted to joint tenants, any of them was the tenant or one of the joint tenants of the dwelling-house concerned under an earlier assured tenancy or, as the case may be, under a tenancy to which Schedule 10 to the Local Government and Housing Act 1989 applied, any reference in paragraph (b) above to the grant of the tenancy is a reference to the grant of that earlier assured tenancy or, as the case may be, to the grant of the tenancy to which the said Schedule 10 applied.

For the purposes of this ground "registered social landlord" has the same meaning as in the Housing Act 1985 (see section 5(4) and (5) of that Act) and "charitable housing trust" means a housing trust, within the meaning of the Housing Associations Act 1985, which is a charity, within the meaning of the Charities Act 1993.

For the purposes of this ground, every acquisition under Part IV of this Act shall be taken to be an acquisition for money or money's worth; and in any case where—

(i) the tenancy (in this paragraph referred to as "the current tenancy") was granted to a person (alone or jointly with others) who, immediately before it was granted, was a tenant under a tenancy of a different dwelling-house (in this paragraph referred to as "the earlier tenancy"), and

(ii) the landlord under the current tenancy is the person who, immediately before that tenancy was granted, was the landlord under the earlier tenancy, and

(iii) the condition in paragraph (b) above could not have been fulfilled with respect to the earlier tenancy by virtue of an acquisition under Part IV of this Act (including one taken to be such an acquisition by virtue of the previous operation of this paragraph),

the acquisition of the landlord's interest under the current tenancy shall be taken to have been under that Part and the landlord shall be taken to have acquired that interest after the grant of the current tenancy.

Ground 7

The tenancy is a periodic tenancy (including a statutory periodic tenancy) which **A2.061** has devolved under the will or intestacy of the former tenant and the proceedings for the recovery of possession are begun not later than twelve months after the death of the former tenant or, if the court so directs, after the date on which, in the opinion of the court, the landlord or, in the case of joint landlords, any one of them became aware of the former tenant's death.

For the purposes of this ground, the acceptance by the landlord of rent from a new tenant after the death of the former tenant shall not be regarded as creating a new periodic tenancy, unless the landlord agrees in writing to a change (as compared with the tenancy before the death) in the amount of the rent, the period of the tenancy, the premises which are let or any other term of the tenancy.

Ground 8

Both at the date of the service of the notice under section 8 of this Act relating to the proceedings for possession and at the date of the hearing—

(a) if rent is payable weekly or fortnightly, at least eight weeks' rent is unpaid;

(b) if rent is payable monthly, at least two months' rent is unpaid;

(c) if rent is payable quarterly, at least one quarter's rent is more than three months in arrears; and

(d) if rent is payable yearly, at least three months' rent is more than three months in arrears;

and for the purpose of this ground "rent" means rent lawfully due from the tenant.

PART II

GROUNDS ON WHICH COURT MAY ORDER POSSESSION

Ground 9

Suitable alternative accommodation is available for the tenant or will be available for him when the order for possession takes effect.

Ground 10

A2.062 Some rent lawfully due from the tenant—

(a) is unpaid on the date on which the proceedings for possession are begun; and

(b) except where subsection (1)(b) of section 8 of this Act applies, was in arrears at the date of the service of the notice under that section relating to those proceedings.

Ground 11

A2.063 Whether or not any rent is in arrears on the date on which proceedings for possession are begun, the tenant has persistently delayed paying rent which has become lawfully due.

Ground 12

Any obligation of the tenancy (other than one related to the payment of rent) has been broken or not performed.

Ground 13

The condition of the dwelling-house or any of the common parts has deteriorated owing to acts of waste by, or the neglect or default of, the tenant or any other person residing in the dwelling-house and, in the case of an act of waste by, or the neglect or default of, a person lodging with the tenant or a sub-tenant of his, the tenant has not taken such steps as he ought reasonably to have taken for the removal of the lodger or sub-tenant.

For the purposes of this ground, "common parts" means any part of a building comprising the dwelling-house and any other premises which the tenant is entitled under the terms of the tenancy to use in common with the occupiers of other dwelling-houses in which the landlord has an estate or interest.

Ground 14

A2.064 The tenant or a person residing in or visiting the dwelling-house—

(a) has been guilty of conduct causing or likely to cause a nuisance or annoyance to a person residing; visiting or otherwise engaging in a lawful activity in the locality, or

(b) has been convicted of—

(i) using the dwelling-house or allowing it to be used for immoral or illegal purposes, or

(ii) an indictable offence committed in, or in the locality of, the dwelling-house.

Ground 14A

The dwelling-house was occupied (whether alone or with others) by a married couple, a couple who are civil partners of each other, a couple living together as husband and wife or a couple living together as if they were civil partners and—

(a) one or both of the partners is a tenant of the dwelling-house,

(b) the landlord who is seeking possession is a non-profit registered provider of social housing, a registered social landlord or a charitable housing trust or, where the dwelling-house is social housing within the meaning of Part 2 of the Housing and Regeneration Act 2008, a profit-making registered provider of social housing,

(c) one partner has left the dwelling-house because of violence or threats of violence by the other towards—

(i) that partner, or

(ii) a member of the family of that partner who was residing with that partner immediately before the partner left, and

(d) the court is satisfied that the partner who has left is unlikely to return.

For the purposes of this ground "registered social landlord" and "member of the family" have the same meaning as in Part I of the Housing Act 1996 and "charitable housing trust" means a housing trust, within the meaning of the Housing Associations Act 1985, which is a charity.

Ground 15

The condition of any furniture provided for use under the tenancy has, in the opinion of the court, deteriorated owing to ill-treatment by the tenant or any other person residing in the dwelling-house and, in the case of ill-treatment by a person lodging with the tenant or by a sub-tenant of his, the tenant has not taken such steps as he ought reasonably to have taken for the removal of the lodger or sub-tenant.

Ground 16

The dwelling-house was let to the tenant in consequence of his employment by **A2.065** the landlord seeking possession or a previous landlord under the tenancy and the tenant has ceased to be in that employment. For the purposes of this ground, at a time when the landlord is or was the Secretary of State, employment by a health service body, as defined in section 60(7) of the National Health Service and Community Care Act 1990, shall be regarded as employment by the Secretary of State.

For the purposes of this ground, at a time when the landlord is or was the Secretary of State, employment by a health service body, as defined in section 60(7) of the National Health Service and Community Care Act 1990, or by a Local Health Board, shall be regarded as employment by the Secretary of State.

Ground 17

The tenant is the person, or one of the persons, to whom the tenancy was granted and the landlord was induced to grant the tenancy by a false statement made knowingly or recklessly by—

    (a) the tenant, or
    (b) a person acting at the tenant's instigation.

PART III

SUITABLE ALTERNATIVE ACCOMMODATION

A2.066   **1.** For the purposes of Ground 9 above, a certificate of the local housing authority for the district in which the dwelling-house in question is situated, certifying that the authority will provide suitable alternative accommodation for the tenant by a date specified in the certificate, shall be conclusive evidence that suitable alternative accommodation will be available for him by that date.

    2. Where no such certificate as is mentioned in paragraph 1 above is produced to the court, accommodation shall be deemed to be suitable for the purposes of Ground 9 above if it consists of either—

    (a) premises which are to be let as a separate dwelling such that they will then be let on an assured tenancy, other than—

        (i) a tenancy in respect of which notice is given not later than the beginning of the tenancy that possession might be recovered on any of Grounds 1 to 5 above, or
        (ii) an assured shorthold tenancy, within the meaning of Chapter II of Part I of this Act, or

    (b) premises to be let as a separate dwelling on terms which will, in the opinion of the court, afford to the tenant security of tenure reasonably equivalent to the security afforded by Chapter I of Part I of this Act in the case of an assured tenancy of a kind mentioned in sub-paragraph (a) above,

and, in the opinion of the court, the accommodation fulfils the relevant conditions as defined in paragraph 3 below.

    3.—(1) For the purposes of parase needs as regards extent are, in the opinion of the court, similar to thograph 2 above, the relevant conditions are that the accommodation is reasonably suitable to the needs of the tenant and his family as regards proximity to place of work, and either—

    (a) similar as regards rental and extent to the accommodation afforded by dwelling-houses provided in the neighbourhood by any local housing authority for persons whose of the tenant and of his family; or
    (b) reasonably suitable to the means of the tenant and to the needs of the tenant and his family as regards extent and character; and

that if any furniture was provided for use under the assured tenancy in question, furniture is provided for use in the accommodation which is either similar to that so provided or is reasonably suitable to the needs of the tenant and his family.

(2) For the purposes of sub-paragraph (1)(a) above, a certificate of a local housing authority stating—

(a) the extent of the accommodation afforded by dwelling-houses provided by the authority to meet the needs of tenants with families of such number as may be specified in the certificate, and

(b) the amount of the rent charged by the authority for dwelling-houses affording accommodation of that extent,

shall be conclusive evidence of the facts so stated.

4.   Accommodation shall not be deemed to be suitable to the needs of the tenant and his family if the result of their occupation of the accommodation would be that it would be an overcrowded dwelling-house for the purposes of Part X of the Housing Act 1985.

5.   Any document purporting to be a certificate of a local housing authority named therein issued for the purposes of this Part of this Schedule and to be signed by the proper officer of that authority shall be received in evidence and, unless the contrary is shown, shall be deemed to be such a certificate without further proof.

6.   In this Part of this Schedule "local housing authority" and "district", in relation to such an authority, have the same meaning as in the Housing Act 1985.

Part IV

Notices Relating to Recovery of Possession

7.   Any reference in Grounds 1 to 5 in Part I of this Schedule or in the following provisions of this Part to the landlord giving a notice in writing to the tenant is, in the case of joint landlords, a reference to at least one of the joint landlords giving such a notice.   **A2.067**

8.—(1) If, not later than the beginning of a tenancy (in this paragraph referred to as "the earlier tenancy"), the landlord gives such a notice in writing to the tenant as is mentioned in any of Grounds 1 to 5 in Part I of this Schedule, then, for the purposes of the ground in question and any further application of this paragraph, that notice shall also have effect as if it had been given immediately before the beginning of any later tenancy falling within sub-paragraph (2) below.

(2) Subject to sub-paragraph (3) below, sub-paragraph (1) above applies to a later tenancy—

(a) which takes effect immediately on the coming to an end of the earlier tenancy; and

(b) which is granted (or deemed to be granted) to the person who was the tenant under the earlier tenancy immediately before it came to an end; and

(c) which is of substantially the same dwelling-house as the earlier tenancy.

(3) Sub-paragraph (1) above does not apply in relation to a later tenancy if, not later than the beginning of the tenancy, the landlord gave notice in writing to the tenant that the tenancy is not one in respect of which possession can be recovered on the ground in question.

9. Where paragraph 8(1) above has effect in relation to a notice given as mentioned in Ground 1 in Part I of this Schedule, the reference in paragraph (b) of that ground to the reversion on the tenancy is a reference to the reversion on the earlier tenancy and on any later tenancy falling within paragraph 8(2) above.

10. Where paragraph 8(1) above has effect in relation to a notice given as mentioned in Ground 3 or Ground 4 in Part I of this Schedule, any second or subsequent tenancy in relation to which the notice has effect shall be treated for the purpose of that ground as beginning at the beginning of the tenancy in respect of which the notice was actually given.

11. Any reference in Grounds 1 to 5 in Part I of this Schedule to a notice being given not later than the beginning of the tenancy is a reference to its being given not later than the day on which the tenancy is entered into and, accordingly, section 45(2) of this Act shall not apply to any such reference.

SCHEDULE 2A

Assured Tenancies: Non-Shortholds

Tenancies excluded by botice

A2.068   1.—(1) An assured tenancy in respect of which a notice is served as mentioned in sub-paragraph (2) below.

(2) The notice referred to in sub-paragraph (1) above is one which—

(a) is served before the assured tenancy is entered into,

(b) is served by the person who is to be the landlord under the assured tenancy on the person who is to be the tenant under that tenancy, and

(c) states that the assured tenancy to which it relates is not to be an assured shorthold tenancy.

2.—(1) An assured tenancy in respect of which a notice is served as mentioned in sub-paragraph (2) below.

(2) The notice referred to in sub-paragraph (1) above is one which—

(a) is served after the assured tenancy has been entered into,

(b) is served by the landlord under the assured tenancy on the tenant under that tenancy, and

(c) states that the assured tenancy to which it relates is no longer an assured shorthold tenancy.

Tenancies containing exclusionary provision

3. An assured tenancy which contains a provision to the effect that the tenancy is not an assured shorthold tenancy.

Tenancies under section 39

4. An assured tenancy arising by virtue of section 39 above, other than one to which subsection (7) of that section applies.

Former secure tenancies

5. An assured tenancy which became an assured tenancy on ceasing to be a **A2.069**
secure tenancy.

Former demoted tenancies

5A. An assured tenancy which ceases to be an assured shorthold tenancy by
virtue of section 20B(2) or (4).

Tenancies under Schedule 10 to the Local Government and Housing Act 1989

6. An assured tenancy arising by virtue of Schedule 10 to the Local
Government and Housing Act 1989 (security of tenure on ending of long
residential tenancies).

Tenancies replacing non-shortholds

7.—(1) An assured tenancy which—

(a) is granted to a person (alone or jointly with others) who, immediately before the tenancy was granted, was the tenant (or, in the
case of joint tenants, one of the tenants) under an assured tenancy
other than a shorthold tenancy ("the old tenancy"),

(b) is granted (alone or jointly with others) by a person who was at
that time the landlord (or one of the joint landlords) under the old
tenancy, and

(c) is not one in respect of which a notice is served as mentioned in
sub-paragraph (2) below.

(2) The notice referred to in sub-paragraph (1)(c) above is one which—

(a) is in such form as may be prescribed,

(b) is served before the assured tenancy is entered into,

(c) is served by the person who is to be the tenant under the assured
tenancy on the person who is to be the landlord under that tenancy
(or, in the case of joint landlords, on at least one of the persons
who are to be joint landlords), and

(d) states that the assured tenancy to which it relates is to be a shorthold tenancy.

8. An assured tenancy which comes into being by virtue of section 5 above
on the coming to an end of an assured tenancy which is not a shorthold
tenancy.

Assured agricultural occupancies

9.—(1) An assured tenancy—

(a) in the case of which the agricultural worker condition is, by **A2.070**
virtue of any provision of Schedule 3 to this Act, for the time
being fulfilled with respect to the dwelling-house subject to the
tenancy, and

(b) which does not fall within sub-paragraph (2) or (4) below.

(2) An assured tenancy falls within this sub-paragraph if—

(a) before it is entered into, a notice—

(i) in such form as may be prescribed, and
(ii) stating that the tenancy is to be a shorthold tenancy,

is served by the person who is to be the landlord under the tenancy on the person who is to be the tenant under it, and

(b) it is not an excepted tenancy.

(3) For the purposes of sub-paragraph (2)(b) above, an assured tenancy is an excepted tenancy if—

(a) the person to whom it is granted or, as the case may be, at least one of the persons to whom it is granted was, immediately before it is granted, a tenant or licensee under an assured agricultural occupancy, and

(b) the person by whom it is granted or, as the case may be, at least one of the persons by whom it is granted was, immediately before it is granted, a landlord or licensor under the assured agricultural occupancy referred to in paragraph (a) above.

(4) An assured tenancy falls within this sub-paragraph if it comes into being by virtue of section 5 above on the coming to an end of a tenancy falling within sub-paragraph (2) above.

SCHEDULE 3

AGRICULTURAL WORKER CONDITIONS

Interpretation

A2.071 **1.**—(1) In this Schedule—

"the 1976 Act" means the meaning as in the 1976 Act; and
"relevant tenancy or Rent (Agriculture) Act 1976;
"agriculture" has the same licence" means a tenancy or licence of a description specified in section 24(2) of this Act.

(2) In relation to a relevant tenancy or licence—

(a) "the occupier" means the tenant or licensee; and
(b) "the dwelling-house" means the dwelling-house which is let under the tenancy or, as the case may be, is occupied under the licence.

(3) Schedule 3 to the 1976 Act applies for the purposes of this Schedule as it applies for the purposes of that Act and, accordingly, shall have effect to determine—

(a) whether a person is a qualifying worker;
(b) whether a person is incapable of whole-time work in agriculture, or work in agriculture as a permit worker, in consequence of a qualifying injury or disease; and
(c) whether a dwelling-house is in qualifying ownership.

The conditions

2. The agricultural worker condition is fulfilled with respect to a dwelling-house subject to a relevant tenancy or licence if–

    (a) the dwelling-house is or has been in qualifying ownership at any time during the subsistence of the tenancy or licence (whether or not it was at that time a relevant tenancy or licence); and

    (b) the occupier or, where there are joint occupiers, at least one of them—

        (i) is a qualifying worker or has been a qualifying worker at any time during the subsistence of the tenancy or licence (whether or not it was at that time a relevant tenancy or licence); or

        (ii) is incapable of whole-time work in agriculture or work in agriculture as a permit worker in consequence of a qualifying injury or disease.

3.—(1) The agricultural worker condition is also fulfilled with respect to a **A2.072** dwelling-house subject to a relevant tenancy or licence if—

    (a) that condition was previously fulfilled with respect to the dwelling-house but the person who was then the occupier or, as the case may be, a person who was one of the joint occupiers (whether or not under the same relevant tenancy or licence) has died; and

    (b) that condition ceased to be fulfilled on the death of the occupier referred to in paragraph (a) above (hereinafter referred to as "the previous qualifying occupier"); and

    (c) the occupier is either–

        (i) the qualifying surviving partner of the previous qualifying occupier; or

        (ii) the qualifying member of the previous qualifying occupier's family.

    (2) For the purposes of sub-paragraph (1)(c)(i) above and sub-paragraph (3) below—

    (a) "surviving partner" means widow, widower or surviving civil partner; and

    (b) a surviving partner of the previous qualifying occupier of the dwelling-house is a qualifying surviving partner if that surviving partner was residing in the dwelling-house immediately before the previous qualifying occupier's death.

    (3) Subject to sub-paragraph (4) below, for the purposes of sub-paragraph (1)(c)(ii) above, a member of the family of the previous qualifying occupier of the dwelling-house is the qualifying member of the family if—

    (a) on the death of the previous qualifying occupier there was no qualifying surviving partner; and

    (b) the member of the family was residing in the dwelling-house with the previous qualifying occupier at the time of, and for the period of two years before, his death.

A2.073

(4) Not more than one member of the previous qualifying occupier's family may be taken into account in determining whether the agricultural worker condition is fulfilled by virtue of this paragraph and, accordingly, if there is more than one member of the family—

(a) who is the occupier in relation to the relevant tenancy or licence, and

(b) who, apart from this sub-paragraph, would be the qualifying member of the family by virtue of sub-paragraph (3) above,

only that one of those members of the family who may be decided by agreement or, in default of agreement by the county court, shall be the qualifying member.

(5) For the purposes of sub-paragraph (2)(a) above—

(a) a person who, immediately before the previous qualifying occupier's death, was living with the previous occupier as his or her wife or husband shall be treated as the widow or widower of the previous occupier, and

(b) a person who, immediately before the previous qualifying occupier's death, was living with the previous occupier as if they were civil partners shall be treated as the surviving civil partner of the previous occupier.

(6) If, immediately before the death of the previous qualifying occupier, there is, by virtue of sub-paragraph (5) above, more than one person who falls within sub-paragraph (1)(c)(i) above, such one of them as may be decided by agreement or, in default of agreement, by the county court shall be treated as the qualifying surviving partner for the purposes of this paragraph.

A2.074 4. The agricultural worker condition is also fulfilled with respect to a dwelling-house subject to a relevant tenancy or licence if—

(a) the tenancy or licence was granted to the occupier or, where there are joint occupiers, at least one of them in consideration of his giving up possession of another dwelling-house of which he was then occupier (or one of joint occupiers) under another relevant tenancy or licence; and

(b) immediately before he gave up possession of that dwelling-house, as a result of his occupation the agricultural worker condition was fulfilled with respect to it (whether by virtue of paragraph 2 or paragraph 3 above or this paragraph);

and the reference in paragraph (a) above to a tenancy or licence granted to the occupier or at least one of joint occupiers includes a reference to the case where the grant is to him together with one or more other persons.

5.—(1) This paragraph applies where—

(a) by virtue of any of paragraphs 2 to 4 above, the agricultural worker condition is fulfilled with respect to a dwelling-house subject to a relevant tenancy or licence (in this paragraph referred to as "the earlier tenancy or licence"); and

(b) another relevant tenancy or licence of the same dwelling-house (in this paragraph referred to as "the later tenancy or licence") is granted to the person who, immediately before the grant, was the occupier or one of the joint occupiers under the earlier tenancy or licence and as a result of whose occupation the agricultural worker condition was fulfilled as mentioned in paragraph (a) above;

and the reference in paragraph (b) above to the grant of the later tenancy or licence to the person mentioned in that paragraph includes a reference to the case where the grant is to that person together with one or more other persons.

(2) So long as a person as a result of whose occupation of the dwelling-house the agricultural worker condition was fulfilled with respect to the earlier tenancy or licence continues to be the occupier, or one of the joint occupiers, under the later tenancy or licence, the agricultural worker condition shall be fulfilled with respect to the dwelling-house.

(3) For the purposes of paragraphs 3 and 4 above and any further application of this paragraph, where sub-paragraph (2) above has effect, the agricultural worker condition shall be treated as fulfilled so far as concerns the later tenancy or licence by virtue of the same paragraph of this Schedule as was applicable (or, as the case may be, last applicable) in the case of the earlier tenancy or licence.

Appendix 3

Housing and Regeneration Act 2008 Schedule 11 Part 2

Housing and Regeneration
Act 2008 c.17

SCHEDULE 11

Possession Orders Relating To Certain Tenancies

Part 2

Replacement of certain terminated tenancies

Circumstances in which replacement tenancies arise

15.—In this Part of this Schedule "an original tenancy" means any secure **A3.001**
tenancy, assured tenancy, introductory tenancy or demoted tenancy—

    (a) in respect of which a possession order was made before the
commencement date, and

    (b) which ended before that date pursuant to the order but not on the
execution of the order.

16.—(1) A new tenancy of the dwelling-house which was let under the original
tenancy is treated as arising on the commencement date between the
ex-landlord and the ex-tenant if—

    (a) on that date—

        (i) the home condition is met, and

        (ii) the ex-landlord is entitled to let the dwelling-house, and

    (b) the ex-landlord and the ex-tenant have not entered into another
tenancy after the date on which the original tenancy ended but
before the commencement date.

(2) The home condition is that the dwelling-house which was let under the
original tenancy—

    (a) is, on the commencement date, the only or principal home of the
ex-tenant, and

    (b) has been the only or principal home of the ex-tenant throughout
the termination period.

(3) In this Part of this Schedule "the termination period" means the period—

    (a) beginning with the end of the original tenancy, and

    (b) ending with the commencement date.

(4) For the purposes of sub-paragraph (2)(a) the dwelling-house is the only or principal home of the ex-tenant on the commencement date even though the ex-tenant is then absent from the dwelling-house as a result of having been evicted in pursuance of a warrant if the warrant is subsequently set aside but the possession order under which it was granted remains in force.

(5) In that case, the new tenancy is treated as arising on the first day (if any) on which the ex-tenant resumes occupation of the dwelling-house as that person's only or principal home.

(6) For the purposes of sub-paragraph (2)(b) any period of time within the termination period is to be ignored if—

   (a) it is a period in which the ex-tenant was absent from the dwelling-house as a result of having been evicted in pursuance of a warrant which was then set aside although the possession order under which it was granted remained in force, and

   (b) the ex-tenant subsequently resumes occupation of the dwelling-house as the ex-tenant's only or principal home.

(7) The appropriate national authority may by order provide for particular cases or descriptions of case, or particular circumstances, where the home condition is met where it would not otherwise be met.

Nature of replacement tenancies

A3.002   17. The new tenancy is to be–

   (a) a secure tenancy if—

      (i) the original tenancy was a secure tenancy, or

      (ii) the original tenancy was an introductory tenancy but no election by the ex-landlord under section 124 of the Housing Act 1996 (c. 52) is in force on the day on which the new tenancy arises,

   (b) an assured shorthold tenancy if the original tenancy was an assured shorthold tenancy,

   (c) an assured tenancy which is not an assured shorthold tenancy if the original tenancy was a tenancy of that kind,

   (d) an introductory tenancy if the original tenancy was an introductory tenancy and an election by the ex-landlord under section 124 of the Housing Act 1996 is in force on the day on which the new tenancy arises,

   (e) a demoted tenancy to which section 20B of the Housing Act 1988 (c. 50) applies if the original tenancy was a demoted tenancy of that kind, and

   (f) a demoted tenancy to which section 143A of the Housing Act 1996 applies if the original tenancy was a demoted tenancy of that kind.

18.—(1) The new tenancy is, subject as follows, to have effect on the same terms and conditions as those applicable to the original tenancy immediately before it ended.

(2) The terms and conditions of the new tenancy are to be treated as modified so as to reflect, so far as applicable, any changes made during the

termination period to the level of payments for the ex-tenant's occupation of the dwelling-house or to the other terms and conditions of the occupation.

(3) The terms and conditions of the new tenancy are to be treated as modified so that any outstanding liabilities owed by the ex-tenant to the ex-landlord in respect of payments for the ex-tenant's occupation of the dwelling-house during the termination period are liabilities in respect of rent under the new tenancy.

(4) The appropriate national authority may by order provide for other modifications of the terms and conditions of the new tenancy.

(5) Nothing in sub-paragraphs (2) to (4) is to be read as permitting modifications of the new tenancy which would not have been possible if the original tenancy had remained a tenancy throughout the termination period.

(6) The terms and conditions of a new secure tenancy which arises by virtue of paragraph 17(a)(ii) are to be treated as modified so far as necessary to reflect the fact that the new tenancy is a secure tenancy and not an introductory tenancy.

19.—(1) Any provision which is made by or under an enactment and relates to a secure tenancy, assured tenancy, introductory tenancy or demoted tenancy applies, subject as follows, to a new tenancy of a corresponding kind.

(2) Any such provision which relates to an introductory tenancy applies to a new tenancy which is an introductory tenancy as if the trial period mentioned in section 125(2) of the Housing Act 1996 (c. 52) were the period of one year beginning with the day on which the new tenancy arises.

(3) Any such provision which relates to a demoted tenancy applies to a new tenancy which is a demoted tenancy as if the demotion period mentioned in section 20B(2) of the Housing Act 1988 (c. 50) or section 143B(1) of the Housing Act 1996 were the period of one year beginning with the day on which the new tenancy arises.

(4) The appropriate national authority may by order modify any provision made by or under an enactment in its application to a new tenancy.

Status of possession order and other court orders

20.—(1) The possession order in pursuance of which the original tenancy **A3.003** ended is to be treated, so far as practicable, as if it applies to the new tenancy.

(2) Any court orders made before the commencement date which—

(a) are in force on that date,

(b) relate to the occupation of the dwelling-house, and

(c) were made in contemplation of, in consequence of or otherwise in connection with the possession order,

are to be treated, so far as practicable, as if they apply to the new tenancy.

Continuity of tenancies

A3.004 **21.**—(1) The new tenancy and the original tenancy are to be treated for the relevant purposes as—

  (a) the same tenancy, and

  (b) a tenancy which continued uninterrupted throughout the termination period.

(2) The relevant purposes are—

  (a) determining whether the ex-tenant is a successor in relation to the new tenancy,

  (b) calculating on or after the commencement date the period qualifying, or the aggregate of such periods, under Schedule 4 to the Housing Act 1985 (c. 68) (qualifying period for right to buy and discount),

  (c) determining on or after the commencement date whether the condition set out in paragraph (b) of Ground 8 of Schedule 2 to that Act is met, and

  (d) any other purposes specified by the appropriate national authority by order.

(3) In proceedings on a relevant claim the court concerned may order that the new tenancy and the original tenancy are to be treated for the purposes of the claim as—

  (a) the same tenancy, and

  (b) a tenancy which continued uninterrupted throughout the termination period.

(4) The following are relevant claims—

  (a) a claim by the ex-tenant or the ex-landlord against the other for breach of a term or condition of the original tenancy—

   (i) in respect of which proceedings are brought on or after the commencement date, or

   (ii) in respect of which proceedings were brought, but were not finally determined, before that date,

  (b) a claim by the ex-tenant against the ex-landlord for breach of statutory duty in respect of which proceedings are or were brought as mentioned in paragraph (a)(i) or (ii), and

  (c) any other claim of a description specified by the appropriate national authority by order.

(5) For the purposes of sub-paragraph (4)(a) proceedings must be treated as finally determined if—

  (a) they are withdrawn,

  (b) any appeal is abandoned, or

  (c) the time for appealing has expired without an appeal being brought.

Compliance with consultation requirements

22.—(1) The fact that—   **A3.005**

    (a) the views of the ex-tenant during the termination period were not sought or taken into account when they should have been sought or taken into account, or

    (b) the views of the ex-tenant during that period were sought or taken into account when they should not have been sought or taken into account,

is not to be taken to mean that the consultation requirements were not complied with.

  (2) The consultation requirements are—

    (a) the requirements under—

        (i) section 105(1) of the Housing Act 1985 (c. 68),

        (ii) paragraphs 3 and 4 of Schedule 3A to that Act,

        (iii) regulations made under section 27AB of that Act which relate to arranging for ballots or polls with respect to a proposal to enter into a management agreement, and

        (iv) section 137(2) of the Housing Act 1996 (c. 52), and

    (b) any other requirements specified by the appropriate national authority by order.

Joint tenancies

23.—(1) In the application of this Part of this Schedule in relation to an orig- **A3.006** inal tenancy which was a joint tenancy, a reference to the dwelling-house being the only or principal home of the ex-tenant is to be treated as a reference to the dwelling-house being the only or principal home of at least one of the ex-tenants of the joint tenancy.

  (2) The appropriate national authority may by order provide for this Part of this Schedule to apply in relation to an original tenancy which was a joint tenancy subject to such additional modifications as may be specified in the order.

Successor landlords

24.—(1) The appropriate national authority may by order provide for this **A3.007** Part of this Schedule to apply, subject to such modifications as may be specified in the order, to successor landlord cases.

  (2) For the purposes of sub-paragraph (1) a successor landlord case is a case, in relation to an original tenancy, where the interest of the ex-landlord in the dwelling-house—

    (a) has been transferred to another person after the end of the original tenancy and before the commencement date, and

    (b) on the commencement date, belongs to the person to whom it has been transferred or a subsequent transferee.

Supplementary

A3.008
25. In determining for the purposes of this Part of this Schedule whether a tenancy has ended, any ending which was temporary because the tenancy was restored in consequence of a court order is to be ignored.

26.—(1) In this Part of this Schedule—

"appropriate national authority" means—

(a) in relation to a dwelling-house in England, the Secretary of State, and

(b) in relation to a dwelling-house in Wales, the Welsh Ministers,

"assured shorthold tenancy" and "assured tenancy" have the same meanings as in Part 1 of the Housing Act 1988 (c. 50) but do not include a demoted tenancy to which section 20B of that Act applies,

"the commencement date" means the day on which section 299 comes into force for purposes other than the purposes of the Secretary of State or the Welsh Ministers making orders under this Part of this Schedule,

"demoted tenancy" means a tenancy to which section 20B of the Act of 1988 or section 143A of the Housing Act 1996 (c. 52) applies,

"dwelling-house"—

(a) in relation to an assured tenancy, or a tenancy to which section 20B of the Act of 1988 applies, has the same meaning as in Part 1 of that Act,

(b) in relation to a tenancy to which section 143A of the Act of 1996 applies, has the same meaning as in Chapter 1A of Part 5 of that Act,

(c) in relation to an introductory tenancy, has the meaning given by section 139 of the Act of 1996, and

(d) in relation to a secure tenancy, has the meaning given by section 112 of the Housing Act 1985 (c. 68),

"ex-landlord" means the person who was the landlord under an original tenancy,

"ex-tenant" means the person who was the tenant under an original tenancy,

"introductory tenancy" has the same meaning as in Chapter 1 of Part 5 of the Act of 1996,

"modification" includes omission,

"new tenancy" means a tenancy which is treated as arising by virtue of paragraph 16,

"original tenancy" has the meaning given by paragraph 15,

"possession order", in relation to a tenancy, means a court order for the possession of the dwelling-house,

"secure tenancy" has the same meaning as in Part 4 of the Act of 1985,

"successor"—

(a) in relation to a new tenancy which is an assured tenancy or which is a demoted tenancy to which section 20B of the Act of 1988 applies, has the same meaning as in section 17 of that Act,

(b) in relation to a new tenancy which is a demoted tenancy to which section 143A of the Act of 1996 applies, has the meaning given by section 143J of that Act,

(c) in relation to a new tenancy which is an introductory tenancy, has the same meaning as in section 132 of the Act of 1996, and

(d) in relation to a new tenancy which is a secure tenancy, has the same meaning as in section 88 of the Act of 1985.

"termination period" has the meaning given by paragraph 16(3).

(2) For the purposes of the definition of "appropriate national authority" in sub-paragraph (1) a dwelling-house which is partly in England and partly in Wales is to be treated—

(a) as being in England if it is treated as situated in the area of a billing authority in England by virtue of regulations under section 1(3) of the Local Government Finance Act 1992 (c. 14) (council tax in respect of dwellings), and

(b) as being in Wales if it is treated as situated in the area of a billing authority in Wales by virtue of regulations under that section.

Index

Disability Discrimination Act 1997
impact on possession proceedings,
24.003
Equality Act 2010, 24.001, 24.002
generally, 24.001
possession claims
suspension, 24.008
postponement, 24.008
rent cases, 27.029
Disclaimer
bankruptcy, 4.018, 4.019
Discretionary powers
agreements, 32.072
consumer credit cases, 32.067
power to impose conditions, 32.071
sale of property, 32.064–32.066
securities, 32.072
suspension of operation of order,
32.071
tenancies granted after the mortgage,
32.074
tenants in occupation, 32.073–32.082
time orders, 32.068
use, 32.058–32.061
variation
agreements, 32.072
securities, 32.072
Disposition of property
meaning, 1.012
registered, 32.078–32.080
Dispute resolution
see **Alternative dispute resolution**
Divorce
status following, 21.003, 21.005
Documents
see also **Evidence**
destruction, 27.006
execution
companies, 1.005
in hands of another party, 27.004
in the hands of a person not a party,
27.005
lost documents, 27.006
Dwelling houses
see **Houses**
Employees
assured tenancies, 17.011
change of employer, 17.005
contracts of employment, 17.004
licensed premises, 17.008
licensees, 17.002
local authorities, 17.007
possession for new employee, 17.009,
17.010
public sector employees, 17.007
regulated tenancies, 17.009

rent
payment, 17.006
requirement to occupy, 17.003
status, 17.001
unfair dismissal, 17.004, 17.005
Enforcement
see also **Damages**; **Unlawful eviction**
contempt of court, 34.002
date of possession
postponement, 34.008
harassment
examples, 35.003
protection from harassment, 35.001
insolvency, 34.006
money judgment
execution, 34.003
notice
applications for warrant, 34.003, 34.004
suspension of warrant, 34.009, 25.037
oppression, 34.012, 34.013
rules, 34.001
setting aside
judgement, 34.010
possession orders, 34.010–34.013
suspended orders
fall, 34.002
grounds for, 34.009
terms, 34.002
unlawful eviction
claims 35.002
damages, 35.001
injunctions to prevent, 3.001
jurisdiction, 35.004
warrants of possession
execution, 34.005
issue, 34.001, 34.002
notice of applications for, 34.003,
34.004
suspension, 28.037, 34.008
time limit, 34.004
warning notice, 34.004
writ for possession, 34.001
Equity
leases, 1.010
Estoppel
basis, 1.008
creation, 1.008
landlords and tenants, 1.008
owners of property, 1.008
surrender by operation of law, 3.024
Eviction
agricultural accommodation, 18.016
harassment
examples, 35.003
protection from harassment, 35.001
unlawful eviction, 35.001–35.004